Essentials of Services Marketing

3rd Edition

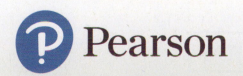

Pearson

Jochen Wirtz

Christopher Lovelock

Harlow, England • London • New York • Boston • San Francisco • Toronto • Sydney • Dubai • Singapore • Hong Kong
Tokyo • Seoul • Taipei • New Delhi • Cape Town • Sao Paulo • Mexico City • Madrid • Amsterdam • Munich • Paris • Milan

Director of Content and Publishing Operations: Angshuman Chakraborty
Head of Publishing and Digital Media: Amarjyoti Dutta
Managing Editor: Yajnaseni Das
Associate Acquisitions Editor: Ananya Srivastava
Associate Project Editor: Paromita Banerjee
Senior Project Editor: Daniel Luiz
Manager, Media Production: M. Vikram Kumar
Senior Manufacturing Controller, Production: Jerry Kataria
Cover Design: Subhashish Roy
Cover image: ©Ociacia/Shutterstock

Pearson Education Limited
Edinburgh Gate
Harlow
Essex CM20 2JE
England

and Associated Companies throughout the world

Visit us on the World Wide Web at:
www.pearsonglobaleditions.com

ISBN 10: 1-292-08995-4
ISBN 13: 978-1-292-08995-9

British Library Cataloguing-in-Publication Data
A catalogue record for this book is available from the British Library

10 9 8 7 6 5 4 3 2 1
21 20 19 18 17

Typeset in Garamond by S4 Carlisle.

Printed and bound by L.E.G.O. S.p.A. Lavis (TN) in Italy.

Brief Contents

To Lorraine, Alexander, and Stefanie, the cool gang who brings Jeannette and me so much love and joy. Wishing you all the happiness and success in life!

JW

About the Authors

As a team, Christopher Lovelock and Jochen Wirtz provide a blend of skills and experience that's ideally suited to writing an authoritative and engaging services marketing text. They have worked together on a variety of projects, including cases, articles, conference papers, as well as *Services Marketing: People, Technology, Strategy* and *Essentials of Services Marketing.*

Jochen Wirtz is Professor of Marketing and Vice Dean, Graduate Studies, at the National University of Singapore (NUS) and an international fellow of the Service Research Center at Karlstad University. Furthermore, he is the founding director of the dual degree UCLA-NUS Executive MBA Program (ranked globally #6 in the *Financial Times* 2016 EMBA rankings), international fellow of the Service Research Center at Karlstad University, and Academic Scholar at the Cornell Institute for Healthy Futures (CIHF) at Cornell University. Dr. Wirtz holds a PhD in services marketing from the London Business School and has worked in the field of services for over 25 years.

Previously, Professor Wirtz was an associate fellow at the Saïd Business School, University of Oxford, from 2008 to 2013, and a founding member of the NUS Teaching Academy (the NUS think tank on education matters) from 2009 to 2015.

Professor Wirtz's research focuses on services marketing and has been published in over 200 academic articles, book chapters, and industry reports. He is an author or co-author of over ten books, including *Services Marketing: People, Technology, Strategy* (8th edition, World Scientific, 2015), co-authored with Professor Lovelock, which has become one of the world's leading services marketing textbooks and has been translated and adapted for over 26 countries and regions, with sales of approximately 800,000 copies. His other books include *Winning in Service Markets* (World Scientific, 2015) and *Flying High in a Competitive Industry: Secrets of the World's Leading Airline* (McGraw Hill, 2009).

In recognition of his excellence in teaching and research, Professor Wirtz has received over 40 awards, including the prestigious Academy of Marketing Science (AMS) 2012 Outstanding Marketing Teacher Award (the highest recognition of teaching excellence by AMS globally) and the top university-level Outstanding Educator Award at NUS. He was also the winner of the inaugural Outstanding Service Researcher Award 2010 and the Best Practical Implications Award 2009, both by Emerald Group Publications. He serves on the editorial review boards of over ten academic journals, including the *Journal of Service Management, Journal of Service Research, Journal of Service Science,* and *Cornell Hospitality Quarterly*, and is also an ad hoc reviewer for the *Journal of Consumer Research* and *Journal of Marketing*. Professor Wirtz chaired the American Marketing Association's biennial Service Research Conference in 2005 when it was held for the first time in Asia.

Professor Wirtz was a banker and took the banking exam at the Chamber of Commerce and Industry in Munich. He has since been an active management consultant, working with international consulting firms including Accenture, Arthur D. Little, and KPMG as well as major service firms in the areas of strategy, business development, and customer feedback systems. He has also been involved in a number of start-ups, including in Accellion (www.accellion.com), AngelLoop (www.angelloop.com), TranscribeMe (www.transcribeme.com), and UP! Your Service (www.upyourservice.com).

Originally from Germany, Professor Wirtz spent seven years in London before moving to Asia. Today, he shuttles between Asia, the United States, and Europe. For further information, visit www.jochenwirtz.com.

The late **Christopher Lovelock** was one of the pioneers of services marketing. He consulted and gave seminars and workshops for managers around the world, with a particular focus on strategic planning in services and managing the customer experience. From 2001 to 2008, he was an adjunct professor at the Yale School of Management, where he taught services marketing in the MBA program.

After obtaining a BCom and an MA in economics from the University of Edinburgh, he worked in advertising with the London office of J. Walter Thompson Co. and then in corporate planning with Canadian Industries Ltd. in Montreal. Later, he obtained an MBA from Harvard and a PhD from Stanford, where he was also a postdoctoral fellow.

Professor Lovelock's distinguished academic career included 11 years on the faculty of the Harvard Business School and two years as a visiting professor at IMD in Switzerland. He has also held faculty appointments at Berkeley, Stanford, and the Sloan School at MIT, as well as visiting professorships at INSEAD in France and The University of Queensland in Australia.

Author or co-author of over 60 articles, more than 100 teaching cases, and 27 books, Professor Lovelock has seen his work translated into 16 languages. He served on the editorial review boards of the *Journal of Service Management, Journal of Service Research, Service Industries Journal, Cornell Hospitality Quarterly,* and *Marketing Management* and was also an ad hoc reviewer for the *Journal of Marketing*.

Widely acknowledged as a thought leader in services, Professor Lovelock has been honored by the American Marketing Association's prestigious Award for Career Contributions in the Services Discipline. This award has been renamed as the SERVSIG Christopher Lovelock Career Contribution Award in his honor. His article co-written with Evert Gummesson, "Whither Services Marketing? In Search of a New Paradigm and Fresh Perspectives," won the AMA's Best Services Article Award in 2005. He had previously also received a best article award from the *Journal of Marketing*. Recognized many times for excellence in case writing, he has twice won top honors in the *Business Week* "European Case of the Year" Award. For further information, visit www.lovelock.com.

About the Contributors of the Cases

Karla Cabrera is a senior researcher at the Service Management Research & Education Group, EGADE Business School, Tecnologico de Monterrey, Mexico.

Mark Colgate is a professor at the University of Victoria, Canada.

Lorelle Frazer is Director of Online and Blended Learning at Griffith Business School, Australia.

James L. Heskett is UPS Foundation Professor of Business Logistics, Emeritus, at Harvard Business School, United States.

Roger Hallowell is Academic Director of Programs at HEC Paris and a former professor at Harvard Business School, United States.

Christopher W. Hart is a former professor at Harvard Business School, United States.

Loizos Heracleous is Chair in Strategy and Organization at Warwick Business School, and Associate Fellow at Oxford University.

Sheryl E. Kimes is a professor of operations management at Cornell University, United States.

Youngme Moon is Senior Associate Dean for Strategy and Innovation and Donald K. David Professor of Business Administration at Harvard Business School, United States.

John Quelch is Charles Edward Wilson Professor of Business Administration at Harvard Business School, United States.

Javier Reynoso is Professor of Service Management and Chair of the Service Management Research & Education Group, EGADE Business School, Tecnologico de Monterrey, Mexico.

Christopher S. Tang is a UCLA Distinguished Professor and the holder of the Edward W. Carter Chain in Business Administration.

Rohit Verma is Dean of External Relations, Cornell University, United States.

Lauren K. Wright is a professor of marketing at California State College, Chico, United States.

Contents

The following cases are available for free download and class distribution on the Instructor's Resource Website for courses that adopt *Essentials of Services Marketing*.

Preface

Services dominate the expanding world economy as never before, and technology continues to evolve in dramatic ways. Established industries and old, illustrious companies decline and may even disappear as new business models and industries emerge. Competitive activity is fierce, with firms often using new strategies and technologies to respond to changing customer needs, expectations, and behaviors. This book has been written in response to the global transformation of our economies to services. Clearly, the skills in marketing and managing services have never been more important!

As the field of services marketing has evolved, so too has this book. This new edition has been revised significantly since the 2nd edition. It captures the reality of today's world, incorporates recent academic and managerial thinking, and illustrates cutting-edge service concepts.

This book is based on *Services Marketing: People, Technology, Strategy*, 8th edition (World Scientific, 2015). It has been significantly condensed and sharpened to provide a crisp introduction to key topics in services marketing. In addition, the case selection, visuals, and design are meant to appeal to undergraduate and polytechnic students.

WHAT'S NEW IN THIS EDITION?

The 3rd edition represents a significant revision. Its contents reflect ongoing developments in the service economy, dramatic developments in technology, new research findings, and enhancements to the structure and presentation of the book in response to feedback from reviewers and adopters.

New Structure, New Topics

▶ Almost all chapters are now structured around an *organizing framework* that provides a pictorial overview of the chapter's contents and line of argument.

▶ New *applications of technology* are integrated throughout the text, ranging from apps, M-commerce and social networks, to robots, artificial intelligence, and biometrics.

▶ Each of the 15 chapters has been revised. All chapters incorporate *new examples* and references to *recent research*. Significant changes in chapter content are highlighted below.

▶ Chapter 1, "**Introduction to Services Marketing**," now explores the nature of the modern service economy more deeply and covers B2B services, outsourcing, and offshoring. Furthermore, the Service-Profit Chain was moved here to serve as a guiding framework for the book (it was featured in Chapter 15 in the previous edition).

▶ Chapter 2, "**Consumer Behavior in a Services Context,**" also covers the post-consumption behaviors, including service quality, its dimensions and measurement (including SERVQUAL), and how quality relates to customer loyalty. This section was in Chapter 14 in the previous edition.

- ▶ Chapter 7, "**Promoting Services and Educating Customers**," is now tightly organized around the 5 Ws model, a new section on the services marketing communications funnel was added, and the coverage of new media (including social media, mobile, apps, and QR codes) was significantly expanded.

- ▶ Chapter 8, "**Designing Service Processes**," has a new section on emotionprints and covers service blueprinting in more depth.

- ▶ Chapter 11, "**Managing People for Service Advantage**," has new sections on a service-oriented culture, how to build a climate for service, and effective leadership in service organization and leadership styles. Part of this content was previously covered in Chapter 15.

- ▶ Chapter 14, "**Improving Service Quality and Productivity**," now integrates key concepts in the main body of the chapter instead of the appendix as in the earlier edition. These are TQM, ISO 9000, Six Sigma, and the Malcolm-Baldrige and EFQM.

- ▶ Chapter 15, "**Building a Service Organization that Wins**," was completely restructured to provide a recap and integration of the key themes of *Services Marketing*, 8th edition. It now features an auditing tool to assess the service level of an organization. It emphasizes the impact of customer satisfaction on long-term profitability and closes with a call to action.

FOR WHAT TYPES OF COURSES CAN THIS BOOK BE USED?

This text is suitable for courses directed at undergraduate and polytechnic students equally. *Essentials in Services Marketing* places marketing issues within a broader general management context. The book will appeal to students heading for a career in the service sector, whether at the executive or management level.

Whatever the job is in the services industry, a person has to understand the close ties that link the marketing, operations, and human resources functions in service firms. With that perspective in mind, we have designed the book so that instructors can make selective use of chapters and cases to teach courses of different lengths and formats in either services marketing or services management.

WHAT ARE THE BOOK'S DISTINGUISHING FEATURES?

The third edition of *ESM* retains some of the key features that have made it successful, and improves on other aspects of the textbook to help students understand services marketing more effectively. These features include the following:

▶ You'll find that this text takes a **strongly managerial perspective**, yet is **rooted in solid academic research**, complemented by memorable frameworks. Our goal is to bridge the all-too-frequent gap between theory and the real world.

▶ The text is **organized around an integrated framework** the reader immediately can relate to. The framework cascades across the entire book. Furthermore, each chapter provides a succinct **chapter overview in pictorial form**.

▶ We worked hard to create a text that is **clear, readable, and focused**.

Figure 1.3 An introduction to services marketing.

PART IV

▶ An **easy-to-read text** that works hand-in-hand with visuals that make important concepts accessible.

▶ A **global perspective**. Examples were carefully selected from America, Europe and Asia.

▶ **Systematic learning approach**. Each chapter has clear **learning objectives**, an **organizing framework that that provides a quick overview** of the chapter's contents and line of argument, and **chapter summaries in bullet form** that condense the core concepts and messages of each chapter.

▶ **Opening vignettes** and **boxed inserts** within the chapters are designed to capture student interest and provide opportunities for in-class discussions. They describe significant research findings, illustrate practical applications of important service marketing concepts, and describe best practices by innovative service organizations.

The following table links the cases to the chapters in the book.

CASES		PRIMARY CHAPTERS
1	Sullivan Ford Auto World	1
2	Dr. Beckett's Dental Office	All chapters
3	Uber	3
4	Banyan Tree	3, 4
5	Kiwi Experience	4, 5, 7
6	The Accra Beach Hotel	6
7	Revenue Management of Gondolas	6
8	Aussie Pooch Mobile	7
9	Shouldice Hospital Limited (Abridged)	8, 9, 10
10	Red Lobster	11
11	Singapore Airlines	11, 15
12	Dr. Mahalee Goes to London	12
13	The Royal Dining Membership Program Dilemma	12
14	Customer Asset Management at DHL in Asia	13
15	Starbucks	11, 12, 14, 15
16	Lux Resorts★	11, 12, 14, 15
17	KidZania	All chapters

SECONDARY CHAPTERS	CONTINENT	COUNTRY	INDUSTRY
2, 10	Americas	United States	Automobile Servicing
	Americas	United States	Medical
4, 5, 7, 12	Asia/Americas	China/United States	Transportation
5, 11	Asia/Global		Resort
3, 11	Oceania	New Zealand	Tourism
9	Americas	Barbados	Resort
	Europe	Italy	Tourism
5	Australia	Australia	Pet Grooming
11, 14	Americas	Canada/United States	Medical
	Americas	United States	Food & Beverage
3, 4, 8	Global		Airline
8	Europe	United Kingdom	Private Banking
6	Asia	Hong Kong	Food and Beverage
	Asia		Logistics
4, 5, 8, 9, 10, 11	Global		Food and Beverage
2, 3	Asia/ Global	Mauritius	Resort
	Global		Edutainment Park

CASES	PRIMARY CHAPTERS

SECONDARY CHAPTERS	CONTINENT	COUNTRY	INDUSTRY
	Americas	United States	Range of B2C Services
3	Asia/Americas	Philippines/United States	Management Consulting/Auditing
	Europe	Eastern Europe	Hotel/Hospitality
	Asia	Philippines	Fast Food
	Global		Online Service
11	Asia/Global		Clothing Retailing
	Asia	Singapore	Food and Beverage
	Asia	Vietnam	Insurance
	Americas	United States	Banking
3	Americas	United States	Nature Conservation
	Asia	Singapore	Industrial Supplies
	Americas	United States	Cable Service
15	Continent Asia	Singapore	Library

What Aids Are Available for Instructors?

We have developed pedagogical aids to help instructors develop and teach courses built around this book and to create stimulating learning experiences for students both in and out of the classroom.

Teaching Aids within the Text

▶ An opening vignette, which highlights key issues discussed in the chapter

▶ Learning objectives and milestone markers for these when a section provides material that meet these learning objectives

▶ Boxed inserts throughout the chapters, which often lend themselves well to in-class discussion

▶ Interesting graphics, photographs, and reproductions of advertisements, which enhance student learning, provide opportunities for discussion, and add a visual appeal

▶ Key words, which help to reinforce important terms and concepts

▶ Chapter summaries, which meet each chapter's learning objectives

▶ Review Questions and Application Exercises located at the end of each chapter

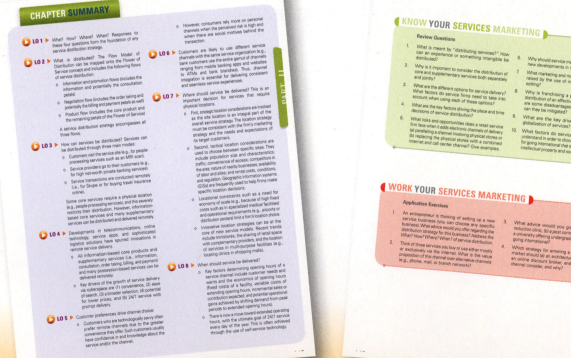

Pedagogical Materials Available from the Publisher

Case Bank: A large set of additional cases that can be used in courses that adopt this textbook. Available in both Word and PDF versions as a resource for instructors. A table shown in the textbook will suggest which cases to pair with which chapters.

Instructor's Manual: A repository of detailed course design and teaching hints, including sample course outlines; chapter-by-chapter teaching suggestions, plus discussion of learning objectives and sample responses to study questions and exercises; suggested student exercises and comprehensive projects (designed for either individual or team work); detailed case teaching notes, including teaching objectives, suggested study questions, in-depth analysis of each question, and helpful hints on teaching strategy designed to aid student learning, create stimulating class discussions, and help instructors create end-of-class wrap-ups and "takeaways."

Test Bank: Multiple choice True/False, short-answer, and essay questions, with page references and difficulty level provided for each question. Contents are classified into general and application. This is available in TestGen format, a test-generating program, which allows instructors to add, edit, or delete questions from the test item file; analyze test results; and organize a database of exams and student results.

PowerPoint Slides: The slides are linked to each chapter and featuring both "word" slides and graphics. All slides have been designed to be clear, comprehensible, and easily readable.

Image Bank: A collection of images in the textbook.

Video Bank: A list of website links that features corporate videos and advertisements to relate concept to application.

EBook: Electronic version of the text that includes useful features such as highlighting and search. It can be viewed on a variety of browsers and devices.

Acknowledgments

Over the years, many colleagues in both the academic and business worlds have provided us with valued insights into the marketing and management of services through their publications, in conference or seminar discussions, and stimulating individual conversations. In addition, both of us have benefited enormously from in-class and after-class discussions with our students and executive program participants.

We're much indebted to those researchers and teachers who helped to pioneer the study of services marketing and management, and from whose work we continue to draw inspiration. Among them are John Bateson of Cass Business School; Leonard Berry of Texas A&M University; Mary Jo Bitner and Stephen Brown of Arizona State University; David Bowen of Thunderbird Graduate School of Management; Richard Chase of the University of Southern California; Bo Edvardsson of University of Karlstad; Pierre Eiglier of Université d'Aix-Marseille III; Raymond Fisk of the Texas State University; Christian Grönroos of the Swedish School of Economics in Finland; Stephen Grove of Clemson University, Evert Gummesson of Stockholm University; James Heskett and Earl Sasser of Harvard University, A. "Parsu" Parasuraman of University of Miami; Roland Rust of the University of Maryland; and Benjamin Schneider formerly of the University of Maryland. We salute, too, the contributions of the late Eric Langeard, Robert Johnston, and Daryl Wyckoff.

Although it's impossible to mention everyone who has influenced our thinking, we particularly want to express our appreciation to the following: Tor Andreassen, Norwegian School of Management; Steve Baron of University of Liverpool; Ruth Bolton of Arizona State University; John Deighton, Theodore Levitt, and Leonard Schlesinger, all currently or formerly of Harvard Business School; Michael Ehret of Nottingham Trent University; Dominik Georgi of Lucerne School of Business; Loizos Heracleous of University of Warwick; Douglas Hoffmann of Colorado State University; Irene Ng of University of Warwick; Jay Kandampully of Ohio State University; Ron Kaufman of UP! Your Service College; Sheryl Kimes of Cornell University; Tim Keiningham of Rockbridge Associate; Jean-Claude Larréché of INSEAD; Jos Lemmink of Maastricht University; Kay Lemon of Boston College; David Maister of Maister Associates; Anna Mattila of Pennsylvania State University; Ulrich Orth of Kiel University; Chiara Orsingher of University of Bologna; Anat Rafaeli of Technion-Israeli Institute of Technology, Ram Ramaseshan of Curtin University; Frederick Reichheld of Bain & Co; Jim Spohrer of IBM; Bernd Stauss formerly of Katholische Universität Eichstät; Christopher Tang of UCLA; Rodoula Tsiotsou of University of Macedonia; Charles Weinberg of the University of British Columbia; Lauren Wright of California State University, Chico; George Yip of London Business School; Ping Xiao of the National University of Singapore; and Valarie Zeithaml of the University of North Carolina.

We've also gained important insights from our co-authors on international adaptations of *Services Marketing*, and are grateful for the friendship and collaboration of Guillermo D'Andrea of Universidad Austral, Argentina; Harvir S. Bansal of University of Waterloo, Canada; Jayanta

Chatterjee of Indian Institute of Technolgy at Kanpur, India; Xiucheng Fan of Fudan University, China; Miguel Angelo Hemzo, Universidade de São Paulo, Brazil; Hean Tat Keh of the University of Queensland, Australia; Luis Huete of IESE, Spain; Laura Iacovone of University of Milan and Bocconi University, Italy; Denis Lapert of Telecom École de Management, France; Barbara Lewis of Manchester School of Management, UK; Xiongwen Lu of Fudan University, China; Paul Maglio of University of California, Merced, USA; Annie Munos, Euromed Marseille École de Management, France; Jacky Mussry of MarkPlus, Inc., Indonesia; Javier Reynoso of Tec de Monterrey, Mexico; Paul Patterson of the University of New South Wales, Australia; Sandra Vandermerwe of Imperial College, London, UK; and Yoshio Shirai of Takasaki City University of Economics, Japan.

It's a pleasure to acknowledge the insightful and helpful comments of reviewers of this and previous editions: Christian Brock, Zeppelin University, Germany; Peter Jones, University of Gloucestershire, United Kingdom; Leung Lai-cheung Leo of Lingnan University, Hong Kong; and Bernardette Jacynta Henry of Universiti Teknologi MARA (UiTM), Sabah, Malaysia; Viktor Magnusson, Linnaeus University, Sweden; and Kai Saldsieder, Pforzheim University of Applied Sciences, Germany. They challenged our thinking and encouraged us to include many substantial changes.

It takes more than authors to create a book and its supplements. Warm thanks are due to the editing and production team who worked hard to transform our manuscript into a handsome published text. They include Ananya Srivastava, Acquisitions Editor; Yajnaseni Das, Managing Editor; and Daniel Luiz, Senior Project Editor.

Finally, we'd like to thank you, our reader, for your interest in this exciting and fast-evolving field of services marketing. If you have interesting research, examples, stories, cases, videos, or any other materials that would look good in the next edition of this book, or any feedback, please do contact us via www.JochenWirtz.com. We'd love to hear from you!

JOCHEN WIRTZ
CHRISTOPHER LOVELOCK

Essentials of
Services Marketing

AT YOUR SERVICE

PART **I**

THE *ESM* FRAMEWORK

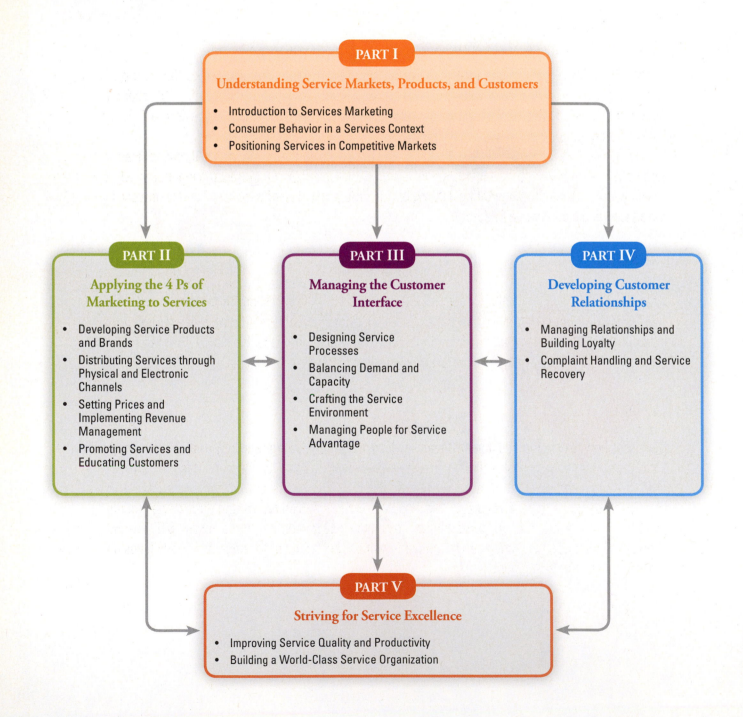

PART I

Understanding Service Markets, Products, and Customers

- Introduction to Services Marketing
- Consumer Behavior in a Services Context
- Positioning Services in Competitive Markets

PART II

Applying the 4 Ps of Marketing to Services

- Developing Service Products and Brands
- Distributing Services through Physical and Electronic Channels
- Setting Prices and Implementing Revenue Management
- Promoting Services and Educating Customers

PART III

Managing the Customer Interface

- Designing Service Processes
- Balancing Demand and Capacity
- Crafting the Service Environment
- Managing People for Service Advantage

PART IV

Developing Customer Relationships

- Managing Relationships and Building Loyalty
- Complaint Handling and Service Recovery

PART V

Striving for Service Excellence

- Improving Service Quality and Productivity
- Building a World-Class Service Organization

Understanding Service Markets, Products, and Customers

Part I lays the building blocks for studying services and learning how one can become an effective service marketer. It consists of the following three chapters:

Chapter 1 Introduction to Services Marketing

Chapter 1 highlights the importance of services in our economies. We also define the nature of services and how they create value for customers without transfer of ownership. The chapter highlights some distinctive challenges involved in marketing services and introduces the 7 Ps of services marketing.

The framework shown in Figure 1.1 on the facing page will accompany us throughout as it forms the basis for each of the four parts in this book. It describes in a systematic manner of what is involved in developing marketing strategies for different types of services. The framework is introduced and explained in Chapter 1.

Chapter 2 Consumer Behavior in a Services Context

Chapter 2 provides a foundation for understanding consumer needs and behavior related to services. The chapter is organized around the three-stage model of service consumption that explores how customers search for and evaluate alternative services, make purchase decisions, experience and respond to service encounters, evaluate service performance, and finally, develop loyalty.

Chapter 3 Positioning Services in Competitive Markets

Discusses how to develop a customer-driven services marketing strategy and how a value proposition should be positioned in a way that creates competitive advantage for the firm. This chapter first links the customer, competitor, and company (commonly referred to as 3 Cs) analysis links to a firm's positioning strategy. The core of the chapter is then organized around the three key elements of positioning—segmentation, targeting and positioning (commonly referred to as "STP")—and shows how firms can segment a service market, position their value proposition and finally focus on attracting their target segment.

introduction to
SERVICES
MARKETING

LEARNING OBJECTIVES (LOs)

By the end of this chapter, the reader should be able to:

▶ **LO 1** Understand how services contribute to a country's economy.

▶ **LO 2** Know the principal industries of the service sector.

▶ **LO 3** Identify the powerful forces that are transforming service markets.

▶ **LO 4** Understand how B2B services improve the productivity of individual firms and drive economic development.

▶ **LO 5** Define services using the non-ownership framework.

▶ **LO 6** Identify the four broad "processing" categories of services.

▶ **LO 7** Be familiar with the characteristics of services and the distinctive marketing challenges they pose.

▶ **LO 8** Understand the components of the traditional marketing mix applied to services.

▶ **LO 9** Describe the components of the extended marketing mix for managing the customer interface.

▶ **LO 10** Appreciate that marketing, operations, and human resource management functions need to be closely integrated in service businesses.

▶ **LO 11** Understand the implications of the Service–Profit Chain for service management.

▶ **LO 12** Know the framework for developing effective services marketing strategies.

Figure 1.1 Tertiary education may be one of the biggest service purchases in life.

OPENING VIGNETTE

Introduction to the World of Services Marketing

Like every reader of this book, you're an experienced service consumer. You use an array of services every day, although some—like talking on the phone, using a credit card, riding a bus, downloading music, using the Internet, or withdrawing money from an ATM—may be so routine that you hardly notice them unless something goes wrong. Other service purchases may involve more thought and be more memorable—for instance, booking a cruise vacation, getting financial advice, or having a medical examination.

Enrolling in college may be one of the biggest service purchases you will ever make. The typical university is a complex service organization that offers not only educational services, but also libraries, student accommodation, health-care, athletic facilities, museums, security, counseling, and career services. On campus, you may find a bookstore, a bank, a post office, a photocopying shop, Internet cafes, a grocery store, entertainment, and more.

Your use of these services is an example of service consumption at the individual or business-to-consumer (B2C) level. Organizations also use many business-to-business (B2B) services, which usually involve purchases on a much larger scale than those made by individuals or households.

Unfortunately, consumers aren't always happy with the quality and value of the services they receive. Both individual and corporate consumers complain about broken promises, poor value for money, rude or incompetent personnel, inconvenient service hours, bureaucratic procedures, wasted time, malfunctioning self-service technologies, complicated websites, or a lack of understanding of their needs.

Suppliers of services, who often face stiff competition, appear to have a very different set of concerns. Many owners and managers complain about how difficult it is to find skilled and motivated employees, to keep costs down and make a profit, or to satisfy customers who, they sometimes grumble, have become unreasonably demanding. Fortunately, there are service companies that know how to please their customers even as they run productive and profitable operations. Often, their services are made available through user-friendly self-service technologies, websites, and apps.

You probably have a few favorite firms whose services you like to purchase. Have you ever stopped to think about the way they succeed in delivering services that meet and sometimes even exceed your expectations? This book will show you how service businesses can be managed to satisfy customers and generate profits at the same time. In addition to studying key concepts, organizing frameworks, and tools of services marketing, you will also be introduced to many examples from firms across the United States and around the world. From the experiences of other firms, you can draw important lessons on how to succeed in increasingly competitive service markets.

Figure 1.2 Happy vacationer on a cruise vacation.

Why Study Services
- Services dominate the global economy
- Most new jobs are generated by services
- Understanding services offers personal competitive advantage

Definition of Services
- Services provide benefits without ownership
- Services are economic activities performed by one party to another. Often time-based, these performances bring about desired results to recipients, objects, or other assets. In exchange for money, time, and effort, service customers expect value from access to labor, skills, expertise, goods, facilities, networks, and systems.

Service Sector Industries
In order of contribution to U.S. GDP:
- Government services
- Real estate
- Business and professional services
- Wholesale and retail trade
- Transport, utilities, and communications
- Finance and insurance
- Healthcare services
- Accommodation and food services
- Arts, entertainment, and recreation services
- Other private sector services

Categories of Services by Type of Processing
- People processing (e.g., passenger transport, hairstyling)
- Possession processing (e.g., freight transport, repair services)
- Mental stimulus processing (e.g., education)
- Information processing (e.g., accounting)

Key Trends

General Trends
- Government policies
- Social changes
- Business trends
- Advances in IT
- Globalization

B2B Services Growth
- Outsourcing
- Offshoring
- Firms increasing focus on core competencies
- Increasing specialization of economies
- Increasing productivity through R&D

Services Pose Distinct Marketing Challenges
Services tend to have four frequently cited characteristics: *i*ntangibility, *h*eterogeneity (variability of quality), *i*nseparability of production and consumption, and *p*erishability of output, or *IHIP* for short. Key implications of these features include:
- Most services cannot be inventoried (i.e., output is perishable)
- Intangible elements typically dominate value creation (i.e., services are physically intangible)
- Services are often difficult to understand (i.e., services are mentally intangible)
- Customers are often involved in co-production (i.e., if people processing is involved, the service in inseparable)
- People (service employees) may be part of the service product and experience
- Operational inputs and outputs tend to vary more widely (i.e., services are heterogeneous)
- The time factor often assumes great importance (e.g., capacity management)
- Distribution may take place through nonphysical channels (e.g., information processing services)

Functions
Need to be tightly integrated as together they shape the customer experience, especially:
- Marketing
- Operations
- Human resources
- Information technology

Service-Profit Chain
Shows the tight links between
- Leadership
- Internal quality and IT
- Employee engagement
- Customer value, satisfaction, and loyalty
- Profitability and growth

Putting Service Strategy into Action
This books is structured around an integrated model of services marketing and management that covers:
- Understanding Service Products, Consumers and Markets
- Applying the 4 Ps of Marketing to Services
- Designing and Managing the Customer Interface using the additional 3 Ps of Services Marketing (Process, People, and Physical Environment)
- Developing Customer Relationships
- Striving for Service Excellence

Figure 1.3 An introduction to services marketing.

WHY STUDY SERVICES?

LO 1
Understand how services contribute to a country's economy.

Consider this paradox: we live in a service-driven economy, yet most business schools continue to teach marketing from a manufacturing perspective. If you have already taken a course in marketing, you have probably learned about marketing manufactured products rather than services. Fortunately, a growing and enthusiastic group of scholars, consultants, and educators, including the authors of this book, has chosen to focus on services marketing. This book aims to provide you with the knowledge and skills that are necessary and relevant in tomorrow's business environment.

Services Dominate the Global Economy

The size of the service sector is increasing in almost all countries around the world. As an economy develops, the relative share of employment between agriculture, industry, and services changes dramatically.[1] Even in emerging economies, the service output represents at least half of the Gross Domestic Product (GDP). Figure 1.4 shows how an economy becomes increasingly service-dominated over time as the per capita income rises. In Figure 1.5, we see that the service sector already accounts for almost two-thirds of the value of the global GDP.

Figure 1.6 shows the relative size of the service sector in various large and small economies. Services account for 65% to 80% of the GDP in most developed nations. One exception is South Korea, a manufacturing-oriented country, whose service sector contributes only 58% to the GDP. Jersey, the Bahamas, and Bermuda—all small islands with a similar economic mix—are home to the world's most service-dominated economies. Luxembourg (86%) has the most service-dominated economy in the European Union. Panama's strong showing (78%) reflects not only the operation of the Panama Canal, but also related services such as container ports, flagship registry, and a free port zone, as well as financial services, insurance, and tourism (Figure 1.7).

On the opposite end of the scale is China (46%), an emerging economy dominated by a substantial agricultural sector as well as booming manufacturing and construction industries. However, China's economic growth is now leading to an increase in demand for business and consumer services.

Most New Jobs Are Generated by Services

Due to the rapid growth of the service sector in virtually all countries around the world, new job creation comes mainly from services. Service jobs do not just refer to relatively

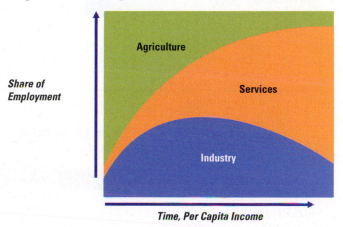

Figure 1.4 Changing structure of employment as an economy develops.

SOURCE
International Monetary Fund, 1997.

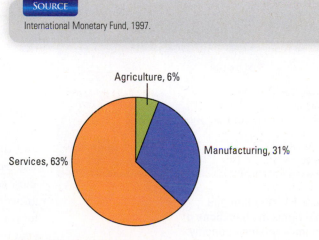

Figure 1.5 Contribution of services industries to GDP globally.

SOURCE
Data from *The World Factbook 2015*, Central Intelligence Agency, www.cia.gov, accessed January 22, 2015.

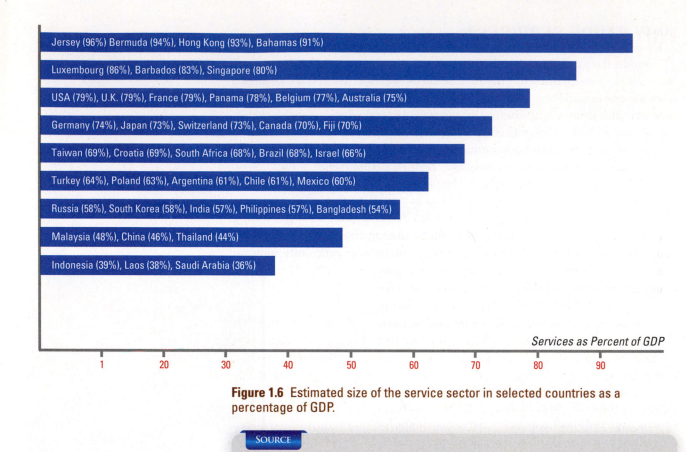

Jersey (96%) Bermuda (94%), Hong Kong (93%), Bahamas (91%)
Luxembourg (86%), Barbados (83%), Singapore (80%)
USA (79%), U.K. (79%), France (79%), Panama (78%), Belgium (77%), Australia (75%)
Germany (74%), Japan (73%), Switzerland (73%), Canada (70%), Fiji (70%)
Taiwan (69%), Croatia (69%), South Africa (68%), Brazil (68%), Israel (66%)
Turkey (64%), Poland (63%), Argentina (61%), Chile (61%), Mexico (60%)
Russia (58%), South Korea (58%), India (57%), Philippines (57%), Bangladesh (54%)
Malaysia (48%), China (46%), Thailand (44%)
Indonesia (39%), Laos (38%), Saudi Arabia (36%)

Services as Percent of GDP

1 20 30 40 50 60 70 80 90

Figure 1.6 Estimated size of the service sector in selected countries as a percentage of GDP.

SOURCE

Data from *The World Factbook 2015*, Central Intelligence Agency, www.cia.gov, accessed January 22, 2015.

Figure 1.7 The Panama Canal forms the backbone of Panama's service economy.

low-paid front-line jobs. Rather, some of the fastest economic growth is in knowledge-based industries, such as professional and business services, education, and healthcare.[2] These well-paid jobs require good educational qualifications and offer attractive careers.

Understanding Services Offers Personal Competitive Advantage

This book is in response to the global transformation of our economies toward services. It discusses the distinctive characteristics of services and the ways in which they affect both customer behavior and marketing strategy. There is a high probability that you will spend most of your working life in service organizations. The knowledge gained from studying this book may create a competitive advantage for your own career, and even encourage you to think about starting your own service business!

WHAT ARE THE PRINCIPAL INDUSTRIES OF THE SERVICE SECTOR?

 **LO 2**

Know the principal industries of the service sector.

What industries make up the service sector, and which are the biggest? The latter may not be the ones you would imagine at first, because this diverse sector includes many services targeted at business customers. Some of these are not very visible unless you happen to work in that industry.

Contribution to Gross Domestic Product

Look at Figure 1.8 to see how much value each of the major service industry groups contributes to the U.S. GDP. Would you have guessed that real estate, rental, and leasing constitute the largest for-profit service industry sector in the United States, accounting for 13% (almost one-eighth) of the GDP in 2013? Over 90% of this figure comes from such activities as renting residential or commercial property; providing realty services to facilitate purchases, sales, and rentals; and appraising property to determine its condition and value. The remaining 10% involves the renting or leasing of a wide variety of other manufactured products, ranging from heavy construction equipment (with or without operators) to office furniture, tents, and party supplies. Another large cluster of services provides for the distribution of physical products. Wholesale and retail trade accounts for about 11.8% of the GDP.

Other substantial industry sectors or subsectors are professional and business services (11.8%), finance and insurance (7.2%), and healthcare (7.1%). Accommodation and food services constitute 2.7% of the GDP. The arts, entertainment, and recreation subsector—which includes such high-profile consumer services as spectator sports, fitness centers, skiing facilities, museums and zoos, performing arts, casinos, golf courses, marinas, and theme parks—collectively represents a mere 1% of the GDP. Nevertheless, in an economy worth over $17.1 trillion, this last group of services was still valued at an impressive $164 billion in 2013.

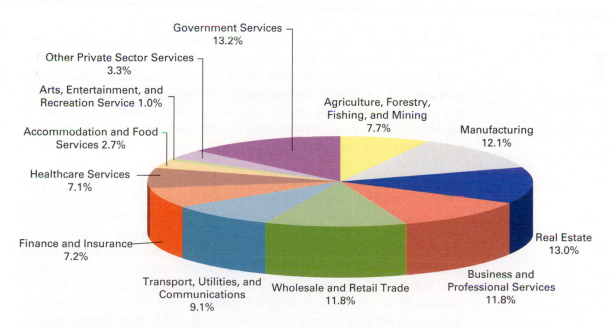

Figure 1.8 Value added by service industry categories to U.S. GDP.

SOURCE

Data from U.S. Department of Commerce, Bureau of Economic Analysis, GDP by Industry Accounts for 2013.

LO 3

Identify the powerful forces that are transforming service markets.

LO 4

Understand how B2B services improve the productivity of individual firms and drive economic development.

POWERFUL FORCES ARE TRANSFORMING SERVICE MARKETS

What are the factors causing this rapid growth of the service sector? Government policies, social changes, business trends, globalization, and advances in information technology and communications are powerful forces that are transforming today's service markets (Figure 1.9). Collectively, these forces reshape demand, supply, and even the way customers buy and use services.

Of these forces, the dramatic development of IT and communications is perhaps the most important. Innovations in big data, cloud computing, user-generated content, mobile communications, networking technologies, artificial intelligence, the Internet of Things, and increasingly app-based self-service technologies have a major impact on the service market. These technologies enable firms to deepen their relationships with customers, offer multi-way information flow and more personalized services, and increase productivity and profitability.[3] More importantly, these new technologies also lead to a vast array of highly innovative business models, ranging from peer-to-peer services (e.g., Airbnb for short-term accommodation and Lending Club for personal loans) and integrators (e.g., Uber, which connects passengers with independent drivers through apps) to crowd-based services (e.g., crowdSPRING, which is a leading provider of logo and graphic design services).

B2B SERVICES AS A CORE ENGINE OF ECONOMIC DEVELOPMENT[4]

A key driver of successful economies is their ecosystem of advanced, competitive, and innovative business services. You may ask, "Why would business services improve the productivity of a manufacturing firm and an economy as a whole?" How good do you think a manufacturing firm is in buying food ingredients; cooking, designing, and running kitchen processes; supervising chefs; and controlling quality and costs in a canteen? The general answer is that the firm would probably not be capable of producing fantastic food, since canteen operations are low-volume and of little importance to the overall business.

Many manufacturing firms have recognized this problem and outsourced their canteen operations, usually via a tendering process with a renewal period of every few years. The winning bidder is likely to be a firm that specializes in running canteens and kitchens across many sites or branches. It focuses on providing food and other services of high quality within a cost-efficient structure. It also makes sense for the firm to invest in process improvements and R&D as the benefits can be reaped across multiple sites. What used to be a neglected support activity within a manufacturing firm thus becomes the core competency of an independent service provider. The same logic applies to almost all non-core activities, assets, goods, and services. Figure 1.10 shows how companies can source services more cost-effectively from third-party providers. McKinsey estimates that such service inputs to manufacturing output are about 20% to 25%, offering much potential for further outsourcing.[5] This development leads to an increasing specialization of our economies with significant improvements in overall productivity and living standards (see Figure 1.11).

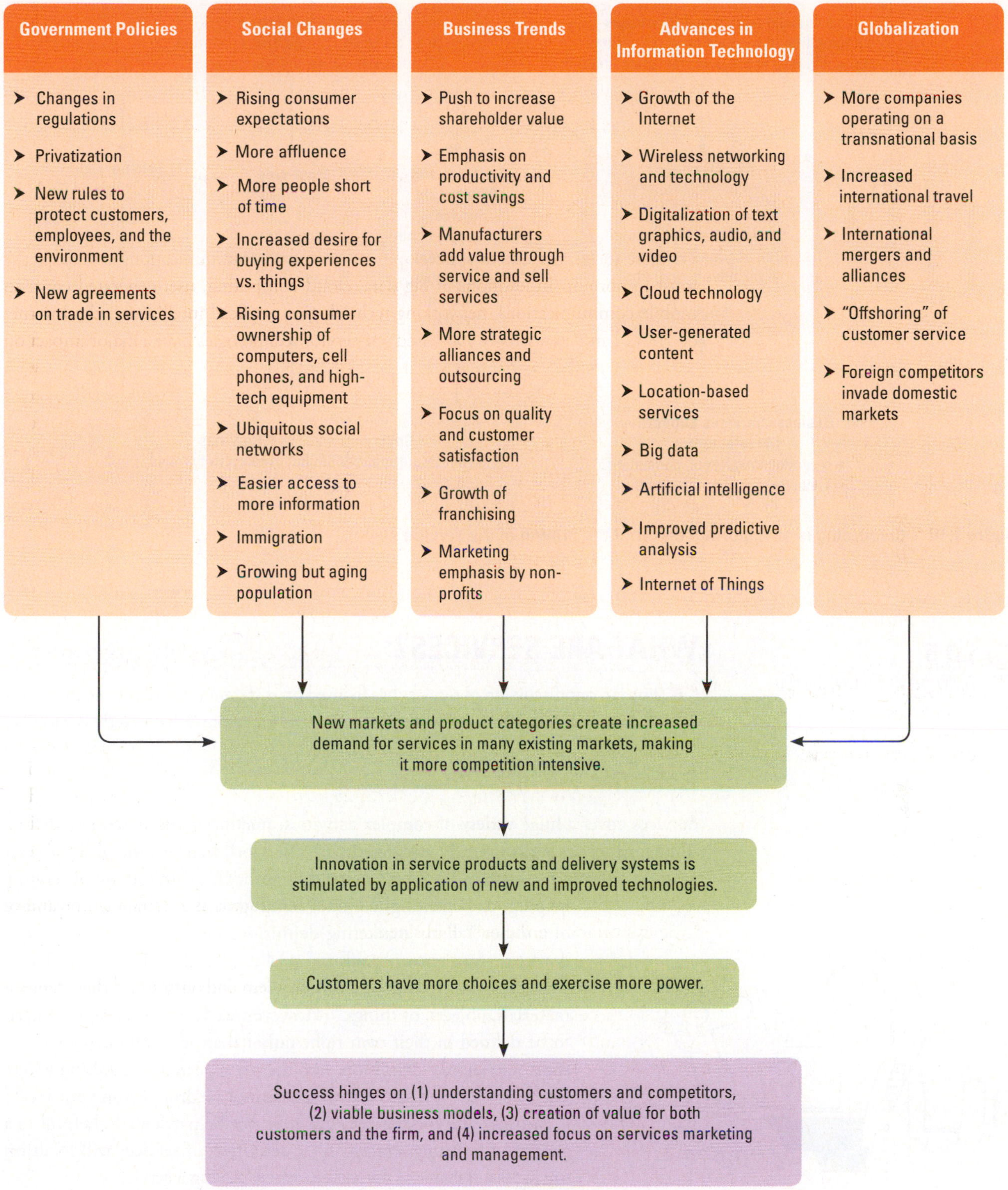

Government Policies	Social Changes	Business Trends	Advances in Information Technology	Globalization
➤ Changes in regulations	➤ Rising consumer expectations	➤ Push to increase shareholder value	➤ Growth of the Internet	➤ More companies operating on a transnational basis
➤ Privatization	➤ More affluence	➤ Emphasis on productivity and cost savings	➤ Wireless networking and technology	➤ Increased international travel
➤ New rules to protect customers, employees, and the environment	➤ More people short of time	➤ Manufacturers add value through service and sell services	➤ Digitalization of text graphics, audio, and video	➤ International mergers and alliances
➤ New agreements on trade in services	➤ Increased desire for buying experiences vs. things	➤ More strategic alliances and outsourcing	➤ Cloud technology	➤ "Offshoring" of customer service
	➤ Rising consumer ownership of computers, cell phones, and high-tech equipment	➤ Focus on quality and customer satisfaction	➤ User-generated content	➤ Foreign competitors invade domestic markets
	➤ Ubiquitous social networks	➤ Growth of franchising	➤ Location-based services	
	➤ Easier access to more information	➤ Marketing emphasis by non-profits	➤ Big data	
	➤ Immigration		➤ Artificial intelligence	
	➤ Growing but aging population		➤ Improved predictive analysis	
			➤ Internet of Things	

New markets and product categories create increased demand for services in many existing markets, making it more competition intensive.

Innovation in service products and delivery systems is stimulated by application of new and improved technologies.

Customers have more choices and exercise more power.

Success hinges on (1) understanding customers and competitors, (2) viable business models, (3) creation of value for both customers and the firm, and (4) increased focus on services marketing and management.

Figure 1.9 Factors stimulating the transformation of the service economy.

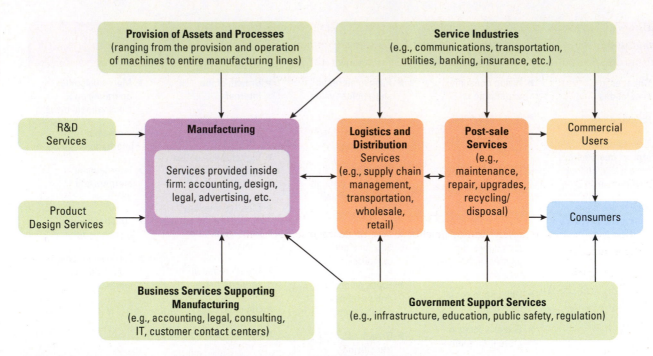

Figure 1.10 Outsourcing is an important driver of the growth of the service sector.

LO 5

Define services using the non-ownership framework.

WHAT ARE SERVICES?

Thus far, our discussion of services has focused on different types of service industries and their development. Now it's time to ask the question: What exactly is a *service*?

Benefits without Ownership

Services cover a huge variety of complex activities, making them difficult to define. The word *service* was originally associated with the work that servants did for their masters. In time, the term came to be defined more broadly as "the action of serving, helping, or benefiting; conduct tending to the welfare or advantage of another."[6] Early marketing definitions described services as "acts, deeds, performances, or efforts" and argued that they had different characteristics from goods, which were defined as "articles, devices, materials, objects, or things."[7] However, we believe that services need to be defined in their own right rather than in relation to goods. A short and snappy definition, like the oft-repeated "something which can be bought and sold but which cannot be dropped on your foot"[8] is amusing and memorable, but may not be particularly helpful as a guide to marketing strategy. Our definition of services will focus on the lack of transfer of ownership when buying a service.

"We found someone overseas who can drink coffee and talk about sports all day for a fraction of what we're paying you."

Figure 1.11 Many services today can be outsourced to lower-cost destinations.

Consider this: you didn't acquire ownership of the hotel room in which you stayed last weekend, you didn't have ownership over the physical therapist who worked on your injured knee, and you didn't receive ownership of the concert you just attended. If you didn't receive a transfer of ownership the last time you purchased a service, then what did you buy?

Christopher Lovelock and Evert Gummesson argue that services involve a form of *rental* through which customers can obtain benefits.[9] We use the term *rent* as a general term to describe payment made for the temporary use of something, or for access to skills and expertise, facilities, or networks (usually for a defined period of time), instead of buying it outright.

We can identify five broad categories within the non-ownership framework of services. These focus on (1) the use of labor, skills, and expertise; (2 to 4) various degrees of use of goods and facilities (exclusive, defined, or shared); and (5) access to and use of networks and systems:

1) **Labor, skills, and expertise rentals.** Here, other people are hired to perform work that customers either cannot or choose not to do themselves. Some of these include:

 o Car repair
 o Medical check-up
 o Management consulting

2) **Rented goods services.** These services allow customers to obtain the exclusive temporary right to use a physical object that they prefer not to own. Examples include:

 o Boats
 o Fancy-dress costumes
 o Construction and excavation equipment

3) **Defined space and facility rentals.** This is when customers obtain the use of a certain portion of a larger facility such as a building, vehicle, or area. They usually share this facility with other customers. Examples of this kind of rental include:

 o A seat in an aircraft
 o A suite in an office building
 o A storage container in a warehouse

4) **Access to shared facilities.** Customers rent the right to share the use of a facility. Such facilities may be a combination of indoors, outdoors, and virtual. Examples include:

 o Theme parks
 o Golf clubs
 o Toll roads (Figure 1.12)

5) **Access to and use of networks and systems.** Customers rent the right to participate in a specified network. Service providers offer a variety of terms for access and use, depending on the needs of customers. Examples include:

 o Telecommunications
 o Utilities and banking
 o Social online networks and games (e.g., *League of Legends*)

Figure 1.12 Customers rent the right to use toll roads.

DEFINITION OF SERVICES

> Services are economic activities performed by one party to another. Often time-based, these performances bring about desired results to recipients, objects, or other assets.
>
> In exchange for money, time, and effort, service customers expect value from access to labor, skills, expertise, goods, facilities, networks, and systems. However, they do not normally take ownership of the physical elements involved.[10]

The difference between ownership and non-ownership has a major impact on marketing strategy. For example, the criteria for a customer's choice of service differ when something is being rented instead of owned. Customers who wish to rent a car for a vacation in Hawaii will probably focus on the ease of making reservations, the rental location and hours, the performance of service personnel, and the maintenance of the vehicles. However, if the customers are looking to own a car, then they are more likely to consider factors such as price, brand image, ease of maintenance, running costs, design, color, and upholstery.

Defining Services

We offer the following comprehensive definition of services based on the non-ownership perspective:

Note that we define services as *economic activities* between two parties, implying an exchange of value between the seller and the buyer in the marketplace. We describe services as *performances* that are most commonly *time-based*. We emphasize that purchasers buy services for *desired results*. In fact, many firms explicitly market their services as "solutions" to the needs of potential customers. Lastly, our definition emphasizes that customers *expect to obtain value* from their service purchases *in exchange for their money, time, and effort*. This value comes from *access to a variety of value-creating elements rather than transfer of ownership*.

Service Products versus Customer Service and After-Sales Service

With the growth of the service economy and the emphasis on adding value-enhancing services to manufactured goods, the line between services and manufacturing becomes increasingly blurred. Many manufacturing firms—from car makers Toyota and aerospace engine producers GE and Rolls-Royce to high-tech equipment manufacturers Samsung and Siemens—are moving aggressively into service businesses. Instead of simply bundling supplementary services with their physical products, quite a few firms are now enhancing certain service elements and marketing them as standalone services (see the example of Toyota in Figure 1.13).

The principles discussed in services marketing are equally applicable to manufacturing firms that increase the service component of their offerings. As Theodore Levitt observed long ago, "There are no such things as service industries. There are only industries whose service components are greater or less than those of other industries. Everybody is in service."[11]

FOUR BROAD CATEGORIES OF SERVICES— A PROCESS PERSPECTIVE

▶ **LO 6**
Identify the four broad "processing" categories of services.

Did you notice that the definition of services emphasizes not only value creation through rental and access, but also the desired results that can be brought about to recipients of the service? There are major differences among services depending on what is being processed. Services can "process" people, physical objects, and data, and the nature of the processing can be tangible or intangible. Tangible actions are performed on people's bodies or to their physical possessions. Intangible actions are performed on people's minds or to their non-physical assets. This gives rise to the classification of services into four broad categories. They are *people processing*, *possession processing*, *mental stimulus processing*, and *information processing* (Figure 1.14)[12]. Let's examine why these four different types of processes often have distinctive implications for marketing, operations, and human resource management.

People Processing

From ancient times, people have sought out services directed at themselves, including transportation, food, lodging, health restoration, and beautification (Figure 1.15). To receive these services, customers must enter the *service factory*, a physical location where people or machines (or both) create and deliver service benefits to customers. Sometimes, service providers are willing to bring the necessary tools of their trade to the customers' preferred location. Implications of people-processing services include:

▶ Service production and consumption are simultaneous, which means that the customers must be physically present in the service factory.

▶ The active cooperation of the customer is required. For example, for a manicure service, you would have to cooperate with the manicurist by specifying what you want, sitting still, and presenting each finger for treatment when requested.

▶ There is a need for managers to think carefully about the location of the service operation, the design of service processes and the service environment, demand and capacity management, and output from the customer's point of view.

Possession Processing

Often, customers ask a service organization to provide tangible treatment for some physical possession, such as a house that has been invaded by insects, a malfunctioning elevator (Figure 1.16), the broken screen of a smartphone, a parcel that needs to be sent to another city, or a sick pet.

Figure 1.13 Services like Toyota's interactive navigation service "T-Connect" move beyond the supplementary into the stand-alone.

Who or What Is the Direct Recipient of the Service?		
Nature of the Service Act	**People**	**Possessions**
Tangible Actions	**People processing** (services directed at people's bodies): • Hairstylist • Passenger Transportation • Healthcare	**Possession processing** (services directed at physical possessions): • Freight Transportation • Laundry and Dry Cleaning • Repair and Maintenance
Intangible Actions	**Mental stimulus processing** (services directed at people's minds): • Education • Advertising PR • Psychotherapy	**Information processing** (services directed at intangible assets): • Accounting • Banking • Legal Services

Figure 1.14 Four broad categories of services.

The implications of such services are:

▶ Production and consumption are not necessarily simultaneous. This allows the service firm greater flexibility in designing such services for cost-efficiency.

▶ Customers tend to be less involved in these services. Their involvement may be limited to dropping off or collecting the item. In such instances, production and consumption can be described as *separable*. In other cases, customers may prefer to be present during service delivery. For example, they may wish to supervise the cutting of the hedge, or comfort the family dog while it receives an injection at the veterinary clinic.

Mental Stimulus Processing

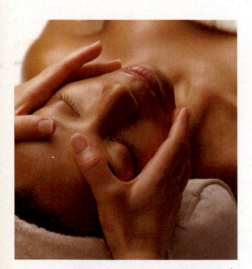

Figure 1.15 A customer getting pampered to look more beautiful.

Mental-stimulus-processing services include education, news and information, professional advice, and some religious activities. Customers are required to invest some time and mental effort to obtain the full benefit of such services. However, they don't necessarily have to be physically present in a service factory. For instance, passengers can sleep through a flight and still arrive at their desired destination. However, if you fall asleep during an online lecture, you won't be any wiser at the end than at the beginning!

As the core content of the services in this category is information-based, it can be digitized and made available via downloads. For instance, the Boston Symphony Orchestra's concerts can be attended live, viewed or heard live, pre-recorded on TV, or sold as digital recordings (Figure 1.17). Key implications that arise from these kinds of services are:

▶ Customers do not have to be physically present in the service factory. They only access the information remotely when they need it.

▶ Services in this category can be "inventoried" for consumption at a later date than their production. The same performance can also be consumed repeatedly.

Information Processing

Figure 1.16 Elevator repair is a possession-processing service.

Information can be processed by information and communications technology (often referred to as ICT), or by professionals. Information is the most intangible form of service output. However, it can be transformed into more permanent and tangible forms such as letters, reports, books, or files in any type of format. Some services that are highly dependent on the effective collection and processing of information are financial and professional services such as accounting (Figure 1.18), law, marketing research, management consulting, and medical diagnosis.

It is sometimes difficult to tell the difference between information and mental stimulus processing services. For example, if a stockbroker analyzes a client's brokerage transactions, it seems like information processing. Yet, when the results of the analysis are used to make a recommendation about the most suitable type of investment strategy, it seems like mental stimulus processing. Therefore, for simplicity, we will periodically combine our coverage of mental-stimulus and information-processing services under the umbrella term of *information-based services*.

SERVICES POSE DISTINCT MARKETING CHALLENGES

▶ LO 7

Be familiar with the characteristics of services and the distinctive marketing challenges they pose.

Can the marketing concepts and practices developed in manufacturing companies be transferred to service organizations where no transfer of ownership takes place? The answer is often "no." Services tend to have different features from goods,

Figure 1.17 Orchestral concerts provide mental stimulation and pleasure.

Figure 1.18 A young couple getting financial advice on buying a new home.

including the frequently cited four characteristics of *i*ntangibility, *h*eterogeneity (variability of quality), *i*nseparability of production and consumption, and *p*erishability of output,[13] or IHIP for short. Table 1.1 explains these characteristics and other common differences between services and goods. Together, these differences cause the marketing of services to differ from that of manufactured goods in several important respects.

It is important to recognize that these differences, while useful generalizations, *do not apply equally to all services.* Intangibility, for example, ranges from tangible-dominant to intangible-dominant (see Figure 1.19 for a scale that presents a variety of examples).[14] Major differences also exist between the four categories of services we discussed in the previous section. For example, customers tend to be part of the service experience only if they have direct contact with service employees. This is usually the case for people-processing services, but not for many information-processing service transactions such as online banking.

THE 7 PS OF SERVICES MARKETING

When developing strategies to market manufactured goods, marketers usually address four basic elements: *p*roduct, *p*lace (or distribution), *p*rice, and *p*romotion (or communication). They are usually referred to as the "4 Ps" of the marketing mix. As is evident from Table 1.1, the nature of services poses distinct marketing challenges. Hence, the 4 Ps of goods marketing are not adequate to deal with the issues arising from marketing services and have to be adapted. We will therefore revisit the traditional 4 Ps of the marketing mix in this book to focus on service-specific issues.

Furthermore, the traditional marketing mix fails to cover the customer interface. We therefore need to extend the marketing mix by adding three Ps associated with service delivery—*process, physical environment,* and *people.* Collectively, these seven elements are referred to as the "7 Ps" of services marketing. Now, let's look briefly at each of the 7 Ps.

LO 8
Understand the components of the traditional marketing mix applied to services.

The Traditional Marketing Mix Applied to Services

Product Elements
Service products lie at the heart of a firm's marketing strategy. If a product is poorly designed, it won't create meaningful value for customers, even if the rest of the 7 Ps are well executed. Thus, the first step is to create a service product that will offer value to target customers and satisfy their needs better than competing alternatives. Service products usually consist of a core product that meets the customers' primary need, and a variety of other elements that help customers use the core product more effectively. Supplementary service elements include providing information, consultation, order taking, hospitality, and handling exceptions.

Place and Time
Service distribution may take place through physical or electronic channels (or both), depending on the nature of the service (see Table 1.1). For example, today's banks offer customers a wide range of distribution channels, including visiting a bank

branch, using a network of ATMs, doing business by telephone, online banking on a desktop, and using apps on a smartphone. In particular, many information-based services can be delivered almost instantaneously to any location in the world that has Internet access. Firms may also deliver their services directly to end-users, or through intermediary organizations that receive a fee or commission to perform certain tasks associated with sales, service, and customer contact. Companies need to decide where and when they can deliver service elements to customers, and the methods and channels they can use.

Distribution of Core versus Supplementary Services. The Internet is reshaping distribution strategies for numerous industries. It can be used to deliver information-based *core products* (those that respond to customers' primary requirements) as well as *supplementary services* that facilitate the purchase and use of physical goods. Examples of information-based core products include online educational programs offered by the Khan Academy and Coursera, and automobile insurance coverage from Progressive Casualty Co.

In contrast, if you buy outdoor gear or book a flight online, the actual delivery of the core product must take place through physical channels. The tent and sleeping bag that you bought from REI (Recreational Equipment Inc.) will be delivered to your home, and you'll have to go to the airport in person to board your United Airlines flight. Much e-commerce activity concerns supplementary services based on the *transfer of information, reservations, and payments,* as opposed to downloading the core product itself.

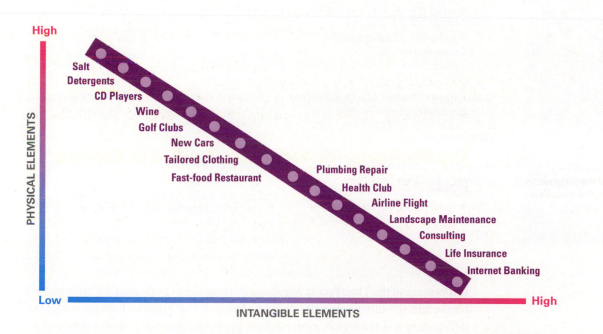

Figure 1.19 Relative value added by physical versus intangible elements in goods and services.

SOURCE

Based on Lynn Shostack, "Breaking Free from Product Marketing," in Journal of Marketing 41: 73–80, April 1977. © Jochen Wirtz

Table 1.1 Managerial implications of eight common features of services.

Difference	Implications	Marketing-related Topics
Most service products cannot be inventoried (i.e., output is perishable).	• Customers may be turned away or have to wait.	• Smooth demand through promotions, dynamic pricing, and reservations. • Work with operations to adjust capacity.
Intangible elements usually dominate value creation (i.e., service is physically intangible).	• Customers cannot taste, smell, or touch these elements and may not be able to see or hear them. • Harder to evaluate service and distinguish from competitors.	• Make services tangible through emphasis on physical clues. • Employ concrete metaphors and vivid images in advertising, branding.
Services are often difficult to visualize and understand (i.e., service is mentally intangible).	• Customers perceive greater risk and uncertainty.	• Educate customers to make good choices, explain what to look for, document performance, offer guarantees.
Customers may be involved in co-production (i.e., if people processing is involved, the service is inseparable).	• Customers interact with providers' equipment, facilities, and systems. • Poor task execution by customers may hurt productivity, spoil service experience, and curtail benefits.	• Develop user-friendly equipment, facilities, and systems. • Train customers to perform effectively; provide customer support.
People may be part of the service experience.	• The appearance, attitude and behavior of service personnel and other customers can shape the experience and affect satisfaction.	• Recruit, train, and reward employees to reinforce the planned service concept. • Target the right customers at the right times; shape their behavior.
Operational inputs and outputs tend to vary more widely (i.e., services are heterogeneous).	• Harder to maintain consistency, reliability, and service quality or to lower costs through higher productivity. • Difficult to shield customers from the results of service failures.	• Set quality standards based on customer expectations; redesign product elements for simplicity and failure-proofing. • Institute good service recovery procedures. • Automate customer-provider interactions; perform work while customers are absent.
The time factor often assumes great importance.	• Customers see time as a scarce resource to be spent wisely, dislike wasting time waiting, and want service at times that are convenient.	• Find ways to compete on speed of delivery, minimize burden of waiting, offer extended service hours.
Distribution may take place through nonphysical channels.	• Information-based services can be delivered through electronic channels such as the Internet or voice telecommunications, but core products involving physical activities or products cannot.	• Seek to create user-friendly, secure websites and free access by telephone. • Ensure that all information-based service elements can be downloaded from site.

Importance of the Time Factor. Speed and convenience of place and time are important for the effective distribution and delivery of services (see Table 1.1). Many services are delivered in real time while customers are physically present. Today's customers are highly time-sensitive. They may be willing to pay extra to save time, such as taking a taxi when a city bus serves the same route (see Figure 1.21). Increasingly, busy customers expect services to be available when it suits them, rather than when it suits the supplier. If one firm responds by offering extended hours, its competitors often feel obliged to follow suit. Nowadays, a growing number of services are available 24/7, and via more delivery channels.

Price and Other User Outlays

Payment is very important in allowing a value exchange to take place. The pricing strategy of firms directly affects the income generated. Pricing strategy is often highly dynamic, with price levels adjusted over time according to factors such as customer segment, time and place of delivery, level of demand, and available capacity.

For customers, price is a key part of the costs they must incur to obtain desired benefits. To calculate whether a particular service is "worth it," they may also go beyond money and assess how much time and effort are involved (see Figure 1.22). Service marketers must not only set prices that target customers are willing and able to pay, but also understand—and seek to minimize, where possible—the other costs that customers incur in using the service. These may include additional monetary costs, time spent, unwanted mental and physical effort, and exposure to negative sensory experiences.

Most Service Products Cannot Be Inventoried. Since services involve actions or performances, they are temporary and perishable. They usually cannot be stocked as inventory for future use (see Table 1.1). Although facilities, equipment, and labor can be held in readiness to create the service, each represents productive capacity and not the product. If there is no demand, unused capacity is wasted and the firm loses the chance to create value from these assets. During periods when demand exceeds capacity, customers may be turned away or asked to wait until later. Service marketers must therefore find ways to match demand levels with the available capacity using dynamic pricing strategies.

Figure 1.20 Time is of the essence—service providers must be swift and smart in their customer interactions.

Figure 1.21 Taking a taxi can save time for busy customers.

Figure 1.22 Money is not the only consideration when measuring the cost of a service.

Promotion and Education

Few marketing programs can succeed without effective communication. It plays three vital roles: (1) providing the necessary information and advice; (2) persuading target customers to buy the service product; and (3) encouraging them to take action at specific times. In services marketing, most communication is educational in nature, especially for new customers. Suppliers need to teach their customers about the benefits of the service, where and when to obtain it, and how to participate in service processes to get the best results.

Services Are Often Difficult to Visualize and Understand as Intangible Elements Tend to Dominate Value Creation. Intangibility consists of both mental and physical dimensions. *Mental intangibility* refers to the difficulty in understanding the value and benefits of a service before purchasing it. In contrast, *physical intangibility* is what cannot be touched or experienced by the other senses.[15] Often, intangible elements such as processes, Internet-based transactions, and the expertise and attitudes of service personnel create maximum value in service performances. When customers can't taste, smell, touch, see, or hear these elements (i.e., when the service is physically intangible), it may be more difficult for them to assess important service features before purchase, or to evaluate the quality of the service performance (see Table 1.1).

It is important for a service firm to create confidence in its experience, credentials, and the expertise of its employees. For example, firms can use physical images and metaphors to promote service benefits and demonstrate their competencies (see Figure 1.23). They must also have well-trained service employees to help prospective customers make good choices, educate them on what to expect both during and after service delivery, and help them to move smoothly through the service process. Documenting performance, explaining what was done and why, and offering guarantees are additional ways to reassure customers. Service firms have much to gain from helping customers to appreciate the service offering. After all, if you know how to use a service well, you'll not only have a better service experience and outcome, but your greater efficiency may boost the firm's productivity, lower its costs, and even enable it to reduce the price you pay.

Customer–Customer Interactions Affect the Service Experience. When you encounter other customers at a service facility, they too can affect your satisfaction. How they're dressed, who they are, and how they behave can reinforce or negate the image a firm is trying to project and the experience it is trying to create. The implications are clear: we need to use marketing communications to attract the right customer segments to the service facility, and to educate them on the proper behavior.

LO 9

Describe the components of the extended marketing mix for managing the customer interface.

The Extended Services Marketing Mix for Managing the Customer Interface

Process

Smart managers know that where services are concerned, *how* a firm does things is as important as *what* it does. Therefore, it is necessary to design and implement effective processes for the creation and delivery of services. Badly designed service processes lead to slow and ineffective service delivery, wasted time, and a disappointing experience for customers.

Operational Inputs and Outputs Can Vary Widely. Operational inputs and outputs tend to vary more widely for services. This makes customer service process management a challenge (see Table 1.1). When a service is delivered face-to-face and consumed as it is produced, final "assembly" must take place in real time. However, operations are often distributed across thousands of sites or branches. In such cases, it is difficult for service organizations to ensure reliable delivery, control quality, and improve productivity. As a former packaged goods marketer once observed after moving to a new position at Holiday Inn:

> We can't control the quality of our product as well as a Procter and Gamble control engineer on a production line can . . . When you buy a box of Tide, you can reasonably be 99 and 44/100% sure that it will work to get your clothes clean. When you reserve a Holiday Inn room, you're sure at some lesser percentage that it will work to give you a good night's sleep without any hassle, or people banging on the walls and all the bad things that can happen in a hotel.[16]

Nevertheless, the best service firms have made significant progress in reducing variability by carefully designing customer service processes, adopting standardized procedures and equipment, implementing rigorous management of service quality, training employees more carefully, and automating tasks previously performed by humans.

Customers Are Often Involved in Co-production. Some services require customers to participate actively in co-producing the service product (see Table 1.1). For example, you're expected to help the investment banker understand what your needs are, the kind of risks you are willing to take, and the expected returns. This will enable the banker to advise you on what to invest in. Increasingly, your involvement takes the form of self-service, often using self-service technologies (SSTs) facilitated by smart machines, telecommunications, and the Internet. Thus, well-designed customer service processes are needed to facilitate service delivery.

Demand and Capacity Need to Be Balanced. Manufacturing can ensure a smooth process flow by having an inventory of materials and parts ready for use. For services, the same thing would mean having customers wait in the service process! Therefore, effective service process management involves the balancing of demand and capacity, the design of waiting systems, and the management of the impact of waiting on the customer's psychology.

Figure 1.23 Services and offerings can be communicated through physical images and metaphors.

Figure 1.24 Co-producing the service: working out at the gym under the direction of a personal trainer.

▶ **LO 10**

Appreciate that marketing, operations, and human resource management functions need to be closely integrated in service businesses.

Physical Environment

If your job is in a service business that requires customers to enter the service factory, you'll also have to spend time thinking about the design of the "servicescape."[17] The appearance of buildings, landscaping, vehicles, interior furnishings, equipment, staff members' uniforms, signs, printed materials, and other visible cues provide tangible evidence of a firm's service quality. The servicescape also facilitates service delivery and guides customers through the service process. Service firms need to manage servicescapes carefully, since they can have a profound impact on customer satisfaction and service productivity.

People

Despite advances in technology, many services will always need direct interaction between customers and service employees (see Table 1.1). You must have noticed many times how the difference between one service supplier and another lies in the attitude and skills of their employees. Service firms need to work closely with their human resources (HR) departments and devote special care to the selection, training, and motivation of their service employees (see Figure 1.25). In addition to possessing the necessary technical skills, these individuals also need good interpersonal skills and a positive attitude.

MARKETING MUST BE INTEGRATED WITH OTHER MANAGEMENT FUNCTIONS

As you think about the 7 Ps, it should quickly become clear that marketers working in a service business cannot expect to operate successfully in isolation from managers in other functions. Marketing, operations, human resources (HR), and information technology (IT) are four management functions that play central and interrelated roles in meeting the needs of service customers: Figure 1.26 illustrates this interdependency.

The operations function is primarily responsible for managing service delivery through equipment, facilities, systems, and many tasks performed by customer-contact employees. In most service organizations, operations managers are actively involved in the design of products and processes and the implementation of programs for improving productivity and quality.

HR is often seen as a staff function, responsible for job definition, recruitment, training, reward systems, and the quality of work life. However, in a well-managed service business, HR managers view these activities from a strategic perspective. They understand that the quality and commitment of the front-line are crucial for gaining competitive advantage. Service organizations cannot afford to have HR specialists who do not understand customers. Marketing and operations activities are more likely to be successful when employees have the necessary skills and training to create and maintain customer satisfaction.

IT is a key function, as many service processes are information heavy. At almost every customer touch-point, real-time information is needed (from customer data to prices and available capacity). Operations, HR, and marketing are critically dependent on IT to manage their functions and create value for the organization's customers.

For these reasons, we don't limit our coverage exclusively to marketing in this book. In many of the chapters, you'll also find us referring to service operations, human resource management, and IT.

THE SERVICE–PROFIT CHAIN

The Service–Profit Chain is a conceptual framework that shows how marketing, operations, HR, and IT are integrated in high-performance service organizations. James Heskett and his colleagues at Harvard argue that when service companies put employees and customers first, there is a major change in the way they manage and measure success. They relate profitability, customer loyalty, and customer satisfaction to the value created by productive employees and supported by customer- and employee-centric operations and technology:

> Top-level executives of outstanding service organizations spend little time setting profit goals or focusing on market share. . . . Instead they understand that in the new economics of service, frontline workers and customers need to be the center of management concern. Successful service managers pay attention to the factors that drive profitability. . . . investment in people, technology that supports frontline workers, revamped recruiting and training practices, and compensation linked to performance for employees at every level.

Figure 1.25 Hospitality is shown through employees wearing smart outfits and a ready smile.

The service–profit chain, developed from analyses of successful service organizations, puts "hard" values on "soft" measures. It helps managers target new investments to develop service and satisfaction levels for maximum competitive impact, widening the gap between service leaders and their merely good competitors.[18]

The service–profit chain, shown in Figure 1.27, demonstrates the links in a managerial process that are essential for success in service businesses.

Table 1.2 summarizes what service leaders must do to manage their organizations effectively. Links 1 and 2 focus on customers. They emphasize the need to identify and understand customer needs, make investments to ensure customer retention, and adopt new performance measures to track variables such as satisfaction and loyalty among both customers and employees. Link 3 focuses on customer value created by the service concept and highlights the need for investments to continually improve both service quality and productivity.

Another set of service leadership behaviors (links 4–7) relates to employees and includes organizational focus on the front-line. The design of jobs should offer greater freedom for employees. Managers with potential should be developed. This category also stresses the idea that paying higher wages can actually decrease labor costs because

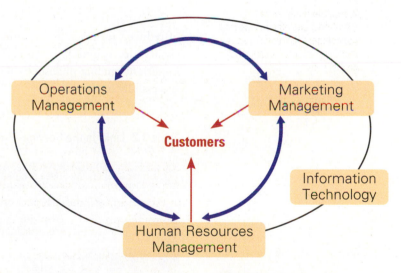

Figure 1.26 Marketing, operations, human resources, and IT must collaborate to serve the customer.

▶ **LO 11**
Understand the implications of the Service–Profit Chain for service management.

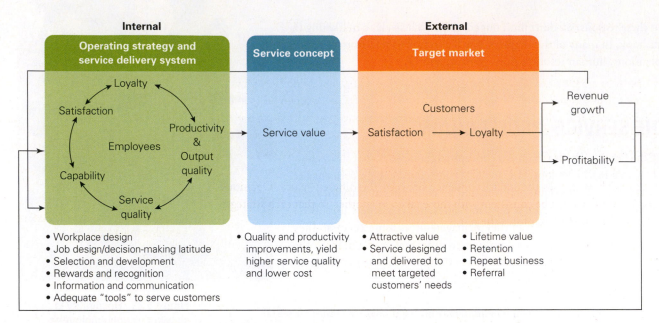

Figure 1.27 The Service–Profit Chain.

SOURCE

From J. L. Heskett, T. O. Jones, G. W. Loveman, W. E. Sasser Jr., and L. A. Schlesinger, "Putting the Service-Profit Chain to Work," Harvard Business School, 1994, p.166.

of reduced turnover, and ensure higher productivity and quality. Underlying the chain's success (link 8) is top management leadership. The service–profit chain is an important guiding philosophy for this book, with core chapters explaining how to successfully implement it.

Table 1.2 Links in the Service–Profit Chain.

1.	Customer loyalty drives profitability and growth
2.	Customer satisfaction drives customer loyalty
3.	Value drives customer satisfaction
4.	Quality and productivity drive value
5.	Employee loyalty drives service quality and productivity
6.	Employee satisfaction drives employee loyalty
7.	Internal quality as delivered by operations and IT drives employee satisfaction
8.	Top management leadership underlies the chain's success.

SOURCE

From J. L. Heskett, T. O. Jones, G. W. Loveman, W. E. Sasser Jr., and L. A. Schlesinger, "Putting the Service-Profit Chain to Work," Harvard Business School, 1994.

A FRAMEWORK FOR DEVELOPING EFFECTIVE SERVICE MARKETING STRATEGIES

▶ **LO 12**
Know the framework for developing effective services marketing strategies.

The 7 Ps and the service–profit chain are integrated into the wider organizing framework of this book. Figure 1.28 presents this organizing framework, which is divided into five parts: (1) *understanding service markets, products, and customers*; (2) *applying the 4 Ps of marketing to services*; (3) *managing the customer interface (i.e., the additional 3 Ps of services marketing)*; (4) *developing customer relationships*; and (5) *striving for service excellence*. Note that the different boxes in the model are linked by arrows. This stresses the interdependence between the different parts. Decisions made in one area must be consistent with those taken in another, so that each strategic element will mutually reinforce the rest.

Figure 1.28 Integrated model of services marketing.

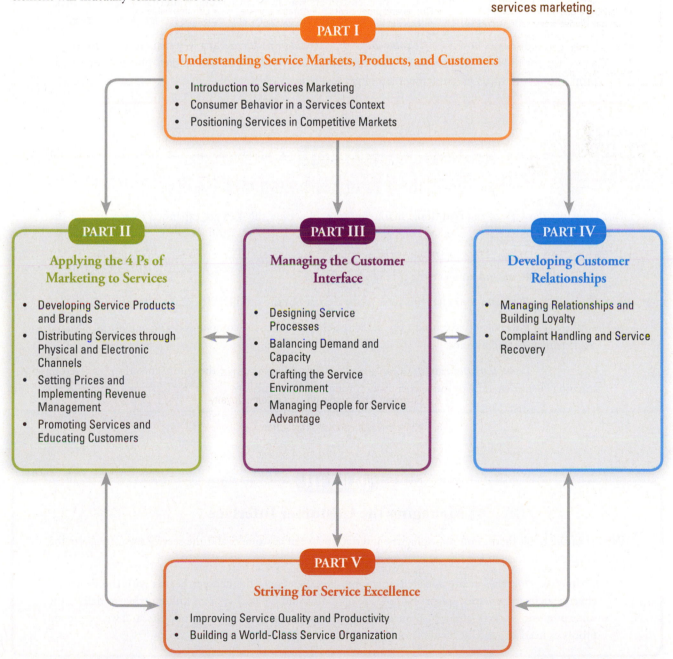

PART I

Understanding Service Markets, Products, and Customers

- Introduction to Services Marketing
- Consumer Behavior in a Services Context
- Positioning Services in Competitive Markets

PART II

Applying the 4 Ps of Marketing to Services

- Developing Service Products and Brands
- Distributing Services through Physical and Electronic Channels
- Setting Prices and Implementing Revenue Management
- Promoting Services and Educating Customers

PART III

Managing the Customer Interface

- Designing Service Processes
- Balancing Demand and Capacity
- Crafting the Service Environment
- Managing People for Service Advantage

PART IV

Developing Customer Relationships

- Managing Relationships and Building Loyalty
- Complaint Handling and Service Recovery

PART V

Striving for Service Excellence

- Improving Service Quality and Productivity
- Building a World-Class Service Organization

The key contents of the five parts of this book are:

PART I

Understanding Service Markets, Products, and Customers

Part I of the book lays the foundation for studying services and learning how to become an effective services marketer.

- Chapter 1—*defines services* and shows how we can create value without transfer of ownership.

- Chapter 2—discusses *consumer behavior* in both high- and low-contact services. The three-stage model of service consumption is used to explore how customers search for and evaluate alternative services, make purchase decisions, experience and respond to service encounters, and evaluate service performance.

- Chapter 3—discusses how a *service value proposition should be positioned* in a way that creates competitive advantage for the firm. The chapter shows how firms can segment a service market, position their value proposition, and focus on attracting their target segment.

PART II

Applying the 4 Ps of Marketing to Services

Part II revisits the 4 Ps of the traditional marketing mix. However, the 4 Ps are expanded to account for the characteristics of services.

- Chapter 4—*Product* includes both the core and supplementary service elements. The supplementary elements facilitate and enhance the core service offering.

- Chapter 5—*Place and time* elements refer to the delivery of the product elements to the customers.

- Chapter 6—*Prices* of services need to be set with reference to costs, competition and value, and revenue management considerations.

- Chapter 7—*Promotion and education* explains the educational nature of the communication involved in teaching customers how to move effectively through service processes.

PART III

Managing the Customer Interface

Part III of the book focuses on managing the interface between customers and the service firm. It covers the additional 3 Ps that are unique to services marketing.

- Chapter 8—*Processes* create and deliver the product elements. The chapter begins with the design of effective delivery *processes*, specifying how the operating and delivery systems link together to deliver the value proposition. Very often, customers are involved in these processes as co-producers, and well-designed processes need to account for that.

- Chapter 9—This chapter also relates to *process management* and focuses on balancing demand and capacity for each step of a customer service process. Marketing strategies for managing demand involve smoothing demand fluctuations, inventorying demand through reservation systems, and formalized queuing.

- Chapter 10—The *servicescape* needs to be engineered to create the right impression and facilitate effective service process delivery. The servicescape provides tangible evidence of a firm's image and service quality.

- Chapter 11—*People* play a key role in services marketing when direct interaction between customers and service personnel is part of the service. The nature of these interactions strongly influences how customers perceive service quality. Hence, service firms devote a significant amount of effort to the recruitment, training, and motivation of employees. The Service Talent Cycle explains how a firm can execute all this effectively.

PART IV

Developing Customer Relationships

Part IV focuses on developing customer relationships and building loyalty.

- Chapter 12—Achieving profitability requires creating *relationships with customers* from the right segments, and then finding ways to build and reinforce their loyalty. This chapter introduces the Wheel of Loyalty, which shows three systematic steps in building customer loyalty. The chapter closes with a discussion of customer relationship management (CRM) systems.

- Chapter 13—A loyal customer base is often built from effective *complaint handling* and *service recovery*. Service guarantees are explored as a powerful way of institutionalizing service recovery, and as an effective marketing tool to signal high-quality service.

PART V

Striving for Service Excellence

Part V focuses on how to develop and transform a firm to achieve service excellence.

- Chapter 14—*Productivity and quality* are strongly related to financial success in services. This chapter focuses on service quality, diagnosing quality shortfalls using the Gaps Model. Customer feedback systems are discussed as an effective tool for systematically listening to and learning from customers. Productivity is also introduced as being closely related to quality.

- Chapter 15—This final chapter discusses how we can move a service organization to higher levels of performance in each functional area.

LO 1 ▶ Services represent an important and growing contribution to most economies in the world. As economies develop, services form the largest part of their GDP. Globally, most new jobs are generated in the service sector.

LO 2 ▶ The principal industries of the service sector include (in order of contribution to GDP):

- o Government services
- o Real estate services
- o Business and professional services
- o Wholesale and retail trade
- o Transport, utilities, and communications services
- o Finance and insurance
- o Healthcare services
- o Accommodation and food services
- o Arts, entertainment, and recreation services

LO 3 ▶ Many forces are transforming our economies, making them more *service-oriented*. They include government policies, social changes, business trends, advances in information technology, and globalization.

LO 4 ▶ Business services allow manufacturing firms and other service organizations to outsource non-core activities, processes, and assets. The benefits include:

- o Economies of scale and scope, and high quality and productivity levels
- o Tight cost and quality control (performance can be benchmarked across many sites)
- o Application of process improvements and R&D

The rapid growth of business services leads to an increasing specialization of advanced economies with significant gains in overall productivity and standards of living.

LO 5 ▶ What exactly is a service? The key distinguishing feature of a service is that it is a form of rental rather than ownership. Service customers obtain the rights to hire the labor, skills, and expertise of personnel; use a physical object or space; or access shared facilities, networks, and systems. Services are performances that bring about the desired results or experience for the customer.

LO 6 ▶ Services vary widely and can be categorized according to the nature of the underlying process. There are four broad categories of services:

- o People processing
- o Possession processing
- o Mental stimulus processing
- o Information processing

Mental stimulus and information processing can collectively be called information-based services.

LO 7 ▶ Services have unique characteristics that make them different from products:

- o Most service products cannot be inventoried (i.e., they are perishable).
- o Intangible elements usually dominate value creation (i.e., they are physically intangible).
- o Services are often difficult to visualize and understand (i.e., they are mentally intangible).
- o Customers may be involved in co-production (i.e., if people processing is involved, the service is inseparable).
- o People may be part of the service experience.
- o Operational inputs and outputs tend to vary widely (i.e., they are heterogeneous).
- o The time factor often assumes great importance.
- o Distribution may take place through non-physical channels.

LO 8 ▶ Due to the unique characteristics of services, the traditional marketing mix of the 4 Ps needs to be amended. Some important amendments are as follows:

- o *Product elements* include not only the core elements, but also supplementary service elements such as the provision of consultation, hospitality, or the handling of exceptions.
- o *Place and time* elements refer to the delivery of the product elements to the customer.
- o *Pricing* includes non-monetary costs to the consumer and revenue management considerations.
- o *Promotion* does not focus only on advertising and promotions, but is also viewed as a form of communication and education that guides customers through service processes.

LO 9 ▶ Services marketing requires three additional Ps that cover management of the customer interface:

- o *Process* refers to the design and management of customer service processes, including managing demand and capacity and related customer waits.
- o *Physical environment*, also known as the servicescape, facilitates process delivery and provides tangible evidence of a firm's image and service quality.
- o *People* covers the recruitment, training, and motivation of service employees to deliver service quality and productivity.

LO 10 ▶ To be successful, marketing, operations, human resource, and IT management functions need to

CHAPTER SUMMARY

be tightly integrated. Integration means that the key deliverables and objectives of the various functions are not only compatible but also mutually reinforcing.

LO 11 ▶ The service–profit chain shows how successful service firms integrate key management functions and deliver high quality performance in several related areas:

o Customer relationships must be managed effectively, and there must be strategies to build and sustain loyalty.

o Value must be created and delivered to the target customers in ways that lead them to see the firm's offerings as superior to competing offerings.

o Service quality and productivity must be continuously improved through better processes, systems and tools, and IT.

o Service employees must be enabled and motivated.

o Top management's leadership needs to drive and support all the components of the service–profit chain.

LO 12 ▶ A framework for services marketing strategy forms the underlying structure of this book. The framework consists of the following five interlinked parts:

o Part I begins with the need for service firms to understand their markets, customers, and competition.

o Part II shows us how to apply the traditional 4 Ps to services marketing.

o Part III covers the 3 Ps of the extended services marketing mix, and shows how to manage the customer interface.

o Part IV illustrates how to develop lasting customer relationships through a variety of tools ranging from the Wheel of Loyalty and CRM to effective complaint management and service guarantees.

o Part V discusses how to improve service quality and productivity. This part closes with a discussion on how change management and leadership can propel a firm to become a service leader.

UNLOCK YOUR LEARNING

LO 1
1. Knowledge-based industries
2. Service science
3. Service sector
4. Service-driven economy

LO 2
1. Contribution to GDP
2. NAICS

LO 3
1. Advances in IT and communications
2. Business trends
3. Globalization
4. Government policies
5. Social change

LO 4
1. Business services
2. Non-core activities
3. Management focus
4. Economies of scale
5. Cost and quality control
6. Process improvements and R&D
7. Specialization of advanced economies

LO 5
1. Acts
2. Deeds
3. Economic activities
4. Efforts

5. Non-ownership
6. Performances
7. Rental

LO 6
1. "Inventoried"
2. Information processing
3. Information-based services
4. Intangible actions
5. Mental stimulus processing
6. People processing
7. Possession processing
8. Tangible actions

LO 7
1. 4 Ps
2. Heterogeneity
3. Inseparability
4. Intangibility
5. Intangible-dominant
6. Perishability
7. Tangible-dominant

LO 8
1. 7 Ps
2. Core products
3. Place and time
4. Price
5. Product elements
6. Promotion and education
7. Service products
8. User outlays

LO 9
1. "Servicescape"
2. Capacity
3. Co-production
4. Demand

5. Operational inputs
6. People
7. Physical environment
8. Process

LO 10
1. Marketing function
2. Operations function
3. Human resources function
4. IT
5. Interfunctional integration

LO 11
1. Customer loyalty
2. Customer satisfaction
3. Productive employees
4. Profitability
5. Service–profit chain
6. Shareholder value
7. Top management leadership

LO 12

1 Complaint handling
2 Customer feedback systems
3 Customer interface
4 Customer relationship management (CRM) systems
5 Customer relationships
6 Delivery processes
7 Gaps Model
8 High-contact services
9 Human resources
10 Low-contact services
11 Marketing
12 Motivating
13 Operations
14 Productive capacity
15 Productivity
16 Quality
17 Recruiting
18 Service excellence
19 Service–profit chain
20 Service recovery
21 Tangible evidence
22 Target segment
23 Training
24 Value proposition
25 Wheel of Loyalty

How well do you know the language of services marketing? Quiz yourself!

⚠ **Not for the academically faint-of-heart**

For each keyword you are able to recall without referring to earlier pages, give yourself a point (and a pat on the back). Tally your score at the end and see if you earned the right to be called—a *services marketeer*.

SCORE

01 – 12   Services Marketing is done a great disservice.

13 – 24   The midnight oil needs to be lit, pronto.

25 – 36   I know what you *didn't* do all semester.

37 – 48   By George! You're getting there.

49 – 60   Now, go forth and market.

61 – 73   There should be a marketing concept named after you.

KNOW YOUR SERVICES MARKETING

Review Questions

1. What are the main reasons for the growing share of the service sector in all major economies of the world?

2. What are the five powerful forces transforming the service landscape, and what impact do they have on the service economy?

3. Why would growth in business services help individual firms and entire economies become more productive?

4. "A service is rented rather than owned." Explain what this statement means, and use examples to support your explanation.

5. Describe the four broad "processing" categories of services, and provide examples for each.

6. What is so special about services marketing that it needs a special approach?

7. "The 4 Ps are all a marketing manager needs to create a marketing strategy for a service business." Prepare a response that argues against this, and support it with examples.

8. Why do the marketing, operations, human resource management, and IT functions need to be closely coordinated in service organizations?

9. What are the implications of the service–profit chain for service management?

10. What are the key elements in the framework for developing effective service marketing strategies?

WORK YOUR SERVICES MARKETING

Application Exercises

1. Visit the websites of the following national statistical bureaus: U.S. Bureau of Economic Analysis (www.bea.gov); Eurostat (ec.europa.eu/eurostat); and the respective websites for your country if they are not covered here. In each instance, obtain data on the latest trends in services as (a) a percentage of the GDP; (b) the percentage of employment accounted for by services; (c) the breakdown of these two statistics by type of industry; and (d) service exports and imports. Looking at these trends, what are your conclusions for the main sectors of these economies and the specific service sectors?

2. Give examples of how Internet and telecommunications technologies (e.g., mobile commerce [M-Commerce] and apps) have changed some of the services you use.

3. Choose a service company you are familiar with, and show how each of the 7 Ps of services marketing applies to one of its service products.

4. Explain how the concepts in Chapter 1 are relevant to the marketing of a religious institution, or a non-profit organization such as World Wildlife Fund.

END**NOTES**

1. Organisation for Economic Co-operation and Development, *The Service Economy* (Paris: OECD, 2000).

2. Marion Weissenberger-Eibl and Daniel Jeffrey Koch, "Importance of Industrial Services and Service Innovations," *Journal of Management and Organization* 13 (2007): 88–101.

3. Roland Rust and Ming-Hui Huang, "The Service Revolution and the Transformation of Marketing Science," *Marketing Science* 33, no. 2 (2014): 206–221.

4. This section is based on: Jochen Wirtz and Michael Ehret, "Service-based Business Models: Transforming Businesses, Industries and Economies," in Raymond P. Fisk, Rebekah Russell-Bennett, and Lloyd C. Harris (eds), *Serving Customers: Global Services Marketing Perspectives* (Melbourne: Tilde University Press, 2013): 28–46. For firms' motivation to use non-ownership services see also: Kristina Wittkowski, Sabine Möller, and Jochen Wirtz, "Firms' Intentions to Use Non-Ownership Services," *Journal of Service Research* 16, no. 2 (2013): 171–185.

5. McKinsey & Company, *Manufacturing the Future: The Next Era of Global Growth and Innovation*, McKinsey Global Institute (November 2012).

6. Lesley Brown, ed., *Shorter Oxford English Dictionary*, 5th edition, 2002.

7. John M. Rathmell, "What Is Meant by Services?" *Journal of Marketing* 30 (October 1966): 32–36.

8. Evert Gummeson (citing an unknown source), "Lip Service: A Neglected Area in Services Marketing," *Journal of Consumer Services* 1 (Summer 1987): 19–22.

9. Christopher H. Lovelock and Evert Gummesson, "Whither Services Marketing? In Search of a New Paradigm and Fresh Perspectives," *Journal of Service Research* 7 (August 2004): 20–41.

10. Adapted from a definition by Christopher Lovelock (identified anonymously as Expert 6, Table II, p. 112) in Bo Edvardsson, Anders Gustafsson, and Inger Roos, "Service Portraits in Service Research: A Critical Review," *International Journal of Service Industry Management* 16, no. 1 (2005): 107–121.

11. From Theodore Levitt, *Marketing for Business Growth*. McGraw-Hill, 1974.

12. These classifications are derived from Christopher H. Lovelock, "Classifying Services to Gain Strategic Marketing Insights," *Journal of Marketing* 47 (Summer 1983): 9–20.

13. Valarie A. Zeithaml, A. Parasuraman, and Leonard L. Berry, "Problems and Strategies in Services Marketing," *Journal of Marketing* 49 (Spring 1985): 33–46.

14. G. Lynn Shostack, "Breaking Free from Product Marketing," *Journal of Marketing* 41 (April 1977): 73–80.

15. John E. G. Bateson, "Why We Need Service Marketing," in O.C. Ferrell, S. W. Brown, and C. W. Lamb Jr. (eds.), *Conceptual and Theoretical Developments in Marketing* (Chicago: American Marketing Association, 1979): 131–146.

16. From Gary Knisely, "Greater Marketing Emphasis by Holiday Inns Breaks Mold," *Advertising Age*, January 15, 1979.

17. The term "servicescape" was coined by Mary Jo Bitner, "Servicescapes: The Impact of Physical Surroundings on Customers and Employees," *Journal of Marketing* 56 (April 1992), 57–71.

18. From J. L. Heskett, T. O. Jones, G. W. Loveman, W. E. Sasser Jr., and L. A. Schlesinger, "Putting the Service-Profit Chain to Work," Harvard Business School, 1994.

consumer behavior in a
SERVICES
CONTEXT

LEARNING OBJECTIVES (LOs)

By the end of this chapter, the reader should be able to:

▶ **LO 1** Understand the three-stage model of service consumption.

▶ **LO 2** Use the multi-attribute model to understand how consumers evaluate and choose between alternative service offerings.

▶ **LO 3** Learn why consumers often have difficulty evaluating services, especially those with many experience and credence attributes.

▶ **LO 4** Know the perceived risks customers face in purchasing services and the strategies firms can use to reduce consumer risk perceptions.

▶ **LO 5** Understand how customers form service expectations and the components of these expectations.

▶ **LO 6** Know the "moment of truth" metaphor.

▶ **LO 7** Contrast how customers experience and evaluate high- versus low-contact services.

▶ **LO 8** Be familiar with the servuction model and understand the interactions that together create the service experience.

▶ **LO 9** Obtain insights from viewing the service encounter as a form of theater.

▶ **LO 10** Know how role, script, and perceived control theories contribute to a better understanding of service encounters.

▶ **LO 11** Describe how customers evaluate services and what determines their satisfaction.

▶ **LO 12** Understand service quality, its dimensions and measurement, and how quality relates to customer loyalty.

Figure 2.1 New York University is the gateway to a brighter future for students like Susan Munro.

OPENING VIGNETTE

Susan Munro, Service Customer[1]

Susan Munro, a final-year business student, had breakfast and then checked the weather app on her iPhone. It predicted rain, so she grabbed an umbrella before leaving the apartment. On the way to the bus stop, she dropped a letter in a mailbox. The bus arrived on schedule. It was the usual driver, who recognized her and greeted her cheerfully as she showed her commuter pass.

On arriving at her destination, Susan walked to the College of Business. Joining a crowd of other students, she found a seat in the lecture theater where her marketing class was held. The professor was a dynamic individual who believed in having an active dialog with the students. Susan made several contributions to the discussion and felt that she had learned a lot from listening to others' analyses and opinions.

After class, Susan and her friends ate lunch at the recently renovated Student Union. It was a well-lit and colorfully decorated food court, featuring a variety of small stores. These included both local suppliers and brand-name fast-food chains, which offered different types of cuisine. There were stores selling sandwiches, crepes, health foods, a variety of Asian cuisine, and desserts. Although Susan wanted a sandwich, there was a long queue at the Subway outlet. Thus, she joined her friends at Burger King and then splurged on a café latte from the Have-a-Java coffee stand. The food court was unusually crowded, perhaps because of the rain. When they finally found a table, they had to clear away the dirty trays. "Lazy slobs!" commented her friend Mark, referring to the previous customers.

After lunch, Susan stopped at the cash machine, inserted her bank card, and withdrew some money. When she remembered that she had a job interview at the end of the week, she telephoned her hairdresser and made an appointment for later. When she left the Student Union, the rain had stopped and the sun was shining.

Susan looked forward to her visit to the hairdresser. The store, which had a bright, trendy décor, was staffed by friendly hairdressers. Unfortunately, the hairstylist was running late, and Susan had to wait for 20 minutes. She used that time to review a human resources course. Some of the other waiting customers were reading magazines provided by the store.

Eventually, it was time for a shampoo, after which the hairstylist proposed a slightly different cut. Susan agreed, although she drew the line at the suggestion that she lighten her hair color. She had never done it before and was unsure about how it would look. She did not want to take the risk just before her job interview. She sat still, watching the process in the mirror and turning her head when asked. She was very pleased with the result and complimented the hairstylist on her work. She tipped the hairstylist and paid at the reception desk.

On the way home, Susan stopped by the dry cleaners to pick up some clothes. The store was rather gloomy and smelled of cleaning solution, and the walls needed repainting. She was annoyed to find that although her silk blouse was ready as promised, the suit that she needed for the interview was not. The assistant, who had dirty fingernails, mumbled an apology in an insincere tone. Although the store was conveniently located and the quality of work was quite good, Susan considered the employees unfriendly and unhelpful, and was unhappy with their service. However, she had no choice but to use them as there were no other dry cleaners nearby.

Back at her apartment building, she opened the mailbox in the lobby. Her mail included a bill from her insurance company. However, it required no action since the payment had been deducted automatically from her MasterCard. She was about to throw away the junk mail when she noticed a flyer promoting a new dry-cleaning store nearby. It even included a discount coupon. She decided to try the new firm and kept the coupon.

Since it was her turn to cook dinner, Susan looked in the kitchen to see what food was available. She sighed when she realized that there was nothing much. She decided to make a salad and call for the delivery of a large pizza.

This story of Susan's day as a service consumer will follow us throughout this chapter to illustrate service-related consumer behavior concepts and theories.

Figure 2.2 Susan is just another customer facing a large selection of services out there.

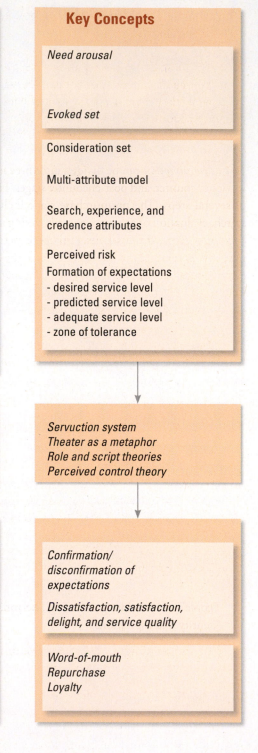

Stages of Service Consumption

1. Pre-purchase Stage

Awareness of need
- Information search
- Clarify needs
- Explore solutions
- Identify alternative service products and suppliers

Evaluation of alternatives (solutions and suppliers)
- Review supplier information (e.g. advertising, brochures, websites)
- Review information from third parties (e.g. published reviews, ratings, comments on the web, blogs, complaints to public agencies, satisfaction ratings, awards)
- Discuss options with service personnel
- Get advice and feedback from third-party advisors and other customers

Make decisions on service purchase and often make reservations

2. Service Encounter Stage

Request service from a chosen supplier or initiate self-service (payment may be upfront or billed later)
Service delivery by personnel or self-service

3. Post-encounter Stage

Evalution of service performance

Future intentions and behaviors

Key Concepts

Need arousal

Evoked set

Consideration set

Multi-attribute model

Search, experience, and credence attributes

Perceived risk
Formation of expectations
- desired service level
- predicted service level
- adequate service level
- zone of tolerance

Servuction system
Theater as a metaphor
Role and script theories
Perceived control theory

Confirmation/ disconfirmation of expectations

Dissatisfaction, satisfaction, delight, and service quality

Word-of-mouth
Repurchase
Loyalty

Figure 2.3 The three-stage model of service consumption.

THE THREE-STAGE MODEL OF SERVICE CONSUMPTION

LO 1

Understand the three-stage model of service consumption.

Susan Munro's story shows consumer behavior in a variety of situations and stages. In marketing, it is very important to understand why customers behave the way they do. How do they make decisions about buying and using a service? What determines their satisfaction with it after consumption? Without this understanding, no firm can hope to create and deliver services that will satisfy customers.

Service consumption can be divided into three main stages. They are the pre-purchase, service encounter, and post-encounter stages. Figure 2.3 shows that each stage consists of several steps. The pre-purchase stage includes awareness of need, information search, evaluation of alternatives, and making a purchase decision. During the service encounter stage, the customer initiates, experiences, and consumes the service. The post-encounter stage includes evaluation of the service performance, which determines future intentions such as wanting to buy again from the same firm and recommending it to friends. The rest of this chapter is organized around the three stages and the related key concepts of service consumption.

PRE-PURCHASE STAGE

The pre-purchase stage begins with *need awareness* and continues through information search and evaluation of alternatives to deciding whether or not to buy a particular service.

Need Awareness

When a person or organization decides to buy or use a service, it is triggered by an underlying need or *need arousal*. The awareness of a need will lead to information search and evaluation of alternatives before a decision is reached. Needs may be triggered by:

- People's unconscious minds (e.g., personal identity and aspirations)

- Physical conditions (e.g., Susan Munro's hunger drove her to Burger King.)

- External sources (e.g., social media or a service firm's marketing activities) (see Figure 2.4)

Susan Munro's need for hair styling, for example, was triggered when she remembered that she had a job interview at the end of the week. She wanted to look her best for the interview. Needs and wants are continuously developing. An example is the need for increasingly novel and innovative service experiences, including extreme sports such as paragliding.

Figure 2.4 As activities such as paragliding are becoming more popular, there is an increase in the number of service providers offering these sports.

Information Search

Once a need has been recognized, customers are motivated to search for solutions to satisfy that need. Several alternatives may come to mind, and these form the *evoked set*. The evoked set can be derived from past experience or external sources such as social media, online reviews and searches, advertising, retail displays, news stories, and recommendations from service personnel, friends, and family. However, a consumer is unlikely to use all the alternatives in the evoked set for decision-making. Only a few alternatives are seriously considered, and these form the *consideration set*. For instance, Susan's consideration set for a quick lunch included the sandwich store and Burger King. During the search process, consumers also learn about service attributes they should consider, and form expectations about how firms in the consideration set are likely to perform on those attributes (see Figure 2.4).

Evaluation of Alternative Services

Once the consideration set and key attributes are understood, the consumer typically makes a purchase decision. In marketing, we often use multi-attribute models to simulate consumer decision making.

Multi-attribute Model

This model holds that consumers use service attributes that are important to them to evaluate and compare the alternative offerings of firms in their consideration set. Each attribute has an importance weight. A higher weight means that the attribute is more important. For example, let's assume that Susan has three alternative dry cleaners in her consideration set. Table 2.1 shows the alternatives as well as the attributes she would use to compare them. The table shows that the quality of the dry cleaning is most important to her, followed by convenience of location, and then price. Susan's final decision can either be guided by the very simple linear compensatory rule, or by the more complex but also more realistic conjunctive rule. Using the same information, Susan can end up choosing different alternatives if she uses different decision rules. It is therefore important for firms to understand through careful market research which rule their target customers are using.

LO 2

Use the multi-attribute model to understand how consumers evaluate and choose between alternative service offerings.

Table 2.1 Modeling consumer choice—Susan Munro's multiattribute model for choosing a dry cleaner.

	Current Dry Cleaner	Campus Dry Cleaner	New Dry Cleaner	Importance Weight
Quality of Dry Cleaning	9	10	10	30%
Convenience of Location	10	8	9	25%
Price	8	10	8	20%
Opening Hours	6	10	9	10%
Reliability of On-time Delivery	2	9	9	5%
Friendliness of Staff	2	8	8	5%
Design of Shop	2	7	8	5%
Total Score	**7.7**	**9.2**	**9.0**	**100%**

Using the linear compensatory rule, Susan mentally computes a global score for each dry cleaner, with scores ranging from 1 to 10. This is done by multiplying the score on each attribute with the importance weight. The scores are then added up. For example, the current dry cleaner would score 9 × 30% for quality of dry cleaning, plus 10 × 25% for convenience of location, plus 8 × 20% for price, etc. If this computation is done for all three alternatives, the current dry cleaner will get a total score of 7.7; the campus dry cleaner, of 9.2; and the new dry cleaner, of 9.0. Therefore, Susan's choice would be the campus dry cleaner.

In the conjunctive rule, the consumer will make the decision based on the total overall score in conjunction with minimum performance levels on one or several attributes. For example, Susan may only consider a dry cleaner that scores a minimum of 9 on convenience of location as she does not want to carry her dry cleaning over longer distances. In that case, her choice is between the current and the new dry cleaner in her neighborhood. She will pick the new dry cleaner because its total score is higher. If none of the brands meets all the cutoffs in a conjunctive model, then Susan may delay making a choice, change the decision rule, or modify the cutoffs.

Service providers can try to influence the decision-making process of their target customers in a number of ways to enhance their chances of being the chosen provider:

▶ Firms need to ensure that their service is in the consideration set, for a firm cannot be chosen without being considered first! This can be done through advertising or viral marketing (see Chapter 7).

▶ Firms can change and correct consumer perceptions. For example, customers may not be aware of the superior performance of the doctors in a clinic in personalized and special care. In such a case, the clinic can focus its communications on correcting customer perceptions.

▶ Firms can also shift importance weights. This can be done by communicating messages that increase the weights of attributes that the firm excels in, and deemphasize those that the firm is not very strong at.

▶ Firms can even introduce new attributes like Hertz did when advertising the environment-friendly car. Consumers who are eco-conscious would then consider the environment aspect when deciding which car rental company to use.

Service Attributes

The multi-attribute model assumes that consumers can evaluate all important attributes before purchase. However, this is often not the case, as some attributes are harder to evaluate than others. There are three types of attributes.[2]

▶ *Search attributes* are tangible characteristics customers can evaluate before purchase. For example, the search attributes for a restaurant include the type of food, location, type of restaurant, and price. These attributes help customers to better understand and evaluate a service, and reduce the sense of uncertainty or risk associated with the purchase.

▶ *Experience attributes* are those that cannot be evaluated before purchase. Customers must "experience" the service before they can assess attributes such as reliability, ease of use, and customer support. For example, you won't know

▶ **LO 3**
Learn why consumers often have difficulty evaluating services, especially those with many experience and credence attributes.

Figure 2.5 Holiday-makers canoeing in Emerald Lake, Yoho National Park, Canada.

how much you actually like the food, the service provided by your waiter, and the atmosphere in a restaurant until you are actually using the service.

Vacations (Figure 2.5), live entertainment performances, and even many medical procedures have high experience attributes. Although people can scroll through websites describing a specific holiday destination, view travel films, read reviews by travel experts and past guests, or hear about the experiences of family members and friends, they cannot really evaluate or feel the dramatic beauty associated with, say, hiking in the Canadian Rockies or snorkeling in the Caribbean until they experience these activities themselves.

Finally, reviews and recommendations cannot possibly account for all situation-specific circumstances. For example, your romantic candlelight dinner at a restaurant may be spoiled if the excellent chef is on a vacation, or if there is a boisterous birthday party at a neighboring table.

▶ **Credence attributes** are characteristics that customers find hard to evaluate even after consumption. Here, the customer is forced to believe or trust that certain tasks have been performed at the promised level of quality. In a restaurant, credence attributes include the hygiene conditions in the kitchen and the quality of the cooking ingredients (e.g., "Do they really use the more expensive olive oil for cooking?").

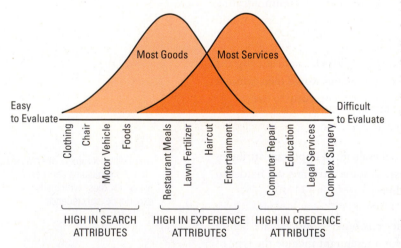

Figure 2.6 How product characteristics affect ease of evaluation.

SOURCE

James H. Donnelly, et al., *Marketing of Services*, reproduced with permission of the American Marketing Association.

It's not easy for a customer to determine the quality of repair and maintenance work performed on a car, and patients can't usually evaluate how well their dentists have performed complex dental procedures. Consider the purchase of professional services such as counseling, surgery, or legal advice. People seek such assistance precisely because they lack the necessary expertise in these fields. How can they be sure that the best possible job was done? Often, it comes down to a matter of having confidence in the service provider's skills and professionalism.

All products can be placed on a continuum ranging from "easy to evaluate" to "difficult to evaluate," depending on whether they are high in search, experience, or credence attributes. As shown in Figure 2.6, most physical goods are located somewhere toward the left of the continuum because they rank high in search attributes. Most services are located from the center to the right of the continuum as they tend to be high in experience and credence attributes.

The harder it is to evaluate a service, the higher is the perceived risk associated with the purchase decision. We will now discuss perceived risk.

Perceived Risk

If you buy physical goods that are unsatisfactory, you can usually return or replace them. With services, this may not be possible. When the hairstylist suggested that Susan lighten her hair color, she declined because she was uncertain about how it would turn out. Her uncertainty increased her *perceived risk*. Perceived risk is usually greater for services that are high in experience and credence attributes, and first-time users are likely to face greater uncertainty. Think about how you felt the first time you had to make a decision about an unfamiliar service, especially one with important consequences, such as choosing a college or a health insurance. It is likely that you were worried about the possibility of not making the best choice. The worse the possible consequences and the more likely they are to occur, the higher the perception of risk. Table 2.2 shows seven categories of perceived risks.

LO 4

Know the perceived risks customers face in purchasing services and the strategies firms can use to reduce consumer risk perceptions.

Table 2.2 Perceived risks in purchasing and using services.

Type of Risk	Examples of Customer Concerns
Functional (unsatisfactory performance outcomes)	• Will this training course give me the skills I need to get a better job? • Could my credit card details be stolen if I register with this website? • Will the dry cleaner be able to remove the stains from this jacket?
Financial (monetary loss, unexpected costs)	• Will I lose money if I make the investment recommended by my stockbroker? • Could my identity be stolen if I make this purchase on the Internet? • Will repairing my car cost more than the original estimate?
Temporal (wasting time, consequences of delays)	• Will I have to wait in line for a long time before I can enter the exhibition? • Will service at this restaurant be so slow that I will be late for my afternoon meeting? • Will the renovations to our bathroom be completed before our friends come to stay with us?
Physical (personal injury or damage to possessions)	• Will there be complications or scars if I go for this cosmetic surgery? • Will the contents of this package get damaged in the mail? • Will I fall sick if I travel abroad on vacation? • Will I get a stomach upset if I eat at this roadside stall?
Psychological (personal fears and emotions)	• How can I be sure that this aircraft will not crash? • Will the consultant make me feel embarrassed or stupid? • Will the doctor's diagnosis upset me?
Social (how others think and react)	• What will my friends think of me if they learned that I registered for the dating service? • Will my relatives approve of the restaurant I have chosen for the family reunion dinner? • Will my business colleagues disapprove of my selection of an unknown law firm?
Sensory (unwanted effects on any of the five senses)	• Will I get a view of the parking lot rather than the beach from my restaurant table? • Will I be kept awake by noise from the guests in the room next door? • Will my room smell of stale cigarette smoke?

Figure 2.7 Winning awards is a cue for service excellence.

People usually feel uncomfortable with perceived risks and use a variety of methods to reduce them, including:

▶ Seeking information from trusted and respected personal sources such as family, friends, and peers.

▶ Using the Web to compare service offerings, search for independent reviews and ratings, and explore discussions on social media.

▶ Relying on a firm that has a good reputation.

▶ Looking for guarantees and warranties.

▶ Visiting service facilities, trying aspects of the service before purchase, and examining tangible cues such as the feel and look of the service setting or awards won by the firm (Figure 2.7).

▶ Asking knowledgeable employees about competing services.

Customers are risk averse and—all else being equal—will choose the service with the lower perceived risk. Therefore, firms need to work proactively on reducing customer risk perceptions. Suitable strategies vary according to the nature of the service and may include the following:

▶ Encourage prospective customers to preview the service through websites and videos and visit the service facilities before purchase.

Figure 2.8 Many caterers organize free food-tasting sessions.

- Offer free trials that are suitable for services with high experience attributes. Many caterers and restaurants offer potential wedding customers free food tasting before making a booking for their wedding banquet (Figure 2.8).

- Advertisement is important for services with high credence qualities and high customer involvement. It helps to communicate the benefits and usage of the service and the ways in which consumers can enjoy the best results. For example, Zurich, an insurance company, uses advertisements to help customers understand what it can do for them (Figure 2.9).

- Display credentials. Professionals such as doctors, architects, and lawyers often display their degrees and other certifications because they want customers to "see" that they are qualified to provide expert service (see Figure 2.10). Many professional firms' websites inform prospective clients about their services, highlight their expertise, and even showcase successful past engagements.

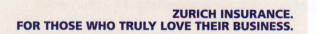

Figure 2.9 Zurich shows customers what it can do for them.

Figure 2.10 Doctor displays his credentials.

▶ **LO 5**

Understand how customers form service expectations and the components of these expectations.

▶ Use *evidence management*, an organized approach where customers are presented with coherent evidence of the company's targeted image and value proposition. This includes the appearance of furnishings, equipment and facilities, and employees' dress and behavior. For example, the bright and trendy décor at the hairdressing salon may have influenced Susan Munro's decision to choose it on her first visit. Now, it probably contributes to her feeling of satisfaction in the end, even though her stylist keeps her waiting for 20 minutes.

▶ Have visible safety procedures that build confidence and trust.

▶ Give customers access to online information about the status of an order or procedure.

▶ Offer service guarantees such as money-back guarantees and performance warranties.

When a company does a good job in managing potential customers' risk perceptions, it reduces uncertainty and increases its own chances of being chosen as the customers' preferred service provider.

Service Expectations

Expectations are formed during the search and decision-making process, and they are heavily shaped by information search and evaluation of alternatives. If you do not have any previous experience with the service, you may base your pre-purchase expectations on online searches and reviews, word of mouth, news stories, or a firm's own marketing efforts.

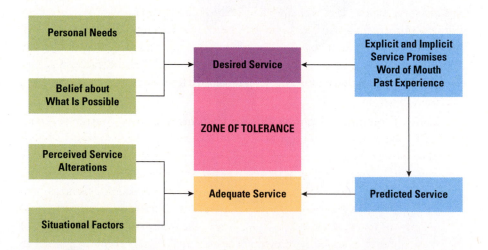

Figure 2.11 Factors influencing customer expectations from the service.

SOURCE

From Valarie A. Zeithaml, Leonard L. Berry and A. Parasuraman, "The Nature and Determinants of Customer Expectations of Service," *Journal of the Academy of Marketing Science*. Springer 1993, pp. 1–12.

Expectations embrace several elements, including desired, adequate, and predicted service, and a zone of tolerance that falls between the desired and adequate service levels.[3] The model in Figure 2.11 shows the factors that influence the different levels of customer expectations. These factors are:

- **Desired service.** This is a "wished for" level of service—a combination of what customers believe can and should be delivered in the context of their personal needs. Desired service can also be influenced by explicit and implicit promises made by service providers, word of mouth, and past experiences.[4] However, most customers are realistic and recognize that a firm can't always deliver the "wished for" level of service. Thus, they have a threshold level of expectations termed *adequate service*, as well as a predicted service level.

Figure 2.12 This photograph creates high expectations for Singapore Airline Suites on its A380 Airbus aircraft.

- **Adequate service.** This is the minimum level of service customers will accept without being dissatisfied.

- **Predicted service.** This is the level of service that customers actually expect to receive. Predicted service can also be affected by service provider promises (Figure 2.12), word of mouth, and past experiences. The predicted service level directly affects how customers define "adequate service" on that occasion. If good service is predicted, the adequate level will be higher than if poorer service is predicted.

Customer predictions of service are often situation-specific. For example, customers visiting a museum on a summer day may expect to see larger crowds if the weather is poor than if the sun is shining. So, a 10-minute wait to buy tickets on a cool, rainy day in summer might not fall below their adequate service level. Another factor that may determine this expectation is the service level anticipated from alternative service providers.

- **Zone of tolerance.** It can be difficult for firms to achieve consistent service delivery at all touch-points across many service delivery channels and thousands of employees. Even the performance of the same service employee is likely to vary from time to time. The extent to which customers are willing to accept this variation is called the zone of tolerance. A very poor performance causes frustration and dissatisfaction, whereas one that exceeds the zone of tolerance can surprise and delight customers. Another way of looking at the zone of tolerance is to think of it as the range of service within which customers don't pay explicit attention to service performance.[5] When service falls outside this range, customers will react, either positively or negatively.

The predicted service level is the most important level for the consumer choice process. Desired and adequate levels and the zone of tolerance are important determinants of customer satisfaction.

Figure 2.13 Consumers have to see whether it is worthwhile to pay a higher price for better seats.

Purchase Decision

After consumers have evaluated possible alternatives by comparing the performances of competing service offerings, assessing the perceived risk associated with each offering, and developing their desired, adequate, and predicted service-level expectations, they are ready to select the option they like best.

Purchase decisions for frequently purchased services are usually quite simple and can be made quickly without too much thought. The perceived risks are low, the alternatives are clear, and, because they have been used before, their characteristics are easily understood. However, in many instances, purchase decisions involve trade-offs. Price is often a key factor. For example, is it worth paying more for a larger room with a better view or a better seat in a theater performance (see Figure 2.13)?

For more complex decisions, trade-offs can involve multiple attributes, as we have seen in the section on consumer choice based on the multi-attribute model. Once a decision is made, the consumer is ready to move to the service encounter stage.

SERVICE ENCOUNTER STAGE

After making a purchase decision, customers move on to the core of the service experience. The service encounter stage involves the direct interaction of the customer with the service firm. We use a number of models and frameworks to understand the consumers' behavior and experience during the service encounter.

LO 6

Know the "moment of truth" metaphor.

Service Encounters Are "Moments of Truth"

Richard Normann borrowed the "moment of truth" metaphor from bullfighting to show the importance of contact points with customers (Figure 2.14):

> [W]e could say that the perceived quality is realized at the moment of truth, when the service provider and the service customer confront one another in the arena. At that moment they are very much on their own. . . . It is the skill, the motivation, and the tools employed by the firm's representative and the expectations and behavior of the client which together will create the service delivery process.[6]

In bullfighting, the life of either the bull or the matador (or possibly both) is at stake. The message in a service context is that at the moment of truth, the relationship between the customer and the firm is at stake.

Jan Carlzon, the former chief executive of Scandinavian Airlines System (SAS), used the "moment of truth" metaphor as a reference point for transforming SAS from an operations-driven business into a customer-driven airline. Carlzon made the following comments about his airline:

Last year, each of our 10 million customers came into contact with approximately five SAS employees, and this contact lasted an average of 15 seconds each time. Thus, SAS is "created" 50 million times a year, 15 seconds at a time. These 50 million "moments of truth" are the moments that ultimately determine whether SAS will succeed or fail as a company. They are the moments when we must prove to our customers that SAS is their best alternative.[7]

Service Encounters Range from High Contact to Low Contact

Services involve different levels of contact with the service operation. Some of these encounters can be very brief and may consist of a few steps, such as when a customer calls a customer contact center or uses a service app. Others may extend over a longer time frame and involve multiple interactions of varying degrees of complexity. For example, a visit to a theme park may last all day. In Figure 2.15, we group services into three levels of customer contact. These represent how much customers interact with service personnel, physical service elements, or both. Although we recognize that the level of customer contact covers a spectrum, it's useful to examine the differences between services at the high and low ends.

Figure 2.14 The service provider is the matador who skillfully manages the service encounter.

LO 7

Contrast how customers experience and evaluate high- versus low-contact services.

▶ **High-contact Services.** Using a high-contact service means that there is direct contact between customers and the firm throughout the service delivery process. When customers visit the facility where the service is delivered, they enter a service "factory". Viewed from this perspective, a hospital is a health treatment factory, and a restaurant is a food service factory. Each of these industries focuses on "processing" people rather than inanimate objects. The marketing challenge is to make the experience appealing for customers both in terms of the physical environment and their interactions with service personnel. During the service delivery process, customers are usually exposed to many physical cues about the organization, such as the exterior and interior of its buildings, equipment and furnishings, appearance and behavior of service personnel, and even other customers. For Susan Munro, the cues at the dry cleaners, such as the gloomy interior and the walls that needed repainting, contributed to her experience of a bad service.

▶ **Low-contact Services.** At the opposite end of the spectrum, low-contact services involve little, if any, physical contact between customers and service providers. Instead, contact takes place at arm's length through electronic or physical distribution channels. For example, customers conduct their insurance and banking transactions by mail, telephone, and Internet. They may also buy a variety of information-based services online rather than from brick-and-mortar stores. In fact, many

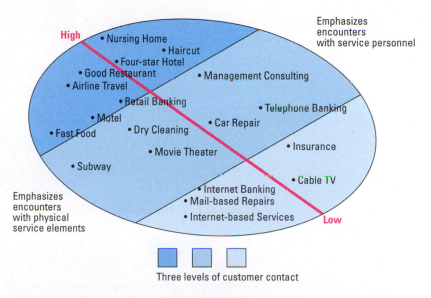

Figure 2.15 Levels of customer contact with service firms.

"I sent you an e-mail and forwarded a copy to your PDA, cell phone, and home computer. I also faxed a copy to your office assistant and laptop. Then I snail-mailed hard copies to you on paper, floppy, and CD. But in case you don't receive it, I'll just tell you what it said..."

Figure 2.16 Today's technology allows services to be conducted at arm's length through electronic or physical distribution channels.

▶ **LO 8**

Be familiar with the servuction model and understand the interactions that together create the service experience.

high-contact and medium-contact services are being transformed into low-contact services as part of a fast-growing trend whereby convenience plays an increasingly important role in consumer choice.

The Servuction System

French researchers Pierre Eiglier and Eric Langeard were the first to conceptualize the service business as a system that integrated marketing, operations, and customers. They coined the term *servuction system* (combining the terms service and production) to describe the part of the service organization's physical environment that is visible to and experienced by customers.[8] The servuction model in Figure 2.17 shows all the interactions that make up a typical customer experience in a high-contact service. Customers interact with the service environment, service employees, and even other customers who are present during the service encounter. Each type of interaction can create value (e.g., a pleasant environment, friendly and competent employees, and other customers who are interesting to observe) or destroy value (e.g., another customer blocking your view in a movie theater). Firms have to "engineer" all interactions to make sure that their customers get the service experience they came for.

The servuction system consists of a technical core and the service delivery system:

▶ **Technical core**—where inputs are processed and the elements of the service product are created. This technical core is typically back-stage and invisible to the customer (e.g., think of the kitchen in a restaurant). As in a theater, the *invisible* components can be termed "backstage" or "back office," while the *visible* components can be termed "frontstage" or "front office."[10] What goes on backstage is usually not of interest to customers unless it directly affects frontstage activities (see Figure 2.18). For example, if a kitchen reads orders wrongly, diners will be upset.

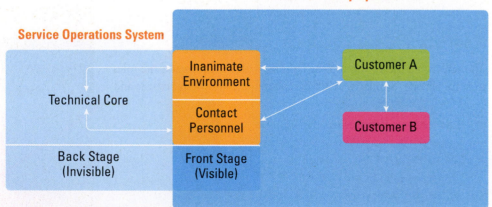

Figure 2.17 The servuction system.

SOURCE

Adapted and Expanded from an original concept by Eric Langeard and Pierre Eiglier, "Services as Systems: Marketing Implications," in Pierre Eiglier, Eric Langeard, Christopher H. Lovelock, John E. G. Bateson, and Robert F. Young (eds.), *Marketing Consumer Services: New Insights* (Cambridge, MA: Marketing Science Institute, Report 77–115, November 1977): 83–103.

- **Service delivery system**—where the final "assembly" takes place and the product is delivered to the customer. This subsystem includes the visible part of the service operations system. Using the theater analogy, the visible front office is like a live theater where the service experience is staged for the customer.

The proportion of the overall service operation that is visible to customers varies according to the level of customer contact. For high-contact services which directly involve the customer, the visible component of the entire service operations tends to be substantial. In contrast, low-contact services usually have most of the service operations system backstage. Frontstage elements are limited to online, telephone, or mail contacts. As customers normally do not see the "factory" where the work is performed, the design and management of such facilities becomes much easier. For example, credit card customers may never have to visit a physical bank—they transact online and may talk to a service employee on the phone only if there is a problem.

Theater as Metaphor for Service Delivery: An Integrative Perspective

Service delivery consists of a series of events that customers experience as a *performance*. The theater is a good metaphor for understanding the creation of service experiences through the servuction system, especially for high-contact service providers[11] (see Figure 2.19). Let us discuss the stage (i.e., service facilities) and the members of the cast (i.e., the front-line personnel):

- **Service facilities.** Imagine service facilities as containing the *stage* on which the drama unfolds.
- **Personnel.** The frontstage personnel are like the members of a cast, playing roles as *actors* in a drama, and supported by a backstage production team. (Figure 2.20).

The theater metaphor also includes the roles of the players on stage and the scripts they have to follow, which we will discuss next.

Role and Script Theories

The actors in a theater need to be familiar with the script and the roles they are playing. Similarly, in service encounters, knowledge of role and script theories can help organizations to better understand, design, and manage both employee and customer behaviors during service encounters.

Role Theory. If we view service delivery from a theatrical perspective, then both employees and customers act out their parts in the performance according to predetermined roles. Stephen Grove and Ray Fisk define a role as "a set of behavior patterns learned through experience and communication, to be performed by an individual in a certain social interaction in order to attain maximum effectiveness in goal accomplishment."[12] Roles have also been defined as combinations of social cues or expectations that guide behavior in a specific setting or context.[13] The satisfaction and productivity of both parties depend on the extent to which each person acts out his or her prescribed role during a service encounter (also called "role congruency").

Figure 2.18 Back office operations are typically not seen by the customer.

 LO 9

Obtain insights from viewing the service encounter as a form of theater.

Figure 2.19 When service facilities and personnel are all in place, the stage is set for a memorable service performance for the customer.

Employees must perform their roles with reference to customer expectations to reduce the risk of dissatisfying customers. Likewise, the customer must "play by the rules" to avoid causing problems for the firm, its employees, and even other customers.

Script Theory. Like a movie script, a service script specifies the sequences of behavior that employees and customers are expected to learn and follow during service delivery. While employees receive formal training, customers learn scripts through experience, communication with others, and designed communications and education.[14] Any deviations from this known script may frustrate both customers and employees.

Many service dramas are tightly scripted (like the flight attendants' scripts for economy class). This reduces variability and ensures uniform quality. Scripts tend to be more flexible for providers of highly customized services—designers, educators, consultants—and may vary by situation and by customer.

Role and Script Theory Complement Each Other. Think of the *roles* played by the professor and the students in the classes that you've attended. Typically, the role of the professor is to deliver a well-structured and interesting lecture that focuses on key topics and engages the students in discussion. The role of the student is to come to class prepared and on time, listen attentively, participate in discussions, and not disrupt the class (Figure 2.21).

By contrast, the opening portion of the *script* for a lecture describes specific actions to be taken by each party. For instance, students should arrive at the lecture hall before the class starts, select a seat, sit down, and open their laptops. The professor then enters, puts notes on the table, turns on the notebook and LCD projector, greets the students, makes preliminary announcements, and starts the class on time. As you can see, the frameworks offered by the two theories are complementary and describe the appropriate behavior during the encounter from two different perspectives.

Perceived Control Theory[15]

The Perceived Control Theory holds that customers have a need for control during the service encounter. The higher the level of perceived control during a service situation, the higher will be their level of satisfaction.[16] The perception of control can be behavioral, decisional, or cognitive.

Behavioral control allows the customer to change the service situation by asking the firm to customize its typical offerings (e.g., asking front-line employees to make special arrangements for a romantic candlelight dinner). Decisional control means that the customer can choose between two or more standardized options without changing either option (e.g., choosing between two tables at a restaurant). Cognitive control is exercised when the customer understands why something is happening (e.g., the flight will be delayed because there is a technical problem with the aircraft) and knows what will happen next (also called predictive control; e.g., knowledge of how long the delay will be). We are often mollified when the service provider keeps us informed about the situation.[17]

The theory of perceived control applies to online services as well. Users of an online service want to know where they are on a website, whether their transaction is being

Figure 2.20 A hotel doorman in a fancy uniform contributes to the performance staged by the guests.

Figure 2.21 Students and professors play well-defined roles during a lecture.

processed, or whether the site has "died" on them (that is why websites usually have a moving icon or processing bar to show that they are working on the transaction). Even self-service machines such as ATMs are designed to make the user feel in control. Did you notice that ATMs make noises to indicate that they are processing your card and haven't simply swallowed it? These sounds are often generated by a chip, as the machine alone would be silent for much of the process.

In short, it is important to design perceived control into service encounters. If processes, scripts, and roles are tightly defined, firms cannot give much behavioral control to customers. However, they can still offer decisional control (e.g., offer two or more fixed options), cognitive control (e.g., explain at great length what is being done and why in high involvement services such as healthcare), and predictive control (e.g., never let the customer wait without indicating how long the wait is likely to be). Perceived control is largely a compensatory additive, which means that a reduction in behavioral control can be compensated through higher decisional and cognitive control.

POST-ENCOUNTER STAGE[18]

The last stage of service consumption is the post-encounter stage, which involves consumers' attitudinal and behavioral responses to the service experience. These include customer satisfaction, service quality perceptions, repeat purchase, and customer loyalty.

Customer Satisfaction

In the post-encounter stage, customers evaluate the service performance they have experienced and compare it with their prior expectations.

The Expectancy-Disconfirmation Model of Satisfaction. Satisfaction is a judgment that follows a series of consumer product interactions. Most customer satisfaction studies are based on the expectancy-disconfirmation model of satisfaction (Figure 2.22).[19] In this model, confirmation or disconfirmation of pre-consumption expectations is the essential determinant of satisfaction.

Where do service expectations in our satisfaction model come from? During the decision-making process, customers assess attributes and risks related to a service offering. They also develop expectations about how the service they choose will perform

LO 11
Describe how customers evaluate services and what determines their satisfaction.

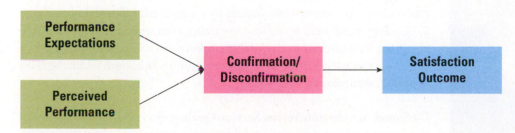

Figure 2.22 The expectancy-disconfirmation model of satisfaction.

SOURCE
Based on Richard L. Oliver and M.E. Sharpe, *Satisfaction: A Behavioral Perspective on the Consumer.* 2nd ed., 2010, p. 120, © Jochen Wirtz.

(i.e., the predicted, desired, and adequate service levels). The zone of tolerance can be narrow and firm if the expectations are related to attributes that are important in the decision-making process. For example, if a customer pays a premium of $350 for a direct flight instead of choosing one that has a four-hour stopover, then he or she will not take it lightly if there is a six-hour flight delay.

During and after consumption, consumers experience the service performance and compare it to their expectations. Satisfaction judgments are then formed on the basis of this comparison. If performance perceptions are worse than expected, it is called *negative disconfirmation*. Susan Munro's expectations were negatively disconfirmed when her blouse was not ready for pick-up at the dry cleaner. This led to her dissatisfaction and her intention to give another dry cleaner a try in the future. If performance is better than expected, it is called *positive disconfirmation*, and if it is as expected, then it is simply called *confirmation of expectations*.

Customers will be reasonably satisfied so long as perceived performance falls within the zone of tolerance, that is, above the adequate service level. If performance perceptions approach or exceed desired levels, customers will be very pleased. Satisfied customers are more likely to make repeat purchases, remain loyal, and spread positive word of mouth. However, if the service experience does not meet their expectations, customers may suffer in silence, complain about poor service quality, or switch to a different provider in the future.

You can see that the attributes used in the decision-making process are used again in the satisfaction evaluation. The satisfaction judgments for individual attributes are aggregated by the consumer to an overall customer satisfaction evaluation. Multi-attribute models help us understand how customer satisfaction is created. Specifically, they help managers to identify the attributes that have a strong impact on overall satisfaction. This is especially important if customers are satisfied with some attributes but dissatisfied with others. Understanding this enables managers to cement the strengths of the firm's services and to focus improvement efforts where they matter most.

 LO 12

Understand service quality, its dimensions and measurement, and how quality relates to customer loyalty.

Service Quality

The intangible nature of services makes them harder to evaluate than goods. In addition, customers often experience the servuction process. Thus, a distinction needs to be drawn between the process of service delivery and the actual output (or outcome) of the service.[20] We define excellent service quality as a high standard of performance that *consistently* meets or exceeds customer expectations. As suggested humorously by the restaurant illustration in Figure 2.23, service quality can be difficult to manage even when failures are tangible in nature. Nevertheless, it is critical to improve service quality and keep it at high levels as it is a key driver of important customer behaviors, including word of mouth, repurchasing, and loyalty.

Customer Satisfaction versus Service Quality. Both customer satisfaction and service quality are determined by comparing customers' expectations with their performance perceptions. However, satisfaction and service quality are very different constructs. Specifically, satisfaction is an evaluation of a single consumption experience. It is a direct and immediate response to that experience and may be seen as a fleeting judgment. In contrast, service quality refers to

Figure 2.23 Service quality is difficult to manage.

relatively stable attitudes and beliefs about a firm. For instance, you may have been dissatisfied with a particular visit to your favorite Starbucks outlet, but you still think that this café is fantastic and offers great service. Of course, satisfaction and quality are linked. Although the perception of a firm's overall service quality is relatively stable, it will change over time in the same direction as transaction-specific satisfaction ratings.[21] And it is service quality that in turn influences repurchase intentions.

Sometimes people also refer to transaction quality (e.g., the quality of food, the friendliness of the server, and the ambiance of a restaurant), which then relates to attribute satisfaction (e.g., satisfaction with the food and service in a restaurant). Both are transaction-specific and determine overall customer satisfaction, which in turn drives service quality beliefs (whether at the attribute or overall level). It is the interchangeable use of these terms that confuses people. However, when we distinguish between transaction-specific judgments and the more stable beliefs and attitudes, the difference in meaning becomes clear.

Note that consumers' repurchase intentions are influenced by their general beliefs about the service quality of the firm rather than by individual, transaction-specific satisfaction judgments formed immediately during and after consumption. Consumers try to predict how good the next service transaction will be. For example, consumers might return to a hairstylist if they think he or she is generally fantastic even if they were unhappy at their last visit. They may view the poor experience as an exception. However, a second or even a third dissatisfaction evaluation will reduce the overall service quality perception of the firm more dramatically and jeopardize repeat visits (see Figure 2.24).

Dimensions of Service Quality. Valarie A. Zeithaml, Leonard Berry, and A. Parasuraman have identified 10 dimensions used by consumers in evaluating service quality (Table 2.3). In subsequent research, they found a high degree of correlation between several of these variables and consolidated them into five broad dimensions:

▶ *Tangibles* (appearance of physical elements)

▶ *Reliability* (dependable and accurate performance)

▶ *Responsiveness* (promptness and helpfulness)

▶ *Assurance* (credibility, security, competence, and courtesy)

▶ *Empathy* (easy access, good communications, and customer understanding)[22]

Measuring Service Quality. To measure service quality, Valarie A. Zeithaml and her colleagues developed a survey instrument called SERVQUAL.[23] It is based on the premise that customers evaluate a firm's service quality by comparing their perceptions of its service with their own expectations. SERVQUAL is seen as a generic measurement tool that can be applied across a broad spectrum of service industries. In its basic form, respondents answer 21 questions that measure their expectations from companies in

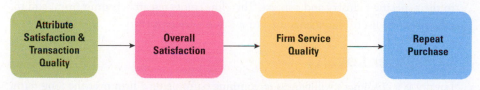

Figure 2.24 From attribute satisfaction to repeat purchase.

Table 2.3 Generic dimensions used by customers to evaluate service quality.

Dimensions of Service Quality	Definition	Sample Illustrations
Tangibles	Appearance of physical facilities, equipment, personnel, and communication materials	Are the hotel's facilities attractive? Is my accountant dressed appropriately? Is my bank statement easy to understand?
Reliability	Ability to perform the promised service dependably and accurately	Does my lawyer call me back when promised? Is my telephone bill free of errors? Is my TV repaired right the first time?
Responsiveness	Willingness to help customers and provide prompt service	When there is a problem, does the firm resolve it quickly? Is my stockbroker willing to answer my questions? Is the cable TV company willing to give me a specific time when the installer will show up?
Assurance • Credibility	Trustworthiness, believability, honesty of the service provider	Does the hospital have a good reputation? Does my stockbroker refrain from pressuring me to trade? Does the repair firm guarantee its work?
• Security	Freedom from danger, risk, or doubt	Is it safe for me to use the bank's ATMs at night? Is my credit card protected against unauthorized use? Can I be sure that my insurance policy provides complete coverage?
• Competence	Possession of the skills and knowledge required to perform the service	Can the bank teller process my transaction without fumbling around? Can my health insurance obtain the information I need when I call? Does the dentist appear to be competent?
• Courtesy	Politeness, respect, consideration, and friendliness of contact personnel	Does the flight attendant have a pleasant demeanor? Are the telephone operators consistently polite when answering my calls? Does the plumber take off muddy shoes before stepping on my carpet?
Empathy • Access	Approachability and ease of contact	How easy is it for me to talk to a supervisor when I have a problem? Does the airline have a 24-hour, toll-free phone number? Is the hotel conveniently located?
• Communication	Listening to customers and keeping them informed in the language they can understand	When I have a complaint, is the manager willing to listen to me? Does my doctor avoid using technical jargon? Does the electrician call when he or she is unable to keep a scheduled appointment?
• Understanding the customer	Making the effort to know customers and their needs	Does someone in the hotel recognize me as a regular guest? Does my financial advisor try to determine my specific financial objectives? Is the moving company willing to accommodate my schedule?

a particular industry on a wide array of specific service characteristics (see Table 2.4). Subsequently, they are asked a matching set of questions on their perceptions of a specific company whose services they have used. When perceived performance ratings are lower than expectations, the service quality is poor. The reverse indicates good quality.

SERVQUAL has been widely used in its generic form as shown in Table 2.4. However, many managers have observed that the measure provides more insights if it is adapted to their specific industry and context. Therefore, most researchers omit from, add to, or change the list of statements used to measure service quality.[24]

Customer Loyalty

Loyalty is a customer's willingness to continue patronizing a firm over the long term, preferably on an exclusive basis, and recommend the firm's products to friends and

Table 2.4 The SERVQUAL scale.

The SERVQUAL scale included five dimensions: tangibles, reliability, responsiveness, assurance, and empathy. Within each dimension, several items are measured. There are many different formats in use, and we show the most basic 21 items for ideal perceptions below. The statements are accompanied by a seven-point scale ranging from "strongly disagree = 1" to "strongly agree = 7".

The firm's performance is measured by rewording the same items (e.g., for item 1 in the table below: "XYZ firm has modern-looking equipment"). The difference between the scores for each item, dimension and for overall service quality is the computed and used as an indicator of a firm's level of service quality.

If measuring both ideal (or expected) and actual performance perceptions is not possible due to time constraints during the interview, both measures can also be combined by using the same 21 items (e.g., "modern-looking equipment") and scale anchors "Lower than my desired service level," "The same as my desired service level," and "Higher than my desired service level."

Tangibles
- Excellent banks (refer to cable TV companies, hospitals, or the appropriate service business throughout the questionnaire) will have modern-looking equipment.
- The physical facilities at excellent banks will be visually appealing.
- Employees at excellent banks will be neat in appearance.
- Materials (e.g. brochures or statements) associated with the service will be visually appealing in an excellent bank.

Reliability
- When excellent banks promise to do something by a certain time, they will do so.
- Excellent banks will perform the service right the first time.
- Excellent banks will provide their services at the time they promise to do so.
- Excellent banks will insist on error-free records.

Responsiveness
- Employees of excellent banks will tell customers exactly when service will be performed.
- Employees of excellent banks will give prompt service to customers.
- Employees of excellent banks will always be willing to help customers.
- Employees of excellent banks will never be too busy to respond to customer requests.

Assurance
- The behavior of employees of excellent banks will instill confidence in customers.
- Customers of excellent banks will feel safe in their transactions.
- Employees of excellent banks will be consistently courteous with customers.
- Employees of excellent banks will have the knowledge to answer customer questions.

Empathy
- Excellent banks will give customers individual attention.
- Excellent banks will have operating hours convenient to all their customers.
- Excellent banks will have employees who give customers personal attention.
- Excellent banks have your best interest at heart.
- The employees of excellent banks will understand the specific needs of their customers.

SOURCE

Based on A. Parasuraman, V.A. Zeithaml, and L. Berry, "SERVQUAL: A Multiple-Item Scale for Measuring Consumer Perceptions of Service Quality," *Journal of Retailing* 64 (1988): 12–40, © Jochen Writz.

associates. Loyalty is an important outcome of customer satisfaction. Customers are not inherently loyal to any one firm! Rather, firms need to give their customers a reason to buy from them and then stay with them. Delivering great service experiences that satisfy customers and build their service quality perceptions is the first and probably the most important step toward building a loyal customer base. Later in this book, we will discuss a number of strategies and tools that are key drivers of loyalty. These include the Wheel of Loyalty in Chapter 12 and complaint management and service recovery in Chapter 13.

LO 1 ▶ Service consumption can be divided into the following three stages: (1) pre-purchase stage, (2) service encounter stage, and (3) post-encounter stage.

o The *pre-purchase stage* consists of the following four steps: (1) need awareness, (2) information search, (3) evaluation of alternative solutions and suppliers, and (4) making a purchase decision.

LO 2 ▶ The following theories help us understand consumer behavior during the pre-purchase stage:

o Recognizing a need motivates customers to search for solutions to satisfy that need. Several alternatives may come to mind, and these form the evoked set. This is further narrowed down to a few alternatives that form the consideration set.

o During the search process, consumers also learn about service attributes they should consider and form expectations about how firms in the consideration set perform on those attributes.

o *Multi-attribute model.* Many decisions involve complex trade-offs along several attributes. The multi-attribute model simulates this decision making by combining customers' attribute performance expectations for each firm in the consideration set and the importance weights of each attribute.

o Two common consumer decision rules in the multi-attribute model are the linear compensatory rule and the conjunctive rule. Given the same attribute ratings, consumers can arrive at different decisions when different decision rules are applied.

o Firms should actively manage key variables in the multi-attribute model to increase the chances of their service being the one chosen.

LO 3 ▶ *Service attributes.* Services are often difficult to evaluate because they tend to have a low proportion of search attributes and a high proportion of experience and credence attributes. Tangible cues become important, and firms need to manage them carefully to shape their customer's expectations and perceptions of experience and credence attributes.

LO 4 ▶ *Perceived risk.* Consumers perceive higher risk when buying services than when buying goods. As customers do not like to take risks, successful firms employ risk reduction strategies such as offering free trials and guarantees.

LO 5 ▶ o *Service expectations.* These are shaped by information search and the evaluation of service attributes. The components of expectations include desired, adequate, and predicted service levels. Between the desired and adequate service levels is the zone of tolerance, within

which customers are willing to accept variation in service levels.

o *Purchase decision.* The outcome of the pre-purchase stage is a purchase decision, based largely on service-level expectations and associated risk perceptions. Many decisions involve complex trade-offs along several attributes, typically including price.

LO 6 ▶ In the *service encounter stage*, the customer initiates, experiences, and consumes the service. A number of concepts and models help us to better understand customer behavior in this stage:

o The "moments of truth" *metaphor* refers to customer touch-points that can make or break a customer relationship.

LO 7 ▶ We distinguish between *high-* and *low-contact services.* High-contact services are challenging as they have many points of contact and moments of truth that have to be managed. In contrast, low-contact services are mostly delivered via websites, equipment (e.g., ATMs), or call centers with relatively few customer interfaces.

LO 8 ▶ o The *servuction model* encompasses a technical core and a service delivery system.

o The *technical core* is backstage and *invisible* to the customers, but what happens backstage can affect the quality of frontstage activities. Therefore, backstage activities have to be coordinated with front-stage activities.

o The *service delivery system* is frontstage and visible to the customer. It encompasses all the interactions that create the service experience. In a high-contact service, it includes customer interactions with the service environment, service employees, and other customers. Each type of interaction can create or destroy value. Firms have to orchestrate all these interactions to create a satisfying service experience.

LO 9 ▶ *Theater can be used as a metaphor for service delivery.* Firms can view their service as the "staging" of a performance with props and actors and manage them accordingly. The props are the service facilities and equipment. The actors are the service employees and customers.

LO 10 ▶ o The actors need to understand their roles and scripts in order to perform their part of the service well. Firms can make use of the *role* and *script* theories to better design, train, communicate, and manage both employee and customer behaviors.

o Consumers have a need to feel in *control.* There are three types of control that can be designed into a service encounter: *behavioral control* (customers can change the service encounter according to their individual preferences), *decisional control* (they can choose between fixed options), and *cognitive control* (they understand what is happening and why, and they know what will happen next; the latter is also called *predictive control*).

o However, if processes, scripts, and roles are tightly defined (e.g., as in fast food or consumer banking), the scope for behavioral control is limited. Here, firms can focus on giving customers more decisional, cognitive, and predictive control.

▶ **LO 11** ▶ In the post-encounter stage, customers evaluate the service performance and compare it to their prior expectations.

o The *expectancy-disconfirmation model of satisfaction* holds that satisfaction judgments are formed by comparing service expectations with performance perceptions.

o Satisfaction is a continuum ranging from great satisfaction to deep dissatisfaction. As long as perceived performance falls within the zone of tolerance (that is, above the adequate service level), customers will be reasonably satisfied. If performance perceptions approach or exceed desired levels, customers will be very satisfied. They will be delighted at unexpectedly high levels of performance. Performance below the adequate service level will result in dissatisfaction.

▶ **LO 12** ▶ o Excellent *service quality* means that a firm *consistently* meets or exceeds customer expectations.

o While customer satisfaction is transaction-specific and refers to a single service experience, service quality refers to a consumer's beliefs and attitudes about the general performance of a firm.

o Consumers use five broad dimensions to evaluate service quality: (1) tangibles, (2) reliability, (3) responsiveness, (4) assurance, and (5) empathy.

o In situations where customer satisfaction and service quality deviate (e.g., "I think the firm in general is great, but the last transaction was poor"), customers use their relatively stable perception of service quality to form their performance expectations for the next purchase. However, a second or third dissatisfaction evaluation will reduce the overall service quality perception of the firm more dramatically and jeopardize repeat visits.

o *SERVQUAL* is a 21-item scale that was designed to measure the five dimensions of service quality. The scale is frequently adapted to the specific context of a particular service, including internet shopping and online services.

UNLOCK YOUR LEARNING

LO 1
1. Consideration set
2. Evaluation of alternatives
3. Evoked set
4. Information search
5. Need arousal
6. Need awareness
7. Pre-purchase stage
8. Service encounter stage
9. Post-encounter stage
10. Purchase decision
11. Service consumption

LO 2
1. Conjunctive rule
2. Linear compensatory rule
3. Multi-attribute model

LO 3
1. Credence attributes
2. Experience attributes
3. Search attributes

LO 4
1. Evidence management
2. Financial risk
3. Functional risk
4. Perceived risk
5. Physical risk

6. Psychological risk
7. Sensory risk
8. Social risk
9. Temporal risk

LO 5
1. Adequate service
2. Desired service
3. Predicted service
4. Purchase decision
5. Service expectations
6. Zone of tolerance

LO 6
1. "moments of truth"

LO 7
1. High-contact services
2. Low-contact services

LO 4
1. Backstage
2. Frontstage
3. Service delivery system
4. Servuction system
5. Technical core

LO 4
1. Performance
2. Personnel
3. Service facilities
4. Theater as metaphor

LO 4
1. Role theory
2. Script theory
3. Perceived control theory

LO 4
1. Confirmation of expectations
2. Expectancy-disconfirmation model of satisfaction
3. Negative disconfirmation
4. Positive disconfirmation
5. Satisfaction

LO 4
1. Service quality
2. Five dimensions of service quality
3. SERVQUAL
4. Customer loyalty

How well do you know the language of services marketing? Quiz yourself!

⚠ **Not for the academically faint-of-heart**

For each keyword you are able to recall without referring to earlier pages, give yourself a point (and a pat on the back). Tally your score at the end and see if you earned the right to be called—a *services marketeer*.

SCORE

01 – 12	Services Marketing is done a great disservice.
13 – 24	The midnight oil needs to be lit, pronto.
25 – 36	I know what you *didn't* do all semester.
37 – 48	By George! You're getting there.
49 – 60	Now, go forth and market.
61 – 73	There should be a marketing concept named after you.

KNOW YOUR SERVICES MARKETING

Review Questions

1. Explain the three-stage model of service consumption.

2. How can customer choice between services in their consideration set be modeled?

3. What is the difference between the linear compensatory rule and the conjunctive rule?

4. Describe search, experience, and credence attributes, and give examples of each.

5. Explain why services tend to be harder for customers to evaluate than goods.

6. Why do consumer's perceptions of risk play an important role in choosing between alternative service offers? How can firms reduce consumer risk perceptions?

7. How are customers' expectations formed? Explain the difference between desired service and adequate service with reference to a service experience you've had recently.

8. What are "moments of truth"?

9. Describe the difference between high-contact and low-contact services, and explain how the nature of a customer's experience may differ between the two.

10. How do the concepts of theater, role theory, and script theory help to provide insights into consumer behavior during the service encounter?

11. Describe the relationship between customer expectations and customer satisfaction.

12. What is service quality? How is it different from customer satisfaction?

13. What are the five dimensions of service quality?

14. How can you measure service quality?

WORK YOUR SERVICES MARKETING

Application Exercises

1. Construct a multi-attribute model to compare three different restaurants for an important celebration in your family. Apply the two different decision rules and determine the choices that arise from that.

2. What are the backstage elements of (a) a car repair facility, (b) an airline, (c) a university, and (d) a consulting firm? Under what circumstances would it be appropriate or even desirable to allow customers to see some of these backstage elements, and how would you do it?

3. Visit the facilities of two competing service firms in the same industry (e.g., banks, restaurants, or gas stations) that you believe have different approaches to service. Compare and contrast their approaches using suitable frameworks from this chapter.

4. Apply the script and role theories to a service of your choice. What insights can you gain that would be useful for management?

5. How can a firm design perceived control into a service encounter? Apply it to one face-to-face and one online encounter.

6. Describe an unsatisfactory encounter you recently experienced with (a) a low-contact service provider via email, mail, or phone and (b) a high-contact, face-to-face service provider. What were the key drivers of your dissatisfaction with these encounters? In each instance, what could the service provider have done to improve the service?

7. How would you define "excellent service quality" for an enquiry/information service provided by your cell phone or electricity service provider? Call a service organization, go through a service experience, and evaluate it against your definition of excellence.

END**NOTES**

1. Adapted and updated from Christopher Lovelock and Lauren Wright, *Principles of Services Marketing and Management*, 2nd ed. (Upper Saddle River, NJ: Prentice Hall, 2001).

2. Valarie A. Zeithaml, "How Consumer Evaluation Processes Differ between Goods and Services," in J. A. Donnelly and W. R. George (eds.), *Marketing of Services* (Chicago: American Marketing Association, 1981): 186–190.

3. Valarie A. Zeithaml, Leonard L. Berry, and A. Parasuraman, "The Behavioral Consequences of Service Quality," *Journal of Marketing* 60 (April 1996): 31–46; R. Kenneth Teas and Thomas E. DeCarlo, "An Examination and Extension of the Zone-of-Tolerance Model: A Comparison to Performance-Based Models on Perceived Quality," *Journal of Service Research* 6, no. 3 (2004): 272–286.

4. Cathy Johnson and Brian P. Mathews, "The Influence of Experience on Service Expectations," *International Journal of Service Industry Management* 8, no. 4 (1997): 46–61.

5. Robert Johnston, "The Zone of Tolerance: Exploring the Relationship between Service Transactions and Satisfaction with the Overall Service," *International Journal of Service Industry Management* 6, no. 5 (1995): 46–61.

6. From Richard Normann, "Service Management: Strategy and Leadership in Service Business." 2nd Edition, John Wiley & Sons, 1991.

7. From Jan Carlzon, "Moments of Truth." Ballinger Publishing Company, 1987.

8. Pierre Eiglier and Eric Langeard, "Services as Systems: Marketing Implications," in Pierre Eiglier, Eric Langeard, Christopher H. Lovelock, John E. G. Bateson, and Robert F. Young (eds.), *Marketing Consumer Services: New Insights* (Cambridge, MA: Marketing Science Institute, Report 77–115, November 1977): 83–103; Eric Langeard, John E. Bateson, Christopher H. Lovelock, and Pierre Eiglier, *Services Marketing: New Insights from Consumers and Managers* (Marketing Science Institute, Report # 81–104, August 1981).

9. Ibid.

10. Richard B. Chase, "Where Does the Customer Fit in a Service Organization?" *Harvard Business Review* 56 (November–December 1978): 137–142; Stephen J. Grove, Raymond P. Fisk, and Joby John, "Services as Theater: Guidelines and Implications," in Teresa A. Schwartz and Dawn Iacobucci (eds), *Handbook of Services Marketing and Management* (Thousand Oaks, CA: Sage, 2000): 21–36.

11. Stephen J. Grove, Raymond P. Fisk, and Joby John, "Services as Theater: Guidelines and Implications," in Teresa A. Schwartz and Dawn Iacobucci (eds.), *Handbook of Services Marketing and Management* (Thousand Oaks, CA: Sage, 2000): 21–36; Steve Baron, Kim Harris, and Richard Harris, "Retail Theater: The 'Intended Effect' of the Performance," *Journal of Service Research* 4 (May 2003): 316–332; Richard Harris, Kim Harris, and Steve Baron, "Theatrical Service Experiences: Dramatic Script Development with Employees," *International Journal of Service Industry Management* 14, no. 2 (2003): 184–199.

12. Stephen J. Grove and Raymond P. Fisk, "The Dramaturgy of Services Exchange: An Analytical Framework for Services Marketing," in L. L. Berry, G. L. Shostack, and G. D. Upah (eds), *Emerging Perspectives on Services Marketing* (Chicago, IL: The American Marketing Association, 1983): 45–49.

13. Michael R. Solomon, Carol Suprenant, John A. Czepiel, and Evelyn G. Gutman, "A Role Theory Perspective on Dyadic Interactions: The Service Encounter," *Journal of Marketing* 49 (Winter 1985): 99–111.

14. Richard Harris, Kim Harris, and Steve Baron, "Theatrical Service Experiences: Dramatic Script Development with Employees," *International Journal of Service Industry Management* 14, no. 2 (2003): 184–199.

15. Parts of this section were adapted from K. Douglas Hoffman and John E. G. Bateson, *Services Marketing: Concepts, Strategies, & Cases*, 4th ed. (Mason, USA: South-Western Cengage Learning, 2011): 100–101.

16. Michael K. Hui and John E. G. Bateson, "Perceived Control and the Effects of Crowding and Consumer Choice on the Service Experience," *Journal of Consumer Research* 18, no. 2 (1991): 174–184; Michael K. Hui and Roy Toffoli, "Perceived Control and Consumer Attribution for the Service Encounter", *Journal of Applied Psychology* 32, no. 9 (2006): 1,825–1,844.

17. Richard B. Chase and Sriram Dasu, "Experience Psychology—A Proposed New Subfield of Service Management," *Journal of Service Management* 25, no. 5 (2014): 574–577.

18. For an excellent and comprehensive review of the extant literature on customer satisfaction and its outcomes see: Richard L. Oliver, *Satisfaction: A Behavioral Perspective on the Consumer*, 2nd ed. (New York: Armonk, M.E. Sharpe, 2010).

19. Richard L. Oliver, "A Cognitive Model of the Antecedents and Consequences of Satisfaction Decisions," *Journal of Marketing Research* 17 (November 1980): 460–469; Eugene W. Anderson and Mary W. Sullivan, "The Antecedents and Consequences of Customer Satisfaction for Firms," *Marketing Science* 12 (Spring 1993): 125–143.

20. Christian Grönroos, *Service Management and Marketing*, 3rd ed. (Chichester, NY: Wiley, 2007).

21. William Boulding, Ajay Kalia, Richard Staelin, and Valarie A. Zeithaml, "A Dynamic Process Model of Service Quality: From Expectations to Behavioral Intentions," *Journal of Marketing Research* 30, no. 1 (1993): 7–27; A. Palmer and M. O'Neill, "The Effects of Perceptual Processes on the Measurement of Service Quality," *Journal of Services Marketing* 17, no. 3 (2003): 254–274.

22. Valarie A. Zeithaml, A. Parasuraman, and Leonard L. Berry, *Delivering Quality Service* (New York: The Free Press, 1990). See also Valarie A. Zeithaml, Mary Jo Bitner, and Dwayne D. Gremler, *Services Marketing: Integrating Customer Focus across the Firm* (New York: McGraw Hill, 2013): 49–105.

23. A. Parasuraman, Valarie A. Zeithaml, and Leonard Berry, "SERVQUAL: A Multiple Item Scale for Measuring Consumer Perceptions of Service Quality," *Journal of Retailing* 64 (1988): 12–40.

24. See, for instance, Anne M. Smith, "Measuring Service Quality: Is SERVQUAL Now Redundant?" *Journal of Marketing Management* 11 (Jan/Feb/April 1995): 257–276; Francis Buttle, "SERVQUAL: Review, Critique, Research Agenda," *European Journal of Marketing* 30, no. 1 (1996): 8–32; Terrence H. Witkowski and Mary F. Wolfinbarger, "Comparative Service Quality: German and American Ratings across Service Settings," *Journal of Business Research* 55 (2002): 875–881; Lisa J. Morrison Coulthard, "Measuring Service Quality: A Review and Critique of Research Using SERVQUAL," *International Journal of Market Research* 46 (Quarter 4, 2004): 479–497.

3

positioning
SERVICES in
COMPETITIVE MARKETS

LEARNING OBJECTIVES (LOs)

By the end of this chapter, the reader should be able to:

▶ **LO 1** Understand how *c*ustomer, *c*ompetitor, and *c*ompany analyses (i.e., the *3 Cs*) help to develop a customer-driven services marketing strategy.

▶ **LO 2** Know the key elements of a positioning strategy (i.e., *STP*) and explain why they are so crucial for service firms.

▶ **LO 3** *S*egment customers on the basis of needs before using other common bases to further identify and profile the segments.

▶ **LO 4** Distinguish between important and determinant attributes for segmentation.

▶ **LO 5** Use different service levels for segmentation.

▶ **LO 6** *T*arget service customers using the four focus strategies for competitive advantage.

▶ **LO 7** *P*osition a service to distinguish it from its competitors.

▶ **LO 8** Understand how to use positioning maps to analyze and develop competitive strategy.

▶ **LO 9** Develop an effective positioning strategy.

OPENING VIGNETTE

Positioning a Chain of Child-care Centers away from the Competition[1]

Roger Brown and Linda Mason met at business school following previous experience as management consultants. After graduation, they operated programs for refugee children in Cambodia and ran a "Save the Children" relief program in East Africa. When they returned to the United States, they saw a need for child-care centers with educational environments that would assure parents of their children's well-being.

Through research, they discovered that the child-care industry in the US had many weaknesses. It lacked regulation, and there were no barriers to entry. The profit margins and economies of scale were low. The industry was also labor intensive and had no clear brand differentiation. Brown and Mason developed a service concept that would allow them to turn these weaknesses into strengths for their own company, Bright Horizons. Instead of marketing their services directly to parents—a one-customer-at-a-time sale—Bright Horizons formed partnerships with companies seeking to create on-site day-care centers for employees with small children. The advantages included:

▶ A powerful, low-cost marketing channel.

▶ A partner/customer who would supply the funds to build and equip the center and would therefore want to help Bright Horizons achieve its goal of delivering high-quality care.

▶ Benefits for parents, who would be attracted to a Bright Horizons center (rather than competing alternatives) because of its nearness to their own workplace, thus lowering travel time and offering greater peace of mind.

Bright Horizons offered a high pay and benefits package to attract the best staff so that they could provide quality service, an aspect that was lacking in many of the other providers. Most traditional approaches to child care either did not have a proper teaching plan or had strict, cookie-cutter lesson plans. Bright Horizons developed a flexible teaching plan called "World at Their Fingertips." Although it had a course outline, it gave teachers control over daily lesson plans.

Bright Horizons sought accreditation for its centers from the National Association for the Education of Young Children (NAEYC) and actively promoted it. Its emphasis on quality allowed it to meet or exceed the highest local and state government licensing standards. As a result, lack of regulation became an opportunity rather than a threat for Bright Horizons and gave it a competitive edge.

With the support and help of its clients, which included many hi-tech firms, Bright Horizons developed several innovative technologies. These included videos of its classrooms that could be streamed to the parents' computers; digitally scanned or photographed artwork; electronic posting of menus, calendars, and student assessments; as well as online student assessment capabilities. All of these served to differentiate Bright Horizons and helped it to stay ahead of the competition.

Bright Horizons sees labor as a competitive advantage. It seeks to recruit and retain the best people. In 2014, it was listed for the fourteenth time as one of the "100 Best Companies to Work for in America" by *Fortune* magazine. By then, Bright Horizons had some 20,000 employees globally and was operating for more than 700 clients in the US, Canada, and Europe. These include the world's leading corporations, hospitals, universities, and government offices. Clients want to hire Bright Horizons as a partner because they know they can trust the staff.

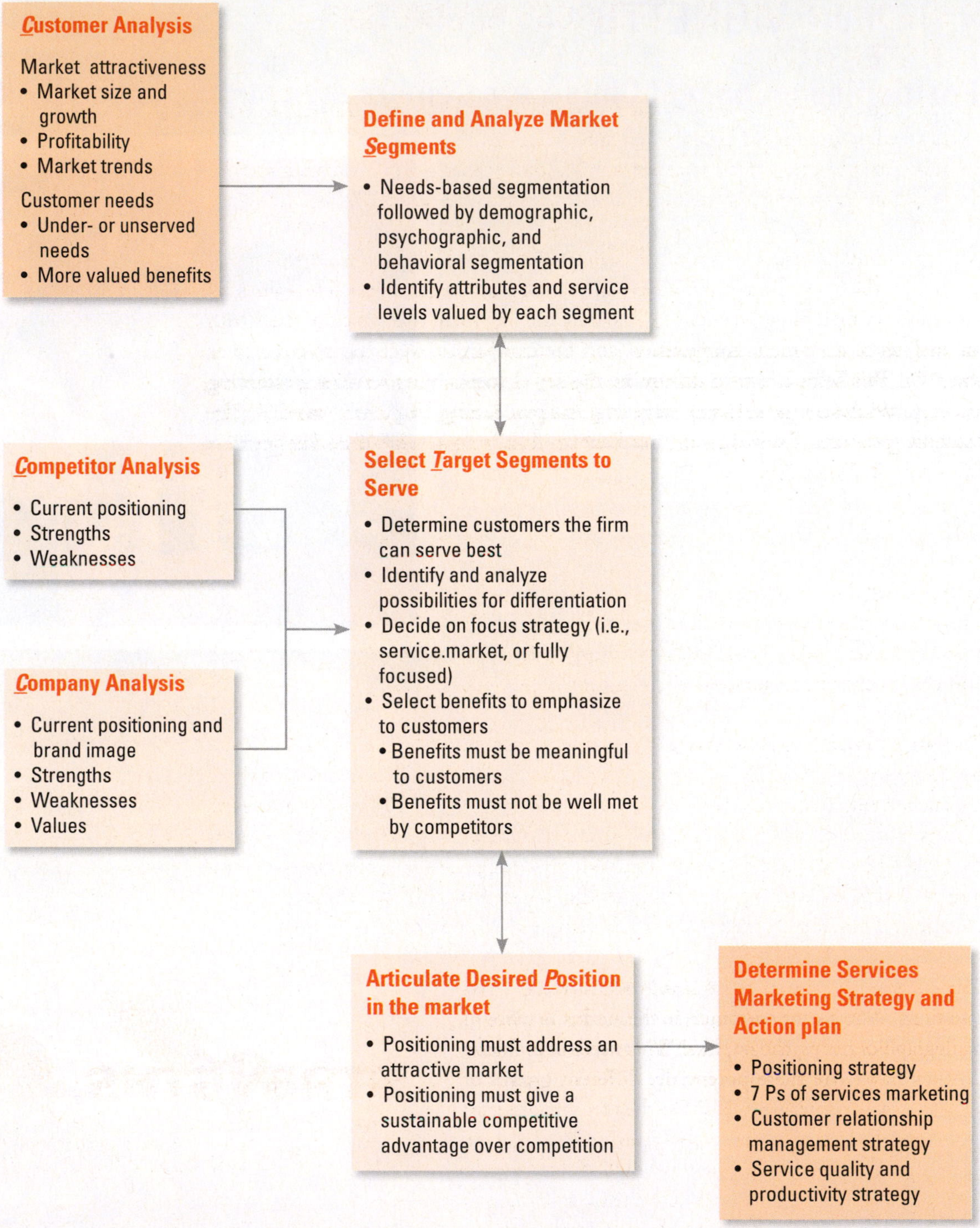

Customer Analysis

Market attractiveness
- Market size and growth
- Profitability
- Market trends

Customer needs
- Under- or unserved needs
- More valued benefits

Define and Analyze Market Segments

- Needs-based segmentation followed by demographic, psychographic, and behavioral segmentation
- Identify attributes and service levels valued by each segment

Competitor Analysis

- Current positioning
- Strengths
- Weaknesses

Select Target Segments to Serve

- Determine customers the firm can serve best
- Identify and analyze possibilities for differentiation
- Decide on focus strategy (i.e., service.market, or fully focused)
- Select benefits to emphasize to customers
  - Benefits must be meaningful to customers
  - Benefits must not be well met by competitors

Company Analysis

- Current positioning and brand image
- Strengths
- Weaknesses
- Values

Articulate Desired Position in the market

- Positioning must address an attractive market
- Positioning must give a sustainable competitive advantage over competition

Determine Services Marketing Strategy and Action plan

- Positioning strategy
- 7 Ps of services marketing
- Customer relationship management strategy
- Service quality and productivity strategy

Figure 3.1 Developing a services marketing positioning strategy.

CUSTOMER-DRIVEN SERVICES MARKETING STRATEGY

▶ **LO 1**
Understand how _c_ustomer, _c_ompetitor, and _c_ompany analyses (i.e., the *3 Cs*) help to develop a customer-driven services marketing strategy.

In an industry with low barriers of entry and a lot of competition, Bright Horizons managed to find a niche position and differentiate itself from other similar firms. As competition intensifies in the service sector, it is becoming ever more important for service organizations to differentiate their products in ways that are meaningful to customers.

Managers need to think systematically about all aspects of the service offering and emphasize the firm's competitive advantage on those attributes that will be valued by customers in their target segment(s). A systematic way to do this typically starts with an analysis of customers, competitors, and the company, collectively referred to as the *3 Cs*. This helps a firm to determine the key elements of its services positioning strategy, which are segmentation, targeting, and positioning, frequently called *STP* by marketing experts. The basic steps involved in identifying a suitable market position are shown in Figure 3.1.

Customer, Competitor, and Company Analysis (3Cs)

Customer Analysis

The customer analysis is typically done first and includes an examination of overall market characteristics. This is followed by an in-depth exploration of customer needs and related customer characteristics and behaviors.

The *market analysis* tries to establish the attractiveness of the overall market and the potential segments within it. Specifically, it looks at the overall size and growth of the market, the margins and profit potential, and demand levels and trends affecting the market. For example, there is a growing segment of wealthy retirees who are interested in traveling but want customized tours with personal guides and itineraries that are not too taxing. Alternative ways of segmenting the market should be considered, and the size and potential of different market segments should be assessed.

The *analysis of customer needs* involves answering a few questions. Who are the customers in the market in terms of demographics and psychographics? What needs or problems do they have? Are there potentially different groups of customers with differing needs? Do they require different service products or different levels of service? What are the service benefits that are valued most by each of these groups? To use the previous example, wealthy retirees wishing to travel value comfort and safety the most and are much less price-sensitive than young families. Sometimes, research shows that certain market segments are "under-served." This means that their needs are not well met by existing suppliers.

Competitor Analysis

The identification and analysis of a firm's competitors can provide a marketing strategist with a sense of their strengths and weaknesses (Figure 3.2). By relating these to the company analysis discussed in the next section, the

Figure 3.2 The SWOT analysis is a popular method in businesses.

strategist should be able to suggest opportunities for differentiation and competitive advantage. Competitor analysis also enables managers to decide which benefits can be emphasized to which target segments.

Company Analysis

The objective of an internal corporate analysis is to identify the organization's strengths in terms of its current brand positioning and image as well as the resources it has (finances, human labor, and physical assets). It also examines the organization's limitations or constraints, and how its values shape the way it does business. Using insights from this analysis, the management should be able to select a limited number of target market segments that can be served with either existing or new services. The core question is: How well can our company and our services address the needs and problems faced by each customer segment?

Segmentation, Targeting, and Positioning (STP)

LO 2

Know the key elements of a positioning strategy (i.e., *STP*) and explain why they are so crucial for service firms.

Linking customer and competitor analysis to company analysis allows the service organization to develop an effective positioning strategy. The basic steps involved in identifying a suitable market position and developing a strategy to reach it are:

▶ Segmentation: This involves dividing the population of possible customers into groups. A *market segment* is composed of a group of buyers who share common characteristics, needs, purchasing behavior, and/or consumption patterns. Once customers with similar needs are grouped together, demographic, geographic, psychographic, and behavioral variables can be used to describe them. Customers in the same segment should have needs that are as similar as possible. In contrast, the needs of customers in different segments should be as different as possible.

▶ Targeting: Once a firm's customers have been segmented, the firm has to assess the attractiveness of each segment and decide which segment(s) would most likely be interested in its service. It must also focus on ways to serve the chosen segment(s) well.

▶ Positioning: This is the unique place that the firm and/or its service offerings occupy in the minds of its consumers. In order to create a unique position for its service, the firm must differentiate the service from those offered by its competitors.

Table 3.1 shows the key elements of a services positioning strategy as well as other related concepts. We will discuss each concept in the remainder of this chapter.

SEGMENTING SERVICE MARKETS

LO 3

*S*egment customers on the basis of needs before using other common bases to further identify and profile the segments.

Segmentation is one of the most important concepts in marketing. Service firms vary widely in their abilities to serve different types of customers. Hence, rather than trying to compete in an entire market, each firm should adopt a strategy of market segmentation. This involves the identification of certain parts or segments of the market that the firm can serve best.

There are many ways to segment a market, and marketing experts typically combine and integrate several approaches. Traditionally, *demographic segmentation* (e.g., based

Table 3.1 Elements and key concepts of a services positioning strategy.

Elements of a Positioning Strategy	Key Concepts

Segmentation	• Segmenting service markets
	• Service attributes and service levels relevant for segmentation
	   – Important versus determinant attributes
	   – Establishing service levels

Targeting	• Targeting service markets through four focus strategies:
	   – Fully focused
	   – Market-focused
	   – Service-focused
	   – Unfocused

Positioning	• Positioning services in competitive markets • Using positioning maps to plot a competitive strategy • Developing an effective positioning strategy

on age, gender, and income) has frequently been used. However, this often does not result in meaningful segmentation as two people in the exact same demographics can exhibit very different buying behaviors. *Psychographic segmentation* has become more popular as it reflects people's lifestyles, attitudes, and aspirations. It can be very useful in strengthening brand identity and creating an emotional connection with the brand. However, it may not necessarily map to behaviors and sales. *Behavioral segmentation* addresses this shortcoming as it focuses on observable behaviors, such as people being non-users, light users, or heavy users. *Needs-based segmentation* focuses on what customers truly want in a service and maps closely to the multi-attribute decision models we discussed in Chapter 2.

You need to recognize that, often, people have different needs and decision-making criteria according to:

▶ The purpose of using the service

▶ The individual who makes the decision

▶ The timing of use (time of day/week/season)

▶ Whether the individual is using the service alone or with a group; and, if the latter, the composition of that group

For companies to effectively segment a market, it is best to start with a deep understanding of customers' needs. The availability of big data and marketing analytics on the cloud enables marketers to collect accurate and detailed information at the individual consumer level. This allows very narrow and specific segmentation analyses.[2] Marketers can overlay this understanding with demographic, psychographic, behavioral, and consumption context variables to further define and describe key segments in a market.[3]

Figure 3.3 Contiki targets young and fun-loving travelers.

Contiki Holiday is an example of a company that uses needs-based segmentation as a foundation and then fine-tunes it with other types of segmentation. It serves a special group of single people who do not want to join tours where there are families. They prefer holidays where they can meet people with similar preferences (needs-based segmentation). Contiki is a worldwide leader in vacation for those in the 18–35 age group (demographic segmentation) (Figure 3.3). Its holiday packages are aimed at fun-loving youths. Contiki further segments its packages in order to cater to different lifestyles and budgets (psychographic segmentation). For example, those going to Europe can choose between "Camping" (for people who are very outgoing and do not mind roughing it out), "Concept/Budget" (for those who want more for their time and money, in backpacker-style accommodation), or "Time out/Superior" (with lots of sightseeing, free time, extra excursions, and stays in superior-class tourist hotels).

LO 4

Distinguish between important and determinant attributes for segmentation.

Important versus Determinant Service Attributes

Consumers usually choose between alternative service offerings on the basis of perceived differences between them. However, the attributes that distinguish competing services from one another may not always be the most important ones. For instance, many travelers rank "safety" as a very important attribute in their choice of an airline. They avoid traveling on airlines with a poor safety reputation. However, a traveler flying on major routes is still likely to have several choices of carriers available that are perceived as equally safe. Hence, safety is not usually an attribute that influences the customer's choice at this point.

Determinant attributes (i.e., those that actually determine buyers' choices between competing alternatives) are often way down on the list of service characteristics that are important to purchasers. However, they are the attributes that help customers to identify significant differences among competing alternatives. For example, convenience of departure and arrival times (Figure 3.4), availability of frequent flyer miles and related loyalty privileges, quality of in-flight service, or the ease of making reservations might be determinant characteristics for business travelers when selecting an airline. For budget-conscious vacation travelers, on the other hand, price might assume primary importance.

In Chapter 2, we saw that consumers may use different decision rules and therefore arrive at different choices even though the

Figure 3.4 Convenient departure times are determinant attributes for business travelers.

important attributes are the same. For example, in Table 2.1 on page 40, the most important attribute is the quality of dry cleaning. However, if the consumer uses the conjunctive rule, depending on what the cut-offs are, the determinant attribute may actually be price, which is the third most important variable. Identifying determinant attributes is therefore crucial for effective positioning that makes a firm's service stand out in the minds of its target customers.

Segmenting Based on Service Levels

After the service attributes to be used for segmentation have been identified, decisions should also be made on the service levels to be offered on each attribute. Some service attributes are easily quantified, whereas others are qualitative. Price, for instance, is a quantitative attribute. However, characteristics such as the quality of personal service in a hotel and the degree of luxury offered are more qualitative. Customers can often be segmented according to their willingness to give up some level of service for a lower price. Price-insensitive customers are willing to pay a relatively high price to obtain higher levels of service on each of the attributes important to them. In contrast, price-sensitive customers will look for an inexpensive service that offers a relatively low level of performance on many key attributes.

LO 5
Use different service levels for segmentation.

TARGETING SERVICE MARKETS

It is usually not realistic for a firm to try to appeal to all potential buyers in a market because customers are varied in their needs, purchasing behavior, and consumption patterns. Moreover, they are often too numerous and widely spread geographically. Service firms also tend to differ greatly in terms of their strengths and weaknesses. Thus, in order to achieve competitive advantage, each company should ideally focus its efforts on those customers it can serve best—its *target segment*.[4]

LO 6
Target service customers using the four focus strategies for competitive advantage.

Achieving Competitive Advantage through Focus

In marketing terms, *focus* means providing a relatively narrow product mix for a particular target segment. The firm identifies the strategically important elements in its service operations and concentrates its resources on them. The extent of a company's focus can be described along two dimensions: market focus and service focus.[5] *Market focus* is the extent to which a firm serves a few or many markets, while *service focus* describes the extent to which a firm offers a few or many services. These two dimensions define the four basic focus strategies (Figure 3.5):

▶ *Fully focused*. A fully focused organization provides a limited range of services (perhaps just a single core product) to a narrow and specific market segment. For example, private jet charter services may focus on high-net-worth individuals or corporations (Figure 3.6). Developing recognized expertise in a well-defined niche allows a firm to charge premium prices and provides protection against would-be competitors. An example of a fully focused firm is Shouldice Hospital, featured in Case 9. The hospital performs only a single surgery (hernia) on otherwise healthy patients (mostly men in the age group of 40–60). Due to its focus, its surgery and service quality are superb.

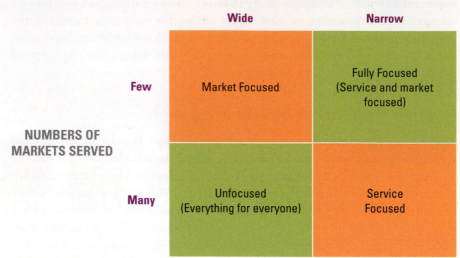

BREADTH OF SERVICE OFFERINGS

	Wide	Narrow
Few	Market Focused	Fully Focused (Service and market focused)
Many	Unfocused (Everything for everyone)	Service Focused

NUMBERS OF MARKETS SERVED

Figure 3.5 Basic focus strategies for services.

SOURCE

From Robert Johnston, "Achieving Focus in Service Organisations," in *The Service Industries Journal* 16(1), pp.10–20. Published by Taylor and Francis, © 1996.

There are key risks associated with pursuing the fully focused strategy. The market may be too small for the firm to get the volume of business needed for financial success. The firm also becomes vulnerable when new alternative products or technologies substitute its own.

▶ **Market focused.** In a market-focused strategy, a company offers a wide range of services to a narrowly defined target segment. Service Insights 3.1 features the example of Rentokil Initial, a provider of business-to-business services. The growing trend of outsourcing services related to facilities maintenance has enabled Rentokil to develop a large range of services for its clients.

Figure 3.6 Private air charter services for VIPs.

Following a market-focused strategy often looks attractive because the firm can sell multiple services to a single buyer. However, before choosing such a strategy, managers need to be sure that their firms can efficiently deliver each of the different services selected.

▶ **Service focused.** Service-focused firms offer a narrow range of services to a fairly broad market (Figure 3.7). Lasik eye surgery clinics and Starbucks coffee shops follow this strategy, serving a broad customer base with a largely standardized product. However, as new segments are added, the firm needs to develop the necessary expertise in serving each segment. Furthermore, this strategy is likely to require a broader sales effort and greater investment in marketing communication—particularly in B2B markets.

▶ **Unfocused.** Finally, many service providers fall into the unfocused category because they try to serve broad markets and provide a wide range of services. Unfocused firms are often "jacks of all trades and masters of none." In general, that's not a good idea, although public utilities and government agencies may be obliged to do so.

Figure 3.7 Warehousing service firms provide logistics solutions for broad markets.

It is recommended that firms have some sort of focus, whether on market segments or on services. How should a firm select which of the three "focused" strategies to pursue? This decision relates back to the 3 Cs, segmentation, and targeting analyses. For example, a market-focused strategy may be appropriate if (a) customers value the convenience of one-stop shopping, (b) the firm is capable of delivering these multiple services better than the competition, and/ or (c) there are significant synergies in selling multiple services to the same customer (as is often the case in B2B services; see Rentokil Initial in Service Insights 3.1), which then enables the firm to either lower the price or provide better service.

A service-focused strategy can work best if the firm has a unique set of capabilities and resources to deliver a particular service exceptionally well or cost-effectively. The firm may then want to use its advantage to deliver the service to a broad market (i.e., many customer segments at the same time).

Finally, a fully focused strategy can deliver superb quality at low costs if a particular segment has very specific needs and requires unique design of the service environment, service processes, and interaction with the firm's front-line employees.

Trade-offs are inherent in focus and excellence. According to Frances Frei and Anne Morriss, there are a lot of heroic people in service organizations who feel compelled to be the best at everything. However, any attempt to do that will almost inevitably lead to mediocrity. The authors argue that excellence requires sacrifice (another way of looking at focus), and service firms should excel where it matters. For example, the Mayo Clinic focuses on reducing the time it takes for patients to schedule an appointment with a doctor, undergo an examination, and receive a diagnosis (to 24 hours or less).

Market-Focused Brand across Multiple Services at Rentokil Initial

With revenue for 2015 at over £2.3 billion, Rentokil Initial is one of the world's largest business-support service companies. The company has about 27,000 employees in over 50 countries where the "Rentokil" and "Initial" brands have come to represent innovation, deep expertise, and consistent quality of service. The UK-based firm has grown and developed from its origins as a manufacturer of rat poison and pesticides for killing wood-destroying beetles. When the firm realized it could make more money by providing a service to kill rodents than by selling products, it shifted to pest control and extermination services.

Through organic growth and acquisitions, Rentokil Initial has developed an extensive product range that includes testing and safety services, security, package delivery, interior plants landscaping (including sale or rental of tropical plants), specialized cleaning services, pest control, uniform rental and cleaning, clinical waste collection and disposal, personnel services, and a washroom solutions service that supplies and maintains a full array of equipment, dispensers, and consumables. The firm sees its core competence as "the ability to carry out high-quality services on other people's premises through well-recruited, well-trained, and motivated staff."

Promoting the use of additional services to existing customers is an important aspect of the firm's strategy. Initial Integrated Services offers clients the opportunity to move beyond the established concept of "bundling" services—bringing together several free-standing support services contracts from one provider—to full integration of services. Clients purchase sector-specific solutions that deliver multiple services, but feature just "one invoice, one account manager, one help desk, one contract, and one motivated service team."

According to former chief executive Sir Clive Thomson:

> Our objective has been to create a virtuous circle. We provide a quality service in industrial and commercial activities under the same brand-name, so that a customer satisfied with one Rentokil Initial Service is potentially a satisfied customer for another. . . .

Although it was considered somewhat odd at the time, one of the reasons we moved into [providing and maintaining] tropical plants [for building interiors] was in fact to put the brand in front of decision makers. Our service people maintaining the plants go in through the front door and are visible to the customer. This contrasts with pest control where no one really notices unless we fail. . . . The brand stands for honesty, reliability, consistency, integrity and technical leadership.

Investment in R&D ensures constant improvement in its many service lines. For example, the company has built the RADAR intelligent rodent trap. RADAR attracts rats and mice into a sealable chamber and kills them humanely by injecting carbon dioxide. Using Rentokil's unique "PestConnect" technology, the trap causes emails to be sent to the customer and the local branch when a rodent is caught. In addition, a Rentokil technician receives a text message identifying which unit has been activated at which customer's premises, and its precise location. PestConnect checks each individual RADAR unit every 10 minutes, 24/7. Getting information in real time enables technicians to remove dead rodents promptly and control future infestations better.

Rentokil Initial's success lies in its ability to position each of its many business services in terms of the company's core brand values, which include providing superior standards of customer care and using the most technologically advanced services and products. The brand image is strengthened through physical evidence, such as distinctive uniforms, vehicle color schemes, and use of the corporate logo.

SOURCES

Based on Clive Thompson, "Rentokil Initial: Building a Strong Corporate Brand for Growth and Diversity," in F. Gilmore (ed.), *Brand Warriors*. London: HarperCollinsBusiness, 1997, pp. g g 123–124.

Figure 3.8 Visa has one simple message globally.

This is important for anxious patients who want to know what is wrong with them as soon as possible. However, the focus on speed does not allow patients to select a specific physician. It is important to decide on areas where the firm does not have to perform as well (i.e., the aspects of the service that the customers care less about). This knowledge allows the firm to utilize its resources to excel in areas that are most important to their target customers.[6]

PRINCIPLES OF POSITIONING SERVICES

Positioning strategy is concerned with creating, communicating, and maintaining distinctive differences that will be noticed and valued by those customers with whom the firm would most like to develop a long-term relationship. Jack Trout distilled the essence of positioning into the following four principles[7]:

LO 7
Position a service to distinguish it from its competitors.

1) A company must establish a position in the minds of its targeted customers.

2) The position should be singular, providing one simple and consistent message (Figure 3.8).

3) The position must set the company apart from its competitors (Figure 3.9).

4) A company cannot be all things to all people—it must focus its efforts.

These principles apply to any type of organization that competes for customers. Firms must understand the principles of positioning in order to develop an effective

"In hindsight, I'd say my first mistake was letting my competitors advertise on my website."

Figure 3.9 For powerful positioning, a firm needs to set itself apart from its competitors.

competitive position. The concept of positioning offers valuable insights by forcing service managers to analyze their firm's existing offerings and provide specific answers to the following six questions:

1) What does our firm stand for in the minds of current and potential customers?

2) What customers do we serve now, and which ones would we like to target in the future?

3) What is the value proposition for each of our current service offerings, and what market segments is each one targeted at?

4) How does each of our service products differ from those of our competitors?

5) How well do customers in the chosen target segments perceive our service offerings as meeting their needs?

6) What changes do we need to make to our service offerings in order to strengthen our competitive position within our target segment(s)?

LO 8

Understand how to use positioning maps to analyze and develop competitive strategy.

One of the challenges in developing a viable positioning strategy is to avoid the trap of investing too much in points of difference that can easily be copied. When Roger Brown and Linda Mason, founders of the Bright Horizons chain of child-care centers featured in the opening vignette of this chapter, were developing their service concept and business model, they took a long, hard look at the industry. Discovering that for-profit child-care companies had adopted low-cost strategies, Brown and Mason selected a different approach that competitors would find very difficult to copy.

Earlier, large companies in need of auditing services typically turned to one of the Big Four accounting firms (Figure 3.10). Now, a growing number of clients are switching to so-called "Tier Two" accounting firms in search of better service, lower costs, or both.[8] Grant Thornton, the fifth largest firm in the industry, has successfully positioned itself as offering easy access to its partners and having "a passion for the business of accounting." Its advertising promotes an award from J. D. Powers ranking it as achieving the "Highest Performance among Audit Firms Serving Companies with up to $12 billion in Annual Revenue."

The **BIG4** accounting firms

Deloitte
PWC
KPMG
Ernst & Young

Figure 3.10 The Big Four accounting firms refer to PricewaterhouseCoopers, Deloitte Touche Tohmatsu, Ernst & Young, and KPMG.

USING POSITIONING MAPS TO PLOT COMPETITIVE STRATEGY

Positioning maps are great tools to visualize a firm's competitive positioning along key aspects of its services marketing strategy, to map developments over time, and to develop scenarios of potential competitor responses. Developing a positioning map—a task sometimes referred to as perceptual mapping—is a useful way of representing consumers' perceptions of alternative products graphically. A map usually has two attributes, although three-dimensional models can be used to show three attributes. When more than three dimensions are needed to describe product performance in a given market, then a series of separate charts needs to be drawn.

Information about a product can be inferred from market data, derived from ratings by representative consumers, or both. If consumer perceptions of service characteristics differ sharply from "reality" as defined by management, then communications efforts may be needed to change these perceptions. We will discuss this in Chapter 7.

An Example of Applying Positioning Maps to the Hotel Industry

The hotel business is highly competitive, especially during seasons when the supply of rooms exceeds demand. Customers visiting a large city find that they have many alternatives to choose from within a particular class of hotels. The degree of luxury and comfort in physical amenities will be one choice criterion; others may include attributes such as location, safety, availability of meeting rooms and a business center, restaurants, a swimming pool and a gym, and loyalty programs for frequent guests (Figure 3.13).

Let's look at an example, based on a real-world situation, of how to apply positioning maps. Managers of the Palace, a successful four-star hotel, developed a positioning map showing their hotel alongside those of their competitors. Their purpose was to get a better understanding of future threats to their established market position in a large city that we will call Belleville.

Figure 3.11 Executives conducting competitive analysis.

Located on the edge of the booming financial district, the Palace was an elegant old hotel that had been renovated and modernized a few years earlier. Its competitors included eight four-star establishments as well as the Grand, one of the city's oldest hotels, with a five-star rating. The Palace had been very profitable in recent years, with an above-average occupancy rate. For many months of the year, it was sold out on weekdays. This reflected its strong appeal to business travelers, who were willing to pay a higher room rate than tourists or conference delegates. However, the general manager and his staff saw problems on the horizon. Planning permissions had recently been granted for four large new hotels in the city, and the Grand had just started a major renovation and expansion project which included the construction of a new wing. There was a risk that customers might see the Palace as falling behind.

To better understand the nature of the competitive threat, the hotel's management team worked with a consultant to prepare charts that displayed the Palace's position in the business traveler market both before and after the entrance of new competition. Four key attributes were selected for study: room price, level of personal service, level of physical luxury, and location.

Figure 3.12 Dubai's Burj Al Arab is favorably positioned along many determinant attributes like personal service, level of physical extravagance, and location.

Data Sources. In this instance, management did not conduct new consumer research. Instead, they got their customer perceptions data from various sources:

▶ Published information.

▶ Data from past surveys done by the hotel.

▶ Reports from travel agents and knowledgeable hotel staff members who frequently interacted with guests.

Information on competing hotels was not difficult to obtain because their locations were known. Information was obtained by:

▶ Visiting and evaluating the physical structures.

▶ Having sales staff who kept themselves informed on pricing policies and discounts.

▶ To evaluate service level, they used the ratio of rooms per employee. It is easily calculated from the published number of rooms and employment data provided to the city authorities.

▶ Data from surveys of travel agents conducted by the Palace provided additional insights on the quality of personal service in each hotel.

Scales and Hotel Ratings. Scales were then created for each attribute, and every hotel was rated on these attributes so that the positioning maps could be drawn:

▶ Price was simple because the average price charged to business travelers for a standard single room at each hotel was already quantified.

▶ The rooms-per-employee ratio formed the basis for a service level scale, with low ratios equated to high service. This rating was then fine-tuned according to the available information on the quality of service actually delivered by each major competitor.

▶ The level of physical luxury was more subjective. The management team identified the hotel that members agreed was the most luxurious (the Grand) as well as the four-star hotel that they viewed as having the least luxurious physical facilities (the Airport Plaza). All other four-star hotels were then rated on this attribute relative to these two benchmarks.

▶ Location was defined using the stock exchange building in the heart of the financial district as a reference point. Past research had shown that a majority of the Palace's business guests were visiting destinations in this area. The location scale plotted each hotel in terms of its distance from the stock exchange. The competitive set of 10 hotels lay within a four-mile, fan-shaped radius, extending from the exchange through the city's principal retail area (where the convention center was also located) to the inner suburbs and the nearby airport.

Two positioning maps were created to portray the existing competitive situation. The first (Figure 3.13) showed the 10 hotels on the dimensions of price and service level; the second (Figure 3.14) displayed them on location and degree of physical luxury.

Findings. Some findings were intuitive, but others provided valuable insights:

▶ A quick glance at Figure 3.13 shows a clear correlation between the attributes of price and service: hotels that offer higher levels of service are relatively more expensive. The shaded bar running from upper left to lower right highlights this relationship, which is not a surprising one (and can be expected to continue diagonally downward for three-star and lesser-rated establishments).

▶ Further analysis shows that there appear to be three groups of hotels within what is already an upscale market category. At the top end, the four-star Regency is

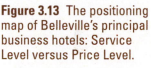

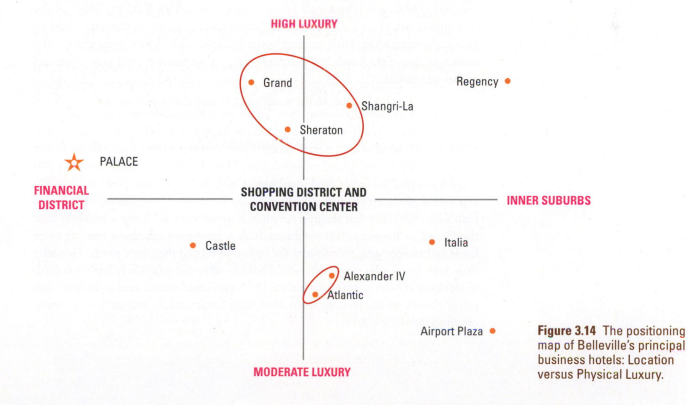

Figure 3.13 The positioning map of Belleville's principal business hotels: Service Level versus Price Level.

close to the five-star Grand. In the middle, the Palace is clustered with four other hotels, and at the lower end, there is another group of three hotels. One surprising insight from this map is that the Palace appears to be charging a lot more (on a relative basis) than its service level would seem to justify. However, since its occupancy rate is very high, guests seem willing to pay the going rate.

Figure 3.14 The positioning map of Belleville's principal business hotels: Location versus Physical Luxury.

Figure 3.15 The kaleidoscopic glass panes of the Montreal Convention Center is a huge draw for hoteliers and other services providers.

▶ Figure 3.14 shows how the Palace is positioned relative to the competition on location and degree of luxury. We don't expect these two variables to be related, and they don't appear to be so. A key insight here is that the Palace occupies a relatively empty portion of the map. It is the only hotel in the financial district—a fact that probably explains its ability to charge more than its service level (or degree of physical luxury) seems to justify.

▶ There are two groups of hotels in the vicinity of the shopping district and convention center (Figure 3.15). There is a relatively luxurious group of three, led by the Grand, and a second group of two offering a moderate level of luxury.

Mapping Future Scenarios to Identify Potential Competitive Responses

The Palace's management team next sought to anticipate the positions of the four new hotels being constructed in Belleville as well as the probable repositioning of the Grand (see Figures 3.16 and 3.17). Predicting the positions of the four new hotels was not difficult for experts in the field, especially as preliminary details of the new hotels had already been released to city planners and the business community.

The construction sites were already known; two would be in the financial district and two in the vicinity of the convention center. Press releases distributed by the Grand had already declared its management's intentions: The "New" Grand would not only be larger, but the renovations would be designed to make it even more luxurious. Moreover, there were plans to add new service features. Three of the newcomers would be linked to international chains, and their strategies could be guessed by examining hotels recently opened in other cities by the same chains. The owners of two of the hotels had declared their plan to position their new properties as five-star hotels.

Pricing was also easy to estimate. New hotels use a formula for setting posted room prices (the prices typically charged to individuals staying on a weeknight in high season). This price is linked to the average construction cost per room at the rate of $1 per night for every $1,000 of construction costs. Thus, a 200-room hotel that costs $80 million to build (including land costs) would have an average room cost of $400,000 and would need to set a price of $400 per room per night. Using this formula, Palace managers concluded that the four new hotels would have to charge a lot more than the Grand or Regency. This would establish a *price umbrella* above existing price levels and thereby give competitors the option of raising their own prices. To justify their high prices, the new hotels would have to offer customers very high standards of service and luxury. At the same time, the New Grand would need to raise its own prices to recover the costs of renovation, new construction, and enhanced service offerings (see Figure 3.16).

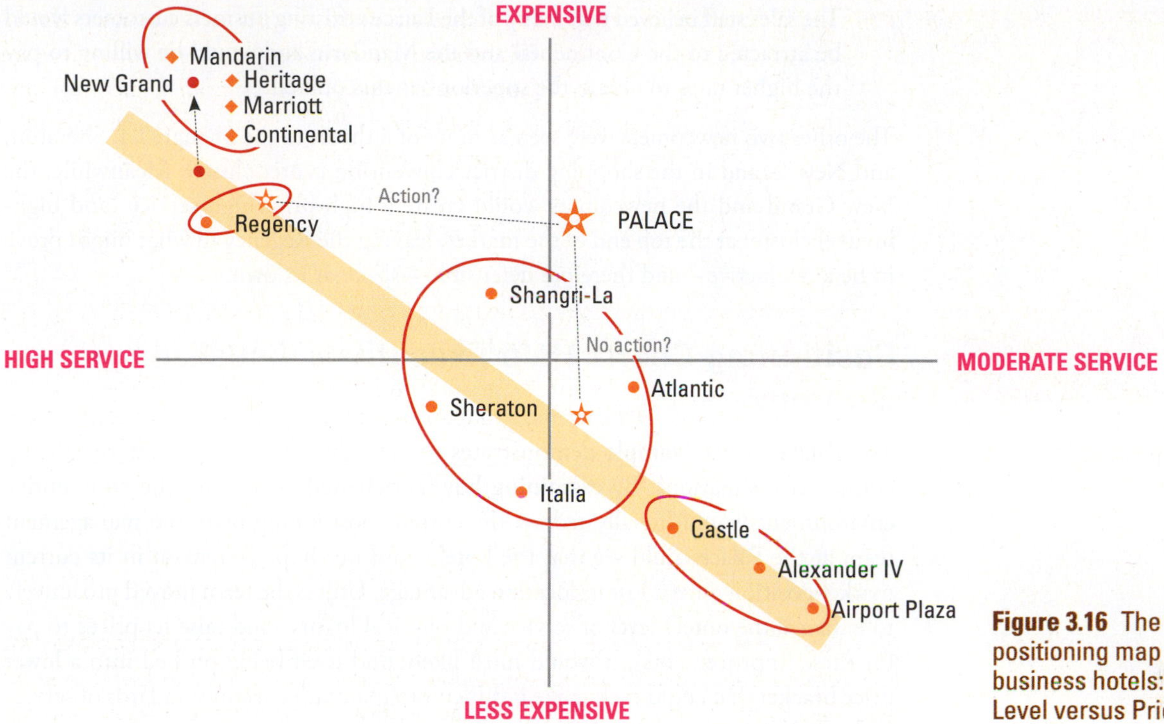

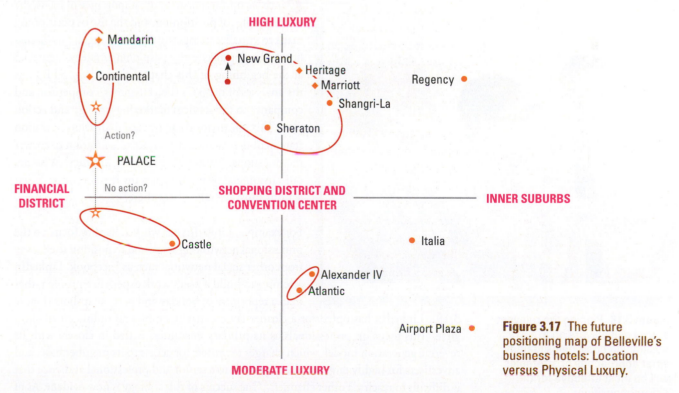

Figure 3.16 The future positioning map of Belleville's business hotels: Service Level versus Price Level.

Assuming no changes by either the Palace or other existing hotels, the effect of the new competition in the market clearly posed a significant threat to the Palace:

▶ It would lose its unique location advantage and become one of three hotels in the immediate vicinity of the financial district (Figure 3.17).

Figure 3.17 The future positioning map of Belleville's business hotels: Location versus Physical Luxury.

▶ The sales staff believed that many of the Palace's existing business customers would be attracted to the Continental and the Mandarin and would be willing to pay the higher rates to obtain the superior benefits offered.

The other two newcomers were seen as more of a threat to the Shangri-La, Sheraton, and New Grand in the shopping district/convention center cluster. Meanwhile, the New Grand and the newcomers would create a high-price/high-service (and high-luxury) cluster at the top end of the market, leaving the Regency in what might prove to be a distinctive—and therefore defensible—space of its own.

Positioning Charts Help Executives Visualize Strategy

The Palace Hotel example demonstrates the insights that come from visualizing competitive situations. By examining how anticipated changes in the competitive environment would literally redraw the current positioning map, the management team at the Palace could see that the hotel could not hope to remain in its current market position once it lost its location advantage. Unless the team moved proactively to enhance the hotel's level of service and physical luxury (and raise its prices to pay for these improvements), it would most likely find itself being pushed into a lower price bracket that could even make it difficult to maintain current standards of service and physical upkeep.

LO 9

Develop an effective positioning strategy.

DEVELOPING AN EFFECTIVE POSITIONING STRATEGY

Since we now understand the importance of focus, the principles of positioning, and the use of positioning maps to visualize competitive positioning, let us discuss how to develop an effective positioning strategy. Figure 3.3 at the beginning of this chapter shows how STP links the analyses of the 3 Cs (i.e., customer, competitor, and company) to the services marketing strategy and action plan. This information can be used to develop a position statement that enables the service organization to answer the questions, "What is our service product? Who are our customers? What do we want it to become? What actions must we take to get there?"

For example, LinkedIn has worked hard to focus on the professional networking space and to position itself away from other social networks such as Facebook. LinkedIn attempts to build a user's work experience profile rather than a repository of holiday and party snapshots (Figure 3.19). LinkedIn has opted for a cleaner layout that resembles an online curriculum vitae. This focus on professionals as its primary customers is tied in closely with its revenue generation model, which charges recruiters for access to its member base, and advertisers for highly targeted placement ads to a senior and professional audience that is difficult to reach via other channels.[9] The success of this strategy is now evident. As of

Figure 3.18 Placing the relevant actors and players on a positioning chart helps identify what approaches or strategies will be most effective for the different positions.

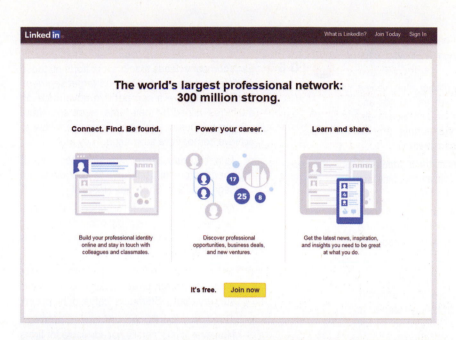

Figure 3.19 LinkedIn positioned itself away from social networks by focusing exclusively on professional networking and career development.

SOURCE

From LinkedIn.com. © LinkedIn Corporation.

2015, with over 300 million members in over 200 countries and territories, LinkedIn is significantly ahead of competitors Viadeo (France) and XING (Germany), which had 70 million and 10 million members, respectively.

There are four basic elements to writing a good positioning statement,[10] and we use the LinkedIn example to illustrate them:

▶ Target audience—the specific group(s) of people that the brand wants to sell to and serve (e.g., professionals as primary target customers, and employers and advertisers as secondary target audiences).

▶ Frame of reference—the category that the brand is competing in (e.g., in the social networking space).

▶ Point of difference—the most compelling benefit offered by the brand that stands out from its competition (e.g., largest network of professionals and recruiters to help advance your career and develop your business acumen and knowledge of the industry).

▶ Reason to believe—proof that the brand can deliver the benefits that are promised (e.g., our network is many times bigger than that of our closest competitor).

The outcome of integrating the 3 Cs and the STP analyses is the positioning statement that defines the desired position of the organization in the marketplace. With this understanding, marketers can now develop a specific plan of action that includes its positioning strategy along the 7 Ps of services marketing, its customer relationship management and loyalty strategies, and its service quality and productivity strategies. The remaining chapters in this book tell you how to do this!

LO 1 ▶ Developing an effective positioning strategy links *customer, competitor,* and *company analysis,* often called the *3 Cs.*

  o *Market analysis* looks at the market attractiveness (e.g., market size and growth, and trends) and customer needs (e.g., desired service levels, level of contact, delivery channels, time of consumption, and price sensitivity).

  o *Competitor analysis* examines the competitors' current positioning, strengths, and weaknesses to spot opportunities for the firm.

  o *Company analysis* focuses on a firm's brand positioning and image, its strengths and weaknesses, and how its values shape the way it does business.

LO 2 ▶ The key elements of developing a customer-driven services marketing strategy are *segmentation, targeting,* and *positioning,* commonly referred to as *STP.*

LO 3 ▶ *Segmentation* is the division of a market into groups. Those customers within the same segment share common service-related needs. Segmentation is often based primarily on customer needs. This enables the firm to focus on what customers truly want and what drives their purchase decisions. Subsequently, demographic, psychographic, and behavioral variables can be used to further define and describe key segments.

LO 4 ▶ In order to segment customers, it is crucial to understand the difference between important and determinant attributes for consumer choice.

  o *Important attributes* are important to the consumer, but they may not be important for the actual buying decision (e.g., safety is important, but all airlines considered by a traveler are seen as safe). If that is the case, such an attribute should not be used as a basis for segmentation.

  o *Determinant attributes* are often further down on the list of service characteristics important to customers. However, they are attributes on the basis of which customers see significant differences between competing alternatives (e.g., convenience of departure times, or quality of in-flight service). Thus, they determine the final purchase decision. Differences among customers regarding determinant attributes are therefore crucial for segmentation.

LO 5 ▶ Once the important and determinant attributes are understood, the management needs to decide which *service level* different customers prefer on each of the attributes. Service levels are often used to differentiate customer segments according to their willingness to trade off price and service level.

LO 6 ▶ Each company needs to focus its efforts on those customers it can serve best—its *target segment.* Firms must have a competitive advantage on attributes valued by their target segment. There are three focused strategies firms can follow to achieve competitive advantage. They are:

  o *Fully focused*: A firm provides a limited range of services (perhaps only one) to a narrow target segment (e.g., Shouldice Hospital).

  o *Market focused*: A firm concentrates on a narrow market segment but offers a wide range of services to address the many diverse needs of that segment (e.g., Rentokil).

  o *Service focused*: A firm offers a narrow range of services to a fairly broad market (e.g., Lasik eye surgery clinics, Starbucks' cafés, or LinkedIn).

  o There is a fourth, the unfocused strategy. However, it is generally not advisable for firms to choose such a strategy as it will require them to spread themselves too thin to remain competitive (e.g., some departmental stores).

LO 7 ▶ Once we have understood determinant attributes and related service levels of our target segment(s), we can decide how to best position our service in the market. *Positioning* is based on establishing and maintaining a distinctive place in the market for a firm's offerings. The essence of positioning is:

  o A company must establish a position in the minds of its targeted customers.

  o The position should be singular, providing one simple and consistent message.

  o The position must set a company apart from its competitors.

  o A company cannot be all things to all people—it must focus its efforts.

LO 8 ▶ *Positioning maps* are an important tool to help firms develop their positioning strategy. They provide a visual way of summarizing customer perceptions of how different services are performing on determinant attributes compared to the competition. They can help firms to see where they might reposition and even anticipate competitors' actions.

LO 9 ▶ The outcome of these analyses is the position statement that articulates the desired position of the firm's offering in the marketplace. With this understanding, marketers can then develop a specific plan of action that includes its positioning strategy along the *7 Ps* of services marketing, its customer relationship management and loyalty strategies, and its service quality and productivity strategies.

UNLOCK YOUR LEARNING

These keywords are found within the sections of each Learning Objective (LO). They are integral to understanding the services marketing concepts taught in each section. Having a firm grasp of these keywords and how they are used is essential to helping you do well on your course, and in the real and very competitive marketing scene out there.

LO 1
1. Customer analysis
2. Company analysis
3. Competitor analysis
4. Customer needs analysis
5. Internal corporate analysis
6. Market analysis

LO 2
1. Market position
2. Positioning
3. Positioning strategy
4. Segmentation
5. Targeting

LO 3
1. Behavioral segmentation
2. Demographic segmentation
3. Needs-based segmentation
4. Psychographic segmentation

LO 4
1. Competing alternatives
2. Decision rules
3. Determinant attributes
4. Important attributes
5. Service attribute

LO 5
1. Qualitative attribute
2. Quantitative attribute
3. Service levels

LO 6
1. Competitive advantage
2. Focus
3. Focus strategies
4. Fully focused strategy
5. Market-focused strategy
6. Service-focused strategy
7. Target segment
8. Unfocused strategy

LO 7
1. Distinctive differences
2. Positioning services

LO 8
1. Competitive responses
2. Future scenarios
3. Perceptual mapping
4. Positioning charts
5. Positioning maps
6. Visualize strategy

LO 9
1. Effective positioning strategy
2. Frame of reference
3. Point of difference
4. Position statement
5. Reason to believe
6. Target audience

How well do you know the language of services marketing? Quiz yourself!

⚠ **Not for the academically faint-of-heart**

For each keyword you are able to recall without referring to earlier pages, give yourself a point (and a pat on the back). Tally your score at the end and see if you earned the right to be called a *services marketeer*.

SCORE

01 – 12	Services Marketing is done a great disservice.
13 – 24	The midnight oil needs to be lit, pronto.
25 – 36	I know what you *didn't* do all semester.
37 – 48	By George! You're getting there.
49 – 60	Now, go forth and market.
61 – 73	There should be a marketing concept named after you.

Review Questions

1. What are the elements of a customer-driven services marketing strategy?

2. What are the most common bases used in segmentation? Provide examples for each of these bases.

3. What is the distinction between important and determinant attributes in consumer purchase decisions?

4. Why should service firms focus their efforts? Describe the basic focus strategies, and give examples of how these work.

5. What are the six questions for developing an effective positioning strategy?

6. How can positioning maps help managers better understand and respond to competitive dynamics?

7. Describe what is meant by positioning strategy. How do the market, customer, internal, and competitive analyses relate to positioning strategy?

WORK **YOUR** SERVICES MARKETING

Application Exercises

1. Select a company of your choice. Identify the variables that the company has used to segment its customers. Support your answers with examples from the company.

2. Provide two examples of service firms that use service levels (other than airlines, hotels, and car rentals) to differentiate their products. Explain the determinant attributes and service levels used to differentiate the positioning of one service from another.

3. Find examples of companies that illustrate each of the four focus strategies discussed in this chapter.

4. Imagine that you have been hired as a consultant to give advice to the Palace Hotel. Consider the options facing the hotel based on the four attributes in the positioning charts (Figures 3.15 and 3.16). What actions do you recommend for the Palace? Explain your recommendations.

5. Choose an industry you are familiar with (such as cell phone services, credit cards, or online music stores) and create a perceptual map showing the competitive positions of different service providers in that industry. Use attributes you believe are determinant attributes. Identify gaps in the market and generate ideas for a potential "blue ocean" strategy.

END NOTES

1. Roger Brown, "How We Built a Strong Company in a Weak Industry," *Harvard Business Review*, February 2001, 51–57; www.brighthorizons.com, accessed February 3, 2015.

2. Roland Rust and Ming-Hui Huang, "The Service Revolution and the Transformation of Marketing Science," *Marketing Science* 33, no. 2 (2014): 206–221.

3. Daniel Yankelovich and David Meer, "Rediscovering Marketing Segmentation," *Harvard Business Review* 84, no. 2 (2006): 122–131. A best-practice example in a B2B context is discussed in: Ernest Waaser, Marshall Dahneke, Michael Pekkarinen, and Michael Weissel, "How You Slice It: Smarter Segmentation for Your Sales Force," *Harvard Business Review* 82, no. 3 (2004): 105–111.

4. George S. Day, *Market Driven Strategy* (New York: The Free Press, 1990): 164.

5. Robert Johnston, "Achieving Focus in Service Organizations," *The Service Industries Journal* 16 (January 1996): 10–20.

6. Frances Frei and Anne Morriss, *Uncommon Service: How to Win by Putting Customers at the Core of Your Business* (Boston, MA: Harvard Business Review Press, 2012).

7. Jack Trout, *The New Positioning: The Latest on the World's #1 Business Strategy* (New York: McGraw-Hill, 1997).

8. Nanette Byrnes, "The Little Guys Doing Large Audits," *BusinessWeek* (August 22/29, 2005): 39.

9. Robert Simons, "Choosing the Right Customer: The First Step in a Winning Strategy," *Harvard Business Review* 92, no. 3 (2014): 49–55; http://www.linkedin.com/company/linkedin, accessed 2 February 2015

10. http://www.brandeo.com/positioning%20statement, accessed February 2, 2015

PART **II**

THE *ESM* FRAMEWORK

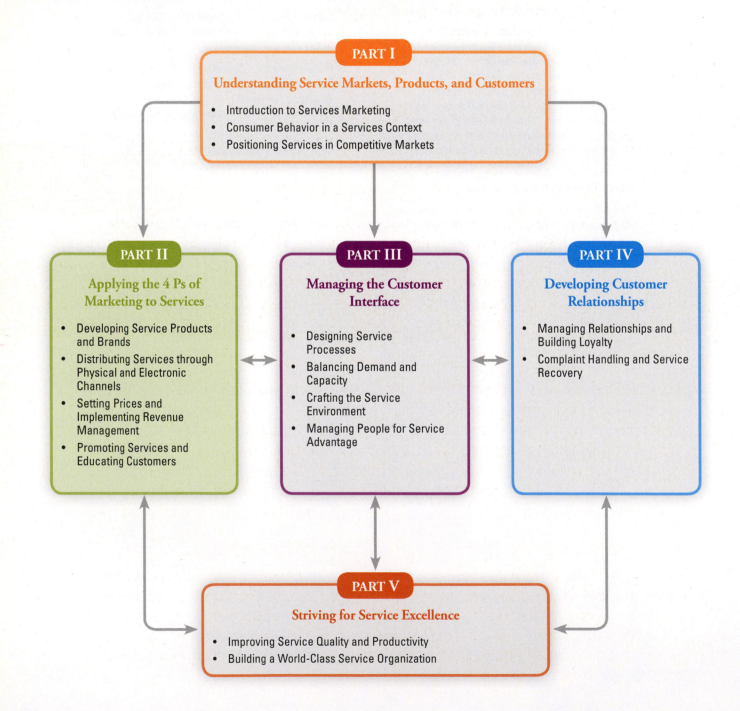

PART I

Understanding Service Markets, Products, and Customers

- Introduction to Services Marketing
- Consumer Behavior in a Services Context
- Positioning Services in Competitive Markets

PART II

Applying the 4 Ps of Marketing to Services

- Developing Service Products and Brands
- Distributing Services through Physical and Electronic Channels
- Setting Prices and Implementing Revenue Management
- Promoting Services and Educating Customers

PART III

Managing the Customer Interface

- Designing Service Processes
- Balancing Demand and Capacity
- Crafting the Service Environment
- Managing People for Service Advantage

PART IV

Developing Customer Relationships

- Managing Relationships and Building Loyalty
- Complaint Handling and Service Recovery

PART V

Striving for Service Excellence

- Improving Service Quality and Productivity
- Building a World-Class Service Organization

Applying the 4 Ps of Marketing to Services

Part II revisits the 4 Ps of the traditional marketing mix (*P*roduct, *P*lace, *P*rice, and *P*romotions). However, the 4Ps are expanded to take into account the specific characteristics of services that make them different from goods marketing. It consists of the following four chapters:

Chapter 4 Developing Service Products and Brands

Discusses the meaningful service concept that includes both the core and supplementary elements. The supplementary elements both facilitate and enhance the core service offering. This chapter also covers branding, tiered servicer products and explains how service firms can build brand equity.

Chapter 5 Distributing Services through Physical and Electronic Channels

Examines the time and place elements. Manufacturers usually require physical distribution channels to move their products. Some service businesses however, are able to use electronic channels to deliver all (or at least some) of their service elements. For the services delivered in real time with customers physically present, speed and convenience of place and time have become important determinants of effective service delivery. This chapter also discussed the role of intermediaries, franchising, and international distribution and market entry.

Chapter 6 Setting Prices and Implementing Revenue Management

Provides an understanding of pricing from both the firm and customer's point of view. For firms, the pricing strategy determines income generation. Service firms need to implement revenue management to maximize the revenue that can be generated from available capacity at any given time. From the customer's perspective, price is a key part of the costs they must incur to obtain the desired benefits. However, the cost to the customer also often includes significant non-monetary costs. This chapter also discusses ethics and fairness in service pricing and how to develop an effective pricing strategy.

Chapter 7 Promoting Services and Educating Customers

Deals with how firms should communicate with their customers about their services through promotion and education. Since customers are co-producers and contribute to how others experience service performances, much communication in services marketing is educational in nature to teach customers how to effectively move through a service process. This chapter covers the service marketing communications funnel, the services marketing communications mix, communications through online, mobile and social networks.

4

developing
SERVICE PRODUCTS and
BRANDS

LEARNING OBJECTIVES (LOs)

By the end of this chapter, the reader should be able to:

▶ **LO 1** Understand what constitutes a service product.

▶ **LO 2** Be familiar with the Flower of Service model.

▶ **LO 3** Know how facilitating supplementary services relate to the core product.

▶ **LO 4** Know how enhancing supplementary services relate to the core product.

▶ **LO 5** Understand branding at the corporate and individual service product levels.

▶ **LO 6** Examine how service firms use different branding strategies.

▶ **LO 7** Understand how branding can be used to tier service products.

▶ **LO 8** Discuss how firms can build brand equity.

▶ **LO 9** Understand what is required to deliver a branded service experience.

▶ **LO 10** List the categories of new service development, ranging from simple style changes to major innovations.

▶ **LO 11** Describe how firms can achieve success in new service development.

Figure 4.1 Starbucks is a familiar brand that even has traditional tea consumers drinking out of its cups.

OPENING VIGNETTE[1]

When you think of a specialty coffee brand, the name that immediately comes to mind is Starbucks. Starbucks attributes its Cinderella success story to three core components: (1) what it believes is the highest-quality coffee in the world; (2) its customer service, which aims to create an uplifting experience every time you walk through the door; and (3) the ambiance of its stores—an upscale, yet inviting environment for those who want to linger.

However, Starbucks has been making many retail and service innovations completely unrelated to coffee. It was one of the first coffee chains to offer free wireless broadband in many of its outlets around the world. Later, it tied up with Apple's iTunes Wi-Fi Music Store so that the songs played at select Starbucks cafés could be browsed, purchased, and downloaded wirelessly onto customers' iPhones or iPads. Since then, Starbucks has continued to experiment with innovative services that its customers may want to use while enjoying their coffee. It launched its Starbucks Digital Network, which offers exclusive movie trailers and a bounty of premium video and other media content. Its Android and Apple apps allow customers to pay, check card balances and reload cards, track stars and redeem rewards, leave digital tips for the barista, find and redeem personalized offers, view menu choices and nutritional content, and much more. Recently, Starbucks incorporated Spotify into its mobile app to allow its baristas and customers to pick the songs played at the shops. According to Howard Schultz, Starbucks' CEO, "By connecting Spotify's world-class streaming platform into our world-class store and digital ecosystem, we are reinventing the way our millions of customers discover music."

Starbucks is a company that has developed service innovations with great success. However, the competition is intense, and Starbucks has to continue reinventing itself to maintain its edge.

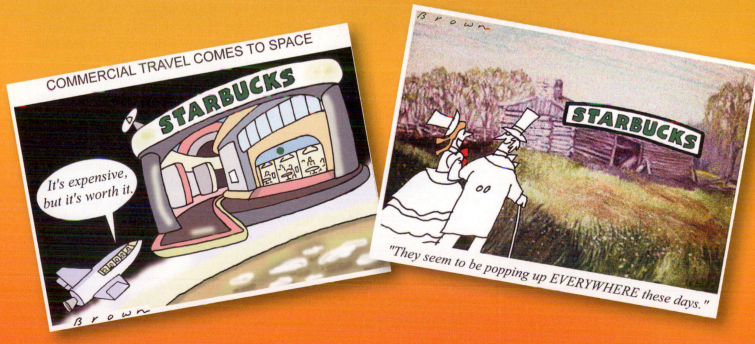

CREATING SERVICE PRODUCTS

In recent years, more and more service firms have started talking about their *products*—a term previously associated largely with manufactured goods. A *product* implies a defined and consistent "bundle of output" as well as the ability to differentiate one bundle of output from another. In a manufacturing context, the concept is easy to understand and visualize. Service firms can also differentiate their products as manufacturers do by offering various product "models." For example, fast-food restaurants display a menu of their products, which are of course highly tangible.

Providers of more intangible services also offer various "models" of products. Usually, these represent an assembly of carefully prescribed value-added supplementary services built around a core product. For instance, credit card companies develop different cards, each of which comes with a distinct bundle of benefits and fees. Likewise, insurance companies offer different types of policies, and universities offer different degree programs composed of a mix of required and elective courses. The objective of product development is to design bundles of output that are distinct and can easily be differentiated from other products.

All service organizations face choices concerning the types of products to be offered and the ways of delivering them to customers. To better understand the nature of services, it's useful to distinguish between the core product and the supplementary elements that facilitate its use and enhance its value for customers.

What Are the Components of a Service Product?

A service product comprises all the elements of the service performance, both physical and intangible, that create value for customers. Experienced service marketers recognize the need to take a holistic view of the entire performance that they want customers to experience. The value proposition must address and integrate three components: (1) *core product*, (2) *supplementary services*, and (3) *delivery processes*.

Core Product. The core product is 'what' the customer is fundamentally buying. When buying a one-night stay in a hotel, the core service is accommodation and security. When paying to have a package delivered, the core service is the timely delivery of the package in perfect condition at the correct address. Thus, a core product is the central component that supplies the principal benefits, solutions, or experience that the customer is seeking. Some core products are highly intangible. Think of credit card and travel insurance products and the innovative design of their features, benefits, and pricing.

Supplementary Services. Delivery of the core product is usually accompanied by a variety of other service-related activities that we collectively refer to as supplementary services. These augment the core product, both facilitating its use and enhancing its value.[2] Core products tend to become commoditized as an industry matures and competition increases. In order to gain competitive advantage, firms often emphasize supplementary services, which can play an important role in differentiating the core product from competing services.

Delivery Processes. The third component in designing a service concept concerns the processes used to deliver the core product and the supplementary services. The design of the service offering must address the following issues:

- How the different service components are delivered to the customer
- The nature of the customers' role in those processes
- How long delivery lasts
- The prescribed level and style of service to be offered

The integration of the core product, supplementary services, and delivery processes is captured in Figure 4.2, which illustrates the components of the service offering for an overnight stay at a luxury hotel. The core product—the overnight rental of a bedroom—has several dimensions. These include the service level; scheduling (how long the room may be used before another payment becomes due); the nature of the process (in this instance, people processing); and the role of customers in terms of what they are expected to do for themselves and what the hotel will do for them (such as making the bed, supplying bathroom towels, and cleaning the room).

Surrounding the core product is a variety of supplementary services. These range from reservations and meals to in-room service elements. The more expensive the hotel, the higher the level of service required of each element. For example, very important guests might be received at the airport and transported to the hotel in a limousine. Check-in arrangements can be made on the way to the hotel. By the time the guests arrive at the hotel, they are ready to be escorted to their rooms, where a butler is on hand to serve them.

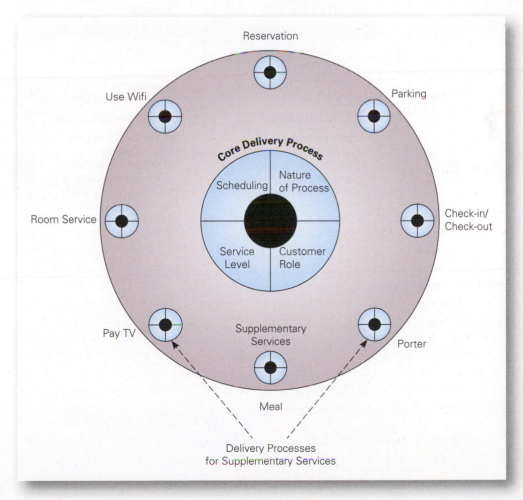

Figure 4.2 Depicting the service offering for an overnight hotel stay.

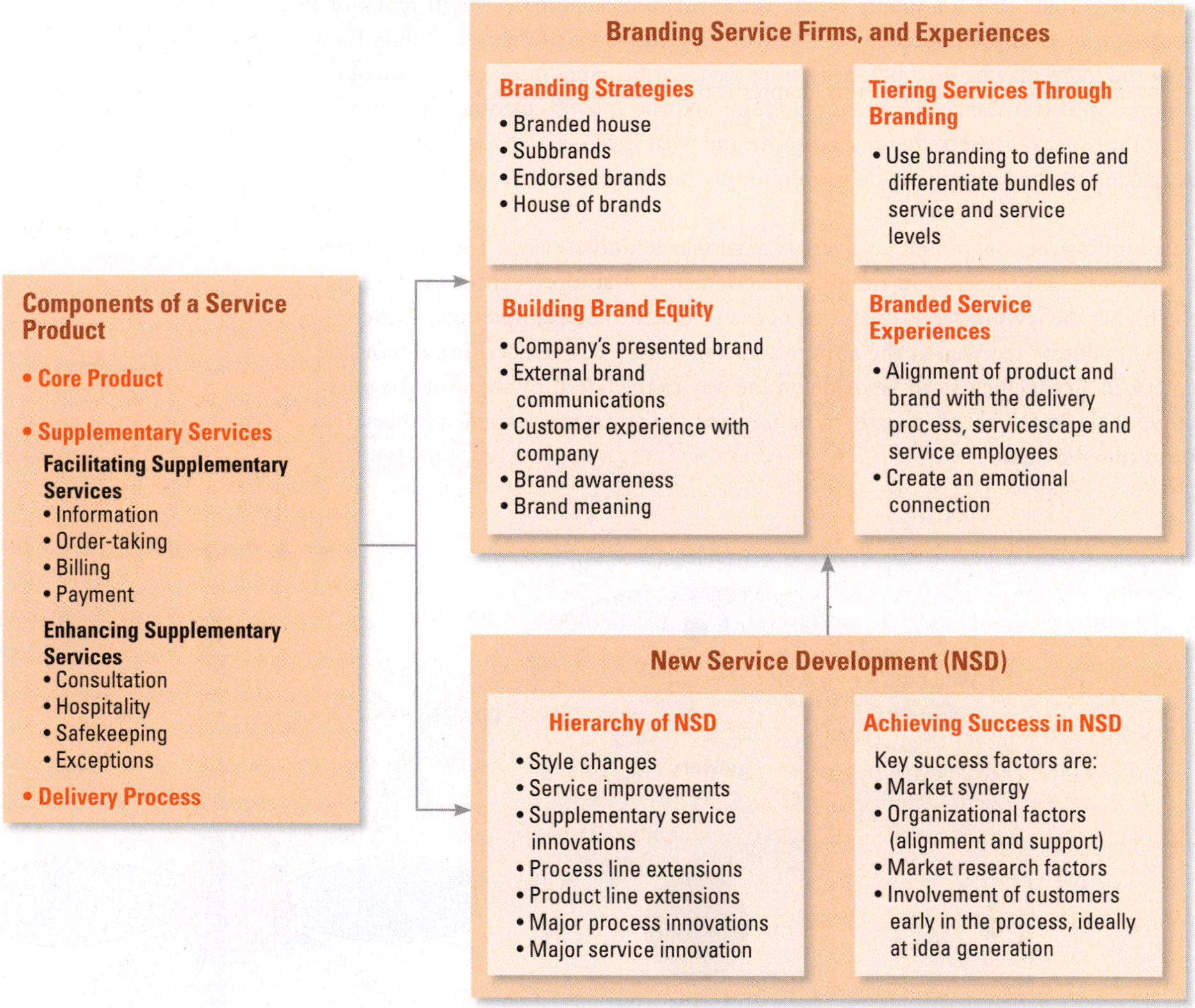

Branding Service Firms, and Experiences

Branding Strategies
- Branded house
- Subbrands
- Endorsed brands
- House of brands

Tiering Services Through Branding
- Use branding to define and differentiate bundles of service and service levels

Building Brand Equity
- Company's presented brand
- External brand communications
- Customer experience with company
- Brand awareness
- Brand meaning

Branded Service Experiences
- Alignment of product and brand with the delivery process, servicescape and service employees
- Create an emotional connection

Components of a Service Product

- **Core Product**

- **Supplementary Services**
  Facilitating Supplementary Services
  - Information
  - Order-taking
  - Billing
  - Payment

  Enhancing Supplementary Services
  - Consultation
  - Hospitality
  - Safekeeping
  - Exceptions

- **Delivery Process**

New Service Development (NSD)

Hierarchy of NSD
- Style changes
- Service improvements
- Supplementary service innovations
- Process line extensions
- Product line extensions
- Major process innovations
- Major service innovation

Achieving Success in NSD
Key success factors are:
- Market synergy
- Organizational factors (alignment and support)
- Market research factors
- Involvement of customers early in the process, ideally at idea generation

Figure 4.3 Overview of the structure of Chapter 4.

Table 4.1 Facilitating and enhancing services provide value to the core product.

Facilitating Services	Enhancing Services
• Information • Order taking • Billing • Payment	• Consultation • Hospitality • Safekeeping • Exceptions

An overview of the structure of this chapter is provided in Figure 4.3.

THE FLOWER OF SERVICE[3]

The Flower of Service consists of the core service and a range of supplementary services. There are potentially dozens of different supplementary services, but almost all of them can be classified into one of the eight clusters shown in Table 4.1. Each of these clusters is identified as either facilitating or enhancing. *Facilitating supplementary services* are required either for service delivery or for aid in the use of the core product. *Enhancing supplementary services* add extra value and appeal for customers (see Table 4.1). For example, consultation and hospitality can be very important supplementary services in a health-care context.

In Figure 4.4, the eight clusters are displayed as petals surrounding the center of a flower. The petals are arranged in a clockwise sequence starting with "information," according to how they are likely to be encountered by customers. In a well-designed and well-managed service product, the petals and core are fresh and well-formed. A badly designed or poorly delivered service is like a flower with missing, wilted, or discolored petals. Even if the core is perfect, the flower looks unattractive.

Facilitating Supplementary Services

Information

To obtain full value from goods or services, customers need relevant information. Information includes the following:

▶ Direction to service site

▶ Schedules/service hours

▶ Price information

▶ Terms and conditions of sale/service (Figure 4.5)

▶ Advice on how to get maximum value from a service

LO 2
Be familiar with the Flower of Service model.

LO 3
Know how facilitating supplementary services relate to the core product.

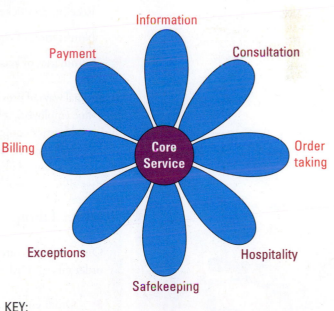

KEY:
Facilitating Supplementary Services
Enhancing Supplementary Services

Figure 4.4 The Flower of Service: A core product surrounded by clusters of supplementary services.

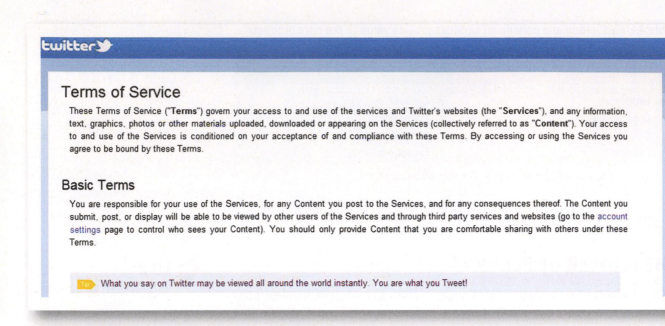

Figure 4.5 Twitter.com provides conditions of service to users.

SOURCE

From Twitter.com © Twitter Inc.

▶ Warnings and advice on how to avoid problems

▶ Confirmation of reservations

▶ Receipts and tickets

▶ Notification of changes

▶ Summaries of account activities

Traditional ways of providing information include using company websites, mobile apps, front-line employees, self-service machines, signs, printed notices, and brochures. Many business logistics companies offer shippers the opportunity to track the movements of their packages, each of which has been assigned a unique identification number (Figure 4.6). For example, Amazon provides its customers with a reference number that allows them to track the goods and know when to expect them.

Figure 4.6 Parcels can be tracked around the world with their identity codes.

Order Taking

Once customers are ready to buy, a key supplementary element comes into play—order taking. Order taking includes:

▶ Order entry
  o On-site order entry
  o Mail/telephone/e-mail/online/mobile app order

▶ Reservations or check-ins
  o Seats/tables/rooms
  o Vehicles or equipment rental
  o Professional appointment (Figure 4.7)

- Applications
  - o Memberships in clubs/programs
  - o Subscription services (e.g., utilities)
  - o Enrolment-based services (e.g., financial credit, college enrolment)

Order entry can be received through sales personnel, by phone and e-mail, online, or through a variety of other sources (Figure 4.8). The process of order taking should be polite, fast, and accurate so that customers do not waste time and endure unnecessary mental or physical effort.

Reservations (including appointments and check-ins) represent a special type of order taking that entitles customers to a specified unit of service.

Technology can be used to make order taking and reservations easier and faster for both customers and suppliers. For example, airlines now make use of ticketless systems based on e-mail and mobile apps. Customers receive a confirmation number when they make the reservation and need only show identification (or the ticket as shown on a mobile app) at the airport to claim their seats and receive a boarding pass.

Banks, insurance companies, and utilities require prospective customers to go through an application process so that they can gather relevant information and screen out those who do not meet basic enrolment criteria.

Figure 4.7 The services of a professional DJ have to be reserved.

Billing

Billing is common to almost all services. Timely billing encourages people to make faster payment. Billing can be:

- ▶ Periodic statements of account activity

- ▶ Invoices for individual transactions

- ▶ Verbal statements of amount due

- ▶ Online or machine display of amount due for self-payment transactions

Perhaps the simplest approach is self-billing, by which the customer tallies up the amount of an order and authorizes a card payment. In such instances, billing and payment are combined into a single act, although the seller may still need to check for accuracy.

Customers usually expect bills to be clear, informative, and itemized in ways that show how the total was computed. Unexplained, arcane symbols that have all the meaning of hieroglyphics on an Egyptian monument do not create a favorable impression of the service firm.

Busy customers hate to be kept waiting for a bill to be prepared in a hotel, a restaurant, or a rental car lot. Many hotels and car rental firms have created express check-out options, taking customers' credit card details in advance and documenting charges later by e-mail. However, accuracy is essential. Even though customers use the express check-outs to save time, they certainly don't want to waste

Figure 4.8 Some restaurants take dining reservations to a whole new level by allowing diners to bypass the traditional call-and-book experience with a mere click.

Figure 4.9 A wireless hand-held terminal allows car rental bills to be printed on the spot.

time later with corrections and refunds. An alternative express check-out procedure is used by some car rental companies. An agent meets customers as they return their cars, checks the mileage on the odometer and the fuel gauge readings, and then prints a bill on the spot using a portable wireless terminal (Figure 4.9).

Payment

In most cases, a bill requires the customer to take action on payment. Exceptions include bank statements and other direct debit-paid services, which show charges that will be deducted from a customer's account.

A variety of payment options exist, but customers expect them to be convenient and easy to use. They include:

▶ Self-service
   o Insert card, cash, or token into machine (Figure 4.10)
   o Transfer funds electronically
   o Mail a check
   o Enter a credit card number online
   o Use online payment systems such as PayPal, Google Wallet, or Bitcoins

▶ Direct to payee or intermediary
   o Cash handling or change giving
   o Check handling
   o Credit/charge/debit card handling
   o Coupon redemption

▶ Automatic deduction from financial deposits
   o Automated systems (e.g., machine-readable tickets that operate entry gates)
   o Pre-arranged automatic deduction for bill payment through direct debit (e.g., for bank loans and post-paid cell phone subscription plans)

LO 4

Know how enhancing supplementary services relate to the core product.

Self-service payment systems, for instance, require insertion of coins, banknotes, tokens, or cards in machines. As equipment breakdowns will destroy the whole purpose of such a system, good maintenance and prompt troubleshooting are essential. Most payment still takes the form of cash or credit cards. Other alternatives include vouchers, coupons, and pre-paid tickets. Electronic means such as PayPal offer a fuss-free and secure way to make payments, especially when shopping is done online.

Enhancing Supplementary Services

Consultation

At its simplest, consultation consists of advice from a knowledgeable service person in response to the request: "What do you suggest?" For example, you might ask your hairstylist for advice on different hairstyles and products. Effective consultation requires an understanding of each customer's current situation before suggesting a suitable course of action. Examples of consultation include:

Figure 4.10 Tokens, cards, and tickets allow self-service payment.

- ► Customized advice

- ► Personal counseling

- ► Tutoring/training in service use

- ► Management or technical consulting (Figure 4.11)

Counseling represents a more subtle approach to consultation because it helps customers understand their situations better and allows them to come up with their "own" solutions and action programs. This approach can be a particularly valuable supplement to services such as health treatment, where part of the challenge is to get customers to make significant lifestyle changes and live healthily. For example, diet centers like Weight Watchers use counseling to help customers change behaviors so that weight loss can be sustained after the initial diet is completed (Figure 4.12).

More formalized efforts to provide management and technical consulting for corporate customers include the "solution selling" associated with expensive industrial equipment and services. The sales engineer researches a customer's situation and offers advice about which particular package of equipment and systems will yield the best results.

Hospitality

Hospitality-related services should ideally reflect pleasure at meeting new customers and greeting old ones when they return. Well-managed businesses try to ensure that their employees treat customers as guests. Courtesy and consideration for customers' needs apply to both face-to-face encounters and telephone interactions. Hospitality elements include:

- ► Greeting

- ► Food and beverages

- ► Toilets and washrooms

- ► Waiting facilities and amenities
    - o Lounges, waiting areas, seating
    - o Weather protection
    - o Magazines, entertainment, newspapers

- ► Transport

Hospitality finds its fullest expression in face-to-face encounters. In some cases, it starts (and ends) with an offer of transport to and from the service site on courtesy shuttle buses. If customers must wait outdoors before the service can be delivered, then a thoughtful service provider will offer weather protection. If customers have to wait indoors, a waiting area with seating and even entertainment (TV, newspapers, or magazines) may be provided to pass the time. Shoppers at Abercrombie & Fitch, a global clothing retailer, are given a cheerful "hello" and "thank you" when they enter and leave the store, even if they do not buy anything (Figure 4.13).

Figure 4.11 An auditor provides a human touch during the process of consultation.

WHEN I SUGGESTED YOU EXERCISE TO SLIM DOWN.. I MEANT ALL OF YOU !

Figure 4.12 Counseling for weight reduction is a form of consultation.

Figure 4.13 Abercrombie & Fitch provides hospitality with a smile.

The quality of the hospitality services offered by a firm plays an important role in determining customer satisfaction. This is especially true for people-processing services because one cannot easily leave the service facility until the core service has been delivered. Private hospitals often seek to enhance their appeal by providing a level of room service that might be expected in a good hotel (Figure 4.14).

Safekeeping

When customers are visiting a service site, they often want assistance with their personal possessions. In fact, unless certain safekeeping services are provided, some customers may not visit at all. Safekeeping includes:

- Child care, pet care (Figure 4.15)
- Parking for vehicles, valet parking
- Coat rooms
- Baggage handling
- Storage space
- Safe deposit boxes
- Security personnel

Responsible businesses pay close attention to safety and security issues for customers who are visiting the firm's premises. Wells Fargo Bank mails a brochure with its bank statements that contains information about how its ATM machines can be used safely. The brochure also educates customers about how to protect their ATM cards and themselves from theft and personal injury. Moreover, the bank makes sure that its machines are in brightly lit, highly visible locations that are equipped with CCTV.

Figure 4.14 High-end hospital chains offer service and rooms like a five-star hotel chain.

Likewise, many services deal with sensitive information (e.g., healthcare providers and financial services). These companies must ensure that their customers' intangible financial assets and privacy are carefully safeguarded (Figure 4.16).

Exceptions

Exceptions involve supplementary services that fall outside the routine of normal service delivery. Astute businesses anticipate such exceptions and develop contingency plans and guidelines in advance. That way, employees will not appear helpless and surprised when customers ask for special assistance. Well-defined procedures make it easier for employees to respond promptly and effectively (Figure 4.17). There are several types of exceptions:

- **Special requests.** A customer may request services that require a departure from normal operating procedures. Common requests relate to personal needs, including care of children, dietary requirements, medical needs, religious observance, and personal disabilities. Such requests are particularly common in the travel and hospitality industries.

► **Problem solving.** Sometimes, normal service delivery (or product performance) fails to run smoothly due to accidents, delay, equipment failure, or difficulty faced by a customer while using a product.

► **Handling of complaints/suggestions/compliments.** This activity requires well-defined procedures. It should be easy for customers to express dissatisfaction, offer suggestions for improvement, or pass on compliments. Likewise, service providers should be able to make an appropriate response quickly (see Chapter 13 on complaint handling and service recovery).

► **Restitution.** Many customers expect to be compensated for serious performance failures. Compensation may take the form of repairs under warranty, legal settlements, refunds, an offer of free service, or any other form of payment-in-kind.

Managers need to keep an eye on the level of exception requests. Too many requests may indicate that standard procedures need revamping. For instance, if a restaurant frequently receives requests for special vegetarian meals that aren't on the menu, it may be time to revise the menu to include at least one or two such dishes. A flexible approach to exceptions is generally a good idea because it reflects responsiveness to customer needs. On the other hand, too many exceptions may compromise safety, negatively impact other customers, and overburden employees.

Figure 4.15 Pet care services are a form of safekeeping.

Managerial Implications

The eight categories of supplementary services that form the Flower of Service collectively provide many options for enhancing core products. Most supplementary services do (or should) represent responses to customer needs. As noted earlier, facilitating services such as information and reservations enable customers to use the core product more effectively. Others are "extras" that enhance the core product or even reduce its non-financial costs (e.g., meals, magazines, and entertainment are hospitality elements that help pass the waiting time). Some elements—notably billing and payment—are, in effect, imposed by the service provider. Even if they are not actively desired by the customer, they still form part of the overall service experience. Any badly handled element may negatively affect customers' perceptions of service quality. The "information" and "consultation" petals illustrate the emphasis in this book on the need for education as well as promotion in communicating with service customers (see Chapter 7 on communications and customer education).

A company's market positioning strategy helps to determine which supplementary services should be included. A strategy of adding benefits to increase customers' perceptions of quality will require more supplementary services than a strategy of competing on price. Furthermore, offering progressively higher levels of supplementary services around a common core may offer the basis for a product line of differentiated offerings, such as the various classes of travel offered by airlines.

Figure 4.16 Security features ensure that online transactions are safe.

The various components of the Flower of Service can serve as a checklist in the continuing search for new ways to augment existing core products and design new offerings. Regardless of which supplementary services a firm decides to offer, all the elements in each petal should receive the care and attention needed to consistently meet defined service standards. That way, the resulting flower will always have a fresh and appealing appearance.

LO 5

Understand branding at the corporate and individual service product levels.

BRANDING SERVICE FIRMS, PRODUCTS, AND EXPERIENCES

Branding plays an important role in services, as explained by Leonard Berry:

> Strong brands enable customers to better visualize and understand intangible products. They reduce customers' perceived monetary, social, or safety risk in buying services, which are difficult to evaluate prior to purchase. Strong brands are surrogates when the company offers no fabric to touch, no trousers to try on, no watermelons or apples to scrutinize, no automobile to test drive.[4]

Branding can be employed at both the corporate and product levels by almost any service business. In a well-managed firm, the corporate brand is not only easily recognized but also has meaning for customers as it stands for a particular way of doing business. Applying brand names to individual products enables the firm to communicate to the target market the distinctive experiences and benefits associated with a specific service concept.

Branding individual service products helps to differentiate one bundle of output from another. An example is Banyan Tree Hotels & Resorts (featured in Case 4), which carefully crafted specified products for its various target segments and branded them as "Heavenly Honeymoon," "Spa Indulgence," or "Intimate Moments."[5] The last is a product specially created for couples celebrating their wedding anniversary. It is presented as a surprise to the spouse. Guests return to find their villas decorated with lit candles, incense burning, flower petals spread throughout the room, satin sheets on the decorated bed, chilled champagne or wine, and a private outdoor pool with a variety of aromatic massage oils to further inspire those intimate moments. The packaging and branding of this product allows Banyan Tree to sell it via its website, distributors, and reservations centers, and to train staff about it at the individual hotels. Without giving the product a name or specifying exactly what it means, marketing, selling, and delivery would not be effective. Let us now look at alternative branding strategies for services.

Figure 4.17 McDonald's well-established procedures let employees respond smartly to customers' requests.

Branding Strategies for Services

Most service organizations offer a line of products rather than a single product. Thus, they must choose from among four broad branding alternatives: branded house (i.e., using a single brand to cover all products and services); house of brands (i.e., using a separate stand-alone brand for each offering); and sub-brands and endorsed brands, which are both some combination of these two extremes.[6] These alternatives are represented as a spectrum in Figure 4.18 and discussed in the following sections.

Branded House. The term *branded house* is used to describe a company, such as the Virgin Group, that applies its brand name to multiple offerings in often unrelated fields.[7] Virgin's core business areas are travel, entertainment, and lifestyle, but it also offers financial services, healthcare, and media and telecommunications services. The danger of such a strategy is that the brand gets overstretched and weakened.

Sub-brands. For *sub-brands*, the corporate or the master brand is the main reference point, but each product has a distinctive name as well. FedEx has been successfully using a sub-branding strategy. When the company decided to rebrand a ground delivery service

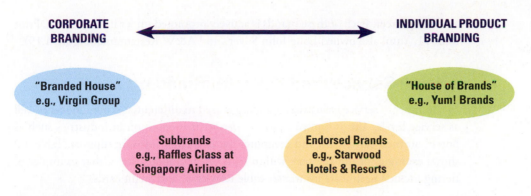

Figure 4.18 The spectrum of branding alternatives.

SOURCE

Based on James Devlin, "Brand Architecture in Services: The Example of Retail Financial Services" *Journal of Marketing Management* 19(9-10) (2003): 1046, © Jochen Wirtz.

it had purchased, it chose the name FedEx Ground and developed an alternative color for the standard logo (purple and green rather than purple and orange). Its goal was to transfer the positive image of reliability and timeliness associated with its air services to its less expensive, small-package ground service. The well-known air service was then rebranded as FedEx Express. The other sub-brands in what the firm refers to as "the FedEx family of companies" include FedEx Home Delivery (delivers to US residential addresses); FedEx Freight (regional, less-than-truckload transportation for heavyweight freight); FedEx Custom Critical (nonstop, door-to-door delivery of time-critical shipments); FedEx Trade Networks (customs brokerage, international freight forwarding, and trade facilitation); Fedex Supply Chain (comprehensive suite of solutions that synchronize the movement of goods); and Fedex Office (office and printing services, technology services, shipping supplies, and packing services located in both city and suburban retail stores).[8]

Endorsed Brands. For *endorsed brands*, the product brand dominates but the corporate name is still featured. Many hotel companies use this approach. They offer a family of sub-brands and/or endorsed brands. For instance, although the Intercontinental Hotel Group is in itself well known, its product brands are dominant. They are: Intercontinental Hotels & Resorts, Crowne Plaza Hotels & Resorts, Hotel Indigo, Holiday Inn, Holiday Inn Club Vacations, Holiday Inn Resort, Holiday Inn Express, Staybridge Suites, Candlewood Suites, Even Hotels, Hualuxe, and its loyalty program IHG Rewards Club.[9]

For a multi-brand strategy to succeed, each brand must promise a distinctive value proposition targeted at a different customer segment. It is important to note that in some instances, segmentation is situation-based. The same individual may have different needs (and willingness to pay) under different circumstances, such as when traveling with family or on business. A multi-brand strategy is aimed at encouraging customers to continue buying from within the brand family. Loyalty programs are often used to encourage this. For instance, loyalty points may be collected in one sub-brand on business travel and redeemed in another on leisure trips.

House of Brands. At the far end of the spectrum is the *house of brands* strategy. A good service example is Yum! Brands Inc., which has more than 40,000 restaurants in 125 countries and sales of $13 billion. While many may not have heard of Yum! Brands, people are certainly familiar with their restaurant brands—Taco Bell, KFC, Pizza Hut, and WingStreet. Each of these brands is actively promoted under its own name. Prior to 2011, Yum! also owned Long John Silver's and A&W Restaurants (Figure 4.19).

Tiering Service Products with Branding

LO 7

Understand how branding can be used to tier service products.

In a number of service industries, branding is used to differentiate core services as well as service levels. This is known as *service tiering*. It is common in industries such as hotels, airlines, car rentals, and computer hardware and software support. Table 4.2 shows examples of the key tiers within each of these industries. Other examples of tiering include healthcare insurance, cable television, and credit cards.

In the airline industry, individual carriers decide what levels of performance should be included with each class of service. Innovative carriers, such as British Airways and Virgin Atlantic, are continually trying to add new service features like business class seats that can be folded into beds for overnight travel. In other industries, tiering often reflects an individual firm's strategy of bundling service elements into a limited number of packages, each priced separately. Let's examine a few examples.

▶ **Avis Car Rental.** Avis focuses on two kinds of customers—consumer customers and business customers. For consumer customers, they tier their service based on different car classes (e.g., sub-compact, compact, intermediate, standard, full size, specialty, signature, premium, luxury, standard elite SUV, intermediate SUV, full-size SUV, premium SUV, convertible, minivan, and passenger van) as well as service. For example, if a customer does not want to drive, they can opt for Avis Chauffeur Drive. The chauffeur not only drives but also acts as a mobile concierge. Business customers have four programs to choose from: small and mid-sized business, entertainment and productions, meeting and group services, and government and military.[10]

▶ **British Airways.** A comprehensive example of strong sub-branding of service tiers in the airline industry comes from British Airways (BA), which offers a number of distinct air travel products. These include First (deluxe service), Club Europe (business class for flights within Europe), Club World (business class for longer international flights), Club World London City (business class for flights between London City and New York JFK), World Traveller Plus (premium economy class), World Traveller (economy class on longer international flights), Euro Traveller (economy class on flights within Europe), and UK Domestic (economy class on flights within the UK). Each BA sub-brand represents a specific service concept and a set of clearly stated product specifications for pre-flight, in-flight, and on-arrival service elements. To provide additional focus on product, pricing, and marketing communications, the responsibility for managing and developing each service is assigned to a separate management team. Through internal training and external communication, staff and passengers are kept informed of the characteristics of each service. Except for the UK Domestic, most aircrafts in BA's fleet are configured in several classes. For instance, the airline's intercontinental fleet of Boeing 777-300s is equipped to serve First, Club World, World Traveller Plus, and World Traveller passengers.

Figure 4.19 KFC and Pizza Hut are just some of the few popular fast food brands under Yum! Brands.

On any given route, all passengers traveling on a particular flight receive the same core product—say, a 10-hour journey from Los Angeles to London—but the nature

Table 4.2 Examples of service tiering.

Industry	Tiers	Key Service Attributes and Physical Elements Used in Tiering
Lodging	Star or diamond rating (5 to 1)	Architecture; landscaping; room size, furnishings, and décor; restaurant facilities and menus; room service hours; array of services and physical amenities; staffing levels; caliber and attitudes of employees
Airline	Classes (intercontinental): first, business, premium economy, economy[a]	Seat pitch (distance between rows), seat width, and reclining capability; meal and beverage service; staffing ratios; check-in speed; departure and arrival lounges; baggage retrieval speed
Car rental	Class of vehicle[b]	Base on vehicle size (from subcompact to full size), degree of luxury, plus special vehicle types (minivan, SUV, convertible)
Hardware and software support	Support levels	Hours and days of service; speed of response; speed of delivering replacement parts; technician-delivered service versus advice on self-service; availability of additional services

a   Only a few airlines offer as many as four classes of intercontinental service; domestic services usually feature one or two classes.
b   Avis and Hertz offer seven classes based on size and luxury, plus several special vehicle types.

and extent of most of the supplementary elements differ widely, both on the ground and in the air. Passengers in Club World, for instance, not only benefit from better tangible elements but also receive more personalized service from airline employees. Moreover, they enjoy faster service on the ground at check-in, passport control in

Overview   Resources

Sun System Service Plans for Solaris

Sun System Service Plans for the Solaris Operating System provide integrated hardware and Solaris OS (or OpenSolaris OS) support service coverage to help keep your systems running smoothly. This single price, complete system approach is ideal for companies running Solaris on Sun hardware.

» Compare Plans Now

Choose from four service plan options to best meet your support needs.

Platinum	Gold	Silver	Bronze
Comprehensive support for mission-critical systems	Enhanced support including 24/7 help desk assistance	Basic business-hours coverage for less-critical systems	Resources and replacement parts for self-maintainers

» Compare Plans Now

Figure 4.20 Sun System service plans for Solaris clearly differentiate service levels.

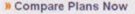

SOURCE

From Oracle.com © Sun Microsystems, Inc.

London (special lines), and baggage retrieval (priority handling). First class passengers are pampered even more.[11]

▶ **Sun's Hardware and Software Support.** Sun, a brand of Oracle, shows how different tiers may be branded in a high-tech, business-to-business product line. The company offers a full range of hardware and software support in a program branded as "SunSpectrum Support."[12] Four different levels of support are available, sub-branded from platinum to bronze (Figure 4.20). The objective is to allow buyers to choose a level of support consistent with their own organization's needs (and willingness to pay), ranging from expensive, mission-critical support at the enterprise level (Platinum Service Plan) to relatively inexpensive assistance with self-service maintenance support (Bronze Service Plan).

▶ Platinum: Mission-critical support with onsite service 24/7 and a two-hour response time.

▶ Gold: Business critical support with onsite service from Monday to Friday, 8 a.m. to 8 p.m.; telephone service 24/7; and a four-hour response time.

▶ Silver: Basic support with onsite service from Monday to Friday, 8 a.m. to 5 p.m.; telephone service from Monday to Friday, 8 a.m. to 8 p.m.; and a four-hour response time.

▶ Bronze: Self-support with phone service from 8 a.m. to 5 p.m.

Building Brand Equity

LO 8

Discuss how firms can build brand equity.

To build a strong brand, we need to understand what contributes to brand equity. Brand equity is the value premium that comes with a brand. It is the additional amount that customers are willing to pay for a branded service over a similar service that has no brand. Figure 4.21 shows the following six key components:

▶ *Company's presented brand*—mainly through advertising, service facilities, and personnel.

▶ *External brand communications*—from word-of-mouth and publicity. These are outside of the firm's control.

▶ *Customer experience with the company*—what the customer goes through when they patronize the company.

▶ *Brand awareness*—the ability to recognize and recall a brand when provided with a cue.

▶ *Brand meaning*—what comes to the customer's mind when a brand is mentioned.

▶ *Brand equity*—the degree of marketing advantage that a brand has over its competitors.

From Figure 4.21, we can see that a company's marketing and external communications help to build brand awareness. However, it is the customer's actual experience with the brand that is more powerful in building brand equity.

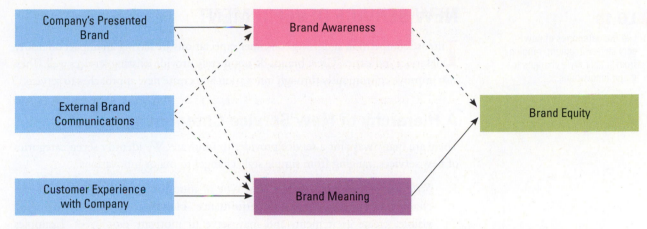

Figure 4.21 A Service-Branding Model. The bold arrows represent strong relationships and the dotted arrows represent weaker relationships.

SOURCE

From Leonard L. Berry, "A Service- Branding Model," *Journal of Academy of Marketing Science* 28(1): 130; published by Springer © 2000.

Delivering Branded Service Experiences

LO 9

Understand what is required to deliver a branded service experience.

Around the world, many financial service firms continue to create and register brand names to distinguish the different accounts and service packages that they offer. Their objective is to transform a series of service elements and processes into a consistent and recognizable service experience, offering a definable and predictable output at a specified price. Unfortunately, there is often little discernible difference—other than name—between one firm's branded offering and another's, and their value propositions may be unclear. Don Shultz emphasizes that "The brand promise or value proposition is not a tag line, an icon, or a color or a graphic element, although all of these may contribute. It is, instead, the heart and soul of the brand. . . ."[13]

An important role for service marketers is to become brand champions, familiar with and responsible for shaping every aspect of the customer's experience. We can relate the notion of a branded service experience to the Flower of Service metaphor by emphasizing the need for consistency in the color and texture of each petal.

Besides designing great service products and giving them a brand name, how can we deliver branded service experiences?[14] To begin with, we must align the service product and brand with the delivery process, and the servicescape and people with the brand proposition. In order to do this, it is important to have great processes in place (see Chapter 8—Designing Service Processes). In addition, the emotional experience of the service can often be created effectively through the servicescape (see Chapter 10—Crafting the Service Environment). The hardest part of crafting the emotional experience is the building of interpersonal relationships where trust is established between the consumers and the firm's employees.[15] Thus, we need to invest in good employees who can deliver the brand experience that creates customer loyalty (see Chapter 11—Managing People for Service Advantage).

LO 10

List the categories of new
service development, ranging
from simple style changes to
major innovations.

NEW SERVICE DEVELOPMENT

Intense competition and rising consumer expectations are having an impact on nearly all service industries. Great brands do not merely provide existing services well. They also improve continuously through innovation and create new approaches to service.[16]

A Hierarchy of New Service Categories

There are many ways for a service provider to innovate. We identify seven categories of new services, ranging from simple style changes to major innovations.

1. *Style changes* represent the simplest type of innovation, typically involving no changes in either processes or performance. However, they are often highly visible, create excitement, and may serve to motivate employees. Examples include redesigning retail branches, websites, or uniforms for service employees.

2. *Service improvements* are the most common type of innovation. They involve small changes in the performance of current products, including improvements to either the core product or to existing supplementary services. For example, the Lydmar hotel in Stockholm has a series of buttons where passengers can choose their music from a choice of garage, funk, and rhythm and blues. This is a simple but unique improvement that can enhance a customer's experience.[17]

3. *Supplementary service innovations* take the form of adding new facilitating or enhancing service elements to an existing core service, or of significantly improving an existing supplementary service. Low-tech innovations for an existing service can be as simple as adding parking at a retail site or agreeing to accept payment via smartphone. Theme restaurants such as the Rainforest Café enhance the core food service with new experiences. The cafés are designed to keep customers entertained with aquariums, live parrots, waterfalls, fiberglass monkeys, talking trees that spout environmentally related information, and regularly timed thunderstorms, complete with lightning.

4. *Process line extensions* often represent distinctive new ways of delivering existing products. The intention is either to offer a different and more convenient experience for existing customers, or to attract new customers who find the traditional approach unappealing. Often, they involve adding a lower-contact distribution channel to an existing high-contact channel, such as having self-service complement delivery by service employees, or creating online or app-based service delivery.

5. *Product line extensions* are additions to a company's current product lines. The first company in a market to offer such a product may be seen as an innovator. These new services may be targeted at existing customers to serve a broader variety of needs, or designed to attract new customers with different needs (or both). For example, a restaurant may extend the product line to offer a menu for dogs, so that both the owners and their dogs can dine in the same restaurant.

6. *Major process innovations* involve the use of new processes to deliver existing core products with additional benefits. For example, online courses are transforming higher education using cutting-edge technology such as the internet and smart devices. Sebastian Thrun launched the for-profit Udacity in 2012 while he was still a tenured professor at Stanford University. Andrew Ng and Daphne

Figure 4.22 Online courses and MOOCS are transforming education.

Koller, also from Stanford, launched Coursera, a non-profit competitor that uses massive open online courses (MOOCS) to completely redesign education (Figure 4.22).

Major redesign was required to make online courses effective and successful. Today, these courses take full advantage of the interactivity of online videos, short assessment tasks, simulations, and discussion forums. Students can watch and work on any part of a course as often as they want until they have internalized the content. According to Salman Khan, founder of Khan Academy and former hedge fund analyst, "if people are meeting, they don't need a lecture; if you don't need them to interact, information should just be in a video or a memo."[18] Online education will clearly mean upheaval for universities around the world. However, for students, education will be transformed.

7. *Major service innovations* are new core products for markets that have not been previously defined. They usually include new service characteristics as well as radical new processes. For example, Amazon diversified into providing on-demand computing power and became a leader in cloud-computing services (Figure 4.23). Other examples are Virgin Galactic and XCOR Aerospace, which hope to create sub-orbital space tourism. Space Adventures, a leading company in the space-flight industry, flew the first space tourist on the Russian Soyuz spacecraft to the International Space Station in 2001. Today, the company

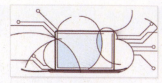
WHAT IS CLOUD COMPUTING?

Learn about the benefits of on-demand IT resources and pay-as-you-go pricing

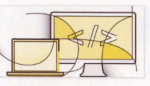
SELF-PACED LABS

Access free self-paced labs and instructional videos

GET STARTED WITH AWS

Learn how to start using AWS in minutes

SOFTWARE FREE TRIALS

Try top software products from AWS Marketplace for free

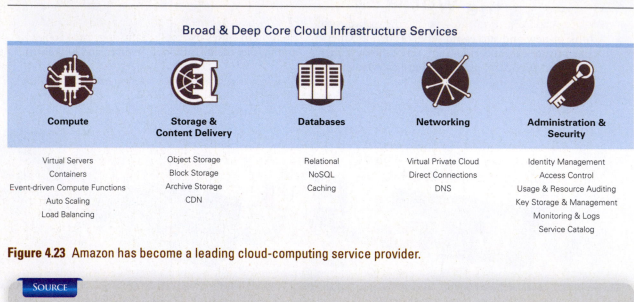

Broad & Deep Core Cloud Infrastructure Services

Compute	Storage & Content Delivery	Databases	Networking	Administration & Security
Virtual Servers	Object Storage	Relational	Virtual Private Cloud	Identity Management
Containers	Block Storage	NoSQL	Direct Connections	Access Control
Event-driven Compute Functions	Archive Storage	Caching	DNS	Usage & Resource Auditing
Auto Scaling	CDN			Key Storage & Management
Load Balancing				Monitoring & Logs
				Service Catalog

Figure 4.23 Amazon has become a leading cloud-computing service provider.

LO 11

Describe how firms can achieve success in new service development.

provides different space experiences, including a lunar mission, orbital space flight, sub-orbital space flight, and space-walk program (Figure 4.24). These experiences do not come cheap. Sub-orbital spaceflights start from over $100,000, and the lunar mission costs $100m per seat.[19]

Major service innovations are relatively rare. More common is the use of new technologies to deliver existing services in new ways, enhance or create new supplementary services, and greatly improve performance on existing ones through process redesign. However, technology is improving so fast that we will soon see major service innovations. This is discussed in Service Insights 4.1.

Achieving Success in New Service Development

Consumer goods have high failure rates, with more than 90% of the 30,000 new products introduced each year ending in failure.[20] Services are not immune to high failure rates either. For example, Delta Airlines was one of several major carriers attempting to launch a separate low-cost carrier designed to compete with discount airlines such as Jet Blue and Southwest Airlines. However, none of these

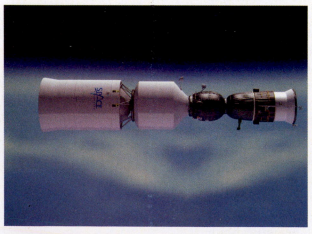

Figure 4.24 Space Adventure provides different experiences to space tourists.

SERVICE INSIGHTS 4.1

Major Service Innovation Enabled by Technology

Digital startups are bubbling up in an astonishing variety of services, penetrating every nook and cranny of our economies and reshaping entire industries. According to Marc Andreessen, a Silicon Valley venture capitalist, "software is eating the world." Just think of new and successful services such as Uber's taxi, private car, and ride-share service (www.uber .com) and AirB&B's platform that lets people rent out their homes for holidays and short-term stays (www.airbnb.com). This digital frenzy has given rise to a global movement, with most big cities—from London to Berlin and Singapore to Shanghai—having sizeable startup ecosystems. There are hundreds of startup schools (i.e., "accelerators") and thousands of co-working spaces where caffeinated folk in their 20s and 30s toil hunched over their laptops. All these ecosystems are highly interconnected and form a global crowd. People travel from city to city, and a few of them spend a semester with "Unreasonable at Sea," an accelerator program on a ship which cruises the world while its passengers work on their business models and write code. "Anyone who writes code can become an entrepreneur—anywhere in the world," says Simon Levene, a venture capitalist in London.

Today's entrepreneurial boom is based on solid foundations. This makes it likely to continue for the foreseeable future. The basic building blocks for digital services (or the "technologies for startup production", in the words of Josh Lerner of Harvard Business School) have become so evolved, cheap, and ubiquitous that they can easily be combined, built upon, and reconfigured. These building blocks include snippets of code that can be copied freely from the internet; easy-to-learn programming frameworks (e.g., Ruby on Rails); services for finding developers (eLance, oDesk), sharing code (GitHub), and testing usability (UserTesting.com); and application programming interfaces (APIs). Others include services that can be used as inputs, such as voice calls (Twilio), maps (Google), and payments (PayPal). Probably the most important are platform services that can host startup services (e.g., Amazon's cloud computing), distribute them (app stores by Apple, Samsung, and Google), and market them (Facebook, Twitter, and LinkedIn).

Thanks to the internet, information on how to build a startup has become easily accessible. Global standards are emerging for all things related to startups, ranging from term sheets for investments to business plans.

Innovation does not stop at the virtual world. Hardware—from processors and cameras to sensors—is getting better, smaller, and cheaper! Technologies such as robots, drones, wearable computers and sensors, self-driving cars, virtual reality, speech recognition, biometrics, artificial intelligence, and the internet will bring opportunities for a wide range of service innovations that will dramatically improve customer experience, service quality, and productivity.

For example, the Henn-na Hotel in Nagasaki, Japan, is run by robots. It aims to have 90% of hotel services provided by robots (Figure 4.25), including porter service, room cleaning, front desk, and other services to reduce costs and ensure comfort. The use of facial recognition to give access to the hotel, rooms, and other facilities is also an effective replacement for cumbersome room card systems.

Never before has technological development been so fast and wide-reaching! It will need highly skilled managers with a deep knowledge of the service consumer and services marketing to translate these opportunities into well-designed service products.

SOURCES

Based on "A Cambrian Moment," *Economist*, January 18, 2014: 4; "The Third Great Wave," *The Economist*, October 4, 2014: 3; "Japan Opens Hotel Run by Robots That Will Welcome Guests, Carry Bags and Even Clean Your Room," *Mail Online*, http://www.dailymail.co.uk/sciencetech/article-2946103/FAULTY-towers-Japan-opens-hotelmulti- ingual-ROBOTS-welcome-guestscarry-bags-clean-room.html, accessed on February 17, 2015.

operations were successful. Many banks have tried to sell insurance products in the hope of increasing the number of profitable relationships with existing customers, but these product extensions have also often failed.

There are various reasons for failure, such as inability to meet a consumer need, inability to cover costs from revenues, and poor execution. For example, a study in the restaurant

Figure 4.25 Robots serve guests at the Henn-na Hotel in Japan.

business found a failure rate of about 26% during the first year, rising to almost 60% within three years.[21] How then can we successfully develop new services? A number of studies have found that the following three factors contribute most to success:[22]

1. *Market synergy*—The new product fits well with the existing image of the firm, its expertise, and its resources. It is better than competing products in terms of meeting customers' needs as the firm has a good understanding of its customers' purchase behavior. It also receives strong support from the firm and its branches during and after the launch.

2. *Organizational factors*—There is strong inter-functional cooperation and coordination. Development personnel are fully aware of why they are involved and of the importance of new products to the company.

3. *Market research factors*—Detailed and scientifically designed market research studies are conducted early in the development process with a clear idea of the type of information to be obtained. A good definition of the product concept is developed before undertaking field surveys.

Furthermore, researchers found that in the idea-generation stage, the nature of submitted ideas differed significantly depending on whether they were created by professional service developers or by customers. Customers' ideas were judged to be more original and to have a higher perceived value for customers. However, these ideas were usually harder to convert into commercial services.[23] The emergence of crowds as innovation partners provides additional opportunities for cost-effective innovation that can lead to new breakthroughs in service development.[24] We will discuss the role of customer feedback in improving and developing (new) services in greater detail in Chapter 8 on process design and Chapter 14 on improving service quality and productivity.

LO 1 ▶ A service product consists of three components:

- o The core product delivers the principle benefits and solutions customers seek.
- o Supplementary services facilitate and enhance the core product.
- o Delivery processes determine how the core and supplementary service elements are being delivered to the customer.

LO 2 ▶ The Flower of Service consists of two components:

- o Core product
- o Supplementary services

As the core product often becomes commoditized, supplementary services can play an important role in differentiating and positioning the core product.

LO 3 ▶ The Flower of Service concept categorizes supplementary services into facilitating and enhancing supplementary services.

- o Facilitating supplementary services are needed for service delivery or help in the use of the core product. They include information, order taking, billing, and payment.

LO 4 ▶ Enhancing supplementary services add value for the customer. They include consultation, hospitality, safekeeping, and dealing with exceptions.

LO 5 ▶ Branding can be used at both the corporate and the individual service levels.

- o The corporate brand is not only easily recognized but also has meaning for the customer as it stands for a particular way of doing business.
- o Branding of individual service products helps firms to differentiate one bundle of output from another. Most service firms offer a line of products, with each product having a different combination of service attributes and performance levels. Branding of individual service products is used to increase the tangibility of the service offering and value proposition.

LO 6 ▶ Firms can use a variety of branding strategies, including:

- o *Branded house*: applying a brand to multiple, often unrelated services (e.g., Virgin Group)
- o *Sub-brands*: using a master brand (often the firm name) with a specific service brand (e.g., FedEx Ground service).
- o *Endorsed brands*: here, the product brand dominates but the corporate brand is still featured (e.g., Starwood Hotels & Resorts).
- o *House of brands*: promoting individual services under their own brand name without the corporate brand (e.g., KFC of Yum! Brands).

LO 7 ▶ In many industries, branding is used to differentiate core services as well as service levels. This is called service tiering. Service tiering is common in industries such as hotels, airlines, car rentals, and credit cards.

LO 8 ▶ Branding is not just about distinctive brand names and market communications.

- o A service firm's presented brand (e.g., through advertising) is more effective in building brand awareness than brand equity.
- o The customer's service experience with the brand (i.e., the moments of truth) is ultimately more powerful in building brand equity.

LO 9 ▶ A branded service experience transforms a series of service elements and processes into a consistent and recognizable service experience. It aligns the service product and brand with the delivery process, and the servicescape and people with the brand proposition.

LO 10 ▶ Firms need to improve and develop new services to maintain a competitive edge. The seven levels in the hierarchy of new service development are:

- o *Style changes*: introducing highly visible changes that create excitement but do not typically involve changes in service performance or processes.
- o *Service improvements*: introducing modest changes in the performance of current products.
- o *Supplementary service innovations*: significantly improving or adding new facilitating or enhancing service elements.
- o *Process line extensions*: developing new ways of delivering existing service products, such as creating self-service options.
- o *Product line extensions*: adding new services that typically deliver the same core service but are specified to satisfy different needs.
- o *Major process innovations*: using new processes to deliver current products, such as adding online courses to traditional classroom-delivered lectures.
- o *Major service innovations:* developing new core products for markets that have not been previously defined. Major service innovations are relatively rare. More common is the use of new technologies to deliver existing services in new ways, enhance or create new supplementary services, and greatly improve performance on existing ones through process redesign.

However, digital startups, quickly improving hardware (from processors and cameras to sensors), and new technologies bring opportunities for service innovations that will dramatically improve customer experience, service quality, and productivity.

 LO 11 ▶ Key factors that enhance the chances of success in new service development are:

o *Market synergy:* The new product fits well with the firm's existing image, expertise, and resources; is better at meeting customers' needs than competing services; and receives strong support during and after the launch from the firm and its branches.

o *Organizational factors:* There is strong cooperation between the different functional areas in a firm. Staff members understand the new product and its underlying processes and are aware of its importance for the firm.

o *Market research:* Customer ideas and research are incorporated at an early stage in the new service design process. There is a clear idea of the type of information to be obtained. A good definition of the product concept is developed before field surveys are undertaken.

UNLOCK YOUR LEARNING

These keywords are found within the sections of each Learning Objective (LO). They are integral to understanding the services marketing concepts taught in each section. Having a firm grasp of these keywords and how they are used is essential to helping you do well on your course, and in the real and very competitive marketing scene out there.

LO 1
1 Core product
2 Bundle of output
3 Delivery processes
4 Supplementary services

LO 2
1 Flower of Service
2 Enhancing supplementary services
3 Facilitating supplementary services

LO 3
1 Information
2 Order taking
3 Billing
4 Payment
5 Reservations
6 Self-service

LO 4
1 Consultation
2 Counseling
3 Exceptions
4 Hospitality
5 Safekeeping
6 Special requests

LO 5
1 Branding

LO 6
1 Branding strategies
2 Branded house
3 Sub-brands
4 Endorsed brands
5 House of brands

LO 7
1 Service tiering

LO 8
1 Brand awareness
2 Brand communications
3 Brand equity
4 Brand meaning
5 Branded experience
6 Presented brand
7 Service-Branding Model

LO 9
1 Branded service experience
2 Value proposition
3 Servicescape

LO 10
1 Major process innovations
2 Major service innovations
3 Process line extensions
4 Product line extensions
5 Service improvements
6 Style changes
7 Supplementary service innovations
8 New service development

LO 11
1 Market research factors
2 Market synergy
3 Organizational factors
4 Success in new service development

How well do you know the language of services marketing? Quiz yourself!

⚠ **Not for the academically faint-of-heart**

For each keyword you are able to recall without referring to earlier pages, give yourself a point (and a pat on the back). Tally your score at the end and see if you earned the right to be called—a *services marketeer*.

SCORE

01 – 12 Services Marketing is done a great disservice.
13 – 24 The midnight oil needs to be lit, pronto.
25 – 36 I know what you *didn't* do all semester.
37 – 48 By George! You're getting there.
49 – 60 Now, go forth and market.
61 – 73 There should be a marketing concept named after you.

Review Questions

1. Explain what is meant by the core product and supplementary services.

2. Explain the Flower of Service concept and identify each of its petals. What insights does this concept provide for service marketers?

3. What is the difference between enhancing and facilitating supplementary services? Give several examples of each type by referring to services you have used recently.

4. How is branding used in services marketing? What is the distinction between a corporate brand such as Marriott and the names of its various inn and hotel chains?

5. How can service firms build brand equity?

6. How can brands be used to tier service products?

7. What are the approaches firms can take to create new services?

8. Why do new services often fail? What are the factors associated with the successful development of new services?

WORK YOUR SERVICES MARKETING

Application Exercises

1. Select a specific service product you are familiar with, and identify its core product and supplementary services. Select a competing service and analyze the differences between the two in terms of the core product and supplementary services.

2. Identify two examples of branding in financial services (e.g., specific types of retail bank accounts or insurance policies), and define their characteristics. How meaningful are these brands likely to be for customers?

3. Select a service firm that you believe is highly successful and has strong brand equity. Conduct a few interviews to find out how consumers experience its service. Use your findings to identify the factors that helped the service firm to build its strong brand equity.

4. Using a firm you are familiar with, analyze what opportunities it might have to create product line extensions for its current and/or new markets. What impact might these extensions have on its present services?

5. Identify two new service developments that have failed. Analyze the causes for their failure.

6. Select a service brand you consider to be outstanding, and explain why you think so. Explore the weaknesses of this brand as well. (You should select an organization you are very familiar with.)

END**NOTES**

1. Bruce Horovitz, "Starbucks Aims beyond Lattes to Extend Brand," *USA Today*, May 18, 2006; Ben Sisariomay, "Starbucks and Spotify Team Up to Program Playlists in Stores," *New York Times*, May 19, 2015: B2; www.starbucks.com, accessed February 17, 2015.

2. The notion of a core service enhanced by supplementary services was advanced by: Pierre Eiglier and Eric Langeard, "Services as Systems: Marketing Implications," in Pierre Eiglier, Eric Langeard, Christopher H. Lovelock, John E. G. Bateson, and Robert F. Young (eds), *Marketing Consumer Services: New Insights* (Cambridge, MA: Marketing Science Institute, 1977): 83–103.

3. The "Flower of Service" concept was first introduced in Christopher H. Lovelock, "Cultivating the Flower of Service: New Ways of Looking at Core and Supplementary Services," in P. Eiglier and E. Langeard (eds.), *Marketing, Operations, and Human Resources: Insights into Services* (Aix-en-Provence, France: IAE, Université d'Aix-Marseille III, 1992): 296–316.

4. From Leonard L Berry, "Cultivating Service Brand Equity," *Academy of Marketing Science* 28, no. 1 (2000): 128–137, © 1994 Academy of Marketing Science.

5. www.banyantree.com, accessed February 17, 2015.

6. James Devlin, "Brand Architecture in Services: The Example of Retail Financial Services," *Journal of Marketing Management* 19 (2003): 1043–1065.

7. David Aaker and Erich Joachimsthaler, "The Brand Relationship Spectrum: The Key to the Brand Challenge," *California Management Review* 42, no. 4 (2000): 8–23.

8. www.fedex.com, accessed February 17, 2015.

9. www.ihgplc.com, accessed February 17, 2015.

10. www.avis.com, accessed February 17, 2015.

11. www.britishairways.com, accessed February 17, 2015.

12. http://www.sun.com/service/serviceplans/sunspectrum/index.jsp, accessed May 7, 2009.

13. From Don E. Schultz, "Getting to the Heart of the Brand," © 2001 American Marketing Management.

14. For an excellent and detailed introduction to the development of customer experience strategies, see: Phillip Klaus, *Measuring Customer Experience: How to Develop and Execute the Most Profitable Customer Experience Strategies* (Palgrave Macmillan, 2014).

15. Sharon Morrison and Frederick G. Crane, "Building the Service Brand by Creating and Managing an Emotional Brand Experience," *Brand Management* 14, no. 5 (2007): 410–421.

16. For an overview of service innovation research, see: Per Carlborg, Daniel Kindström, and Christian Kowalkowski, "The Evolution of Service Innovation Research: A Critical Review and Synthesis," *The Service Industries Journal* 34, no. 5 (2014): 373–398.

17. Talk by Rory Sutherland, "Sweat the Small Stuff," http://www.ted.com/talks/lang/eng/rory_sutherland_sweat_the_small_stuff.html, accessed February 17, 2015.

18. "Life's Work, Salman Khan," *Harvard Business Review* 92, no. 1/2 (2014): 124.

19. http://www.spaceadventures.com/, accessed February 17, 2015.

20. Clayton M. Christenson, Scott Cook, and Taddy Hall, "Marketing Malpractice: The Cause and the Cure," *Harvard Business Review* (December 2005): 4–12.

21. H. G. Parsa, John T. Self, David Njite, and Tiffany King, "Why Restaurants Fail," *Cornell Hotel and Restaurant Administration Quarterly* 46 (August 2005): 304–322.

22. Scott Edgett and Steven Parkinson, "The Development of New Financial Services: Identifying Determinants of Success and Failure," *International Journal of Service Industry Management* 5, no. 4 (1994): 24–38; Michael Ottenbacher, Juergen Gnoth, and Peter Jones, "Identifying Determinants of Success in Development of New High-Contact Services," *International Journal of Service Industry Management* 17, no. 4 (2006): 344–363.

23. Peter R. Magnusson, Jonas Matthing, and Per Kristensson, "Managing User Involvement in Service Innovation: Experiments with Innovating End Users," *Journal of Service Research* 6 (November 2003): 111–124; Jonas Matthing, Bodil Sandén, and Bo Edvardsson, "New Service Development: Learning from and with Customers," *International Journal of Service Industry Management* 15, no. 5 (2004): 479–498.

24. Kevin J. Boudreau and Karim R. Lakhani, "Using the Crowd as an Innovation Partner," *Harvard Business Review* 91, no. 4 (2013): 61–69.

SERVICES through PHYSICAL and ELECTRONIC CHANNELS

LEARNING OBJECTIVES (LOs)

By the end of this chapter, the reader should be able to:

LO 1 Know the four key questions that form the foundation of any service distribution strategy: What? How? Where? When?

LO 2 Describe the three interrelated flows that show *what* is being distributed.

LO 3 Know *how* services can be distributed using three main options, and understand the importance of distinguishing between the distribution of core and supplementary services.

LO 4 Recognize the issues of delivering services through electronic channels, and discuss the factors that have fueled the growth of service delivery via cyberspace.

LO 5 Understand the determinants of customers' channel preferences.

LO 6 Know the importance of channel integration.

LO 7 Describe the *where* (place) decisions of physical channels, and be familiar with the strategic and tactical location considerations.

LO 8 Describe the *when* (time) decisions of physical channels and the factors that determine extended operating hours.

LO 9 Understand the role, benefits, and costs of using intermediaries in distributing services.

LO 10 Know why franchising is such a common way of delivering services to end users.

LO 11 Understand the challenges of distribution in large domestic markets.

LO 12 Be familiar with the forces that drive service firms to go international.

LO 13 Appreciate the special challenges of distributing services internationally.

LO 14 Explain the determinants of international market entry strategies.

OPENING VIGNETTE

Being Global in an Instant? . . . Or Does It Take Forever?

Some services spread like wildfire and at incredible speed. For example, Lauren Luke's *panacea81* has become one of the world's most popular YouTube channels in less than 12 months. Today, it has over 135 million views. Luke's short video tutorials showing viewers how to apply make-up for various occasions have made her an Internet celebrity. She was named the most influential make-up mentor by *Allure* magazine. Related services, including the British make-up artist's website, have been hugely successful.[1] In a similar manner, diverse business models such as Airbnb, Uber, TripAdvisor, and Coursera went global within a few years.

Other services, however, may take decades to achieve global distribution. Think of how long it took Starbucks or supply chain solution providers such as FedEx or DHL to achieve a global presence! These contrasting examples show the diversity of the service sector as well as the importance of differentiating information-processing and people- or possession-processing services. While the former can be distributed rapidly, the latter require development of facilities in every market where presence is sought. There is also a need for the growing firm to deal with local labor, building, food hygiene regulations, and more. That requires a lot of finances and management time! Just think about all the decisions that had to be made by Starbucks so that its service would be accessible around the world.

Figure 5.1 Lauren Luke's make-up videos on YouTube are viewed by millions of people globally.

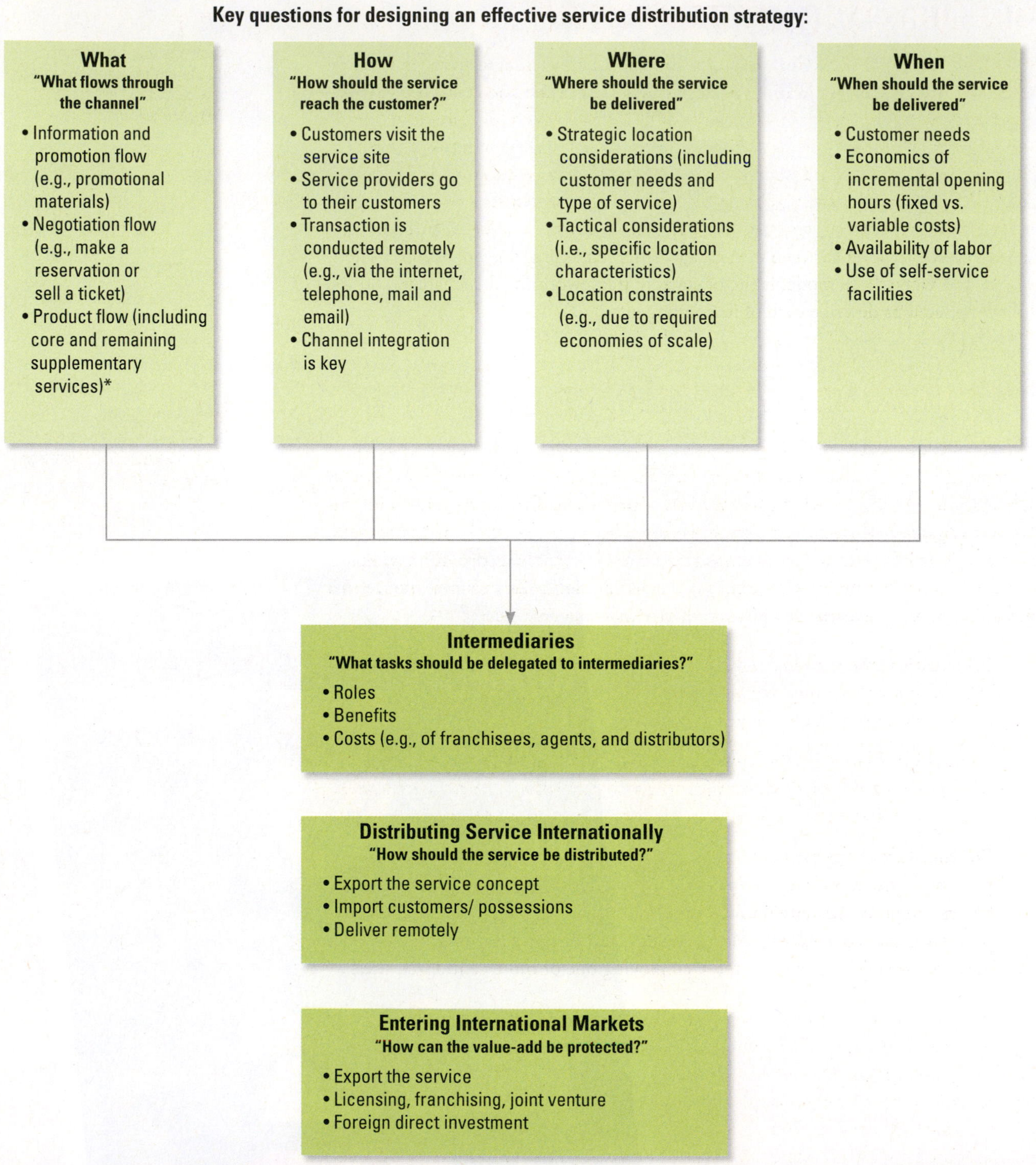

Key questions for designing an effective service distribution strategy:

What
"What flows through the channel"

- Information and promotion flow (e.g., promotional materials)
- Negotiation flow (e.g., make a reservation or sell a ticket)
- Product flow (including core and remaining supplementary services)*

How
"How should the service reach the customer?"

- Customers visit the service site
- Service providers go to their customers
- Transaction is conducted remotely (e.g., via the internet, telephone, mail and email)
- Channel integration is key

Where
"Where should the service be delivered"

- Strategic location considerations (including customer needs and type of service)
- Tactical considerations (i.e., specific location characteristics)
- Location constraints (e.g., due to required economies of scale)

When
"When should the service be delivered"

- Customer needs
- Economics of incremental opening hours (fixed vs. variable costs)
- Availability of labor
- Use of self-service facilities

Intermediaries
"What tasks should be delegated to intermediaries?"

- Roles
- Benefits
- Costs (e.g., of franchisees, agents, and distributors)

Distributing Service Internationally
"How should the service be distributed?"

- Export the service concept
- Import customers/ possessions
- Deliver remotely

Entering International Markets
"How can the value-add be protected?"

- Export the service
- Licensing, franchising, joint venture
- Foreign direct investment

*Note that information and negotiations are types of supplementary services, but were listed separately here to emphasize their importance in any service distribution strategy.

Figure 5.2 The Flow Model of Service Distribution.

DISTRIBUTION IN A SERVICES CONTEXT

What? How? Where? When? Responses to these four questions form the foundation of any service distribution strategy. They determine the customer's service experience, which is a function of how the different elements of the Flower of Service (see Chapter 4) are distributed and delivered through physical and electronic channels. We summarize these questions in the Flow Model of Service Distribution in Figure 5.2. The "what" determines what exactly will flow through the distribution channel (i.e., information, negotiation, and the core and supplementary services). A distribution strategy needs to cover for each of these flows the remaining three questions of how, where, and when. This model is the organizing framework for this chapter, and the following sections describe each of its components.

▶ **LO 1**

Know the four key questions that form the foundation of any service distribution strategy: What? How? Where? When?

WHAT IS BEING DISTRIBUTED?

If you mention distribution, many people are likely to think of moving boxes through physical channels to distributors and retailers for sale to end users. However, in services, there is often nothing to move. Experiences, performances, and solutions are not physically shipped and stored. Meanwhile, informational transactions are increasingly conducted via electronic channels. How, then, does distribution work in a services context? In a typical service sales cycle, distribution embraces three interrelated flows that partially address the question of *what* is being distributed:

▶ **LO 2**

Describe the three interrelated flows that show *what* is being distributed.

▶ **Information and promotion flow:** This refers to the distribution of information and promotion materials related to the service offer. The objective is to get the customer interested in buying the service.

▶ **Negotiation flow:** This involves reaching an agreement on the service features and configuration as well as the terms of the offer so that a purchase contract can be closed. Often, the objective is to sell the *right* to use a service (e.g., sell a reservation or a ticket).

▶ **Product flow:** Many services, especially those involving people processing or possession processing, require physical facilities for delivery. Here, distribution strategy requires the development of a network of local sites. For information-processing services such as internet banking and distance learning, the product flow can be via electronic channels, employing one or more centralized sites.

It is important to distinguish between the distribution of core and supplementary services. Many core services require a physical location, and this severely restricts distribution. For instance, you can only consume Club Med holidays at Club Med Villages, and a live performance of a Broadway show must take place at a theater in Manhattan (until it goes on tour). However, many of the supplementary services can be distributed widely and cost-effectively via other means. Prospective Club Med customers can get information and consultation from a travel agent face-to-face, online, by phone, or by e-mail. They can then use one of these channels to make a booking. Similarly, theater tickets can be purchased through an agency without the need for an advance trip to the physical facility itself.

Table 5.1 Six options for service delivery.

Nature of Interaction between Customer and Service Organization	Availability of Service Outlets	
	Single Site	**Multiple Sites**
Customer goes to service organization	• Theater • Car service workshop	• Café house chain • Car rental chain
Service organization comes to customer	• House painting • Mobile car wash	• Mail delivery • Auto club road service
Customer and service organization transact remotely (mail or electronic communication)	• Credit card company • Local TV station	• Broadcast network • Telephone company

LO 3

Know *how* services can be distributed using three main options, and understand the importance of distinguishing between the distribution of core and supplementary services.

Figure 5.3 Tree pruning is a service that has to be provided on-site.

HOW SHOULD A SERVICE BE DISTRIBUTED?

Here, a key question is: Does the service or the firm's positioning strategy require customers to be in direct physical contact with its personnel, equipment, and facilities? (As we saw in Chapter 1, this is unavoidable for people-processing services but may not be necessary for other categories.) If so, do customers have to visit the facilities of the service organization, or will the service organization send personnel and equipment to customers' own sites? Alternatively, can transactions between provider and customer be completed through the use of either telecommunications or physical channels of distribution? (The three possible options are shown in the first column of Table 5.1.) For each of these three options, should the firm maintain just a single outlet or offer to serve customers through multiple outlets at different locations?

Customers Visit the Service Site

For services that require customers to visit service sites, firms need to consider key factors such as costs (e.g., rental), customer catchment areas, convenience of service outlet locations for the customer, and operational hours. Elaborate statistical analyses (including retail gravity models) are used to help firms make decisions on where to locate supermarkets or similar large stores relative to the homes and workplaces of future customers.

Service Providers Go to Their Customers

For some types of services, the service provider visits the customer. When do they do this?

▶ Going to the customer's site is unavoidable when the object of the service is some immovable physical item, such as a tree that has to be pruned (Figure 5.3) or a house that requires pest-control treatment.

▶ There may be a profitable niche in serving individuals who are willing to pay a premium for the convenience of receiving personal visits or home delivery. Think of Domino's Pizza's delivery service or Starbucks's new system of delivery to office buildings. The latter was launched in 2015 in Manhattan and Seattle, with workers in the Empire State Building being the first to enjoy the convenience of having their favorite Espresso Frappuccino Blended Coffee and other energy boosters delivered directly to their desks.

Another example is that of a young veterinary doctor who has built her business around house calls to care for sick pets. She has found that customers are glad to pay more money for a service that not only saves them time but is also less stressful for their pets, compared to waiting in a crowded veterinary clinic full of other animals and their worried owners.

▶ In remote areas like Alaska or Canada's Northwest Territory, service providers often fly to visit their customers because the latter find it extremely difficult to travel. Australia is famous for its Royal Flying Doctor Service, in which physicians fly to make house calls at farms and sheep stations in the outback.

▶ In general, service providers are more likely to visit corporate customers at their premises than individuals in their homes. This reflects the larger volume associated with business-to-business (B2B) transactions.

A growing service activity involves the rental of both equipment and labor at the customer's site for special occasions or in response to customers who need to expand their capacity during busy periods. Service Insights 5.1 describes the B2B services of Aggreko, an international company that rents generating and cooling equipment around the world.

The Service Transaction Is Conducted Remotely

Developments in telecommunications, online technology, and sophisticated logistics solutions have spurred many new approaches to service delivery. A customer may never see the service facilities or meet service personnel face-to-face when dealing with a firm through remote transactions. Service encounters with personnel are more likely via a customer contact center, mail, email, chat, or Twitter. If physical products, documents, or other tangibles (e.g., credit cards or membership cards) need to reach a customer, logistics providers offer service firms integrated, reliable, and cost-effective solutions. Examples of service transactions at arm's length are:

▶ Repair services for small pieces of equipment sometimes require customers to ship the product to a maintenance facility, where it is serviced and then returned by mail (with the option of paying extra for express shipment). Many service providers offer solutions with the help of integrated logistics firms such as FedEx, TNT, or UPS. These solutions range from storage and express delivery of spare parts for aircraft (B2B delivery) to pickup of defective cell phones from customers' homes and return of the repaired phones to the customers (B2C pickup and delivery, also called "reverse logistics").

▶ Any information-based product can be delivered instantaneously through the internet to apps on smart devices such as phones and tablets (Figure 5.4).

When you look at the eight petals of the Flower of Service, you can see that no fewer than five supplementary services are information based (Figure 5.5). Information, consultation, order-taking, billing, and payment (e.g., via credit card) can all be transmitted using online channels. Service businesses that involve physical core products, such as retailing and repair, are also closing physical branches and shifting delivery of many supplementary services to the internet. They rely on speedy business logistics to enable a strategy of arm's-length transactions with their customers (Figure 5.6).

LO 4
Recognize the issues of delivering services through electronic channels, and discuss the factors that have fueled the growth of service delivery via cyberspace.

Figure 5.4 Financial advice can be delivered through the internet.

Power and Temperature Control for Rent

You probably think of electricity as coming from a distant power station and of air conditioning and heating as fixed installations. How would you deal with the following challenges?

- At the 2014 FIFA World Cup in Brazil, temporary power was required to support the broadcasting of 64 matches in 12 host cities to over three billion people worldwide.

- A tropical cyclone has devastated the small mining town of Pannawonica in Western Australia, destroying everything in its path, including power lines. Electrical power must be restored as soon as possible so that the town and its infrastructure can be rebuilt.

- In Amsterdam, organizers of the World Championship Indoor Windsurfing competition need to power 27 wind turbines that will be installed along the length of a huge indoor pool to create winds of 20–30 mph (32–48 km/h).

- A U.S. Navy submarine needs a shore-based source of power when it is docked at a remote Norwegian port.

- Sri Lanka faces a great shortage of electricity-generating capability after water levels fall dangerously low at major hydroelectric dams due to insufficient monsoon rains two years in a row.

- Hotels in Florida need to be dried out following water damage from a hurricane.

- A large, power-generating plant in Oklahoma urgently seeks temporary capacity to replace one of its cooling towers, destroyed in a tornado the previous day.

- The Caribbean island of Bonaire requires a temporary power station to stabilize its grid after fire damages the main power plant and causes widespread blackouts.

These are all challenges that have been faced and met by a company called Aggreko, which describes itself as "The World Leader in Temporary Utility Rental Solutions." Aggreko serves customers around the world and generates $2.4 billion in revenue. It rents a "fleet" of mobile electricity generators, oil-free air compressors, and temperature control devices ranging from water chillers and industrial air conditioners to giant heaters and dehumidifiers.

Aggreko's customer base is dominated by large companies and government agencies. Although much of its business comes from predicted needs, such as backup operations during planned factory maintenance or the filming of a James Bond movie, the firm is ready to resolve problems that arise unexpectedly from emergencies or natural disasters.

Much of the firm's rental equipment is contained in sound-proofed, box-like structures that can be shipped anywhere in the world to create the specific type and level of electrical power output or climate-control capability required by the client. Consultation, installation, and ongoing technical support add value to the core service. Emphasis is placed on solving customer problems rather than simply renting equipment. While some customers have a clear idea of their needs in advance, others require advice on how to develop innovative and cost-effective solutions to what may be unique problems. Still others are desperate to restore power that has been lost because of an unexpected

disaster. In the last instance, speed is essential because downtime can be extremely expensive and lives may depend on the promptness of Aggreko's response.

In order to deliver its service, Aggreko has to ship its equipment to the customer's site. Following the Pannawonica cyclone, Aggreko's West Australian team swung into action, rapidly setting up some 30 generators ranging from 60–750 kVA, plus cabling, refueling tankers, and other equipment. The generators were transported by four "road trains," each comprising a giant tractor unit pulling three 40-foot (13 m) trailers. Technicians and additional equipment were flown in on two Hercules aircraft. The Aggreko technicians remained on site for six weeks, providing service 24/7 while the town was being rebuilt.

SOURCE

Aggreko's "International Magazine," 1997, www.aggreko.com, accessed February 21, 2015.

Web and app-delivered services are becoming increasingly sophisticated and more user friendly. They often simulate the services of a well-informed sales assistant by steering customers toward items that are likely to be of interest. Some even provide the opportunity for "live" dialog with helpful customer service personnel via e-mail or chat. Important factors that attract customers to online services are:

▶ Convenience

▶ Ease of search (obtaining information and searching for desired items or services)

▶ A broader selection

▶ Potential for better prices

▶ 24/7 service with prompt delivery. This is particularly appealing to customers whose busy lives leave them short of time.

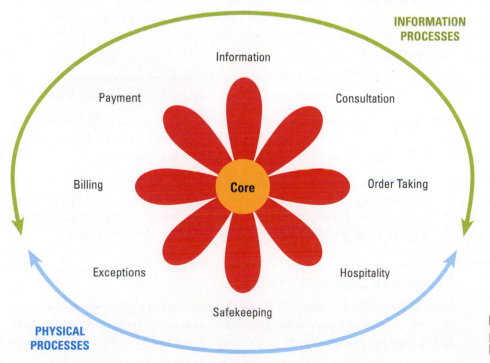

Figure 5.5 Information and physical processes of the Flower of Service.

©Glasbergen
glasbergen.com

"OUR COMPETITION LAUNCHED THEIR WEB SITE, STOLE ALL OUR CUSTOMERS AND PUT US OUT OF BUSINESS WHILE YOU WERE IN THE JOHN."

Figure 5.6 Many companies have moved their customers to online channels.

The distribution of information, consultation, and order taking (or reservations and ticket sales) has reached extremely sophisticated levels in some global service industries (such as the hotel, airline, and car rental industries), requiring a number of carefully integrated channels targeted at key customer segments. For instance, Starwood Hotels & Resorts Worldwide—whose nearly 1,200 hotels include such brands as St. Regis, W Hotel, Westin, Le Méridien, and Sheraton—has more than 33 global sales offices (GSOs) around the world to manage customer relationships with key global accounts (Figure 5.7). Each GSO offers a one-stop solution to corporate travel planners, wholesalers, meeting planners, incentive houses, and major travel organizations.[2] The company also operates customer contact centers strategically placed around the globe to cover all time zones and key language requirements. You only need to call one toll-free number to book any Starwood hotel. Alternatively, you can reserve rooms through electronic channels, including www.starwoodhotels.com and its app called SPG, which stands for Starwood Preferred Guest.

Channel Preferences Vary among Customers

The use of different channels to deliver the same service drastically affects the nature of the service experience for the customer. Although electronic self-service channels tend to be the most cost-effective, not all customers like to use them. This means that if we want to move customers to new electronic channels, we may require different strategies for different segments.[3] We also need to recognize that some proportion of customers will never voluntarily change from their preferred high-contact delivery environments. Recent research has explored how customers choose among personal, impersonal, and self-service channels and has identified the following key drivers:[4]

LO 5

Understand the determinants of customers' channel preferences.

▶ For services that are complex and have a high perceived risk, people tend to rely on personal channels. For example, customers are happy to apply for credit cards using remote channels but prefer a face-to-face transaction when obtaining a mortgage.

▶ Individuals with greater confidence in and knowledge about a service and/or the channel are more likely to use impersonal and self-service channels (Figure 5.8).

▶ Customers who look for the functional aspects of a transaction prefer more convenience. This often means the use of impersonal and self-service channels. Customers with social motives tend to use personal channels.

▶ Convenience is a key driver of channel choice for the majority of consumers. A customer's search for convenience is not confined to the purchase of core products. It also extends to convenient times and places and easy access to supplementary services, especially information, reservations, and problem solving.

LO 6

Know the importance of channel integration.

Channel Integration Is Key

Channel integration is essential for the successful delivery of a service through multiple channels.[5] Consumers are now using smart devices as well as traditional channels (e.g., ATMs, branches, and call centers). It is therefore important for service organizations to

Figure 5.7 Starwood Hotels & Resorts Worldwide manages integrated channels at a global level to offer customers a one-stop experience.

deliver a seamless and consistent user experience across all channels. New delivery channels have frequently created an inconsistent and disjointed experience for many customers.

Finally, service providers have to be careful when channels are priced differently. Increasingly, customers take advantage of price variations among channels and markets, a strategy known as channel arbitrage.[6] For example, customers can ask the expensive full-service broker for advice (and perhaps place a small order) and then conduct the bulk of their trades via the much lower-priced discount broker. Service providers need to develop effective pricing strategies that will enable them to deliver value and capture it through the appropriate channel.

WHERE SHOULD A SERVICE FACILITY BE LOCATED?[7]

A physical site location requires a sizable investment and a long-term commitment. As a site often involves long leases and high investments, a firm cannot easily move to another site. Even if sunk costs are written off, moving to another location may cause the firm to lose a proportion of loyal customers and employees.

How then should service managers make decisions on the places *where* service is delivered? Frequently, a two-step approach is used. In the first step, strategic location

LO 7

Describe the *where* (place) decisions of physical channels, and be familiar with the strategic and tactical location considerations.

Figure 5.8 Frequent travellers are often willing to use self-check-in to avoid queues.

considerations are developed to help identify the general types of location a service firm should aim for. In the second step, tactical considerations are used to choose between specific sites of a similar type that fit the overall location strategy.

Strategic Location Considerations

To develop a location strategy, a firm should start by understanding customer needs and expectations, competitive activity, and the nature of the service operation. As we noted earlier, the distribution strategies used for some of the supplementary service elements may differ from those used to deliver the core product. For instance, as a customer, you're probably willing to go to a particular location at a specific time to attend a sporting or entertainment event. However, it is likely that you want greater flexibility and convenience when reserving a seat in advance. Thus, you may expect the reservations service to be open for extended hours, to offer booking and credit card payment by phone or the Web (Figure 5.9), and to deliver tickets through postal or electronic channels.

Figure 5.9 Customers respond well to services that allow them to make reservations with ease and convenience.

Likewise, firms in competitive industries should make it easy for people to access frequently purchased services.[8] Examples include retail banks and fast-food restaurants. However, customers may be willing to travel further from their homes or workplaces to access specialty services (Figure 5.10).

In general, firms have to achieve a balance between ease of access and convenience for their customers and the cost of providing that

Figure 5.10 Millions of people from around the world were willing to travel to Shanghai to see the World Expo.

access and convenience. Markets can often be segmented by accessibility preferences and price sensitivity. While some segments are willing to pay premium for ease of access and convenience, others prefer to travel and spend time for a lower price.

Tactical Location Considerations

In the second step for selecting a specific site, key factors that need to be considered include:

▶ Population size and characteristics (i.e., to assess density and number of target customers that could be served with this site)

▶ Pedestrian and vehicular traffic and its characteristics (i.e., to assess number of target customers passing a site)

▶ Convenience of access for customers (e.g., public transportation, availability of parking)

▶ Competitors in this area

▶ Nature of nearby businesses and stores

▶ Availability of labor

▶ Availability of site locations, rental costs and contractual conditions (e.g., length of lease, legal restrictions), and regulations (e.g., on zoning and opening hours)

Firms often use geographic information system (GIS) tools to find locations with the most desirable attributes and derive the sales potential of these sites. Such tools combine

Applying the 4 Ps of Marketing to Services **129**

maps with key location data, including population demographics, purchase data, and listing of current and proposed competitor locations. Starbucks is an example of a firm that uses GIS software as part of its site selection. Patrick O'Hagan, Starbucks' manager of global market planning, said:

> My team provides analytics, decision support, business intelligence, and geo-spatial intelligence to our real-estate partners. . . . we need tools that provide decision support to answer critical questions—what's going on in this trade area; what are general retail trends in this area; where are competitors; who are those competitors; where is business generated; where's the highest traffic volume; where are people living; where are they working; and how are they travelling to work?[9]

Innovative Location Strategies

Innovative distribution strategies can be at the core of powerful new service models. We highlight location strategies for ministores and multi-purpose facilities in the following sections. Accessibility is a key component of the value propositions of both these types of services.

Ministores. An interesting innovation among multi-site service businesses involves creating numerous small service factories to maximize geographic coverage. Here are some examples:

▶ Automated kiosks offer many of the functions of a bank branch in a self-service machine that can be located within stores, hospitals, colleges, airports, and office buildings. Another example is the use of automated vending machines for the purchase of stamps and the payment of bills (Figure 5.11).

▶ Another approach involves separating the front and back stages of the operation. Taco Bell's innovative K-Minus strategy involves restaurants without kitchens.[10] Meals are shipped from a central location where food preparation takes place.

▶ Increasingly, firms offering one type of service business are purchasing space from another provider in a complementary field. Perhaps you've noticed small bank branches inside supermarkets and food outlets such as Dunkin Donuts and Subway sharing space with a fast-food restaurant such as Burger King.

Figure 5.11 Automated kiosks selling stamps are a form of ministore.

Locating in Multi-purpose Facilities. The most obvious locations for consumer services are close to where customers live or work. Modern buildings are often designed to be multi-purpose, featuring not only office or production space but also such services as a bank (or at least an ATM), a restaurant, a hair salon, several stores, and maybe a health club (Figure 5.12).

Figure 5.12 Many office buildings now include shops.

Whole new business models are now based on colocation strategies. Walgreens, a pharmacy chain in the United States, is increasingly locating clinics in shopping malls in an attempt to offer convenient and low(er)-cost health services. These clinics look like a doctor's office but do not operate like one. Patients can check waiting times online before coming to the store, see a nurse for a diagnosis in a private room, and use touch screens at kiosks to pick up prescriptions and pay for them. The pharmacists devote their time to patients' questions, whereas pharmacy clerical work is done centrally in a separate location. Some doctors and their lobbyists huff that such clinics are doomed to provide substandard health care. However, there is little evidence of this. A study by RAND found that retail clinics were less expensive for treating common health conditions without any apparent loss in quality.[11]

Interest is growing in locating retail and other services on transportation routes and in bus, rail, and air terminals. Most major oil companies have developed chains of small retail stores to complement the fuel pumps at their service stations. They offer customers the convenience of one-stop shopping for fuel, vehicle supplies, food, and a selection of basic household products. Truck-stops on major highways often include laundry centers, restrooms, ATMs, internet access, restaurants, and inexpensive accommodation in addition to a variety of vehicle maintenance and repair services.

LO 8

Describe the *when* (time) decisions of physical channels and the factors that determine extended operating hours.

WHEN SHOULD SERVICE BE DELIVERED?

Previously, most retail and professional services in industrialized countries followed a traditional schedule of being available about 40 or 50 hours a week. This routine reflected social norms (and even legal requirements or union agreements) as to what were appropriate hours for people to work and for enterprises to sell things. Historically, Sunday opening was strongly discouraged in most Christian cultures and often prohibited by law, reflecting a long tradition based on religious practice. The situation inconvenienced working people, who had to shop either during their

SERVICE INSIGHTS 5.2

Factors That Encourage Extended Operating Hours

At least five factors are driving the move toward extended operating hours and seven-day operations. The trend that originated in the United States and Canada has since spread to many other countries around the world.

- *Pressure from consumers.* Dual-income families and single wage earners who live alone need time outside normal working hours to shop and use other services. Other customers like to enjoy the convenience of shopping and carrying out their service transactions at any time of the day or week. When one store or firm in any given area extends its hours to meet the needs of these market segments, competitors often feel the need to follow suit. Chain stores have frequently led the way.

- *Changes in legislation.* Support has declined for the traditional religious view that a specific day (Sunday in predominantly Christian cultures) should be legalized as a day of rest for one and all, regardless of religious affiliation. In multicultural societies, the designation of a particular day as special has become a moot point. For observant Jews and Seventh Day Adventists, Saturday is the Sabbath; for Muslims, Friday is the holy day; and agnostics or atheists are presumably indifferent. In recent years, there has been a gradual erosion of such legislation in Western nations.

- *Economic incentives to improve asset utilization.* As a great deal of capital is often tied up in service facilities, the incremental cost of extending hours tends to be relatively modest. If the extension of

operating hours reduces crowding and increases revenues, it is economically attractive. There are costs involved in shutting down and reopening a facility such as a supermarket. Climate control and some lighting must be left running all night, and security personnel must be paid 24/7. Thus, even if the number of extra customers served is minimal, there are both operational and marketing advantages to remaining open 24 hours.

- *Availability of employees to work during "unsocial" hours.* Changing lifestyles and a desire for part-time employment have created a growing labor pool of people who are willing to work evenings and nights. They include students looking for part-time work outside classroom hours, people working a second job, parents juggling child-care responsibilities, and others who simply prefer to work by night and relax or sleep by day.

- *Automated self-service facilities.* Self-service equipment has become increasingly reliable and user-friendly. Many machines now accept card- and cellphone-based payments in addition to coins and banknotes. Therefore, the installation of unattended machines may be an economically feasible alternative for locations that cannot support a staffed facility. Unless a machine requires frequent servicing or is particularly vulnerable to vandalism, the incremental cost of going from limited hours to 24-hour operation is minimal. In fact, it may be simpler to leave machines running continuously than to turn them on and off.

lunch breaks or on Saturdays. Today, the situation has changed. For some highly responsive operations, 24/7 service has become the standard—24 hours a day, 7 days a week, around the world.

Key factors determining the opening hours of a service facility are (1) customer needs and wants and (2) the economics of opening hours. In the latter, the fixed costs of the facility and the variable costs of extending opening hours (including labor and energy costs) are weighted against the expected contribution generated from incremental sales and potential operational benefits (e.g., shifting demand from peak periods to extended opening hours). For a more detailed overview of the factors behind the move to more extended hours, see Service Insights 5.2.

THE ROLE OF INTERMEDIARIES

Should a service organization deliver all aspects of its service itself, or should it involve intermediaries to take on certain parts of service delivery? In practice, many service organizations find it cost effective to outsource certain aspects of distribution. Most frequently, this delegation concerns supplementary service elements. For instance, despite their increased use of telephone call centers and the internet, cruise lines and resort hotels still rely on travel agents to handle a significant portion of their customer interactions. These include giving out information, taking reservations, accepting payment, and ticketing.

LO 9

Understand the role, benefits, and costs of using intermediaries in distributing services.

Benefits and Costs of Alternative Distribution Channels

How should a service provider work in partnership with one or more intermediaries to deliver a complete service package to customers? In Figure 5.13, we use the Flower of Service framework to show how the core product and certain supplementary

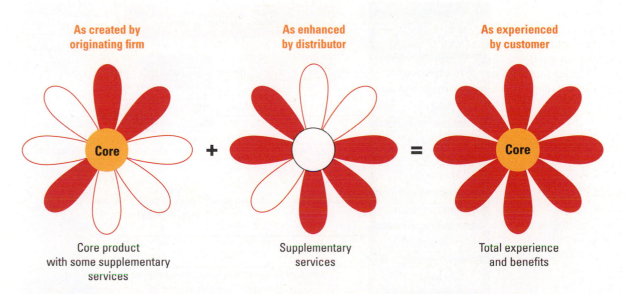

As created by originating firm

Core

Core product with some supplementary services

+

As enhanced by distributor

Supplementary services

=

As experienced by customer

Core

Total experience and benefits

Figure 5.13 Splitting responsibilities for service delivery.

elements such as information, consultation, and exception are delivered by the original supplier. The delivery of other supplementary services is delegated to an intermediary to complete the offering as experienced by the customer. The challenge for the original supplier is to act as guardian of the overall process, ensuring that each element offered by intermediaries fits the overall service concept to create a consistent and seamless branded service experience.

Intermediaries are also frequently used to add reach and generate business. Think of the various sales and reservation channels that are used in the travel industry (see Figure 5.14). Each channel offers different benefits and has vastly different costs. The distribution channel having the lowest cost would be the service firm's own website (incremental costs are typically less than $1 per sales transaction), followed by its call-center-based central reservations systems (typically between $5 to $25 per sales transaction; note that one sales transaction can involve more than one call). Retail travel agents usually charge 10% commission, and tour operators typically mark up 20% to 30% of the transaction value. The most expensive channels are often online distributors such as Expedia and Priceline, which can charge up to 30% of the transaction value. Therefore, many service firms that have achieved brand equity aim to migrate their customers and sales to lower-cost channels in order to circumvent or remove intermediaries. This process is also called disintermediation.

Swissôtel Hotels & Resorts executed an entire campaign to switch transactions to direct distribution channels by increasing online bookings, especially among the important business traveler segment. Within seven months of launch, its revamped website (www.swissotel.com) more than doubled online revenues. Apart from the enhanced express reservation functions (with fewer clicks), user-friendly navigation, and online promotions and incentives, the hotel company's "Best Rate Guarantee" was a key driver of its success.[12]

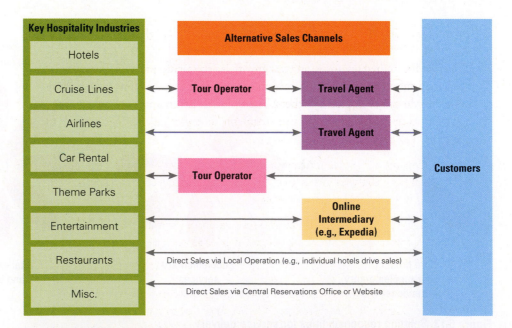

Figure 5.14 Alternative sales channels in the hospitality industry.

Leading low-cost carriers often rely on direct sales channels to minimize distribution costs. For example, easyJet claims to have almost 100% of its customer bookings through its website, which provides "guaranteed best prices to over 140 destinations." Likewise, Southwest Airlines says that its website is the "only place to find Southwest Airlines fares online."[13]

The role, benefits, and costs of every intermediary have to be carefully considered when designing a firm's distribution strategy. Franchising is one of the most commonly used distribution strategies in services. We will now discuss it in detail.

Franchising

LO 10

Know why franchising is such a common way of delivering services to end users.

Franchising has become a popular way to expand delivery of an effective service concept embracing all of the 7 Ps (see Chapter 1) to multiple sites. A franchisor recruits entrepreneurs who are willing to invest their time, effort, and equity in managing a previously developed service concept. In return, the franchisor provides training on how to operate and market the business, sells necessary supplies, and provides promotional support at a national or regional level. Local marketing activities are typically paid for by the franchisee but must adhere to copy and media guidelines prescribed by the franchisor.[14]

The International Franchise Association, the world's oldest and largest organization representing franchising worldwide, has defined the term as follows:

> A franchise is the agreement or license between two legally independent parties which gives: (a) a person or group of people (franchisee) the right to market a product or service using the trademark or trade name of another business (franchisor); (b) the franchisee the right to market a product or service using the operating methods of the franchisor; (c) the franchisee the obligation to pay the franchisor fees for these rights; and (d) the franchisor the obligation to provide rights and support to franchisees.[15]

Franchising is a particularly attractive strategy for service firms when:

▶ The firm has limited resources, and fast growth is necessary to preempt competition. Service firms often have little protection beyond their brand as almost everything else they do can be copied by others. The firm that first manages to achieve top-of-mind awareness among the target segments for a particular category tends to become the market leader in the long run.

▶ The long-term commitment of the store manager is crucial. Franchisees tend to be highly motivated to ensure high customer satisfaction, build customer loyalty, and run high-quality service operations.

▶ Local knowledge is important. Franchisees tend to be from the local community and can therefore be highly effective in dealing with local authorities (e.g., during the construction and renovation of facilities), labor markets, media, and customers.

Although franchising is still most commonly associated with fast-food restaurants (for an example, see Figure 5.15), the concept has been applied to a wide variety of both consumer and B2B services and now spans some 300 different product categories. The fastest-growing categories of concepts are related to health and fitness, publications,

Figure 5.15 Costa Coffee is a popular British coffeehouse franchise.

security, and consumer services. The franchise industry accounts for approximately 50% of all retail sales and services in the United States. One out of every 12 businesses is a franchised business. Some 900,000 franchise businesses in the United States provide jobs for more than 18 million people and create over $2.1 trillion in economic activity. Among the cases featured in this book is "Aussie Pooch Mobile," which describes a successful Australia-based franchised dog-washing service (see Case 8). In your own role as a consumer, you probably patronize more franchises than you realize (see Table 5.2).

From a franchisee perspective, a longitudinal study in the restaurant industry has shown that buying a franchise is on average more profitable than starting an independent restaurant.[16] Nevertheless, there is a high drop-out rate among franchisors in the early years of a new franchise system. One-third of all systems fail within the first four years, and no less than three-quarters of all franchisors cease to exist after 12 years.[17] Success factors for franchisors include:

▶ The ability to achieve a larger size with a more recognizable brand name

▶ Offering franchisees fewer supporting services but longer-term contracts

▶ Having lower overhead per outlet

▶ Providing accurate and realistic information about expected characteristics of franchise operations and the support given

▶ Building a cooperative rather than a controlling relationship[18]

As growth is very important to achieve an efficient scale, some franchisors adopt a strategy known as "master franchising." Master franchisees are often individuals who have already succeeded as operators of one or several individual franchise outlets. They have the responsibility of recruiting, training, and supporting franchisees within a given geographic area.

While franchising has many success stories, it also has some disadvantages:

▶ The delegation of activities to franchisees entails some loss of control over the delivery system and, thereby, over how customers experience the actual service.

▶ Ensuring that an intermediary adopts exactly the same priorities and procedures prescribed by the franchisor is difficult, yet it's vital to effective quality control. Franchisors usually seek to exercise control over all aspects of the service performance through a contract that specifies adherence to tightly defined service standards, procedures, scripts, and physical presentation.

▶ As franchisees gain experience, they may start to resent the various fees they pay the franchisor and believe that they can operate the business better without the constraints imposed by the agreement. The resulting disputes often lead to legal fights between the two parties.

Table 5.2 The top 10 franchises in the USA in 2015 and their start-up costs.

Rank	Franchise Name	Description	Startup Costs
1	Hampton Hotels	Hotels	$4M–14M
2	Anytime Fitness	Health and Fitness	$79K–371K
3	Subway	Fast Food	$117K–263K
4	Jack in the Box	Fast Food	$1M–2M
5	Supercuts	Hair Salon	$114K–234K
6	Jimmy John's Franchise, LLC	Fast Food	$331K–520K
7	Servpo	Restoration	$139K–187K
8	Denny's Inc.	Restaurant	$1M–3M
9	Pizza Hut, Inc.	Fast Food	$297K–2M
10	7-Eleven Inc.	Convenience Store	$37K–2M

SOURCE

Based on "Top Franchises from Entrepreneur's Franchise 500 List," https://www.entrepreneur.com/franchise 500, © Jochen Wirtz.

Other Intermediaries

Service intermediaries take on many forms in terms of their role, structure, legal status, and relationship with the service firm (often referred to as "principle"). Franchising is one of the most common distribution strategies used, but a range of alternative distribution intermediaries are also available. One option is to license another supplier to act on the original supplier's behalf and deliver the core product. Trucking companies regularly make use of independent agents (Figure 5.16) instead of locating company-owned branches in each of the different cities they serve. They may also choose to contract with independent "owner-operators" who drive their own trucks.

Other service distribution agreements can be contractual, such as those used in financial services. A bank seeking to move into investment services will often act as the distributor of mutual fund products created by an investment firm that lacks extensive distribution channels of its own. Many banks also sell insurance products underwritten by an insurance company. They collect a commission on the sale but are normally not involved in handling claims.

THE CHALLENGE OF DISTRIBUTION IN LARGE DOMESTIC MARKETS

LO 11

Understand the challenges of distribution in large domestic markets.

There are important differences between marketing services within a compact geographic area and in a federal nation covering a large geographic area, such as the United States, Canada, or Australia. In the latter case, physical logistics immediately become more challenging for many types of services because of the distances involved and the existence of multiple time zones. Multiculturalism is also an issue because of

Figure 5.16 Trucking companies license jobs to local firms in remote areas.

the growing proportion of immigrants and the presence of indigenous peoples. Firms that market across Canada have to work in two official languages, English and French (the latter is spoken throughout Quebec, where it is the only official language; in parts of New Brunswick, which is officially bilingual; and in northeastern Ontario). Finally, within each country, there are differences between the laws and tax rates of the various states or provinces and those of the respective federal governments. The challenges in Australia and Canada, however, pale in comparison to those facing service marketers in the mega-economy of the United States.

Visitors from overseas who tour the United States are often overwhelmed by the immense size of the country, surprised by the diversity of its people, astonished by the climatic and topographic variety of the landscape, and impressed by the scale and scope of some of its business undertakings. Consider some of the statistics. Marketing at a national level in the "lower 48" states of the United States involves dealing with a population of some 300 million people and transcontinental distances that exceed 2,500 miles (4,000 km). If Hawaii and Alaska are included, the market embraces even greater distances, covering six time zones, incredible topographic variety, and all climatic zones from arctic to tropical. From a logistical standpoint, serving customers in all 50 states might seem at least as complex as serving customers throughout, say, Europe, North Africa, and the Middle East, were it not for the fact that the United States has an exceptionally well-developed communications, transportation, and distribution infrastructure.

The United States is less homogeneous than national stereotypes might suggest. As a federal nation, it has a diverse patchwork of government practices. In addition to observing federal laws and paying federal taxes, service businesses operating nationwide may also need to conform to relevant state and municipal laws and plan for variations in tax policies from one state to another. However, U.S. law firms operating in multiple states may find this exposure an advantage when expanding overseas. As cities, counties, and special districts (such as regional transit authorities) have taxing authority in many states, there are also thousands of variations in sales tax across the United States!

As the population in the United States becomes increasingly mobile and multicultural, market segmentation issues are also becoming more complex for U.S. service marketers operating on a national scale. They encounter growing populations of immigrants (as well as visiting tourists) who speak many languages, led by Spanish. U.S. economic statistics show a wider range of household incomes and personal wealth (or lack thereof) than almost anywhere else on Earth. Faced with an enormous and diverse domestic marketplace, most large U.S. service companies simplify their marketing and management tasks by targeting specific market segments (refer to Chapter 3). While some firms segment on a geographic basis, others target certain groups based on demographics, lifestyle, needs, or—in a corporate context—industry type and company size. Smaller firms wishing to operate nationally usually choose to seek out narrow market niches, a task made easier today by the ubiquitous reach of the internet. However, the largest national service operations face tremendous challenges as they seek to serve multiple segments across a huge geographic area. They must strike a balance between standardization of strategies across all the elements embraced by the 7 Ps and adaptation to different segments and local market conditions. Decisions are especially challenging when they concern high-contact services in which customers visit the delivery site.

DISTRIBUTING SERVICES INTERNATIONALLY

LO 12
Be familiar with the forces that drive service firms to go international.

Many firms distribute their services internationally, including CNN, Reuters, Google, AMEX, Starbucks, Hertz, Citibank, and McKinsey. What are the driving forces pushing these firms to go international or even global? How should service companies enter new markets?

Factors Favoring Adoption of Transnational Strategies

Several forces or *industry drivers* influence the trend toward globalization and the creation of transnationally integrated strategies.[19] As applied to services, these forces are market drivers, competition drivers, technology drivers, cost drivers, and government drivers. Their relative significance may vary according to the type of service.

Market Drivers. Market factors that stimulate the move toward transnational strategies include common customer needs across many countries, global customers who demand consistent service from suppliers around the world, and the availability of international channels in the form of efficient physical supply chains or electronic networks.

As large corporate customers become global, they often seek to standardize and simplify the suppliers used in different countries for a wide array of B2B services. For instance, they may seek to minimize the number of auditors they use around the world, expressing a preference for the "Big Four" accounting firms (i.e., PricewaterhouseCoopers, Deloitte Touche Tohmatsu, Ernst & Young, and KPMG) that can apply a consistent approach (within the context of the national rules prevailing within each country of operation). Similarly, the development of global logistics and supply chain management capabilities

Figure 5.17 As populations change, many firms are targeting groups based on demographics, lifestyle, needs, etc.

among such firms as DHL, FedEx, and UPS has encouraged many manufacturers to outsource responsibility for their logistics function to a single firm (Figure 5.18). In each instance, there are real advantages in consistency, ease of access, consolidation of information, and accountability.

Competition Drivers. The presence of competitors from different countries, the interdependence of countries, and the transnational policies of the competitors are among the key competition drivers that exercise a powerful force in many service industries. Firms may be obliged to follow their competitors into new markets in order to protect their positions elsewhere.

Technology Drivers. Technology drivers tend to center around advances in information technology. These may include enhanced performance and capabilities in telecommunications, computerization, and software; miniaturization of equipment; and the digitization of voice, video, and text so that everything can be stored, manipulated, and transmitted in the digital language of computers. For information-based services, the growing availability of broadband telecommunication channels with their capability of moving vast amounts of data at great speed is playing a major role in opening up new markets.

Cost Drivers. There may be economies of scale to be gained from operating on a global basis. Sourcing efficiencies also result from favorable logistics and lower costs in certain countries. Improved performance and lower operating costs for telecommunications and transportation facilitate entry into international markets. The effects of these drivers vary according to the level of fixed costs required to enter an industry and the potential for cost savings. However, cost drivers may be less applicable for services that are primarily people-based. When most elements of the service factory are replicated in multiple locations, scale economies tend to be lower and experience curves flatter.

Figure 5.18 DHL combines multiple transport modes to create integrated logistics solutions for its global customer base.

Government Drivers. Government policies can serve to encourage or discourage the development of a transnationally integrated strategy. Among these drivers are favorable trade policies, compatible technical standards, and common marketing regulations. For instance, the actions taken by the European Commission to create a single market throughout the EU are a stimulus to the creation of pan-European service strategies in numerous industries.

Furthermore, the World Trade Organization's (WTO) focus on the internationalization of services has pushed governments around the world to create more favorable regulatory environments for transnational service strategies. The power of the drivers for internationalization can be seen in the case of the Qantas airliner arriving in Hong Kong as described in Service Insights 5.3.

Many of the factors driving internationalization and the adoption of transnational strategies also promote the trend to have nationwide operations. The market, cost, technological, and competitive forces that encourage creation of nationwide service businesses or franchise chains are often the same as those that subsequently drive some of the same firms to operate transnationally.

SERVICE INSIGHTS 5.3

Flight to Hong Kong: A Snapshot of Globalization

A white and red Boeing 777-300ER, sporting the flying kangaroo of Qantas, banks low over Hong Kong's crowded harbor as it nears the end of its 10-hour flight from Australia. Once it lands, the aircraft taxis past a kaleidoscope of tail-fins representing airlines from more than a dozen different countries on several continents—just a sample of all the carriers that offer their services to this remarkable city.

The passengers include business travelers and tourists as well as returning residents. After passing through immigration and customs, most visitors head first for their hotels, many of which belong to global chains (some of them Hong Kong-based). Some travelers pick up cars reserved earlier from Hertz or one of the other well-known rental car companies offering facilities at the airport. Others take the fast train into the city. Tourists on packaged vacations actively look forward to enjoying Hong Kong's renowned Cantonese cuisine. Parents, however, are resigned to the fact that their children demand to eat at the same fast-food chains that can be found back home. Many of the more affluent tourists plan to go shopping not only in distinctive Chinese jewelry and antiques stores but also in the internationally branded luxury stores that can be found in most world-class cities.

What brings business travelers to this SAR ("special administrative region") of China? Many are negotiating supply contracts for manufactured goods ranging from clothing and toys to computer components. Others have come to market their own goods and services. Some are in the shipping or construction businesses, while others work in an array of service industries ranging from telecommunications to entertainment and international law. The owner of a large Australian tourism operation has come to negotiate a deal for package vacations on Queensland's famous Gold Coast. The Brussels-based Canadian senior partner of a Big

Four accounting firm is half-way through a grueling round-the-world trip. His task is to persuade the offices of an international conglomerate to consolidate its global auditing business with his firm alone. An American executive and her British colleague, both working for a large Euro-American telecom partnership, are hoping to achieve similar goals by convincing a multinational corporation to employ their firm for managing all of its telecommunications activities worldwide. More than a few of the passengers either work for international banking and financial service firms or have come to Hong Kong, one of the world's most dynamic financial centers, to seek financing for their own ventures.

The Boeing's freight hold carries not only passengers' bags but also cargo for delivery to Hong Kong and other Chinese destinations. The freight includes mail, Australian wine, some vital spare parts for an Australian-built high-speed ferry operating out of Hong Kong, a container full of brochures and display materials about the Australian tourism industry for an upcoming trade promotion, and a variety of other high-value merchandise. Waiting at the airport for the aircraft's arrival are local Qantas personnel, baggage handlers, cleaners, mechanics and other technical staff, customs and immigration officials, and people who have come to greet individual passengers. A few of them are Australians, but most are local Hong Kong Chinese, many of whom have never traveled very far afield. However, in their daily lives, they patronize banks, fast-food outlets, retail stores, and insurance companies whose brand names—promoted by global advertising campaigns—may be equally familiar to their expatriate relatives living in countries such as Australia, Britain, Canada, Singapore, and the United States. Welcome to the world of global services marketing!

LO 13

Appreciate the special challenges of distributing services internationally.

Barriers to International Trade in Services

The marketing of services internationally has been the fastest-growing segment of international trade.[20] Transnational strategy involves the integration of strategy formulation and its implementation across all countries in which the company elects to do business. Barriers to entry, which have historically been a serious problem for foreign firms wishing to do business abroad, are slowly diminishing. The passage of free trade legislation in recent years has been an important facilitator of transnational operations. Notable developments include NAFTA, linking Canada, Mexico, and the United States; Latin American economic blocs such as Mercosur and Pacto Andino; and the European Union, now 28 countries strong.

Despite the efforts of the WTO and its predecessor General Agreement on Trade and Tariffs (GATT), it remains difficult for some services to operate successfully in international markets. Airline access is a sore point, as many countries require bilateral (two-country) agreements for establishing new routes. If one country is willing to allow entry by a new carrier but the other is not, access will be blocked. Moreover, capacity limits at certain major airports lead to denial of new or additional landing rights for foreign airlines. Both passenger and freight transport are affected by such restrictions.

Financial, healthcare, and telecommunications service markets are typically very highly regulated, and this makes it difficult for international players to enter these markets. Companies that enter more mundane markets, such as Uber in the taxi market (Figure 5.19) and AirBnB in the accommodation space, try to offer a global reservation service and connect this with local facilities and/or micro entrepreneurs. However, they often face regulatory roadblocks. The incumbents in these industries are used to regulatory protection and fight back by lobbying regulators in many markets. Ironically, they often use customer protection and service standards as arguments against the new entrants (e.g., passenger safety, security, and insurance in the case of taxi services). In the end, customers will vote with their feet and put pressure on their regulators. Thus, incumbent operators will have to improve their service and probably cut prices as well, and local governments will work on a regulatory framework that accommodates innovative business models.

Figure 5.19 Uber's business model involves offering a global service that connects with local drivers.

How to Enter International Markets

LO 14
Explain the determinants of international market entry strategies.

The strategy that is most suitable for entering a new international market depends on (1) how a firm can protect its intellectual property (IP) and control its key sources of value creation, and (2) whether the level of desired interaction with the customer is high or low (see Figure 5.20).

A firm can export a service if its intellectual property and value-creation sources can be protected through copyright or other legal means and the level of customer contact required is low. In such cases, there is little risk of losing the business to local competitors, distributors, or other local partners. Examples include database services (e.g., Thomson Reuters' Web of Science and Social Sciences Citation Index-related services), online news (e.g., those offered by CNN or the *Financial Times*), online advertising (e.g., as sold globally by Google or Facebook), and the downloading of music, films, ebooks and software. If these firms do establish a local presence in international markets, it is usually to organize their local corporate sales and marketing rather than deliver the service itself. For example, Google, Facebook, and LinkedIn have sales teams in many countries that sell their advertising services.

Some services such as fast food, global hotel chains, and courier services allow a firm to control its intellectual property and sources of value creation. This is done through branding; the creation of a global customer base; and access to global resources, capabilities, and networks. Without these, it would be difficult or even impossible for the firm to deliver the service at the level expected by customers. Here, customer contact is often at a moderate level. Firms in this category can expand globally through

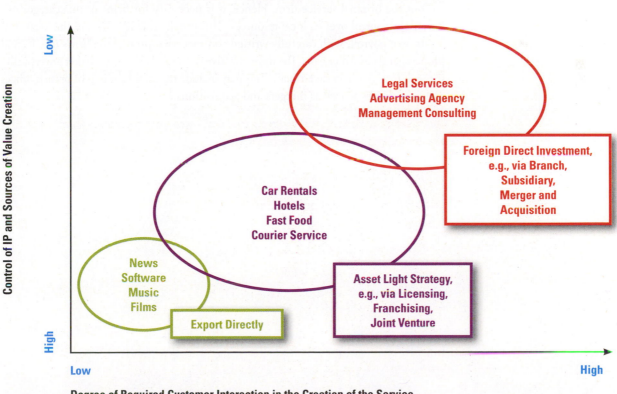

Figure 5.20 How to go international?

licensing, franchising, or joint ventures without losing control. For example, brands such as Starbucks and Hard Rock Café add value, and outlets without these brands don't have the same attraction for customers. Large global hotel chains like Starwood Hotels & Resorts or Hilton "own" millions of customer relationships through their loyalty programs and global sales offices. These offices then feed business to locally owned and operated properties that need customer traffic from the global chain.

To cite another example, a global courier service firm has global resources, capabilities, and an extensive network. However, a local courier service provider can neither source inbound shipments from around the world nor deliver outbound shipments on a global level. Thus, the global courier service firm can safely appoint a local agent without having to fear that this agent will at some point become a competitor.

Finally, there are services where the added value comes mainly from the skills and knowledge of the service provider. In such cases, a high degree of customer contact is needed to deliver value. These are often knowledge-based, professional services. Examples include creative design of advertising campaigns and management consulting projects. For such services, value is typically created by the firm's employees through their knowledge and the relationships they have built with their clients. It is difficult to control the sources of value creation for such services. For example, if a firm works through a licensee or joint-venture partner, it is possible that the partner will be able to deliver the service without the support of the firm after a few years of operation (once the necessary skills have been transferred). When this happens, the partner is likely to show increasing resistance to paying licensing fees or sharing profits. It is then likely to renegotiate the terms of the venture, and can even threaten to go 'independent' and cut out the original service firm. Hence, it is necessary for firms in this category to have tight control over its local resources. This usually includes having the local staff on its own payroll, with carefully written contracts that protect the firm's intellectual property and customer base. The most effective ways to enter a new market are typically through foreign direct investment. This may include the establishment of branch offices and subsidiaries as well as mergers and acquisitions.[21]

CHAPTER SUMMARY

LO 1 ▶ *What? How? Where? When?* Responses to these four questions form the foundation of any service distribution strategy.

LO 2 ▶ What is distributed? The Flow Model of Distribution can be mapped onto the Flower of Service concept and includes the following flows of service distribution:

- o Information and promotion flows (includes the information and potentially the consultation petals)
- o Negotiation flow (includes the order taking and potentially the billing and payment petals as well)
- o Product flow (includes the core product and the remaining petals of the Flower of Service)

A service distribution strategy encompasses all three flows.

LO 3 ▶ How can services be distributed? Services can be distributed through three main modes:

- o Customers visit the service site (e.g., for people-processing services such as an MRI scan).
- o Service providers go to their customers (e.g., for high net-worth private banking services).
- o Service transactions are conducted remotely (i.e., for Skype or for buying travel insurance online).

Some core services require a physical location (e.g., people-processing services), and this severely restricts their distribution. However, information-based core services and many supplementary services can be distributed and delivered remotely.

LO 4 ▶ Developments in telecommunications, online technology, service apps, and sophisticated logistics solutions have spurred innovations in remote service delivery.

- o All information-based core products and supplementary services (i.e., information, consultation, order taking, billing, and payment) and many possession-based services can be delivered remotely.
- o Key drivers of the growth of service delivery via cyberspace are (1) convenience, (2) ease of search, (3) a broader selection, (4) potential for lower prices, and (5) 24/7 service with prompt delivery.

LO 5 ▶ Customer preferences drive channel choice:

- o Customers who are technologically savvy often prefer remote channels due to the greater convenience they offer. Such customers usually have confidence in and knowledge about the service and/or the channel.

- o However, consumers rely more on personal channels when the perceived risk is high and when there are social motives behind the transaction.

LO 6 ▶ Customers are likely to use different service channels with the same service organization (e.g., bank customers use the entire gamut of channels ranging from mobile banking apps and websites to ATMs and bank branches). Thus, channel integration is essential for delivering consistent and seamless service experiences.

LO 7 ▶ *Where* should service be delivered? This is an important decision for services that require physical locations.

- o First, strategic location considerations are involved as the site location is an integral part of the overall service strategy. The location strategy must be consistent with the firm's marketing strategy and the needs and expectations of its target customers.
- o Second, tactical location considerations are used to choose between specific sites. They include population size and characteristics; traffic; convenience of access; competitors in the area; nature of nearby businesses; availability of labor and sites; and rental costs, conditions, and regulation. Geographic information systems (GISs) are frequently used to help firms make specific location decisions.
- o Locational constraints such as a need for economy of scale (e.g., because of high fixed costs such as in specialized medical facilities) and operational requirements (e.g., airports or distribution centers) limit a firm's location choice.
- o Innovative location strategies can be at the core of new service models. Recent trends include ministores, the sharing of retail space with complementary providers, and the location of services in multi-purpose facilities (e.g., locating clinics in shopping malls).

LO 8 ▶ When should service be delivered?

- o Key factors determining opening hours of a service channel include customer needs and wants and the economics of opening hours (fixed costs of a facility, variable costs of extending opening hours, incremental sales or contribution expected, and potential operational gains achieved by shifting demand from peak periods to extended opening hours).
- o There is now a move toward extended operating hours, with the ultimate goal of 24/7 service every day of the year. This is often achieved through the use of self-service technology.

- o Information-based core and supplementary services can be offered 24/7. Recent technological developments link CRM systems, mobile telephones, apps, websites, and smart cards to provide increasingly convenient and sophisticated electronic services.

▶ **LO 9** ▶ Service firms frequently use intermediaries to distribute some of the supplementary services. For example, cruise lines still use travel agencies to provide information, take reservations, collect payment, and often bundle complementary services such as air travel.

- o Service organizations may find it cost effective to outsource certain tasks. Intermediaries often add reach and generate incremental sales.

- o However, there are vast cost differences between channels, with a firm's own website typically costing a fraction of transactions via intermediaries such as Travelocity in the travel industry. A careful cost-benefit analysis is needed, which generally leads strong brands to shift transactions towards their own channels. Brands that lack recognition and reach rely more on intermediaries.

- o In either case, the challenge for the service firm is to ensure that the overall service experience is seamless and meets the consumer's expectations.

▶ **LO 10** ▶ Franchising is frequently used to distribute even the core service. There are advantages and disadvantages to franchising:

- o It allows fast growth. Franchisees are highly motivated to ensure customer orientation as well as high-quality and cost-effective service operations.

- o Disadvantages of franchising include the firm's loss of control over the delivery system and the customers' service experience. Hence, franchisors often enforce strict quality controls over all aspects of the operation.

▶ **LO 11** ▶ Large domestic markets (e.g., the United States, Canada, and Australia) are less homogeneous than national stereotypes suggest. Careful market segmentation, focusing on specific segments and balancing standardization and adaptation strategies enhance a firm's chances of succeeding in developing large national service penetration.

▶ **LO 12** ▶ Five important forces that drive service firms to go international are:

- o Market drivers (e.g., customers expect a global presence)

- o Competitive drivers (e.g., competitors become global and put pressure on domestic firms)

- o Technology drivers (e.g., the internet allows global distribution and cost arbitrage)

- o Cost drivers (e.g., economies of scale push towards adding markets)

- o Government drivers (e.g., countries joining the World Trade Organization have to open many service sectors to international competition)

▶ **LO 13** ▶ Regulation remains a major challenge for many services that have highly regulated markets (such as air travel, health care, and financial services). New business models in more mundane markets (such as Uber in the taxi market and Airbnb in the accommodation market) also face stiff regulatory hurdles around the world.

▶ **LO 14** ▶ The strategy for entering international markets depends on (1) how a firm can control its intellectual property (IP) and its sources of value creation and (2) the degree of customer interaction required for the creation of the service

- o If the value lies in the IP, then the service can simply be exported directly (as for e-books, music, and software).

- o If IP control and customer contact requirements are moderate, then licensing, franchising, or joint ventures may be used.

- o If a high degree of interaction is required, and the control of IP is low, then foreign direct investments may be effective. These may include the establishment of branches and subsidiaries as well as mergers and acquisitions.

UNLOCK YOUR LEARNING

These keywords are found within the sections of each Learning Objective (LO). They are integral to understanding the services marketing concepts taught in each section. Having a firm grasp of these keywords and how they are used is essential to helping you do well on your course, and in the real and very competitive marketing scene out there.

LO 1
1. Service distribution strategy
2. Flow Model of Service Distribution

LO 2
1. Information flow
2. Negotiation flow
3. Product flow
4. Promotion flow

LO 3
1. Convenience
2. Customer visits the service site
3. Location-specific services
4. Operational hours
5. Service providers visit their customers

LO 4
1. Remote transactions
2. Reverse logistics

LO 5
1. Channel choice
2. Channel preferences
3. Impersonal channels
4. Personal channels
5. Self-service channels

LO 6
1. Channel integration
2. Channel arbitrage

LO 7
1. Strategic location considerations
2. Tactical considerations
3. Ease of access
4. Automated kiosks
5. Back-stage elements
6. Ministores
7. Multi-purpose facilities

LO 8
1. 24/7 service
2. Extended opening hours
3. Self-service equipment

LO 9
1. Intermediaries
2. Alternative distribution channels
3. Outsourcing
4. Disintermediation

LO 10
1. Licensing
2. Franchisee
3. Franchising
4. Franchisor
5. Master franchising
6. Contractual agreements

LO 11
1. Large domestic markets
2. Multiculturalism
3. Market segmentation
4. Market niches

LO 12
1. Transnational strategies
2. Industry drivers
3. Technology drivers
4. Competition drivers
5. Cost drivers
6. Market drivers
7. Government drivers
8. Economies of scale
9. Sourcing efficiencies
10. Marketing regulations

LO 13
1. Free trade legislation
2. Barriers to entry
3. Regulatory protection
4. Regulatory framework
5. Innovative business models

LO 14
1. Branch office
2. Control
3. Customer contact
4. Branding
5. Foreign direct investment
6. Intellectual property
7. Joint ventures
8. Mergers and acquisitions
9. Subsidiary
10. Value creation

How well do you know the language of services marketing? Quiz yourself!

⚠️ **Not for the academically faint-of-heart**

For each keyword you are able to recall without referring to earlier pages, give yourself a point (and a pat on the back). Tally your score at the end and see if you earned the right to be called a *services marketeer*.

SCORE

01 – 12	Services Marketing is done a great disservice.
13 – 24	The midnight oil needs to be lit, pronto.
25 – 36	I know what you *didn't* do all semester.
37 – 48	By George! You're getting there.
49 – 60	Now, go forth and market.
61 – 73	There should be a marketing concept named after you.

PART II

Review Questions

1. What is meant by "distributing services?" How can an experience or something intangible be distributed?

2. Why is it important to consider the distribution of core and supplementary services both separately and jointly?

3. What are the different options for service delivery? What factors do service firms need to take into account when using each of these options?

4. What are the key factors driving the place and time decisions of service distribution?

5. What risks and opportunities does a retail service firm face when it adds electronic channels of delivery (a) paralleling a channel involving physical stores or (b) replacing the physical stores with a combined internet and call center channel? Give examples.

6. Why should service marketers be concerned with new developments in mobile communications?

7. What marketing and management challenges are raised by the use of intermediaries in a service setting?

8. Why is franchising a popular way to expand distribution of an effective service concept? What are some disadvantages of franchising, and how can they be mitigated?

9. What are the key drivers for the increasing globalization of services?

10. What factors do service companies need to understand in order to choose a distribution strategy for going international that still allows it to control its intellectual property and sources of value creation?

WORK YOUR SERVICES MARKETING

Application Exercises

1. An entrepreneur is thinking of setting up a new service business (you can choose any specific business). What advice would you offer regarding the distribution strategy for this business? Address the What? How? Where? When? of service distribution.

2. Think of three services you buy or use either mostly or exclusively via the internet. What is the value proposition of this channel over alternative channels (e.g., phone, mail, or branch network)?

3. What advice would you give to (a) a weight reduction clinic, (b) a pest control company, and (c) a university offering undergraduate courses about going international?

4. Which strategy for entering a new international market should (a) an architectural design firm, (b) an online discount broker, and (c) a satellite TV channel consider, and why?

END**NOTES**

1. http://en.wikipedia.org/wiki/Lauren_Luke and www.bylaurenluke.com, accessed February 21, 2015.

2. Jochen Wirtz and Jeannette P. T. Ho, "Westin in Asia: Distributing Hotel Rooms Globally," in Jochen Wirtz and Christopher H. Lovelock (eds), *Services Marketing in Asia—A Case Book* (Singapore: Prentice Hall, 2005): 253–259; www.starwoodhotels.com, accessed February 21, 2015.

3. Recent research on the adoption of self-service technologies includes: Matthew L. Meuter, Mary Jo Bitner, Amy L. Ostrom, and Stephen W. Brown, "Choosing among Alternative Service Delivery Modes: An Investigation of Customer Trial of Self-Service Technologies," *Journal of Marketing* 69 (April 2005): 61–83; James M. Curran and Matthew L. Meuter, "Self-Service Technology Adoption: Comparing Three Technologies," *Journal of Services Marketing* 19, no. 2 (2005): 103–113.

4. The section was based on the following research: Nancy Jo Black, Andy Lockett, Christine Ennew, Heidi Winklhofer, and Sally McKechnie, "Modelling Consumer Choice of Distribution Channels: An Illustration from Financial Services," *International Journal of Bank Marketing* 20, no. 4 (2002): 161–173; Leonard L. Berry, Kathleen Seiders, and Dhruv Grewal, "Understanding Service Convenience," *Journal of Marketing* 66, no. 3 (July 2002): 1–17; Jiun-Sheng C. Lin and Pei-ling Hsieh, "The Role of Technology Readiness in Customers' Perception and Adoption of Self-Service Technologies," *International Journal of Service Industry Management* 17, no. 5 (2006): 497–517.

5. Madhumita Banerjee, "Misalignment and Its Influence on Integration Quality in Multichannel Services," *Journal of Service Research* 17, no. 4 (2014): 460–474.

6. Paul F. Nunes and Frank V. Cespedes, "The Customer Has Escaped," *Harvard Business Review* 81, no. 11 (2003): 96–105.

7. Locating a service outlet is in many ways akin to locating a retail facility. A detailed discussion on location in a retail context is provided in: Barry Berman and Joel R. Evans, *Retail Management: A Strategic Approach*, 12th ed. (Upper Saddle River, New Jersey: Prentice Hall, 2013). Of particular interest are Chapter 9 ("Trading-Area Analysis") and Chapter 12 ("Site Selection"). Parts of this section were adapted from these two chapters.

8. Michael A. Jones, David L. Mothersbaugh, and Sharon E. Beatty, "The Effects of Locational Convenience on Customer Repurchase Intentions across Service Types," *Journal of Services Marketing* 17, no. 7 (2004): 701–712.

9. From Erin Harris, "Inside Starbucks' GIS Strategy," © 2011 Jameson Publishing.

10. James L. Heskett, W. Earl Sasser Jr., and Leonard A. Schlesinger, *The Service Profit Chain* (New York: The Free Press, 1997): 218–220.

11. *The Economist*, "Health Care in America: Medicine at the Mall," April 6, 2013: 66.

12. www.swissotel.com and www.eyefortravel.com/node/9187, accessed February 25, 2015.

13. www.easyjet.com/en/cheap-flights and www.southwest.com/flight, accessed February 24, 2015.

14. For a special issue on franchising in services that features the latest academic thinking on this topic, see: *The Service Industries Journal*. Special Double Issue: Franchising in Services, editors: Domingo Ribeiro and Gary Akehurst, 2014, Vol. 34, No. 9–10; and *Journal of Retailing*. Special Issue: Franchising and Retailing, editors Rajiv P. Dant, Marko Grünhagen and Josef Windsperger 2011, Vol. 87, No. 3.

15. Based on International Franchise Association, www.franchise.org, accessed February 18, 2015.

16. Melih Madanoglu, Kyuho Lee, and Gary J. Castrogiovanni, "Franchising and Firm Financial Performance among U.S. Restaurants," *Journal of Retailing* 87, no. 3 (2011): 406–417.

17. Scott Shane and Chester Spell, "Factors for New Franchise Success," *Sloan Management Review* 39 (Spring 1998): 43–50.

18. Firdaus Abdullah and Mohd Rashidee Alwi, "Measuring and Managing Franchisee

Satisfaction: A Study of Academic Franchising," *Journal of Modelling in Management* 3, no. 2 (2008): 182–199. For more research on factors that affect the success of franchises, see: Markus Blut, Christof Backhaus, Tobias Heussler, David M. Woisetschläger, Heiner Evanschintzky, and Dieter Ahlert, "What to Expect after the Honeymoon: Testing a Lifecycle Theory of Franchise Relationships," *Journal of Retailing* 87, no. 3 (2011): 306–319.

19. Christopher H. Lovelock and George S. Yip, "Developing Global Strategies for Service Businesses," *California Management Review* 38 (Winter 1996): 64–86; May Aung and Roger Heeler, "Core Competencies of Service Firms: A Framework for Strategic Decisions in International Markets," *Journal of Marketing Management* 17 (2001): 619–643; Rajshekhar G. Javalgi and D. Steven White, "Strategic Challenges for the Marketing of Services Internationally," *International Marketing Review* 19, no. 6 (2002): 563–581.

20. Jochen Wirtz, Sven Tuzovic, and Michael Ehret, "Global Business Services: Increasing Specialization and Integration of the World Economy as Drivers of Economic Growth," *Journal of Service Management* 26, no. 4 (2015): 565-587.

21. Sandra Vandermerwe and Michael Chadwick, "The Internationalization of Services," *The Services Industries Journal* 9, no. 1 (January 1989): 79–93.

setting prices and

IMPLEMENTING
REVENUE
MANAGEMENT

LEARNING OBJECTIVES (LOs)

By the end of this chapter, the reader should be able to:

▶ **LO 1** Recognize that effective pricing is central to the financial success of service firms.

▶ **LO 2** Outline the foundations of a pricing strategy as represented by the pricing tripod.

▶ **LO 3** Define different types of financial costs and explain the limitations of cost-based pricing.

▶ **LO 4** Understand the concept of net value and know how gross value can be enhanced through value-based pricing and reduction of related monetary and non-monetary costs.

▶ **LO 5** Describe competition-based pricing and situations where service markets are less price-competitive.

▶ **LO 6** Define revenue management and describe how it works.

▶ **LO 7** Discuss the role of rate fences in effective revenue management.

▶ **LO 8** Be familiar with the issues of ethics and consumer concerns related to service pricing.

▶ **LO 9** Understand how fairness can be designed into revenue management policies.

▶ **LO 10** Discuss the six questions marketers need to answer to design an effective service-pricing strategy.

Figure 6.1 Dynamic pricing, a strategy to price the same product differently to different customers at various times, has gained popularity in many industries.

OPENING VIGNETTE

Dynamic Pricing Is Here to Stay[1]

Service firms often face the problem of maximizing revenue and capacity, and one way to do this is through dynamic pricing. But what exactly is dynamic pricing? Have you had the experience of chatting with your neighbor on a plane and discovering that the two of you paid very different prices for the same air ticket in the same class of seats? That's dynamic pricing at work.

Dynamic pricing is a pricing strategy that varies prices for different customers at different times on the basis of demand conditions. It is commonly used in the airline industry but has also gained popularity in other industries. For example, the Eagles, the highest-selling American band in U.S. history, started a system of increasing the prices of the best seats and lowering the prices of cheaper seats for a show organized in early 2010 in Sacramento, California. Their highest-priced tickets cost $250, but the cheapest ticket was priced as low as $32. They cooperated with Live Nation Entertainment Inc. to use dynamic pricing for their tickets. Ten categories of ticket prices were set based on anticipated demand. In this way, the band hoped to fill more seats and at the same time make the tickets more affordable for fans.

Lion King's success in turning its once-shaky fortunes around and becoming one of Broadway's top grossing shows has been largely attributed to dynamic pricing. Similarly, the San Francisco Giants, a professional baseball team, sold 25,000 extra tickets during the first year in which they experimented with dynamic pricing. It earned them an extra $500,000 in revenue. Officials from the Major League Baseball and the National Basketball Association expect dynamic pricing to become the norm for the sporting industry.

Companies like ScoreBig Inc. are hoping to tap into this trend. It has been estimated that about 25–35% of seats for sports events and 40–50% of concert tickets remain unsold every year. ScoreBig Inc. aims to become the Priceline.com in this space by using demand-based dynamic pricing to help find buyers for these tickets.

Companies in diverse industries such as sports, hotels, airlines, and car rental have been able to benefit greatly from using dynamic pricing. Such a strategy allows companies to increase revenues, allocate their resources more effectively, and focus on improving customer experience. Thus, dynamic pricing is certainly here to stay!

Figure 6.2 Major League Baseball is increasingly embracing dynamic pricing.

LO 1

Recognize that effective pricing is central to the financial success of service firms.

EFFECTIVE PRICING IS CENTRAL TO FINANCIAL SUCCESS

The creation of a viable service requires a business model that allows for the costs of creating and delivering the service. It also includes a margin for profits, to be recovered through realistic pricing and revenue management strategies. However, the pricing of services is complicated. Consider the bewildering fee schedules of many consumer banks or cell phone service providers, or try to understand the fluctuating fare structure of a full-service airline. Universities talk about tuition, professional firms collect fees, banks impose interest and service charges, brokers charge commissions, some expressways impose tolls, utilities set tariffs, and insurance companies determine premiums. In this chapter, you will learn how to set an effective pricing and revenue management strategy that fulfills the promise of the value proposition so that a value exchange takes place (i.e., the consumer decides to buy the service). An overview of this chapter is provided in Figure 6.3.

Objectives for Establishing Prices

Any pricing strategy must be based on a clear understanding of a company's pricing objectives. The most common high-level pricing objectives are summarized in Table 6.1.

LO 2

Outline the foundations of a pricing strategy as represented by the pricing tripod.

PRICING STRATEGY STANDS ON THREE FOUNDATIONS

Once the pricing objectives are understood, we can focus on pricing strategy. The foundations of pricing strategy can be described as a tripod, with costs to the provider, competitors' pricing, and value to the customer as the three legs (Figure 6.4). In the pricing tripod, the costs a firm needs to recover usually set a minimum price or price floor for a specific service offering. The customer's perceived value of the offering sets a maximum price or price ceiling.

The prices charged by competing services typically determine where within the floor-to-ceiling range the price can be set. Let's look at each leg of the pricing tripod in greater detail, starting with costs to the provider.

LO 3

Define different types of financial costs and explain the limitations of cost-based pricing.

Cost-Based Pricing

It's usually harder to determine the financial costs of creating a process or intangible real-time performance than of producing a physical good. In addition, service organizations typically have a higher ratio of fixed costs to variable costs than manufacturing firms (Figure 6.5). Service businesses with high fixed costs include those with expensive physical facilities (such as hospitals or colleges), a fleet of vehicles (such as airlines or trucking companies), or a network (such as railroads, telecommunications, and gas pipeline companies).

Establishing the Costs of Providing Service. Even if you have already taken a marketing course, you may find it helpful to review how service costs can be estimated using fixed, semi-variable, and variable costs. It is also important to understand how the

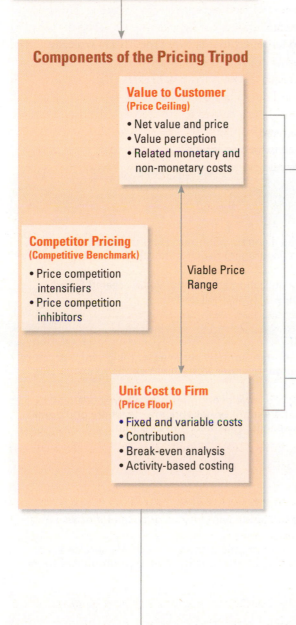

Objectives of Service Pricing

- Gain Profit and cover costs
- Build demand and develop a user base
- Support positioning strategy

Components of the Pricing Tripod

Value to Customer
(Price Ceiling)

- Net value and price
- Value perception
- Related monetary and non-monetary costs

Competitor Pricing
(Competitive Benchmark)

- Price competition intensifiers
- Price competition inhibitors

Viable Price Range

Unit Cost to Firm
(Price Floor)

- Fixed and variable costs
- Contribution
- Break-even analysis
- Activity-based costing

Revenue Management

When Should RM Be Used?

- Fixed capacity and high fixed costs
- Variable and uncertain demand
- Varying customer price sensitivity

How to Apply RM?

- Predict demand by segment
- Reserve capacity for high-yield customers
- Maximise revenue per available space and time unit (RevPAST)
- "Pick up" competitor pricing through booking pace in the RM system
- Implement price segmentation through "rate fences"

Rate Fences

- Physical fences
  - Basic product
  - Amenities
  - Service level
- Non-Physical fences
  - Transaction characteristics
  - Consumption characteristics
  - Buyer characteristics

Fairness and Ethical Concerns in Service Pricing

Ethical Concerns

- Service pricing is complex
- Confusiopology
- Fees: Crime and punishment

Design Fairness into RM

- Clear, logical and fair prices and rate fences
- Frame rate fences as discounts
- Communicate benefits of RM
- "Hide" discounts
- Take care of loyal customers
- Use service recovery to deal with overbooking

Putting Service Pricing into Practice

- How much should be charged?
- What should be the basis of pricing?
- Who should collect payment and where?
- When should payment be made?
- How should payment be made?
- How should prices be communicated?

Figure 6.3 Organizing framework for the pricing of services.

Table 6.1 Objectives for the pricing of services.

Revenue and Profit Objectives

Gain Profit

- Make the largest possible long-term contribution or profit.
- Achieve a specific target level, but do not seek to maximize profits.
- Maximize revenue from a fixed capacity by varying prices and target segments over time. This is typically done using revenue management systems.

Cover Costs

- Cover fully allocated costs, including corporate overhead.
- Cover costs of providing one particular service, excluding overhead.
- Cover incremental costs of selling one extra unit or serving one extra customer.

Patronage and User-Base-Related Objectives

Build Demand

- Maximize demand (when capacity is not a restriction), provided a certain minimum level of revenue is achieved (e.g., many non-profit organizations are focused on encouraging usage rather than revenue, but they still have to cover costs).
- Achieve full capacity utilization, especially when high capacity utilization adds to the value created for all customers (e.g., a "full house" adds excitement to a theater play or basketball game).

Develop a User Base

- Encourage trial and adoption of a service. This is especially important for new services with high infrastructure costs as well as for membership-type services that generate large revenues from their continued usage after adoption (e.g., cell phone service subscriptions or life insurance plans).
- Build market share and/or a large user base, especially if there are large economies of scale that can lead to a competitive cost advantage (e.g., if development or fixed costs are high) or network effects where additional users enhance the value of the service for the existing user base (e.g., Facebook and LinkedIn).

Strategy-Related Objectives

Support Positioning Strategy

- Help and support the firm's overall positioning and differentiation strategy (e.g., as a price leader or as a premium quality provider).
- Promote a "we-will-not-be-undersold" positioning, whereby a firm promises the best possible service at the best possible price. That is, the firm wants to communicate that the offered quality of service products cannot be bought at a lower cost elsewhere.

Support Competitive Strategy

- Discourage existing competitors from expanding their capacity.
- Discourage potential new competitors from entering the market.

notions of contribution and break-even analysis can help in making pricing decisions (see the Marketing Review on p. 159).

Activity-Based Costing.[2] For service firms with high fixed costs and complex product lines with shared infrastructure (e.g., retail banking) (Figure 6.7), it may be worthwhile to consider the more complex activity-based costing (also called "ABC") approach. It is a more accurate way to allocate indirect costs or overheads.

When determining the indirect cost of a service, a firm looks at the resources needed to perform each activity. It then allocates an indirect cost to the service based on the quantities and types of activities required to create and deliver the service. Thus, resource expenses (or indirect costs) are linked not only to physical volume but also to the variety and complexity of services produced. If the activity-based costing approach is implemented well, firms will be in a better position to estimate the costs of their various services, activities, and processes. The net result is a management tool that can help companies to pinpoint the profitability of different services, channels, market segments, and even individual customers.

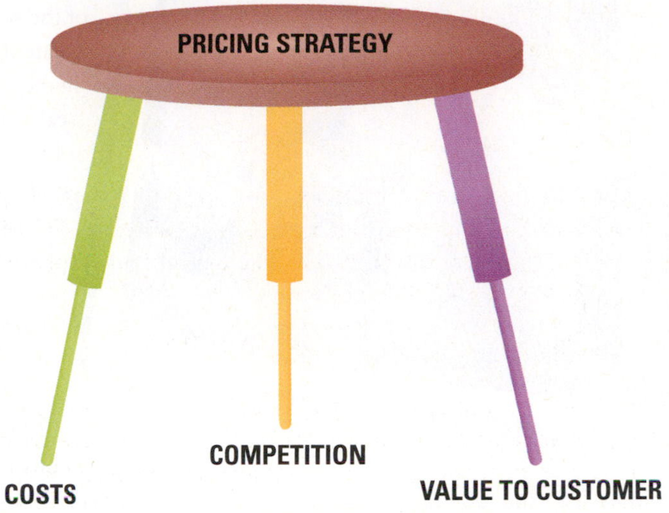

Pricing Implications of Cost Analysis. To make a profit, a firm must set its price high enough to recover the full costs of producing and marketing the service and add a sufficient margin to yield the desired profit at the predicted sales volume.

Managers in businesses with high fixed and marginal variable costs may feel that they have tremendous pricing flexibility. This may prompt them to set low prices to boost sales. Some firms promote *loss leaders*, which are services sold at less than full cost to attract customers. It is hoped that these customers will then be tempted to buy more profitable service offerings from the same organization in the future. However, if all relevant costs are not recovered, service businesses will have no profit at the end of the year and may even go bankrupt. Hence, firms that compete on low prices need to have a very good understanding of their cost structure and of the sales volumes needed to break even.

Value-Based Pricing

Another leg of the pricing tripod is value to the customer. No customer will pay more for a service than he or she thinks it is worth. Marketers need to understand how customers perceive service value in order to set an appropriate price.

Understanding Net Value. When customers purchase a service, they weigh the perceived benefits of the service against the perceived costs they will incur. However, customer definitions of value may be highly personal and idiosyncratic. Valarie Zeithaml proposes four broad expressions of value:

▶ Value is a low price.

▶ Value is whatever I want in a product.

▶ Value is the quality I get for the price I pay.

▶ Value is what I get for what I give.[3]

In this book, we focus on the fourth category and use the term *net value*, which is the sum of all the perceived benefits (gross value) minus the sum of all the perceived costs

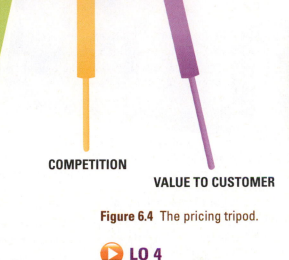

Figure 6.4 The pricing tripod.

Labels on figure: PRICING STRATEGY / COSTS / COMPETITION / VALUE TO CUSTOMER

▶ **LO 4**

Understand the concept of net value and know how gross value can be enhanced through value-based pricing and reduction of related monetary and non-monetary costs.

Figure 6.5 Train services have very high infrastructure costs; variable costs of transporting an additional passenger are insignificant.

Figure 6.6 Housekeeping services contribute to the cost of hotel rooms.

of the service. The greater the positive difference between the two, the greater the net value. You can think of calculations that customers make in their minds as being similar to weighing with a pair of old-fashioned scales, with product benefits in one tray and the costs associated with obtaining those benefits in the other tray (Figure 6.9). When customers evaluate competing services, they are basically comparing the relative net values (see also multi-attribute models in Chapter 2, where we discuss how to quantify net value through a scoring system).

Managing the Perception of Value.[4] Since value is subjective, not all customers have the skills or knowledge to judge the quality and value they receive. This is true especially for credence services (discussed in Chapter 2), the quality of which customers cannot assess even after consumption. Marketers of services such as strategy consulting and specialized hospitals must find ways to communicate the time, research, professional expertise, and attention to detail that go into, for example, completing a best-practice-consulting project. This is because the invisibility of back-stage facilities and labor makes it hard for customers to see what they're getting for their money. Therefore, the service provider has to manage their perception of value.

Consider a home owner who calls an electrician to repair a defective circuit. The electrician arrives, carrying a small bag of tools. He disappears into the closet where the circuit board is located, finds the problem, replaces a defective circuit breaker, and presto! Everything works. A mere 20 minutes have elapsed. A few days later, the home owner is horrified to receive a bill for $150, most of which covers labor charges. Not surprisingly, customers are often left feeling they have been taken advantage of—take a look at Blondie's reaction to the plumber in Figure 6.10.

Effective communications and even personal explanations are needed to help customers understand the value they receive. Customers often fail to recognize the fixed costs that

Figure 6.7 Service firms such as retail banks assign resources to activities based on the actual consumption by each activity.

MARKETING REVIEW

Understanding Costs, Contribution, and Break-Even Analysis

Fixed costs are economic costs that a supplier would continue to incur (at least in the short run) even if no services were sold. These costs are likely to include rent, depreciation, utilities, taxes, insurance, salaries and wages for managers and long-term employees, security, and interest payments.

Variable costs refer to the economic costs associated with serving an additional customer, such as making an additional bank transaction or selling an additional seat on a flight. In many services, such costs are very low. For instance, very little labor or fuel cost is involved in transporting an extra passenger on a flight. In a theater, the cost of seating an extra patron is close to zero. More significant variable costs are associated with such activities as serving food and beverages or installing new parts when undertaking repairs because they often include providing costly physical products in addition to labor. However, a firm cannot be considered profitable simply because it sells a service at a price that exceeds its variable cost. There are still fixed and semi-variable costs to be recouped.

Semi-variable costs fall in between fixed and variable costs. They represent expenses that rise or fall in a step-wise fashion as the volume of business increases or decreases. Examples include adding an extra flight to meet increased demand on a specific route or hiring a part-time employee to work in a restaurant on busy weekends.

Contribution is the difference between the variable cost of selling an extra unit of service and the money received from the buyer of that service. It goes to cover fixed and semi-variable costs before creating profits.

Determining and allocating economic costs can be a challenging task in some service operations because of the difficulty in deciding how to assign fixed costs in a multi-service facility, such as a hospital. For instance, certain fixed costs are associated with running the emergency department in a hospital. In addition, there are other fixed costs involved in the running of the hospital as a whole. How much of the hospital's fixed costs should be allocated to the emergency department? A hospital manager might use one of several approaches to calculate the emergency department's share of overhead costs. These could include (1) the percentage of total floor space it occupies, (2) the percentage of employee hours or payroll it accounts for, or (3) the percentage of total patient-contact hours involved. Each method is likely to yield a totally different fixed-cost allocation. One method might show the emergency department to be very profitable, while the other might flag it as a loss-making operation.

Break-even analysis allows managers to know the sales volume at which a service will become profitable. This is called the break-even point. The necessary analysis involves dividing the total fixed and semi-variable costs by the contribution obtained on each unit of service. For example, if a 100-room hotel needs to cover fixed and semi-variable costs of $2 million a year, and the average contribution per room-night is $100, then the hotel will need to sell 20,000 room-nights per year out of a total annual capacity of 36,500. If prices are cut by an average of $20 per room-night (or if variable costs rise by $20), the contribution will drop to $80, and the hotel's break-even volume will rise to 25,000 room-nights.

business owners need to recoup. The electrician in our earlier example has to cover the costs for his office, telephone, insurance, vehicles, tools, fuel, and office support staff. The variable costs of a home visit are also higher than they appear. To the 20 minutes spent at the house, 15 minutes of driving each way might be added, plus 5 minutes each to unload and reload the necessary tools and supplies from the van. Thus, the labor time devoted to this call is effectively tripled to a total of 60 minutes. The firm still has to add a margin in order to make a profit.

Reducing Related Monetary and Non-Monetary Costs

From a customer's point of view, the price charged by a supplier is only part of the costs involved in buying and using a service. There are other *costs of service*, which are made up of the *related monetary* and *non-monetary costs*.

Related Monetary Costs. Customers often incur significant financial costs in searching for, purchasing, and using the service. These go above and beyond the purchase price paid to the supplier. For instance, the cost of an evening at the theater for a couple with young children far exceeds the price of the two tickets because it can include such expenses as hiring a babysitter, travel, parking, food, and beverages.

Figure 6.8 Budget airlines like easyJet set low prices to encourage higher sales. As a consequence, the need high load factors to break even.

Non-monetary Costs. Non-monetary costs reflect the time, effort, and discomfort associated with the search, purchase, and use of a service. There are four distinct categories of non-monetary costs: time, physical, psychological, and sensory costs.

▶ *Time costs* are part of the service delivery. Today's customers are reluctant to waste time on non-enjoyable and non-value-adding activities such as traveling to a government office and waiting in a queue. Many people loathe visiting government offices to obtain passports, driving licenses, or permits, not because of the fees involved but because of the time "wasted."[5]

▶ *Physical costs* (like effort, fatigue, and discomfort) may be part of the costs of obtaining services, especially if (1) customers must go to the service factory, (2) waiting and long queues are involved, (3) body treatments are involved (e.g., medical treatments, piercing, or waxing) (Figure 6.11), and/or (4) delivery is through self-service.

▶ *Psychological costs* such as mental effort (e.g., filling in account-opening forms that request lots of detailed information), perceived risk and anxiety ("Is this the best treatment?", "Is he the right surgeon?", or "Is this the best mortgage for me?") (Figure 6.12), cognitive dissonance ("Was it good to sign up for this life insurance or this annual gym membership?"), and feelings of inadequacy and fear ("Will I be smart enough to succeed in this MBA program?") are sometimes attached to buying and using a particular service.

▶ *Sensory costs* relate to unpleasant sensations affecting any of the five senses. In a service environment, these costs may include putting up with crowding, noise, unpleasant smells, drafts, excessive heat or cold, uncomfortable seating, and visually unappealing environments.

Figure 6.9 Net value equals perceived benefits minus perceived costs.

As shown in Figure 6.13, service users can incur costs during any of the three stages of the service consumption model as introduced in Chapter 2. Consequently, firms have to consider (1) *search costs*, (2) *purchase and service encounter costs*, and (3) *post-purchase* or *after costs*.

A firm can create competitive advantage and increase consumer value by minimizing non-monetary and related monetary costs. Possible approaches include:

- Working with operations experts to reduce the time required to complete service purchase, delivery, and consumption; becoming "easy-to-do-business-with."

- Minimizing unwanted psychological costs of service at each stage by eliminating or redesigning unpleasant or inconvenient procedures, educating customers on what to expect, and retraining staff to be friendlier and more helpful.

- Eliminating or minimizing unwanted physical effort, notably during search and delivery processes. Improving signage and "road mapping" in facilities and on webpages can help customers find their way and prevent them from getting lost and frustrated.

- Decreasing unpleasant sensory costs of service, such as by creating more attractive visual environments, reducing noise, installing more comfortable furniture and equipment, and curtailing offensive smells.

- Suggesting ways in which customers can reduce associated monetary costs, including discounts with partner suppliers (e.g., parking) or the online delivery of services that previously required personal visits.

> Perceptions of net value may vary widely among customers. Most services have at least two segments—one that spends time to save money and another that spends money to save time. Therefore, many service markets can be segmented by sensitivity to time savings and convenience versus price sensitivity.[6] Consider Figure 6.14, which identifies a choice of three clinics available to an individual who needs to obtain a routine chest X-ray. Each offering involves not only varying dollar prices but also different time and effort costs. Depending on the customer's priorities, non-monetary costs may be as important, or even more important, than the price charged by the service provider.

Competition-Based Pricing

The last leg of the pricing tripod is competition. Firms with relatively undifferentiated services need to monitor what competitors are charging and price their services accordingly. When customers see little or no difference between competing offerings, they may simply choose what they perceive to be the cheapest. In such a situation, the firm with the lowest cost per unit of service enjoys an enviable market advantage and often assumes *price leadership* (i.e., one firm acts as the price leader, with others taking their cue from this company). You can sometimes see this phenomenon at the

LO 5

Describe competition-based pricing and situations where service markets are less price-competitive.

Figure 6.10 Blondie seeks her money's worth from the plumber.

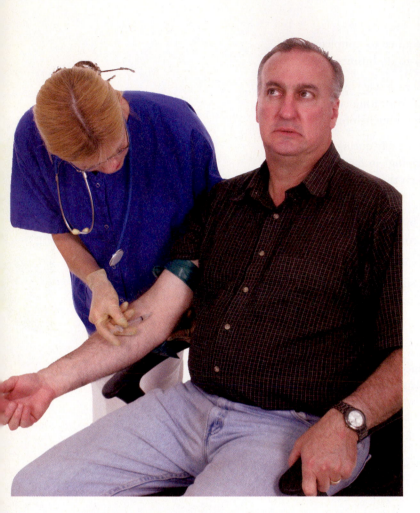

Figure 6.11 Anxiety is an important psychological cost in medical treatment.

"As an alternative to the traditional 30-year mortgage, we also offer an interest-only mortgage, balloon mortgage, reverse mortgage, upside down mortgage, inside out mortgage, loop-de-loop mortgage, and the spinning double axel mortgage with a triple lutz."

Figure 6.12 Does adding options always create value? Or can it confuse the customer?

local level when several gas stations compete within a short distance of one another. As soon as one station raises or lowers its prices, the others follow suit.

Price-Competition Intensifiers. Price-competition intensifies with:

▶ Increasing number of competitors,

▶ Increasing number of substituting offers,

▶ Wider distribution of competitor and/or substitution offers, and

▶ Increasing surplus capacity in the industry.

Price-Competition Inhibitors. Although some service industries can be fiercely competitive (e.g., airlines and online banking), not all are, especially when one or more of the following circumstances reduce price competition:

▶ **Non-price-related costs of using competing alternatives are high.** When saving time and effort are of equal or greater importance to customers than price in selecting a supplier, the intensity of price competition is reduced. Competing services have their own sets of related monetary and non-monetary costs. Therefore, the actual prices charged sometimes become secondary for competitive comparisons (as shown in Figure 6.14).

▶ **Personal relationships matter.** For services that are highly personalized and customized, such as hairstyling (Figure 6.15) or family medical care, relationships with individual providers are often very important to customers and discourage them from responding to competing offers. Many global banks, for example, prefer to focus on wealthy customers in order to form long-term personal relationships with them.

▶ **Switching costs are high.** When it takes effort, time, and money to switch providers, customers are less likely to take advantage of competing offers.[7] Cell phone service providers often require one- or two-year contracts from their subscribers and charge significant financial penalties for early cancellation of service. Likewise, life insurance firms charge administrative fees or cancellation charges when policy holders want to cancel their policy within a certain time period.

▶ **Time and location specificity reduces choice.** When people want to use a service at a specific location or at a particular time (or perhaps both), they usually find that they have fewer options. This reduces price competition.[8]

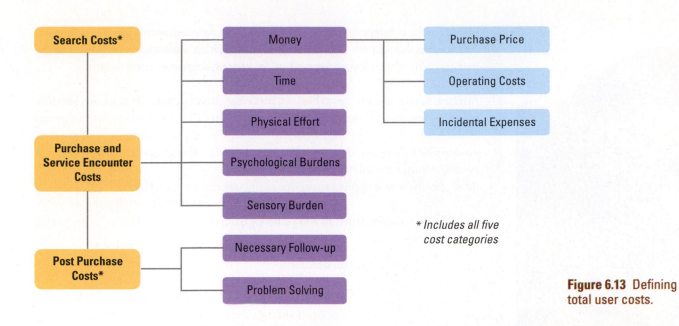

* Includes all five
cost categories

Figure 6.13 Defining total user costs.

PART II

Firms that always react to competitors' price changes run the risk of pricing *lower* than might really be necessary. A better strategy is to take into account the entire cost of each competing offering to customers. This includes all related monetary and non-monetary costs as well as potential switching costs. Managers should also assess the impact of distribution, time, and location factors and estimate the available capacity of competitors before deciding what response is appropriate.

Revenue Management: What It Is and How It Works[9]

Many service businesses now focus on strategies to maximize the revenue (or contribution) that can be obtained from the available capacity at any given point in time. Revenue

LO 6
Define revenue management and describe how it works.

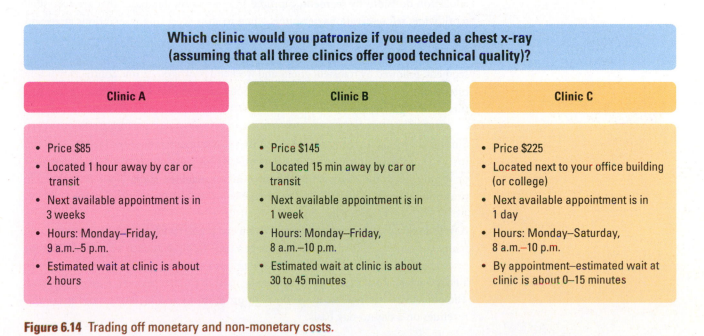

Which clinic would you patronize if you needed a chest x-ray (assuming that all three clinics offer good technical quality)?		
Clinic A	**Clinic B**	**Clinic C**
• Price $85	• Price $145	• Price $225
• Located 1 hour away by car or transit	• Located 15 min away by car or transit	• Located next to your office building (or college)
• Next available appointment is in 3 weeks	• Next available appointment is in 1 week	• Next available appointment is in 1 day
• Hours: Monday–Friday, 9 a.m.–5 p.m.	• Hours: Monday–Friday, 8 a.m.–10 p.m.	• Hours: Monday–Saturday, 8 a.m.–10 p.m.
• Estimated wait at clinic is about 2 hours	• Estimated wait at clinic is about 30 to 45 minutes	• By appointment–estimated wait at clinic is about 0–15 minutes

Figure 6.14 Trading off monetary and non-monetary costs.

Figure 6.15 Personalized hairstyling may prevent customers from switching to competing providers.

management is important in value creation as it ensures better capacity utilization and reserves capacity for higher-paying segments. It's a sophisticated approach to the management of supply and demand under varying degrees of constraint.

Airlines, hotels, and car rental firms in particular, have become adept at varying their prices in response to the price sensitivity and needs of different market segments at different times of the day, week, or season. Hospitals, restaurants, golf courses, on-demand IT services, data-processing centers, concert organizers (Figure 6.16), and even non-profit organizations are also increasingly using revenue management. It is most effective when applied to service businesses characterized by:

▶ High fixed-cost structure and relatively fixed capacity, which result in perishable inventory

▶ Variable and uncertain demand

▶ Varying customer price sensitivity

Reserving Capacity for High-Yield Customers

In practice, revenue management (also known as yield management) involves setting prices according to predicted demand levels among different market segments. The least price-sensitive segment is the first to be provided capacity. As higher-paying segments often book closer to the time of actual consumption, firms need a disciplined approach to save capacity for them instead of simply selling on a first-come, first-served basis. For example, business travelers often reserve airline seats, hotel rooms, and rental cars on short notice, but vacationers may book leisure travel months in advance, and convention organizers often block hotel space years in advance of a big event.

Figure 6.17 illustrates capacity allocation in a hotel setting, where demand from different types of customers varies not only by the day of the week but also by season. These allocation decisions by segment, captured in reservation databases that are accessible worldwide, tell reservations personnel when to stop accepting reservations at certain prices, even though many rooms may still remain un-booked. Loyalty program members (mainly business travelers paying high corporate rates) are obviously a very desirable segment, followed by transient guests and weekend packages. Airline contracts typically offer the lowest rates per room as airlines book large volumes far in advance and can therefore negotiate attractive rates.

Similar charts can be constructed for most capacity-constrained businesses. In some instances, capacity is measured in terms of seats for a given performance, seat-miles, or room-nights; in others it may be in terms of machine time, labor time, billable professional hours, vehicle miles, or storage volume, whichever is the scarce resource.

A well-designed revenue management system can predict with reasonable accuracy how many customers will use a given service at a specific time at each of several different price levels. It can then block the relevant amount of capacity at each level (known as a *price bucket*). This information can also be used to predict periods of excess capacity. The objective is to increase usage through promotions and incentives and maximize revenues on a day-to-day basis.

In the case of airlines, these models integrate massive historical databases on past passenger travel and can forecast demand of up to one year in advance for each individual departure. The revenue manager, who may be assigned specific routes at a large airline, checks the actual pace of bookings (i.e., sales at a given time before departure) at fixed intervals and compares it with the forecasted pace. If significant deviations exist between actual and forecasted demand, the manager will adjust the size of the inventory buckets. For example, if the *booking pace* for a higher-paying segment is greater than expected, additional capacity is taken away from the lowest-paying segment and allocated to the higher-paying segment in order to maximize the revenues from the flight. Service Insights 6.1 shows how revenue management has been implemented at American Airlines, which has long been an industry leader in this field.

How Can We Measure the Effectiveness of a Firm's Revenue Management?

Many capacity-constrained service organizations use percentage of capacity sold as a basic indicator of success. For instance, airlines talk of "load factor," hotels of "occupancy rate," and hospitals of "census." Similarly, professional firms monitor the proportion of their partners' and associates' time that counts as "billable hours." However, by

Figure 6.16 As golf courses have a high fixed cost structure, it benefits them to implement revenue management.

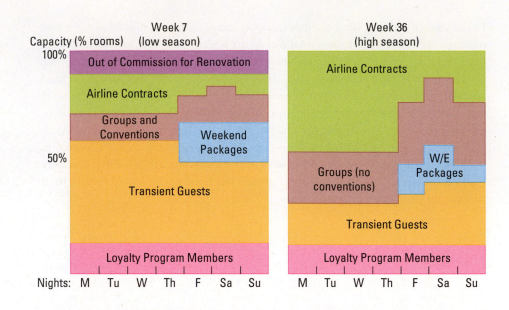

Figure 6.17 Setting capacity allocation targets by segment for a hotel.

themselves, these percentages tell us little about the relative profitability of the business attracted, since high usage rates may simply be a reflection of heavy discounting.

Success in revenue management is generally defined as maximizing the revenue per available capacity for a given space and time unit (RevPAST). For example, airlines seek to maximize revenue per available seat kilometer (RevPASK); hotels try to maximize their revenue per available room night (RevPAR); and performing arts centers try to maximize their revenue per available seat performance. These indices show the interplay between capacity utilization and average rate or price achieved. They can be tracked over time and benchmarked across firms as well as operating units within a service firm (e.g., across hotel properties in a larger chain).

How Does Competitors' Pricing Affect Revenue Management?

As revenue management systems monitor booking pace, they indirectly pick up the effects of competitors' pricing. For example, if an airline prices a flight too low, it will experience a higher booking pace, and its cheaper seats will fill up quickly. That is generally not desirable, because customers who book late but pay higher fares will not be able to get their seats confirmed and will therefore fly on competing airlines. If the initial pricing is too high, the firm will get too low a share of early booking segments (which still tend to offer a reasonable yield) and may later have to offer deeply discounted "last-minute" tickets to sell excess capacity. Some of the sales of distressed inventory (as it is called in the industry) may take place through reverse auctions, using intermediaries such as Priceline.com.

Price Elasticity

For revenue management to work effectively, there must be two or more segments that attach different values to the service and have different price elasticities. The concept of elasticity describes how sensitive demand is to changes in price. It is computed as follows:

Pricing Seats on Flight AA333

Revenue management departments use sophisticated software and powerful computers to forecast, track, and manage each flight separately on a given date. Let's look at American Airlines (AA) Flight 333, a popular flight from Chicago to Phoenix, Arizona, which departs daily at 4:50 pm on the 1,440 mile (2,317 km) journey.

The 124 seats in coach (economy class) are divided into different fare categories, referred to by revenue management specialists as "buckets." There is enormous variation in ticket prices among these seats: round-trip fares range from $298 for a bargain excursion ticket (with various restrictions and a cancellation penalty attached) all the way up to an unrestricted fare of $1,065. Seats are also available at an even higher price of $1,530 in the small first-class section. Scott McCartney tells us how ongoing analysis by the computer program changes the allocation of seats among each of the seven buckets in economy class:

> In the weeks before each Chicago–Phoenix flight, American's revenue management system constantly adjusts the number of seats in each bucket, taking into account tickets sold, historical ridership patterns, and connecting passengers likely to use the route as one leg of a longer trip.

If advance bookings are slim, American adds seats to low-fare buckets. If business customers buy unrestricted fares earlier than expected, the revenue management system takes seats out of the discount buckets and preserves them for the last-minute bookings predicted by the system.

With 69 of 124 coach seats already sold four weeks before one recent departure of Flight AA333, American's revenue management system began to limit the number of seats in lower-priced buckets. A week later, it totally shut off sales for the bottom three buckets that were priced $300 or less. To a Chicago customer looking for a cheap seat, the flight was "sold out."

A day before departure, with 130 passengers booked for the 124-seat flight, American still offered four seats at full fare because its revenue management system indicated that 10 passengers were likely not to show up or to take other flights. Flight AA333 departed full, and no one was bumped.

Although Flight AA333 for that date is now history, it has not been forgotten. The booking experience for this flight was saved in the memory of the revenue management system to help the airline do an even better job of forecasting in the future.

SOURCE

Source: Based on Scott McCartney, "Ticket Shock: Business Fares Increase Even as Leisure Travel Keeps Getting Cheaper," *The Wall Street Journal* 3 (November 1997): A1, A10; http://www.aa.com, accessed March 2, 2015. Note that flight details and prices are illustrative only.

$$\text{Price elasticity} = \frac{\text{Percentage change in demand}}{\text{Percentage change in price}}$$

When price elasticity is at "unity," sales of a service rise (or fall) by the same percentage that price falls (or rises). If a small change in price has a big impact on sales, demand for that product is said to be price elastic. If a change in price has little effect on sales, demand is described as price inelastic. The concept is illustrated in the simple chart presented in Figure 6.18, which shows the price elasticity for two segments—one with a highly elastic demand and the other with a highly inelastic demand. To allocate and price capacity effectively, the revenue manager needs to find out how sensitive

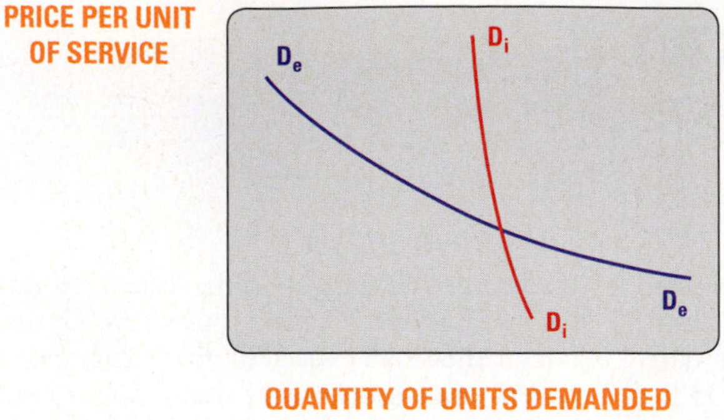

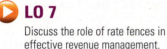

PRICE PER UNIT OF SERVICE

D_e

D_i

D_i

D_e

QUANTITY OF UNITS DEMANDED

$$\text{Price elasticity} = \frac{\text{Percentage change in demand}}{\text{Percentage change in price}}$$

D_e: Demand is *price elastic*. Small changes in price lead to big changes in demand.
D_i: Demand for service is *price inelastic*. Big changes in price have little impact on demand.

Figure 6.18 Illustration of price elasticity.

demand is to price and what net revenues will be generated at different price points for each target segment.

LO 7

Discuss the role of rate fences in effective revenue management.

Designing Rate Fences

Inherent in revenue management is the concept of *price customization*—that is, charging different customers different prices for what is actually the same product. As noted by Hermann Simon and Robert Dolan,

> The basic idea of price customization is simple: Have people pay prices based on the value they put on the product. Obviously you can't just hang out a sign saying "Pay me what it's worth to you," or "It's $80 if you value it that much but only $40 if you don't." You have to find a way to segment customers by their valuations. In a sense, you have to "build a fence" between high-value customers and low-value customers so the "high" buyers can't take advantage of the low price.[10]

How can a firm make sure that customers who are willing to pay higher prices are unable to take advantage of lower price buckets? Properly designed rate fences allow customers to self-segment on the basis of service characteristics and willingness to pay. Rate fences help companies to restrict lower prices to customers who are willing to accept certain restrictions on their purchase and consumption experiences.

Fences can be either physical or non-physical. Physical fences refer to tangible product differences related to the different prices, such as the seat location in a theater (Figure 6.19), the size and furnishing of a hotel room, or the product bundle (e.g., first class is better than economy). In contrast, non-physical fences refer to differences in consumption, transaction, or buyer characteristics, but the service is basically the same (e.g., an economy-class seat or service remains the same, irrespective of whether a person bought a heavily discounted ticket or paid the full fare for it). Examples of non-physical fences include having to book a certain length of time ahead, not being able to cancel or change a booking (or having to pay cancellation or change penalties), or having to stay over a weekend night. Examples of common rate fences are shown in Table 6.2.

Figure 6.19 Expect higher prices for seats that have a better view of your favorite, musical like *Cats*.

In summary, on the basis of a detailed understanding of customer needs, preferences, and willingness to pay, product and revenue managers can design effective products comprising the core service, physical product features (physical fences), and non-physical product features (non-physical fences). In addition, a good understanding of the demand curve is needed so that "buckets" of inventory can be assigned to the various products and price categories. An example from the airline industry is shown in Figure 6.20.

FAIRNESS AND ETHICAL CONCERNS IN SERVICE PRICING

LO 8

Be familiar with the issues of ethics and consumer concerns related to service pricing.

Do you sometimes have difficulty understanding the cost of using a service? Do you believe that many prices are unfair? If so, you're not alone.[11]

Service Pricing Is Complex

Pricing for services tends to be complex and hard to understand. Comparisons across providers may even require complex spreadsheets or mathematical formulas. Consumer advocates sometimes allege that service suppliers deliberately choose this complexity to reduce price competition. They don't want customers to be able to determine which firm offers the best value for money and therefore reduce price competition. In fact, complexity makes it easy (and perhaps more tempting) for firms to engage in unethical behavior.

Table 6.2 Key categories of rate fences.

Rate Fences	Examples
Physical (product-related) fences	
• Basic product	• Class of travel (business/economy class) • Size of rental car • Size and furnishing of a hotel room • Seat location in a theater or a stadium
• Amenities	• Free breakfast at a hotel, airport pick up, etc. • Free golf cart at a golf course • Valet parking
• Service level	• Priority wait-listing, separate check-in counters with no or only short queues • Improved food and beverage selection • Dedicated service hotlines • Personal butler • Dedicated account management team
• Other physical characteristics	• Table location pricing (e.g., restaurant table with view in a high-rise building), seat location pricing (e.g., a window or aisle seat in an aircraft cabin) • Extra legroom on an airline
Non-Physical Fences	
Transaction Characteristics	
• Time of booking or reservation	• Discounts for advance purchase
• Location of booking or reservation	• Passengers booking air tickets for an identical route in different countries are charged different prices (e.g., prices tend to be higher at an airline's hub because of higher frequency flights and more direct flights). • Customers making reservations online are charged a lower price than those making reservations by phone.
• Flexibility of ticket usage	• Fees/penalties for canceling or changing a reservation (up to loss of entire ticket price) • Non-refundable reservation fees
Consumption Characteristics	
• Time or duration of use	• Happy-hour offer in a bar, early-bird special in a restaurant before 6:00pm, and minimum required spending during peak periods • Must stay over a Saturday night for a hotel booking • Must stay at least for five nights
• Location of consumption	• Price depends on departure location, especially in international travel. • Prices vary by location (between cities, or between the city center and the edges of the city).

(continued)

Table 6.2 Key categories of rate fences. (continued)

Buyer Characteristics	
• Frequency or volume of consumption	• Members of certain loyalty tiers with the firm (e.g., platinum members) get priority pricing, discounts, or loyalty benefits • Season tickets
• Group membership	• Child, student, and senior citizen discounts • Affiliation with certain groups (e.g., alumni) • Membership with the firm's loyalty program • Corporate rates
• Size of customer group	• Group discounts based on size of group
• Geographic location	• Local customers are charged lower rates than tourists. • Customers from certain countries are charged higher prices.

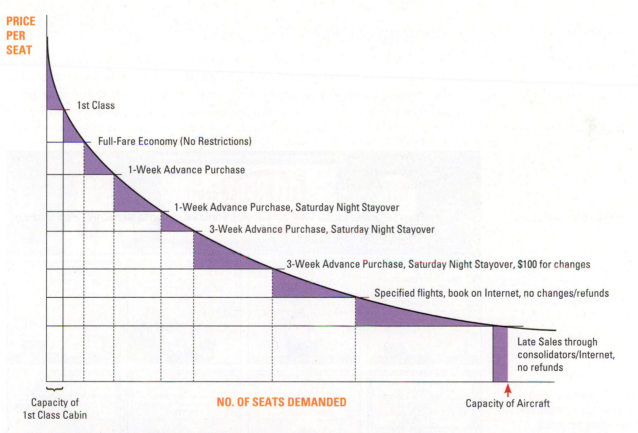

PART II

For example, cell phone companies have a confusing variety of plans to meet the distinct needs and usage patterns of different market segments. Plans can be national, regional, or purely local in scope. Monthly fees vary according to the number of minutes and mobile data capacity selected in advance. There can be separate allowances for peak

* Dark areas denote amount of consumer surplus (goal of segmented pricing is to reduce this).

Figure 6.20 Relating price buckets to the demand curve.

and off-peak minutes. Overtime minutes and "roaming minutes" on other carriers are charged at higher rates. Some plans allow unlimited off-peak calling, while others have free incoming calls. Data plans (including features such as being allowed to roll over unused mobile data to the next month), hand-set subsidies for new phones, roaming fees, family and bundled plans that can include several cell phones and other mobile devices, landlines, and internet services add further to this complexity. In addition, many people find it difficult to forecast their own usage, and this makes it even harder for them to compute comparative prices when evaluating competing suppliers whose fees are based on a variety of usage-related factors.

It seems no coincidence that the humorist Scott Adams (creator of Dilbert) exclusively used service examples when he "branded" the future of pricing as "confusiology." Adams remarks:

> You would think this would create a price war and drive prices down to the cost of providing it (that's what I learned between naps in my economics classes), but it isn't happening. The companies are forming efficient confusopolies so customers can't tell who has the lowest prices. Companies have learned to use the complexities of life as an economic tool.[12]

One of the roles of effective government regulation, says Adams, should be to discourage this tendency of certain service industries to develop into "confusopolies" (see also Figure 6.21).

Piling on the Fees

Not all business models are based on generating income from sales. Today, there is a growing trend of imposing fees that have little to do with usage. In the United States, the car rental industry has attracted some notoriety for advertising bargain rental prices and then telling customers on arrival that other fees such as collision insurance and

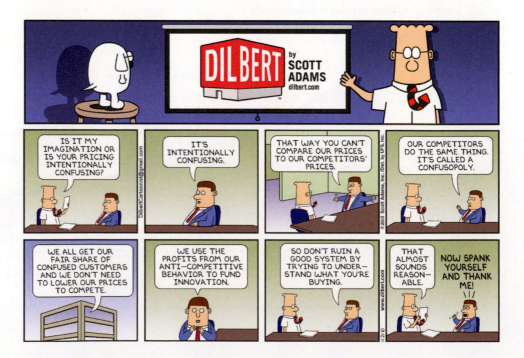

Figure 6.21 Firms would rather confuse customers than compete on price. How far can firms go before such behavior becomes unethical?

personal insurance are compulsory. In some Florida resort towns, there were so many "hidden extras" for car rentals at one point that people started joking: "The car is free, the keys are extra!"[13]

There has also been a trend of adding (or increasing) fines and penalties. Banks have been heavily criticized for using penalties as an important revenue-generating tool rather than as a means to educate customers and achieve compliance with payment deadlines (Figure 6.22). Chris Keeley, a New York University student, used his debit card to buy $230 worth of Christmas gifts. His holiday mood soured when he received a notice from his bank that he had overdrawn his checking account. Although his bank authorized each of his seven transactions, it charged him a fee of $31 per payment, totaling $217 for only $230 in purchases. Keeley maintained that he had never requested the so-called overdraft protection on his account. He wished his bank had rejected the transactions, for he could simply have paid by credit card. He fumed, "I can't help but think they wanted me to keep spending money so that they could collect these fees."[14]

It's possible to design fees and even penalties in ways that do not seem unfair to customers. Service Insights 6.2 describes what drives customers' fairness perceptions with service fees and penalties.

Designing Fairness into Revenue Management

Like pricing plans and fees, revenue management practices can be perceived as highly unfair. Therefore, a well-implemented revenue management strategy cannot mean blind pursuit of short-term yield maximization. The following approaches can help firms to reconcile revenue management practices with customers' fairness perceptions, satisfaction, trust, and goodwill:[15]

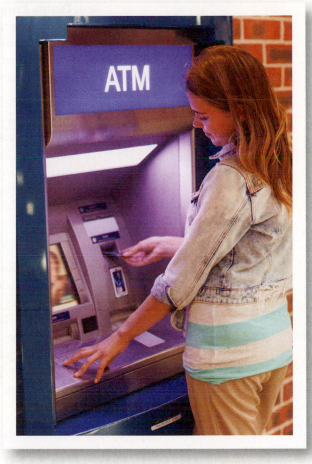

Figure 6.22 Consumers may be unaware of the high penalty fees imposed on overdrafts.

LO 9

Understand how fairness can be designed into revenue management policies.

Figure 6.23 Limousine service providers usually charge for no-shows.

- **Design Price Schedules and Fences That Are Clear, Logical, and Fair.** Firms should proactively spell out all fees and expenses (e.g., no-show or cancellation charges) clearly in advance so that there are no surprises (Figure 6.23). A related approach is to develop a simple fee structure so that customers can easily understand the financial implications of a specific usage situation.

- **Use High Published Prices and Frame Fences as Discounts.** Rate fences framed as customer gains (i.e., discounts) are generally perceived as fairer than those framed as customer losses (i.e., surcharges) even if the situations are economically equivalent. For example, a customer who patronizes her hair salon on Saturdays may perceive the salon as profiteering if she finds herself facing a weekend surcharge. However, she is likely to find the higher weekend price more acceptable if the salon advertises its peak weekend price as the published price and offers a $5 discount for weekday haircuts. Furthermore, a high published price helps to increase the reference price and related quality perceptions.

- **Communicate Consumer Benefits of Revenue Management.** Marketing communications should position revenue management as a win-win practice. By providing different prices and value propositions, firms can enable a broader spectrum of customers to self-segment and enjoy the service. For example, higher prices can be charged for the best seats in a theater because some people are willing and able to pay more for a better location. This also makes it possible to sell other seats at lower prices. When customers become more familiar with certain revenue management practices, unfairness perceptions are likely to decrease over time.[16]

SERVICE INSIGHTS 6.2

Crime and Punishment: How Customers Respond to Fines and Penalties

Various types of "penalties" are part and parcel of many pricing schedules. Their function is to discourage undesirable consumer behaviors, ranging from late fees for DVD rentals to cancellation charges for hotel bookings and charges for late credit card payments. Customer responses to penalties can be highly negative, thereby causing them to switch providers and spread poor word-of-mouth. Young Kim and Amy Smith conducted an online survey using the Critical Incident Technique (CIT) in which 201 respondents were asked to recall a recent penalty incident, describe the situation, and complete a set of structured questions based on how they felt and responded to the incident. The results of the survey showed that negative consumer responses can be reduced significantly if the service provider follows these three guidelines:

1 **Make penalties relative to the crime committed.** The survey showed that

customers' negative reaction to a penalty increased greatly when they perceived that the penalty was out of proportion to the "crime" committed. Their negative feelings were further aggravated if they were "surprised" by the sudden imposition of the penalty or unaware of the magnitude of the fee. These findings suggest that firms can reduce negative customer responses significantly by exploring which amounts are seen as reasonable or fair for a given "customer lapse." They must also communicate their fines/fees effectively before a chargeable incident occurs. For example, in a banking context, this may be done through a clearly explained fee schedule. When a customer opens an account or buys additional services, front-line staff should explain the potential fines or fees that are associated with various "violations" (such as overdrawing beyond the authorized limits, bounced checks, or late payments).

2 **Consider causal factors and customize penalties.** The study showed that customers' perceptions of fairness were lower and negative responses were higher when they perceived the causes that led to the penalty to be out of their control ("I mailed the check on time—there must have been a delay in the postal system") than when they felt these causes to be within their control and really their fault (e.g., "I forgot to mail the check"). To increase the perception of fairness, firms may want to identify common penalty cases that are typically out of the customer's control and allow the front line to waive or reduce such fees.

In addition, it was found that customers who generally observe all the rules and have not paid fines in the past react more negatively if they are fined. One respondent said, "I have always made timely payments and have never been late with a payment—they should have considered this fact and waived the fee." Service firms can improve fairness perceptions by taking into account customers' previous penalties and offering different treatments based on past behavior. For instance, they may waive the fine for the first incident, and at the same time communicate to the customer that the fee will be charged for future incidents.

3 **Focus on fairness and manage emotions during penalty situations.** Consumers' responses are heavily driven by their fairness perceptions. Customers are likely to perceive a penalty as excessive and respond negatively if they find that it is out of proportion to the damage or extra work inflicted on the service firm. One consumer complained, "I thought this particular penalty [credit card late payment] was excessive. You are already paying high interest; the penalty should have been more in line with the payment. The penalty was more than the payment!" Considering customers' perceptions of fairness might mean, for example, that the late fee for keeping a DVD or library book should not exceed the potentially lost rental fees during that period.

Service companies can also make penalties seem fairer by providing adequate explanations and justifications for the penalty. Ideally, penalties should be imposed for the good of other customers (e.g., "We kept the room for you even though we could have given it to another guest on our wait list") or the community (e.g., "Others are already waiting for this book to be returned") but not as a means for generating significant profit. Finally, front-line employees should be trained in how to handle customers who have become angry or distressed as a result of penalties and complain about them (see Chapter 13 for recommendations on how to deal with such situations).

SOURCE

Source: From Young "Sally" K. Kim and Amy K. Smith, "Crime and Punishment: Examining Customers' Responses to Service Organizations' Penalties," *Journal of Service Research* 8(2): 162–180, © 2005 Springer.

▶ **"Hide" Discounts through Bundling, Product Design, and Targeting.** Bundling a service into a package effectively obscures the discounted price. When a cruise line includes the price of air travel or ground transportation in the cruise package (Figure 6.24), the customer knows only the total price and not the cost of the individual components. Bundling usually makes price comparisons between the bundles and its components impossible and thereby side-steps potential unfairness perceptions and reductions in reference prices.[17]

Service products can be designed to hide discounts. Instead of varying the prices of food (which are difficult to increase once they have been lowered), restaurants can vary the product. For example, restaurants can offer smaller portions for lower-cost set lunches and impose a minimum spending level during peak periods. Thus, menu prices will not be changed, and price perceptions of diners will be unaffected. These two tactics give restaurants flexibility in adjusting effective revenue per seat to demand levels.[18]

▶ **Take Care of Loyal Customers.** Revenue management systems can be programmed to incorporate "loyalty multipliers" for regular customers so that reservations systems can give them "special treatment" status at peak times, even when they are not paying premium rates.

▶ **Use Service Recovery to Compensate for Overbooking.** Many service firms overbook to compensate for anticipated cancellations and no-shows. Profits increase, but so too does the incidence of being unable to honor reservations. Being "bumped" by an airline or "walked" by a hotel can lead to a loss of customer loyalty and adversely affect a firm's reputation.[19] It's therefore important to back up overbooking programs with well-designed service recovery procedures, such as:

1) **Giving customers a choice between retaining their reservation or receiving compensation** (e.g., many airlines practice voluntary off-loading at check-in against cash compensation and a later flight).

2) **Providing sufficient advance notice so that customers are able to make alternative arrangements** (e.g., pre-emptive off-loading and rescheduling to another flight the day before departure, often in combination with cash compensation).

3) **If possible, offering a substitute service that delights customers** (e.g., upgrading a passenger to business or first class on the next available flight, often in combination with options 1 and 2 above).

Figure 6.24 Cruise packages bundle land tours into their total package price.

A Westin beach resort has found that it can free up capacity by offering guests who are departing the next day the choice of spending their last night in a luxury hotel near the airport or in the city at no cost. Guest feedback on the free room, upgraded service, and a night in the city after a beach holiday has been very positive. From the hotel's perspective, this practice trades the cost of getting a one-night stay in another hotel against that of turning away a multiple-night guest arriving that same day.

PUTTING SERVICE PRICING INTO PRACTICE

▶ LO 10

Discuss the six questions marketers need to answer to design an effective service-pricing strategy.

The first thing a manager has to realize is that service pricing is multi-faceted. There are other important decisions to be made that have a major impact on the behavior and value perceptions of customers. Table 6.3 summarizes the questions service marketers need to ask themselves to develop a well-thought-out pricing strategy. Let's look at each in turn.

How Much Should Be Charged?

Realistic decisions on pricing are critical for financial solvency. The pricing tripod model discussed earlier (refer to Figure 6.4) provides a useful starting point. First, all the relevant economic costs need to be recovered at different sales volumes, and these set the relevant floor price. Next, the elasticity of demand of the service (from the perspectives of the providers as well as the customers) helps to set a "ceiling" price for any given market segment. Finally, firms need to analyze the intensity of price competition among the providers before they come to a final price.

More recently, auctions and dynamic pricing have become increasingly popular as a way of pricing according to demand and the value perceptions of customers. This can be seen in the examples of dynamic pricing in the internet environment in Service Insights 6.3.

What Should Be the Specified Basis for Pricing?

It's not always easy to define a unit of service as the specified basis for pricing. For instance, should price be based on completing a promised service task or on admission to a service performance? Should it be time-based—for instance, using an hour of a lawyer's time? Alternatively, should it be related to a monetary value linked to the service delivery (e.g., a commission as a percentage of the transaction value)?

Some service prices are tied to the consumption of physical resources such as food, drinks, water, or natural gas. Transport firms have traditionally charged by distance, with freight companies using a combination of weight or cubic volume and distance to set their rates (Figure 6.25). For some services, prices may include separate charges for access and usage. Research suggests that access or subscription fees are important drivers of adoption and customer retention, whereas usage fees are much more important drivers of actual usage.[20] Consumers of hedonic services such as amusement parks tend to prefer flat rates for access rather than payment by individual usage. This is because they don't like to be reminded of the pain of paying while they are enjoying the service. This is also called the taximeter effect as customers don't want to "hear" the price ticking upward—it lowers their consumption enjoyment![21]

Table 6.3 Issues to consider when developing a service pricing schedule.

1.	**How much should be charged for the service?** • What costs is the organization attempting to recover? Is the organization trying to achieve a specific profit margin or return on investment by selling this service? • How sensitive are customers to various prices? • What prices are charged by competitors? • What discount(s) should be offered from basic prices? • Are psychological pricing points (e.g., $4.95 versus $5.00) customarily used? • Should auctions and dynamic pricing be used?
2.	**What should be the basis of pricing?** • Execution of a specific task • Admission to a service facility • Units of time (hour, week, month, year) • Percentage commission on the value of the transaction • Physical resources consumed • Geographic distance covered, weight or size of object serviced • Outcome of service or cost-saving generated for the client • Should each service element be billed independently? • Should a single price be charged for a bundled package? • Should discounting be used for selective segments? • Is a freemium pricing strategy beneficial?
3.	**Who should collect payment and where?** • The organization that provides the service collects payment either at the location of service delivery or at arm's length (e.g., by mail, by phone, or online). • A specialist intermediary (travel or ticket agent, bank, retail, etc.) with a convenient retail outlet location. • How should the intermediary be compensated for this work—by a flat fee or by percentage commission?
4.	**When should payment be made?** • In advance or after service delivery? • In a lump sum or by installments over time?
5.	**How should payment be made?** • Cash (exact change or not?) • Tokens (where can these be purchased?) • Stored value card • Check (how to verify?) • Electronic funds transfer • Charge card (credit or debit) • Credit account with service provider • Vouchers • Third-party payment (e.g., insurance company or government agency)?
6.	**How should prices be communicated to the target market?** • Through which communication medium? (advertising, signage, electronic display, salespeople, customer service personnel) • What message content (how much emphasis should be placed on price?) • Can the psychology of pricing presentation and communications be used?

Dynamic Pricing on the Internet

Dynamic pricing—also known as customized or personalized pricing—is a version of the age-old practice of price discrimination. It is popular with service providers because of its potential to increase profits and at the same time provide customers with what they value. E-tailing, or retailing over the internet, lends itself well to this strategy because changing prices electronically is a simple procedure. Dynamic pricing enables service firms to charge different customers different prices for the same product based on information collected about their purchase history, preferences, price sensitivity, and so on. However, customers may not be happy.

E-tailers are often uncomfortable about admitting to the use of dynamic pricing because of the ethical and legal issues associated with price discrimination. Customers of Amazon.com were upset when they learned that the online mega-store was not charging everyone the same price for the same movie DVDs in its early days of e-commerce. A study of online consumers by the University of Pennsylvania's Annenberg Public Policy Center found that 87% of respondents did not think dynamic pricing was acceptable.

Reverse Auctions

Travel e-tailers such as Priceline.com and Hotwire. com follow a customer-driven pricing strategy known as a reverse auction. Each firm acts as an intermediary between potential buyers (who ask for quotations for a product or service) and multiple suppliers (who quote the best price they're willing to offer). Buyers can then compare the offers and choose the supplier that best meets their needs. For example, if a buyer is looking for a flight and accommodation package, search results often show a variety of package combinations one can choose from. All the different airlines and hotels are listed by brand, and the price of each package is listed clearly.

Different business models underlie these services. Although some are provided freely to end users, most e-tailers either receive a commission from the supplier or do not pass on their whole savings to their customers. Others charge customers a fixed fee or a percentage of the savings.

Traditional Auctions

Other e-tailers, such as eBay, uBid, or OnlineAuction, follow the traditional online auction model in which bidders place bids for an item and compete with each other to determine who buys it. Marketers of both consumer and industrial products use such auctions to sell obsolete or overstocked items, collectibles, rare items, and second-hand merchandise. This form of retailing has become very successful since it was launched by eBay in 1995.

Shopbots and Meta-search Engines Help Consumers to Benefit from Dynamic Pricing

Consumers now have tools of their own to prevent themselves from being taken advantage of by practices of dynamic pricing. One approach involves using shopbots and meta-search engines to compare prices and find the cheapest options available. Shopbots, or shopping robots, are basically intelligent agents that automatically collect price and product information from multiple vendors. A customer has only to visit a shopbot site, such as Dealtime.com, and run a search for the product he/she wants. In the travel industry, Kayak is a leading meta-search engine. These shopbots instantly query all the associated service providers to check availability, features, and price. The results are then presented in a comparison table. Different shopbots have links to different retailers. There is even a shopbot site called MegaShopBot.com, which searches for deals within the best shopbots!

There's little doubt that dynamic pricing is here to stay. With further advances in technology and wider application, its reach will extend to more and more service categories.

SOURCES

Sources: Based on Laura Sydell, "New Pricing Plan Soon to Be at Play For Online Music," July 27, 2009, http://www.npr.org/templates/story/story.php?storyId=111046679&ft=1&f=1006, accessed March 2, 2015; Jean-Michel Sahut, "The Impact of Internet on Pricing Strategies in the Tourism Industry," *Journal of Internet Banking and Finance* 14(1) (2009): 1–8; "Promotional Pricing: Dynamic Pricing," from "Setting Price: Part 2 Tutorial," KnowThis. com (2015), http://www.knowthis.com/setting-price-part-2/promotional-pricing-dynamic-pricing, accessed March 2, 2015; Thad Rueter, "The Price Is Right—Then It's Not." (2014), https://www.internetretailer.com/2014/08/04/price-rightthen-its-not-2?p=1, accessed March 2, 2015; Max Starkov and Tara Dyer, "Meta Search Marketing: The New Revenue Frontier in Hospitality" (2013), http://blog.hebsdigital.com/meta-search-marketing-the-new-revenuefrontier-in-hospitality, accessed March 12, 2015, © Jochen Wirtz.

In B2B markets in particular, innovative business models charge on the basis of outcomes rather than on services provided. For example, Rolls-Royce's Power-by-the-Hour service does not charge for services such as maintenance, repairs, and materials. Its charges are based on the outcome of these activities, that is, the number of flying hours.[22] In effect, generated cost savings are shared between the provider and their client.

Price Bundling. An important question for service marketers is whether to charge an inclusive price for all elements (referred to as a "bundle") or to price each element separately. If customers prefer to avoid making many small payments, bundled pricing may be best. In other cases, itemized pricing is preferable. Bundled prices offer firms a certain level of guaranteed revenue from each customer while providing customers a clear idea in advance of how much they can expect to pay. Unbundled pricing provides customers with the freedom to choose what to buy and pay for. However, customers may be angered if they discover that the actual price of what they consume, inflated by all the "extras," is substantially higher than the advertised base price that attracted them in the first place.[23]

Discounting. Selective price discounting targeted at specific market segments can offer important opportunities to attract new customers and fill capacity that would otherwise go unused. However, unless it is used with effective rate fences that allow specific segments to be targeted cleanly, a strategy of discounting should be approached with caution.

Figure 6.25 Shipment of goods are typically charged by a combination of distance (miles, kilometers, or zones) and weight or size (such as cubic volume).

Freemium. Over the past decade, "freemium" (a combination of "free" and "premium") has become a popular pricing strategy for online and mobile services. Users get the basic service at no cost (typically funded by advertising) and can upgrade to a richer functionality for a subscription fee. If you have shared files on Dropbox, networked on LinkedIn, or streamed music from Spotify, you have experienced this business model first hand. As marginal costs for technology and bandwidth are dropping, freemium models are likely to become more attractive.[24]

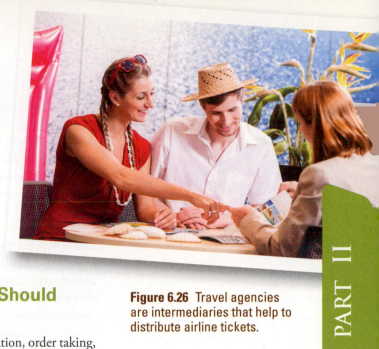

Figure 6.26 Travel agencies are intermediaries that help to distribute airline tickets.

Who Should Collect Payment and Where Should Payment Be Made?

As discussed in Chapter 4, supplementary services include information, order taking, billing, and payment. However, service delivery sites are not always conveniently located. Airports, theaters, and stadiums, for instance, are often situated far from where potential customers may live or work. When consumers need to purchase such services and no convenient online channel is available, it is beneficial to use intermediaries that are more conveniently located. Therefore, firms sometimes delegate these services to intermediaries, such as travel agents who make hotel and transport bookings and collect payment from customers (see Figure 6.26), or ticket agents who sell seats for theaters, concert halls, and sports stadiums.

When Should Payment Be Made?

Two basic ways are to ask customers to pay in advance (as with an admission charge, an airline ticket, or postage stamps) or to bill them once service delivery has been completed (as with restaurant bills and repair charges). Occasionally, a service provider may ask for an initial payment in advance of service delivery, with the balance due later (Figure 6.27). This approach is quite common for expensive repair and maintenance jobs that require the firm—often a small business with limited working capital—to buy and pay for materials.

Advance payment implies that the buyer is paying before the benefits of the service are received. However, pre-payments may offer advantages to the customer as well as the provider. Sometimes, it is inconvenient to pay each time a regularly patronized service—such as the postal service or public transport—is used. To save time and effort, customers may prefer the convenience of buying a book of stamps or a monthly travel pass.

Finally, the timing of payment can determine usage patterns. From an analysis of the payment and attendance records of a Colorado-based health club, John Gourville and Dilip Soman found that members' usage patterns were closely related to their payment schedules. For instance, their use of the club was highest during the months immediately following payment and then slowed down steadily until the next payment. Members with monthly payment plans used the health club much more consistently and were more likely to renew their memberships, perhaps because each month's payment encouraged them to use what they were paying for (Figure 6.28).[25]

"Unless we receive the outstanding balance within ten days, we will have no choice but to destroy your credit rating, ruin your reputation, and make you wish you were never born. If you have already sent the seven cents, please disregard this notice."

Figure 6.27 Some firms do not leave their customers with much flexibility in dealing with late payment.

Gourville and Soman conclude that the timing of payment can be used more strategically to manage capacity utilization. For instance, if a golf club wants to reduce demand during its busiest time, it can bill its fees long before the season begins (e.g., in January rather than in May or June). The members' pain of payment will have faded by the time the peak summer months arrive, thereby reducing their need to get their "money's worth." A reduction in demand during the peak period would then allow the club to increase its overall membership.

Conversely, timing of payment can also be used to boost consumption. Consider the Boston Red Sox (i.e., the famous American professional baseball team) season ticket holders, who are billed five months before the season starts. To build attendance and strong fan support throughout the season, Red Sox could spread out this large annual payment to, say, four installments that coincide with their games. The team would garner a high game attendance and fan support, and their fans might prefer the lower and financially more manageable installments.

How Should Payment Be Made?

There are many different forms of payment. Cash may appear to be the simplest method, but it raises security problems and is inconvenient when exact change is required to operate machines. Credit and debit cards can be used around the world as their acceptance has become almost universal. Other payment procedures include tokens or vouchers as supplements to (or instead of) cash.

Service marketers should remember that the simplicity and speed with which payment is made may influence the customer's perception of overall service quality. Pre-payment systems based on cards that store value on a magnetic strip or in a microchip embedded within are now coming into broader usage. Contactless payment systems based on credit and debit cards with radio-frequency identification (RFID) technology are increasingly

Figure 6.28 Payment schedules can drive health club usage and renewal of membership!

being used. Starbucks launched a smartphone cum app-based payment system that is integrated with its My Starbucks Reward Program, which allows its customers to earn special discounts and freebies. Soon, order taking will be integrated to cut wait time at the counter. Apple users can even pay by holding their device to the point-of-sale system and authenticating the transaction using the phone's Touch ID fingerprint sensor (Figure 6.29). Suppliers of these systems claim that transactions can be up to twice as fast as conventional cash, credit, or debit card purchases.

Figure 6.29 Apple Pay aims to make payment simple.

PART II

SERVICE INSIGHTS 6.4

The Psychology of Menu Pricing in Restaurants

- Have you ever wondered why you choose certain dishes on the menu and not others? It could be due to the way the dish is displayed on the menu. Menu psychology is a growing field of research. Menu engineers and consultants conduct research on the most effective ways to design a menu, including layout and pricing information, in the hope that the diner will spend more money. What can we do to get people to spend more money and order items with high profit margins?

- It is best to avoid using a currency symbol ($, €, etc.) when showing prices on the menu. Prices that come with dollar signs will cause customers to spend less money than when there are no dollar signs.

- Prices that end with "9," like $9.99, make diners feel that they are getting value for money. This is favorable for a low price and good value positioning but should not be used by high-end restaurants.

- Prices should be placed at the end of the description of an item and should not be highlighted in any way.

- The most expensive item should be placed at the top of the menu so that the prices of the other items look lower in comparison.

- The most profitable item on the menu should be placed at the top right hand corner of the page because people tend to look there first.

- A longer description of a dish tends to encourage people to order it. Therefore, menus can be designed to have detailed and appetizing descriptions of dishes that are more profitable and shorter descriptions of those that are less profitable.

- How should dishes be named? It has been shown that people are encouraged to order items that are named after mothers, grandmothers, and other relatives (e.g., Aunty May's beef stew).

The next time you select a dish from the menu, you may want to stop and see how it is displayed. This will help you determine whether you have been swayed towards a dish that the restaurant wants you to order.

SOURCE

Sources: Based on Sarah Kershaw, "In Search of a Formula to Entice Mind, Stomach and Wallet," *The New York Times*, December 23, 2009, © Jochen Wirtz.

How Should Prices Be Communicated to the Target Markets?

The final task is to decide how the organization's pricing policies can best be communicated to its target market(s). People need to know the price they are expected to pay for a service offering before they purchase it. They may also need to know how, where, and when that price is payable. This information must be presented in intelligible and unambiguous ways so that customers will not be misled and question the ethical standards of the firm. Managers must decide whether or not to include information on pricing in advertisements for the service. It may be suitable to relate the price to the costs of competing products. Salespeople and customer service representatives should

Figure 6.30 Customers may be paying more than they should for their hospital stay.

be able to give immediate and accurate responses to customer queries about pricing, payment, and credit. Good signage at retail points of sale will save staff members from having to answer basic questions on prices.

The methods used to communicate prices are important and shape buying behavior. For example, in a restaurant context, menu psychology looks at how diners respond to pricing information on a menu (see Service Insights 6.4).

Finally, when the price is presented in the form of an itemized bill, marketers should make sure that it is both accurate and easy to understand. Hospital bills, which may run to several pages and contain dozens or even hundreds of items, have frequently been criticized for their inaccuracy (Figure 6.30). Hotel bills, despite containing fewer entries, are also notoriously inaccurate. One study estimated that business travelers in the United States may be overpaying for their hotel rooms by half-a-billion dollars a year, with 11.6% of all bills incorrect, resulting in an average overpayment of $11.36.[26]

LO 1 ▶ Effective pricing is central to the financial success of service firms. The key objectives for establishing prices can be to (1) gain profits and cover costs, (2) build demand and develop a user base, and/or (3) support the firm's positioning strategy. Once a firm sets its pricing objectives, it needs to decide on its pricing strategy.

LO 2 ▶ The foundations of a pricing strategy are the three legs of the pricing tripod:

o The costs the firm needs to recover set the minimum or floor price.

o The customer's perceived value of the offering sets a maximum or ceiling price.

o The price charged for competing services determines where, within the floor-to-ceiling range, the price can be set.

LO 3 ▶ The first leg of the pricing tripod is the cost to the firm.

o Costing services is often complex. Services frequently have high fixed costs, varying capacity utilization, and large shared infrastructures that make it difficult to establish unit costs.

o If services have a large proportion of variable and/or semi-variable costs, cost-accounting approaches work well (e.g., the use of contribution and break-even analysis).

o However, activity-based costing (ABC) is often more appropriate for complex services with shared infrastructure.

LO 4 ▶ The second leg of the pricing tripod is value to the customer.

o Net value is the sum of all the perceived benefits (gross value) minus the sum of all the perceived costs of a service. Customers will only buy the service if the net value is positive. The net value can be enhanced by increasing value and/or by reducing costs.

o Since value is perceived and subjective, it can be enhanced through communication and education to help customers better understand the value they receive.

o In addition to the price customers pay for the service, costs include related monetary costs (e.g., the taxi fare to the service location) and non-monetary costs (e.g., time, physical, psychological, and sensory costs) during the search, purchase and service encounter, and post-purchase stages. Firms can enhance net value by reducing these related monetary and non-monetary costs.

LO 5 ▶ The third leg of the pricing tripod is competition.

o Price competition can be fierce in markets with relatively similar services. Here, firms need to closely observe what competitors charge and price accordingly.

o Price competition intensifies with the (1) number of competitors, (2) number of substituting offers, (3) distribution density of competitor and substitution offers, and (4) amount of surplus capacity in the industry.

o Price competition is reduced if one or more of the following applies: (1) Non-price-related costs of using competing alternatives are high; (2) personal relationships are important; and (3) switching costs are high, and service consumption is time and location specific.

LO 6 ▶ Revenue management (RM) increases revenue for the firm through better use of capacity and reservation of capacity for higher-paying segments. Specifically, revenue management:

o Designs products using physical and non-physical rate fences, and prices them for different segments according to their specific reservation prices.

o Sets prices according to predicted demand levels of different customer segments.

o Works best in service businesses characterized by (1) high fixed costs and perishable inventory, (2) several customer segments with different price elasticities, and (3) variable and uncertain demand.

o Measures success by revenue per available capacity for a given space and time unit (RevPAST). For example, airlines seek to maximize revenue per available seat kilometer (RevPASK), while hotels try to maximize their revenue per available room night (RevPAR).

LO 7 ▶ Well-designed rate fences are needed to define "products" for each target segment so that customers who are willing to pay higher prices for a service are unable to take advantage of lower price buckets. Rate fences can be physical and non-physical:

o Physical fences refer to tangible product differences related to different prices (e.g., seat location in a theater, size of a hotel room, or service level).

o Non-physical fences refer to consumption (e.g., having to stay over a weekend at a hotel), transaction (e.g., two weeks' advance booking with cancellation and change penalties), or buyer characteristics (e.g., student and group discounts). The service experience is identical across fence conditions although different prices are charged.

LO 8 ▶ Customers often have difficulties understanding service pricing (e.g., RM practices and their many fences and fee schedules). Service firms need to be careful that their pricing does not become so complex and full of hidden fees that customers perceive them as unethical and unfair.

LO 9 ▶ The following ways help firms to improve customers' fairness perceptions:

o Design price schedules and fences that are clear, logical, and fair.

o Use published prices and frame fences as discounts.

o Communicate consumer benefits of revenue management.

o "Hide" discounts through bundling, product design, and targeting.

o Take care of loyal customers.

o Use service recovery or deal with overbooking.

LO 10 ▶ Service marketers need to consider seven questions to develop a well-thought-out pricing strategy. The questions are:

o How much should be charged?

o What should be the specified basis for pricing?

o Who should collect payment, and where should payment be made?

o When should payment be made?

o How should payment be made?

o How should prices be communicated to the target markets?

UNLOCK YOUR LEARNING

These keywords are found within the sections of each Learning Objective (LO). They are integral to understanding the services marketing concepts taught in each section. Having a firm grasp of these keywords and how they are used is essential to helping you do well on your course, and in the real and very competitive marketing scene out there.

LO 1
1. Pricing strategy
2. Pricing objectives
3. Profit
4. Demand
5. User base

LO 2
1. Value-based pricing
2. Competitive pricing
3. Minimum price
4. Floor
5. Maximum price
6. Ceiling
7. Pricing tripod
8. Costs
9. Competition
10. Value to customer

LO 3
1. Cost-based pricing
2. Fixed costs
3. Variable costs
4. Semi-variable costs
5. Cost-accounting
6. Activity-based costing
7. Indirect costs
8. Resource expenses
9. Contribution
10. Economic costs
11. Break-even analysis
12. Price sensitivity

LO 4
1. Value-based pricing
2. Net value
3. Perceived benefits
4. Perceived costs
5. Perception of value
6. Monetary costs
7. Non-monetary costs
8. Time costs
9. Physical costs
10. Psychological costs
11. Sensory costs
12. Search costs
13. Purchase costs
14. Service-encounter costs
15. Post-purchase costs

LO 5
1. Competition-based pricing
2. Price leadership
3. Non-price-related costs
4. Relationships
5. Switching costs
6. Time specificity
7. Location specificity

LO 6
1. Revenue management
2. Perishable inventory
3. Yield management
4. Distressed inventory
5. Reverse auctions
6. Price elasticity
7. Price elastic
8. Price inelastic
9. Price bucket

LO 7
1. Rate fences
2. Price customization
3. Physical fences
4. Non-physical fences
5. "Buckets" of inventory
6. Transaction characteristics
7. Consumption characteristics
8. Buyer characteristics

PART II

How well do you know the language of services marketing? Quiz yourself!

⚠ **Not for the academically faint-of-heart**

For each keyword you are able to recall without referring to earlier pages, give yourself a point (and a pat on the back). Tally your score at the end and see if you earned the right to be called—a *services marketeer*.

SCORE

0 – 18	Services Marketing is done a great disservice.
19 – 36	The midnight oil needs to be lit, pronto.
37 – 54	I know what you *didn't* do all semester.
55 – 72	A close shave with success.
73 – 90	Now, go forth and market.
91 – 95	There should be a marketing concept named after you.

Review Questions

1. Why is the pricing of services more difficult than the pricing of goods?

2. How can the pricing tripod approach to service pricing be useful in setting a good pricing point for a particular service?

3. How can a service firm compute its unit costs for pricing purposes? How does predicted and actual capacity utilization affect unit costs and profitability?

4. What is the role of non-monetary costs in a business model, and how do they relate to the consumer's value perceptions?

5. Why can't we compare competitor prices dollar-for-dollar in a service context?

6. What is revenue management? How does it work? Which types of service operations benefit most from good revenue management systems, and why?

7. Explain the difference between physical and non-physical rate fences using suitable examples.

8. Why are ethical concerns important issues when designing service pricing and revenue management strategies? What are potential consumer responses to service pricing or policies that are perceived as unfair?

9. How can we charge different prices to different segments without customers feeling cheated? How can we even charge the same customer different prices at different times, contexts, and/or occasions and at the same time be seen as fair?

10. What are the six key decisions managers need to make when designing an effective pricing schedule?

WORK YOUR SERVICES MARKETING

Application Exercises

1. Select a service organization of your choice, and find out what its pricing policies and methods are. In what respects are they similar to or different from what has been discussed in this chapter?

2. Review recent bills you have received from service businesses, such as those for telephone services, car repair, cable TV, and credit cards. Evaluate each one against the following criteria: (a) general appearance and clarity of presentation, (b) easily understood terms of payment, (c) avoidance of confusing terms and definitions, (d) appropriate level of detail, (e) unanticipated ("hidden") charges, (f) accuracy, and (g) ease of access to customer service in case of problems or disputes.

3. How might revenue management be applied to (a) a professional service firm (e.g., a law firm), (b) a restaurant, and (c) a golf course? What rate fences would you use and why?

4. Explore two highly successful business models that are based on innovative service pricing and/or revenue management strategies, and identify two business models that failed because of major issues in their pricing strategy. What general lessons can you learn from your analysis?

5. Consider a service of your choice, and develop a comprehensive pricing schedule. Apply the six questions marketers need to answer for designing an effective pricing schedule.

ENDNOTES

1. Joshua Brustein, "Star Pitchers in a Duel? Tickets Will Cost More," *The New York Times*, June 27, 2010; Adam Satariano, "Eagles Pinch Scalpers with Live Nation Price Hikes (Update 1)," *Businessweek*, February 24, 2010; Ethan Smith, "Start-Up Scoops Up Unsold Tickets," *The Wall Street Journal*, December 16, 2010; Patrick Healy, "Ticket Pricing Puts 'Lion King' Atop Broadway's Circle of Life," *The New York Times*, March 17, 2014: A1.

2. This section is based on: Robin Cooper and Robert S. Kaplan, "Profit Priorities from Activity-Based Costing," *Harvard Business Review* 69, no. 3 (May–June 1991): 130–135; Robert S. Kaplan and Steven R. Anderson, "Time-Driven Activity Based Costing," *Harvard Business Review* (November 2004).

3. From "Consumer Perceptions of Price, Quality, and Value: A Means-End Model and Synthesis of Evidence," in *Journal of Marketing* 52, pp. 2–21, © 1988 American Marketing Association.

4. Parts of this section are based on: Leonard L. Berry and Manjit S. Yadav, "Capture and Communicate Value in the Pricing of Services," *Sloan Management Review* 37 (Summer 1996): 41–51.

5. It has been shown that music piracy can be reduced by making the purchase and use of music more convenient. Ironically, the use of digital rights management (DRM), which aims to reduce unauthorized copying and piracy, actually increases piracy not because of consumers' unwillingness to pay but because of the inconvenience entailed in using DRM protected files. See: Rajiv K. Sinha, Fernando S. Machado, and Collin Sellman, "Don't Think Twice, It's All Right: Music Piracy and Pricing in a DRM-Free Environment," *Journal of Marketing* 74, no. 2 (2010): 40–54.

6. Leonard L. Berry, Kathleen Seiders, and Dhruv Grewal, "Understanding Service Convenience," *Journal of Marketing* 66 (July 2002): 1–17. For examining the trade-off between price and effort (i.e., self-service), see: Lan Xia and Rajneesh Suri, "Trading Effort for Money: Consumers' Cocreation Motivation and the Price of Service Options," *Journal of Service Research* 17, no. 2 (2014): 229–242.

7. Jochen Wirtz, Ping Xiao, Jeongwen Chiang, and Naresh Malhotra, "Contrasting Switching Intent and Switching Behavior in Contractual Service Settings," *Journal of Retailing* 90, no. 4 (2014): 463–480.

8. Kristina Heinonen, "Reconceptualizing Customer Perceived Value: The Value of Time and Place," *Managing Service Quality* 14, no. 3 (2004): 205–215.

9. For a review of the extant revenue management literature, see: Sheryl E. Kimes and Jochen Wirtz, "Revenue Management: Advanced Strategies and Tools to Enhance Firm Profitability," *Foundations and Trends in Marketing* 8, no 1 (2015): 1-68.

10. From Hermann Simon and Robert J. Dolan, "Price Customization," in *Marketing Management* 7, © 1998 Harvard Business School.

11. Lisa E. Bolton, Luk Warlop, and Joseph W. Alba, "Consumer Perceptions of Price (Un)Fairness," *Journal of Consumer Research* 29, no. 4 (2003): 474–491; Lan Xia, Kent B. Monroe, and Jennifer L. Cox, "The Price is Unfair! A Conceptual Framework of Price Fairness Perceptions," *Journal of Marketing* 68 (October 2004): 1–15.

12. From Scott Adams, "The Dilbert Future: Thriving on Business Stupidity in the 21st Century," © 1997 HarperBusiness.

13. Ian Ayres and Barry Nalebuff, "In Praise of Honest Pricing," *Sloan Management Review* 45 (Fall 2003): 24–28.

14. Dean Foust, "Protection Racket? As Overdraft and Other Fees Become Huge Profit Sources for Banks, Critics See Abuses," *Business Week* 5 (February 2005): 68–89.

15. Parts of this section are based on: Jochen Wirtz, Sheryl E. Kimes, Jeannette P. T. Ho, and Paul Patterson, "Revenue Management: Resolving Potential Customer Conflicts," *Journal of Revenue and Pricing Management* 2, no. 3 (2003): 216–228.

16. Jochen Wirtz and Sheryl E. Kimes, "The Moderating Role of Familiarity in Fairness Perceptions of Revenue Management Pricing," *Journal of Service Research* 9, no. 3 (2007): 229–240.

17. Judy Harris and Edward A. Blair, "Consumer Preference for Product Bundles: The Role of Reduced Search Costs," *Journal of the Academy of Marketing Science* 34, no. 4 (2006): 506–513.

18. Rafi Mohammed, "A Better Way to Make Deals on Meals," *Harvard Business Review* (January–February 2011): 25.

19. Florian V. Wangenheim and Tomas Bayon, "Behavioral Consequences of Overbooking Service Capacity," *Journal of Marketing* 71, no. 4 (October 2007): 36–47.

20. Peter J. Danaher, "Optimal Pricing of New Subscription Services: An Analysis of a Market Experiment," *Marketing Science* 21 (Spring 2002): 119–129; Gilia E. Fruchter and Ram C. Rao, "Optimal Membership Fee and Usage Price Over Time for a Network Service," *Journal of Services Research* 4, no. 1 (2001): 3–14.

21. Fabian Uhrich, Jan H. Schumann, and Florian von Wangenheim, "The Impact of Consumption Goals on Flat-Rate Choice: Can "Hedonizing" a Service Increase Customers' Propensity to Choose a Flat Rate?" *Journal of Service Research* 16, no. 2 (2012): 216–230.

22. Irene C.L. Ng, David Xing Ding, and Nick Yip, "Outcome-based Contracts as New Business Model: The Role of Partnership and Value-driven Relational Assets," *Industrial Marketing Management* 42, no. 5 (2013): 730–743; Irene C.L. Ng, Roger Maull, and Nick Yip, "Outcome-based Contracts as a Driver for Systems Thinking and Service-Dominant Logic in Service Science: Evidence from the Defence Industry," *European Management Journal* 27, no. 6 (2009): 377–387.

23. Eoghan Macguire, "'Hidden' Airline Charges: Dirty Tricks or Customer Choice?", CNN (2012), http://edition.cnn.com/2012/07/10/travel/airline-charges/index.html, accessed February 27, 2015.

24. Vineet Kumar, "Making 'Freemium' Work," *Harvard Business Review* 92, no. 5 (2014): 27–29.

25. John Gourville and Dilip Soman, "Pricing and the Psychology of Consumption," *Harvard Business Review* 9 (September 2002): 90–96.

26. See, for example: Anita Sharpe, "The Operation Was a Success; The Bill Was Quite a Mess," *The Wall Street Journal*, September 17, 1997: 1; Gary Stoller, "Hotel Bill Mistakes Mean Many Pay Too Much," *USA Today*, July 12, 2005.

LEARNING OBJECTIVES (LOs)

By the end of this chapter, the reader should be able to:

LO1 Know the 5 Ws of the Integrated Service Communications Model; i.e., *W*ho, *W*hat, Ho*w*, *W*here, and *W*hen.

LO2 Be familiar with the three broad target audiences (i.e., "*W*ho") for any service communications program.

LO3 Understand the most common strategic and tactical service communications objectives ("*W*hat").

LO4 Be familiar with the *Services Marketing Communications Funnel* and the key objectives in that funnel.

LO5 Know a few important roles that service marketing communications can assume.

LO6 Understand the challenges of service communications and know how they can be overcome ("Ho*w*").

LO7 Be familiar with the *Services Marketing Communications Mix* ("*W*here").

LO8 Know the communications mix elements of the traditional marketing communication channels.

LO9 Know the role of the internet, mobile phones, apps, QR codes, and other electronic media in service marketing communications.

LO10 Know the communications mix elements available via service delivery channels.

LO11 Know the communications mix elements that originate from outside the firm.

LO12 Understand when communications should take place ("*W*hen"), how budgets for service communications programs may be set, and how these programs may be evaluated.

LO13 Appreciate ethical and consumer-privacy-related issues in service marketing communications.

LO14 Understand the role of corporate design in communications.

LO15 Know the importance of Integrated Marketing Communications to deliver a strong brand identity.

OPENING VIGNETTE

Oscar Is Having the Time of His Life[1]

Employees of the Kilronan Castle Hotel in Ireland found a bright orange and yellow monkey soft toy that had been left behind in a linen bin. Instead of putting it in the lost-property shelf, the employees had the great idea of starting a social media campaign to reunite Oscar (the name they gave to the toy) with his rightful owner. They had a lot of fun during the process, as can be seen in the photos they uploaded on Facebook!

The photos showed Oscar living a life of luxury at the hotel, enjoying afternoon teas and beauty treatments and even having a buffet prepared for him by the executive chef. The message was that although Oscar was lost and looking for his owner, he was having the time of his life at the luxurious castle hotel. It almost seemed as though he didn't mind not being found for a little while longer! Have a look online to know whether he was eventually reunited with his owner.

While the employees did hope that Oscar's owner would come forward, the significant social media publicity their campaign generated for the Kilronan Castle Hotel is undeniable. Speed, creativity, and fun are some of the attributes that can make a social media campaign go viral.

LO 1

Know the 5 Ws of the Integrated Service Communications Model; i.e., **W**ho, **W**hat, Ho**w**, **W**here, and **W**hen.

INTEGRATED SERVICE MARKETING COMMUNICATIONS

The "Oscar" campaign in our opening vignette was successful in creating a following on Facebook because the hotel's employees were quick and innovative. Social media has become an integral part of many service organizations. This chapter focuses on how to plan and design an effective marketing communications strategy for services.

An effective service marketing communications strategy starts with a good understanding of the service product and its prospective buyers. It is essential to understand target market segments and their exposure to different media, consumers' awareness of the service product and their attitudes toward it, and how easily they can evaluate the product's characteristics before purchase or during and after consumption. Important decisions include determining the content, structure, and style of the message to be communicated; its manner of presentation; and the media most suited for transmitting it to its intended audience.

The Integrated Service Communications Model represented in Figure 7.2 incorporates all these considerations and serves as the organizing framework for this chapter. It starts with the "5 Ws" model, which offers a useful checklist for marketing communications planning:

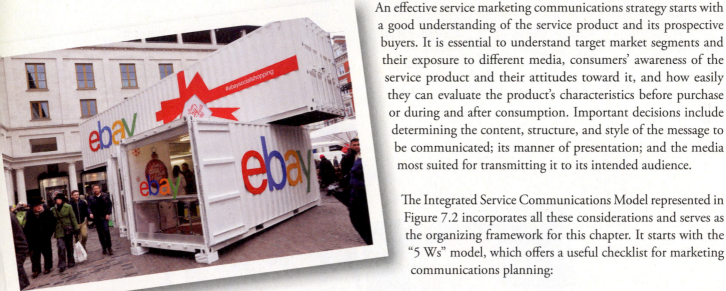

Figure 7.1 'EBay Social Shopping' uses product recommendations from social networks including Facebook, Twitter and Instagram to help people make decisions about Christmas presents.

1) <u>*Who*</u> is our target audience?
2) <u>*What*</u> do we need to communicate and achieve?
3) <u>*How*</u> should we communicate this?
4) <u>*Where*</u> should we communicate this?
5) <u>*When*</u> do the communications need to take place?

Let's first consider the issues of defining the target audience (i.e., the "*who*") and specifying communication objectives ("*what*"), as these are the key strategic communications decisions to be made. Then we'll review the tactical decisions of the service communications plan that are required for the implementation of the communications strategy. These decisions relate to the wide array of communication channels available to service marketers ("*where*"), the ways of overcoming service-specific challenges of communications ("*how*"), and the proper scheduling of communication activities ("*when*"). Additional considerations included in our model are discussed in the subsequent sections. They include the available budget for the execution of a communications program, the methods of measuring and evaluating its performance, ethics and consumer privacy, and corporate design. In the final section, we'll discuss how all communications across channels should be aligned using Integrated Marketing Communications.

LO 2

Be familiar with the three broad target audiences (i.e., "**W**ho") for any service communications program.

DEFINING THE TARGET AUDIENCE

Prospects, users, and employees represent the three broad target audiences for any service communications strategy:

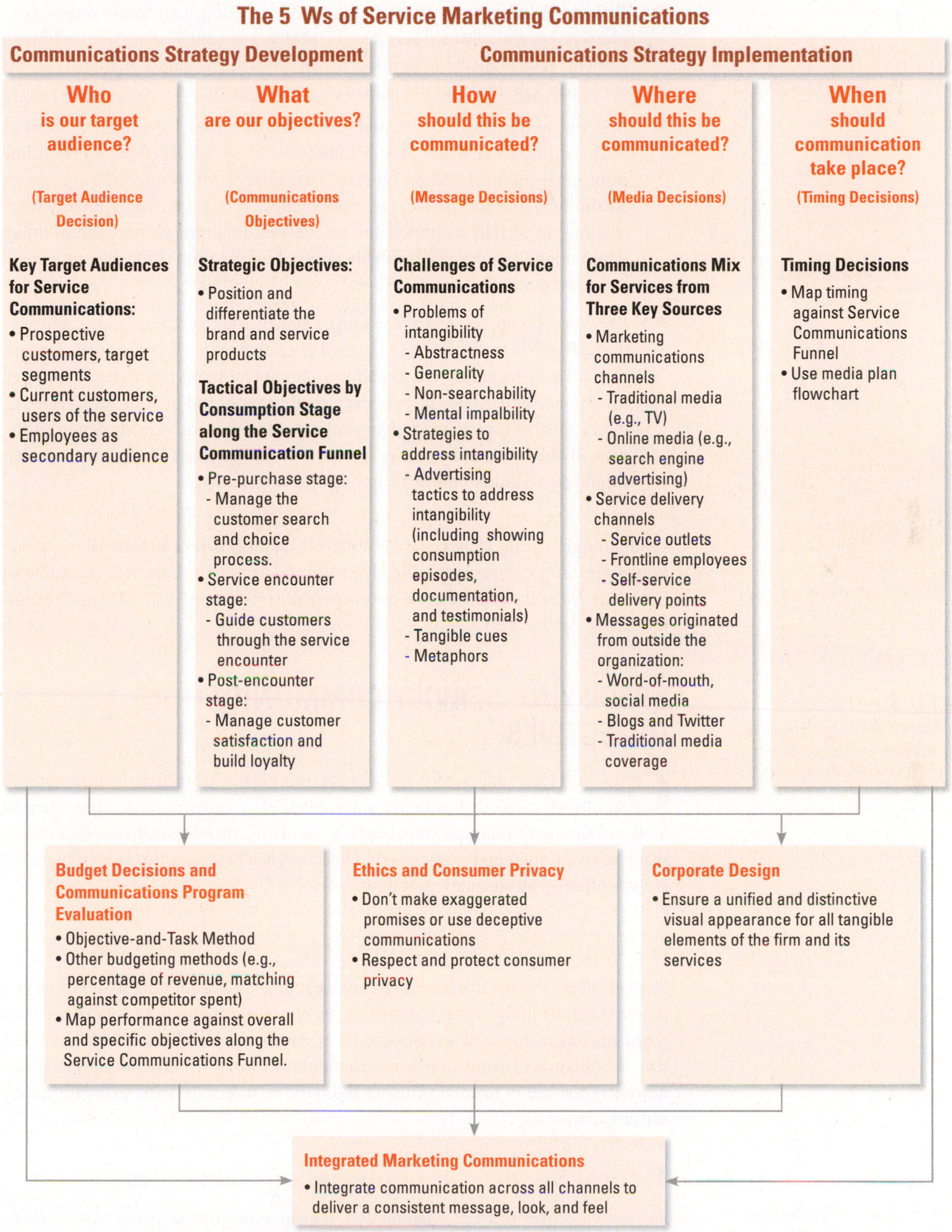

The 5 Ws of Service Marketing Communications

Communications Strategy Development		Communications Strategy Implementation		
Who is our target audience? (Target Audience Decision)	**What** are our objectives? (Communications Objectives)	**How** should this be communicated? (Message Decisions)	**Where** should this be communicated? (Media Decisions)	**When** should communication take place? (Timing Decisions)

Key Target Audiences for Service Communications:
- Prospective customers, target segments
- Current customers, users of the service
- Employees as secondary audience

Strategic Objectives:
- Position and differentiate the brand and service products

Tactical Objectives by Consumption Stage along the Service Communication Funnel
- Pre-purchase stage:
  - Manage the customer search and choice process.
- Service encounter stage:
  - Guide customers through the service encounter
- Post-encounter stage:
  - Manage customer satisfaction and build loyalty

Challenges of Service Communications
- Problems of intangibility
  - Abstractness
  - Generality
  - Non-searchability
  - Mental impalbility
- Strategies to address intangibility
  - Advertising tactics to address intangibility (including showing consumption episodes, documentation, and testimonials)
  - Tangible cues
  - Metaphors

Communications Mix for Services from Three Key Sources
- Marketing communications channels
  - Traditional media (e.g., TV)
  - Online media (e.g., search engine advertising)
- Service delivery channels
  - Service outlets
  - Frontline employees
  - Self-service delivery points
- Messages originated from outside the organization:
  - Word-of-mouth, social media
  - Blogs and Twitter
  - Traditional media coverage

Timing Decisions
- Map timing against Service Communications Funnel
- Use media plan flowchart

Budget Decisions and Communications Program Evaluation
- Objective-and-Task Method
- Other budgeting methods (e.g., percentage of revenue, matching against competitor spent)
- Map performance against overall and specific objectives along the Service Communications Funnel.

Ethics and Consumer Privacy
- Don't make exaggerated promises or use deceptive communications
- Respect and protect consumer privacy

Corporate Design
- Ensure a unified and distinctive visual appearance for all tangible elements of the firm and its services

Integrated Marketing Communications
- Integrate communication across all channels to deliver a consistent message, look, and feel

Figure 7.2 Integrated Service Communications Model.

▶ *Prospects*: As marketers of consumer services do not usually know prospects in advance, they typically need to employ a traditional communications mix comprising elements such as media advertising, online advertising, public relations, and the use of purchased lists for direct mail or telemarketing.

▶ *Users*: In contrast to prospects, more cost-effective channels are often available to reach existing users. These may include cross- or up-selling efforts by front-line employees, point-of-sale promotions, information distributed during service encounters, and location-based mobile apps. If the firm has a membership relationship with its customers and a database containing contact and profiling information, it can distribute highly targeted information through apps, e-mail, messages, direct mail, or telephone.

▶ *Employees*: Employees serve as a secondary audience for communication campaigns through public media.[2] A well-designed campaign targeted at customers can also be motivating for employees. The advertising content shows them what is promised to customers and thereby helps to shape their behavior and performance. However, there's a risk of generating cynicism among employees and actively demotivating them if the communication in question promotes levels of performance that employees regard as unrealistic or impossible to achieve.

Communications directed specifically at staff are typically part of an internal marketing campaign using company-specific channels, and hence they are not accessible to customers. We will discuss internal communications in Chapter 11 ("Managing People for Service Advantage").

LO 3

Understand the most common strategic and tactical service communications objectives ("*W*hat").

SPECIFYING SERVICE COMMUNICATION OBJECTIVES

Once the target audience for a service has been clearly identified, the firm needs to specify what exactly it wants to achieve with this audience. At the most general level, marketing communications objectives are to inform, educate, persuade, remind, shape behavior, and build relationships. Objectives can be strategic or tactical in nature and are often an amalgamation of both.

Strategic Service Communications Objectives

Strategic objectives include building a service brand and positioning it and its service products against competition. Companies use marketing communications to persuade target customers that their service product offers a better solution for customer needs than the offerings of competing firms. Communication efforts serve not only to attract new users but also to maintain contact and build relationships with an organization's existing customers.

LO 4

Be familiar with the Services Marketing Communications Funnel and the key objectives in that funnel.

Tactical Service Communications Objectives

Tactical objectives relate to shaping and managing customers' perceptions, beliefs, attitudes, and behavior during any of the three stages of the service consumption process we discussed in Chapter 2 (i.e., the pre-purchase, service encounter, and post-encounter stages). In the Services Marketing Communications Funnel (Figure 7.3),

Three-Stage Model of Service Consumption	Common Communication Objectives along the Services Marketing Communications Funnel	Key Consumer Behavior Concepts and Theories

Pre-purchase Stage

Awareness of need
- Information search
- Clarify needs
- Explore solutions
- Identify alternative service products

Evaluation of alternatives
- Review supplier information (e.g., advertising, website)
- Review information from third parties (e.g., published reviews, ratings, blogs)
- Discuss options with service personnel
- Get advice from third-parties
- Make purchase decision

Customer Acquisition
- Move customers along the key stages of the sales funnel
- Build awareness, knowledge and interest in the service or brand
  - Encourage to explore the firm's website or social media sites
  - Register for your online newsletter, service updates, or YouTube channel
- Develop liking, preference and conviction for the service or brand
  - Compare a service favorably with competitors' offerings
  - Convince potential customers about the firm's superior performance on determinant attributes
- Encourage potential customers to purchase
  - Reduce perceived risk by providing information and service guarantees
  - Encourage trial by offering promotional incentives
- Create memorable images of brands and services
- Stimulate and shift demand to match capacity

Pre-purchase Stage
- Need arousal
- Evoked set
- Consideration set
- Multi-attribute choice model
- Search, experience, and credence attributes
- Perceived risk
- Formation of expectations
- Purchase decision

Service Encounter Stage
- Request service from the chosen supplier or initiate self-service
- Experience the service encounter

Service Encounter Management
- Familiarize customers with service processes in advance of use (e.g., what to prepare and expect)
- Guide customers through the service process
- Manage customer behavior and perceptions during the service encounter (e.g., teach roles, script for queuing, inject perceived control)
- Manage quality perceptions
- Cross sell and upsell services

Service Encounter Stage
- Moments of truth
- Service encounters
- Servuction system
- Theater as metaphor
- Role and script theories
- Perceived control theory

Post-encounter Stage
- Evaluation of service performance
- Future intentions
- Future behaviors

Customer Engagement
- Manage customer satisfaction
- Manage service quality perceptions
- Build loyalty
- Encourage WOM (offline and online)
- Encourage referrals
- Build a brand community

Post-encounter Stage
- Confirmation/disconfirmation of expectations
- Dissatisfaction, satisfaction and delight
- Service quality
- WOM and referrals
- Online reviews
- Repurchase
- Customer loyalty

Figure 7.3 Common communications objectives along the Service Marketing Communications Funnel.

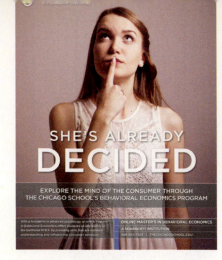

Figure 7.4 This advertisement for the Chicago School creates awareness and interest.

Figure 7.5 Communication can be used to manage customers at the pre-purchase stage (top), the service encounter stage (middle), and the post purchase stage (bottom).

we show how common tactical communications objectives map against the three stages of service consumption (see the left column in Figure 7.3) and related key consumer behavior concepts and theories (see the right column in Figure 7.3).

You may be familiar with models that deal with the pre-purchase phase. These are generally referred to as the sales funnel (or purchase funnel from the customer's perspective). There are also models that depict the stages a consumer typically passes through as he/she proceeds from not being aware of a product to actually buying it. Probably the oldest model of this type is "AIDA," standing for *A*wareness, *I*nterest, *D*esire, and *A*ction. It explains how customers move from cognitive (awareness) to affective (interest and desire) and finally to behavioral (action) responses.[3] The AIDA model has stood the test of time and is still used. The *hierarchy-of-effects model* is an extension of the AIDA model and is now the most widely used framework to describe this process. It starts with a cognitive stage of awareness and knowledge (Figure 7.4); followed by an affective stage that leads to liking, preference, and conviction; and, finally, a behavioral stage of buying.[4]

The Services Marketing Communications Funnel is aligned to the AIDA and hierarchy-of-effects models in the pre-purchase stage and extends them by incorporating a wider range of service-specific objectives. Furthermore, as neither of the two models covers the service encounter and post-encounter stages, we have added service communications objectives relating to these two stages in Figure 7.3. For example, many services are membership-type or contractual in nature and therefore include a host of post-encounter behaviors that can be shaped by communications.

The Services Marketing Communications Funnel starts with a broad target audience at the top (i.e., all prospects in the firm's target segments) and narrows down to customers who actually buy and consume the service. Even for loyalty initiatives, firms typically do not target all their customers with the same intensity. The focus tends to be on their "platinum" or premium customers with high purchase volumes (see also Chapter 12: "Managing Relationships and Building Loyalty").

Figure 7.3 also shows that communications objectives can be highly specific and can address any aspect of service-consumer behavior. Do go back to Chapter 2 ("Consumer Behavior in a Service Context") and consider how communications can be used to shape consumer behavior in the direction desired by the firm in any of the three stages (Figure 7.5).

▶ How can communications be used in the pre-purchase stage to trigger a need, get a service into the evoked and consideration sets, reduce perceived risk, and shape multi-attribute-model-type processing (e.g., shifting attribute-performance perceptions, attribute weightings, and decision rules in favor of the firm's services)?

▶ How can communications be employed during the service encounter stage to shape performance perceptions, help customers move effectively through the service encounter, shape quality perceptions, teach service roles and scripts, and inject perceived control into the service encounter?

▶ How can communications be used in the post-encounter stage to shape customer satisfaction and service-quality evaluations and encourage word of mouth, referrals, repurchase, and loyalty?

A discussion of all possible objectives that can be derived from the Services Marketing Communications Funnel is beyond the scope of this chapter. However, we highlight a few important communications objectives in the following sections.

Promote Tangible Cues to Communicate Quality. Even if customers understand what a service is supposed to do, they may find it hard to differentiate the offerings of different suppliers. Companies can use concrete cues to communicate service performance by highlighting the quality of equipment and facilities and by emphasizing employee characteristics such as qualifications, experience, commitment, and professionalism. Some performance attributes are easier or more appropriate to communicate than others. Airlines and hospitals do not advertise safety because even the suggestion that things might go wrong makes many people nervous. Instead, they approach this ongoing customer concern indirectly by communicating the high quality of their people, facilities, equipment, and processes.

Add Value through Communication Content. Information and consultation are important ways to add value to a product. Prospective customers may need information and advice about what service options are available to them (Figure 7.6); where and when these services are available; how much they cost; and what specific features, functions, and service benefits they have. (See the Flower of Service framework in Chapter 4, which illustrates how this information can add value.)

Facilitate Customer Involvement in Service Production. When customers are actively involved in service production, they need training to perform well just as employees do. Marketers often use sales promotions as incentives to encourage customers to make the necessary changes in their behavior. For example, giving price discounts or running lucky draws are some ways to encourage customers to switch to self-service.

Promote the Contribution of Service Personnel and Back-stage Operations. High-quality performance, front-line staff, and back-stage operations can be important differentiators for services. In high-contact services, front-line personnel are central to service delivery. Their presence makes the service more tangible and, in many cases, more personalized.

Advertising, brochures, websites, and videos on YouTube can also show customers the work that goes on "back-stage" to ensure good service delivery. Highlighting the expertise and commitment of employees whom customers normally never encounter may enhance trust in the organization's competence and commitment to service quality. For example, Starbucks has publicity materials and videos that show customers what service personnel do behind the scenes. Starbucks shows how coffee beans are cultivated, harvested, and produced and specifically highlights its use of the finest and freshest ingredients (Figure 7.7).

Stimulate and Shift Demand to Match Capacity. Low demand outside peak periods is a serious problem for service industries with high fixed costs, such as hotels. One strategy is to run promotions that offer extra value (such as room upgrades or free

LO 5
Know a few important roles that service marketing communications can assume.

PART II

Figure 7.6 Firms such as travel agencies need to provide customers with information and advice about what options are available to them.

Figure 7.7 The Starbucks websites has stories about what goes on behind the scenes in creating a new blend of coffee.

LO 6

Understand the challenges of service communications and know how they can be overcome ("How").

breakfasts) to encourage demand without decreasing price. When demand increases, the number of promotions can be reduced or eliminated. (See also Chapter 6 on revenue management and Chapter 9 on managing demand.)

Advertising and sales promotions can also help to shift usage from peak- to lower-demand periods and thereby match demand with the available capacity at a given time.

CRAFTING EFFECTIVE SERVICE COMMUNICATION MESSAGES

Now that we've discussed service communications objectives, let's explore some of the communications challenges service firms face when developing their communications messages. For goods and services alike, messages have to break through the clutter, as communication can only succeed if it gains the attention of its target group. Marketers have to make decisions regarding what they want to say (i.e., message content) and how they can say it (i.e., message structure and format). The ways of designing messages and creative strategies for service marketing communications programs are also determined to a significant extent by the differences between services and goods. The intangibility of most services is one such difference that is discussed in the next section.

Problems of Intangibility

As services are performances rather than objects, their benefits can be difficult to communicate to customers. This is especially the case when the service in question does not involve tangible actions performed on customers or their possessions. Intangibility creates four problems for marketers seeking to promote its attributes or benefits: abstractness, generality, non-searchability, and mental impalpability. Each problem has important implications for service communications:[5]

- *Abstractness.* Abstract concepts such as financial security or investment-related matters (Figure 7.8), expert advice, or safe transportation do not have one-to-one correspondence with physical objects. It can therefore be challenging for marketers to connect their services to these intangible concepts.

- *Generality.* This refers to items that comprise a class of objects, persons, or events—for instance, airline seats, flight attendants, and cabin service. As there may be physical objects that can show these services, abstractness is not a problem. However, such services are not specific enough. Thus, even though most consumers know what these services are, it is difficult for marketers to create a unique value proposition to communicate what makes a specific offering distinctly different from, and superior to, competing offerings.

Figure 7.8 Julius Bar, a Swiss private bank, shows how the intangibility of providing balanced solutions can be communicated.

- *Non-searchability.* This refers to the fact that many service attributes cannot be searched or inspected before they are purchased. Physical service attributes, such as the appearance of a health club and the type of equipment installed, can be checked in advance, but the experience of working with the trainers can only be determined through extended personal involvement.

- *Mental impalpability.* Many services are complex, multi-dimensional, or novel. This makes it difficult for consumers—especially new prospects—to understand what the experience of using them will be like and what benefits will result from the experience.

Overcoming the Problems of Intangibility

How should service messages be communicated? The intangibility of service presents problems for advertising that need to be overcome. Table 7.1 suggests specific communications strategies marketers can follow to overcome each of the four problems created by the intangibility of services.

In addition to the strategies presented in Table 7.1, firms can use tangible cues and metaphors to overcome the four challenges of intangibility. Both these methods help to communicate intangible service attributes and benefits to potential customers.

Table 7.1 Advertising strategies for overcoming intangibility.

Intangibility Problem	Advertising Strategy	Description
Abstractness	Service consumption episode	Capture and show typical customers benefiting from the service; e.g., by smiling in satisfaction at a staff member going out of his way to help.
Generality		
• For objective claim	System documentation	Document facts and statistics about the service delivery system. For example, the UPS website states that the company has 227 aircraft in operation.
	Performance documentation	Document and cite past service performance statistics, such as the number of packages that have been delivered on time.
• For subjective claim	Service performance episode	Present actual service delivery being performed by the service personnel. The video mode is best for showing this.
Non-searchability	Consumption documentation	Obtain and present testimonials from customers who have experienced the service.
	Reputation documentation	If the service is high in credence attributes, document the awards received or the qualifications of the service provider.
Mental impalpability	Service process episode	Present a clear step-by-step documentation of what exactly will happen during the service experience.
	Case history episode	Present an actual case history of what the firm did for a specific client and how it solved the client's problem.
	Service consumption episode	Present a story or depiction of a customer's experience with a service.

PART II

Figure 7.9 The Merrill Lynch bull represents the firm's strong commitment to the financial performance of its clients.

Tangible Cues. Commonly used strategies in advertising include the use of tangible cues whenever possible, especially for services that involve few tangible elements. It's also helpful to include "vivid information" that catches the audience's attention and produces a strong, clear impression on the senses, especially for services that are complex and highly intangible.[6] For example, many business schools feature successful alumni to make the benefits of their education tangible and communicate what their programs could do for prospective students in terms of career advancement, salary increases, and lifestyle.

Use Metaphors. Some companies have created metaphors that are tangible in nature to help communicate the benefits of their service offerings and to emphasize key points of differentiation. The Merrill Lynch bull has been a symbol for the wealth manager's business philosophy, which suggests both a bullish market and a strong commitment to the financial performance of its clients (Figure 7.9).

Where possible, advertising metaphors should highlight *how* service benefits are actually provided. Consulting firm AT Kearney emphasizes that it includes all management levels in seeking solutions, not just higher-level management. One of its advertisements showed bear traps across the office floor, drawings attention to the way in which the company differentiates its service through careful work with all levels in its client organizations, thus avoiding the problems left behind by other consulting firms who work mostly with senior management.

LO 7

Be familiar with the Services Marketing Communications Mix ("*W*here").

THE SERVICES MARKETING COMMUNICATIONS MIX

After understanding our target audience, our specific communications objectives, and our message strategy, we now need to select a mix of cost-effective communication channels (Figure 7.10). Most service marketers have access to numerous forms of communication, referred to collectively as the Services Marketing Communications Mix. Different communication elements have distinctive capabilities relative to the types of messages they can convey and the market segments most likely to be exposed to them. The communications mix needs to be optimized to achieve the best possible results for a given budget.

Figure 7.11 provides an overview of the wide range of communications channels available to service firms. Note that these channels can be categorized in several ways. For example, service employees are part of the service delivery point but also act as media for personal communications. We have placed each element of the communications mix under the most suitable category for the purpose of discussing the overall media strategy of service organizations.

There are, of course, other ways to categorize these channels. Often, they are split into non-personal (e.g., advertising) and personal (e.g., direct marketing and personal communications) media. They may also be divided into traditional media (e.g., TV, print, and outdoor) and online media (e.g., online advertising, social media, and mobile communications). Each type of media has its own strengths and weaknesses and can be

Figure 7.10 Services marketing involves numerous forms of communication.

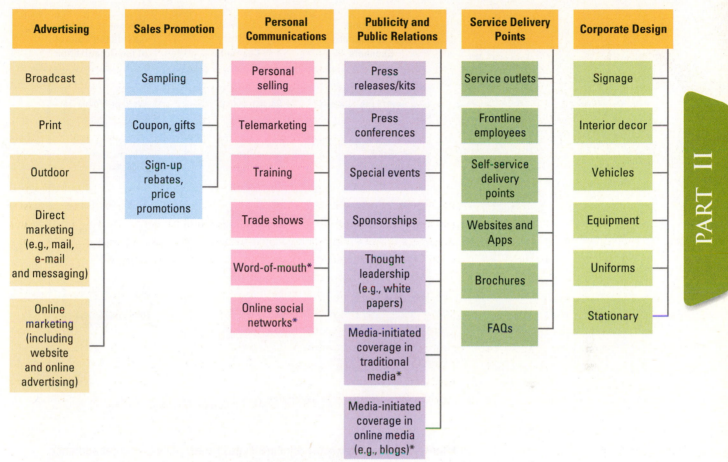

Advertising	Sales Promotion	Personal Communications	Publicity and Public Relations	Service Delivery Points	Corporate Design
Broadcast	Sampling	Personal selling	Press releases/kits	Service outlets	Signage
Print	Coupon, gifts	Telemarketing	Press conferences	Frontline employees	Interior decor
Outdoor	Sign-up rebates, price promotions	Training	Special events	Self-service delivery points	Vehicles
Direct marketing (e.g., mail, e-mail and messaging)		Trade shows	Sponsorships	Websites and Apps	Equipment
		Word-of-mouth*	Thought leadership (e.g., white papers)	Brochures	Uniforms
Online marketing (including website and online advertising)		Online social networks*	Media-initiated coverage in traditional media*	FAQs	Stationary
			Media-initiated coverage in online media (e.g., blogs)*		

* **Denotes communications originated from outside the organization.**

Figure 7.11 The Services Marketing Communications Mix.

used for different objectives. For example, non-personal mass media tend to be effective for creating awareness and positioning the service, whereas personal communications can be highly effective for explaining complex service information, reducing risk perceptions, and persuading the consumer to buy the service. Communications in the servicescape (e.g., signs and posters) can be used to manage consumer behavior during the service encounter. They relate to consumer activities such as queuing, following the service script, and trying new services (i.e., cross-selling). Direct marketing is highly cost-effective in the post-encounter stage. It encourages customers to come back and to recommend the service to their friends and family.

Communications Originate from Different Sources

As shown in Figure 7.12, the Services Marketing Communications Mix featured in Figure 7.12 can be divided into three broad categories based on sources of communications. These are (1) marketing communications channels, which include traditional media and online channels; (2) service delivery channels; and (3) messages that originate from outside the organization.[7] Let's look at key options within each of these three originating sources. We will discuss traditional media and online media separately as they have vastly different characteristics and applications.

PART II

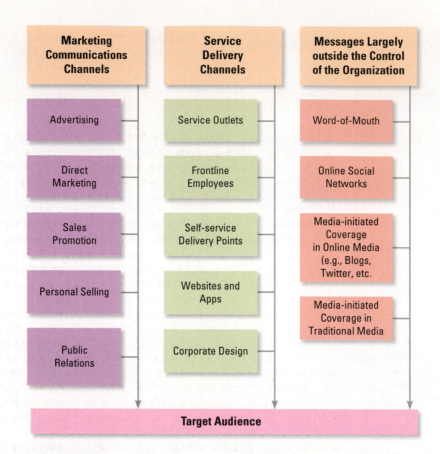

Marketing Communications Channels	Service Delivery Channels	Messages Largely outside the Control of the Organization
Advertising	Service Outlets	Word-of-Mouth
Direct Marketing	Frontline Employees	Online Social Networks
Sales Promotion	Self-service Delivery Points	Media-initiated Coverage in Online Media (e.g., Blogs, Twitter, etc.
Personal Selling	Websites and Apps	Media-initiated Coverage in Traditional Media
Public Relations	Corporate Design	

Target Audience

Figure 7.12 Three key sources of messages received by the target audience.

Messages Transmitted through Traditional Marketing Channels

Service marketers have a wide array of communication tools at their disposal (as shown in Figure 7.12). Let's briefly review the principal elements.

Advertising. A wide array of paid advertising media is available, including broadcast (TV and radio), print (magazines and newspapers), movie theaters, and many types of outdoor media (posters, billboards, electronic message boards, and the exteriors of buses or bicycles). Some media are more focused than others, targeting specific geographic areas or audiences with a particular interest. Advertising messages delivered through mass media are often reinforced by direct marketing tools such as mailings, telemarketing, or e-mail.

How can a firm hope to stand out from the crowd? Longer, louder commercials and larger-format ads are not the answer. Marketers are trying to be more creative with their advertising to make their messages more effective (Figure 7.13). For example, when customers have low involvement with a service, firms should focus on more emotional appeals and the service experience itself.[8] Some advertisers stand out by using clever messaging, interesting stories, striking designs, or a distinctively different format. Some firms are now placing advertisements in video games and online role-playing games. These can be dynamic advertisements if the games are connected to the internet.

Direct Marketing. This category embraces such tools as mailings, e-mail, and text messaging. These channels allow firms to send personalized messages to highly targeted micro-segments. Direct strategies usually succeed when marketers possess a detailed database of information about prospects and customers.

LO 8
Know the communications mix elements of the traditional marketing communication channels.

Advances in on-demand technologies such as e-mail spam filters, TiVo, podcasting, and pop-up blockers allow consumers to decide how, when, and by whom they prefer to be reached. A 30-second television spot interrupts a viewer's favorite program, and a telemarketing call interrupts a meal. Thus, customers increasingly use such technologies to save their time. Customer resistance to advertising gives rise to *permission marketing*, where customers are encouraged to "raise their hands" and agree to learn more about a company and its products in anticipation of receiving useful marketing information or something else of value. Instead of annoying prospects by interrupting their personal time, permission marketing allows customers to self-select into the target segments.

By reaching out only to individuals who have expressed prior interest in receiving a certain type of message, permission marketing enables service firms to build stronger relationships with their customers. For instance, people can be invited to register at the firm's website or download an app and state what type of information they would like to receive.

Many service firms have increased their focus on permission-based marketing because of its high effectiveness. Falling prices and the improving quality of customer relationship management (CRM) systems, big data, social media, and communications technology are other factors that power permission-based marketing. To see how some firms have implemented excellent permission-based marketing strategies, you may register yourself at Amazon.com or Hallmark. com and download their apps.

Sales Promotion. Sales promotions may be seen as a form of communication with an incentive. They are usually specific to a time period, price, or customer group (and sometimes all three, as in direct marketing). Typically, they are employed for short-term objectives, such as to accelerate the purchase decision or motivate customers to use a specific service sooner, in greater volume with each purchase, or more frequently.[9] Sales promotions for service firms (samples, coupons and other discounts, gifts, and competitions with prizes) increase sales during periods when demand would otherwise be weak. They also speed up the introduction and acceptance of new services and generally encourage customers to act faster than they would in the absence of any promotional incentive.[10] However, sales promotions need to be used with care because research shows that customers acquired through sales promotions may have lower repurchase rates and lifetime values.[11]

Figure 7.13 When QR codes were introduced, advertisers moved quickly to use them to differentiate their ads and make them more engaging.

A few years ago, SAS International Hotels devised an interesting sales promotion plan targeted at older customers. If a hotel had vacant rooms, guests over 65 years of age could get a discount equivalent to their years (e.g., a 75-year-old could save 75% of the normal room price). All went well until a Swedish guest checked into one of the SAS chain's hotels in Vienna, announced his age as 102, and asked to be paid 2% of the room rate in return for staying the night. This request was granted, whereupon the spry centenarian challenged the general manager to a game of tennis—and got

"I read someplace that eye contact is a very important business skill."

Figure 7.14 Body language is important to persuade customers of the superiority of one's brand.

that, too. (The results of the game, however, were not disclosed!) In this case, a clever promotional strategy led to a humorous, widely reported story that placed the hotel chain in a favorable light.

Personal Selling. This refers to inter-personal encounters in which efforts are made to educate customers and promote a particular brand or product (Figure 7.14). Many firms, especially those marketing business-to-business services, maintain a sales team or employ agents and distributors to undertake personal selling efforts on their behalf. For services that are bought less often, such as property, insurance, and funeral services, the firm's representative may act as a consultant to help buyers make their selections. For industrial and professional firms that sell relatively complex services, customer may have an account manager they can turn to for advice, education, and consultation.

However, face-to-face selling to new prospects is expensive. A lower-cost alternative is *telemarketing*, involving the use of the telephone to reach prospective customers. At the consumer level, there is growing frustration with the intrusive nature of telemarketing, which is often timed to reach people when they are home in the evening or during weekends (Figure 7.15).

Public Relations. Public relations (PR) involves efforts to stimulate positive interest in an organization and its products by sending out news releases, holding press conferences, staging special events, and sponsoring news-worthy activities put on by third parties. A basic element in PR strategy is the preparation and distribution of press releases (including photos and/or videos) that feature stories about the company, its products, and its employees.

"Before you hang up, Mrs. Johnson, are you aware that you can lose up to 50 pounds a year by listening to telemarketers instead of eating your dinner?"

Figure 7.15 Telemarketers call in the evenings.

Firms can also gain wide exposure through sponsorship of sporting events and other high-profile activities such as the Olympics and the World Cup for soccer. Banners, decals, and other visual displays in these events provide continuous visibility to the corporate name and symbol. Furthermore, unusual activities can present opportunities to promote a company's expertise. FedEx gained a lot of positive publicity when it safely transported two giant pandas from Chengdu, China, to the National Zoo in Washington, D.C. The pandas flew in specially designed containers aboard a FedEx aircraft renamed "FedEx PandaOne." In addition to press releases, the company also featured information about the unusual shipment on a special page on its website (Figure 7.16).

Messages Transmitted Online

Online and mobile advertising using the internet, social media, and apps allows companies to complement and sometimes even substitute traditional communications channels at a reasonable cost.

Company's Website. Marketers use their own websites for a variety of communications tasks:

▶ Creating consumer awareness and interest

▶ Providing information and consultation

LO 9

Know the role of the internet, mobile phones, apps, QR codes, and other electronic media in service marketing communications.

- Allowing two-way communications with customers through e-mail and chat rooms

- Encouraging product trial

- Enabling customers to place orders

- Measuring the effectiveness of specific advertising or promotional campaigns

Marketers must also address other factors that affect website "stickiness" (i.e., whether visitors are willing to spend time on the site and will revisit it in the future), such as downloading speed. A sticky site is:

- *High in quality content.* A site needs to contain relevant and useful content so that visitors can find what they are looking for.

- *Easy to use.* It must be easy for visitors to find their way around the site. Good navigation, proper signposting, and a site structure that is neither over-complicated nor too big are essential. Customers do not get lost in good sites!

- *Quick to download.* Viewers don't want to wait and often give up if it takes them too long to download pages from a site. Good sites have "light" content that can be downloaded quickly, whereas bad sites are slow.

- *Updated frequently.* Good sites look fresh and up to date. They include recently posted information that visitors find relevant and timely.[12]

Online Advertising. There are two main types of online advertising: banner advertising and search engine advertising.

- **Banner Advertising.** Many firms pay to place advertising banners and buttons on portals such as Yahoo or CNN; social media websites such as Facebook and LinkedIn; and apps, online games, and advertising-funded content websites. The usual goal is to draw online traffic to the advertiser's own site. In many instances, websites include advertising messages from other marketers with services that are related but not competing. For example, Yahoo's stock-quotes page has a sequence of advertisements for various financial service providers.

  Getting a large number of exposures ("eyeballs") for a banner (Figure 7.17) (a thin horizontal ad running across all or part of a web page), a skyscraper (a long skinny ad running vertically down one side of a website), or a button doesn't necessarily lead to an increase in awareness, preference, or sales for the advertiser. Even if a visitor does click through to the advertiser's site, his/her action might not result in sales. Consequently, there is now more emphasis on advertising contracts that link fees to marketing-relevant behavior by these visitors (such as providing the advertiser with some information about themselves or making a purchase). More and more internet advertisers pay only if a visitor to the host site clicks through to the advertisers' site. This is similar to the idea of paying for the delivery of junk mail only if the recipients read it.[13]

- **Search Engine Advertising.** Search engines let advertisers know exactly what consumers want through their keyword search. Advertisers can then target

Figure 7.16 FedEx transported two giant pandas to the National Zoo in Washington, D.C.

Figure 7.17 Web banners function like traditional banners; i.e., by turning consumers' attention to the product or service and selling a pitch through service provider and consumer interaction

relevant marketing communications directly at these consumers. Search engine advertising is currently the most popular online advertising instrument,[14] and Google is the leader in this space (see Service Insights 7.1). Firms like Bing and Yahoo! are also seeking to increase their market share.

A key advantage of online advertising is that it provides a very clear and measurable return on investment, especially when compared to other forms of advertising. The link between advertising costs and the customers who were attracted to a company's website or offer is trackable, particularly in performance-priced online advertising (e.g., pay per click). Contrast this to traditional media advertising on TV or in magazines, where it is notoriously difficult to assess the success of and investment return from an advertisement. Advertisers have several options. They can:

▶ Buy top rankings in the display of search results through "pay-for-placement." Since users expect the rankings to reflect the best fit with the keywords used in the search, Google's policy is to shade paid listings that appear at the top of the rankings column and identify them as "sponsored links." Pricing for these ads and placements can be based on either the number of impressions (i.e., eyeballs) or click-throughs. As sponsored links aim to connect to customers just before they make a purchase decision, some firms buy keywords that are closely related to their competitors' offerings. This allows them to "poach" customers and free ride on the market created by other firms.[15]

▶ Pay for the targeted placement of ads in keyword searches related to their offer.

▶ Sponsor a short text message with a click-through link located next to the search results.

▶ Pay for performance-priced online advertising. The advertiser is charged on the basis of pre-agreed results of their communication campaign. These could include actions such as registration on a website, download of a brochure, and even sales.

▶ Regularly conduct search engine optimization (SEO) of the firm's website. SEO improves the ranking of a website in organic (i.e., unsponsored) search lists. Doing this should be a "no brainer" as firms do not have to spend advertising dollars to get the attention of potential customers. However, SEO only works well if the website is well designed, contains relevant information, and is aligned with the interests of target customers.[16]

Moving from Impersonal to Personal Communications. Communication experts distinguish between impersonal communications (where messages move only in one direction and are generally targeted at a large group of customers and prospects rather than at a single individual) and personal communications (such as personal selling, telemarketing, and word of mouth). Technology, however, has created a gray area between personal and impersonal communications. Think about the e-mail messages you've received that contained a personal salutation and perhaps some reference to your specific situation or past use of a particular product. Similarly, interactive software can simulate a two-way conversation. For example, a few firms are beginning to experiment with Web-based agents; i.e., on-screen simulations that move, speak, and even change expression.

The widespread use of smart mobile devices and social networking platforms has given firms unprecedented opportunities to communicate with their customers and even facilitate relevant communications between customers. Based on the analysis of customer data, highly targeted and personalized services and messages can be generated for each customer. These messages supplement or replace traditional marketing communications.[17] For a brief description of important new media and their implications, see Service Insights 7.2.

SERVICE INSIGHTS 7.1

Google: The Online Marketing Powerhouse

Larry Page and Sergey Brin, who were both fascinated by mathematics, computers, and programming from an early age, founded Google in 1998 while they were Ph.D. students at Stanford University. Seven years later, following Google's successful public offering, they had become multi-billionaires, and Google itself had become one of the world's most valuable companies.

The grand vision of the company is "to organize the world's information and make it universally accessible and useful." The utility and ease of its search engine has made it immensely successful, and its popularity has increased almost entirely through word of mouth from satisfied users. Few company names become verbs, but to "google" has now entered common usage in English.

Google's popularity has made it a highly targeted advertising medium. It allows advertisers two important ways to reach their customers—through sponsored links and content ads.

Sponsored links appear at the top of search results on Google's website. Google prices its sponsored links service on a "cost-per-click" basis using a sealed-bid auction (where advertisers submit bids for a search term without knowing the bids of other advertisers for the same term). Prices depend on the popularity of the search terms with which the advertiser wants to be associated. Heavily used terms such as "MBA" are more expensive than less popular terms such as

Figure 7.18 Google HQ at Mountain View, California.

"MSc in Business." Advertisers can easily keep track of their ad performance using the reports in Google's online account-control center.

Google allows *content ads* to be highly targeted in a number of ways via its Google AdWords service. Ads can be placed next to search results on Google.com (they are, for example, displayed as banner ads). These ads allow businesses to connect with potential customers at the precise moment when they are looking at related topics or even specific product categories. Firms buy the opportunity to be associated with particular search categories or terms. To explore this part of Google's advertising business model, just "google" a few words and observe what appears on your screen in addition to the search results.

AdWords also allows advertisers to display their ads on websites that are part of the Google content network rather than only on Google.com. This means that these ads are not initiated by a search but are simply displayed when a user browses a website. Such ads are called "placement-targeted ads." Advertisers can specify either individual websites or website content (e.g., about travel or baseball). Placement targeting allows advertisers to hand-pick their target audiences, which can be really large (e.g., all baseball fans in the United States or even in the world) or small and focused (e.g., people interested in fine dining in the Boston area). Google places the ads alongside relevant content on its partners' websites. For example, if you read an article on a partner website, you will see an ad block at the foot of the article. These ads have been dynamically targeted by Google to match the content of that article. The same ads can appear on Google.com alongside searches, but they are distributed in a different way here and appear on websites of publishers of all sizes in the Google partner network.

AdWords is complemented by a second service called AdSense, which represents the other side of Google's advertising model. AdSense is used by website owners who wish to make money by displaying ads on their websites. In return for allowing Google to display relevant ads on their content pages, these website owners receive a share of the advertising revenue generated. AdSense has created advertising income streams for thousands of small and medium online publishers and blog sites, making those businesses sustainable. Although big media companies such as the *New York Times* and CNN also use AdSense, it generates a smaller portion of their total online advertising revenue compared to the typical niche web or blog site.

Google's ability to deliver an advertising medium that is highly targeted, contextual, and results-based has been very attractive to advertisers and has led to rapid revenue growth and profits. It's no surprise that Google's success frightens other advertising media.

Integrating online and traditional media. The complexity of integrating various media can be understood in a budget carrier context. The largest budget carriers in the United States (Southwest Airlines), Europe (Ryanair), and Asia (AirAsia) have different advertising strategies, but their common goal is to have travelers book flights directly at their own websites. Southwest Airlines integrates heavy TV advertising in its communications mix. Ryanair focuses heavily on search engine optimization and buys strategic keywords for its online ad campaigns. AirAsia has been highly active on various social media platforms such as Twitter and Facebook to update its followers on a regular basis, push promotions, and collect customer feedback. Although the communications campaign of each airline has a different emphasis, most budget carriers use all of the channels shown in Figure 7.21 to drive online traffic to its website and generate ticket sales.

LO 10

Know the communications mix elements available via service delivery channels.

Messages Transmitted through Service Delivery Channels

Unlike most goods marketers, service firms typically control the point-of-sale and service-delivery channels. These give service firms particularly powerful and cost-effective

New Media and Their Implications for Marketing Communications

Technology has created exciting new communication channels that offer important opportunities for targeting. Among the key developments are mobile advertising, mobile apps, Web 2.0, social media and social networks, and podcasting.

Mobile Advertising[18]

Mobile advertising through cell phones and other mobile wireless devices is one of the fastest-growing forms of advertising and is expected to exceed $ 62.8 billion by 2017. Mobile advertising is quite complex, as it can include the internet, video, text, gaming, music, and much more. For example, advertisements can come in the form of text messages, advertisements in mobile games, and videos. Mobile advertising and the use of global positioning systems allow customers to receive targeted advertisements with discounts when they walk into a shopping mall and visit a particular store. The most prevalent type is still mobile display advertising (MDA), which takes the form of banners on mobile web pages and in mobile applications. For consumers, mobile advertising may stand for greater convenience and relevance. However, it might also mean the invasion of privacy.

2D codes, better known as QR ("quick response") codes, appear on many ads. Consumers who are interested may take a photo of the code with their smart phone and get connected to an in-store promotion, coupons, or a real world treasure hunt. For firms, QR codes bridge offline and online communication channels. They also help to funnel potential customers from other media to the firm's online channels.

Figure 7.19 QR code for the URL of the English Wikipedia main page.

Mobile Apps

Apps have become increasingly popular tools to help customers navigate extended service encounters and get the most out of the experience. At the same time, they pursue the firm's objectives, such as cross-selling, up-selling, demand management, and queuing. For example, major cruise lines such as Disney, Norwegian, and Royal Caribbean have their own apps to help passengers navigate their large ships and explore their on-board entertainment options, spa services, and ports of call.[19]

Web 2.0, Social Media, and Social Networking[20]

Web 2.0 technology helps the rise of user-generated content and combines it with the power of peer-to-peer communications. It is an umbrella term for various media including Facebook (the grandpa of social networks), Google+, LinkedIn, YouTube, Vine, Twitter, Instagram, Snapchat, Pinterest, Wikipedia, Flickr, and other social networks. In Web 2.0, content is generated, updated, and shared by multiple users. Social networking is the fastest growing media behavior online.

Service firms use social media for various purposes, including learning from the market, targeting potential customers, creating a buzz, and shaping customer behavior. They do this by advertising on social media, listening to what is being discussed, and selectively participating in conversations. Marketers need to understand the importance of social media and carefully integrate them into their communications mix.

Figure 7.20 YouTube's headquarters is in this office building at 901 Cherry Avenue, San Bruno, California

Podcasting

Podcasting comes from the words "iPod" and "broadcasting." It refers to a group of technologies for distributing audio or video programs over the internet using a publisher/subscriber model. Podcasting gives broadcast radio or television programs a method of distribution. Once someone has subscribed to a certain feed, they will automatically receive new "episodes" that become available.

Podcasting has several forms. These include video podcasting for the delivery of video clips, mobilecast for downloads onto a cell phone, and blogcast for the attachment of audio or video files to a blog. It is beneficial to include podcasting as part of a firm's marketing communications program because a listener who has subscribed to a specific show is evidently interested in the topic. Hence, podcasts can reach a wide audience of listeners who have a narrow focus (more like "narrowcasting" than broadcasting). When the advertising message is more targeted, there is a higher return on investment for the advertising dollars spent.

communications opportunities. Specifically, messages can be transmitted through service outlets, front-line employees, self-service delivery points, and location-enabled apps.

Service Outlets. Both planned and unintended messages reach customers through the service delivery environment. Impersonal messages can be distributed in the form of banners, posters, signage, brochures, video screens, and audio. As we will discuss in Chapter 10 ("Crafting the Service Environment"), the physical design of the service outlet or *servicescape* sends important messages to customers.[21] Interior architects and corporate design consultants can design the servicescape in such a way as to coordinate the visual elements of the interiors and exteriors. This will communicate and strengthen the positioning of the firm and shape the customers' service experiences in positive ways (Figure 7.22).

Front-line Employees. Employees in front-line positions may serve customers face-to-face, by telephone, or via e-mail. Communications from front-line staff take the form of the core service and a variety of supplementary services, including providing information, giving advice,[22] taking reservations, receiving payments, and solving problems.

Front-line employees have a very important part to play. As discussed in Chapter 4, brand equity is created largely through a customer's personal experience with the service firm rather than through mass communications. (The latter is more suitable for creating awareness and interest.) Furthermore, many service firms encourage their customer-service staff to cross-sell additional services or up-sell to higher value services. Tony Hsieh has an interesting perspective on how to use customer contact centers for brand building (see Service Insights 7.3).

Self-Service Delivery Points. ATMs, vending machines, websites, and service apps are all examples of self-service delivery points. Promoting self-service delivery requires clear signage, step-by-step instructions (perhaps through diagrams or animated videos) on how to operate the equipment, and user-friendly design. Self-service delivery points

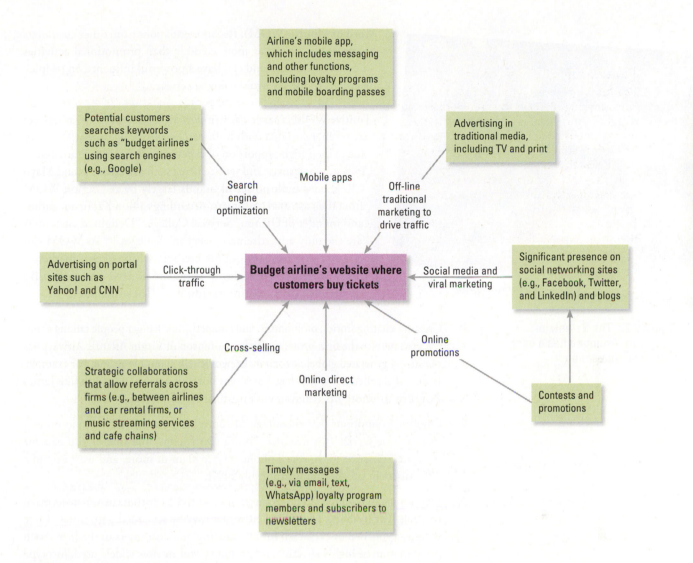

Figure 7.21 Budget carriers are excellent at integrating a vast array of (mostly online) channels to drive ticket sales on their websites.

can often be used effectively in communications with current and potential customers, especially to cross-sell services and promote new services. Similarly, location-enabled apps can guide customers through complex servicescapes (such as cruise ships, airports, hospitals, and shopping malls) in addition to selling services and providing information to customers.

Messages Originating from Outside the Organization

Some of the most powerful messages about a company and its products come from outside the organization and are not controlled by the marketer. They include word of mouth (both in person and in electronic form on social media), online reviews on third-party websites, blogs, Twitter, and media coverage.

▶ LO 11

Know the communications mix elements that originate from outside the firm.

Word of Mouth (WOM). Recommendations from other customers are generally viewed as more credible than promotional activities initiated by the firm and can have a powerful influence on people's decisions to use (or avoid using) a service.

Positive WOM is particularly important for service firms, as services are often associated with high perceived risk by potential buyers due to their high proportion of experience and credence attributes. In fact, many successful service firms such as Starbucks and Mayo Clinic have built powerful brands largely by relying on WOM from their satisfied customers. According to Ron Kaufman, author and founder of UP Your Service! College, "Delighted customers are the only advertisement everyone believes."[23] As WOM can act as a powerful and highly credible selling agent, marketers use a variety of strategies to stimulate positive and persuasive comments from existing customers.[24] These include:

▶ Creating exciting stories, promotions, and competitions that get people talking about the great service the firm provides. Richard Branson of Virgin Atlantic Airways has repeatedly generated global news to make people talk about his airline. For example, Branson abseiled off a 407-feet Las Vegas hotel dressed in a tuxedo like James Bond to promote his (then new) Virgin America airline.

▶ Offering promotions that encourage customers to persuade others to join them in using the service (for instance, "bring two friends, and one of you eats for free," or "subscribe to three cell phone service plans or more, and we'll extend a 35% discount off the family's monthly bill").

▶ Developing referral reward programs that incentivize existing customers to make referrals. For instance, an existing customer may be rewarded with units of free service, a voucher, or even cash for introducing new customers to the firm. Such programs can be highly effective and profitable and are now widely used. Just type "recommend a friend program" into your browser, and you will get hundreds of millions of hits.[25] Such programs work offline (e.g., clubs, credit card companies, and even diving schools use it) and online (think of Dropbox's highly effective viral incentive scheme; see Figure 7.25).

▶ Referencing other purchasers and knowledgeable individuals; for instance: "We have done a great job for ABC Corp., and if you wish, feel free to talk to Mr. Cabral, their MIS manager, who oversaw the implementation of our project."

▶ Presenting and publicizing testimonials. Advertisements and websites sometimes feature comments from satisfied customers (Figure 7.26).

▶ Providing opportunities for, supporting, and responding to online reviews. Positive postings help a firm's brand equity and sales, but these may be damaged by negative reviews.

A firm's communications strategy should be to encourage satisfied customers to post positive reviews. Ideally, dissatisfied customers should be able to complain to the firm and get a service recovery (see Chapter 13: "Complaint Handling and Service Recovery"), so that they don't have to go online to vent their frustration. A small hair-styling shop tried to achieve this by posting the

SERVICE INSIGHTS 7.3

Using the Call Center for Building Brand Equity

Have you ever tried to call Google, eBay, or even Amazon (the company that owns Zappos)? More likely than not, the phone number is buried many links deep, if it can be found at all! Zappos takes the exact opposite approach and puts its customer-service hotline at the top of every single page on its website.

Tony Hsieh, the founding CEO of the highly successful multi-billion-dollar e-tailer Zappos, thinks it is funny that when he attends marketing conferences, he hears companies talking about bombarding customers with thousands of advertising messages every day. Although he acknowledges the buzz about social media, he feels that "as unsexy and low-tech as it may sound, the telephone is one of the best branding devices out there. You have the customer's undivided attention for five to ten minutes, and if you get the interaction right, what we've found is that the customer remembers this experience for a very long time." He explains: "A lot of people may think it's strange that an internet company would be so focused on the telephone, when only 5 percent of our sales happen by phone. But we've found that on average, our customers telephone us at least once at some point, and if we handle the call well, we have an opportunity to create an emotional impact and a lasting memory. We receive thousands of phone calls and e-mails every day, and we view each one of them as an opportunity to build the Zappos brand … Our philosophy has been that most of the money we might ordinarily have spent on advertising should be invested in customer service, so that our customers will do the marketing for us through word of mouth."

Many service firms view their call centers through an expense-minimizing lens. They focus on managing

Figure 7.23 Zappos CEO Tony Hsieh stresses the importance of telephone calls in building relationships with customers

average handling times; i.e., the number of calls an agent can handle in a day. This makes reps worry about how quickly they can get a customer off the phone. In the eyes of Zappos, this is not a way of delivering great service. Zappos's longest phone call came from a customer who wanted the rep's help to go through what seemed like thousands of pairs of shoes. The call lasted for almost six hours. Zappos reps don't up-sell or use scripts, and handling customer calls is viewed as an investment in marketing and branding rather than an expense. Hsieh's view is that call centers are "a huge untapped opportunity for most companies, not only because it can result in word-of-mouth marketing, but because of its potential to increase the lifetime value of the customer."

Based on Tony Hsieh, "How I Did It:

SOURCE

Based on Tony Hsieh, "How I Did It: Zappos's CEO on Going to Extremes for Customers," *Harvard Business Review* 88(7–8) (2010): 41–45; Tony Hsieh, *Delivering Happiness: A Path to Profits, Passion, and Purpose.* Grand Central Publishing, 2010.

following sign at the exit: "If you like our service, please tell a friend; if you don't like it, please tell us."

▶ Supporting brand communities. This can be done online with relatively low costs.[26] See, for example, the successful online brand communities supported by Oracle in Figure 7.27.

In addition to WOM, we also have "word of mouse," or viral marketing. The internet has accelerated the spread of personal influence, causing it to evolve into a viral marketing phenomenon that businesses can ill afford to ignore. Virtually every online start-up relies on viral marketing. Similarly, eBay and other electronic auction firms rely on users to rate sellers and buyers. This enables them to build trust in the items offered on their websites and thereby facilitate transactions between strangers who, without access to such peer ratings, might be reluctant to transact on these sites.

Figure 7.24 Word of mouth can be an effective promotional tool.

Besides e-mail, WOM is spread by service reviews on third-party websites, chat, social media, and online communities that have the potential for global reach in a matter of days! New types of social networks are constantly emerging, and they all feed into the online ecosystem where consumers share their experiences. Successful companies from all over the world take advantage of this trend.

Blogs, Twitter, and Other Social Media as a Type of Online WOM. Web logs, usually referred to as blogs, have become ubiquitous. Blogs are web pages best described as online journals, diaries, or news listings where people can post anything about whatever they like. Their authors, known as bloggers, usually focus on narrow topics, and quite a few of them have become self-proclaimed experts in certain fields. There are a growing number of travel-oriented sites, ranging from Hotelchatter.com (focused on boutique hotels) and CruiseDiva.com (reporting on the cruise industry) to pestiside.hu ("the daily dish of cosmopolitan Budapest").

How do I earn bonus space for referring friends to Dropbox?

You can get extra space by inviting your friends to try out Dropbox. If a friend uses your invitation to sign up for an account, installs the Dropbox desktop app on a computer, and signs in to the app, both of you will receive bonus space.

- **Basic accounts** get 500 MB per referral. You can earn up to 16 GB in referrals.
- **Pro (paid) accounts** get 1 GB per referral and can earn up to 32 GB of **extra** space in referrals.

Figure 7.25 Dropbox's online referral reward program.

SOURCE
© Dropbox, Inc.

Figure 7.26 Many online restaurant guides rely heavily on user testimonials.

Marketers are interested in the way blogs have developed into a new form of social interaction on the internet—a massively distributed but completely connected conversation covering every imaginable topic, including consumers' experiences with service firms and their recommendations on avoiding or patronizing certain firms. A by-product of this online communication is the creation of a set of hyperlinks between weblogs. These links allow customers to share information with others and influence their opinions on a brand or product. If you Google the terms "Citibank and blog" or "Charles Schwab and blog," you will see an entire list of blogs or blog entries relating to these service firms. As a result, service firms are increasingly monitoring blogs and viewing them as a form of immediate market research and feedback. Some service companies have even started their own blogs; see for example Google's blog at http://googleblog.blogspot.com (Figure 7.28).

Blogs and other online media such as Twitter can be seen as lying in between WOM (there are millions of bloggers who do not have too many followers, and the function they perform is akin to traditional WOM) and online media (some bloggers have a large following, similar to popular media). Marketers can treat the WOM part of the spectrum through their standard referral programs and WOM initiatives. However, bloggers who have a large following are dealt with in the same way as publishers of traditional media. These bloggers are important players who need to be treated with respect and engaged at eye level.

Twitter is a social networking and microblogging service that allows its users to post updates or read other users' updates. These updates are up to 140 characters in length and can be sent and received through the Twitter website, SMS, or external applications. Service firms use Twitter in various ways. Comcast, the U.S. cable service provider, has set up @comcastcares to answer customer queries in real time. Zappos's CEO interacts

Figure 7.27 Oracle successfully supports online brand communities.

with his customers as if they were friends. The celebrity Ashton Kutcher interacts with his fans while on the move. The airline branding firm SimpliFlying holds special trivia quizzes and competitions for its followers on Twitter in order to establish itself as a thought leader in its niche.

Media Coverage. Although the online world is rapidly increasing in importance, coverage on traditional media cannot be neglected. Newsworthy events are often discussed first in the online world, but they reach the broader masses only after they are picked up and reported in the traditional media.

LO 12

Understand when communications should take place ("**W**hen"), how budgets for service communications programs may be set, and how these programs may be evaluated.

TIMING DECISIONS OF SERVICES MARKETING COMMUNICATIONS

Goods such as champagne, jewelry, and Christmas pudding are heavily promoted in the three months leading up to Christmas because almost half of their annual sales happen during this period. Service firms, in contrast, are capacity constrained and do not generally promote during heavy usage periods. Rather, timing is closely matched to the various perceptions and behaviors the firm wants to manage in the service

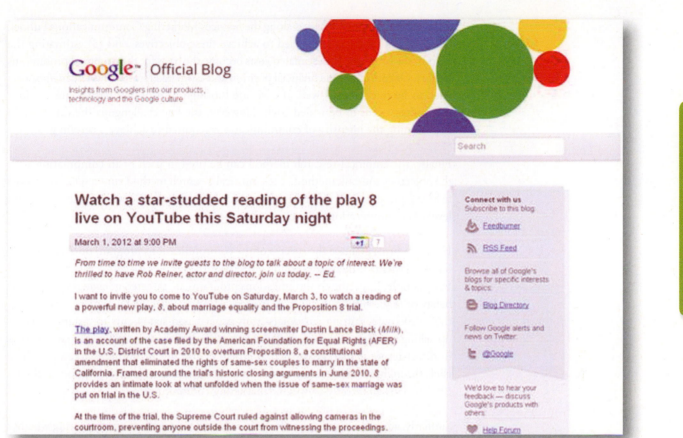

Figure 7.28 Google has its own blog.

communications funnel. Often, different communications channels are used to move a customer along from awareness and preference all the way to the post-consumption stage.

The timing of communications is typically managed with the help of a media-plan flowchart which looks like a large Excel spreadsheet and provides a bird's-eye view of where and when communication has been planned.

BUDGET DECISIONS AND PROGRAM EVALUATION[27]

 LO 13

Appreciate ethical and consumer-privacy-related issues in service marketing communications.

Most service firms will allocate a greater budget to services marketing communications if they believe that it will increase sales and profits. However, the optimal point of communications expenditure is difficult to predict, and setting the budget is one of the hardest decisions to make. In practice, service firms use a number of methods to determine their communications budget, including allocating a percentage of sales or profit, matching competitors' expenditure, and using last year's budget (or adding to or subtracting from it, depending on the success of last year's communications and the firm's future plans).

The most logical method, however, is the objective-and-task method, which is also known as the budget build-up method. This method entails three steps: (1) defining the communications objectives along the Services Marketing Communications Funnel, (2) determining the tasks needed to achieve these objectives, and (3) estimating the costs of the program. The estimated costs become the basis for the proposed promotions budget. Of course, a firm's financial position and estimated returns on these investments need to be integrated as well. If costs are too high or expected returns are too low, the budget needs to be scaled back. However, the key challenge is the difficulty in determining the intensity of communications required to achieve a certain goal.

Finally, the empirical-research method can be used in itself or in combination with the objective-and-task method. The empirical-research method runs a series of tests or field experiments with different communications budgets to determine the optimum level of communications spent.

How can firms evaluate the success of the communications program once the budget has been spent? If there are specific objectives, the level of success is easy to measure. For example, if specific communications programs are targeted at changing customer behavior (e.g., shifting usage away from peak hours, teaching customers how to keep their PINs safe, shifting customers from paper-based statements to e-statements, or up-selling to a higher-level service), the results are directly measurable. The same applies to direct-response marketing such as e-mail campaigns or online marketing, where click-through, newsletter sign-ups, followers, registrations, lead generation, and sales can be matched directly to specific marketing communications.

Similarly, advertising and research agencies have become experts at measuring whether wider communications objectives (e.g., awareness, knowledge, and preference) have been achieved. However, the effect of market communications on sales and profit is notoriously hard to measure. A key reason is that marketing communications is only one of the many drivers that determine sales. These drivers may range from service features and service quality to price and competitor activities.

ETHICAL AND CONSUMER PRIVACY ISSUES IN COMMUNICATIONS

LO 14

Understand the role of corporate design in communications.

We have been focusing on how to reach, persuade, and manage the behavior of prospects and customers. However, firms also need to consider the ethical and privacy issues associated with communications, especially because certain aspects of marketing such as advertising, selling, and sales promotion lend themselves very easily to misuse (and even abuse). The fact that customers often find it hard to evaluate services makes them more dependent on marketing communications for information and advice. Communication messages frequently include promises about the benefits that customers will receive and the quality of service delivery. If these promises are broken, customers are left disappointed.[28]

Some unrealistic service promises result from poor internal communications between operations and marketing personnel concerning the level of service performance that customers can reasonably expect. In other instances, unethical advertisers and salespeople deliberately make exaggerated promises to secure sales. Finally, there are deceptive promotions that lead people to think that they have a much higher chance of winning prizes or awards than is really the case. Fortunately, many consumer-watchdog groups are on the lookout for these deceptive marketing practices. They include consumer-protection agencies, trade associations within specific industries, and journalists seeking to expose cheating and misrepresentation.

A different type of ethical issue concerns unwanted intrusion by aggressive marketers into people's personal lives. The increase in telemarketing, direct mail, e-mail, and messaging is frustrating for those who receive unwanted sales communications.

To address the growing hostility toward these practices, both government agencies and trade associations have acted to protect consumers. In the United States, the Federal Trade Commission's National Do Not Call Registry enables consumers to remove their home and mobile numbers from telemarketing lists for a five-year period. People who continue to receive unauthorized calls from commercial telemarketers can file a complaint, and the telemarketing firm can be subjected to heavy fines for such violations.[29] Similarly, the Direct Marketing Association helps consumers remove their names from mailing, telemarketing, and e-mail lists.[30]

THE ROLE OF CORPORATE DESIGN

So far, we have focused on communications media and content but not much on design. Corporate design is essential to ensure that a consistent style and message is communicated through all the channels in a firm's communications mix. Corporate design is particularly important for companies operating in competitive markets where it's necessary to stand out from the crowd and be instantly recognizable in different locations. Have you noticed how some companies stand out in your mind because of the colors used by them, the widespread application of their logos, the uniforms worn by their employees, or the design of their physical facilities?

Many service firms employ a unified and distinctive visual appearance for all tangible elements to facilitate recognition and reinforce a desired brand image. Corporate design strategies are usually created by external consulting firms and include stationery and promotional materials, retail signage, uniforms, and color schemes for painting vehicles, equipment, and building interiors. The objective is to provide a unifying and recognizable theme that links all the firm's operations in a branded service experience through the strategic use of physical evidence. Companies can do that by using the following approaches either individually or in combination:

▶ Companies in the highly competitive express-delivery industry tend to use their names as a central element in their corporate design. When Federal Express changed its trading name to the more modern "FedEx," it featured the new name in a distinctive new logo.

▶ Many companies use a trademarked symbol rather than a name as their primary logo. Shell makes a pun of its English name by displaying a yellow scalloped shell on a red background. This has the advantage of making its vehicles and service stations instantly recognizable. McDonald's "Golden Arches" is said to be the most widely recognized corporate symbol in the world. It is featured at all touch points—in restaurants, on employee uniforms and packaging, and in all the company's communications materials.

- Some companies have succeeded in creating tangible, recognizable symbols to associate with their corporate brand names. Animal motifs are common physical symbols for services. Examples include the eagles of the U.S. Postal Service and AeroMexico, the lions of ING Bank and the Royal Bank of Canada, the ram of the investment firm T. Rowe Price, and the Chinese dragon of Hong Kong's Dragonair.

- Many companies use colors in their corporate designs. If we look at gasoline retailing, we see BP's immediately recognizable bright green and yellow service stations; Texaco's red, black, and white; and Sunoco's blue, maroon, and yellow.

LO 15

Know the importance of Integrated Marketing Communications to deliver a strong brand identity.

INTEGRATED MARKETING COMMUNICATIONS

Have you ever visited a service branch after seeing a new, exciting service promotion being touted on a firm's website, only to find that the counter staff was not aware of this promotion and couldn't sell it to you? What went wrong? In many service firms, different departments look after different aspects of the firm's market

Figure 7.29 The Golden Arches at the Times Square McDonald's restaurant in New York.

Table 7.2 Corporate design strategies.

Examples of Corporate Design Strategies			
Name as central element	**Trademarked symbol**	**Tangible recognizable symbol**	**Distinctive color used in corporate design**
FedEx	McDonald's "Golden Arches"	U.S. Postal Service's eagle	BP's bright green and yellow service stations
DHL	Shell's yellow scalloped shell	ING Bank's lion	The fire brick color of the dragon

communications. For example, the marketing department is in charge of advertising, the PR department of public relations, functional specialists of a company's website and its direct marketing and promotions activities, operations of customer service, and human resources of training. The service failure described above is due to lack of effective coordination among these various departments.

With so many channels delivering messages to customers and prospects, it becomes more and more important for firms to adopt the concept of Integrated Marketing Communications (IMC). IMC ties together and reinforces all communications to deliver a strong brand identity. This means that a firm's various media deliver the same messages and have the same look and feel, and the communications from the different media become parts of a single, overall message about the service firm and its products. Firms can achieve this by giving ownership of IMC to a single department (e.g., marketing) or by appointing a marketing communications director who has overall responsibility for all of the firm's market communications.

CHAPTER SUMMARY

 LO1 ▶ **S**ervice marketers need to design an effective communications strategy. To do this, they can use the Integrated Service Communications Model as a guiding framework. The model is organized around the 5 Ws, which are:

o **W**ho is our target audience? Are they prospects, users, and/or employees?

o **W**hat do we need to communicate and achieve? Do the objectives relate to consumer behavior in the pre-purchase, service encounter, or post-encounter stage?

o Ho**w** should we communicate this? How can we overcome the challenges caused by the intangibility of services?

o **W**here should we communicate this? Which media mix should we use?

o **W**hen should the communications take place?

LO2 ▶ There are three broad target audiences (**W**ho) of service communications. They are (1) prospects, who can be reached via traditional communications media as in goods marketing; (2) current users, who can be reached via more cost-effective communication channels such as the firm's service delivery channels (e.g., service employees, branch networks, account statements, and self-service channels); and (3) employees as a secondary audience who can be highly motivated with the right communications messaging.

LO3 ▶ At the most generic level, marketing communications objectives (**W**hat) are to inform, educate, persuade, remind, shape behavior, and build relationships. Communications objectives can be strategic or tactical in nature and are typically an amalgamation of both.

o *Strategic objectives* include building brand equity, positioning a brand against competition, and re-positioning it.

LO4 ▶ *Tactical objectives* can be organized according to the *Services Marketing Communications Funnel*, which details a range of potential objectives using the three-stage model of service-consumer behavior as a guiding framework. The funnel illustrates that communications objectives can be highly specific and can address any aspect of service consumption behavior in the (1) pre-purchase stage (e.g., emphasize the importance of attributes the firm outperforms, and reduce perceived risk), (2) service-encounter stage (e.g., guide customers through the service process, encourage proper queuing behavior, and manage performance perceptions), and (3) post-encounter stage (e.g., shape customer satisfaction and encourage referral and loyalty behaviors).

LO5 ▶ Examples of a few important roles that service marketing communications can assume are:

o Promote the tangible cues to communicate quality.

o Add value through communication content (e.g., provide information and consultation as discussed in the Flower of Service model).

o Facilitate customer involvement in production.

o Promote the contribution of service personnel.

o Stimulate and shift demand to match capacity.

LO6 ▶ Ho**w** can services best be communicated? The intangibility of services presents certain challenges for communications. These are:

o Abstractness: There is no one-to-one correspondence with a physical object.

o Generality: Items are part of a class of persons, objects, or events and are not specific to the firm's performance.

o Non-searchability: Services cannot be inspected or searched before purchase.

o Mental impalpability: Services are difficult to understand and interpret.

There are a number of ways to overcome the communications problems posed by intangibility.

o Abstractness: Use service consumption episodes and show typical customers experiencing the service.

o Generality: For objective claims, use system documentation showing facts and statistics about the service delivery system and the firm's performance (including past performance statistics, such as the percentage of packages delivered on time). For subjective claims, use service performance episodes where the actual service delivery being performed by service personnel is shown.

o Non-searchability: Use consumption documentation; i.e., obtain testimonials from customers who have experienced the service. For services high in credence attributes, use reputation documentation, which shows the awards received or the qualifications of the service provider.

o Impalpability: Use service process episodes by presenting what exactly will happen during the service experience; or case history episodes of what the firm did for a client and how it solved the client's problem; or a service consumption episode showing a customer's experience with a service.

Two additional ways to help overcome the problems of intangibility are:

o Emphasize tangible cues such as the employees, facilities, certificates and awards, and customers of the firm.

o Use metaphors to communicate the value proposition. For example, Prudential uses the Rock of Gibraltar as a symbol of corporate strength.

LO7 ▶ To reach our target audiences and achieve the communications objectives, we can use a variety of communications channels (**W**here), including:

o Traditional marketing channels (e.g., advertising, direct marketing, online advertising), apps, and social media (e.g., Web 2.0).

o Service-delivery channels (e.g., service outlets, front-line employees, service apps, and self-service websites).

o Messages originating from outside the organization (e.g., word of mouth, social media, blogs, and coverage in traditional media).

LO8 ▶ The traditional marketing channels include advertising, public relations, direct marketing (including permission marketing), sales promotions, and personal selling. These communication elements are typically used to help companies create a distinctive position in the market and reach prospective customers.

LO9 ▶ Online communications channels include the firm's websites and online advertising (e.g., banner advertising and search engine advertising and optimization).

o Developments in technology are driving innovations such as permission marketing and exciting possibilities of highly-targeted communications using online and mobile advertising, apps, Web 2.0, social media, and podcasting.

LO10 ▶ Service firms usually control service-delivery channels and point-of-sale environments that offer them cost-effective ways of reaching their current customers (e.g., through its service employees, service outlets, and self-service delivery points).

LO11 ▶ Some of the most powerful messages about a company and its services originate from outside the organization and are not controlled by the marketer. They include traditional word of mouth, blogs, Twitter and other social media, and coverage in traditional media.

o Recommendations from other customers are generally viewed as more credible than firm-initiated communications and are sought by prospects, especially for high-risk purchases.

o Firms can stimulate word of mouth from its customers through a number of means, such as by creating exciting promotions, developing referral reward programs, referencing customers, and presenting testimonials. All of these are increasingly being shifted to the online environment.

LO12 ▶ Unlike goods marketing, where much of the communication happens before periods of heavy buying (e.g., before Christmas), service firms typically cannot cater to additional demand during peak periods. Therefore, communications is usually connected to the specific objectives and their timing in the Services Marketing Communications Funnel (**W**hen). Budget decisions and performance management are mapped against these objectives (if the objective-and-task method is used).

LO13 ▶ When designing their communications strategy, firms need to bear in mind ethical and privacy issues such as failure to fulfill promises or intrusion into people's private lives (e.g., through telemarketing or e-mail campaigns). Firms must protect the privacy and personal data of customers and prospects.

LO14 ▶ Besides communication media and content, corporate design is key to achieving a unified image in customers' minds. Good corporate design uses a unified and distinctive visual appearance for tangible elements, including all elements of the Services Marketing Communications Mix, stationery, retail signage, uniforms, vehicles, equipment, and building interiors.

LO15 ▶ With so many channels delivering messages to customers and prospects, it becomes crucial for firms to adopt the concept of Integrated Marketing Communications (IMC).

UNLOCK YOUR LEARNING

These keywords are found within the sections of each Learning Objective (LO). They are integral to understanding the services marketing concepts taught in each section. Having a firm grasp of these keywords and how they are used is essential to helping you do well on your course, and in the real and very competitive marketing scene out there.

LO 1
1 Integrated Service Communications Model
2 5 Ws
3 Communications strategy
4 Strategy implementation

LO 2
1 Target audience
2 Users
3 Employees
4 Prospects

LO 3
1 Service communications objectives
2 Strategic objectives
3 Service brand

LO 4
1 Tactical objectives
2 Service consumption
3 Services Marketing Communications Funnel
4 Sales funnel
5 Service-encounter management
6 Customer acquisition
7 Customer engagement
8 AIDA
9 Hierarchy-of-effects model
10 Cognitive stage
11 Affective stage
12 Behavioral stage

LO 5
1 Tangible cues
2 Service performance
3 Customer involvement
4 Information
5 Consultation
6 Communication content
7 Back-stage operations
8 Service personnel
9 Add value
10 Shift demand
11 Capacity

LO 6
1 Intangibility
2 Non-searchability
3 Mental impalpability
4 Generality
5 Abstractness
6 Performance documentation
7 System documentation
8 Reputation documentation
9 Consumption documentation
10 Service consumption episode
11 Service performance episode
12 Service process episode
13 Case history episode
14 Metaphors

LO 7
1 Advertising
2 Corporate design
3 Instructional materials
4 Services Marketing Communications Mix
5 Personal communications
6 Public relations
7 Publicity
8 Sales promotion
9 Non-personal mass media
10 Direct marketing
11 Service-delivery points

LO 8
1 Micro-segments
2 On-demand technologies
3 Permission marketing
4 Telemarketing
5 Personal selling
6 Press releases

LO 9
1. AdWords
2. Banner advertising
3. Click-throughs
4. Company's website
5. Content ads
6. Eyeballs
7. Google
8. Internet
9. Mobile advertising
10. Online advertising
11. Website "stickiness"
12. Podcasting
13. Search engine advertising
14. AdSense
15. Social media and networks
16. Sponsored links
17. Mobile apps
18. Web 2.0
19. YouTube
20. Placement-targeted ads

LO 10
1. ATMs
2. Front-line employees
3. Self-service delivery points
4. Service outlets
5. Servicescape
6. Vending machines
7. Service apps

LO 11
1. Blogs
2. Media coverage
3. Online communities
4. Referencing
5. Referral reward programs
6. Online reviews
7. Testimonials
8. Twitter
9. Viral marketing
10. Word of mouth

LO 12
1. Budget decisions
2. Timing
3. Objective-and-task method
4. Program evaluation
5. Estimated costs
6. Empirical-research method

LO 13
1. Consumer privacy
2. Ethical issues
3. Do Not Call Registry
4. Promises
5. Intrusion
6. Unethical advertisers

LO 14
1. Colors
2. Uniforms
3. Logos
4. Symbols
5. Branded service experience

LO 15
1. Brand identity
2. Integrated Marketing Communications

How well do you know the language of services marketing? Quiz yourself!

⚠ **Not for the academically faint-of-heart**

For each keyword you are able to recall without referring to earlier pages, give yourself a point (and a pat on the back). Tally your score at the end and see if you earned the right to be called—a *services marketeer*.

SCORE

0 – 18	Services Marketing is done a great disservice.
19 – 36	The midnight oil needs to be lit, pronto.
37 – 54	I know what you *didn't* do all semester.
55 – 72	A close shave with success.
73 – 90	Now, go forth and market.
91 – 95	There should be a marketing concept named after you.

Review Questions

1. What are the 5 Ws along which the Integrated Service Communications Model is structured?

2. What are the three broad target audiences of service communications?

3. In what ways do the objectives of services communications differ substantially from those of goods marketing? Describe four common educational and promotional objectives in service settings, and provide a specific example for each of the objectives you list.

4. What can you learn from the Services Marketing Communications Funnel?

5. What are some challenges in service communications? How can they be overcome?

6. Why is the marketing communications mix larger for service firms than for firms that market goods?

7. What roles do personal selling, advertising, and public relations play in (a) attracting new customers to visit a service outlet and (b) retaining existing customers?

8. What are the different forms of online marketing? Which do you think would be the most effective online-marketing strategies for (a) an online broker and (b) a new high-end club in Los Angeles?

9. Why is permission-based marketing gaining so much focus in service firms' communications strategies?

10. Why is word of mouth important for the marketing of services? How can a service firm that is the quality leader in its industry induce and manage word of mouth?

11. How can companies use corporate design to differentiate themselves?

12. What are the potential ways to implement IMC?

WORK YOUR SERVICES MARKETING

Application Exercises

1. Which elements of the Services Marketing Communications Mix would you use for each of the following scenarios? Explain your answers.

   ▶ A newly established hair salon in a suburban shopping center

   ▶ An established restaurant facing declining patronage because of new competitors

   ▶ A large, single-office accounting firm in a major city that primarily serves business clients and wants to grow its client base aggressively

2. Identify one advertisement (or other means of communications) that is aimed mainly at managing consumer behavior in the (a) choice, (b) service-encounter, and (c) post-consumption stage. Explain how the advertisements try to achieve their objectives, and discuss how effective they may be.

3. Legal and accounting firms now advertise their services in many countries. Search for a few advertisements and review the following: What do these firms do to cope with the intangibility of their services? What could they do better? How do they deal with consumer quality and risk perceptions, and how could they improve this aspect of their marketing?

4. Discuss the significance of search, experience, and credence attributes for the communications strategy of a service provider. Assume that the objective of the communications strategy is to attract new customers.

5. If you were exploring your current university or researching the degree program you are now in, what could you learn from blogs and any other online word of mouth you can find? How would that information influence the decision of a prospective applicant to your university? Given that you are an expert on the school and the degree you are pursuing, how accurate is the information you found online?

6. Identify an advertisement that runs the risk of attracting mixed segments to a service business. Explain why this may happen, and state any negative consequences that could result.

7. Describe and evaluate recent public relations efforts made by service organizations in connection with three or more of the following: (a) launching a new offering, (b) opening a new facility, (c) promoting an expansion of existing services, (d) announcing an upcoming event, or (e) responding to a negative situation that has arisen. (Pick a different organization for each category.)

8. What tangible cues could a diving school or a dentistry clinic use to position itself as appealing to upscale customers?

9. Explore the websites of a management consulting firm, an internet retailer, and an insurance company. Assess them for ease of navigation, content, and visual design. What, if anything, would you change about each site?

10. Register at Amazon.com and Hallmark.com and analyze their permission-based communications strategy. What are their marketing objectives? Evaluate their permission-based marketing for a specific customer segment of your choice. Mention what is excellent, what is good, and what could be improved.

11. Conduct a Google search for (a) MBA programs and (b) vacation (holiday) resorts. Examine two or three contextual ads triggered by your searches. What are they doing right, and what can be improved?

ENDNOTES

1. Kilronan Castle, "OSCAR," Facebook album, https://www.facebook.com/media/set/?set=a.913675381980829.1073741840.125951937419848&type=3; "Oscar the Lost Teddy Is Having the Time of His Life and Lapping Up the Luxury at This Irish Castle Waiting on His Owners," Evoke.ie, http://www.evoke.ie/news/oscar-the-lost-teddy-is-having-the-time-of-his-life-and-lapping-up-the-luxury-at-this-irish-castle-waiting-on-his-owners; *MavSocial*, "Fun + Engagement = Superb Social Media Campaigns," http://mavsocial.com/fun-engagement-superb-social-media-campaigns, accessed March 12, 2015.

2. Daniel Wentzel, Sven Henkel, and Torsten Tomczak, "Can I Live Up to That Ad? Impact of Implicit Theories of Ability on Service Employees' Responses to Advertising," *Journal of Service Research* 13, no. 2 (2010): 137–152.

3. Edward K. Strong, "Theories of Selling," *Journal of Applied Psychology* 9, no. 1 (1925): 75–86.

4. Robert J. Lavidge and Gary A. Steiner, "A Model for Predictive Measurement of Advertising Effectiveness," *Journal of Marketing* 25 (October 1961): 59–62.

5. Banwari Mittal, "The Advertising of Services: Meeting the Challenge of Intangibility," *Journal of Service Research* 2 (August 1999): 98–116; Banwari Mittal and Julie Baker, "Advertising Strategies for Hospitality Services," *Cornell Hotel and Restaurant Administration Quarterly* 43 (April 2002): 51–63.

6. Donna Legg and Julie Baker, "Advertising Strategies for Service Firms," in C. Surprenant (ed.), *Add Value to Your Service* (Chicago: American Marketing Association, 1987): 163–168. See also: Donna J. Hill, Jeff Blodgett, Robert Baer, and Kirk Wakefield, "An Investigation of Visualization and Documentation Strategies in Service Advertising," *Journal of Service Research* 7 (November 2004): 155–166; Debra Grace and Aron O'Cass, "Service Branding: Consumer Verdicts on Service Brands," *Journal of Retailing and Consumer Services* 12 (2005): 125–139.

7. Adrian Palmer, *Principles of Services Marketing*, 6th ed. (London: McGraw-Hill, 2011): 450.

8. Penelope J. Prenshaw, Stacy E. Kovar, and Kimberly Gladden Burke, "The Impact of Involvement on Satisfaction for New, Nontraditional, Credence-based Service Offerings," *Journal of Services Marketing* 20, no. 7 (2006): 439–452.

9. Gila E. Fruchter and Z. John Zhang, "Dynamic Targeted Promotions: A Customer Retention and Acquisition Perspective," *Journal of Service Research* 7 (August 2004): 3–19.

10. Ken Peattie and Sue Peattie, "Sales Promotion: A Missed Opportunity for Service Marketers," *International Journal of Service Industry Management* 5, no. 1 (1995): 6–21.

11. Michael Lewis, "Customer Acquisition Promotions and Customer Asset Value," *Journal of Marketing Research* 43, no. 2 (2006): 195–203.

12. Paul Smith and Dave Chaffey, *eMarketing Excellence* (Oxford, UK: Elsevier Butterworth-Heinemann, 2005): 173.

13. "The Future of Advertising: The Harder Hard Sell," *The Economist*, June 24, 2004.

14. Nadia Abou Nabout, Markus Lilienthal, and Bernd Skiera, "Empirical Generalizations in Search Engine Advertising," *Journal of Retailing* 90, no. 2 (2014): 206–216.

15. Amin Sayedi, Kinshuk Jerath, and Kannan Srinivasan, "Competitive Poaching in Sponsored Search Advertising and Its Strategic Impact on Traditional Advertising," *Marketing Science* 33, no. 4 (2014): 586–608.

16. Ron Berman and Zsolt Katona, "The Role of Search Engine Optimization in Search Marketing," *Marketing Science* 32, no. 4 (2013): 644–651.

17. Roland Rust and Ming-Hui Huang, "The Service Revolution and the Transformation of Marketing Science," *Marketing Science* 33, no. 2 (2014): 206–221.

18. Yakov Bart, Andrew T. Stephen, and Miklos Sarvary, "Which Products Are Best Suited to Mobile Advertising? A Field Study of Mobile Display Advertising Effects on Consumer Attitudes and Behaviors," *Journal of Marketing Research* 51 (June 2014): 270–285.

19. Stephanie Rosenbloom, "Apps to Help Navigate Cruise Lines," *The New York Times* (2015): TR2.

20. V. Kumar and Rohan Mirchandani, "Increasing the ROI of Social Media Marketing," *Sloan Management Review* 54, no. 1 (2012): 55–61; Roxane Divol, David Edelman, and Hugo Sarrazin, "Demystifying Social Media," *McKinsey Quarterly* (April 2012).

21. Mary Jo Bitner, "Servicescapes: The Impact of Physical Surroundings on Customers and Employees," *Journal of Marketing* 56 (April 1992): 57–71.

22. Kathleen Seiders, Andrea Godfrey Flynn, Leonard L. Berry, and Kelly L. Haws, "Motivating Customers to Adhere to Expert Advice in Professional Services: A Medical Service Context," *Journal of Service Research* 18, no. 1 (2015): 39–58.

23. Ron Kaufman, "Lift Me UP! Service with a Smile: World-Class Quips and Action Tips to Brighten Up Your Services!" (Kaufman Professional Services, 2005).

24. Jochen Wirtz and Patricia Chew, "The Effects of Incentives, Deal Proneness, Satisfaction and Tie Strength on Word-of-Mouth Behaviour," *International Journal of Service Industry Management* 13, no. 2 (2002): 141–162; Tom J. Brown, Thomas E. Barry, Peter A. Dacin, and Richard F. Gunst, "Spreading the Word: Investigating Antecedents of Consumers' Positive Word-of-Mouth Intentions and Behaviors in a Retailing Context," *Journal of the Academy of Marketing Science* 33, no. 2 (2005): 123–138; John E. Hogan, Katherine N. Lemon, and Barak Libai, "Quantifying the Ripple: Word-of-Mouth and Advertising Effectiveness," *Journal of Advertising Research* (September 2004): 271–280; Jonah Berger and Raghuram Iyengar, "Communication Channels and Word of Mouth: How the Medium Shapes the Message," *Journal of Consumer Research* 40 (October 2013): 567–579.

25. Phillipp Schmitt, Bernd Skiera, and Christophe Van den Bulte, "Referral Programs and Customer Value," *Journal of Marketing* 75, no. 1 (2011): 46–59; V. Kumar, J. Andrew Petersen, and Robert P. Leone, "Driving Profitability by Encouraging Customer Referrals: Who, When, and How," *Journal of Marketing* 74, no. 5 (2010): 1–17.

26. Jochen Wirtz, Anouk den Ambtman, Josee Bloemer, Csilla Horváth, B. Ramaseshan, Joris Van De Klundert, Zeynep Gurhan Canli, and Jay Kandampully, "Managing Brands and Customer Engagement in Online Brand Communities," *Journal of Service Management* 24, no. 3 (2013): 223–244.

27. This section draws on: Philip Kotler and Gary Armstrong, "Chapter 14: Communicating Customer Value: Integrated Marketing Communications Strategy," in *Principles of Marketing*, 15th ed. (Upper Saddle River, New Jersey: Pearson Education, 2014): 426–453; William F. Arens, Michael F. Weigold, and Christian Arens, "Marketing and IMC Planning," in *Contemporary Advertising & Integrated Marketing Communications*, 14th ed. (New York: McGraw Hill, 2013): 263–267.

28. Louis Fabien, "Making Promises: The Power of Engagement," *Journal of Services Marketing* 11, no. 3 (1997): 206–214.

29. https://www.donotcall.gov/default.aspx, accessed March 21, 2015.

30. https://www.dmachoice.org, accessed March 21, 2015.

III

THE *ESM* FRAMEWORK

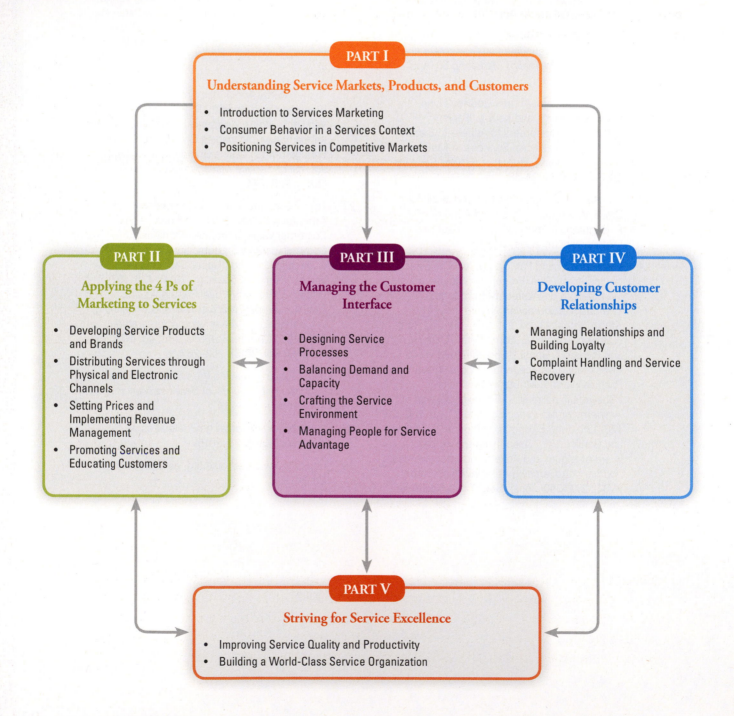

PART I

Understanding Service Markets, Products, and Customers

- Introduction to Services Marketing
- Consumer Behavior in a Services Context
- Positioning Services in Competitive Markets

PART II

Applying the 4 Ps of Marketing to Services

- Developing Service Products and Brands
- Distributing Services through Physical and Electronic Channels
- Setting Prices and Implementing Revenue Management
- Promoting Services and Educating Customers

PART III

Managing the Customer Interface

- Designing Service Processes
- Balancing Demand and Capacity
- Crafting the Service Environment
- Managing People for Service Advantage

PART IV

Developing Customer Relationships

- Managing Relationships and Building Loyalty
- Complaint Handling and Service Recovery

PART V

Striving for Service Excellence

- Improving Service Quality and Productivity
- Building a World-Class Service Organization

MANAGING THE CUSTOMER INTERFACE

Part III focuses on managing the interface between customers and the service organization. It covers the additional 3 Ps (*P*rocess, *P*hysical environment, and *P*eople) that are unique to services marketing. It consists of the following four chapters:

Chapter 8 Designing Service Processes

It begins with design of an effective service delivery process, specifying how operating and delivery systems link together to create the promised value proposition. Very often, customers are actively involved in service creation, especially if acting as co-producers, and the process becomes their experience.

Chapter 9 Balancing Demand and Capacity

Chapter 9 still relates to process management and focuses on the widely fluctuating demand and how to balance the level and timing of customer demand against available productive capacity. Well-managed demand and capacity leads to smooth processes with less waiting time for customers. Marketing strategies for managing demand involve smoothing demand fluctuations and inventorying demand through reservation systems and formalized queuing. Understanding customer motivations in different segments is one of the keys to successful demand management.

Chapter 10 Crafting the Service Environment

Chapter 10 focuses on the physical environment, which is also known as the servicescape. It needs to be engineered to create the right impression and facilitate effective delivery of service processes. The servicescape needs to be managed carefully, because it can have a profound impact on customers' impressions, guide their behavior throughout the service process, and provide tangible clues of a firm's service quality and positioning.

Chapter 11 Managing People for Service Advantage

Chapter 11 introduces people, who are a defining element of many services. Many services require direct interaction between customers and contact personnel. The nature of these interactions strongly influences how customers perceive service quality. Hence, service firms devote a significant amount of effort to recruiting, training and motivating their employees. Satisfied and engaged employees who perform well are often a source of competitive advantage for a firm.

8 designing SERVICE PROCESSES

LEARNING OBJECTIVES (LOs)

By the end of this chapter, the reader should be able to:

LO 1 Know the difference between a service experience and a service process.

LO 2 Tell the difference between flowcharting and blueprinting.

LO 3 Develop a blueprint for a service process with all the typical design elements in place.

LO 4 Understand how to use fail-proofing to design fail points out of service processes.

LO 5 Know how to set service standards and performance targets for customer service processes.

LO 6 Appreciate the importance of consumer perceptions and emotions in service process design.

LO 7 Explain the necessity for service process redesign.

LO 8 Understand how service process redesign can help improve both service quality and productivity.

LO 9 Understand the levels of customer participation in service processes.

LO 10 Be familiar with the concept of service customers as "co-creators" and the implications of this perspective.

LO 11 Understand the factors that lead customers to accept or reject new self-service technologies (SSTs).

LO 12 Know how to manage customers' reluctance to change their behaviors in service processes, including the adoption of SSTs.

Redesigning Customer Service in a Small Hospital Practice[1]

Things were not going smoothly at Family Medicine Faculty Practice (FMFP), a small practice within a hospital system. Its patients were frequently placed on hold for a long time when they called; there was a lack of available and convenient appointment slots; and there were often lengthy delays before patients could move from the crowded waiting room to the clinical area in order to see their doctors.

Dr. Schwartz, the medical director, and Dr. Bryan, the assistant medical director, decided to change this situation and engaged Coleman Associates, a consulting firm that specializes in redesigning processes. Over the course of four days, a Coleman Associates team worked closely with the clinic's staff on-site and radically redesigned work processes. It was an amazing transformation! The redesign started on a Monday afternoon, and by Friday morning the Faculty Practice was operating in a wholly new way.

The Redesigned Service Model

FMFP had 12 staff members, of whom nine were support staff and three were physicians. The clinic was considered lean with only three support staff per physician, which is much lower than the national average of 4.8. A central part of the redesign involved staff members being reorganized into three Patient Care Teams. Each Patient Care Team consisted of a clinician, a medical assistant, and a receptionist who acted like a one-stop shop for all the patients in their care. The Patient Care Teams handled all tasks related to their patients, including walk-ins, collection of co-payments, filing of medical charts, confirmation of the next day's appointments, checking of insurance eligibility, and other patient transactions.

The three Patient Care Teams shared three "back-office" staff members who had the redesigned roles of a medical records staffer, a phone attendant, and a flowmaster. The medical records staffer was in charge of getting medical charts 24 hours in advance of clinic sessions and filing lab results in charts on a real-time basis so that no work would be left to accumulate. If a patient phoned FMFP for an appointment, the call would be answered by the phone attendant and passed on to the relevant Patient Care Team

receptionist. There were further plans to create direct lines to each Patient Care Team in the future so that the traffic to the phone attendant could be eliminated. The flowmaster was in charge of moving patients from the front waiting room into the exam rooms and out again as smoothly and rapidly as possible. The flowmaster communicated with each Patient Care Team's medical assistant to get an estimate of the wait time for each patient. Basically, the flowmaster solved any flow problems occurring in the clinic to keep the visit cycle time within 45 minutes for 90% of all visits.

The receptionists in each Patient Care Team were given wireless phones so that they could receive patient calls even while filing medical charts from visits already completed. Charts were filed immediately after visits to reduce the incidence of lost charts. During the booking of appointments, if a patient had a question the receptionist could not answer, the latter would communicate directly via walkie-talkie with the Patient Care Team's medical assistant to get an immediate answer. This system allowed work to be handled on a real-time basis rather than stacked up to be dealt with later.

New tools and equipment helped to stretch FMFP's available resources. For example, digital floor scales were placed in every exam room to weigh adult patients quickly and privately so that there would be no need for an extra stop at a vitals station. In fact, all work was done in the exam room, and this reflected the following redesign principle: "Organize our work around the patient, not the patient around our work."

As the staff members gained more experience by working together every day in their Patient Care Teams, they also became stronger and more adept at handling variations in patient flow. Stacks of paper seemingly melted during the week when work was redesigned.

FMFP's staff members worked harder than ever, but they were also thrilled with the results and the compliments they received from delighted patients regarding the new service processes.

LO 1

Know the difference between a service experience and a service process.

LO 2

Tell the difference between flowcharting and blueprinting.

Figure 8.1 Baggage collection is one of the last steps in an air-travel service process.

WHAT IS A SERVICE PROCESS?

From the customer's perspective, services are experiences, such as calling a customer contact center or visiting a library. From the organization's perspective, services are processes that have to be designed and managed to create the desired customer experience. Processes describe the method and sequence in which service operating systems work and specify how they link together to create the value proposition promised to customers. Badly designed processes are likely to annoy customers because they often result in slow, frustrating, and poor-quality service delivery. They also make it difficult for front-line employees to do their jobs well, result in low productivity, and increase the risk of service failures. This chapter discusses how service processes can be designed and improved to deliver the promised value proposition. (See Figure 8.2 for the chapter overview.)

DESIGNING AND DOCUMENTING SERVICE PROCESSES

The first step in designing or analyzing any process is to document or describe it. *Flowcharting* and *blueprinting* are two key tools that we use for documenting and redesigning existing service processes and designing new ones. How do we distinguish between flowcharting and blueprinting in a service context? A flowchart describes an existing process, often in a fairly simple form. Specifically, flowcharting is a technique for displaying the nature and sequence of the different steps involved when a customer "flows" through the service process. By flowcharting the sequence of encounters that customers have with a service organization, we can gain valuable insights into the nature of an existing service. Figures 8.3 and 8.4 display two simple flowcharts that demonstrate what is involved in each of the featured services.

Blueprinting is a more complex form of flowcharting and specifies in detail how a service process is constructed. Service blueprints map customer, employee, and service-system interactions. They show the full customer journey from service initiation to final delivery of the desired benefit, which can include many steps and service employees from different departments. For example, a cable service may involve a sales agent, an installation team, and a call center employee to do the scheduling, and back-office agents to set up billing and payment. All these employees are responsible for a trouble-free installation.[2] Thus, blueprints show key customer actions, the ways in which customers and employees from different departments interact (called the line of interaction), the front-stage actions by the service employees, and how these are supported by back-stage activities and systems.

Developing a Service Blueprint

How should you get started on developing a service blueprint? First, you need to identify all the key activities involved in creating and delivering the service in question. You must then specify the linkages between these activities. Initially, it's best to keep activities relatively aggregated in order to define the "big picture." This can be done by developing a simple flowchart that documents the process from the customer's perspective. You can refine any given activity by "drilling down" to obtain a higher level of detail. In an airline context, for instance, the passenger activity of "boarding

Service Processes
- Are the service experience from the customer's perspective
- Are the architecture of service from the firm's perspective

Mapping and Designing Service Processes

Flowcharting of Service Processes
- Maps a service process
- Shows the nature and sequence of steps involved
- Is an easy way to visualize the customer experience

Blueprinting of Service Processes
- A more complex form of flowcharting
- Shows how a service process is constructed
- Maps the customer, employee, and service system interactions
- Design elements:
  - Front-stage activities
  - Physical evidence
  - Line of visibility
  - Backstage activities
  - Support processes and supplies
  - Potential fail points
  - Common customer waits
  - Service standards and targets
  - Details pre-process, inprocess, and post-process stages of service delivery

Process Design Considerations
- Use poka-yokes to design fail points out of processes
- Set service standards and targets to manage processes
- Design customer emotions into the process:
  - Start strong
  - Build an improving trend
  - Create a peak
  - Get bad experiences over with early
  - Segment pleasure, combine pain
  - Finish strong

Redesigning Service Processes

Indicators for Redesign Need
- Excessive information exchange
- High degree of control activities
- Increased processing of exceptions
- Growing number of customer complaints about inconvenient and unnecessary procedures

Objectives of Redesign
- Reduced number of service failures
- Reduced cycle time
- Enhance productivity
- Increased customer satisfaction

How to Redesign Service Processes?
- Examine the blueprint with key stakeholders (including customers, frontline and back office employees, and IT) and see how to reconstruct, rearrange and substitute tasks
- Eliminate non-value adding steps
- Address bottlenecks, balance process
- Shift to self-service

Manage Customer Participation in Service Processes

Customers as Co-Creators
- Educate, train, and motivate customers to do their part well
- Use customer poka-yokes to reduce failures caused by customers
- Consider peer-to-peer problem solving as part of online brand communities

Self-Service Technologies (SSTs)
- Customer benefits
  - Convenience and speed
  - Control, information, and customization
  - Cost savings
- Disadvantages and barriers
  - Poorly designed SSTs
  - Unreliable SSTs
  - Poor service recovery procedures
  - Inadequate customer education
- Assessing and improving SSTs
  - Does the SST work reliably?
  - Is the SST better than the interpersonal alternative?
  - If it fails, are systems in place to recover the service?

Managing Customers' Reluctance to Change
- Develop customers' trust
- Understand customers' habits and expectations
- Pre-test new procedures and equipment
- Publicise the benefits
- Teach customers to use innovations and promote trial
- Monitor performance and improve the SST

Figure 8.2 Chapter overview: Designing and managing service processes.

Figure 8.3 Flowchart for delivery of motel service.

the aircraft" actually represents a series of actions and can be decomposed into such steps as waiting for seat rows to be announced, giving the agent one's boarding pass for verification, walking down the jetway, entering the aircraft, letting the flight attendant verify the boarding pass, finding a seat, stowing the carry-on bag, and sitting down.

The next step is to add the more detailed documentation of a blueprint. Typical service blueprints have the following design characteristics:[3]

▶ **Front-stage activities.** These map the overall customer experience, the desired inputs and outputs, and the sequence in which the delivery of that output should take place.

▶ **Physical evidence of front-stage activities.** This is what the customer can see and use to assess service quality.

▶ **Line of visibility.** A key characteristic of service blueprinting is that it distinguishes between what customers experience "front stage" and the activities of employees and support processes "back stage," where customers can't see them. Between the two lies what is called the *line of visibility*. When a firm clearly understands the line of visibility, it is better able to manage physical and other evidence for front-stage activities in order to give customers the desired experience and quality signals.

▶ **Back-stage activities.** These must be performed to support a particular front-stage step.

▶ **Support processes and supplies.** Many support processes involve a lot of information. The information needed at each step in the blueprint is usually provided by information systems. If the front-line staff does not have the right information at its fingertips, processes such as online broking or borrowing a book from a library can't be completed. Supplies are also necessary for many services. For example, car rental services need to have vehicles, global positioning systems (GPSs), and child seats.

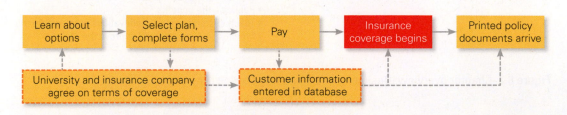

Figure 8.4 Flowchart for delivery of health insurance service.

- **Potential fail points.** Blueprinting gives managers the chance to identify potential *fail points* in the process. These are points at which there is a risk of things going wrong and service quality being diminished. When managers are aware of these fail points, they are better able to design them out of a process (e.g., by using poka-yokes, as discussed later in this chapter). They can also develop back-up plans for service recovery for failures that are not preventable (e.g., departure delays due to bad weather).

- **Identifying customer waits.** Blueprints can also pinpoint stages in the process at which customers commonly have to wait (Figure 8.5), potentially for an excessively long time. These can then be designed out of the process. If that is not always possible, firms can implement strategies to make waits less unpleasant for customers (see the strategies discussed in Chapter 9 on managing demand and capacity).

- **Service standards and targets.** These reflect customer expectations and should be established for each front-stage activity. They include specific times set for the completion of each task and the acceptable wait times between different customer activities. Developing service blueprints gives marketing and operational personnel detailed process knowledge that can then be used to develop standards.

Figure 8.5 Long waiting lines indicate operational problems that need to be addressed.

Blueprinting the Restaurant Experience: A Three-Act Performance

To illustrate how blueprinting of a high-contact, people-processing service can be done, we examine the experience of a dinner for two at Chez Jean, an upscale restaurant that enhances its core food service with a variety of other supplementary services (Figure 8.6, pages 242–245).

Most service processes can be divided into three main steps:

1) Pre-process stage, where preliminaries occur, such as making a reservation, parking the car, getting seated, and being presented with the menu.

2) In-process stage, where the main purpose of the service encounter is accomplished, such as enjoying the food and drinks in a restaurant.

3) Post-process stage, where the activities necessary for the closing of the encounter happen, such as getting the check and paying for the dinner.

It is important to differentiate these stages, as customers tend to have different objectives and sensitivities in each stage. For instance, they want efficiency and convenience in the pre- and post-process stages, which are typically not the core of the service (e.g., a convenient way to get a reservation and make the payment). The in-process stage has to deliver the core benefits of the service.

In Figure 8.6, we use a more "theatrical" three-act structure to represent the three stages. This connects to the theatre analogy discussed in Chapter 2 and emphasizes the dramatic element in the experience of this service process.

PART III

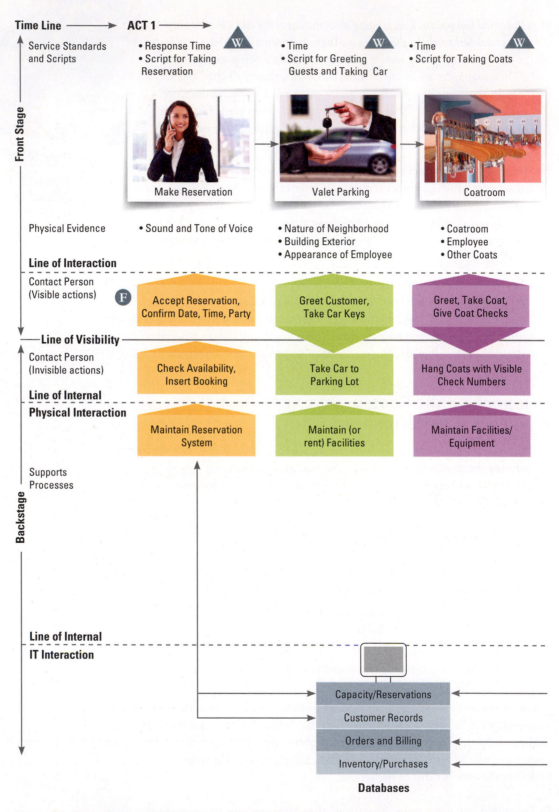

Figure 8.6 Blueprinting a full-service restaurant experience.

ACT II →

- Time
- Order Accuracy
- Script for Serving Drinks

- Punctuality vs. Reservation
- Script for Seating

- Time
- Script for Greeting Guests, Taking Order

- Time
- Script for Wine Service

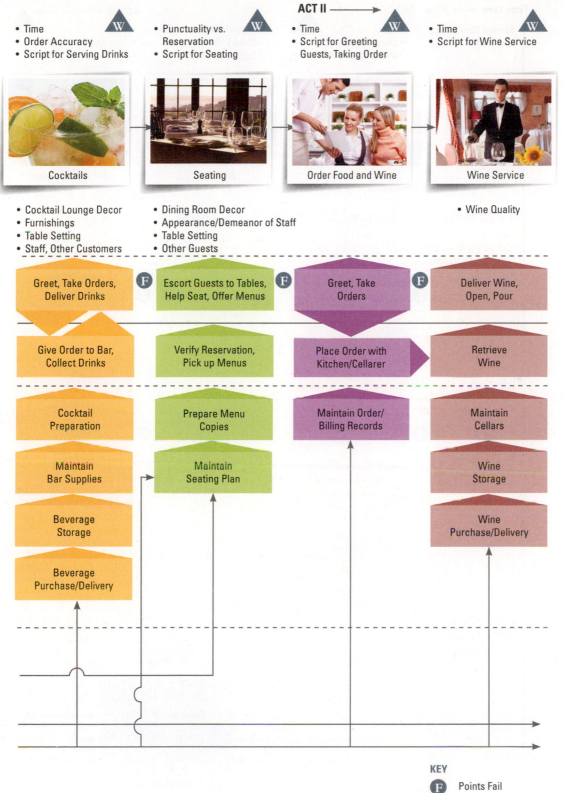

Cocktails | Seating | Order Food and Wine | Wine Service

- Cocktail Lounge Decor
- Furnishings
- Table Setting
- Staff, Other Customers

- Dining Room Decor
- Appearance/Demeanor of Staff
- Table Setting
- Other Guests

- Wine Quality

Greet, Take Orders, Deliver Drinks **F** | Escort Guests to Tables, Help Seat, Offer Menus **F** | Greet, Take Orders **F** | Deliver Wine, Open, Pour

Give Order to Bar, Collect Drinks | Verify Reservation, Pick up Menus | Place Order with Kitchen/Cellarer | Retrieve Wine

Cocktail Preparation | Prepare Menu Copies | Maintain Order/Billing Records | Maintain Cellars

Maintain Bar Supplies | Maintain Seating Plan | | Wine Storage

Beverage Storage | | | Wine Purchase/Delivery

Beverage Purchase/Delivery

KEY

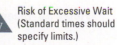 **F** Points Fail

W Risk of Excessive Wait (Standard times should specify limits.)

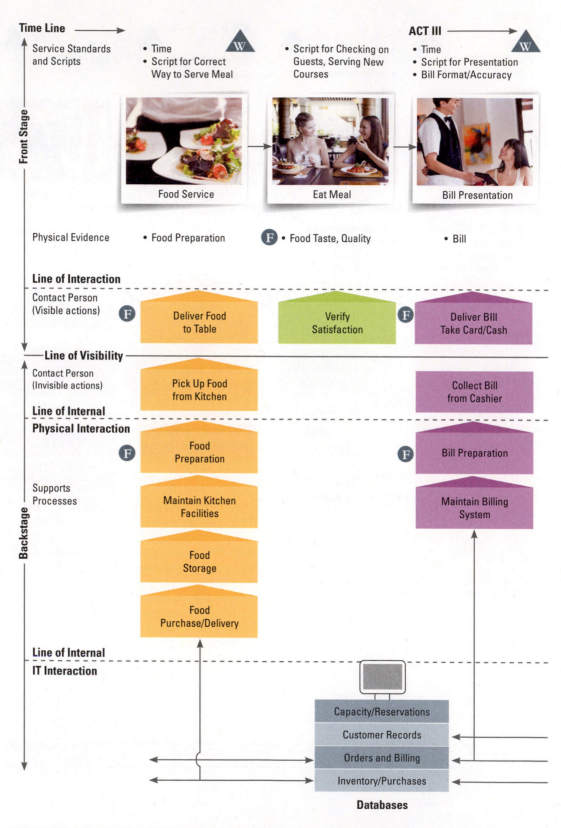

Figure 8.6 Blueprinting a full-service restaurant experience (continued).

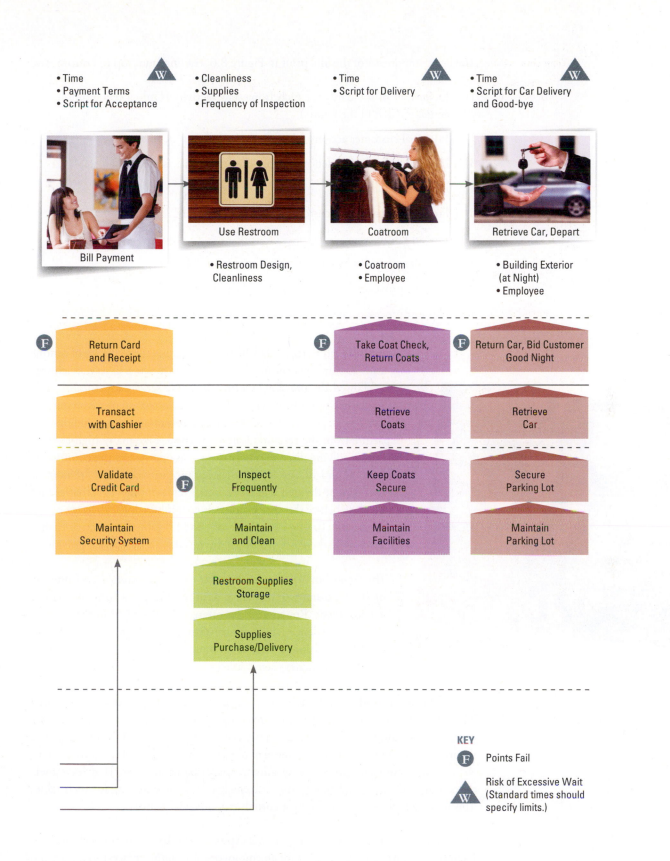

- Time
- Payment Terms
- Script for Acceptance

- Cleanliness
- Supplies
- Frequency of Inspection

- Time
- Script for Delivery

- Time
- Script for Car Delivery and Good-bye

Bill Payment

Use Restroom
- Restroom Design, Cleanliness

Coatroom
- Coatroom
- Employee

Retrieve Car, Depart
- Building Exterior (at Night)
- Employee

Return Card and Receipt

Take Coat Check, Return Coats

Return Car, Bid Customer Good Night

Transact with Cashier

Retrieve Coats

Retrieve Car

Validate Credit Card

Inspect Frequently

Keep Coats Secure

Secure Parking Lot

Maintain Security System

Maintain and Clean

Maintain Facilities

Maintain Parking Lot

Restroom Supplies Storage

Supplies Purchase/Delivery

KEY

F Points Fail

W Risk of Excessive Wait (Standard times should specify limits.)

PART III

The key components of the blueprint in Figure 8.6, reading from top to bottom, are:

1) Definition of standards for each front-stage activity (Only a few examples are actually stated in the figure.)

2) Principal customer actions (illustrated by pictures)

3) Physical and other evidence for front-stage activities (stated for all steps)

4) Line of interaction

5) Front-stage actions by customer-contact personnel

6) Line of visibility

7) Back-stage actions by customer-contact personnel

8) Support processes involving other service personnel

9) Support processes involving information technology

Reading from left to right, the blueprint prescribes the sequence of actions over time. To emphasize the involvement of human actors in service delivery, we've followed the practice (adopted by some service organizations) of using pictures to illustrate each of the 14 principal steps involving our two customers, beginning with making a reservation and concluding with departure from the restaurant after the meal. Like many high-contact services involving discrete transactions—as opposed to the continuous delivery found in, say, utility or insurance services—the "restaurant drama" can be divided into three "acts," representing (1) activities that take place before the core product is encountered, (2) delivery of the core product (in this case, the meal), and (3) subsequent activities that occur while the customer is still involved with the service provider.

The "stage" or *servicescape* includes both the exterior and interior of the restaurant. Front-stage actions take place in a very visual environment. Restaurants are often quite theatrical in their use of physical evidence (such as furnishings, décor, uniforms, lighting, and table settings). They also employ background music to create a themed environment that matches their market positioning (Figure 8.7).

Figure 8.7 Two hosts welcome diners in a servicescape that clearly communicate the restaurant's positioning.

Act I—Prologue and Introductory Scenes. In this particular drama, Act I begins with a customer making a reservation by telephone. In theatrical terms, the telephone conversation can be likened to a radio drama, with impressions being created by the nature of the respondent's voice, the speed of response, and the style of the conversation. When our customers arrive at the restaurant, a valet parks their car. They leave their coats in the coatroom and enjoy a drink in the bar area while waiting for their table. The act concludes with them being escorted to a table and seated.

These five steps constitute the couple's initial experience of the restaurant performance. Each step involves an interaction with an employee—by phone or face-to-face. By the time the two customers reach their table in the dining room, they've been exposed to several supplementary services. They have also encountered a sizeable cast of characters, including five or more contact personnel and many other customers.

Standards can be set for each service activity, but these should be based on a good understanding of guest expectations (remember our discussion in Chapter 2 on how expectations are formed). Below the line of visibility, the blueprint identifies key actions to ensure that each front-stage step is performed in a manner that meets or exceeds customer expectations. These actions include recording reservations; handling customers' coats; preparing and delivering food; maintaining the facilities and equipment; training and assigning staff for each task; and using information technology to access, input, store, and transfer relevant data.

Act II—Delivery of the Core Product. As the curtain rises on Act II, our customers are finally about to experience the core service they came for. For simplicity, we've condensed the meal into just four scenes. In practice, reviewing the menu and placing the order are two separate activities, and meal service proceeds on a course-by-course basis. If you were actually running a restaurant yourself, you'd need to go into greater detail to identify each of the many steps involved in what is often a tightly scripted drama. Assuming all goes well, the two guests will have an excellent meal, nicely served in a pleasant atmosphere. However, if the restaurant fails to satisfy their expectations during Act II, it is going to be in serious trouble. There are numerous potential fail points. Is the menu information accurate? Is everything listed on the menu actually available this evening? Will explanations and advice be given in a friendly and non-condescending manner for guests who have questions about specific menu items or are unsure about which wine to order?

After our customers decide on their meals, they place their orders with the server, who must then pass on the details to personnel in the kitchen, bar, and billing desk. Mistakes in transmitting information are a frequent cause of quality failures in many organizations. A wrong entry into a hand-held wireless ordering device can lead to incorrect preparation or delivery of the wrong items altogether.

In the subsequent scenes of Act II, our customers may evaluate not only the quality of food and drink—the most important dimension of all—but also how promptly it is served (not too quickly, for guests do not want to feel rushed!) and the style of service. Even if the server performs the job correctly, the experience of the customer can still be spoiled if the server is disinterested, unfriendly, or has an overly casual behavior.

Act III—The Drama Concludes. The meal may be over, but a lot is still taking place both front stage and back stage as the drama moves to its close. The core service has now been delivered, and we'll assume that our customers are happily digesting. Act III should be short. The action in each of the remaining scenes should move smoothly, quickly, and pleasantly, with no shocking surprises at the end. Most customers' expectations would probably include the following:

▶ An accurate, intelligible bill is presented promptly as soon as the customer requests it (Figure 8.8).

▶ Payment is handled politely and expeditiously (with all major credit cards accepted).

▶ The guests are thanked for their patronage and invited to come again.

Figure 8.8 The billing process should be quick and painless to ensure customer convenience.

- Customers visiting the restrooms find them clean and properly supplied.

- The right coats are promptly retrieved from the coatroom.

- The customer's car is brought to the door without much of a wait and in the same condition as when it was left. The attendant thanks them again and bids them a good evening.

Identifying Fail Points

Running a restaurant is a complex business and a lot can go wrong. A good blueprint should draw attention to those points in the service delivery process where things are particularly at risk of going wrong. From a customer's perspective, the most serious fail points, marked in our blueprint by **F**, are those that will result in failure to access or enjoy the core product. They involve reservation (Could the customer get through by phone? Was a table available at the desired time and date? Was the reservation recorded accurately?) and seating (Was a table available when promised?).

Since service delivery takes place over time, there is also the possibility of delays between specific actions that require the customers to wait. Common locations for such waits are identified on the blueprint by **W**. Excessively long waits will annoy customers. In practice, every step in the process—both front stage and back stage—has some potential for failures and delays. In fact, failures often lead directly to delays (e.g., reflecting orders that were never passed on) or time spent correcting mistakes.

David Maister coined the acronym OTSU ("opportunity to screw up") to stress the importance of thinking about all the things that might go wrong in delivering a particular type of service.[4] It's only by identifying all the possible OTSUs associated with a particular process that service managers can put together a delivery system that is designed to avoid such problems.

Fail-Proofing to Design Fail Points out of Service Processes

LO 4

Understand how to use fail-proofing to design fail points out of service processes.

Once fail points have been identified, careful analysis of the reasons for failure in service processes is necessary. This analysis often reveals opportunities for designing fail points out of processes in order to reduce or even eliminate the risk of errors.[5]

One of the most useful Total Quality Management (TQM) methods in manufacturing is the application of *poka-yokes* or fail-safe methods to prevent errors in the manufacturing processes. The term poka-yoke is derived from the Japanese words "poka" (inadvertent errors) and "yokeru" (to prevent). Richard Chase and Douglas Steward introduced this concept to fail-safe service processes.[6] Server poka-yokes ensure that service employees do things correctly, as asked, in the right order and at the right speed. For instance, surgical instrument trays have individual indentations for each instrument. For any given operation, all of the instruments are nested in their appropriate spots within the tray. This ensures that the surgeon does not close the incision without removing all the instruments from the patient. (Figure 8.9)

Some service firms use poka-yokes to design frequently occurring service failures out of service processes and to ensure that certain steps or standards in the customer–staff interaction are followed. A bank ensures eye contact by requiring tellers to record the customer's eye color on a checklist at the start of a transaction. At one restaurant, servers place round coasters in front of diners who have ordered a decaffeinated coffee and square coasters in front of the others. Starbucks baristas are trained to repeat their customers' orders to ensure that the correct coffee is served.

Designing poka-yokes is part art and part science. It can be used to design frequently occurring service failures out of service processes and to ensure that certain service standards or service steps are followed. Most of the procedures seem trivial, but this is actually a key advantage of this method. A three-step approach for effectively using poka-yokes includes systematically collecting data on problem occurrence, analyzing the root causes, and establishing preventive solutions. We describe this process later in this chapter in the context of preventing failures caused by customers (see Service Insights 8.1).

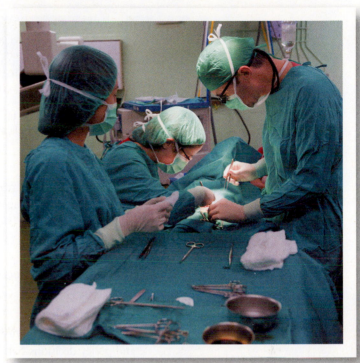

Figure 8.9 The practice of poka-yoke is observed in the operating room.

 LO 5

Know how to set service standards and performance targets for customer service processes.

Setting Service Standards and Targets

The service blueprint, combined with discussions with customers and front-line employees, helps firms to see which service and process attributes are important to customers at each touch point. Through both formal research and on-the-job experience, service managers can learn the nature of customer expectations at each step in the process. As outlined in Chapter 2, customers' expectations range across a spectrum—referred to as the zone of tolerance—from desired service (an ideal) to a threshold level of merely adequate service.

Those aspects of the service process that require the attention of management (i.e., attributes that are most important to customers and most difficult to manage) should be the basis for setting standards. Service providers should design sufficiently high standards for each step to satisfy and even delight customers. If that's not possible, then they will need to modify customer expectations. These standards might include time parameters, the script for a technically correct performance, and prescriptions for appropriate style and demeanor. Our restaurant blueprint shows key standards for each touch point.

As the axiom goes, "What is not measured is not managed." Standards must be expressed in ways that permit objective measurement. Process performance needs to be monitored against standards, and compliance targets need to be determined. Even soft and intangible (but important) service attributes need to be made measurable. This is often achieved by using service process indicators that try to capture the essence of these attributes or at least approximate them. For example, in a retail banking context, the attribute "responsiveness" can be operationalized as "processing time to approve a

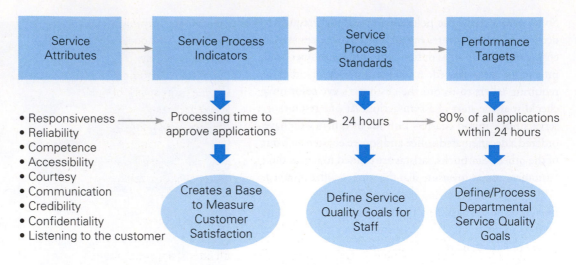

Figure 8.10 Setting standards and targets for customer-service processes.

loan application." Service standards are then ideally based on customer expectations and policy decisions (which in turn are based on how these expectations can be met cost effectively). In cases where standards do not meet customer needs, expectations need to be managed.

Finally, performance targets define specific process and/or team performance targets (e.g., 80% of all applications within 24 hours) for which team leaders will be held accountable. Figure 8.10 shows the relationship between indicators, standards, and targets.

The distinction between standards and performance targets is important. The setting of standards and targets is highly sensitive and political because they are subsequently used for evaluating staff, branch, and/or team performance. By separating standards and targets, the firm can be "hard" about reflecting customer expectations in the performance standards but "realistic" about what the teams can actually deliver.

In practice, management can stand firm on setting the right standards (i.e., according to customer needs and expectations) and go easy on negotiating performance targets that reflect operational reality (i.e., it may not be possible to consistently achieve the standards). This separation of standards and targets can be important for three reasons. First, the correct (i.e., customer-driven) standards get communicated to and internalized by the organization. Second, when implemented well, process owners and department or branch managers can raise their performance levels over time to bring them more in line with customer expectations. Third, it facilitates buy-in and support for the (tough) service standards as it also provides latitude to management and staff.[7]

 LO 6

Appreciate the importance of consumer perceptions and emotions in service process design.

Consumer Perceptions and Emotions in Service Process Design[8]

Service processes need to be designed with emotional intelligence. Sriram Dasu and Richard Chase have highlighted key principles for sequencing service encounters based on their in-depth research on designing emotionally smart processes:[9]

1) **Start strong.** Service firms should ideally try to provide consistently high performances at each step. However, in reality, many service performances are inconsistent. Nevertheless, it is always important to start and finish strong. The opening scenes of a service drama are particularly important because customers' first impressions can affect their evaluations of quality during later stages of the service delivery. Their perceptions of their service experiences tend to be cumulative. If a couple of things go badly at the outset, customers may simply walk out. Even if they stay, they may now be looking for other things that aren't quite right. On the other hand, if the first few steps go really well, their zone of tolerance may increase. Thus, they may be more willing to overlook minor mistakes later during the service performance.

2) **Build an improving trend.** People in general like things to keep moving in a positive direction. Thus, a service encounter that is perceived to start at an adequate level but then builds in quality is generally rated better than one that starts well but declines at the end.

3) **Create a peak.** If you want to improve the perception of your service, you are better off making one step sensational and the other steps merely adequate. Customers tend to remember the peak! For example, Sea World in Orlando, Florida, could spend a lot more money on various attractions, but the thing that counts—the signature Shamu the Whale show—must be done to perfection.

4) **Get bad experiences over with early.** Unpleasant news (e.g., about delays), discomfort (e.g., as part of medical treatments), unpleasant tasks (e.g., completing registration forms), and unavoidable long waits should occur early during the service experience. This way, customers avoid the dread of pain or aggravation, and the negative aspects of their experience are less likely to dominate the memory of the entire service encounter.

5) **Segment pleasure, combine pain.** Since an event is perceived as longer when it is segmented or broken up into separate steps, service processes should extend the feeling of pleasurable experiences by dividing them. They should also combine unpleasant experiences into a single event as far as possible.

6) **Finish strong.** Performance standards should not be allowed to fall off towards the end of service delivery. Rather, the finish should be strong. Think of rock concerts, which always conclude with big hits, or comedians, who save their best jokes for the end. Fireworks close with an amazing array of colors lighting the sky and a deafening finale. Ending on a high note is an important aspect of every service encounter, even if it is just a cheerful and affirmative: "Have a nice day!"

SERVICE PROCESS REDESIGN

Service processes become outdated over time as changes in technology, customer needs, added service features, new service offerings, and even changes in legislation make existing processes inefficient or irrelevant. There are many symptoms that indicate the processes are not working well and need to be redesigned. They include:

▶ A lot of information exchange with the customer and between different service units (implying that the available data is not useful)

▶ A high ratio of checking or control activities to value-adding activities

LO 7

Explain the necessity for service process redesign.

- Increased processing of exceptions
- Growing number of customer complaints about inconvenient and unnecessary procedures

LO 8

Understand how service process redesign can help improve both service quality and productivity.

Service Process Redesign Should Improve Both Quality and Productivity

Managers in charge of service process redesign projects should look for opportunities to achieve a quantum leap in both productivity and service quality. Examining service blueprints is an important step in identifying such opportunities and redesigning the ways in which tasks are performed. Redesign efforts typically focus on achieving the following four key objectives. Ideally, all four should be achieved simultaneously.

1) Reduced number of service failures

2) Reduced cycle time from customer initiation of a service process to its completion

3) Enhanced productivity

4) Increased customer satisfaction

Service process redesign often involves reconstruction, rearrangement, and substitution of service processes. These efforts typically include:[10]

- **Examining the service blueprint with key stakeholders.** By closely examining blueprints of existing services, managers can identify problems in a service process and discover ways to improve it. Each of the stakeholders in a process (i.e., customers, front-line employees, support staff, and IT teams) should be invited to review the blueprint with the purpose of brainstorming for ideas on how to improve the process. This involves identification of missing or unnecessary steps and changes in sequence. Stakeholders also highlight ways in which developments in information technology, equipment, and new methods offer advantages.

  Avis, for example, conducts research each year on the factors that are most important to people who rent cars. The company breaks down the car rental process into more than 100 incremental steps, including making reservations, finding the pick-up counter, getting to the car, driving it, returning it, paying the bill, and so forth. As Avis knows customers' key concerns, it claims it can quickly identify ways to improve their satisfaction while also driving the firm's productivity.

- **Eliminating non-value-adding steps.** Often, activities at the front-end and back-end processes of services can be streamlined with the goal of focusing on the benefit-producing part of the service encounter. For example, a customer wanting to rent a car is not interested in filling out forms, processing payment, or waiting for the returned car to be checked. Service redesign tries to eliminate such non-value-adding steps (from the customer's perspective). Some car rental companies now allow customers to rent a car online and pick it up from a designated car park (a large electronic board lists the name of the customer, the car, and the parking lot number). The key is in the car, and the only interaction with a car rental employee is at the exit of the car park, where the customer's driving license is checked and the contract signed (with the customer confirming the condition of the car). When returning the car, the customer simply parks it in an allocated area at the rental company's car park. The key is dropped into a safe deposit box, and the final bill is deducted from a pre-determined customer credit card and e-mailed to the billing address. The customer does not have to come into contact with service personnel.

► **Addressing bottlenecks in the process.**[11] Bottlenecks and resulting customer waits are a feature of many service processes. It is the step in the service process with the lowest throughput rate that determines the effective capacity of the entire process. For an efficient process, all steps should ideally have the same capacity so that none of the stations forms a bottleneck or is idle. The objective is to design a balanced process in which the processing times of all the steps are approximately the same, and consumers "flow" smoothly through the process without having to wait at any one step.

Determining the processing time and capacity for each step in the blueprint allows one to see the actual capacity available at each step. One way to identify bottlenecks is to simply observe where customers have to wait. Once bottlenecks have been identified, management can address them by devoting more and better resources and/or redesigning the process and its tasks to increase capacity (see also Chapter 9, "Balancing Demand and Capacity," for other ways to manage service capacity).

► **Shifting to self-service.** Significant productivity and sometimes even service quality gains can be achieved by increasing self-service (Figure 8.11). For example, many restaurants replace their menu with an iPad so that customers can perform self-service ordering. An app shows all the delicious food available with lots of drill-down information if desired. It also allows diners to send their orders directly to the kitchen. At the back end, the app links to the restaurant's point-of-sale system to complete the order. Many apps also have features that up-sell menu items and combine dishes with recommended side orders.

Although not self-service in the traditional sense, robots will increasingly be deployed to serve customers. Customers need to learn how to feel comfortable while interacting with robots just as they learned to interact with ATMs and websites. For example, the Bank of Tokyo-Mitsubishi UFJ in Tokyo will use robots to greet their customers, answer basic questions, and guide them to the correct service counter. Nao, a 58-cm-tall robot model, can analyze customers' facial expressions and behaviors and answer most basic questions related to customer service. According to bank spokesman Kazunobu Takahara: "We can ramp up communication with our customers by adding a tool like this." The robot costs around $8,000, a fraction of the costs of having front-line employees performing these tasks. It has been programmed to speak 19 languages in preparation for the Tokyo 2020 Olympics![12]

Figure 8.11 Nao will soon greet customers at the Bank of Tokyo-Mitsubishi UFJ. It speaks several languages and can read the facial expressions of customers.

LO 9

Understand the levels of customer participation in service processes.

LO 10

Be familiar with the concept of service customers as "co-creators" and the implications of this perspective.

CUSTOMER PARTICIPATION IN SERVICE PROCESSES

Service process redesign for productivity and efficiency often requires customers to become more involved in the delivery of the service. Blueprinting helps to specify the role of customers and identify the extent of contact between them and service providers.

Customers as Service Co-Creators

Customer participation refers to the actions and resources supplied by customers during service production, including mental, physical, and even emotional inputs.[13] Some degree of customer participation in service delivery is unavoidable in many services involving real-time contact between customers and providers.

Increasingly, customers are viewed as service co-creators. Value is created when the customer and service providers interact during the production, consumption, and delivery of the service. This means that customers are actively participating in the process, and that their performance affects the quality and productivity of output. Therefore, service firms need to look at how customers can contribute effectively to value creation. Firms also need to educate and train customers so that they have the skills and the motivation needed to perform their tasks well.[14]

Reducing Service Failures Caused by Customers

Stephen Tax, Mark Colgate, and David Bowen found that customers cause about one-third of all service problems.[15] Therefore, firms should focus on preventing customer failures. This is discussed in Service Insights 8.1.

Figure 8.12 Doctor–patient relationships must be mutually cooperative for effective treatment.

LO 11

Understand the factors that lead customers to accept or reject new self-service technologies (SSTs).

SELF-SERVICE TECHNOLOGIES

The ultimate form of involvement in service production is for customers to undertake a specific activity themselves, using facilities or systems provided by the service supplier. In effect, the customer's time and effort replace those of a service employee. In the case of internet- and app-based services, customers even provide their own terminals (Figure 8.13).

Consumers are faced with an array of self-service technologies (SSTs) that allow them to produce a service without the direct involvement of service employees. SSTs include automated banking terminals, self-service scanning at supermarket checkouts, self-service gasoline pumps, automated telephone systems such as phone banking, automated hotel checkout, self-service train ticketing machines (Figure 8.14), and numerous internet- and app-based services.

A Three-Step Approach to Preventing Customer Failures

Fail-safe methods (or poka-yokes) need to be designed not only for employees but also for customers, especially when customers participate actively in the creation and delivery processes. Customer poka-yokes focus on preparing the customer for the encounter (including getting them to bring the right materials for the transaction and to arrive on time, if applicable), understanding and anticipating their role in the service transaction, and selecting the correct service or transaction.

A good way is to use the following three-step approach to prevent customer-generated failures:

1 Systematically collect information on the most common failure points.

2 Identify their root causes. It is important to note that an employee's explanation may not be the true cause. Instead, the cause must be investigated from the customer's point of view. Human causes of customer failure include lack of required skills, failure to understand their role, and insufficient preparation. Some processes are complex and unclear. Other causes may include weaknesses in the design of the servicescape or self-service technology (e.g., "unfriendly" user machines and websites).

3 Create strategies to prevent the failures that have been identified. The five strategies listed below may need to be combined for maximum effectiveness.

(a) **Redesign the customer involvement in the process.** (e.g., redesign customers' role as well as processes). For example, aircraft lavatory doors must be locked in order for the lights to be switched on. ATMs use beepers so that customers do not forget to retrieve their cards at the end of their transaction. In future, customer identification with cards and PINs at ATMs is likely to be replaced by biometric identification (e.g., retina reading combined with voice recognition). This will design the problems of lost cards or forgotten PINs out of the service process and increase customer convenience.

(b) **Use technology.** For example, some hospitals use automated systems that send short text messages or e-mails to patients to confirm and remind them of their appointments and offer information on how an appointment may be rescheduled if required.

(c) **Manage customer behavior.** For example, one may print dress-code requests on invitations, send reminders of dental appointments, or print user guidelines on customer cards (e.g., "Please have your account and PIN ready before calling our service reps").

(d) **Encourage "customer citizenship."** For example, customers can help one another to prevent failure, as in weight-loss programs.

(e) **Improve the servicescape.** For example, many firms forget that customers need user-friendly directional signs to help them find their way around, failing which they might become frustrated.

Helping customers to avoid failure can become a source of competitive advantage, especially when companies increasingly use self-service technologies.

SOURCE

Source: Based on Stephen S. Tax, Mark Colgate, and David E. Bowen, "How to Prevent Customers from Failing," *MIT Sloan Management Review* 47 (Spring 2006), pp. 30–38.

Many companies have developed strategies to encourage customers to serve themselves through the internet and mobile apps. They hope to divert customers from using more expensive alternatives such as face-to-face contact with employees, use of intermediaries such as brokers and travel agents, or voice-to-voice telephony.

Increasingly, customers also help each other in peer-to-peer problem solving. This is facilitated by online brand communities and firm-hosted platforms. Research has shown that encouraging customers to help themselves by posting their questions and to help others by responding to peer questions reduces the resources a firm has to expend on traditional customer-support services. Promoting peer-to-peer customer interactions is a strategic lever to increase the efficiency and effectiveness of a firm's support service.[16]

"I'm setting up a Facebook page, but how do I sniff my friends over the Internet?"

Figure 8.13 Many internet-based services require customers to serve themselves.

Customer Benefits and Adoption of Self-Service Technology

Significant investments in time and money are required for firms to design, implement, and manage SSTs. Thus, it's critical for service marketers to understand how consumers decide between using an SST option and relying on a human provider. Multiple attitudes drive customer intentions to use a specific SST. These include overall attitudes toward related service technologies; attitudes toward the specific service firm and its employees; and the overall perceived benefits, convenience, costs, and ease of using an SST. Firms need to recognize that SSTs present both advantages and disadvantages for their customers. Key advantages of using SSTs include:[17]

▶ Greater convenience, including time savings, faster service, flexibility of timing (e.g., through 24/7 availability), and flexibility of location (e.g., many ATMs). Customers love SSTs when the latter can bail them out of difficult situations, often because SST machines are conveniently located and accessible 24/7.

▶ Greater control over service delivery, more information, and higher perceived level of customization.

▶ Lower prices and fees.

Figure 8.14 Tourists appreciate easy-to-understand instructions when traveling abroad and making payment for train tickets.

Success at the customer interface requires an understanding of what target customers want from an interaction. Sometimes, a well-designed SST can deliver better service than a human being. Many SSTs enable users to get detailed information and complete transactions faster than they could through face-to-face encounters or telephone contact.

However, there are always some consumers who feel uncomfortable with SSTs and prefer to deal with people. Even after an initial trial, not all customers will continue using an SST. It is important that the first trial is satisfying, so that customers feel confident about using the SST effectively in the future. If this is not the case, customers are likely to fall back on traditional services provided by front-line employees.

Customer Disadvantages and Barriers of Adoption of Self-Service Technology

Customers hate SSTs when they fail. Users get angry if self-service machines are out of service, PINs are rejected, websites are down, or tracking numbers do not work. Even when SSTs do work, customers may get frustrated by poorly designed technologies that make service processes difficult to understand and use. A common complaint is difficulty in navigating one's way around a website or completing online registrations and forms that keep rejecting their entries (Figure 8.15).

The challenge for the service firm is to design SSTs to be as "idiot proof" as possible, mitigate common customer errors, use customer poka-yokes, and even design service recovery processes for customers so that they can help themselves if things go wrong.[18]

Figure 8.15 Customers feel frustrated when they get stuck in poorly designed online self-service processes.

Assessing and Improving SSTs

Mary Jo Bitner suggests that managers should put their firms' SSTs to the test by asking the following basic questions:[19]

▶ **Does the SST work reliably?** Firms must make sure that SSTs work as promised and that the design is user-friendly for customers. Southwest Airlines' online ticketing has set a high standard for simplicity and reliability. It boasts the highest percentage of online ticket sales among all airlines—clear evidence of customer acceptance.

▶ **Is the SST better than the inter-personal alternative?** If an SST doesn't save time and money or provide ease of access, customers will continue to use the familiar inter-personal choice. Amazon.com's success reflects its efforts to create a highly personalized yet efficient alternative to visiting a retail store.[20] Today, it has become the most preferred way of browsing and buying books. The rapid growth of e-books will only accelerate this trend.

▶ **Are there systems in place to recover the service if the SST fails?** It's critical for firms to provide systems, structures, and recovery technologies that will enable prompt service recovery when things go wrong (Figure 8.16). Supermarkets that have installed self-service checkout lanes usually assign one employee to monitor the lanes. This practice combines security with customer assistance. In telephone-based service systems, well-designed voicemail menus include an option for customers to reach a customer-service representative.

SERVICE INSIGHTS 8.2

Managing Customers' Reluctance to Change

Customer resistance to changes in familiar processes and long-established behavior patterns can thwart attempts to improve productivity and even quality. The following six steps can help smooth the path of change.

1   **Develop customer trust.** It's more difficult to introduce productivity-related changes when people are distrustful of the initiator, as they often are in the case of large, seemingly impersonal institutions. Customers' willingness to accept change may be closely related to the degree of goodwill they bear towards the firm.

2   **Understand customers' habits and expectations.** People often get into a routine of using a particular service, with certain steps being taken in a specific sequence. In effect, they have their own individual service script or flowchart in mind. Innovations that disrupt deeply rooted routines are likely to face resistance. Aligning new processes more closely with customers' habits and expectations enhances the chances of success.

3.   **Pre-test new procedures and equipment.** To determine probable customer response to new procedures and equipment, marketing researchers can employ concept and laboratory testing and/or field testing. If service personnel are going to be replaced by automatic equipment, it's essential to create designs that customers of almost all types and backgrounds will find easy to use. Even the phrasing of instructions needs careful thought. Unclear or complex instructions may discourage customers with poor reading skills.

4.   **Publicize the benefits.** Introduction of self-service equipment or procedures requires consumers to perform part of the task themselves. Although this additional "work" may be associated with such benefits as extended service hours, time savings, and (in some instances) monetary savings, these benefits are not necessarily obvious and have to be promoted.

5.   **Teach customers to use innovations and promote trial.** The firm should assign service personnel to demonstrate new equipment and answer questions. Providing reassurance as well as educational assistance is a key element in gaining acceptance for new procedures and technology. The costs of such demonstration programs can be spread across multiple outlets by moving staff members from one site to another if the innovation is rolled out sequentially across the various locations. For web-based innovations, firms can consider providing access to e-mail, chat, or even telephone-based assistance. Promotional incentives such as price discounts, loyalty points, or lucky draws may also help to stimulate trial.

6.   **Monitor performance and continue to seek improvements.** Introducing quality and productivity improvements is an ongoing process, especially for SSTs. It is important to monitor utilization, frequency of transaction failures (and their fail points), and customer complaints over time. Service managers have to work hard for the continuous improvement of SSTs so that they can achieve their full potential and are not allowed to flag.

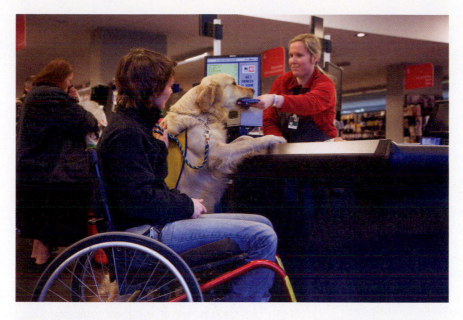

Figure 8.16 Departmental stores normally have employees on standby near self-checkout lanes to assist if there are problems.

Managing Customers' Reluctance to Change

If a firm seeks to increase customer participation in a service process or shift the process entirely to self-service using SSTs, it must take steps to change customer behavior. This is often a difficult task, as customers resent being forced to use SSTs. Service Insights 8.2 identifies ways of addressing customer resistance to change, particularly when the innovation is a radical one. Once the nature of a change has been decided, marketing communications can help prepare customers for the change by explaining its rationale and benefits. Customers must also be educated on what they will need to do differently in the future.

▶ **LO 12**

Know how to manage customers' reluctance to change their behaviors in service processes, including the adoption of SSTs.

PART III

LO 1 ▶ From the customer's perspective, services are experiences. From the organization's perspective, services are the processes that are designed and managed to create the desired experience for customers. Processes are the underlying architecture of services.

LO 2 ▶ Flowcharting is a technique for displaying the nature and sequence of the different steps involved in delivering a service to the customer. It is a simple way to visualize the total customer service experience. Blueprinting is a more complex form of flowcharting that specifies in detail how service processes are constructed, including what is visible to the customer and what goes on in the back office. Blueprints facilitate the detailed design and redesign of customer service processes.

LO 3 ▶ A blueprint typically has the following design elements:

o *Front-stage activities* that map the overall customer experience, the desired inputs and outputs, and the sequence in which delivery of that output should take place.

o *Physical evidence* that the customer can see and use to assess service quality.

o *Line of visibility* that clearly separates what customers experience and see front stage from the back-stage processes customers can't see.

o *Back-stage activities* that must be performed to support a particular front-stage step.

o *Support processes* that are typically provided by information systems and *supplies* that are needed for front- and back-stage activities.

o *Fail points* at which there is a risk of things going wrong and affecting service quality. Fail points should be designed out of a process (e.g., via the use of poka-yokes), and firms should have back-up plans for failures that are not preventable.

o Common *customer waits* in the process, including potential points of excessive waits. These should preferably be designed out of the process. If that is not possible, firms can implement strategies to make waits less unpleasant.

o *Service standards and targets* that reflect customer expectations. These should be established for each activity. They include specific times to be set for the completion of each task and the acceptable wait between two consecutive customer activities.

LO 4 ▶ A good blueprint identifies fail points where things can go wrong. Fail-safe methods, also called poka-yokes, can then be designed to prevent such failures (by both employees and customers) and/or ensure service recovery. A three-step approach can be used to develop poka-yokes:

o Collect information on the most common fail points.

o Identify the root causes of those failures.

o Create strategies to prevent the failures that have been identified.

LO 5 ▶ Service blueprints help to set service standards that are high enough to satisfy customers. As standards need to be measurable, subjective or intangible service attributes must also be operationalized. This can often be achieved through service process indicators that capture the essence of these attributes or at least approximate them. Once standards have been decided, performance targets can be set.

LO 6 ▶ Service processes need to be designed with emotional intelligence. Key principles involved in the sequencing of services are:

o Start strong. The opening scenes of a service drama are particularly important, because customers' first impressions can affect their evaluations of quality during the later stages of service delivery.

o Build an improving trend. All things being equal, it is better to start a little lower and build higher than to start a little higher and fall off at the end.

o Create a peak. Customers tend to remember the peak!

o Get bad experiences over with early. If this is done, negative aspects of the experience are less likely to dominate the customer's memory of the entire service encounter.

o Segment pleasure, combine pain. Service processes should extend the feeling of pleasurable experiences by dividing them. Unpleasant experiences should be combined into a single event as far as possible.

o Finish strong. Ending on a high note is an important aspect of every service encounter, even if it is just a cheerful and affirmative "Have a nice day."

LO 7 ▶ Changes in technology, customer needs, and service offerings require customer service processes to be redesigned periodically. Symptoms indicating that a process is not working well include:

o A lot of information exchange (implying that the data available is not useful)

o A high ratio of checking or control activities to value-adding activities

o Increased processing of exceptions

o Growing numbers of customer complaints about inconvenient and unnecessary procedures

LO 8 ▶ Service process redesign efforts aim to:

o Reduce the number of service failures

o Reduce cycle time

o Improve productivity

o Increase customer satisfaction

Service process redesign involves the reconstruction, rearrangement, or substitution of service processes. These efforts typically include:

o Examining the service blueprint with key stakeholders (Customers, front-line employees, support staff, and IT teams are invited to review the blueprint and brainstorm for ideas on how to improve the process.)

o Eliminating non-value adding steps

o Reducing bottlenecks and balancing process capacity

o Shifting to self-service

LO 9 ▶ Customer participation is required in many service processes and has to be managed.

LO 10 ▶ Customers are often involved in service processes as co-producers and can therefore be thought of as "service co-creators." Their performance affects the quality and productivity of output. Therefore, service firms need to educate and train customers so that they have the skills and motivation needed to perform their tasks well.

LO 11 ▶ The ultimate form of customer involvement is self-service. Most people welcome SSTs that offer more convenience (i.e., time savings, faster service, 24/7 availability, and more locations); cost savings; and better control, information, and customization. However, poorly designed technology and inadequate education in how to use SSTs can cause customers to reject them. Three basic questions can be used to assess an SST's potential for success and to improve it:

o Does the SST work reliably?

o Is the SST better for customers than other service delivery alternatives?

o Are there systems in place to recover the service if the SST fails?

LO 12 ▶ Increasing the customers' participation level in a service process or shifting the process entirely to self-service requires the firm to change customer behavior. There are six steps to guide this process and reduce customer reluctance to change:

o Develop customer trust.

o Understand customers' habits and expectations.

o Pre-test new procedures and equipment.

o Publicize the benefits of changes.

o Teach customers to use innovations and promote trial.

o Monitor performance and continue to seek improvements.

PART III

UNLOCK YOUR LEARNING

These keywords are found within the sections of each Learning Objective (LO). They are integral to understanding the services marketing concepts taught in each section. Having a firm grasp of these keywords and how they are used is essential to helping you do well on your course, and in the real and very competitive marketing scene out there.

LO 1
1 Service processes
2 Service operating systems
3 Value propositions

LO 2
1 Flowcharting
2 Blueprinting
3 Line of interaction
4 Front-stage actions
5 Service initiation
6 Back-stage systems

LO 3
1 Pre-process stage
2 Core product
3 Customer waits
4 Drama
5 Excessive waits
6 Fail points
7 In-process stage
8 Post-process stage

9 OTSU
10 Line of visibility
11 Service blueprints
12 Service standards
13 Servicescape
14 Supplementary services
15 Supplies
16 Support processes
17 Targets

LO 4
1 Fail-proofing
2 Poka-yokes
3 Total Quality Management

LO 5
1 Customer expectations
2 Process performance
3 Service process indicators
4 Zone of tolerance
5 Touch points

LO 6
1 Consumer perceptions
2 Peak
3 Emotions
4 Service process design
5 Improving trend

LO 7
1 Control activities
2 Value-adding activities
3 Information exchange
4 Exceptions
5 Service process redesign
6 Customer complaints

LO 8
1 Cycle time
2 Robots
3 Non-value-adding steps
4 Productivity
5 Self-service
6 Service quality
7 Stakeholders
8 Bottlenecks

LO 9 1 Customer participation

2 Contact

 LO 10 1 Co-creators

2 Customer failures

3 Customer citizenship

4 Customer behavior

5 Root causes

6 Value creation

7 Technology

 LO 11 1 Peer-to-peer problem solving

2 Convenience

3 Online brand communities

4 Service recovery processes

5 Firm-hosted platforms

6 App-based services

7 Internet-based services

8 Customer-support services

9 Self-service technologies

10 Perceived benefits

LO 12 1 Customer resistance to change

2 Customer trust

3 Educational assistance

4 Innovations

5 Promotional incentives

6 Demonstration programs

7 Field testing

8 Concept and laboratory testing

PART III

How well do you know the language of services marketing? Quiz yourself!

⚠ **Not for the academically faint-of-heart**

For each keyword you are able to recall without referring to earlier pages, give yourself a point (and a pat on the back). Tally your score at the end and see if you earned the right to be called—a *services marketeer*.

SCORE

0 – 16	Services Marketing is done a great disservice.
17 – 32	The midnight oil needs to be lit, pronto.
33 – 48	I know what you *didn't* do all semester.
49 – 64	A close shave with success.
65 – 80	Now, go forth and market.
81 – 85	There should be a marketing concept named after you.

Review Questions

1. How does blueprinting help us to better understand the service process from the perspectives of the key actors (i.e., customers and the employees from different service departments and functional areas) in a serviced process?

2. What are the typical design elements of a service blueprint?

3. How can fail-safe methods be used to reduce service failures?

4. Why is it important to develop service standards and targets?

5. How can consumer perceptions and emotions be considered in the design of service processes?

6. Why is periodic service process redesign necessary? What are the typical symptoms that indicate a service process is not working well?

7. What are the four key objectives of service process redesign?

8. What efforts are typically involved in service process redesign?

9. Why does the customer's role as a co-creator need to be designed into service processes?

10. Explain what factors make customers like and dislike self-service technologies (SSTs).

11. How can you test whether an SST has the potential to be successful, and what can a firm do to increase its chances of customer adoption?

WORK YOUR SERVICES MARKETING

Application Exercises

1. Review the blueprint of the restaurant visit in Figure 8.6. Identify several possible "OTSUs" ("opportunity to screw up") for each step in the front-stage process. Consider possible causes underlying each potential failure, and suggest ways to eliminate or minimize these problems.

2. Prepare a blueprint for a service with which you are familiar. On completion, consider (a) the tangible cues or indicators of quality from the customers' perspective (keeping the line of visibility in mind); (b) whether all steps in the process are necessary; (c) the extent to which standardization is possible and advisable throughout the process; (d) the location of potential fail points and how they could be designed out of the process; (e) what service recovery procedures could be introduced; and (f) the potential measures of process performance.

3. Think about what happens in a doctor's office when a patient comes for a physical examination. How much participation is needed from the patient in order for the process to work smoothly? If a patient refuses to cooperate, how can that affect the process? What can the doctor do in advance to ensure that the patient cooperates in the delivery of the process?

4. Observe supermarket shoppers who use self-service checkout lanes, and compare them to those who use the services of a checker. What differences do you observe? How many of those conducting self-service scanning appear to run into difficulties, and how do they resolve their problems?

5. Identify three situations in which you use self-service delivery. For each situation, explain your motivation for using self-service delivery rather than having service personnel do it for you.

6. What actions could a bank take to encourage more customers to transact via the internet, apps, and ATMs instead of visiting a branch?

7. Identify one website that is exceptionally user-friendly and another that is not. What are the factors that make for a satisfying user experience in the first instance and a frustrating one in the second? Specify recommendations for improvements in the second website.

ENDNOTES

1. www.patientvisitredesign.com, accessed April 30, 2015.

2. Alex Rawson, Ewan Duncan, and Conor Jones, "The Truth about Customer Experience: Touchpoints Matter, but It's the Full Journey That Really Counts," *Harvard Business Review* 91, no. 9 (2013): 90–98.

3. G. Lynn Shostack, "Designing Services That Deliver," *Harvard Business Review* (January–February 1984): 133–39; Jane Kingman-Brundage, "The ABCs of Service System Blueprinting," in M. J. Bitner and L. A. Crosby (eds.), *Designing a Winning Service Strategy* (Chicago: American Marketing Association, 1989): 30-33; Lia Patrício, Raymond P. Fisk, and João Falcãe Cunha, "Designing Multi-Interface Service Experiences: The Service Experience Blueprint," *Journal of Service Research* 10, no. 4 (2008): 318–334.

4. David Maister, now President of Maister Associates, coined the term OTSU while teaching at Harvard Business School.

5. For descriptions of how poka-yokes can be used to improve business operations see: Sameer Kumar, Brett Hudson, and Josie Lowry, "Consumer Purchase Process Improvements in E-tailing Operations," *International Journal of Productivity and Performance Management* 59, no. 4 (2010): 388–403.

6. This section is based in part on: Richard B. Chase and Douglas M. Stewart, "Make Your Service Fail-Safe," *Sloan Management Review* 35 (Spring 1994): 35–44.

7. This section was adapted from: Jochen Wirtz and Monica Tomlin, "Institutionalizing Customer-Driven Learning through Fully Integrated Customer Feedback Systems," *Managing Service Quality* 10, no. 4 (2000): 205–215.

8. Parts of this section were based on: Sriram Dasu and Richard B. Chase, *The Customer Service Solution: Managing Emotions, Trust, and Control to Win Your Customer's Business* (New York: McGraw Hill, 2013). This book provides an excellent overview on designing service processes with emotional intelligence.

9. Adapted from: Dasu and Chase, *The Customer Service Solution*, 134–135. We added the item "start strong" based on: Richard B. Chase and Sriram Dasu, "Experience Psychology: A Proposed New Subfield of Service Management," *Journal of Service Management* 25, no. 5 (2014): 574–577.

10. This section is partially based on: Leonard L. Berry and Sandra K. Lampo, "Teaching an Old Service New Tricks: The Promise of Service Redesign," *Journal of Service Research* 2, no. 3 (2000): 265–275.

11. Parts of this section were adapted from: Robert Johnston, Graham Clark, and Michael Shulver, *Service Operations Management: Improving Service Delivery*, 4th ed. (Essex, United Kingdom: Pearson Education, 2012).

12. Atsuko Fukase, "Robots to Greet Customers at Japanese Bank," *The Wall Street Journal*, January 13, 2015; http://blogs.wsj.com/japanrealtime/2015/01/13/robots-to-greet-customers-at-japanese-bank, accessed May 3, 2015.

13. Amy Risch Rodie and Susan Schultz Klein, "Customer Participation in Services Production and Delivery," in T. A. Schwartz and D. Iacobucci (eds.) *Handbook of Service Marketing and Management* (Thousand Oaks, CA: Sage Publications, 2000): 111–125.

14. Stephen L. Vargo and Robert F. Lusch, "Service-Dominant Logic: Continuing the Evolution," *Journal of the Academy of Marketing Science* 36, no. 1 (2008): 1–10.

15. Stephen S. Tax, Mark Colgate, and David E. Bowen, "How to Prevent Customers from Failing," *MIT Sloan Management Review* 47 (Spring 2006): 30–38.

16. Sterling A. Bone, Paul W. Fombelle, Kristal R. Ray, and Katherine N. Lemon, "How Customer Participation in B2B Peer-to-Peer Problem-Solving Communities Influences the Need for Traditional Customer Service," *Journal of Service Research* 18, no. 1 (2015): 23–38.

17. Pratibha A. Dabholkar, "Consumer Evaluations of New Technology-Based Self-Service Options: An Investigation of Alternative Models of Service Quality," *International Journal of Research in Marketing* 13 (1996): 29–51; David G. Mick and Susan Fournier, "Paradoxes of

Technology: Consumer Cognizance, Emotions, and Coping Strategies," *Journal of Consumer Research* 25 (September 1998): 123–43; Mary Jo Bitner, Stephen W. Brown, and Matthew L. Meuter, "Technology Infusion in Service Encounters," *Journal of the Academy of Marketing Science* 28, no. 1 (2000): 138–149; Maria Åkesson, Bo Edvardsson, and Bård Tronvoll, "Customer Experience from a Self-Service System Perspective," *Journal of Service Management* 25, no. 5 (2014): 677–698.

18. Zhen Zhu, Cheryl Nakata, K. Sivakumar, and Dhruv Grewal, "Fix It or Leave It? Customer Recovery from Self-Service Technology Failures," *Journal of Retailing* 89, no. 1 (2013): 15–29.

19. Mary Jo Bitner, "Self-Service Technologies: What Do Customers Expect?" *Marketing Management* 10, no. 1 (Spring 2001): 10–11.

20. Brad Stone, *The Everything Store: Jeff Bezos and the Age of Amazon* (New York: Little, Brown and Company, 2013).

PART III

balancing DEMAND and CAPACITY

LEARNING OBJECTIVES (LOs)

By the end of this chapter, the reader should be able to:

▶ **LO 1** Know the different demand–supply situations that fixed-capacity firms may face.

▶ **LO 2** Describe the building blocks of dealing with the problem of fluctuating demand.

▶ **LO 3** Understand what is meant by *productive capacity* in a service context.

▶ **LO 4** Be familiar with the basic ways to *manage capacity*.

▶ **LO 5** Recognize that demand patterns vary by segment and examine how segment-specific variations in demand may be predicted.

▶ **LO 6** Be familiar with the five basic ways to *manage demand*.

▶ **LO 7** Understand how to use the marketing mix elements of price, product, place, and promotion to smooth out fluctuations in demand.

▶ **LO 8** Know how to use waiting lines and queuing systems to inventory demand.

▶ **LO 9** Understand how customers perceive waits and how waiting may be made less burdensome for them.

▶ **LO 10** Know how to use reservations systems to inventory demand.

▶ **LO 11** Be familiar with strategic approaches to utilize residual surplus capacity even after all other options of matching demand and capacity have been exhausted.

OPENING VIGNETTE

Summer on the Ski Slopes

Earlier, ski resorts used to shut down once the snow on the mountain slopes melted and skiing became impossible. The chair lifts stopped operating, the restaurants closed, and the lodges were locked and shuttered until the next winter. Over time, however, some ski operators recognized that a mountain offers summer pleasures as well. They began to keep lodges and restaurants open for hikers and picnickers. Some even built alpine slides—curving tracks in which wheeled toboggans could run from the top of the mountain to the base—and thus created demand for tickets on the ski lifts.

The arrival of the mountain biking craze created opportunities for equipment rentals as well as chair-lift rides. Killington Resort in Vermont has long encouraged summer visitors to ride to the summit, enjoy the view, and eat at the mountain-top restaurant. Now, it also runs a booking business in renting mountain bikes and related equipment (such as helmets). Beside the base lodge, where racks of skis are available for rent in winter, the summer visitor can now choose from rows of mountain bikes. Usually, bikers use the specially equipped chair lifts to carry their bikes to the top of the mountain and then ride them down marked trails. Once in a while, a biker reverses the process and chooses to ride up the mountain. Serious hikers do the same thing. They climb to the top through trails, get refreshments at the restaurant, and then take the chair lift back down to the base.

Most large ski resorts look for a variety of additional ways to attract guests to their hotels and rental homes during the summer. Mont Tremblant in Québec, for instance, is located beside an attractive lake. In addition to swimming and other water sports on the lake, the resort offers visitors activities like a championship golf course, tennis, rollerblading, and specially designed activities for children. Hikers and mountain bikers come to ride the lifts up the mountain. This is a wonderful example of how service development and marketing can generate demand for otherwise idle service capacity!

Hiking at Snowbird Ski and Summer Resort

Skiing at Snowbird Ski and Summer Resort

FLUCTUATIONS IN DEMAND THREATEN PROFITABILITY

Many services with limited capacity face wide swings in demand. In the opening vignette, this wide swing of demand is caused by seasonal change. This is a problem because service capacity usually cannot be kept aside for sale at a later date. The effective use of expensive productive capacity is one of the secrets of success in such businesses. The goal should be to utilize staff, labor, equipment, and facilities as *productively* as possible. By working with managers in operations and human resources, service marketers may be able to develop strategies to balance demand and capacity in ways that create benefits for customers and generate profits for the business at the same time. (Figure 9.1)

Figure 9.1 Keeping a balance between demand and capacity is a win-win for business owners and customers.

⊳ LO 1

Know the different demand–supply situations that fixed-capacity firms may face.

From Excess Demand to Excess Capacity

For fixed-capacity firms, the problem is a familiar one. "It's either feast or famine for us!" sighs the manager. "In peak periods, we're disappointing prospective customers by turning them away. And in low periods, our facilities are idle, our employees are standing around looking bored, and we're losing money." In other words, demand and supply are not in balance.

At any given moment, a fixed-capacity service may face one of four conditions (see Figure 9.2):

▶ *Excess demand*—The level of demand exceeds maximum available capacity, with the result that some customers are denied service and business is lost.

▶ *Demand exceeds optimum capacity*—No one is turned away, but conditions are crowded, service quality deteriorates, and customers are likely to feel dissatisfied.

▶ *Demand and supply are well balanced at the level of optimum capacity*—Staff and facilities are busy without being overworked, and customers receive good service without delays.

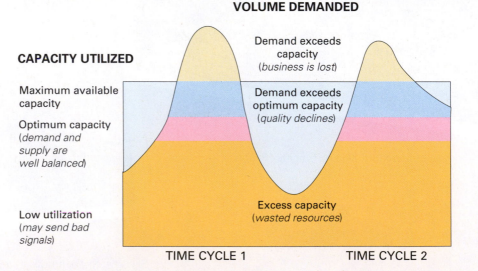

Figure 9.2 Implications of variations in demand relative to capacity.

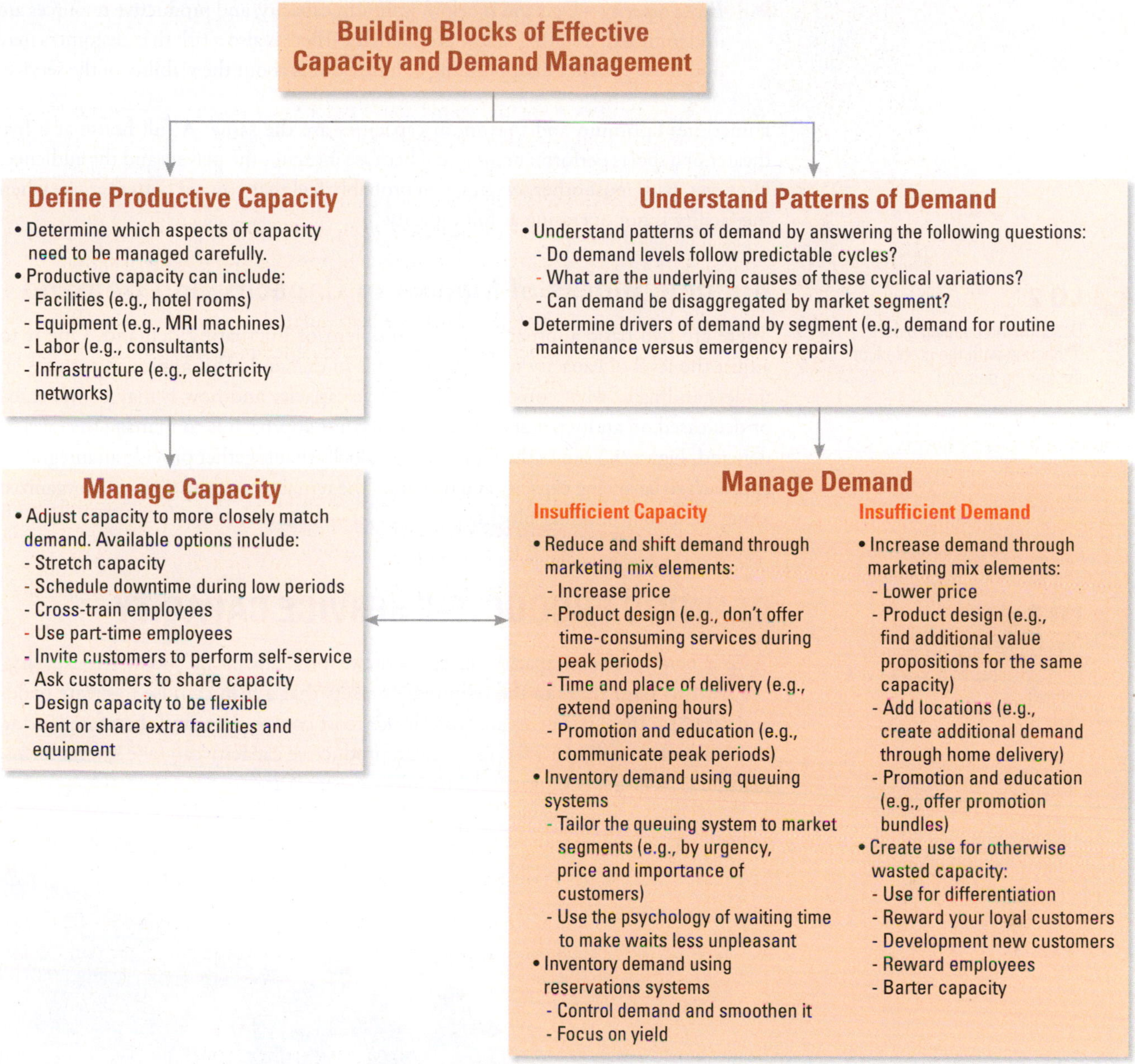

Building Blocks of Effective Capacity and Demand Management

Define Productive Capacity

- Determine which aspects of capacity need to be managed carefully.
- Productive capacity can include:
  - Facilities (e.g., hotel rooms)
  - Equipment (e.g., MRI machines)
  - Labor (e.g., consultants)
  - Infrastructure (e.g., electricity networks)

Understand Patterns of Demand

- Understand patterns of demand by answering the following questions:
  - Do demand levels follow predictable cycles?
  - What are the underlying causes of these cyclical variations?
  - Can demand be disaggregated by market segment?
- Determine drivers of demand by segment (e.g., demand for routine maintenance versus emergency repairs)

Manage Capacity

- Adjust capacity to more closely match demand. Available options include:
  - Stretch capacity
  - Schedule downtime during low periods
  - Cross-train employees
  - Use part-time employees
  - Invite customers to perform self-service
  - Ask customers to share capacity
  - Design capacity to be flexible
  - Rent or share extra facilities and equipment

Manage Demand

Insufficient Capacity

- Reduce and shift demand through marketing mix elements:
  - Increase price
  - Product design (e.g., don't offer time-consuming services during peak periods)
  - Time and place of delivery (e.g., extend opening hours)
  - Promotion and education (e.g., communicate peak periods)
- Inventory demand using queuing systems
  - Tailor the queuing system to market segments (e.g., by urgency, price and importance of customers)
  - Use the psychology of waiting time to make waits less unpleasant
- Inventory demand using reservations systems
  - Control demand and smoothen it
  - Focus on yield

Insufficient Demand

- Increase demand through marketing mix elements:
  - Lower price
  - Product design (e.g., find additional value propositions for the same capacity)
  - Add locations (e.g., create additional demand through home delivery)
  - Promotion and education (e.g., offer promotion bundles)
- Create use for otherwise wasted capacity:
  - Use for differentiation
  - Reward your loyal customers
  - Development new customers
  - Reward employees
  - Barter capacity

Figure 9.3 Building blocks of effective capacity and demand management.

▶ *Excess capacity*—Demand is below optimum capacity, and productive resources are underutilized, resulting in low productivity. There is also a risk that customers may find the experience disappointing or have doubts about the viability of the service.

Sometimes optimum and maximum capacities are the same. A full house at a live theater or a sports performance is grand because it excites the players and the audience. However, with most other services, you probably feel that you get better service when the facility is not operating at full capacity.

 LO 2

Describe the building blocks of dealing with the problem of fluctuating demand.

Building Blocks of Managing Capacity and Demand

There are two basic approaches to the problem of fluctuating demand. One is to adjust the level of capacity to meet variations in demand. This approach requires an understanding of what constitutes productive capacity and how it may be increased or decreased on an incremental basis. The second approach is to manage the level of demand. Figure 9.3 shows the four building blocks that together provide an integrative approach to balancing capacity and demand. The remainder of this chapter is organized along these four building blocks.

LO 3

Understand what is meant by *productive capacity* in a service context.

DEFINING PRODUCTIVE SERVICE CAPACITY

When we refer to capacity management, we implicitly mean "productive capacity." This term refers to the resources or assets that a firm can use to create goods and services. These resources are typically key cost components and therefore need to be managed carefully. In a service context, productive capacity can take several forms, including facilities, equipment, labor, and infrastructure.

Figure 9.4 Cinemas have to follow strict safety regulations on seating capacity in case of fire emergencies.

1. **Facilities** are critical to capacity management and can be divided into two categories—those that are designed to "hold" customers and those that hold goods. The former are used for people-processing services or mental-stimulus-processing services. Examples include medical clinics, hotels, passenger aircraft, and college classrooms. The primary capacity constraint is likely to be in terms of furnishings such as beds, rooms, or seats (Figure 9.4). The latter relate to facilities designed for storing or processing goods that either belong to customers or are being offered to them for sale. Examples include pipelines, warehouses, parking lots (Figure 9.5), and railroad freight wagons.

2. **Equipment** used to process people, possessions, or information may embrace a huge range of items and can be very situation specific. Diagnostic equipment (Figure 9.6), airport security detectors, and toll gates are among the many items whose absence in sufficient numbers can bring service to a crawl.

3. **Labor** is a key element of productive capacity in all high-contact services and many low-contact ones (Figure 9.7). If staffing levels are not sufficient, either customers are kept waiting or service becomes rushed.

4. **Infrastructure** capacity can also be critical. Many organizations require access to sufficient capacity in public or private infrastructure to be able to deliver quality service to their own customers. Capacity problems of this nature may include congested airways that lead to air-traffic restrictions on flights, traffic jams on major highways, and power failures.

MANAGING CAPACITY

▶ **LO 4**
Be familiar with the basic ways to *manage capacity*.

Although service firms may encounter capacity limitations due to varying demand, there are a number of ways in which capacity can be adjusted to reduce the problem.

Stretching Capacity Levels

Some capacity is elastic in its ability to absorb extra demand. Here, the same level of capacity is used to serve more people. For example, a subway car may normally offer 40 seats and allow standing room for another 60 passengers with enough handrail and floor space for all. Yet, at rush hour, perhaps up to 200 people can squeeze into the same subway car (albeit under sardine-like conditions) (Figure 9.8). Similarly, the capacity of service personnel can be stretched. Staff may be able to work at high levels of efficiency for short periods of time. However, they would quickly tire and begin to provide poor service if they had to work that fast for a prolonged period of time.

Another way to stretch capacity is to use facilities for longer periods. For example, some banks extend their opening hours during weekdays and even open on weekends. Universities may offer evening classes, weekend programs, and summer semester programs.

Lastly, the average amount of time customers (or their possessions) spend in process may be reduced. Sometimes, this is achieved by minimizing slack time. For example,

Figure 9.5 Car parks "store" customers' cars temporarily when they are out shopping.

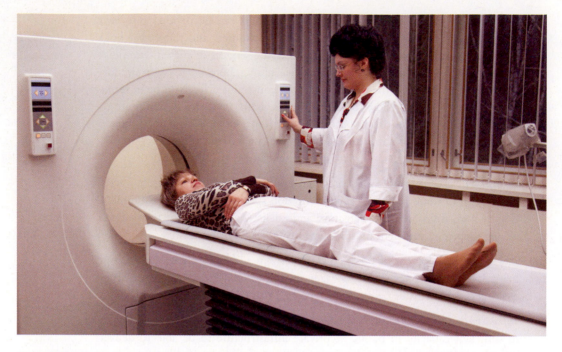

Figure 9.6 Productive capacity is expressed in terms of available hours for MRI scanning equipment.

a restaurant can buzz tables, seat arriving diners, and present menus fast. The bill can be presented promptly to a group of diners relaxing at their table after a meal. In other instances, it may be achieved by cutting back the level of service, such as by offering a simpler menu at busy times of the day.

Adjusting Capacity to Match Demand

Unlike stretching capacity, adjusting capacity involves tailoring the overall level of capacity to match variations in demand. There are several actions that managers can take to adjust capacity as needed.[1] These actions range from those that are easy to implement to those that are more difficult:

▶ *Schedule downtime during periods of low demand.* To make sure that 100% capacity is available during peak periods, maintenance, repair, and renovations should be conducted when demand is expected to be low. Employees should also take their holidays during such periods.

▶ *Cross-train employees.* Even when the service delivery system appears to be operating at full capacity, some physical elements—and their attendant employees—may be underutilized. If employees are cross-trained to perform a variety of tasks, they can be shifted to bottleneck points as needed to increase total capacity. In supermarkets, for instance, the manager may call on stockers to operate cash registers when lines become too long. Likewise, during slow periods, the cashiers may be asked to help stock shelves (Figure 9.9).

Figure 9.7 Restaurants need to ensure sufficient manpower to meet customer demands.

- *Use part-time employees.* Many organizations hire extra workers during their busiest periods. Examples include postal workers and retail store associates during the Christmas season and additional hotel employees for major conventions.

- *Invite customers to perform self-service.* If the number of employees is limited, capacity can be increased by involving customers in the co-production of certain tasks. One way to do this is by adding self-service technologies, such as electronic kiosks at the airport for airline ticketing and check-in or automated check-out stations at supermarkets.

- *Ask customers to share.* Capacity can be stretched by asking customers to share a unit of capacity normally meant for one individual. For instance, at busy airports and train stations, where the supply of taxis is sometimes insufficient to meet demand, travelers going in the same direction may be given the option of sharing a ride at a reduced rate.

- *Create flexible capacity.* Sometimes, the problem lies not in the overall capacity but in the mix available to serve the needs of different market segments. One solution is to design flexible physical facilities. For example, all the tables in a restaurant can be two-seaters. When necessary, two tables can be combined to seat four, or three tables combined to seat six.

- *Rent or share extra facilities and equipment.* To reduce expenditure on fixed assets, a service business may be able to rent extra space or machines at peak times. Two firms with complementary demand patterns may enter into formal sharing agreements. For example, some universities rent out student accommodation to visitors during the peak holiday season when their own students have their summer break and the first-year students have not moved into the campus yet.

Figure 9.8 Rush-hour crowd stretches the capacity of train services.

LO 5

Recognize that demand patterns vary by segment and examine how segment-specific variations in demand may be predicted.

UNDERSTAND PATTERNS OF DEMAND

Now let's look at the other side of the equation. In order to effectively manage demand for a particular service, managers need to understand that demand often differs by market segment. Random fluctuations are usually caused by factors beyond management's control. However, analysis will sometimes reveal that a predictable demand cycle for one segment is concealed within a broader, seemingly random pattern. For instance, a repair and maintenance shop that services industrial electrical equipment may already know that a certain proportion of its work consists of regularly scheduled contracts to perform preventive maintenance (Figure 9.10). The rest may come from "walk-in" business and emergency repairs. Although it might seem hard to predict or control the timing and volume of such work, further analysis might show that walk-in business is more prevalent on some days of the week than others. For example, emergency repairs are frequently requested following damage sustained during thunderstorms (which tend to be seasonal in nature and can often be forecast a day or two in advance). If a firm understands its service demand patterns, it can schedule less preventive maintenance work on days with high anticipated demand so that it can take on more profitable emergency repairs.

Figure 9.9 Supermarket employees are cross-trained as cashiers and stockers.

To understand the patterns of demand by segment, we should begin by getting some answers to a series of important questions about the patterns of demand and their underlying causes (Table 9.1).

Most cycles influencing demand for a particular service vary in length from one day to 12 months. In many instances, multiple cycles operate simultaneously. For example, demand levels for public transport may vary by time of day (highest during commute hours), day of week (less travel to work on weekends but more leisure travel), and season (more travel by tourists in summer). (Figure 9.11)

No strategy for smoothing demand is likely to succeed unless it is based on an understanding of why customers from a specific market segment choose to use the service when they do. For example, it's difficult for hotel staff to convince business travelers to stay in the hotel on Saturday nights, since few executives do business over the weekend. Hotel managers may do better to promote weekend use of their facilities for conferences or pleasure travel. Attempts to get commuters to shift their travel to off-peak periods will probably fail, since such travel is determined by people's employment hours. Instead, efforts should be made to persuade employers to adopt flextime or staggered working hours.

Figure 9.10 Scheduled maintenance checks at a power plant.

Table 9.1 Questions about demand patterns and their underlying causes.

1. **Do demand levels follow a predictable cycle?**
   If so, is the duration of the *demand cycle*
   • One *day* (varies by hour)?
   • One *week* (varies by day)?
   • One *month* (varies by day or by week)?
   • One *year* (varies by month or by season or reflects annual public holidays)?
   • Another period?

2. **What are the underlying causes of these cyclical variations?**
   • Employment schedules
   • Billing and tax payment/refund cycles
   • Wage and salary payment dates
   • School hours and vacation
   • Seasonal changes in climate
   • Occurrence of public or religious holidays
   • Natural cycles, such as coastal tides

3. **Do demand levels seem to change randomly?**
   If so, could the underlying causes be
   • Day-to-day changes in the weather?
   • Health events whose occurrence cannot be pinpointed exactly?
   • Accidents, fires, and certain criminal activities?
   • Natural disasters (e.g., earthquakes, storms, mudslides, and volcanic eruptions)?

4. **Can demand for a particular service over time be disaggregated by market segment to reflect such components as follows?**
   • Use patterns by a particular type of customer or for a particular purpose
   • Variations in the net profitability of each completed transaction

Figure 9.11 In summer, many tourists flock to Cologne, Germany, to take in its rich heritage.

Keeping good records of each transaction helps enormously when it comes to analyzing demand patterns based on past experience. Good practice-queuing systems supported by sophisticated software can automatically track customer-consumption patterns by type of customer, service requested, and date and time of day. Where relevant, it is also useful to record weather conditions and other special factors (a strike, an accident, a big convention in town, a price change, launch of a competing service, etc.) that might have influenced demand.

MANAGING DEMAND

LO 6
Be familiar with the five basic ways to *manage demand*.

Once we have understood the demand patterns of the different market segments, we can proceed to the management of demand. There are five basic approaches:

- ▶ Take no action, and leave demand to find its own levels.
- ▶ Reduce demand during peak periods.
- ▶ Increase demand during low periods.
- ▶ Inventory demand using a queuing system.
- ▶ Inventory demand using a reservations system.

The first approach, *take no action*, has the virtue of simplicity but little else. Eventually, customers learn from experience or word of mouth when they should stand in line to use a service and when it will be available without delay. However, they may also learn to find a competitor who is more responsive. Low off-peak utilization cannot be improved unless action is taken. The other four proactive approaches are therefore more superior and profitable strategies.

Table 9.2 links these five approaches to the two problem situations of excess demand and excess capacity. Many service businesses face both situations at different points and should consider the use of the interventionist strategies described.

Table 9.2 Alternate demand-management strategies for different capacity situations.

Approaches to Manage Demand	CAPACITY SITUATION	
	Insufficient Capacity (Excess demand)	Insufficient Demand (Excess Capacity)
Take no action	• Unorganized queuing results (may irritate customers and discourage future use).	• Capacity is wasted (customers may have a disappointing experience for services such as theater).
Manage demand through marketing mix elements	Reduce demand in peak periods: • Higher prices will increase profits. • Change product elements (e.g., don't offer time-consuming services during peak times). • Modify time and place of delivery (e.g., extend opening hours). • Communication can encourage use in other time slots (can this effort be focused on less profitable and less desirable segments?). • Note that demand from highly profitable segments should still be stimulated and priority to capacity should be given to those segments. Demand reduction and shifting should primarily be focused on lower yield segments.	Increase demand in low periods: • Lower prices selectively (try to avoid cannibalizing existing business; ensure that all relevant costs are covered) • Change product elements (find alternative value propositions for service during low seasons) • Use communications and variation in products and distribution (but recognize extra costs, if any, and make sure that appropriate trade-offs are made between profitability and use levels).
Inventory demand using a queuing system	• Match appropriate queue configuration to service process. • Consider priority system for most desirable segments and make other customer shift to off-peak period. • Consider separate queues based on urgency, duration and premium pricing of service. • Shorten customer's perceptions of waiting time and make their waits more comfortable.	• Not applicable, but the queuing system can still collect data on number and type of transactions and customers served. The same applied to reservations systems below.
Inventory demand using a reservations system	• Focus on yield and reserve capacity for less price-sensitive customers. • Consider a priority system for important segments. • Make other customers shift to off-peak periods.	• Clarify that capacity is available and let customers make reservation at their preferred time slot.

Marketing Mix Elements Can Be Used to Shape Demand Patterns

LO 7

Understand how to use the marketing mix elements of price, product, place, and promotion to smooth out fluctuations in demand.

Several marketing mix variables can be used to stimulate demand during periods of excess capacity and decrease or shift demand during periods of insufficient capacity. Price is often the first variable to be proposed for bringing demand and supply into balance (Figure 9.12). However, changes in product, distribution strategy, and communication efforts can also be used to reshape demand patterns. Although each element is discussed separately, effective demand-management efforts often require simultaneous changes in several elements.

Use Price and Non-monetary Costs to Manage Demand. One of the most direct ways to balance supply and demand is through the use of pricing. The lure of lower prices may encourage at least some people to change the timing of their behavior. Non-monetary costs may also have a similar effect. For instance, customers who dislike spending time waiting in crowded and unpleasant conditions will try to come during less busy times.

For the monetary price of a service to be effective as a demand-management tool, managers must understand how the quantity of service demanded responds to increases or decreases in the price per unit at a particular point in time. It's important to determine whether the demand curve for a specific service varies sharply from one time period to another. For instance, will the same person be willing to pay more for a weekend stay in a hotel in Cape Cod in summer than in winter (when the temperatures can be freezing)? The answer is probably "yes." If so, very different pricing schemes may be needed to fill capacity during each time period.

Complicating matters further, there are typically separate demand curves for different segments within each time period (e.g., business travelers are usually less price sensitive than tourists). When capacity is limited, however, the goal in a profit-seeking business should be to ensure that maximum capacity is utilized by the most profitable segments available (see the discussion on revenue management in Chapter 6).

Change Product Elements. Sometimes, pricing alone will be ineffective in managing demand. The opening vignette is a good case in point. Skiers would not buy lift tickets at any price for use on a midsummer day when there are no skiing opportunities. It is the same for a variety of other seasonal businesses (Figure 9.13). Thus, educational institutions offer weekend and summer programs for adults and senior citizens. Small pleasure boats offer cruises in the summer and a dockside venue for private functions in winter months. These firms recognize that no amount of price discounting is likely to develop business out of season, and that a new service product targeted at different segments is needed to encourage demand.

There can even be variations in the product offering during the course of a 24-hour period. Some restaurants mark the passage of the hours with changing menus and levels of service, variations in lighting and décor, opening and closing of the bar, and the presence or absence of entertainment. The goal is to appeal to different needs within the same group of customers, to reach out to different

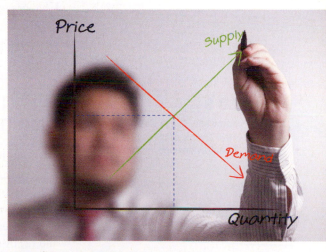

Figure 9.12 Managers are instrumental in pricing a product or a service.

Figure 9.13 Bed and breakfast inns are dependent on the seasonal tide of tourists.

customer segments, or to do both, according to the time of the day. Product elements can also be changed to increase capacity during peak periods. For example, the lunch menu is designed to contain dishes that can be prepared rapidly during the busy lunch period.

Modify Place and Time of Delivery. Rather than seeking to modify demand for a service that continues to be offered at the same time in the same place, firms can also respond to market needs by modifying the time and place of delivery. The following basic options are available:

▶ *Vary the times when the service is available.* This strategy reflects changing customer preference by day of week, by season, and so forth. Theaters and cinema complexes often offer matinees on weekends when people have more leisure time throughout the day. Shops may extend their hours in the days leading up to Christmas or during school holiday periods.

▶ *Offer the service to customers at a new location.* One approach is to operate mobile units that take the service to customers, rather than requiring them to visit fixed-site service locations. Mobile car-wash service and in-office tailoring services are examples of this. A cleaning and repair firm that wishes to generate business during low-demand periods might offer free pickup and delivery of movable items that need servicing.

Promotion and Education. Even if other variables of the marketing mix remain unchanged, communication efforts alone may be able to help smooth demand. Signage, advertising, publicity, and sales messages can be used to educate customers about the timing of peak periods and encourage them to make use of the service at off-peak times when there will be fewer delays.[2] Examples include U.S. Postal Service requests to "Mail Early for Christmas," public transport messages urging non-commuters such as shoppers or tourists to avoid the crush conditions of the commute hours, and communications from sales reps of industrial maintenance firms informing customers when preventive maintenance work can be done quickly.

Changes in pricing, product characteristics, and distribution must be communicated clearly. If a firm wants to obtain a particular response to variations in marketing mix elements, it must, of course, inform customers fully about their options.

LO 8

Know how to use waiting lines and queuing systems to inventory demand.

INVENTORY DEMAND THROUGH WAITING LINES AND QUEUING SYSTEMS

As we have seen in the previous section, there are a variety of tactics for bringing demand and supply into balance. Demand is typically inventoried in such situations. This can be done in two ways: (1) by asking customers to wait in line (usually on a "first-come, first-served" basis) or by offering them more advanced queuing systems (e.g., systems that take urgency, price, or importance of the customer into account) and (2) by offering customers the opportunity of reserving or booking service capacity in advance. We will discuss wait lines and other queuing systems in this section and reservation systems in the next.

Waiting Is a Universal Phenomenon

Waiting is something that occurs everywhere. Waiting lines—known to operations researchers (and also the British) as "queues"—occur whenever the number of arrivals at a facility exceeds the capacity of the system to process them. In a very real sense, queues are a symptom of unresolved capacity-management problems.

Nobody likes to wait or to be kept waiting (Figure 9.14). It's boring, time-wasting, and sometimes physically uncomfortable, especially if there is nowhere to sit or if you are outdoors. Almost every organization faces the problem of waiting lines somewhere in its operation. People are kept waiting on the phone; they line up with their supermarket carts to check out their grocery purchases; they sit in their cars waiting to enter drive-in car washes or to pay at toll booths. Some physical queues are geographically dispersed. Travelers wait at many different locations for the taxis they have ordered by phone to arrive and pick them up.

Physical and inanimate objects wait for processing too. Customers' e-mails sit in the inboxes of customer service staff; appliances wait to be repaired; and checks wait to be cleared at a bank. In each instance, a customer may be waiting for the outcome of that work—an answer to an e-mail, an appliance that is working again, and a check credited to a customer's balance.

Managing Waiting Lines

Reducing customer waiting time often requires a multi-pronged approach. This is evidenced by the approach taken by Disney, which is described in Service Insights 9.1. Increasing capacity simply by adding more space or more staff is not always the

Figure 9.14 Processing applies to physical and inanimate objects as much as it does to people.

Disney Turns Queue Management into a Science

Have you ever been in a queue at Disneyland? Very often, we may not realize how long we have been waiting, because there are many sights to enjoy as we queue. We may be watching a video, playing with interactive technology and touch screens stationed along the way, looking at other customers enjoying themselves, reading the various posters on the wall, and enjoying comfort in the form of fans and shade to help cool off. As our waits are occupied and comfortable, we may not realize that a long time has passed. The line management at Disney's theme parks is an extension of their entertainment philosophy!

For example, at Disney World's Dumbo the Flying Elephant ride, children and their parents can play in an interactive room that resembles a circus tent. While playing, they are also waiting for a buzzer to signal that it is their turn to proceed to the outdoor line for the ride. The children playing in the tent don't have the perception that they are waiting in line, but that is what they are doing!

Disney has taken management of waiting lines to another level. At Walt Disney World, there is a Disney Operational Command Center, where the technicians monitor the queues to make sure that they are not too long and that the people are moving along. To them, patience is not a virtue in the theme park business. Inside the Command Center, they have computer programs, video cameras, digital maps of the park, and other tools to help them to spot areas where the queues might be too long. If there is a problem with any queue, they will send a staff member to fix it immediately. The problem may be dealt with in several ways. For

example, they may send a Disney character to entertain the waiting customers. Alternatively, they may deploy more capacity. For example, if there is a long queue for the boat ride, more boats can be deployed to make the queue move faster. Disney World is divided into different lands. If one land is less crowded than another, they may re-route a mini-parade towards that area. This will prompt the crowds to follow, and the crowd distribution will become more even. Disney has also added video games to waiting areas.

With the Command Center in place, the average number of rides a visitor to Magic Kingdom normally takes has increased from 9 to 10. Disney is now experimenting with ways of using smartphone technology and the Walt Disney World® app to manage waiting lines. It does all this in the hope that customers will not be frustrated by the waits and will return more often.

Figure 9.15 Disney World's Dumbo the Flying Elephant ride.

best solution in situations where customer satisfaction must be balanced against cost considerations. Managers should consider a variety of ways, including:

1. Rethinking the design of the queuing system (i.e., queue configuration and virtual waits).

2. Tailoring the queuing system to different market segments (e.g., by urgency, price, or importance of the customer).

3. Managing customers' behavior and their perceptions of the wait (i.e., using psychology of waiting to make waits less unpleasant).

4. Installing a reservations system (e.g., use reservations, booking, or appointments to distribute demand).

5. Redesigning processes to shorten the time of each transaction (e.g. by installing self-service machines).

Points 1–4 are discussed in the next few sections of this chapter. Point 5 is discussed in Chapter 8 on customer service process redesign.

Different Queue Configurations

There are many different types of queues, and the challenge for managers is to select the most appropriate type. Figure 9.16 shows diagrams of several types that you have probably experienced yourself.

▶ *Single-line, sequential stages*. In such queues, customers proceed through several serving operations, as in a cafeteria. Bottlenecks may occur at any stage where the process takes longer to execute than at previous stages. Many cafeterias have lines at the cash register because the cashier takes longer to calculate how much you owe and to return change than the servers take to slap food on your plate.

▶ *Parallel lines to multiple servers*. These offer more than one serving station, allowing customers to select one of several lines in which to wait. Fast-food restaurants usually have several serving lines in operation at busy times of the day, with each station offering the full menu. The disadvantage of this design is that lines may not move at equal speed. How many times have you chosen what looked like the shortest line only to watch in frustration as the lines on either side of you moved twice as fast as yours?

▶ *Single line to multiple servers*. This type of waiting line is commonly known as a "snake." It solves the problem of parallel lines to multiple servers moving at different speeds. It is commonly used in post offices and at airport check-ins (Figure 9.17).

▶ *Designated lines*. These involve assigning different lines to specific categories of customers. Examples include express lines (for instance, for 5 items or less) and regular lines at supermarket check-outs and different check-in stations for first-class, business-class, and economy-class airline passengers.

▶ *Take a number*. This allows customers to sit down and relax or to guess how long the wait will be and do something else in the meantime. Users of this method include large travel agents, government offices, and outpatient clinics in hospitals.

> *Wait list.* Restaurants often have wait lists where customers put their names down (along with the party size). They must then wait until their name is announced. There are four common ways of wait listing: (1) party size seating, where the number of people is matched to the size of the table; (2) VIP seating, which involves giving special rights to favored customers; (3) call-ahead seating, which allows people to telephone before arrival to hold a place on the wait list; and (4) large party reservations. If customers are familiar with wait listing techniques, they are likely to see them as fair. However, VIP seating is viewed as especially unfair by guests who don't enjoy priority treatment.[3]

Research suggests that selecting the most suitable type of queue is important for customer satisfaction. Anat Rafaeli and her colleagues found that the layout of queues in a waiting area can produce feelings of injustice and unfairness in customers. Customers who waited in parallel lines to multiple servers were significantly more agitated and dissatisfied with the fairness of the service delivery process than those who waited in a

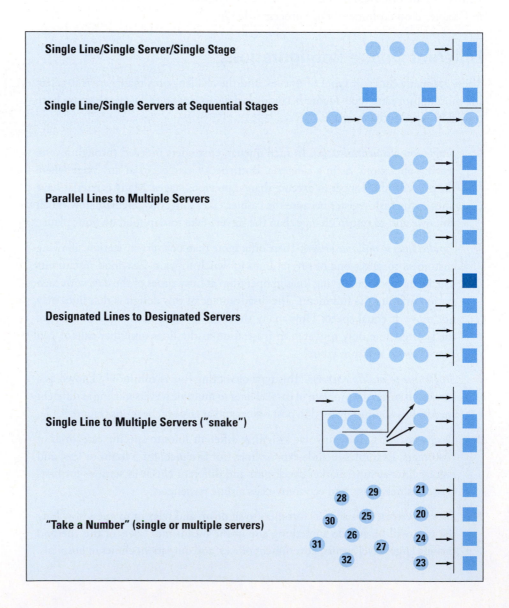

Figure 9.16 Alternative queue configurations.

single line ("snake") to access multiple servers. This result was despite the fact that both groups of customers waited for the same duration and were involved in completely fair service processes.[4]

Virtual Waits

One of the problems associated with waiting in line is the waste of customers' time. The "virtual queue" strategy is a creative way of taking the physical waiting out of the wait altogether. Customers register their place in line on a terminal, which estimates the time at which they should return to claim their place at the head of the virtual line.[5] Sushi Tei, a restaurant chain, has implemented a self-service touch-screen terminal where guests can simply select the party size (thereby allowing the restaurant to match table sizes), enter their cell-phone number, and then go shopping (Figure 9.18). Diners receive a text message that confirms their booking, and the message contains a link that allows them to view in real time the number of parties still ahead of them in the queue. They are called by an automated system five minutes before their table is available. They can confirm their booking (press "1"), ask for an additional 15 minutes to return to the restaurant (press "2"), or cancel their booking if they have made alternative plans (press "3"). The restaurant has a long queue every weekend evening, but it can extend the time it operates at full capacity on busy days. The system also encourages customers to remain loyal.

The concept of virtual queues has many potential applications. Cruise ships, all-inclusive resorts, and restaurants can use this strategy if customers are willing to provide their cell-phone numbers or remain within buzzing range of a firm-operated pager system. Service Insights 9.2 describes the virtual queuing systems used in two very different industries: a theme park and a call center.

Queuing Systems Can Be Tailored to Market Segments

Although the basic rule in most queuing systems is "first come, first served," not all queuing systems are organized in this way. Market segmentation is sometimes used to design queuing strategies that set different priorities for different types of customers. Allocation to separate queuing areas may be based on any of the following:

▶ *Urgency of the job.* At many hospital emergency units, a nurse is assigned to greet incoming patients and decide which patients require priority medical treatment and which patients can safely be asked to register and wait for their turn.

▶ *Duration of service transaction.* Banks, supermarkets, and other retail services often have "express lanes" for shorter, less complicated tasks.

▶ *Payment of a premium price.* Airlines usually offer separate check-in lines for first-class, business-class, and economy-class passengers. The ratio of personnel to passengers is higher in the first- and business-class lines, resulting in reduced waits for those

Waiting in a Virtual Queue

Disney is well known for its efforts to give visitors information on how long they may have to wait to ride a particular attraction at one of its theme parks. It also entertains guests while they are waiting in line. However, the company realized that the long waits at its most popular attractions were still a major source of dissatisfaction. They created an innovative solution to this problem by introducing the system of virtual queues.

The virtual-queue concept was first tested at Disney World. At the most popular attractions, guests were allowed to register their place in line with a computer. They could then use the wait time to visit other places in the park. Surveys showed that guests who used the new system spent more money, saw more attractions, and were significantly more satisfied than others. After further refinement, the system—now named Fastpass—was introduced at the five most popular attractions at Disney World. It was subsequently extended to all Disney parks worldwide and is now used by more than 50 million guests a year.

Fastpass is easy to use. When guests approach a Fastpass attraction, they are given two clear choices: to obtain a Fastpass ticket there and return at a designated time or to wait in a stand-by line. Signs indicate how long the wait is likely to be in each instance. The wait time for each line tends to be self-regulating, because a large difference between the two will cause more people to choose the shorter line. In practice, the virtual wait tends to be slightly longer than the physical one. To use the Fastpass option, guests insert their park admission ticket into a special turnstile and receive a Fastpass ticket stating a return time. Guests have some flexibility because the system allows them a 60-minute window beyond the printed return time.

Call centers also use different types of virtual queuing systems. The "first-in, first-out"

queuing system is very common. When callers call in, they hear a message that informs them of the estimated wait time for the call to be taken by an agent. The caller can (1) wait in the queue and get connected to an agent when his turn arrives or (2) choose to receive a call back. If the caller chooses the second option, he has to enter his telephone number and tell his name. He then hangs up the phone and his virtual place in the queue is kept. The system calls the customer back when he is nearly at the head of the queue, and he is subsequently attended to by an agent.

In both situations, the customer is unlikely to complain. In the first situation, it is the customer's choice to wait in the queue, and he can still do something else as he already knows the estimated wait time. In the second situation, the person does not have to wait too long for the agent after the call back. The call center also benefits because there are fewer frustrated customers who may take up the valuable time of the agents by complaining about how long they had to wait. In addition, firms can reduce aborted or missed calls from customers.

who have paid more for their tickets. At some airports, premium passengers may also enjoy faster lanes for the security check.

▶ *Importance of the customer.* Members of frequent flyer clubs often get priority wait listing. For example, the next seat that becomes available is given to a platinum card holder of the airline's loyalty program. These members can also jump the queue with priority access to call centers. Even when travelling economy class, members of frequent flyer clubs can use the shorter business-class check-in lines.

CUSTOMER PERCEPTIONS OF WAITING TIME

▶ **LO 9**
Understand how customers perceive waits and how waiting may be made less burdensome for them.

People don't like wasting their time on unproductive activities any more than they like wasting money. Customer dissatisfaction with delays in receiving service can often stimulate strong emotions, including anger.[6] In fact, it has been found that customers who are dissatisfied with the wait need to be more satisfied with the service to have the same level of loyalty as customers who are satisfied with the wait.[7]

The Psychology of Waiting Time

Research shows that people often think they have waited longer for a service than they actually have (Figure 9.19).[8] David Maister and other researchers have the following suggestions on how to use the psychology of waiting to make waits less stressful and unpleasant:[9]

▶ *Unoccupied time feels longer than occupied time.* When you are sitting around with nothing to do, time seems to crawl. The challenge for service organizations is to give customers something to do or to distract them while they are waiting (Figure 9.20). Some restaurants manage the waiting problem by inviting dinner guests to have a look at the menu or enjoy a drink in the bar until their table is ready. BMW car owners can wait in comfort in BMW service centers where waiting areas are furnished with designer furniture, plasma TVs, Wi-Fi hotspots, magazines, and freshly brewed cappuccinos. Many customers even bring their own entertainment in the form of a cell phone with messaging and games or an iPad.

▶ *Solo waits feel longer than group waits.* It is nice to wait with people whom you know, and talking to them is one way of passing the time while waiting. However, not everyone is comfortable talking to a stranger.

▶ *Physically uncomfortable waits feel longer than comfortable waits.* "My feet are killing me!" is one of the most frequently heard comments when people are forced to stand in line for a long time. Waiting also seems more burdensome if the temperature is too high or too low.

▶ *Pre- and post-process waits feel longer than in-process waits.* Waiting to buy a ticket to enter a theme park is different from waiting to ride on a roller coaster once you're in the park.

▶ *Unfair waits are longer than equitable waits.* Perceptions about what is fair or unfair sometimes vary from one culture or country to another. In the United States, Canada, or Britain, for example, people expect everybody to wait their

"Ever have one of those days when one millionth of a nanosecond feels like an eternity?"

Figure 9.19 While waiting, time can seem to pass very slowly.

Figure 9.20 Keeping occupied by reading magazines will make the wait for the spa treatment seem shorter.

turn in line and are likely to get irritated if they see others jumping ahead or being given priority for no apparent reason. When people perceive the wait as fair, the negative effect of waiting is reduced.

▶ ***Unfamiliar waits seem longer than familiar ones.*** Frequent users of a service know what to expect and are less likely to worry while waiting. New or occasional users, by contrast, are often nervous. They wonder not only about the probable length of the wait but also about what is likely to happen next.

▶ ***Uncertain waits are longer than known, finite waits.*** Although any wait may be frustrating, we can usually adjust mentally to a wait of known length. It's the unknown that keeps us on edge. (Figure 9.21)

▶ ***Unexplained waits are longer than explained waits.*** Have you ever been in a subway or an elevator that has stopped for no apparent reason without anyone telling you why? In addition to uncertainty about the length of the wait, there's added anxiety about what is going to happen.

▶ ***Anxiety makes waits seem longer.*** Can you remember waiting for someone to show up at the arranged meeting time or rendezvous and worrying about whether you had gotten the time or location correct? While waiting in unfamiliar locations, people often worry about their personal safety.

▶ ***The more valuable or important the service, the longer people will wait.*** People will queue up overnight under uncomfortable conditions to get good seats to a major concert or sports event expected to sell out fast.

LO 10
Know how to use reservations systems to inventory demand.

INVENTORY DEMAND THROUGH RESERVATIONS SYSTEMS

As an alternative or in addition to waiting lines, reservations systems can be used to inventory demand (Figure 9.22). If you ask someone what services come to their mind when you talk about reservations, they will probably cite airlines, hotels, restaurants, car rentals, and theaters. Use synonyms like "bookings" or "appointments," and they may add haircuts, visits to professionals such as doctors and consultants, vacation rentals, and service calls to fix anything from a broken refrigerator to a malfunctioning laptop. Reservations systems have many benefits:

▶ Customer dissatisfaction due to excessive waits can be avoided. One aim of reservations is to guarantee that the service will be available when customers want it. Customers who hold reservations should be able to count on avoiding a queue because they have been guaranteed service at a specific time.

▶ Reservations allow demand to be controlled and smoothed out in a more manageable way. A well-organized reservations system allows the firm to deflect demand for a service from a first-choice time to earlier or later times, from one class of service to another ("upgrades" and "downgrades"), and even from first-choice locations to alternative ones. Such measures contribute to higher capacity utilization.

- Reservations systems enable the implementation of revenue management and serve to pre-sell a service to different customer segments (see Chapter 6 on revenue management). Since these are unpredictable, higher prices can be charged to obtain higher margins.

- Data from reservations systems also help organizations to prepare operational and financial projections for future periods. Systems vary from a simple appointments book with handwritten entries for a doctor's office to a central, computerized data bank for an airline's global operations.

The challenge in designing reservations systems is to make them fast and user-friendly for both staff and customers. Many firms now allow customers to make their own reservations on a self-service basis via their websites and smartphones. However, problems arise when customers fail to show or when service firms overbook. Marketing strategies for dealing with these operational problems include requiring a deposit, canceling non-paid reservations after a certain time, and providing compensation to victims of overbooking. These strategies have been discussed in Chapter 6 on revenue management.

Reservations Strategies Should Focus on Yield

Increasingly, service firms are looking at their "yield"—that is, the average revenue received per unit of capacity. Yield analysis forces managers to recognize the opportunity cost of selling capacity for a given date to a customer from one market segment when another might subsequently yield a higher rate. Think about the following problems facing sales managers for different types of service organizations with capacity limitations:

Figure 9.21 Uncertain wait for a delayed flight can cause frustration.

- Should a hotel accept an advance booking from a tour group of 200 room nights at $140 each when some of these same room nights might possibly be sold later at short notice to business travelers at the full posted rate of $300?

- Should a railroad with 30 empty freight cars accept an immediate request for a shipment worth $1,400 per car, or should it hold the cars for a few more days in the hope of getting priority shipment that would be twice as valuable?

- Should a print shop process all jobs on a "first-come, first-served" basis with a guaranteed delivery time for each job, or should it charge a premium rate for "rush" work and tell customers with "standard" jobs to expect some variability in completion dates?

Decisions on such problems deserve to be handled with a little more sophistication than just resorting to the "bird in the hand is worth two in the bush" formula. Good information based on detailed records of past usage and supported by current market intelligence is essential for the proper allocation of capacity among different segments. The decision to accept or reject business should be based on realistic estimates of the probability of obtaining higher rated business. Firms should also be aware of the need to maintain established (and desirable) customer relationships. We have discussed the more sophisticated use of revenue-management systems for allocating capacity to different "rate buckets" and setting prices in Chapter 6 ("Setting Prices and Implementing Revenue Management").

Figure 9.22 Most libraries have a reservation system for books, magazines, and audio-visual materials.

LO 11

Be familiar with strategic approaches to utilize residual surplus capacity even after all other options of matching demand and capacity have been exhausted.

CREATE ALTERNATIVE USE FOR OTHERWISE WASTED CAPACITY

Even after the professional management of capacity and demand, most service firms will still experience periods of excess capacity. However, not all unsold productive capacity has to be wasted, as alternative "demand" can be created by innovative firms. Many firms take a strategic approach to the disposition of anticipated surplus capacity, allocating it in advance to build relationships with customers, suppliers, employees, and intermediaries.[10] Possible uses for otherwise wasted capacity include:

▶ *Use capacity for service differentiation.* When capacity utilization is low, service employees can go all the way to truly wow their customers. A firm that wants to build customer loyalty and market share should use a slack in operations to focus on outstanding customer service.

▶ *Reward your best customers and build loyalty.* This can be done through special promotions as part of a loyalty program, while ensuring that existing revenues are not cannibalized.

▶ *Customer and channel development.* Provide free or heavily discounted trials for prospective customers and for intermediaries who sell to end customers.

▶ *Reward employees.* In certain industries such as restaurants, beach resorts, or cruise lines, capacity can be used to reward employees and their families. This can improve employee satisfaction, build loyalty, and raise performance levels by providing employees with an understanding of the service as experienced from the customer's perspective.

▶ *Barter free capacity.* Service firms can often save costs and increase capacity utilization by bartering capacity with their own suppliers. Among the most widely bartered services are advertising space or airtime, airline seats, and hotel rooms.

LO 1 ▶ At any given moment, a firm with limited capacity can face different demand–supply situations:

o Excess demand

o Demand that exceeds optimum capacity

o Well-balanced demand and supply

o Excess capacity

If demand and supply are not in balance, firms will have idle capacity during low periods but will have to turn away customers during peak periods. This situation impedes the efficient use of productive assets and erodes profitability. Firms therefore need to try and balance demand and supply by adjusting capacity and/or demand.

LO 2 ▶ The building blocks for effective capacity and demand management are:

o Define productive capacity.

o Use capacity-management tools.

o Understand demand patterns and drivers by customer segment.

o Use demand-management tools.

LO 3 ▶ When we refer to capacity management, we implicitly mean productive capacity. There are several different forms of productive capacity in services:

o Physical facilities for processing customers

o Physical facilities for processing goods

o Physical equipment for processing people, possessions, or information

o Labor

o Infrastructure

LO 4 ▶ *Capacity* can be managed in a number of ways:

Stretching capacity: Some capacity is elastic and can be used to serve more people. Examples include crowding in a subway car, extended operating hours, or faster customer processing.

Adjusting capacity: The overall level of service can be adjusted to match demand more closely. This can be done by:

o Scheduling downtime during low periods

o Cross-training employees

o Using part-time employees

o Inviting customers to perform self-service

o Asking customers to share capacity

o Designing capacity to be flexible

o Renting or sharing extra facilities and equipment

LO 5 ▶ To manage *demand* effectively, firms need to understand demand patterns and drivers by market segment. Different segments often exhibit different demand patterns (e.g., routine maintenance versus emergency repairs). Once firms have an understanding of the demand patterns of their market segments, they can use marketing strategies to reshape those patterns.

LO 6 ▶ Demand can be managed in the following five basic ways:

o Take no action, and leave demand to find its own levels.

o Reduce demand during peak periods.

o Increase demand during low periods.

o Inventory demand using a queuing system.

o Inventory demand using a reservations system.

LO 7 ▶ Marketing mix elements can be used in the following ways to help smooth out fluctuations in demand:

o Use price and non-monetary customer costs to manage demand.

o Change product elements to attract different segments at different times.

o Modify the place and time of delivery (e.g., through extended opening hours).

o Use communication efforts for promotion and education (e.g., "Mail Early for Christmas").

LO 8 ▶ *Waiting lines* and *queuing systems* help firms inventory demand over short periods of time. There are different types of queues with their respective advantages and applications. Queuing systems include single line with sequential stages, parallel lines to multiple servers, single line to multiple servers, designated lines, taking a number, and wait lists.

Not all queuing systems are organized on a "first-come, first-served" basis. Rather, good systems often segment waiting customers by:

o Urgency of the job (e.g., hospital emergency units)

o Duration of the service transaction (e.g., express lanes)

o Premium service based on a premium price (e.g., first-class check-in counters)

o Importance of the customer (e.g., frequent travelers get priority wait listing)

PART III

LO 9 ▶ Customers don't like wasting their time waiting. Firms need to understand the *psychology of waiting* and take active steps to make waiting less frustrating. We discussed 10 possible steps, including:

- o Keeping customers occupied or entertained while waiting,
- o Informing customers about how long the wait is likely to be,
- o Providing them with an explanation of why they have to wait, and
- o Avoiding perceptions of unfair waits.

LO 10 ▶ Effective *reservations systems* inventory demand over a longer period of time and offer several benefits. They:

- o Help customers to avoid queues, thereby reducing dissatisfaction due to excessive waits.
- o Allow the firm to control demand and smooth it out.
- o Enable the use of revenue management to increase yield (by reserving scarce capacity for higher-paying segments rather than just selling off capacity on a "first-come, first-served" basis).

LO 11 ▶ Even after the professional management of capacity and demand, most service firms will still experience periods of excess capacity. Firms can take a strategic approach to the use of surplus capacity, including:

- o Use capacity for service differentiation. When capacity utilization is low, service employees can go all the way to truly wow their customers.
- o Reward your best customers and build loyalty (e.g., through special promotions as part of a loyalty program).
- o Customer and channel development (e.g., provide free or heavily discounted trials).
- o Reward employees (e.g., excess capacity in restaurants, beach resorts, or cruise lines can be used to reward loyal employees and their families).
- o Barter free capacity (e.g., service firms can barter excess capacity for advertising space, airline seats, and hotel rooms).

UNLOCK YOUR LEARNING

These keywords are found within the sections of each Learning Objective (LO). They are integral to understanding the services marketing concepts taught in each section. Having a firm grasp of these keywords and how they are used is essential to helping you do well on your course, and in the real and very competitive marketing scene out there.

LO 1
1. Excess capacity
2. Excess demand
3. Fixed-capacity service
4. Maximum capacity
5. Optimum capacity

LO 2
1. Building blocks
2. Manage capacity
3. Manage demand
4. Productive capacity
5. Fluctuating demand

LO 3
1. Equipment
2. Infrastructure
3. Labor
4. Physical facilities
5. Resources

LO 4
1. Adjusting capacity
2. Capacity limitations
3. Slack time
4. Cross-train employees
5. Downtime
6. Flexible capacity
7. Part-time employees
8. Self-service
9. Stretching capacity

LO 5
1. Market segment
2. Demand patterns
3. Consumption patterns
4. Queuing systems

How well do you know the language of services marketing? Quiz yourself!

⚠ **Not for the academically faint of heart**

For each keyword you are able to recall without referring to earlier pages, give yourself a point (and a pat on the back). Tally your score at the end and see if you earned the right to be called—a *services marketeer*.

SCORE

0 – 15	Services Marketing is done a great disservice.
16 – 30	The midnight oil needs to be lit, pronto.
31 – 45	I know what you *didn't* do all semester.
46 – 60	A close shave with success.
61 – 75	Now, go forth and market.
76 – 78	There should be a marketing concept named after you.

Review Questions

1. What is the difference between ideal capacity and maximum capacity? Provide examples of a situation where (a) the two might be the same and (b) the two are different.

2. Describe the building blocks for managing capacity and demand.

3. What is meant by productive capacity in services?

4. Why is capacity management particularly important for service firms?

5. What actions can firms take to adjust capacity to match demand more closely?

6. How can firms identify the factors that affect demand for their services?

7. What actions can firms take to adjust demand to match capacity more closely?

8. How can marketing mix elements be used to reshape demand patterns?

9. What do you see as the advantages and disadvantages of the different types of queues for an organization serving large numbers of customers? For which type of service might each of the queuing types be more suitable?

10. How can firms make waiting more pleasant for their customers?

11. What are the benefits of having an effective reservations system?

12. How can service firms use residual service capacity after all strategies of matching supply and demand have been exhausted?

WORK YOUR SERVICES MARKETING

Application Exercises

1. Explain how flexible capacity can be created in each of the following situations: (a) a local library, (b) an office-cleaning service, (c) a technical support help desk, (d) an Interflora franchise.

2. Identify some specific examples of firms in your community (or region) that significantly change their product and/or marketing mix in order to increase patronage during low demand periods.

3. Select a service organization of your choice, identify its particular patterns of demand with reference to the checklist provided in Table 9.1, and answer the following: (a) What is the nature of this service organization's approach to capacity and demand management? (b) What changes would you recommend in relation to its management of capacity and demand, and why?

4. Review the 10 suggestions on the psychology of waiting. Which are the most relevant in (a) a supermarket; (b) a city bus stop on a rainy, dark evening; (c) a doctor's office; and (d) a ticket line for a football game expected to be a sell-out.

5. Give examples, based on your own experience, of a reservations system that worked really well and of one that worked really badly. Identify and examine the reasons for the success and failure of these two systems. What recommendations would you make to both firms to improve (or further improve in the case of the good example) their reservation systems?

PART III

ENDNOTES

1. Based on material in James A. Fitzsimmons and M. J. Fitzsimmons, *Service Management: Operations, Strategy, and Information Technology,* 6th ed. (New York: Irwin McGraw-Hill, 2008); W. Earl Sasser, Jr., "Match Supply and Demand in Service Industries," *Harvard Business Review* 54 (November–December 1976): 133–140.

2. Kenneth J. Klassen and Thomas R. Rohleder, "Using Customer Motivations to Reduce Peak Demand: Does It Work?" *The Service Industries Journal* 24 (September 2004): 53–70.

3. Kelly A. McGuire and Sheryl E. Kimes, "The Perceived Fairness of Waitlist-Management Techniques for Restaurants," *Cornell Hotel and Restaurant Administration Quarterly* 47 (May 2006): 121–134.

4. Anat Rafaeli, G. Barron, and K. Haber, "The Effects of Queue Structure on Attitudes," *Journal of Service Research* 5 (November 2002): 125–139.

5. Duncan Dickson, Robert C. Ford, and Bruce Laval, "Managing Real and Virtual Waits in Hospitality and Service Organizations," *Cornell Hotel and Restaurant Administration Quarterly* 46 (February 2005): 52–68.

6. Ana B. Casado Diaz and Francisco J. Más Ruiz, "The Consumer's Reaction to Delays in Service," *International Journal of Service Industry Management* 13, no. 2 (2002): 118–140.

7. Frederic Bielen and Nathalie Demoulin, "Waiting Time Influence on the Satisfaction–Loyalty Relationship in Services," *Managing Service Quality* 17, no. 2 (2007): 174–193.

8. Jay R. Chernow, "Measuring the Values of Travel Time Savings," *Journal of Consumer Research* 7 (March 1981): 360–371. Note that this entire issue of *Journal of Consumer Research* was devoted to the consumption of time.

9. This section is based on: David H. Maister, "The Psychology of Waiting Lines," in J. A. Czepiel, M. R. Solomon, and C. F. Surprenant (eds) *The Service Encounter* (Lexington, MA: Lexington Books/D.C. Heath, 1986): 113–123; Peter Jones and Emma Peppiat, "Managing Perceptions of Waiting Times in Service Queues," *International Journal of Service Industry Management* 7, no. 5 (1996): 47–61; Clay M. Voorhees, Julie Baker, Brian L. Bourdeau, E. Deanne Brocato, and J. Joseph Cronin, Jr., "Moderating the Relationships among Perceived Waiting Time, Anger and Regret," *Journal of Service Research* 12, no. 2 (November 2009): 138–155; Kelly A. McGuire, Sheryl E. Kimes, Michael Lynn, Madeline E. Pullman, and Russell C. Lloyd, "A Framework for Evaluating the Customer Wait Experience," *Journal of Service Management* 21, no. 3 (2010): 269–290.

10. Irene C. L. Ng, Jochen Wirtz, and Khai Sheang Lee, "The Strategic Role of Unused Service Capacity," *International Journal of Service Industry Management* 10, no. 2 (1999): 211–238.

LEARNING OBJECTIVES (LOs)

By the end of this chapter, the reader should be able to:

LO 1 Recognize the four core purposes service environments fulfill.

LO 2 Know the theoretical underpinning from environmental psychology that helps us to understand how customers and employees respond to service environments.

LO 3 Be familiar with the integrative servicescape model.

LO 4 Know the three main dimensions of the service environment.

LO 5 Discuss the key ambient conditions and their effects on customers.

LO 6 Determine the roles of spatial layout and functionality.

LO 7 Understand the roles of signs, symbols, and artifacts.

LO 8 Know how service employees and other customers are part of the servicescape.

LO 9 Explain why designing an effective servicescape has to be done holistically and from the customer's perspective.

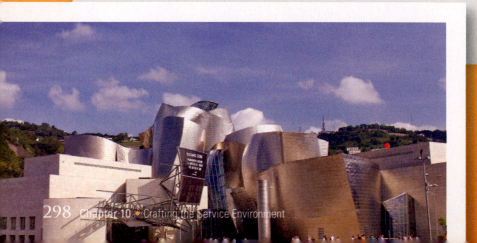

Figure 10.1 The contemporary curves of the Guggenheim have drawn in both praise and crowds in large quantities.

OPENING VIGNETTE

Guggenheim Museum in Bilbao[1]

When the Guggenheim Museum in Bilbao in northern Spain opened its doors to the public, praise poured in from all over the world. The museum, hailed "the greatest building of our time," was designed by Frank Gehry, the influential and famous Canadian-American architect. Its fascinating architecture put Bilbao on the world map as a tourist destination. Before that, most people had never heard of Bilbao, which was once an industrial area with a shipyard, large warehouse districts, and a river choked with waste from the factories that lined its shores. The construction of the museum was the first step in the city's redevelopment plan, and it succeeded in transforming the entire city. In fact, such a transformation is now commonly referred to as the "Bilbao effect." Scholars are studying the Bilbao effect to understand how this kind of "wow-effect architecture" can help to transform a city.

The design features of the museum have a number of meanings and messages. The museum is shaped like a ship and blends in with the environment of the river. It is a combination of regular forms built in stone and curved forms made of titanium. The huge glass walls allow natural light to penetrate the museum and provide visitors inside the building with a view of the surrounding hills. Outside, the titanium panels have been arranged to look like fish scales in order to enhance the image of being by the Nervion River. Visitors are also greeted by a 43-foot-tall terrier topiary made of pots of fresh pansies and a huge spider sculpture called "Maman" by the leading twentieth-century sculptor Louise Bourgeoris.

From the museum's huge, metal-domed atrium, patrons can visit 19 other galleries connected by curved walkways, glass lifts, and stairways. Even the design of the galleries is meant to hint at what visitors can expect inside. The rectangular galleries have limestone-covered walls. The rectangle is a more conventional shape, and these galleries hold the classic art collections. The irregularly shaped galleries hold collections of selected living artists. In addition, there are special galleries without structural columns where large works of art can be displayed. Each gallery thus forms a specially designed and planned servicescape.

While not all servicescapes are great works of architecture, the Guggenheim Museum in Bilbao is certainly one such specimen. It is an attention-drawing medium that shapes the expectations of its visitors. They can look forward to an awesome experience at the museum.

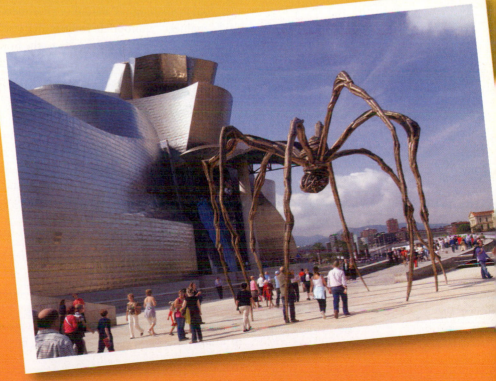

Figure 10.2 The extraordinary design of the Guggenheim Museum has drawn large amounts of praise and crowds.

PART III

SERVICE ENVIRONMENTS—AN IMPORTANT ELEMENT OF THE SERVICES MARKETING MIX

The physical service environment plays a key role in shaping the service experience and enhancing (or undermining) customer satisfaction. Organizations such as hospitals, hotels, restaurants, and the offices of professional service firms have come to recognize that the service environment is an important element of their services marketing mix and overall value proposition.

The process of designing the service environment is an art that takes a lot of time and effort, and it can be expensive to implement. Service environments, also called servicescapes, relate to the style and appearance of the physical surroundings and other experiential elements encountered by customers at service delivery sites. Figure 10.3 provides an overview of the key topics covered in this chapter.

LO 1

Recognize the four core purposes service environments fulfill.

WHAT IS THE PURPOSE OF SERVICE ENVIRONMENTS?

The four main purposes of servicescapes are: (1) to shape customers' experiences and behaviors; (2) to signal quality and to position, differentiate, and strengthen the brand; (3) to be a core component of the value proposition; and (4) to facilitate the service encounter and enhance both service quality and productivity.

Shape Customers' Service Experiences and Behaviors

For organizations that deliver high-contact services, the design of the physical environment and the way in which tasks are performed by customer-contact personnel play a vital role in shaping the nature of customers' experiences. Physical surroundings help to "engineer" appropriate feelings and reactions in customers and employees, which in turn can help to build loyalty to the firm.[2]

Signal Quality and Position, Differentiate, and Strengthen the Brand

Services are often intangible, and customers cannot assess their quality well. Thus, customers use the service environment as an important quality proxy, and firms take great pains to signal quality and portray the desired image.[3] Perhaps you've seen the reception areas of successful professional service firms such as investment banks or management consulting firms. The décor and furnishings tend to be elegant and are designed to impress.

Like most people, you probably infer higher merchandise quality if the goods are displayed in an environment with a prestige image rather than in one that creates a discount feel.[4] Consider Figure 10.4, which shows the lobbies of two different types of hotels that cater to very different target segments. The former caters to younger travelers who have low budgets, while the latter is designed to appeal to a more mature, affluent, and prestigious clientele, including business travelers. Each of these two servicescapes

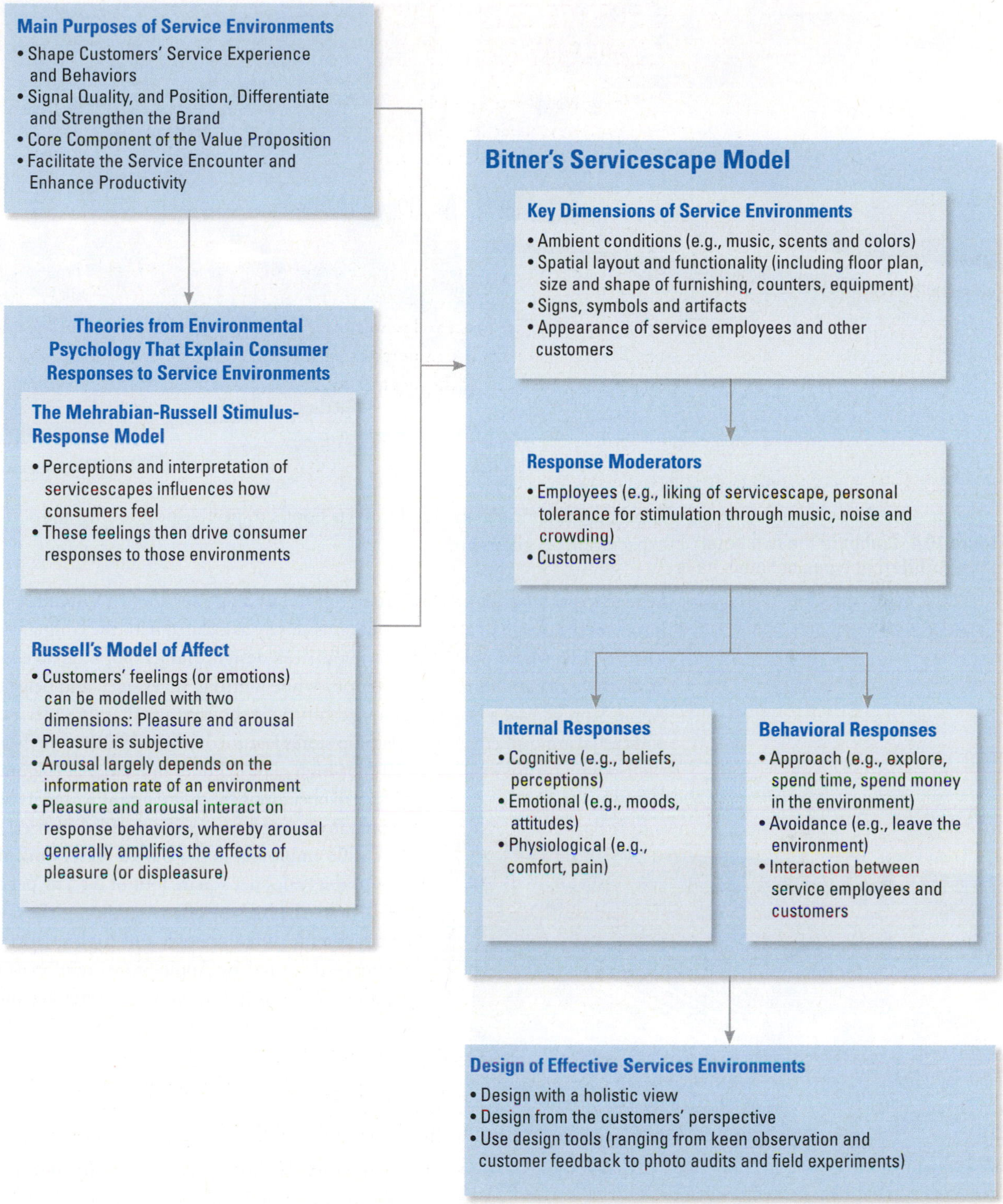

Main Purposes of Service Environments

- Shape Customers' Service Experience and Behaviors
- Signal Quality, and Position, Differentiate and Strengthen the Brand
- Core Component of the Value Proposition
- Facilitate the Service Encounter and Enhance Productivity

Theories from Environmental Psychology That Explain Consumer Responses to Service Environments

The Mehrabian-Russell Stimulus-Response Model

- Perceptions and interpretation of servicescapes influences how consumers feel
- These feelings then drive consumer responses to those environments

Russell's Model of Affect

- Customers' feelings (or emotions) can be modelled with two dimensions: Pleasure and arousal
- Pleasure is subjective
- Arousal largely depends on the information rate of an environment
- Pleasure and arousal interact on response behaviors, whereby arousal generally amplifies the effects of pleasure (or displeasure)

Bitner's Servicescape Model

Key Dimensions of Service Environments

- Ambient conditions (e.g., music, scents and colors)
- Spatial layout and functionality (including floor plan, size and shape of furnishing, counters, equipment)
- Signs, symbols and artifacts
- Appearance of service employees and other customers

Response Moderators

- Employees (e.g., liking of servicescape, personal tolerance for stimulation through music, noise and crowding)
- Customers

Internal Responses

- Cognitive (e.g., beliefs, perceptions)
- Emotional (e.g., moods, attitudes)
- Physiological (e.g., comfort, pain)

Behavioral Responses

- Approach (e.g., explore, spend time, spend money in the environment)
- Avoidance (e.g., leave the environment)
- Interaction between service employees and customers

Design of Effective Services Environments

- Design with a holistic view
- Design from the customers' perspective
- Use design tools (ranging from keen observation and customer feedback to photo audits and field experiments)

Figure 10.3 Designing the service environment.

Figure 10.4 Compare the two hotel lobbies. Different types of hotels have very different target segments.

clearly communicates and reinforces its hotel's respective positioning and sets service expectations as guests arrive.

Servicescapes often play an important role in building a service firm's brand image. For instance, the design of Starbucks outlets is closely associated with the company's brand identity. Likewise, Apple is famous for its sleek design, and its shops are no exception. With their airy and minimalist interiors, white lighting, silver steel, and beige timber, Apple Stores create a bright, open, and futuristic servicescape that provides a carefree and casual atmosphere. Apple's flagship stores feature dramatic locations such as inside the Louvre in Paris or under a 40-foot-high glass cylinder in Shanghai (Figure 10.5).

Apple's retail operations are an important part of its business. The company has 453 retail stores in 16 countries; 30,000 of its 43,000 employees in the United States work at Apple Stores, and its sales per square foot of $4,551 per annum in 2014 were the highest of any retailer in the country![5] The consistent, differentiated, and high-quality service experience delivered by Apple Stores reinforces Apple's brand image and is in line with the upmarket and high-quality positioning of its products (Figure 10.5).

Core Component of the Value Proposition

The servicescape can even be a core component of a firm's value proposition. Resort hotels are a perfect illustration of this principle. Club Med's villages, designed to create a totally carefree atmosphere, may have provided the original inspiration for "getaway" holiday environments. New destination resorts are not only far more luxurious than Club Med but also draw inspiration from theme parks to create fantasy environments, both indoors and outdoors. Perhaps the most extreme examples can be found in Las Vegas. Facing competition from numerous casinos

Figure 10.5 The Shanghai Apple store.

in other locations, Las Vegas has repositioned itself away from being a purely adult destination to become a somewhat more wholesome resort where families too can have fun. The gambling is still there, but many of the huge hotels recently built (or rebuilt) have been transformed by the addition of visually attractive features such as erupting "volcanoes" (Figure 10.6) mock sea battles; and striking reproductions of Paris, the pyramids of Egypt, and Venice and its canals.

Facilitate the Service Encounter and Enhance Productivity

Service environments are often designed to facilitate the service encounter and increase productivity. In fast-food restaurants and school cafeterias, strategically located tray-return stands and notices on walls remind customers to return their trays. Finally, Service Insights 10.1 shows how the design of hospitals helps patients to recover and employees to perform better.

THE THEORY BEHIND CONSUMER RESPONSES TO SERVICE ENVIRONMENTS

We now understand why service firms put so much effort into the design of the service environment. However, why does the service environment have such important effects on people and their behaviors? The field of environmental psychology studies how people respond to particular environments. We can apply the theories from this field to better understand and manage customer behavior in different service settings.

▶ **LO 2**
Know the theoretical underpinning from environmental psychology that helps us to understand how customers and employees respond to service environments.

Figure 10.6 At the Mirage Hotel and Casino in Las Vegas, an erupting volcano is part of the servicescape.

Feelings Are a Key Driver of Customer Responses to Service Environments

Two important models help us better understand consumer responses to service environments. The first, the Mehrabian-Russell Stimulus-Response Model, holds that our feelings are central to how we respond to different elements in the environment. The second, Russell's Model of Affect, focuses on how we can better understand those feelings and their effects on response behaviors.

The Mehrabian-Russell Stimulus-Response Model. Figure 10.7 displays a simple yet fundamental model of how people respond to environments. The model holds that the conscious and unconscious perception and interpretation of the environment influence how people feel in that setting.[6] These feelings, rather than perceptions or thoughts, drive customer behavior. Similar environments can lead to very different feelings and subsequent responses. For example, we may dislike being in a crowded department store with lots of other customers, find ourselves unable to get what we want as fast as we wish, and thus seek to avoid that environment. We don't do this simply because there are a lot of people around us. Rather, we are deterred by the unpleasant feeling of crowding and of not being able to get what we want fast enough. However, if we are not in a rush, we may feel pleased and excited about being part of the crowd during seasonal festivities in the very same environment. This may make us want to stay and enjoy the experience.

In environmental-psychology research, the typical outcome variable studied is the "approach" or "avoidance" of an environment. Of course, in services marketing, we can

Figure 10.7 Model of environmental responses.

The Hospital Servicescape and Its Effects on Patients and Employees[8]

Thankfully, most of us do not have to stay in hospitals. If such a situation arises, we hope our stay will allow us to recover in a suitable environment. But what is considered suitable in a hospital?

During their stay in a hospital, patients may contract infections, feel stressed by contact with many strangers yet bored without much to do, dislike the food, or be unable to rest well. All these factors may delay a patient's recovery. Research has shown that greater care in designing the hospital servicescape reduces these risks and contributes to the well-being and recovery of patients as well as the welfare and productivity of staff. The recommendations include:

- *Provide single-bed rooms.* These can lower the number of infections caught in the hospital, improve rest and sleep quality by lessening disturbance caused by other patients sharing the room, increase patient privacy, facilitate social support by families, and even improve communication between staff and patients.

- *Reduce noise levels.* This leads to decreased stress levels for staff and improved sleep for patients.

- *Provide distractions for patients.* These could include areas of greenery that the patients can see; personalized television with headphones so that others do not get disturbed; internet access for tablets and smart phones; and perhaps a reading room cum library with newspapers, magazines, and books. Such facilities can aid patient recovery.

- *Improve lighting, especially access to natural light.* A lighted environment increases cheerfulness in the building. Natural lighting can reduce the length of a patient's stay in the hospital. Staff members also work better under proper lighting and make fewer errors.

- *Improve ventilation and air filtration.* This can reduce the transmission of airborne viruses and improve air quality in the building.

- *Develop user-friendly "way-finding" systems.* Hospitals are complex buildings, and first-time or infrequent visitors are often frustrated when they cannot find their way, especially when rushing to see a loved one who has been hospitalized.

- *Design the layout* of patient-care units and the location of nurse stations to reduce unnecessary walking within the building and the resultant exhaustion and waste of time. The quality of patient care can be improved in this way. Well-designed layouts also enhance staff communication and activities.

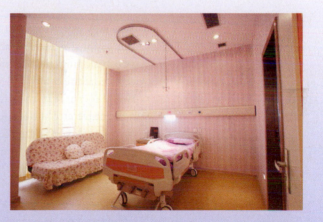

SOURCE

Source: Based on R. Ulrich, X. Quan, C. Zimring, A. Joseph, and R. Choudhary, "The Role of the Physical Environment in the Hospital of the 21st Century: A Once-in-a-Lifetime Opportunity," report to the Center for Health Design for the Designing the 21st Century Hospital Project, funded by the Robert Wood Johnson Foundation (September 2004).

PART III

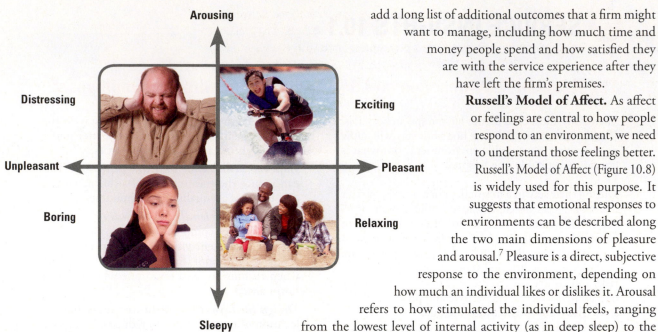

Figure 10.8 The Russell Model of Affect.

add a long list of additional outcomes that a firm might want to manage, including how much time and money people spend and how satisfied they are with the service experience after they have left the firm's premises.

Russell's Model of Affect. As affect or feelings are central to how people respond to an environment, we need to understand those feelings better. Russell's Model of Affect (Figure 10.8) is widely used for this purpose. It suggests that emotional responses to environments can be described along the two main dimensions of pleasure and arousal.[7] Pleasure is a direct, subjective response to the environment, depending on how much an individual likes or dislikes it. Arousal refers to how stimulated the individual feels, ranging from the lowest level of internal activity (as in deep sleep) to the highest levels of adrenaline in the bloodstream (such as when bungee-jumping). The arousal quality of an environment is much less subjective than its pleasure quality. Arousal quality depends largely on the information rate or load of an environment. For example, environments are stimulating (i.e., have a high information rate) when they are complex, include motion or change, and have novel and surprising elements. A low-rate, relaxing environment has the opposite characteristics.

You may ask: How can all my feelings and emotions be explained by only two dimensions? Russell separated the cognitive or thinking part of emotions from these two basic underlying emotional dimensions. Thus, the emotion of anger due to a service failure could be described in terms of high arousal and high displeasure, which would locate it in the distressing region in our model. This is then combined with a cognitive attribution process. When a customer attributes a service failure to the firm, the powerful cognitive attribution process feeds directly into high arousal and displeasure. Similarly, most other emotions can be dissected into their cognitive and affective components.

The strength of Russell's Model of Affect is its simplicity, as it allows a direct assessment of how customers feel when they are in the service environment. Therefore, firms can set targets for the affective states they want their customers to be in. For example, a roller-coaster operator wants its customers to feel excited. A spa may want customers to feel relaxed, a bank pleasant, and so on.

Affective and Cognitive Processes. Affect can be caused by sensations, perceptions, and cognitive processes of any degree of complexity. However, the more complex a cognitive process becomes, the more powerful is its potential impact on affect. For example, a customer's disappointment with the service level and food quality in a restaurant (a complex cognitive process in which perceived quality is compared to previously held service expectations) cannot be compensated by a simple cognitive process such as the subconscious perception of pleasant background music. However, this doesn't mean that simple cognitive processes such as the subconscious perception of scents or music are unimportant. In practice, the large majority of people's service encounters are routine, with little high-level cognitive processing. We tend to function on "auto pilot" and follow our service scripts during routine transactions such as using a bus or subway or entering a fast-food restaurant or a bank. Most of the time, it is the simple cognitive processes that determine how people feel in the service setting. However, if higher levels of cognitive processes are triggered—for instance, through something surprising in the service environment—then it's the interpretation of this surprise that determines people's feelings.[9]

Behavioral Consequences of Affect. At the most basic level, pleasant environments result in approach behaviors and unpleasant ones in avoidance. Arousal amplifies the basic effect of pleasure on behavior. If the environment is pleasant, increasing arousal can generate excitement and lead to a stronger positive response. Conversely, if a service environment is inherently unpleasant, increasing arousal levels will move customers into the "distressed" region. For example, loud fast-paced music increases the stress levels of shoppers trying to make their way through crowded aisles on a pre-Christmas Friday evening. In such situations, retailers should try to lower the information load of the environment.

Finally, customers have strong affective expectations from some services. Think of such experiences as a romantic candle-lit dinner in a restaurant, a relaxing spa visit, or an exciting time at the stadium or the dance club. When customers have strong affective expectations, the environment must be designed to match those expectations.[10]

The Servicescape Model—An Integrative Framework

Building on the basic models in environmental psychology, Mary Jo Bitner developed a comprehensive model that she named the "servicescape."[11] Figure 10.9 shows the main dimensions she identified in service environments: ambient conditions; space/ functionality; and signs, symbols, and artifacts. As individuals tend to perceive these dimensions holistically, the key to effective design is how well each individual dimension fits together with everything else.

Bitner's model shows that there are customer- and employee-response moderators. This means that the same service environment can have different effects on different customers, depending on who the customer is and what he/she likes. Beauty lies in the eyes of the beholder and is subjective. For example, rap music or an opera may be sheer pleasure to some customer segments and torture to others.

An important contribution of Bitner's model is the inclusion of employee responses to the service environment. After all, employees spend much more time there than customers. It's important for designers to be aware of how a particular environment enhances the productivity of front-line personnel and the quality of service that they deliver.

Internal customer and employee responses can be grouped into cognitive responses (e.g., quality perceptions and beliefs), emotional responses (e.g., feelings and moods), and physiological responses (e.g., pain and comfort). These internal responses lead to overt behavioral responses such as avoiding a crowded supermarket or responding positively to a relaxing environment by remaining there longer and spending extra money on impulse purchases. The behavioral responses of customers and employees must be shaped in ways that aid the production and purchase of high-quality services.

LO 3
Be familiar with the integrative servicescape model.

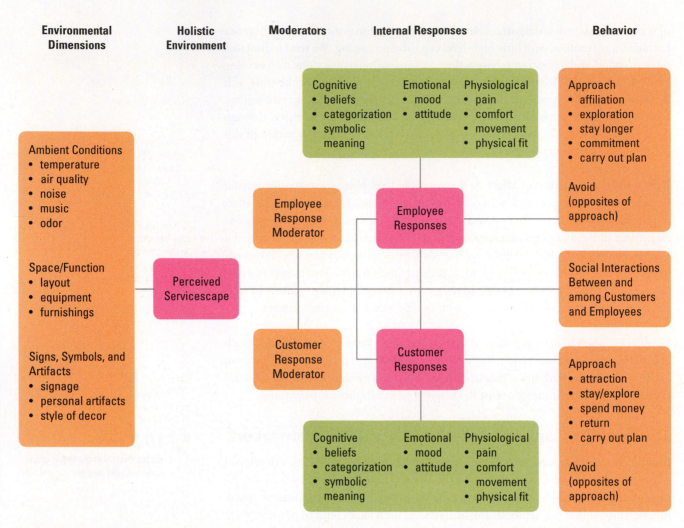

Figure 10.9 The servicescape model.

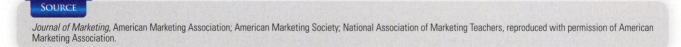

SOURCE

Journal of Marketing, American Marketing Association; American Marketing Society; National Association of Marketing Teachers, reproduced with permission of American Marketing Association.

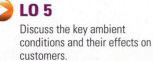

LO 4

Know the three main dimensions of the service environment.

LO 5

Discuss the key ambient conditions and their effects on customers.

DIMENSIONS OF THE SERVICE ENVIRONMENT

Service environments are complex and have many design elements. In Table 10.1, for example, you can see an overview of the design elements that might be encountered in a retail outlet. In this section, we focus on the main dimensions of the service environment in the servicescape model—ambient conditions; space and functionality; and signs, symbols, and artifacts.[12]

The Effect of Ambient Conditions

Ambient conditions refer to those characteristics of the environment that pertain to your five senses. Even when they're not noted consciously, they may still affect a person's emotional well-being, perceptions, and even attitudes and behaviors. They

Table 10.1 Design elements of a retail store environment.

Dimensions	Design Elements	
Exterior facilities	• Architectural style • Height of building • Size of building • Color of building • Exterior walls and exterior signs • Storefront • Marquee • Lawns and gardens	• Window displays • Entrances • Visibility • Uniqueness • Surrounding stores • Surrounding areas • Congestion • Parking and accessibility
General interior	• Flooring and carpeting • Color schemes • Lighting • Scents • Odors (e.g., tobacco smoke) • Sounds and music • Fixtures • Wall composition • Wall textures (paint, wallpaper) • Ceiling composition	• Temperature • Cleanliness • Width of aisles • Dressing facilities • Vertical transportation • Dead areas • Merchandise layout and displays • Price levels and displays • Cash register placement • Technology, modernization
Store layout	• Allocation of floor space for selling, merchandise, personnel, and customers • Placement of merchandise • Grouping of merchandise • Workstation placement • Placement of equipment • Placement of cash register	• Waiting areas • Traffic flow • Waiting queues • Furniture • Dead areas • Department locations • Arrangements within departments
Interior displays	• Point-of-purchase displays • Posters, signs, and cards • Pictures and artwork • Wall decorations • Theme setting • Ensemble	• Racks and cases • Product display • Price display • Cut cases and dump bins • Mobiles
Social dimensions	• Personnel characteristics • Employee uniforms • Crowding	• Customer characteristics • Privacy • Self-service

are composed of literally hundreds of design elements and details that must work together to create the desired service environment. Ambient conditions are perceived both separately and holistically. They include music, sounds and noise, scents and smells, color schemes and lighting, and temperature and air movement (Figure 10.10). The clever design of these conditions can elicit desired behavioral responses among consumers. Let us now discuss a number of important ambient dimensions, starting with music.

Figure 10.10 Live folk music may enhance the diners' experience.

Music. Music can have a powerful effect on perceptions and behaviors in service settings, even if it is played at barely audible volumes. The various structural characteristics of music such as tempo, volume, and harmony are perceived holistically, and their effect on internal and behavioral responses is moderated by respondent characteristics (e.g., younger and older people often respond differently to the same piece of music).[13]

Numerous research studies have found that fast tempo and high-volume music increases arousal levels, which can then cause customers to increase the pace of various behaviors.[14] People tend to adjust their pace, either voluntarily or involuntarily, to match the tempo of music. This means that restaurants can speed up table turnover and serve more diners during busy lunch hours by increasing the tempo and volume of the music. They can also play slow beat music at a softer volume to keep evening diners longer in the restaurant and increase beverage revenues. A restaurant study conducted over eight weeks showed that customers who dined in a slow-music environment spent longer in the restaurant than individuals in a fast-music condition. As a result, beverage revenue increased substantially when slow-beat music was played.[15]

Likewise, studies have shown that shoppers walked less rapidly and increased their level of impulse purchases when slow music was played.[16] In situations that require the customer to wait for the service, the effective use of music may shorten the perceived waiting time and increase customer satisfaction. Relaxing music proved effective in lowering stress levels in a hospital's surgery waiting room.[17]

Figure 10.11 Classical music can be used to deter vandals and loiterers.

Providing the right mix of music to restaurants, retail stores, and even call centers has become an industry in its own right. Mood Media, the market leader in this space, provides music to over 300,000 commercial locations in the United States. It tailors its playlists to outlets such as Christian bookstores, black barber shops, and bilingual malls where Anglo and Hispanic customers mingle. It also uses "day parting" to target music to various client segments such as day-time mothers or after-school teens.[18] Would it surprise you to learn that music can also be used to deter the wrong type of customer? Many service environments, including subway systems, supermarkets, and other publicly accessible locations, attract individuals who are not bona fide customers. Some are jaycustomers (see Chapter 12), whose behavior causes problems for a firm's management as well as its target customers. In the United Kingdom, an increasingly popular strategy for driving such individuals away is to play classical music, which is apparently unpleasant to the ears of vandals and loiterers (Figure 10.11). Co-op, a U.K. grocery chain, has been playing classical music outside its outlets to stop teenagers from hanging around and intimidating customers. Steve Broughton of Co-op reports that the company's staff members are equipped with a remote control and "can turn the music on if there's a situation developing and they need to disperse people."[19]

Scent. The ambient scent or smell that pervades an environment may or may not be perceived consciously by customers and is not related to any particular product. Scent can have a strong impact on mood, feelings, evaluations, purchase intentions, and in-store behaviors.[20] We experience the power of smell when we are hungry and get a whiff of freshly baked croissants long before we pass a local bakery. This smell makes us aware of our hunger and points us to the solution. Likewise, the smell of freshly baked cookies on Main Street in Disney's Magic Kingdom relaxes customers and provides a feeling of warmth, while the smell of potpourri in Victoria's Secret stores creates the ambience of a lingerie closet.

Olfaction researcher Alan R. Hirsch, M.D. of the Smell & Taste Treatment and Research Foundation based in Chicago, is convinced that at some point in the future we will understand scents so well that we will be able to use them to manage people's behaviors.[21] Service marketers are interested in how to make you hungry and thirsty in the restaurant, relax you in a dentist's waiting room, and energize you to work out harder in a gym. In aromatherapy, it is generally accepted that scents have special characteristics and can be used to solicit certain emotional, physiological, and behavioral responses (Figure 10.12). Table 10.2 shows the generally assumed effects of specific scents on people. Research has shown

Figure 10.12 Aromatherapy can induce a state of relaxation and rejuvenation.

Table 10.2 Aromatherapy: The effects of selected fragrances on people.

Fragrance	Aroma Type	Aromatherapy Class	Traditional Use	Potential Psychological Effect on People
Eucalyptus	Camphoraceous	Toning, stimulating	Deodorant, antiseptic, soothing agent	Stimulating and energizing
Lavender	Herbaceous	Calming, balancing, soothing	Muscle relaxant, soothing agent, astringent	Relaxing and calming
Lemon	Citrus	Energizing, uplifting	Antiseptic, soothing agent	Soothing energy levels
Black pepper	Spicy	Balancing, soothing	Muscle relaxant, aphrodisiac	Balancing people's emotions

that scents can have a significant impact on customers' perceptions, attitudes, and behaviors in service settings. For example:

▶ Gamblers plunked 45% more quarters into slot machines when a Las Vegas casino was scented with a pleasant artificial smell. When the intensity of the scent was increased, spending jumped by 53%.[22]

▶ People were more willing to buy Nike sneakers and pay more for them (an average of $10.33 more per pair) when they tried on the shoes in a floral-scented room. The same effect was observed even when the scent was so faint that people could not detect it (i.e., the scent was perceived unconsciously).[23]

Service firms have recognized the power of scent and increasingly make it a part of their brand experience. For example, Westin Hotels uses a white tea fragrance throughout its lobbies, and Sheraton scents its lobbies with a combination of fig, clove, and jasmine. As a response to the trend of scenting servicescapes, professional service firms have entered the scent marketing space. For example, Ambius, a Rentokil Initial company, offers scent-related services such as "sensory branding," "ambient scenting," and "odor remediation" for retail, hospitality, healthcare, financial services, and other services. Firms can outsource their servicescape scenting to Ambius, which offers one-stop solutions ranging from consulting and designing exclusive signature scents for a service firm to managing the ongoing scenting of all the outlets of a chain.[24] Clients of Mood Media, a leading provider of music, scents, and signage for commercial establishments, can choose their ideal ambient scent from a 1,500-strong scent library![25]

Color. In addition to music and scent, researchers have found that colors have a strong impact on people's feelings. Color "is stimulating, calming, expressive, disturbing, impressional, cultural, exuberant, symbolic. It pervades every aspect of our lives, embellishes the ordinary, and gives beauty and drama to everyday objects."[26]

The de facto system used in psychological research is the Munsell System, which defines colors in the three dimensions of hue, value, and chroma.[27] *Hue* is the pigment of the color (i.e. the name of the color: red, orange, yellow, green, blue, or violet). *Value* is the degree of lightness or darkness of the color, relative to a scale that extends from pure black to pure white. *Chroma* refers to hue intensity, saturation, or brilliance. High chroma colors have a high intensity of pigmentation and are perceived as rich and vivid, whereas low chroma colors are perceived as dull.

Hues are classified into warm colors (red, orange, and yellow) and cold colors (blue and green), with orange being the warmest and blue being the coldest. These colors can be used to manage the warmth of an environment. For example, if a violet is too warm, you can cool it off by reducing the amount of red. If a red is too cold, you can warm it up by giving it a shot of orange. Warm colors are associated not only with elated mood states and arousal but also with heightened anxiety. Cool colors reduce arousal levels and can elicit emotions such as peacefulness, calmness, love, and happiness.[28] Table 10.3 summarizes common associations and responses to colors.

Research in a service environment context has shown that despite differing color preferences, people are generally drawn to warm-color environments (Figure 10.13). Warm colors encourage fast decision making and are best suited for low-involvement

Table 10.3 Common associations and human responses to colors.

Color	Degree of Warmth	Nature Symbol	Common Association and Human Responses to Color
Red	Warm	Earth	High energy and passion; can excite and stimulate emotions, expressions, and warmth
Orange	Warmest	Sunset	Emotions, expressions, and warmth
Yellow	Warm	Sun	Optimism, clarity, intellect, and mood enhancing
Green	Cool	Growth, grass and trees	Nurturing, healing, and unconditional love
Blue	Coolest	Sky and ocean	Relaxation, serenity, and loyalty
Indigo	Cool	Sunset	Meditation and spirituality
Violet	Cool	Violet flower	Spirituality, reduces stress, can create an inner feeling of calm

service purchase decisions or impulse buying. Cool colors are favored when consumers need time to make high-involvement purchase decisions.[29]

Recent examples of effective color and lighting are the new cabin designs in the Boeing 787 Dreamliner and Airbus A350 models. In the past, cabin lights were either turned on or off, but the new light-emitting diode (LED) technology has made a wider lighting palette available. Designers are now illuminating the cabin in all kinds of hues and asking questions such as: "Does a pinkish-purple glow soothe and calm passengers when boarding better than an amber warmth?" or "Can lighting be used to prevent jet lag as much as possible?" The Finnair A350 cabin has two dozen light settings for the different stages of a long-haul flight. It also features a roughly 20-minute long "sunset" and aligns colors with the destination (e.g., warmer, amber colors when flying into Asia and cooler "Nordic blue" hues when arriving in Finland). Similarly, Virgin Atlantic has a few main settings on its 787 flights, including rose-champagne for boarding, purple-pink for drinks, amber for dinner, a silver glow for overnight sleep, and a waking color. According to Nik Lusardi, design manager at Virgin Atlantic: "We've always wanted to create a different kind of atmosphere aboard our aircraft and light plays exactly into our hands. . . . You can get people energized or you can relax people very, very quickly."[30]

► LO 6

Determine the roles of spatial layout and functionality.

Spatial Layout and Functionality

In addition to ambient conditions, spatial layout and functionality are other key dimensions of the service environment. These are particularly important because a service environment generally has to fulfill specific purposes and customer needs.

Figure 10.13 Many stores use warm colors to encourage impulse purchases.

Figure 10.14 Uncomfortable chairs in a lecture theater make it harder for students to concentrate.

 **LO 7**

Understand the roles of signs, symbols, and artifacts.

Spatial layout refers to the floor plan; the size and shape of furnishings, counters, and potential machinery and equipment; and the ways in which these are arranged. *Functionality* refers to the ability of these items to facilitate the performance of service transactions. Both dimensions affect the user-friendliness of the facility and its ability to serve customers well. Tables that are too close in a café, counters in a bank that lack privacy, uncomfortable chairs in a lecture theatre (Figure 10.14), and lack of car-parking space can all leave negative impressions on customers. They also affect the service experience, buying behavior, and, consequently, the business performance of the service facility.

Signs, Symbols, and Artifacts

Many things in the service environment act as explicit or implicit signals to communicate the firm's image, help customers find their way (e.g., to certain service counters, departments, or the exit), and convey the service script (e.g., for a queuing system). In particular, first-time customers will automatically try to draw meaning from the environment to guide them through the service processes.[31]

Examples of explicit signals include signs, which can be used (1) as labels (e.g., to indicate the name of the department or counter), (2) for giving directions (e.g., to certain service counters, the entrance and the exit, or lifts and toilets), (3) for communicating the service script (e.g., take a queue number and wait for your number to be called, or clear the tray after your meal), and (4) for reminders about behavioral rules (e.g., to demarcate smoking/no-smoking areas or to instruct viewers to switch off their mobile devices during a performance). Signs are often used to teach behavioral rules in service settings. Singapore is sometimes ironically referred to as a "fine" city because it strictly enforces rules in many service settings, especially in public buildings and public transport (Figure 10.15). However, the sign in Figure 10.16 is more creative and perhaps equally effective. Some signs are quite interesting and may be obvious, but other signs require the person to think a little in order to understand the meaning (Figure 10.17). Table 10.4 provides an overview of the benefits well-designed signage can provide to customers and service organizations.

Figure 10.15 Prohibition sign in the Singapore MRT subway.

Figure 10.16 This sign uses a creative message to manage visitor behavior.

The challenge for servicescape designers is to use signs, symbols, and artifacts to guide customers clearly through the process of service delivery and to teach the service script in as intuitive a manner as possible. This task assumes particular importance in servicescapes with a high proportion of new or infrequent customers (e.g., airports and hospitals) and/or a high degree of self-service (e.g., a self-service bank branch). Customers become disoriented when they cannot derive clear signals from a servicescape. This leads to anxiety and uncertainty about how to proceed and obtain the desired service. Think about the last time you were in a hurry and tried to find your way through an unfamiliar hospital, a shopping center, or a large government office where the signs and other directional cues were not intuitive to you. At many service facilities, customers' first point of contact is likely to be the car park. Service Insights 10.2 emphasizes how the principles of effective environment design apply even in such a mundane environment.

People Are Part of the Service Environment Too

The appearance and behavior of both service personnel and customers can strengthen the impression created by a service environment or weaken it. Dennis Nickson and his colleagues use the term "aesthetic labor" to capture the importance of the physical image of service personnel who serve customers directly.[32] Employees at Disney theme parks are called cast members. They may be acting as Cinderella or one of Snow White's seven dwarfs, or even as park cleaner or manager of Buzz Lightyear's Tomorrowland booth. In each case, they must dress to look the part and then "perform" for the guests.

Likewise, marketing communications may seek to attract customers who will not only appreciate the ambience created by the service provider but will also actively enhance it by their own appearance and behavior. In hospitality and retail settings, newcomers often survey the array of existing customers before deciding whether to patronize the establishment.

Putting It All Together

Although individuals often perceive particular aspects or individual design features of an environment, it is the total configuration of all those design features that determines consumer responses.

Design with a Holistic View

Whether a dark, glossy wooden floor is the perfect flooring in a servicescape depends on everything else in that service environment. These include the type, color scheme, and materials of the furniture; the lighting; the promotional materials; and the overall brand perception and positioning of the firm. Servicescapes have to be seen holistically. No dimension of the design can be optimized in isolation, because everything depends on everything else.

Figure 10.17 Confusing signs can lead people nowhere.

LO 8

Know how service employees and other customers are part of the servicescape.

LO 9

Explain why designing an effective servicescape has to be done holistically and from the customer's perspective.

Table 10.4 Benefits of well-designed signage for customers and service organizations.

For Customers	For the Service Organization
• Be informed, up-to-date, oriented, free to move about, guided along prepared paths, emotionally stimulated	• Direct, inform and manage the flow and the behavior of customers
• Created familiarity with the service scape	• Improve the quality of service provided and increase customer satisfaction
• Helps to participate with greater ease in the service process	• Reduce information-giving by frontline Employees
• Increases confidence and reassurance while following signage; provides higher levels of perceived control during the service encounter	• Help frontline employees to work with fewer Interruptions
• Reduces tension, confusion, lostness, wrong turns and requests for information	• Attract and excite curiosity, help to strengthen the corporate image
• Reduces time to reach the desired goal as efficiently as possible	• Differentiate the firm from the competition

SOURCES

Adapted from Angelo Bonfani, "Towards an Approach to Signage Management Quality (SMQ)," *Journal of Services Marketing* 27(4): 312–321. © 2013 Emerald Group Publishing Limited.

The process of planning the overall design of a service environment is an art. Therefore, professional designers tend to focus on specific types of servicescapes. For example, a handful of famous interior designers do nothing but create hotel lobbies around the world. Similarly, there are design experts who focus exclusively on restaurants, bars, and clubs; cafés and bistros; retail outlets; healthcare facilities; and so forth.

Design from a Customer's Perspective

Many service environments are built with an emphasis on aesthetic values. Designers sometimes forget the most important factor to consider when designing service environments—the customers who will be using them. Ron Kaufman, the founder of Up Your Service! College, experienced the following design flaws in two new high-profile service environments:

▶ "A new Sheraton Hotel had just opened in Jordan without clear signage that would guide guests from the ballrooms to the restrooms. The signs that did exist were etched in muted gold on dark marble pillars. More 'obvious' signs were apparently inappropriate amidst such elegant décor. Very swish, very chic, but who were they designing it for?"

▶ "At a new airport lounge in a major Asian city, a partition of colorful glass hung from the ceiling. My luggage lightly brushed against it as I walked inside. The entire partition shook and several panels came undone. A staff member hurried over and began carefully reassembling the panels. (Thank goodness nothing broke.) I apologized profusely. 'Don't worry,' she replied, 'This happens all the time.'" An airport lounge is a heavy traffic area. People are always moving in and out. Kaufman keeps asking "What were the interior designers thinking? Who were they designing it for?"

Guidelines for Parking Design

Car parks play an important role at many service facilities. The effective use of signs, symbols, and artifacts in a parking lot or garage helps customers find their way, manages their behavior, and portrays a positive image of the sponsoring organization.

- *Friendly warnings.* All warning signs should communicate a customer benefit. The following sign is an example: "Fire lane—for everyone's safety we ask you not to park in the fire lane."

- *Safety lighting.* Good lighting that penetrates all areas makes life easier for customers and enhances safety. Firms may want to draw attention to this feature with notices stating that "Parking lots have been specially lit for your safety."

- *Help customers remember where they left their vehicle.* Forgetting where one left the family car in a large parking structure can be a nightmare. Many car parks have adopted color-coded floors to help customers remember which level they parked on. In addition, many car parks also mark sections with special symbols such as different kinds of animals. This helps customers to remember not only the level but also the section where the car is parked. Boston's Logan Airport has gone two steps further. Each level has been assigned a theme associated with Massachusetts, such as Paul Revere's Ride, Cape Cod, or the Boston Marathon. An image is attached to each theme—a male figure on horseback, a lighthouse, or a female runner. While waiting for the elevator at a particular level, travelers hear a few bars of music that are tied to the theme for that level. For instance, the Boston Marathon floor uses the theme music from *Chariots of Fire*, an Oscar-winning movie about an Olympic runner.

- *Maternity parking.* Handicapped parking spaces are often required by law, but vehicles must have special stickers in order to be parked in these spaces. A few thoughtful organizations have special parking spaces for expectant mothers that are marked with a blue/pink stork. This strategy demonstrates a sense of caring and an understanding of customer needs.

- *Fresh paint.* Curbs, cross walks, and lot lines should be repainted regularly before any cracking, peeling, or disrepair becomes evident. Proactive and frequent repainting gives positive cleanliness cues and projects a positive image.

Figure 10.18 The environmental design of shopping centers affects the shopping experience.

"I am regularly amazed," declared Kaufman, "by brand new facilities that are obviously user 'unfriendly'!" He draws the following key learning point: "It's easy to get caught up in designing new things that are 'cool' or 'elegant' or 'hot'. But if you don't keep your customer in mind throughout, you could end up with an investment that's not."[33]

Along a similar vein, Alain d'Astous explored environmental aspects that irritate shoppers. His findings highlighted the following problems:

▶ *Ambient conditions* (ordered by level of irritation):
  o The store is not clean.
  o It is too hot inside the store or the shopping center.
  o The music inside the store is too loud.
  o The store smells bad.

▶ *Environmental design variables*:
  o There is no mirror in the dressing room.
  o Customers are unable to find what they need.
  o Directions within the store are inadequate.
  o The arrangement of store items has been changed in a way that confuses customers.

SERVICE INSIGHTS 10.3

Design of Disney's Magic Kingdom

Walt Disney was one of the undisputed champions in the field of service environment design. His tradition of amazingly careful and detailed planning has become a hallmark of his company and is visible everywhere in its theme parks. For example, Main Street is angled to make it seem longer upon entry into the Magic Kingdom than it actually is. Myriad facilities and attractions are strategically inclined and located at each side of the street to make people look forward to the relatively long journey to the Castle. However, when one looks down the slope from the Castle back towards the entrance, Main Street appears shorter. This relieves exhaustion, rejuvenates guests, and even encourages strolling (thereby eliminating the problem of traffic congestion due to too many buses).

The meandering sidewalks with multiple attractions keep guests entertained, as they can participate in the planned activities and even watch other guests. Trash bins are plentiful and always in sight to convey the message that littering is prohibited. The repainting of facilities is a routine procedure that signals a high level of maintenance and cleanliness.

Disney's servicescape design and upkeep help to script customer experiences and create pleasure and satisfaction for guests not only in its theme parks but also in its cruise ships and hotels.

o   The store is too small.

o   Customers lose their way in a large shopping center.[34] (Figure 10.18)

Contrast Kaufman's experiences and d'Astou's findings with the Disney example in Service Insights 10.3. One can clearly see how detailed attention to the design of the service environment can make a difference.

Tools to Guide Servicescape Design

A manager can use several tools to determine how customers use the servicescape, which of its aspects irritate them, and which aspects they like. Some of these are as follows:

▶   *Keen observation* of customers' behavior and responses to the service environment by management, supervisors, branch managers, and front-line staff.

Table 10.5 A visit to the movies: the service environment as perceived by the customer.

Steps in the Service Encounter	Design of the Service Environment	
	Exceeds Expectations	**Fails Expectations**
Locate a parking lot	Ample room in a bright place near the entrance, with a security officer protecting your valuables	Insufficient parking spaces, so patrons have to park in another lot
Queue up to obtain tickets	Strategic placement of mirrors, posters of upcoming movies, and entertainment news to ease perception of long wait, if any; movies and time slots easily seen; ticket availability clearly communicated	A long queue and having to wait for a long while; difficult to see quickly what movies are being shown at what time slots and whether tickets are still available
Check tickets to enter the theater	A very well-maintained lobby with clear directions to the theater and posters of the movie to enhance patrons' experience	A dirty lobby with rubbish strewn and unclear or misleading directions to the movie theater
Go to the restroom before the movie starts	Sparkling clean, spacious, brightly lit, dry floors, well stocked, nice décor, clear mirrors wiped regularly	Dirty, with an unbearable odor; broken toilets; no hand towels, soap, or toilet paper; overcrowded; dusty and dirty mirrors
Enter the theater and locate your seat	Spotless theater; well designed with no bad seats; sufficient lighting to locate your seat; spacious, comfortable chairs, with drink and popcorn holders on each seat; and a suitable temperature	Rubbish on the floor, broken seats, sticky floor, gloomy and insufficient lighting, burned-out exit signs
Watch the movie	Excellent sound system and film quality, nice audience, an enjoyable and memorable entertainment experience overall	Substandard sound and movie equipment, uncooperative audience that talks and smokes because of lack of "No Smoking" and other signs; a disturbing and unenjoyable entertainment experience overall
Leave the theater and return to the car	Friendly service staff greet patrons as they leave; an easy exit through a brightly lit and safe parking area, back to the car with the help of clear lot signs	A difficult trip, as patrons squeeze through a narrow exit, unable to find the car because of no or insufficient lighting

- ▶ ***Feedback and ideas from front-line staff and customers*** using a variety of research tools ranging from social media and suggestion boxes to focus groups and surveys.

- ▶ ***Photo audit*** is a method of asking customers (or mystery shoppers) to take photographs of their service experience. These photographs can be used later as a basis for further interviews of their experience or included as part of a survey about the service experience.[35]

- ▶ ***Field experiments*** can be used to manipulate specific dimensions in an environment so that their effects can be observed. For instance, researchers can experiment with various types of music and scents and then measure the time and money customers spend in the environment. Laboratory experiments with pictures, videos, or other ways to simulate real-world service environments (such as virtual tours via computer) can be effectively used to examine the impact of changes in design elements that cannot be easily manipulated in a field experiment. Examples include testing of different color schemes, spatial layouts, or styles of furnishing.

- ▶ ***Blueprinting*** or flowcharting (described in Chapter 8) can be extended to include the physical evidence in the environment. Design elements and tangible cues can be documented as the customer moves through each step of the service delivery process. Photos can supplement the map to make it more vivid.

Table 10.5 shows an examination of a customer's visit to a movie theater. It identifies how the different environmental elements at each step exceeded or failed to meet expectations. The service process was broken up into steps, decisions, duties, and activities, all designed to take the customer through the entire service encounter. The more a service company can see, understand, and experience the same things as its customers, the better equipped will it be to realize errors in the design of its environment and to improve what is already functioning well.

LO 1 ▶ Service environments fulfill four core purposes. Specifically, they:

- Shape customers' experiences and behaviors.
- Play an important role in determining customer perceptions of the firm and its image and positioning. Customers often use the service environment as an important quality signal.
- Can be a core part of the value proposition (as for theme parks and resort hotels).
- Facilitate the service encounter and enhance productivity.

LO 2 ▶ Environmental psychology provides the theoretical underpinning for understanding the effects of service environments on customers and service employees. There are two key models:

- The Mehrabian-Russell Stimulus-Response model holds that environments influence peoples' affective state (or emotions and feelings), which in turn drives their behavior.
- Russell's Model of Affect holds that affect can be modeled with the two interacting dimensions of pleasure and arousal. Together, they determine whether people approach an environment and spend time and money in it or whether they avoid it.

LO 3 ▶ The servicescape model, which builds on the aforementioned theories, represents an integrative framework that explains how customers and service staff respond to key environmental dimensions.

LO 4 ▶ The servicescape model emphasizes three dimensions of the service environment:

- Ambient conditions (including music, scents, and colors)
- Spatial layout and functionality
- Signs, symbols, and artifacts

LO 5 ▶ Ambient conditions refer to those characteristics of the environment that pertain to our five senses. Even when not consciously perceived, they can still affect people's internal and behavioral responses. Important ambient dimensions include:

- Music: Its tempo, volume, harmony, and familiarity shape behavior by affecting emotions and moods. People tend to adjust their pace to match the tempo of the music.
- Scent: Ambient scent can stir powerful emotions and relax or stimulate customers.

- Color: Colors can have strong effects on people's feelings, with warm (e.g., red and orange) and cold colors (e.g., blue) having different impacts. Warm colors are associated with elated moods, while cold colors are linked to peacefulness and happiness.

LO 6 ▶ Effective spatial layout and functionality are important for making the service operation more efficient and enhancing its user friendliness.

- Spatial layout refers to the floor plan; the size and shape of furnishings, counters, and potential machinery and equipment; and the ways in which they are arranged.
- Functionality refers to the ability of these items to facilitate service operations.

LO 7 ▶ Signs, symbols, and artifacts help customers to draw meaning from the environment and guide them through the service process. They can be used to:

- Label facilities, counters, or departments
- Show directions (e.g., to the entrance, exit, elevator, or toilet)
- Communicate the service script (e.g., take a queuing number and wait for it to be called)
- Reinforce behavioral rules (e.g., "please turn your cell phones to silent mode")

LO 8 ▶ The appearance and behavior of service employees and other customers in a servicescape can be part of the value proposition and can reinforce (or undermine) the positioning of the firm.

LO 9 ▶ Service environments are perceived holistically. Therefore, no individual aspect can be optimized without considering everything else. The process of designing service environments is an art rather than a science.

- Due to this challenge, professional designers tend to specialize on specific types of environments, such as hotel lobbies, clubs, health-care facilities, and so on.
- The best service environments are designed not only on the basis of aesthetic considerations but, more importantly, with the customer's perspective in mind. The purpose is to guide customers smoothly through the service process.
- Tools that can be used to design and improve servicescapes include careful observation, feedback from employees and customers, photo audits, field experiments, and blueprinting.

PART III

UNLOCK YOUR LEARNING

These keywords are found within the sections of each Learning Objective (LO). They are integral to understanding the services marketing concepts taught in each section. Having a firm grasp of these keywords and how they are used is essential to helping you do well on your course, and in the real and very competitive marketing scene out there.

LO 1
1 Differentiation
2 Enhance productivity
3 Service quality
4 Brand image
5 Positioning
6 Service environments
7 Servicescapes
8 Service expectations
9 Shape customers' experiences
10 Value proposition
11 Service encounter

LO 2
1 Affective expectations
2 Affective processes
3 Approach
4 Arousal
5 Avoidance
6 Behavioral consequences
7 Cognitive processes
8 Feelings
9 Environmental psychology
10 Mehrabian-Russell Stimulus-Response Model
11 Pleasure

12 Consumer responses
13 Russell's Model of Affect

LO 3
1 Bitner
2 Cognitive responses
3 Emotional responses
4 Internal responses
5 Physiological responses
6 Behavioral responses
7 Servicescape model

LO 4
1 Dimensions of the service environment
2 Design elements

LO 5
1 Ambient conditions
2 Ambient scenting
3 Aromatherapy
4 Brilliance
5 Chroma
6 Color
7 Hue
8 Music
9 Odor remediation
10 Saturation
11 Scent
12 Sensory branding
13 Value

LO 6
1 Functionality
2 Spatial layout

LO 7
1 Artifacts
2 Parking design

3 Signs
4 Symbols
5 Service script
6 Explicit signals
7 Behavioral rules

LO 8
1 Aesthetic labor
2 People

LO 9
1 Feedback
2 Blueprinting
3 Customer's perspective
4 Environmental design variables
5 Field experiments
6 Flowcharting
7 Holistic view
8 Observation
9 Photo audit
10 Servicescape design

How well do you know the language of services marketing? Quiz yourself!

⚠️ **Not for the academically faint-of-heart**

For each keyword you are able to recall without referring to earlier pages, give yourself a point (and a pat on the back). Tally your score at the end and see if you earned the right to be called—a *services marketeer*.

SCORE

0 – 11	Services Marketing is done a great disservice.
12 – 22	The midnight oil needs to be lit, pronto.
23 – 33	I know what you *didn't* do all semester.
34 – 44	A close shave with success.
45 – 55	Now, go forth and market.
56 – 60	There should be a marketing concept named after you.

Review Questions

1. What are the four main purposes service environments fulfill?

2. Describe how the Mehrabian-Russell Stimulus-Response Model and Russell's Model of Affect explain consumer responses to a service environment.

3. What is the relationship or link between Russell's Model of Affect and the servicescape model?

4. Why do different customers and service staff respond very differently to the same service environment?

5. Explain the dimensions of ambient conditions and the ways in which each can influence customer responses to the service environment.

6. What are the roles of signs, symbols, and artifacts?

7. What are the implications of the fact that service environments are perceived holistically?

8. What tools are available for aiding our understanding of customer responses and for guiding the design and improvement of service environments?

WORK YOUR SERVICES MARKETING

Application Exercises

1. Identify firms from three different service industries where the service environment is a crucial part of the overall value proposition. Analyze and explain in detail the value that is being delivered by the service environment in each of the three industries.

2. Visit a service environment, and have a detailed look around. Experience the environment, and try to understand how the various design elements shape what you feel and how you behave in that setting.

3. Select a bad and a good waiting experience, and contrast the two situations with respect to the service environment and the other people waiting.

4. Visit a self-service environment and analyze how the design dimensions guide you through the service process. Which elements do you find most effective, and which seem least effective? How can the environment be improved to make the "way-finding" process easier for self-service customers?

5. Take a camera and conduct a photo audit of a specific servicescape. Photograph examples of excellent and very poor design features. Develop concrete suggestions on how this environment could be improved.

PART III

ENDNOTES

1. Beatriz Plaza, "The Bilbao Effect," *Museum News* (September–October 2007): 13–15, 68; Denny Lee, "Bilbao, 10 Years Later," *The New York Times*, 23 September 2007, http://www .nytimes.com/2007/09/23/travel/23bilbao. html?pagewanted=all&_r=0, accessed April 25, 2015; *The Economist*, "The Bilbao Effect: If You Build It, Will They Come?" December 21, 2013: 5.

2. Madeleine E. Pullman and Michael A. Gross, "Ability of Experience Design Elements to Elicit Emotions and Loyalty Behaviors," *Decision Sciences* 35, no. 1 (2004): 551–578.

3. Anja Reimer and Richard Kuehn, "The Impact of Servicescape on Quality Perception," *European Journal of Marketing* 39, no. 7/8 (2005): 785–808.

4. Julie Baker, Dhruv Grewal, and A. Parasuraman, "The Influence of Store Environment on Quality Inferences and Store Image," *Journal of the Academy of Marketing Science* 22, no. 4 (1994): 328–339.

5. Barbara Thau, "Apple and the Other Most Successful Retailers by Sales per Square Foot," *Forbes*, May 20, 2014, http://www.forbes.com/ sites/barbarathau/2014/05/20/apple-and-the- other-most-successful-retail-stores-by-sales- per-square-foot/, accessed April 25, 2015; Yukari Iwatani Kane and Ian Sherr, "Secrets from Apple's Genius Bar: Full Loyalty, No Negativity," *The Wall Street Journal*, June 12, 2011, http://www .wsj.com/articles/SB100014240527023045631045 76364071955678908, accessed April 25, 2015.

6. Robert J. Donovan and John R. Rossiter, "Store Atmosphere: An Environmental Psychology Approach," *Journal of Retailing* 58, no. 1 (1982): 34–57.

7. James A. Russell, "A Circumplex Model of Affect," *Journal of Personality and Social Psychology* 39, no. 6 (1980): 1161–1178.

8. For a review of the literature on hospital design effects on patients, see: Karin Dijkstra, Marcel Pieterse, and Ad Pruyn, "Physical Environmental Stimuli That Turn Healthcare Facilities into Healing Environments through Psychologically Mediated Effects: Systematic Review," *Journal of Advanced Nursing* 56, no. 2 (2006): 166–181. See also the painstaking effort the Mayo Clinic has made to lower noise levels in its hospitals: Leonard L. Berry and Kent D. Seltman, *Management Lessons from Mayo Clinic: Inside One of the World's Most Admired Service Organizations* (McGraw-Hill, 2008): 171–172. For a study on the effects of hospital servicescape design on service workers' job stress, job satisfaction, and commitment to the firm, see: Janet Turner Parish, Leonard L. Berry, and Shun Yin Lam, "The Effect of the Servicescape on Service Workers," *Journal of Service Research* 10, no. 3 (2008): 220–238.

9. Jochen Wirtz and John E. G. Bateson, "Consumer Satisfaction with Services: Integrating the Environmental Perspective in Services Marketing into the Traditional Disconfirmation Paradigm," *Journal of Business Research* 44, no. 1 (1999): 55–66.

10. Jochen Wirtz, Anna S. Mattila, and Rachel L. P. Tan, "The Moderating Role of Target-Arousal on the Impact of Affect on Satisfaction: An Examination in the Context of Service Experiences," *Journal of Retailing* 76, no. 3 (2000): 347–365; Jochen Wirtz, Anna S. Mattila, and Rachel L. P. Tan, "The Role of Desired Arousal in Influencing Consumers' Satisfaction Evaluations and In-Store Behaviours," *International Journal of Service Industry Management* 18, no. 2 (2007): 6–24.

11. Mary Jo Bitner, "Servicescapes," 57–71.

12. For a comprehensive review of experimental studies on the atmospheric effects, refer to: L.W. Turley and Ronald E. Milliman, "Atmospheric Effects on Shopping Behavior: A Review of the Experimental Literature," *Journal of Business Research* 49 (2000): 193–211.

13. Steve Oakes, "The Influence of the Musicscape within Service Environments," *Journal of Services Marketing* 14, no. 7 (2000): 539–556.

14. Morris B. Holbrook and Punam Anand, "Effects of Tempo and Situational Arousal on the Listener's Perceptual and Affective Responses to Music," *Psychology of Music* 18 (1990): 150–162; S. J. Rohner and R. Miller, "Degrees of Familiar and Affective Music and Their Effects on State Anxiety," *Journal of Music Therapy* 17, no. 1 (1980): 2–15.

15. Laurette Dubé and Sylvie Morin, "Background Music Pleasure and Store Evaluation Intensity Effects and Psychological Mechanisms," *Journal of Business Research* 54 (2001): 107–113.

16. Clare Caldwell and Sally A. Hibbert, "The Influence of Music Tempo and Musical Preference on Restaurant Patrons' Behavior," *Psychology and Marketing* 19, no. 11 (2002): 895–917.

17. For a review of the effects of music on various aspects of consumer responses and evaluations, see: Steve Oakes and Adrian C. North, "Reviewing Congruity Effects in the Service Environment Musicscape," *International Journal of Service Industry Management* 19, no. 1 (2008): 63–82.

18. See www.moodmedia.com for in-store music solutions provided by Mood Media.

19. This section is based on: "Classical Music and Social Control: Twilight of the Yobs," *The Economist*, January 8, 2005: 48.

20. Eric R. Spangenberg, Ayn E. Crowley, and Pamela W. Henderson, "Improving the Store Environment: Do Olfactory Cues Affect Evaluations and Behaviors?" *Journal of Marketing* 60 (April 1996): 67–80; Paula Fitzgerald Bone and Pam Scholder Ellen, "Scents in the Marketplace: Explaining a Fraction of Olfaction," *Journal of Retailing* 75, no. 2 (1999): 243–262; Jeremy Caplan, "Sense and Sensibility," *Time* 168, no. 16 (2006): 66–67.

21. Alan R. Hirsch, *Dr. Hirsch's Guide to Scentsational Weight Loss* (UK: Harper Collins, 1997): 12–15; http://www.smellandtaste.org/, accessed April 25, 2015.

22. Alan R. Hirsch, "Effects of Ambient Odors on Slot Machine Usage in a Las Vegas Casino," *Psychology and Marketing* 12, no. 7 (1995): 585–594.

23. Alan R. Hirsch and S. E. Gay, "Effect on Ambient Olfactory Stimuli on the Evaluation of a Common Consumer Product," *Chemical Senses* 16 (1991): 535.

24. See Ambius's website for details of its scent marketing, ambient scenting, and sensory branding services at: http://www.ambius.com/ambius-catalogs/scent/index.html, accessed April 24, 2015.

25. *The Economist*, "Christmas Music: Dreaming of a Hip-Hop Christmas," December 14, 2013: 36.

26. Linda Holtzschuhe, *Understanding Color: An Introduction for Designers*, 3rd ed. (New Jersey: John Wiley, 2006): 51.

27. Albert Henry Munsell, *A Munsell Color Product* (New York: Kollmorgen Corporation, 1996).

28. Heinrich Zollinger, *Color: A Multidisciplinary Approach* (Zurich: VHCA; Weinheim: Wiley-VCH, 1999): 71–79.

29. Joseph A. Bellizzi, Ayn E. Crowley, and Ronald W. Hasty, "The Effects of Color in Store Design," *Journal of Retailing* 59, no. 1 (1983): 21–45.

30. Justin Bachman, "Airlines Add Mood Lighting to Chill Passengers Out: New Boeing and Airbus Models Offer Cabin Designers Splashy Ways to Engage Passengers with Light," *Bloomberg Business* (2015), http://www.bloomberg.com/news/articles/2015-04-22/airlines-add-mood-lighting-to-chill-passengers-out, accessed April 24, 2015.

31. For an excellent review of the quality of signage management, see: Angelo Bonfani, "Towards an Approach to Signage Management Quality (SMQ)," *Journal of Services Marketing* 27, no. 4 (2013): 312–321.

32. Dennis Nickson, Chris Warhurst, and Eli Dutton, "The Importance of Attitude and Appearance in the Service Encounter in Retail and Hospitality," *Managing Service Quality* 2 (2005): 195–208.

33. Ron Kaufman, "Service Power: Who Were They Designing it for?" Newsletter, May 2001, http://ronkaufman.com.

34. Alan d'Astous, "Irritating Aspects of the Shopping Environment," *Journal of Business Research* 49 (2000): 149–156.

35. Madeleine E. Pullman and Stephani K. A. Robson, "Visual Methods: Using Photographs to Capture Customers' Experience with Design," *Cornell Hotel and Restaurant Administration Quarterly* 48, no. 2 (2007): 121–144.

CHAPTER 11

managing people for SERVICE ADVANTAGE

LEARNING OBJECTIVES (LOs)

By the end of this chapter, the reader should be able to:

- **LO1** Explain why service employees are so important for the success of a firm.
- **LO2** Understand the factors that make the work of front-line staff demanding and often difficult.
- **LO3** Describe the cycles of failure, mediocrity, and success in human resources for service firms.
- **LO4** Understand the key elements of the Service Talent Cycle for successful human resource management in service firms.
- **LO5** Know how to attract, select, and hire the right people for service jobs.
- **LO6** Explain the key areas in which service employees need training.
- **LO7** Understand the role of internal marketing and communications.
- **LO8** Understand why empowerment is so important in many front-line jobs.
- **LO9** Explain how to build high-performance service delivery teams.
- **LO10** Know how to integrate teams across departments and functional areas.
- **LO11** Know how to motivate and energize service employees so that they will deliver service excellence and productivity.
- **LO12** Understand what a service-oriented culture is.
- **LO13** Know the difference between service climate and culture, and describe the determinants of a climate for service.
- **LO14** Explain the qualities of effective leaders in service organizations.
- **LO15** Understand different leadership styles and realize the importance of role modeling and focusing the entire organization on the front line.

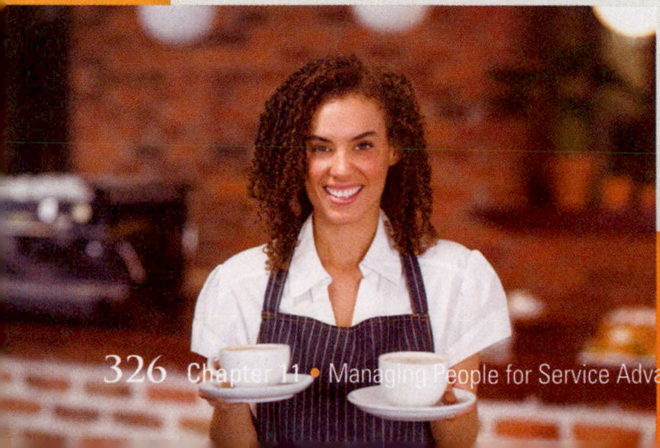

Figure 11.1 A waitress's pride in her professionalism earns her admiration and respect from customers and co-workers.

Cora Griffith: The Outstanding Waitress[1]

Cora Griffith, a waitress for the Orchard Café at the Paper Valley Hotel in Appleton, Wisconsin, is superb in her role! She is appreciated by first-time customers, famous among her regular customers, and revered by her co-workers. Cora loves her work, and it shows. Comfortable in a role that she believes is right for her, Cora follows nine rules of success:

1. **Treat Customers Like Family.** First-time customers are not allowed to feel like strangers. Cheerful and proactive, Cora smiles, chats, and includes everyone at the table in the conversation. She is as respectful to children as she is to adults and makes it a point to learn and use everyone's name. "I want people to feel like they're sitting down to dinner right at my house. I want them to feel they're welcome, that they can get comfortable, that they can relax. I don't just serve people, I pamper them."

2. **Listen First.** Cora has developed her listening skills to the point that she rarely writes down customers' orders. She listens carefully and provides a customized service: "Are they in a hurry? Do they have a special diet? Do they like their selection cooked in a certain way?"

3. **Anticipate Customers' Wants.** Cora refills beverages and brings extra bread and butter in a timely manner. One regular customer who likes honey with her coffee gets it without having to ask. "I don't want my customers to have to ask for anything, so I always try to anticipate what they might need."

4. **Simple Things Make the Difference.** Cora manages the details of her service, monitoring the cleanliness of the utensils and their correct placement. The napkins must be folded just right. She inspects each plate in the kitchen before taking it to the table. She provides crayons for children so that they can draw pictures while waiting for the meal. "It's the little things that please the customer," she says.

5. **Work Smart.** Cora scans all her tables at once, looking for opportunities to combine tasks. "Never do just one thing at a time," she advises. "And never go from the kitchen to the dining room empty-handed. Take coffee or iced tea or water with you." When she refills one glass of water, she refills others. When clearing one plate, she clears others. "You have to be organized, and you have to keep in touch with the big picture."

6. **Keep Learning.** Cora makes an ongoing effort to improve existing skills and learn new ones.

7. **Success Is Where You Find It.** Cora is content with her work. She finds satisfaction in pleasing her customers, and she enjoys helping other people enjoy. Her attitude is a positive force in the restaurant. She is hard to ignore. "If customers come to the restaurant in a bad mood, I'll try to cheer them up before they leave." Her definition of success is: "To be happy in life."

8. **All for One, One for All.** Cora has been working with many of the same co-workers for more than eight years. The team members support one another on the crazy days when 300 conventioneers come to the restaurant for breakfast at the same time. Everyone pitches in and helps. The wait staff cover for one another; the managers bus the tables; the chefs garnish the plates. "We are like a little family," Cora says. "We know each other very well and we help each other out. If we have a crazy day, I'll go in the kitchen towards the end of the shift and say, 'Man, I'm just proud of us. We really worked hard today.'"

9. **Take Pride in Your Work.** Cora believes in the importance of her work and in the need to do it well. "I don't think of myself as 'just a waitress' . . . I've chosen to be a waitress. I'm doing this to my full potential, and I give it my best. I tell anyone who's starting out: 'take pride in what you do'. You're never just an anything, no matter what you do. You give it your all . . . and you do it with pride."

Cora Griffith is a success story. She is loyal to her employer and dedicated to her customers and co-workers. A perfectionist who seeks continuous improvement, Cora's enthusiasm for her work and her unflagging spirit create an energy that radiates through the restaurant. She is proud of being a waitress, proud of "touching lives." She says: "I have always wanted to do my best. However, the owners really are the ones who taught me how important it is to take care of the customer and who gave me the freedom to do it. The company always has listened to my concerns and followed up. Had I not worked for the Orchard Café, I would have been a good waitress, but I would not have been the same waitress."

PART III

LO 1

Explain why service employees are so important for the success of a firm.

SERVICE EMPLOYEES ARE EXTREMELY IMPORTANT

The quality of a service firm's people—especially those working in customer-facing positions—plays a crucial role in determining market success and financial performance. Front-line employees are a key input for delivering service excellence and maintaining the firm's competitive positioning and advantage. The market and financial results of managing people effectively for service advantage can be phenomenal. That's why the *People* element of the 7 Ps is so important.

Highly capable and motivated people are at the center of service excellence and productivity. Cora Griffin in our opening vignette is a powerful demonstration of a front-line employee delivering high-quality service and at the same time having high job satisfaction. Most of Cora Griffin's nine rules of success are the result of good HR strategies for service firms. After reading this chapter, you will know how to manage human resources effectively in service firms to get satisfied, loyal, motivated, and productive service employees. The organizing framework for this chapter is provided in Figure 11.2.

Service Personnel as a Source of Customer Loyalty and Competitive Advantage

Almost everybody can recount some horror story of a dreadful experience they have had with a service business. If pressed, many of these same people can also recount a really good service experience. Service personnel usually feature prominently in such dramas. They either come across as uncaring, incompetent, mean-spirited villains or as heroes who went out of their way to help customers by anticipating their needs and resolving problems in a helpful and empathetic manner. You probably have your own set of favorite stories featuring both villains and heroes. If you're like most people, you probably talk more about the former than the latter.

From a customer's perspective, the encounter with service staff is probably the most important aspect of a service. From the firm's perspective, the service levels and the way service is delivered by front-line personnel can be an important source of differentiation as well as competitive advantage. The front line is particularly important for the firm's customers as well as its competitive positioning because it:

▶ **Is a core part of the product.** Often, the service employees are the most visible element of the service. They deliver the service and affect service quality greatly.

▶ **Is the service firm.** Front-line employees represent the service firm. From a customer's perspective, they are the firm.

▶ **Is the brand.** Front-line employees and the service they provide are often a core part of the brand. The employees usually determine whether the brand promise is delivered.

▶ **Affects sales.** Service personnel are often critically important for generating sales, cross-sales, and up-sales.

Frontline Employees Are Important

- Are a core part of the service product
- Are the service firm in the eyes of the customer
- Are a core part of the brand, deliver the brand promise
- Sell, cross-sell, and up-sell
- Are a key driver of customer loyalty
- Determine productivity

HR in Service Firms Is Challenging

Frontline Work Is Difficult and Stressful

- Boundary-spanning positions
- Link the inside of the organization to the outside world
- Have conflicting roles that cause role stress:
  - Organization/client conflict
  - Person/role conflict
  - Inter-client conflict
- Require emotional labor

Basic Models of HR in Service Firms

- Cycle of Failure
  - Low pay, low investment in people, high staff turnover
  - Result in customer dissatisfaction, defection and low margins
- Cycle of Mediocrity
  - Large bureaucracies; offer job security but little scope in the job itself
  - No incentives to server customers well
- Cycle of Success
  - Heavy investment in recruitment, development and motivation of frontline employees
  - Employees are engaged and productive
  - Customers are satisfied and loyal, margins are improved

How to Get HR Right: The Service Talent Cycle

Hire the Right People

- Be the preferred employer and compete for talent market share
- Intensify the selection process to identify the right people for the organization and given job
  - Conduct multiple structured interviews
  - Observe candidate behavior
  - Use personality tests
  - Give applicants a realistic preview of the job

Enable the Frontline

Training and Development

- Conduct extensive training on:
  - Organizational culture, purpose and strategy
  - Interpersonal and technical skills
  - Product/service knowledge
- Reinforce training to shape behaviors
- Use internal communications/marketing to shape the service culture and behaviors
- Professionalize the frontline

Empower the Frontline

- Provide discretion to find solutions to service problems and customization of service delivery
- Set appropriate levels of empowerment depending on the business model and customer needs
- Empowerment requires: (1) information about performance, (2) knowledge that enables contribution to performance, (3) power to make decisions, and (4) performance-based rewards.

Organize Frontline Employees into Effective Service Delivery Teams

- Use cross-functional teams that can service customers from end-to-end
- Structure teams for success (including set goals, carefully select members with the right skills)
- Integrate teams across departments and functional area (e.g., cross-postings, and internal campaigns such as "walk a mile in my shoes" and "a day in the field")

Motivate the Frontline

- Energize and motivate employees with a full set of rewards
- Rewards should include pay, performance bonuses, satisfying job content, feedback and recognition, and goal accomplishment

Service Culture, Climate, and Leadership

Service Culture

- Shared perceptions of what is important in an organization
- Shares values and beliefs of why those things are important

Climate for Service

- Climate is culture translated into policies, practices, and procedures
- Shared perception of practices and behaviors that get rewarded

Leadership

- Qualities of effective leaders
- Leadership styles that focus on basics versus transformation
- Strong focus on frontline

Figure 11.2 Organizing framework: Managing people for service advantage.

Touching your heart

Meet LOTTE in global cities, boasting of
unparalleled reputation and lavish services.

LOTTE
HOTELS & RESORTS

Big Privilege and the Best Rates through www.lottehotel.com

Figure 11.3 Service personnel
represent the firm and often
build personal relationships
with their customers.

▶ **LO 2**

Understand the factors that
make the work of front-line staff
demanding and often difficult.

▶ **Is a key driver of customer loyalty.** Front-line employees play
a key role in anticipating customers' needs, customizing the
service delivery, and building personalized relationships with
customers (Figure 11.3).[2]

▶ **Determines productivity.** Front-line employees have a great
influence on the productivity of front-line operations.

The success stories of Cora Griffith and many other employees showing
discretionary effort have reinforced the truism that highly motivated
people are at the core of service excellence.[3]

The intuitive importance of the effect of service employees on customer
loyalty was integrated and formalized by James Heskett and his colleagues
in their pioneering research on what they call the Service-Profit Chain
(Chapter 1 illustrates the chain in greater detail). It demonstrates the
chain of relationships among (1) employee satisfaction, retention,
and productivity; (2) service value; (3) customer satisfaction and
loyalty; and (4) revenue growth and profitability for the firm.[4] Unlike
manufacturing, "shop-floor workers" in services (i.e., front-line staff)
are in constant contact with customers, and there is solid evidence
showing that employee satisfaction and customer satisfaction are
highly correlated.[5] Therefore, this chapter focuses on how to have
satisfied, loyal, and productive service employees who care.

FRONT-LINE WORK IS DIFFICULT AND STRESSFUL

The Service-Profit Chain needs high-performing, satisfied employees to achieve
service excellence and customer loyalty. However, these customer-facing employees
work in some of the most demanding jobs in service firms. An example is the story of a
JetBlue flight attendant who abruptly quit his job after 28 years of service. Apparently,
he was fed up after being sworn at by a difficult passenger due to a bag problem. He
scolded the passenger publicly over the airplane intercom, announced that he had had
enough, and opened the emergency slide to get off the plane.[6] This incident, which
soon went viral, shows how stress can affect a person at work. Let's discuss the main
reasons why these jobs are so demanding.

Service Jobs Are Boundary-Spanning Positions

Literature on organizational behavior refers to service employees as *boundary spanners*.
They link the inside of an organization to the outside world by operating at the
boundary of the company. Boundary spanners often have conflicting roles because of
the position they occupy. Customer-contact personnel in particular must attend to
both operational and marketing goals. This multiplicity of roles in service jobs often
leads to role conflict and role stress, which we will discuss next.[7]

Sources of Role Conflict

There are three main causes of role conflict and role stress in front-line positions:
organization/client, person/role, and inter-client conflicts.

Organization/Client Conflict. Customer-contact personnel must attend to operational as well as marketing goals. They are expected to delight customers, which takes time. However, they also have to be fast and efficient at operational tasks. They are often expected to do selling, cross-selling, and up-selling as well.

Finally, customer-contact personnel can even be responsible for enforcing rate integrity and pricing schedules that might be in direct conflict with customer satisfaction (e.g., "I am sorry, but we don't serve ice water in this restaurant. We do have an excellent selection of still and carbonated mineral waters."). This type of conflict where service employees have to choose between enforcing the company's rules and satisfying customer demands is also called the two-bosses dilemma. The problem is especially acute in organizations that are not customer oriented.

Person/Role Conflict. Service staff may have conflicts between what their job requires them to do and their own personalities, self-perception, and beliefs. For example, the job may require staff to smile and be friendly even to rude customers. (See also the section on jay customers in Chapter 12.) V. S. Mahesh and Anand Kasturi note from their consulting work with service organizations around the world that thousands of front-line employees consistently tend to describe customers with a pronounced negative flavor. They frequently use words and phrases such as "over-demanding," "unreasonable," "refuse to listen," "always want everything their way, immediately," and "arrogant."[8]

Providing quality service requires an independent, warm, and friendly personality. These traits are more likely to be found in people with higher self-esteem. However, many front-line jobs are seen as low-level jobs requiring little education and offering low pay and very little career advancement. Organizations must move away from this image by "professionalizing" their front-line jobs to make them consistent with staff's self-perception. Failure to do this may lead to person/role conflicts.

Inter-client Conflict. Conflicts between customers are not uncommon (e.g., smoking in non-smoking sections, jumping queues, talking on a cell phone in a movie theater, or being excessively noisy in a restaurant). Usually, service employees are summoned to call the offending customer to order. This is a stressful and unpleasant task, as it is difficult and often impossible to satisfy both sides.

In short, front-line employees may perform triple roles: satisfying customers, delivering productivity, and generating sales. Although employees may experience conflict and stress, they are still expected to smile and be friendly toward customers. We call this emotional labor, which in itself is an important cause of stress. Let us look at emotional labor in greater detail in the next section.

Emotional Labor

The term *emotional labor* was first used by Arlie Hochschild in her book *The Managed Heart*.[9] Emotional labor arises when a discrepancy exists between the way front-line employees actually feel and the emotions that management requires them to show in front of customers. The employees are expected to have a cheerful disposition and to be genial, compassionate, sincere, or even self-effacing. These emotions can be conveyed through facial expressions, gestures, intonation, and words. Although some service firms make an effort to recruit employees with such characteristics, there will

Figure 11.4 Emotional labor and forced smiles can be difficult for service employees.

inevitably be situations in which employees are required to suppress their true feelings in order to conform to customer expectations (Figure 11.4). As Pannikkos Constanti and Paul Gibbs point out, "the power axis for emotional labor tends to favor both the management and the customer, with the front line employee . . . being subordinate," thereby creating a potentially exploitative situation.[10]

The stress of emotional labor is nicely illustrated in the following (probably apocryphal) story. A flight attendant was approached by a passenger with "Let's have a smile." She replied, "Okay. I'll tell you what, first you smile and then I'll smile, okay?" He smiled. "Good. Now hold that for 15 hours," she said and walked away.[11] Figure 11.5 captures emotional labor with humor.

Firms need to be aware of ongoing emotional stress among their employees. They should make sure that their employees are trained to deal with this stress, cope with pressure from customers, and get support from their team leaders. If not, employees will use a variety of ways to resist the stress of emotional labor.[12]

Service Sweatshops

Rapid developments in information technology are permitting service businesses to make radical improvements in business processes and even completely re-engineer their operations. These developments sometimes result in wrenching changes in the nature of work for existing employees. In some instances, the deployment of new technology and methods can dramatically change the nature of the work environment. In other instances, face-to-face contact is replaced by the use of the internet or services provided by call centers. Firms have redefined and relocated jobs, created new employee profiles for recruiting purposes, and sought to hire employees with a different set of qualifications.

When well designed, such jobs can be rewarding. They often offer parents and students flexible working hours and part-time jobs (some 50% of call-center workers are single mothers or students). In fact, it has been shown that part-time workers are more satisfied with their work as customer service representatives (CSRs) than full-time staff

Figure 11.5 Dilbert encounters emotional labor at the bank.

Figure 11.6 Work in customer contact centers is intense! Yet, the performance of customer service representatives often determines how a firm's service quality is perceived by customers.

and perform just as well.[13] However, these jobs often place employees in an electronic equivalent of the old-fashioned sweatshop. Even in well-managed call centers, the work is intense (see Figure 11.6), with CSRs expected to deal with up to two calls a minute (including trips to the toilet and breaks) under a high level of monitoring. There is also significant stress from customers themselves, because many are irate at the time of contact.

Research on call centers has found that intrinsically motivated agents suffer less customer stress.[14] As we will discuss in this chapter, some of the keys to success in this area involve screening applicants (to make sure they already know how to present themselves well on the telephone and have the potential to learn additional skills), training them carefully, and giving them a well-designed working environment.

CYCLES OF FAILURE, MEDIOCRITY, AND SUCCESS

Let's look at the big picture of how poor, mediocre, and excellent firms set up their front-line employees for failure, mediocrity, or success. All too often, poor working environments translate into dreadful service, with employees treating customers the way their managers treat them. Businesses with high employee turnover are often stuck in what has been termed the "Cycle of Failure." Others which offer job security but little scope for personal initiative and are heavily rule- and procedure-based may suffer from an equally undesirable "Cycle of Mediocrity." However, if managed well, there is potential for a virtuous cycle in service employment called the "Cycle of Success."[15]

LO 3

Describe the cycles of failure, mediocrity, and success in human resources for service firms.

The Cycle of Failure

In many service industries, the search for productivity is carried out with a vengeance. Work routines are simplified, and workers are hired as cheaply as possible to perform repetitive tasks that require little or no training. Among consumer services, departmental stores, fast-food restaurants, and call-center operations are often cited as examples in which this problem abounds (although there are notable exceptions). The Cycle of Failure captures the implications of such a strategy with its two concentric but interactive cycles: one involving failures with employees and the second involving those with customers (Figure 11.7).

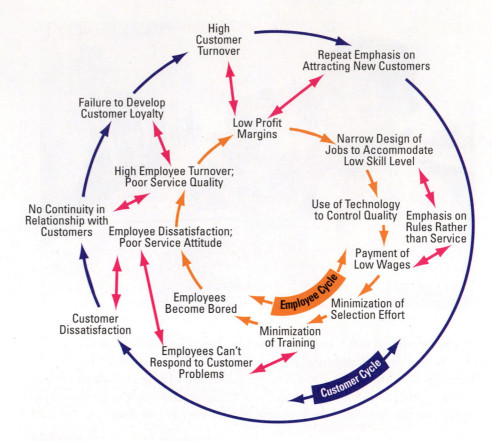

Figure 11.7 The Cycle of Failure.

The *Employee Cycle of Failure* begins with a narrow design of jobs to accommodate low skill levels, an emphasis on rules rather than service, and the use of technology to control quality. Low wages are paid, and there is very little investment in employee selection and training. Consequences include bored employees who lack the ability to respond to customer problems, become dissatisfied, and develop a poor service attitude. The results for the firm are low service quality and high employee turnover. The cycle repeats itself due to weak profit margins and the hiring of more badly paid employees to work in this unrewarding atmosphere (Figure 11.8).

The *Customer Cycle of Failure* begins with heavy organizational emphasis on attracting new customers. These customers become dissatisfied with employee performance and the lack of continuity that results from high staff turnover. As these customers fail to become loyal to the supplier, they turn over as quickly as the staff. This necessitates an ongoing search for new customers to maintain sales volume. The departure of discontented customers is especially worrying in the light of what we know about the greater profitability of a loyal customer base. (See Chapter 12 on customer loyalty.)

Figure 11.8 Employees in the Cycle of Failure are bored and dissatisfied.

Managers' excuses and justifications for perpetuating the Cycle of Failure tend to focus on employees:

▶ "You just can't get good people nowadays."

▶ "People today just don't want to work."

▶ "To get good people would cost too much, and you can't pass on these cost increases to customers."

▶ "It's not worth training our front-line people when they leave you so quickly."

▶ "High turnover is simply an inevitable part of our business. You've got to learn to live with it."[16]

Too many managers ignore the long-term financial effects of low-pay/high-turnover human resource strategies. Part of the problem is the failure to measure all relevant costs. In particular, three key cost variables are often omitted: (1) the cost of constant recruiting, hiring, and training (which is as much a time cost for managers as a financial cost); (2) the lower productivity of inexperienced new workers; and (3) the costs of constantly attracting new customers. Two revenue variables are also frequently ignored: (1) future revenue streams that might have continued for years but are lost when unhappy customers take their business elsewhere and (2) the potential income lost from prospective customers who are turned off by negative word of mouth. Finally, there are less easily quantifiable costs of disruptions to service while a job remains unfilled or when a departing employee's knowledge of the business is lost (potentially along with his/her customers).

The Cycle of Mediocrity

The Cycle of Mediocrity is another potentially vicious employment cycle. (See Figure 11.9.) You are most likely to find it in large, bureaucratic organizations. These are often typified by state monopolies, industrial cartels, or regulated oligopolies in which there's little market pressure from more agile competitors to improve performance. Moreover, the fear of entrenched unions may discourage management from adopting more innovative labor practices.

In such environments, service delivery standards tend to be prescribed by rigid rule books that focus on standardizing service and operational efficiencies and preventing both employee fraud and favoritism toward specific customers. Job responsibilities tend to be narrowly and unimaginatively defined, tightly categorized by grade and scope of responsibilities, and further rigidified by union work rules. Salary increases and promotions are largely based on how long the person has been working in the organization. Successful performance in a job is often measured by the absence of mistakes rather than by high productivity or outstanding customer service. Training focuses on learning the rules and the technical aspects of the job rather than on improving human interactions with customers and co-workers. Since employees are given very little freedom to do their work in the way they think is necessary or suitable, jobs tend to be boring and repetitive (Figure 11.10). However, unlike the Cycle of Failure, most positions provide adequate pay and often good benefits combined with high job security. Thus, employees are reluctant to leave. This lack of mobility is compounded by an absence of marketable skills that would be valued by organizations in other fields.

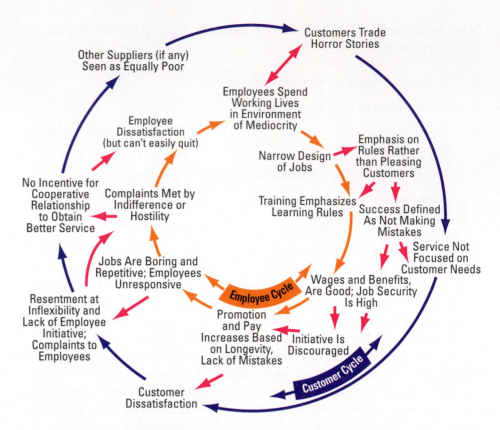

Figure 11.9 The Cycle of Mediocrity.

Customers find such organizations frustrating to deal with. They can even become resentful when faced with bureaucratic hassles, lack of service flexibility, and the unwillingness of employees to make an effort to serve them well. There is little incentive for customers to cooperate with the organization to achieve better service. When they complain to employees who are already unhappy, the poor service attitude becomes worse. Employees may then protect themselves through mechanisms such as withdrawal into indifference, playing overtly by the rule book, or countering rudeness with rudeness.

The Cycle of Success

Some firms reject the assumptions underlying the cycles of failure or mediocrity. Instead, they take a long-term view of financial performance and seek to prosper by investing in their people in order to create a "Cycle of Success" (Figure 11.11).

As with failure or mediocrity, success applies to both employees and customers. Better pay and benefits attract good-quality staff. Broadened job designs are accompanied by training and empowerment practices that allow front-line staff to control quality. With more focused recruitment, intensive training, and better wages, employees are likely to be happier in their work and provide higher quality service. Lower turnover means that regular customers appreciate the continuity in service relationships and are more likely to remain loyal. With greater customer loyalty, profit margins tend to be higher, and the organization is free to focus its marketing efforts on reinforcing customer loyalty through customer-retention strategies. These are usually much more profitable than strategies for attracting new customers. A powerful demonstration of a front-line employee working in the Cycle of Success is waitress Cora Griffin (featured in the opening vignette of this chapter).

Figure 11.10 Employees in the Cycle of Mediocrity are not very productive and motivated.

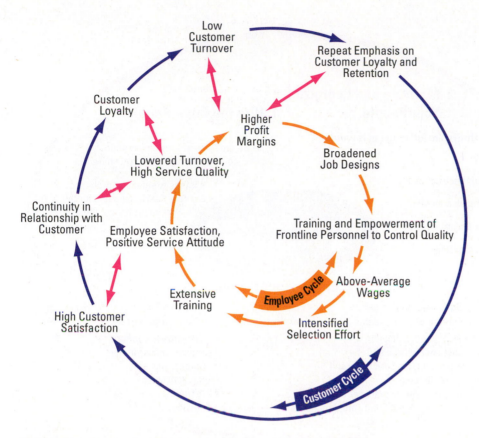

Figure 11.11 The Cycle of Success.

HUMAN RESOURCE MANAGEMENT—HOW TO GET IT RIGHT?

Any rational manager would like to operate in the Cycle of Success. In this section, we'll discuss HR strategies that can help service firms to move towards that goal. Specifically, we'll discuss how firms can hire, motivate, and retain engaged service employees who are willing and able to deliver service excellence, productivity, and sales. Figure 11.12 shows the Service Talent Cycle, which is our guiding framework for successful HR practices in service firms.

Hire the Right People

Employee satisfaction is necessary but not sufficient for having high-performing staff. As Jim Collins said, "The old adage 'People are the most important asset' is wrong. The *right* people are your most important asset."[17] We would like to add: "...and the wrong people are a liability that is often difficult to get rid of." Firms should therefore start by hiring the right people. This includes competing for applications from the best employees in the labor market and selecting the best candidates from this pool for the specific jobs to be filled.

▶ LO 4

Understand the key elements of the Service Talent Cycle for successful human resource management in service firms.

▶ LO 5

Know how to attract, select, and hire the right people for service jobs.

Leadership that
- Fosters a strong climate for service with a passion for service and productivity
- Drives values that inspire, energize and guide service providers and leads by example
- Focuses the entire organization on supporting the frontline

3. Motivate and Energize Your People
- **Utilize the full range of rewards**
- Pay
- Performance bonuses
- Satisfying job content
- Feedback and recognition
- Goal accomplishment

Service Excellence & Productivity

1. Hire the Right People
- Be the preferred employer and compete for talent market share
- Intensify selection process to hire the right people for the organization and the given job

2. Enable Your People
- **Build high performance service delivery teams**
  - Ideally cross functional, customer centric structure
  - Develop team structures and skills that work
  - Integrate teams across departments and functional areas
- **Empower the Frontline**
- **Extensive Training and Development on**
  - Organizational culture, purpose, and strategy
  - Interpersonal and technical skills
  - Product/service knowledge

Figure 11.12 The Service Talent Cycle: Getting HR right in service firms.

"I'm offering you a six-figure salary. Three figures on the 15th of the month and three figures on the 30th."

Figure 11.13 A firm does not need to pay top dollars to attract top performers.

Be the Preferred Employer. To be able to select and hire the best people, a service firm must be able to encourage potential employees to apply for a job with the firm and then accept its job offer in preference over others. Service firms have a brand identity in the labor market as well. Potential candidates tend to seek companies that are good to work for and have an image that's congruent with their own values and beliefs.[18] Job seekers regularly approach current and former employees for information and can easily learn about salaries, benefits, working climate, and even interview questions.[19] A lot of internal company information can also be found online. For example, Glassdoor.com had over 410,000 company and job reviews by 2014, providing potential employees good insights into what it would be like to work for a particular firm.[20] Thus, a firm must first compete for talent market share. The global consulting firm McKinsey & Company calls this "the war for talent."[21]

To effectively compete in the labor market means having an attractive value proposition for prospective employees. The firm must have a good image in the community as a place to work. It must also be seen as delivering high-quality products and services and being a good corporate citizen, so that employees feel proud to be part of the team. Furthermore, the compensation package for the best people cannot be below average. In our experience, it takes a salary in the range of the 60th to the 80th percentile of the market to attract top performers to top companies (Figure 11.13). However, a firm does not have to be a top paymaster if other important aspects of the value proposition are attractive. In short, understand the needs of your target employees and get your value proposition right.

Select the Right People. There's no such thing as the perfect employee (Figure 11.14). Different positions are often best filled by people with different skill sets, styles, and personalities. Different brands have different personalities, and a good employee–brand fit makes it natural for employees to deliver service that supports the firm's espoused image. As a result, customers perceive their behavior as authentic.[22] The recruitment and selection processes should be explicitly designed to encourage a good employee–brand fit.[23] This can be done by:

"Allen is an incredible, wonderful, fun, generous, exciting, kind, loving, brilliant, very special human being. This personal reference from your dog is quite impressive."

Figure 11.14 There's no such thing as a perfect employee.

▶ using recruitment advertising to explicitly display key brand attributes and firm positioning and to encourage potential candidates to reflect on their fit with the firm,

▶ designing selection methods to convey brand values and allowing employees to make a self-assessment of their fit, and

▶ ensuring that recruiters are proactively looking out for brand fit and potential misfit.

For example, the Walt Disney Company assesses prospective employees in terms of their potential brand fit (Is magic, fun, and happiness your world?) as well as their on-stage or back-stage work. The jobs of on-stage workers (known as cast members) are given to people who have the appearance, personality, and skills to match the job.

What makes outstanding service performers so special? Often, it is the things that are intrinsic to people and *cannot* be taught. As one study of high performers observed, qualities such as energy, charm, detail orientation, work ethic, and neatness are instilled early on and can merely be enhanced with on-the-job training or incentives.[24] In addition, HR managers have discovered that while good manners and the need to smile and make eye contact can be taught, warmth itself cannot. The only realistic solution is to ensure that the organization's recruitment criteria favor candidates with naturally warm personalities. As Jim Collins emphasizes, "The right people are those who would exhibit the desired behaviors anyway, as a natural extension of their character and attitude, regardless of any control and incentive system."[25]

The logical conclusion is that service firms should devote great care to attracting and hiring the right candidates. The top companies are increasingly using employee analytics to improve their ability to attract and retain the best talent. Employee analytics are similar to customer analytics; for example, they are able to predict who would be a better performer. Firms can also use analytics to place the right employees in the right job.[26] Let's review some tools that can help you identify the right candidates for a given firm and job and, perhaps even more importantly, reject those candidates that do not fit.

Tools to Identify the Best Candidates[27]

Excellent service firms use a number of approaches to identify the candidates with the best fit in their applicant pool. These approaches include interviewing applicants, observing their behavior, conducting personality tests, and providing them with a realistic job preview.

Figure 11.15 Is the "similar-to-me" bias coming into play?

"Gerald works very well with others and functions cooperatively in a group setting. Got any references more recent than your third grade report card?"

Figure 11.16 References are a good way to assess past behavior.

Use Multiple, Structured Interviews. To improve hiring decisions, successful recruiters like to employ structured interviews built around job requirements and to use more than one interviewer. People tend to be more careful in their judgments when they know that another individual is also judging the same applicant. Another advantage of using two or more interviewers is that it reduces the risk of the "similar-to-me" bias—we all like people who are similar to ourselves (Figure 11.15).

Observe Candidate Behavior. The hiring decision should be based on the behavior that recruiters observe and not just the words they hear. As John Wooden said: "Show me what you can do, don't tell me what you can do. Too often, the big talkers are the little doers."[28] Behavior can be directly or indirectly observed by using behavioral simulations or assessment-center tests. These use standardized situations to see whether applicants display the kinds of behavior that the firms' clients would expect. In addition, past behavior is the best predictor of future behavior. Hire the person who has won service excellence awards, received many compliment letters, and has great references from past employers (Figure 11.16).

Conduct Personality Tests. Many managers hire employees based on personality. Personality tests help to identify traits that are related to a particular job. For

Figure 11.17 Au Bon Pain allows candidates to get a taste of the real job before the final selection interview.

example, willingness to treat customers and colleagues with courtesy, consideration, and tact; perceptiveness of customer needs; and the ability to communicate accurately and pleasantly are traits that can be measured. It's better to hire upbeat and happy people, because customers report higher satisfaction when being served by more satisfied staff.[29] Research has also shown that certain traits such as being hardworking and believing in one's capability to manage situations result in strong employee performance and service quality. Hiring decisions based on such tests tend to be accurate, especially in identifying and rejecting unsuitable candidates.[30]

For example, the Ritz-Carlton Hotels Group uses personality profiles on all job applicants. Employees are selected on the basis of their natural predisposition for working in a service context. Inherent traits such as a ready smile, a willingness to help others, and an affinity for multi-tasking enable them to go beyond learned skills. An applicant to Ritz-Carlton shared her experience of going through the personality test for a job as a junior-level concierge at the Ritz-Carlton Millenia Singapore. Her best advice was: "Tell the truth. These are experts; they will know if you are lying." She added:

> On the big day, they asked if I liked helping people, if I was an organized person and if I liked to smile a lot. "Yes, yes and yes," I said. But I had to support it

with real life examples. This, at times, felt rather intrusive. To answer the first question for instance, I had to say a bit about the person I had helped—why she needed help, for example. The test forced me to recall even insignificant things I had done, like learning how to say hello in different languages, which helped to get a fix on my character.[31]

Apart from intensive interview-based psychological tests, cost-effective internet-based testing kits are available. Here, applicants enter their test responses into a Web-based questionnaire. The prospective employer receives the analysis, the suitability of the candidate, and a hiring recommendation. Developing and administering such tests has become a significant service industry in its own right. SHL Talent Measurement (a unit of CEB) is an example of a company that supplies such assessment products in 30 languages to over 20,000 organizations around the world.[32]

Give Applicants a Realistic Preview of the Job.[33] During the recruitment process, service companies should let candidates know the reality of the job, thereby giving them a chance to "try on the job" and assess whether it's a good fit or not. At the same time, recruiters can observe how candidates respond to the job's realities. Some candidates may withdraw if they realize that the job is not a good match for them. At the same time, the company can manage new employees' expectations from their job. Many service companies adopt this approach. For example, Au Bon Pain, a chain of French bakery cafés, lets applicants work for two paid days in a café prior to the final selection interview. Here, managers can observe candidates in action, and candidates can assess whether they like the job and the work environment (Figure 11.17).

See Service Insights 11.1 on how Southwest Airlines uses a combination of interviews and other selection tools to identify the right candidates from its vast pool of applicants.

SERVICE INSIGHTS 11.1

Hiring at Southwest Airlines

Southwest Airlines hires people with the right attitude and with a personality that matches its corporate personality. Humor is the key. Herb Kelleher, Southwest's legendary former CEO and now chairman, said, "I want flying to be a helluva lot of fun!" "We look for attitudes; people with a sense of humor who don't take themselves too seriously. We'll train you on whatever it is you have to do, but the one thing Southwest cannot change in people is inherent attitudes." Southwest has one fundamental, consistent principle—to hire people with the right spirit. Southwest looks for people with other-oriented, outgoing personalities—individuals who can become part of an extended family of people who work hard and have fun at the same time.

Southwest's painstaking approach to interviewing continues to evolve in the light of experience. It is perhaps at its most innovative in the selection of flight attendants. A day-long visit to the company usually begins with applicants gathered in a group. Recruiters watch how well they interact with each other. Another chance for such observation will come at lunch time.

This is followed by a series of personal interviews. Each candidate has three one-on-one "behavioral-type" interviews during the course of the day. Based on input from supervisors and peers in a given job category, interviewers target eight to ten dimensions for each position. For a flight attendant, these might include a willingness to take initiative, compassion, flexibility, sensitivity, sincerity, a customer-service orientation, and a predisposition to be a team player. Even humor is "tested." Prospective employees are typically asked, "Tell me how you recently used your sense of humor in a work environment. Tell me how you have used humor to defuse a difficult situation."

Southwest describes the ideal interview as "a conversation" in which the goal is to make candidates comfortable. "The first interview of the day tends to be a bit stiff, the second is more comfortable, and by the third they tell us a whole lot more. It's really hard to fake it under those circumstances." The three interviewers don't discuss candidates during the day but compare notes afterwards to reduce the risk of bias.

To help select people with the right attitude, Southwest invites supervisors and peers (with whom future candidates will be working) to participate in the process of in-depth interviewing and selection. In this way, existing employees feel a sense of responsibility for mentoring new recruits and helping them to become successful in the job (rather than wondering, as an interviewer put it, "who hired this turkey?"). More unusually, Southwest invites its own frequent flyers to participate in the initial interviews for flight attendants and to tell the candidates what they, the passengers, value.

The interviewing team asks a group of potential employees to prepare a five-minute presentation about themselves, giving them plenty of time to prepare. As the presentations are delivered, the interviewers don't just watch the speakers. They watch the audience as well to see which applicants are using the time to work on their own presentations and which are enthusiastically cheering on and supporting their potential co-workers. Unselfish people who will support their team mates are the ones who catch Southwest's eyes, not the applicants who are tempted to polish their own presentations while others are speaking.

By hiring the right attitude, the company is able to foster the so-called Southwest spirit—an intangible quality in people that causes them to want to do whatever it takes and to want to go that extra mile whenever they need to. Southwest itself goes the extra mile for its employees and has never laid anyone off, even after it decided to close reservations centers in three cities in 2004 to cut costs. Management knows that the airline's culture is a key competitive advantage.

Train Service Employees Actively

If a firm has good people, investments in training and development can yield outstanding results. Having a good career-development program for employees helps them to feel that they are being valued and taken care of and motivates them to work to meet customers' needs. This results in customer satisfaction, loyalty, and profitability for the firm.[34] Service champions show a strong commitment to training in words, dollars, and actions. Employees of Apple retail stores, for example, are given intensive training on how to interact with customers, how to phrase words in a positive way, and what to say when customers are emotional. Employees are supposed to help customers solve problems rather than merely sell products.[35] As Benjamin Schneider and David Bowen put it, "The combination of attracting a diverse and competent applicant pool, utilizing effective techniques for hiring the most appropriate people from that pool, and then training the heck out of them would be gangbusters in any market."[36]

LO 6

Explain the key areas in which service employees need training.

Training Contents. There are many aspects of a firm that service employees need to be trained on. Service employees need to learn:

▶ **Organizational Culture, Purpose, and Strategy.** Start strong with new hires, and focus on getting emotional commitment to the firm's core strategy. Promote core values such as commitment to service excellence, responsiveness, team spirit, mutual respect, honesty, and integrity. Use managers to teach, and focus on "what," "why," and "how" rather than on the specifics of the job.[37] For example, new recruits at Disneyland attend the "Disney University Orientation." It starts with a detailed discussion of the company history and philosophy, the service standards expected of cast members, and a comprehensive tour of Disneyland's operations.[38]

▶ **Interpersonal and Technical Skills.** Interpersonal skills tend to be generic across service jobs and include visual communications skills such as making eye contact, listening attentively, understanding body language and facial expressions, and reading customers' needs. Technical skills include all the required knowledge related to processes (e.g., how to handle a merchandized return) and machines (e.g., how to operate the terminal or cash machine) and rules and regulations related to customer service processes. Creativity in designing solutions and solving problems is also required in non-routine encounters and service recovery. Both technical and interpersonal skills are *necessary*, but neither alone is enough for optimal job performance (Figure 11.18).[39]

▶ **Product/Service Knowledge.** Knowledgeable staff members are a key aspect of service quality. They must be able to explain product features effectively and position the product correctly. At an Apple retail store, for example, all the products are openly displayed for customers to try them out. Staff members need to be able to answer questions about the product's features, usage, and other aspects of the service such as maintenance, service bundles, etc. (Figure 11.19)

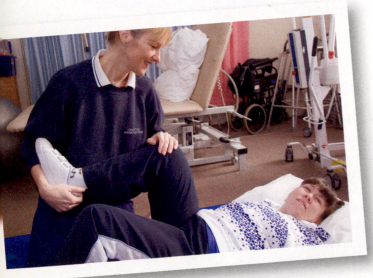

Figure 11.18 A physiotherapist displaying technical competence as well as a warm and friendly smile.

Reinforce Training to Shape Behaviors. Training has to result in observable changes in behavior. Learning is not only about becoming smarter but also about changing behaviors and improving decision making. To achieve this, practice and reinforcement are needed. Supervisors play a crucial role by following up regularly on learning objectives (for instance, meeting with staff to reinforce key lessons from recent complaints and compliments). (Figure 11.20)

Another example of constant reinforcement is Ritz-Carlton's approach. It translated the key product and service requirements of its customers into the Ritz-Carlton Gold Standards, which include a credo, a motto, three steps of service, and 12 service values. Ritz-Carlton's service values are split into different levels.

Service values 10, 11, and 12 represent functional values such as safety, security, and cleanliness. Ritz-Carlton refers to the next level of excellence as emotional engagement, which covers values 4 through 9. They relate to learning and professional growth of its employees, teamwork, service, problem solving and service recovery, innovation, and continuous improvement. Beyond the

Figure 11.19 A salesperson helping a purchaser choose a lamp fixture in a hardware store.

guests' functional needs and emotional engagement is the third level, which relates to values 1, 2, and 3 and is called "the Ritz-Carlton Mystique." This level aims to create unique, memorable, and personal guest experiences, which Ritz-Carlton believes can only occur when employees deliver on the guests' expressed and unexpressed wishes and needs and strive to build life-time relationships between Ritz-Carlton and its guests. The three levels are reflected in the Sixth Diamond in Ritz-Carlton's Gold Standards as a new benchmark in the hospitality industry for achieving both employee and customer engagement.[40]

Tim Kirkpatrick, Director of Training and Development in Ritz-Carlton's Boston Common Hotel, said, "The Gold Standards are part of our uniform, just like your name tag. But remember, it's just a laminated card until you put it into action."[41] Every morning briefing includes a discussion directly related to the standards in order to reinforce them. The aim of these discussions is to keep the Ritz-Carlton philosophy at the center of its employees' minds.

Internal Communications to Shape the Service Culture and Behaviors. In addition to having a strong training platform, it takes a significant communications effort to shape the service culture and get the message to the troops. Service leaders use multiple tools to build their service culture, ranging from internal marketing and training to core principles and company events and celebrations. Internal communications to employees (often also referred to as *internal marketing*) play a vital role in maintaining and nurturing a corporate culture founded on specific service values.

Well-planned internal-marketing efforts are especially necessary in large service businesses that operate in widely dispersed sites, sometimes around the world. Even when employees work far from the head office, they still need to be kept informed about new policies, changes in service features, and new quality initiatives. Communications may also be

LO 7
Understand the role of internal marketing and communications.

Figure 11.20 Morning briefings by a supervisor offer effective training opportunities.

needed to nurture team spirit and support common corporate goals across national frontiers. Consider the challenge of maintaining a unified sense of purpose at the overseas offices of companies such as Citibank, Air Canada, Marriott, or Starbucks, where people from different cultures who speak different languages must work together to create consistent levels of service.

Effective internal communications are an excellent complementary tool to training that can help ensure efficient and satisfactory service delivery; achieve productive and harmonious working relationships; and build employee trust, respect, and loyalty. Commonly used media include internal newsletters and magazines; videos; intranets; e-mail; face-to-face briefings; and promotional campaigns using displays, prizes, and recognition programs.

Professionalizing the Front Line. Training and learning are necessary to professionalize the front line and move these individuals away from the common (self-)image of being in low-end jobs that have no significance. Well-trained employees feel and act like professionals. A waiter who knows about food, cooking, wines, dining etiquette, and ways of effectively interacting with customers (even complaining ones) feels professional, has a high self-esteem, and is respected by his customers. Training and internal communications are therefore extremely effective in reducing person/role stress and in enabling and energizing front-line employees.

"We're not selling galvanized steel plumbing washers. We're selling the galvanized steel plumbing washers experience!"

GLASBERGEN

Figure 11.21 Effective internal communication can reinforce a unified corporate culture across widely dispersed sites.

Empower the Front Line [42]

After being the preferred employer, selecting the right candidates, and training them well, the next step is to empower the front line and encourage them to show proactive customer service performance that can go beyond the call of duty. Virtually all breakthrough service firms have legendary stories of employees who recovered failed service transactions or walked the extra mile to make a customer's day or avoid some kind of disaster for that client. To allow this to happen, employees have to be empowered.

LO 8

Understand why empowerment is so important in many front-line jobs.

SERVICE INSIGHTS 11.2

Empowerment at Nordstrom

Van Mensah, a men's clothes sales associate at Nordstrom, received a disturbing letter from one of his loyal customers. The gentleman had purchased some $2,000 worth of shirts and ties from Mensah and mistakenly washed the shirts in hot water, causing all of them to shrink. He was writing to Mensah to ask for his professional advice on how to deal with this predicament. (The gentleman did not complain and readily conceded that the mistake was his.) Mensah immediately called the customer and offered to replace those shirts with new ones at no charge. He asked the customer to mail the other shirts back to Nordstrom at the firm's expense. "I didn't have to ask for anyone's permission to do what I did for that customer," said Mensah. "Nordstrom would rather leave it up to me to decide what's best."

Middlemas, a Nordstrom veteran, said to employees, "You will never be criticized for doing too much for a customer, you will only be criticized for doing too little. If you're ever in doubt as to what to do in a situation, always make a decision that favors the customer before the company." Nordstrom's Employee Handbook confirms this. It reads:

Welcome to Nordstrom

We're glad to have you with our Company. Our number one goal is to provide outstanding customer service.

Set both your personal and professional goals high. We have great confidence in your ability to achieve them.

Nordstrom Rules:

Rule#1: Use your good judgment in all situations. There will be no additional rules. Please feel free to ask your department manager, store manager, or division general manager any question at any time.

Source: Patrick D. McCarthy and Robert Spector, "The Nordstrom Way to Customer

SOURCE

Patrick D. McCarthy and Robert Spector, "The Nordstrom Way to Customer Service Excellence: The Handbook For Becoming the 'Nordstrom' of Your Industry," reproduced with permission of John Wiley & Sons.

PART III

Nordstrom trains and trusts its employees to do the right thing and empowers them to do so. Its employee handbook has only one rule: "Use good judgment in all situations." (See Service Insights 11.2: "Empowerment at Nordstrom.")

There is a fine line between going the extra mile for a customer and "service sweethearting," whereby employees unnecessarily and often illicitly waive bills or give freebees to boost their unit's satisfaction rating or avoid a confrontation with a customer who is in the wrong[43] (see also the section on jaycustomers in Chapter 13). It is therefore important for employees to be self-directed and to use good judgment, especially in service firms. As front-line employees frequently operate on their own in face-to-face encounters with their customers, it tends to be difficult for managers to closely monitor their behavior.[44]

For many services, providing employees with greater discretion (and training in how to use their judgment) enables them to provide superior service on the spot rather than take time to get permission from supervisors. Empowerment looks to front-line staff to find solutions to service problems and make appropriate decisions about customizing service delivery. It is therefore not surprising that research has linked high empowerment to higher customer satisfaction.[45]

When Are High Levels of Empowerment Appropriate? Advocates claim that the empowerment approach is more likely to yield motivated employees and satisfied customers than the "production-line" alternative in which management designs a relatively standardized system and expects workers to execute tasks within narrow guidelines. However, David Bowen and Edward Lawler suggest that different situations may require different solutions. According to them, "both the empowerment and production-line approaches have their advantages . . . and . . . each fits certain situations. The key is to choose the management approach that best meets the needs of both employees and customers." Not all employees are necessarily eager to be empowered, and many employees do not seek personal growth within their jobs. They would prefer to work according to specific directions rather than to use their own initiative. Research has shown that a strategy of empowerment is most likely to be appropriate when most of the following factors are present within the organization and its environment:

▶ The firm offers personalized, customized service and is based on competitive differentiation.

▶ The firm has extended relationships with customers rather than short-term transactions.

▶ The organization uses technologies that are complex and non-routine in nature.

▶ Service failures are often non-routine and cannot be designed out of the system. Front-line employees have to respond quickly to recover the service.

▶ The business environment is unpredictable, and surprises are to be expected.

▶ Existing managers are comfortable with letting employees decide independently for the benefit of both the organization and its customers.

▶ Employees have a strong need to grow and deepen their skills in the work environment, are interested in working with others, and have good interpersonal and group process skills.[46]

Requirements for Empowering the Front Line. The production-line approach to managing people is based on the well-established *control* model of organization design and management. There are clearly defined roles, top-down control systems, hierarchical pyramid structures, and an assumption that the management knows best. Empowerment, by contrast, is based on the *involvement* (or *commitment*) model, which assumes that employees can make good decisions and produce good ideas for operating the business if they are properly socialized, trained, and informed. This model also assumes that employees can be internally motivated to perform effectively, and that they are capable of self-control and self-direction.

Schneider and Bowen emphasize that "empowerment isn't just 'setting the frontline free' or 'throwing away the policy manuals.' It requires the systematic redistribution of four key ingredients throughout the organization from the top downwards."[47] These are:

▶ *Information* about organizational, team, and individual performance (e.g., operating results and measures of competitive performance)

▶ *Knowledge* that enables employees to understand and contribute to organizational, team, and individual performance (e.g., problem-solving skills)

▶ *Power* to make decisions that influence work procedures and organizational direction (e.g., through quality circles and self-managing teams) at the higher level and transaction-specific decisions (e.g., decisions regarding customization and service recovery) at the micro level

▶ *Rewards* based on organizational, team, and individual performance (e.g., bonuses, profit sharing, and stock options)

In the control model, the four features are concentrated at the top of the organization, while in the involvement model these features are pushed down through the organization. In restaurants, for example, management often schedules servers for shifts they would rather not take. Worse still, the least productive servers can be scheduled on the most profitable shifts. To solve both issues, the Boston-based restaurant chain Not Your Average Joe's pushed all four features of empowerment to the front line. The restaurant developed a performance-rating system that tracks and communicates sales and customer satisfaction data (measured by tips or directly) for each server (giving them information and knowledge). Based on their ranking, employees can now self-select their preferred shifts and restaurant sections through a self-service online system (providing them with decision-making power and rewards). This system empowers and rewards high performers, fosters a culture of performance, saves each restaurant manager between three to five hours of scheduling work per week, and makes restaurants more profitable.[48]

Levels of Employee Involvement. The empowerment and production-line approaches are at the opposite ends of a spectrum that reflects increasing levels of employee involvement as additional information, knowledge, power, and rewards are pushed down to the front line. Management needs to determine the appropriate level of empowerment for its business model and customers' needs. Empowerment can take place at several levels:

▶ *Suggestion involvement* empowers employees to make recommendations through formalized programs. McDonald's, often portrayed as an archetype of the production-line approach, listens closely to its front line. Did you know that innovations ranging from the Egg McMuffin to methods of wrapping burgers without leaving a thumb print on the bun were invented by employees?

▶ *Job involvement* represents a dramatic opening up of job content. Jobs are redesigned to allow employees to use a wider array of skills. Employees require training to cope with the added demands accompanying this form of empowerment. Supervisors also need to be reoriented from directing the group to facilitating its performance in supportive ways.

▶ *High involvement* gives even the lowest-level employees a sense of involvement in the company's overall performance. Information is shared. Employees develop skills in team work, problem solving, and business operations. They participate in work-unit management decisions and are a source of learning and innovation for the organization.[49]

Southwest Airlines is an example of a high-involvement company promoting common sense and flexibility. It trusts its employees and gives them the latitude, discretion, and authority they need to do their jobs. The airline has eliminated inflexible work rules and rigid job descriptions so that its people can assume ownership for getting the job done and enabling flights to leave on time, regardless of whose "official" responsibility it is. This gives employees the flexibility to help each other when needed. As a result, they adopt a "whatever-it-takes" mentality. Southwest mechanics and pilots feel free to help ramp agents load bags. When a flight is running late, it's not uncommon to see pilots helping passengers in wheelchairs to board the aircraft, assisting operations agents by taking boarding passes, or helping flight attendants clean the cabin between flights. All of these actions are their way of adapting to the situation and taking ownership for getting customers on board more quickly. In addition, Southwest employees apply common sense rather than rules when it's in the best interests of the customer.

LO 9

Explain how to build high-performance service delivery teams.

Build High-Performance Service-Delivery Teams

A team has been defined as "a small number of people with complementary skills who are committed to a common purpose, set of performance goals, and approach for which they hold themselves mutually accountable."[50] The nature of many services requires people to work in teams, often across functions, in order to offer seamless customer service.

Traditionally, many firms were organized by functional structures under which, for example, one department is in charge of consulting and selling (e.g., selling a subscription contract with a cell phone), another is in charge of customer service (e.g., activation of value-added services, changes of subscription plans), and a third is in charge of billing. This structure prevents internal service teams from viewing end customers as their own. It can also mean poorer teamwork across functions, slower service, and more errors. When customers have service problems, they easily fall between the cracks (Figure 11.22).

The Power of Teamwork in Services. Teams, training, and empowerment go hand-in-hand. Effective teams and their leaders facilitate communication among team members, sharing of knowledge, and alignment.[51] By operating like small, independent units, service teams take on more responsibility and require less supervision than more traditionally organized customer service units. Furthermore, teams often set higher performance targets for themselves than supervisors would. Within a good team, the pressure to perform is high.[52]

Some academics even feel that too much emphasis is placed on hiring "individual stars," and too little attention is paid to hiring staff with good team abilities and the motivation to work cooperatively. Stanford professors Charles O'Reilly and Jeffrey Pfeffer emphasize that how well people work in teams is often as important as how good people are, and that stars can be outperformed by others through superior teamwork.[53]

Team ability and motivation are crucial for the effective delivery of many types of services, especially those involving individuals who play specialist roles. For example, healthcare services heavily depend on the effective teamwork of many specialists (see Figure 11.23).

"We're a Limited Partnership. We're limited by Allen's pessimism, Elizabeth's abrasive personality, and Dave's refusal to work weekends."

Figure 11.22 Lack of cooperation within a team will cause problems for the company.

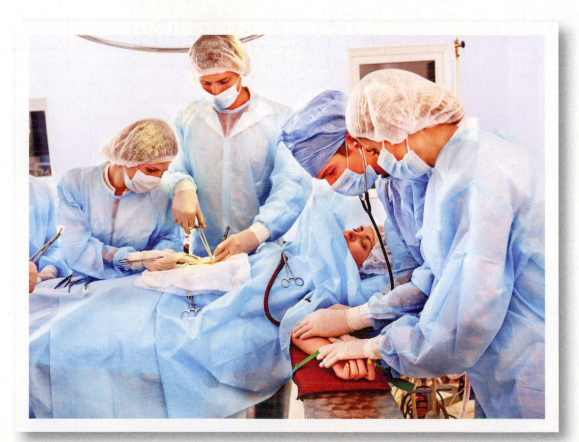

Figure 11.23 Surgical teams work under particularly demanding conditions.

Structure Service-Delivery Teams for Success. It's not easy to make teams function well. If people are not prepared for teamwork, and the team structure isn't set up right, a firm risks having initially enthusiastic team members who lack the competencies that teamwork requires. The skills needed include not only cooperation, listening to others, coaching, and encouraging one another but also an understanding of how to air differences, tell one another hard truths, and ask tough questions. All of these require training. Management also needs to set up a structure that will move the teams towards success. This includes the following:[54]

▶ Identify what the team will achieve. Goals need to be defined and shared with the team members.

▶ Select team members with care. All the skills needed to achieve the goal must be found within the team.

▶ Monitor the team and its team members, and provide feedback. This aligns individual and team goals with those of the organization.

▶ Keep team members informed of goal achievement, update them, and reward them for their efforts and performance.

▶ Coordinate and integrate with other teams, departments, and functions to achieve the overall company objectives. (See the next section for details.)

LO 10

Know how to integrate teams across departments and functional areas.

Integrate Teams across Departments and Functional Areas

Even if service delivery teams work well, we find many firms in which individuals and teams from different departments and functional areas have conflicts with each other. Marketers may see their role as one of continually adding value to the product offering, enhancing its appeal to customers, and stimulating sales. Operations managers, however, may see their job as cutting down on "extras" to reflect the reality of service constraints (such as staff and equipment) and the need to control cost. HR wants to control head count and payroll, and IT is struggling with many changing demands as it often controls the information backbone of many service processes.

Part of the challenge for service management is to ensure that different departments and functions cooperate with each other. Potential ways to reduce conflict and break down the barriers between departments include:

1) Transferring individuals internally to other departments and functional areas, allowing them to develop a more holistic perspective and view issues from the different perspectives of the various departments.

2) Establishing cross-departmental and cross-functional project teams (e.g., for new service development or customer service process redesign).

3) Having cross-departmental and cross-functional service delivery teams.

4) Appointing individuals whose job is to integrate specific objectives, activities, and processes between departments. For example, Robert Kwortnik and Gary Thompson suggest forming a department in charge of "service experience management" that integrates marketing and operations.[55]

5) Carrying out internal marketing, training, and integration programs. (See the Southwest Airlines example in the following paragraphs).

6) Having top management's commitment to ensure that the overarching objectives of all departments are integrated.

A great example of a firm with a strong culture and strong integration across functions is Southwest Airlines, which continuously uses new and creative ways to strengthen its culture. Southwest's Culture Committee members are zealots when it comes to the continuation of the firm's family feel. The committee represents everyone from flight attendants and reservationists to top executives. As one participant observed, "The Culture Committee is not made up of Big Shots; it is a committee of Big Hearts." Culture Committee members are not out to gain power. They use the power of the Southwest spirit to connect people to the cultural foundations of the company. The committee works behind the scenes to foster Southwest's commitment to its core values. The following are examples of events held to reinforce Southwest's culture.

Figure 11.24 Rewarding employees according to their performances is essential for the success of a business.

▶ **Walk a Mile in My Shoes.** This program helped Southwest employees to gain an appreciation for other people's jobs. Employees were asked to visit a different department on their day off and to spend a minimum of six hours on the "walk." These participants were rewarded not only with transferable round-trip passes but also with goodwill and better morale.

▶ **A Day in the Field.** This activity is practiced throughout the company all year long. For example, Barri Tucker, then a senior communications representative in the executive office, once joined three flight attendants working a three-day trip. This allowed Tucker to experience the company from a new angle and hear directly from customers. She was able to see how important it was for corporate headquarters to support Southwest's front-line employees.

▶ **Helping Hands.** Southwest sent out volunteers from around the system to lighten the load of employees in the cities where Southwest was in direct competition with United's Shuttle. This not only built momentum and strengthened the troops for the battle with United but also helped rekindle the fighting spirit of Southwest employees.[56]

Motivate and Energize People[57]

Once a firm has hired the right people, trained them well, empowered them, and organized them into effective service delivery teams, how can it ensure that they are engaged and will deliver? Staff performance is a function of ability and motivation. Effective hiring, training, empowerment, and teams give a firm able people; and performance appraisal and reward systems are key to motivating them. Service staff must get the message that they will be rewarded if they provide quality service efficiently. Motivating and rewarding strong service performers are some of the most effective ways of retaining them (Figure 11.24). Staff members quickly realize that those who get promoted are truly outstanding service providers, and those who do not deliver at the customer level get fired.

However, service businesses often fail because they do not utilize the full range of available rewards effectively. Many firms think in terms of money as reward, but money

LO 11

Know how to motivate and energize service employees so that they will deliver service excellence and productivity.

PART III

does not always function as an effective motivator. Receiving a fair salary is a hygiene factor rather than a motivating factor. Paying more than what is seen as fair only has short-term motivating effects. In contrast, bonuses that are contingent on performance have to be earned again and again and tend to be more lasting in their effectiveness. Other, more lasting rewards are the job content, recognition and feedback, and goal accomplishment.

Job content. People are motivated and satisfied when they know that they are doing a good job. They feel good about themselves and like to reinforce that feeling. This is true especially if the job:

- Has a variety of different activities
- Requires the completion of "whole" and identifiable pieces of work
- Is seen as significant in the sense that it has an impact on the lives of others
- Comes with autonomy and flexibility
- Provides direct and clear feedback on how well employees did their work (e.g., grateful customers and sales performance)

Feedback and recognition. Humans are social beings, and they derive a sense of identity and belonging to an organization from the recognition and feedback they receive from the people around them—their customers, colleagues, and superiors. If employees are recognized and thanked for service excellence outside formal performance-appraisal meetings, they will want to continue achieving such excellence. Awards such as "star employee of the month" recognize excellent performances and can be highly motivating.

Positive emotions are contagious. Employees are highly satisfied and motivated when they work in jobs that allow them to make a positive impact on others. Hence, putting employees in touch with end users and letting them hear positive feedback from customers can be very motivating.[58] Positive effects were observed even when front-line employees simply saw pictures of customers or read stories of exceptional experiences customers had.[59]

Figure 11.25 When people are focused on goal achievement, it will motivate and energize them.

Goal achievement. Goals that are well-communicated and specific, difficult but attainable, and accepted by the staff are strong motivators (Figure 11.25). They focus people's energy and result in higher performance than no goals, vague goals ("do your best"), or goals that are impossible to achieve.

The following are important points to note for effective goal setting:

- When goals are seen as important, achieving the goals is a reward in itself.
- Goal accomplishment can be used as a basis for giving rewards, including bonuses, feedback, and recognition as part of formal performance appraisals. Feedback and recognition from peers can be given faster, more cheaply, and more effectively than pay. They have the additional benefit of gratifying an employee's self-esteem.

- Service employee goals that are specific and difficult must be set publicly to be accepted. Although goals must be specific, they can be something intangible (such as improved employee-courtesy ratings).

- Goal accomplishment and progress reports (feedback) must be public events if they are to gratify employees' self-esteem.

- It is mostly unnecessary to specify the means to achieve goals. Feedback on progress while pursuing the goal performs a corrective function. Thus, goal pursuit will result in goal accomplishment even in the absence of other rewards.

Charles O'Reilly and Jeffrey Pfeffer conducted in-depth research on how some companies succeed over long periods of time in highly competitive industries without having the usual sources of competitive advantage such as barriers of entry or proprietary technology. They concluded that these firms did not succeed by winning the war for talent (although they were hiring very carefully) "but by fully using the talent and unlocking the motivation of the people" they already had in their organizations.[60]

SERVICE CULTURE, CLIMATE, AND LEADERSHIP

So far, we have discussed the nuts and bolts of human resources in service firms. We will now take a look at the leader's role in nurturing an effective service culture within the organization. Let's start by defining culture and climate for service.

Building a Service-Oriented Culture[61]

> **LO 12**
> Understand what a service-oriented culture is.

Firms that strive to deliver service excellence need a strong service culture that is continuously reinforced and developed by management to achieve alignment with the firm's strategy. *Organizational culture* concerns the basic assumptions and values that guide organization action. It includes:

- Shared perceptions or themes regarding what is important in the organization

- Shared values about what is right and wrong

- Shared understanding about what works and what doesn't work

- Shared beliefs and assumptions about *why* these beliefs are important

- Shared styles of working and relating to others

Transforming an organization to develop and nurture a new culture along each of these five dimensions is no easy task for even the most gifted leader. It's doubly difficult when the organization is part of an industry that prides itself on deeply-rooted traditions. The firm may have many different departments run by independent-minded professionals in different fields who are attuned to how they are perceived by fellow professionals in the same field at other institutions. This situation is often found in such pillars of the non-profit world as colleges and universities, major hospitals, and large museums.

Leonard Berry advocates a value-driven leadership that inspires and guides service providers.[62] Leadership should bring out the passion for serving. It should also tap the creativity of service providers, nourish their energy and commitment, and give them a fulfilling working life. An essential feature of a strong service culture is a belief in the importance of delivering superior customer value and service excellence. Some of the core values Berry found in excellent service firms included innovation, joy, teamwork, respect, integrity, and social profit. These values are part of the firm's culture. Berry further boils down the definition of *service culture* to two points:

▶ Shared perceptions of *what* is important in an organization, and

▶ Shared values and beliefs about *why* those things are important.

It is the responsibility of the leaders to create a service culture with values that inspire, energize, and guide service providers.

LO 13

Know the difference between service climate and culture, and describe the determinants of a climate for service.

A Climate for Service[63]

While culture is more overarching and value focused, *organizational climate* is the part of the organization's culture that can be felt and seen. Employees gain their understanding of what is important by noting what the company and its leaders do rather than what they say. They form their perceptions on the basis of the daily experiences they have with the firm's human resources; operations; marketing; and IT policies, practices, and procedures. What they experience is culture translated into more concrete aspects that can be experienced by the employees. This in turn drives employee behavior and customer outcomes. In short, a climate represents the shared perceptions of employees about the practices, procedures, and types of behavior that get supported and rewarded in a particular setting.

As a climate must relate to something specific—for instance, to service, support, innovation, or safety—multiple climates often coexist within a single organization. Essential features of a climate for service include clear marketing goals and a strong drive to be the best in delivering superior customer value or service quality.[64]

LO 14

Explain the qualities of effective leaders in service organizations.

Qualities of Effective Leaders in Service Organizations

Leaders are responsible for creating a culture and climate for service. Why are some leaders more effective than others in bringing about a desired change in culture and climate?

Many commentators have written on the topic of leadership. It has even been described as a service in its own right. The late Sam Walton, founder of the Wal-Mart retail chain, highlighted the role of managers as "servant leaders."[65] The following are some qualities that effective leaders in a service organization should have:

▶ Leaders should love their business. Excitement about the business will encourage them to pass on the art and secrets of operating it to others.

▶ Many outstanding leaders are driven by a set of core values that are related to service excellence and performance.[66] Service quality is seen as a key foundation for success.

▶ Leaders must recognize the key part played by employees in delivering service. Service leaders need to believe in the people who work for them and pay special attention to communication with employees.

- Effective leaders are able to ask great questions and get answers from the team rather than dominate the decision-making process.[67]

- Leaders must be able to role model the behaviors they expect from their teams.

- Effective leaders have a talent for communicating with others in a way that is easy to understand. They know their audiences and are able to communicate even complicated ideas in simple terms that are accessible to all.[68] Effective communication is a key skill that inspires an organization to create success.

Leadership Styles, Focus on the Basics, and Role Modeling

Service climate research has contrasted two leadership styles: management of the "basics" versus transformational leadership that sets strategy and drives change.[69] Research has shown that the persistent management of the basics and endless details create a strong climate for service. Leaders who demonstrate commitment to service quality, set high standards, recognize and remove obstacles, and ensure the availability of the resources required to do it create a strong climate for service. This basic leadership style seems mundane compared to transformational leadership, yet according to James Heskett and his colleagues, both are needed. Leaders must recognize the "importance of the mundane" even as they provide a strong service vision that inspires and motivates the troupes.[70]

One of the traits of successful leaders is their ability to focus the organization on the basics and role model the behavior they expect from managers and other employees. Often, this requires the approach known as "management by walking around," popularized by Thomas Peters and Robert Waterman in their book *In Search of Excellence*.[71] When Herb Kelleher was CEO of Southwest Airlines, no one was surprised to see him turn up at a Southwest maintenance hangar at 2 o'clock in the morning or even to encounter him working an occasional stint as a flight attendant. Walking around involves regular visits (sometimes unannounced) to various areas of the company's operation. This approach provides insights into back-stage as well as front-stage operations. Leaders can observe and meet both employees and customers and see how corporate strategy is implemented at the front line. Periodically, this approach may cause leaders to recognize that changes in a firm's strategy are needed. Encountering the CEO on such a visit can also be motivating for service personnel and provides an opportunity for role modeling good service. Service Insights 11.3 describes how the CEO of a major hospital learned the power of role modeling early in his tenure.

Focusing the Entire Organization on the Front Line

A strong service culture is one where the entire organization focuses on the front line. The organization understands that the front line is the lifeline of the business, and that today's as well as tomorrow's revenues are largely driven by what happens during the service encounter. In firms with a passion for service, members of the top management show that the front line is crucially important to them by being informed and actively involved. They achieve this by regularly talking to and working with front-line staff and customers. Mark Frissora, CEO of the car-rental company Hertz, expressed this as follows:

LO 15

Understand different leadership styles and realize the importance of role modeling and focusing the entire organization on the front line.

PART III

A Hospital President Learns the Power of Role Modeling

During his 30-year tenure as president of Boston's Beth Israel Hospital (now Beth Israel-Deaconess Medical Center), Mitchell T. Rabkin, MD, was known for regularly making informal visits to all parts of the hospital. "You learn a lot from management by walking around," he said. "And you're also seen. When I visit another hospital and am given a tour by its CEO, I watch how that CEO interacts with other people, and what the body language is in each instance. It's very revealing. Even more, it's very important for role modeling." To reinforce this point, Dr Rabkin liked to tell the following story:

People learn to *do* as a result of the way they see you and others *behave*. An example from the Beth Israel that's now almost apocryphal—but *is* true—is the story of the bits of litter on the floor.

One of our trustees, the late Max Feldberg, head of the Zayre Corporation, asked me one time to take a walk around the hospital with him and inquired,

"Why do you think there are so many pieces of paper scattered on the floor of this patient care unit?"

"Well, it's because people don't pick them up," I replied.

He said, "Look, you're a scientist. We'll do an experiment. We'll walk down this floor and we'll pick up every other piece of paper. And then we'll go upstairs, there's another unit, same geography, statistically the same amount of paper, but we won't pick up anything."

So this 72-year old man and I went picking up alternate bits of the litter on one floor and nothing on the other. When we came back 10 minutes later, virtually all the rest of the litter on the first floor had been removed and nothing, of course, had changed on the second.

And "Mr. Max" said to me, "You see, it's not because *people* don't pick them up, it's because *you* don't pick them up. If you're so fancy that you can't bend down and pick up a piece of paper, why should anybody else?"

SOURCE

Source: Originally published in Christopher Lovelock, *Product Plus: How Product + Service = Competitive Advantage* (New York: McGraw-Hill, 1994).

I often hear people say, "As a CEO, you can't get too involved in the day-to-day operations of your business. That's micromanaging." My response is, "I have to get 'too involved' in the business because I'm setting the strategy. If I don't understand the business, then I'm a poor manager and I've failed as a leader." It's critical that leaders spend a lot of time where the work actually gets done.[72]

Many actually spend significant amounts of time at the front line serving customers. For example, Disney World's management spends two weeks every year in front-line staff jobs such as sweeping streets, selling ice-cream, or working as the ride attendant to gain a better understanding of what really happens on the ground.[73] Service leaders are not only interested in the big picture but also focus on the details of the service. They see opportunities in nuances that competitors might consider trivial, and they believe that the way the firm handles little things sets the tone for how it handles everything else.

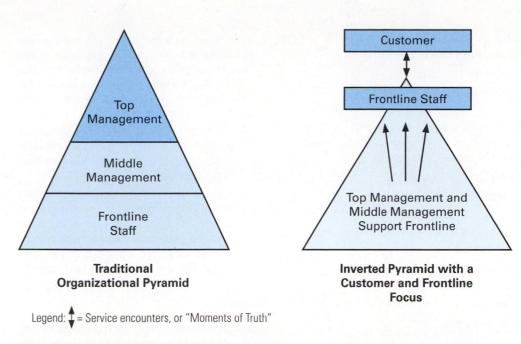

Traditional
Organizational Pyramid

Inverted Pyramid with a
Customer and Frontline
Focus

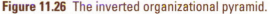

Legend: ↕ = Service encounters, or "Moments of Truth"

Figure 11.26 The inverted organizational pyramid.

Zappos focuses all new recruits on the front line by ensuring that everyone who is hired in its headquarters goes through the same training as their call-center employees (called the "Customer Loyalty Team"). Every accountant, lawyer, or software developer hired by the firm goes through exactly the same training program (regardless of seniority). It takes four weeks and covers the company history, the importance of customer service, the long-term vision of the company, and Zappos's philosophy about company culture. Following this training, all new recruits work for two weeks in the call center taking customer calls. According to CEO Tony Hsieh, "this goes back to our belief that customer service shouldn't just be a department, it should be the entire company."[74]

Figure 11.26 shows the inverted pyramid that highlights the importance of the front line. It demonstrates that the role of top management and middle management is to support the front line in their task of delivering service excellence to their customers.

LO1 ▶ Service employees are extremely important for the success of a service firm because they:
- o Are a core part of the service product.
- o Represent the service firm in the eyes of the customer.
- o Are a core part of the brand as they deliver the brand promise.
- o Generate sales, cross-sales, and up-sales.
- o Are a source of customer loyalty.
- o Determine the productivity of front-line operations.

LO2 ▶ The work of front-line employees is difficult and stressful because they are in boundary-spanning positions that often entail:
- o Organization/client conflicts
- o Person/role conflict
- o Inter-client conflicts
- o Emotional labor and stress

LO3 ▶ We use three types of cycles involving front-line employees and customers to describe how firms can be set up for failure, mediocrity, or success:
- o The Cycle of Failure involves a strategy of low pay and high employee turnover. It results in high customer dissatisfaction and defections, which in turn depress profit margins.
- o The Cycle of Mediocrity is typically found in large bureaucracies, offering job security but not much scope in the job itself. There is no incentive to serve customers well.
- o Successful service firms operate in the Cycle of Success, where employees are satisfied with their jobs and are productive. As a consequence, customers are satisfied and loyal. Higher profit margins allow investment in the recruitment, development, and motivation of the right front-line employees.

LO4 ▶ The Service Talent Cycle is a guiding framework for successful HR strategies in service firms, helping them to move their firms into the Cycle of Success. Implementing the Service Talent Cycle correctly will give firms highly motivated and productive employees who are willing and able to deliver service excellence and go the extra mile for their customers. It has four key prescriptions:
- o Hire the right people.
- o Enable front-line employees.
- o Motivate and energize them.
- o Have a leadership team that fosters a climate for service, walks the talk, and emphasizes and supports the front line.

LO5 ▶ Firms need to attract, select, and hire the right people for their firm and any given service job. Best-practice HR strategies start with the recognition that the labor market is highly competitive in many industries. In order to compete for talent, a firm must:
- o Work on being seen as a preferred employer, so that it can receive a large number of applications from the best potential candidates in the labor market.
- o Carefully select new employees so that they fit both job requirements and the organization's culture. The best suited candidates can be selected using screening methods such as multiple structured interviews, observation, personality tests, and realistic job previews.

LO6 ▶ To enable their front-line employees, firms need to:

Conduct extensive training on (1) the organizational culture, purpose, and strategy; (2) interpersonal and technical skills; and (3) product/service knowledge.

LO7 ▶ Use internal communications (also referred to as "internal marketing") to reinforce the firm's service culture and convey the message to everyone in the company. An effective mix of internal communications tools should be used (e.g., e-mails; magazines; videos; briefings; and promotional campaigns using displays, prices, and recognition programs).

LO8 ▶ Empower the front line so that they can respond with flexibility to customer needs, non-routine encounters, and service failures. Empowerment and training will give employees the authority, skills, and self-confidence to use their own initiative in delivering service excellence.
- o Empowerment needs to be set at the appropriate level for the business model and customer needs. It ranges from the low level of empowerment in the "production-line" approach for highly standardized services to a high level of decision authority for the front line in more complex and customized services.
- o Empowerment requires systematically distributing four key features: (1) information about organizational, team, and individual performance; (2) knowledge that enables employees to understand and contribute to performance; (3) power to make decisions; and (4) performance-based rewards.

LO9 ▶ Organize front-line employees into effective (often cross-functional) service delivery teams that can serve their customers from end to end.

LO10 ▶ Integrate service delivery teams across departments and functional areas. To be successful, the marketing, operations, human resources, and IT management functions need to be tightly integrated so that they can work together in well-coordinated ways. Integration means that the key deliverables and objectives of the various functions are not only compatible but also mutually reinforcing.

Ways to improve integration include (1) internal transfers across functional areas; (2) cross-functional project teams; (3) cross-functional service delivery teams; (4) appointing individuals to integrate objectives, activities, and processes between departments; (5) training, internal marketing, and campaigns (such as "walk a mile in my shoes" and "a day in the field"); and (6) management commitment to ensure that the overarching objectives of all functions are integrated.

LO11 ▶ Finally, energize and motivate employees with a full set of rewards ranging from pay, performance bonuses, satisfying job content, feedback, and recognition to goal accomplishment.

LO12 ▶ A *service culture* describes the basic assumptions and values that guide organizational action. It can be boiled down to two points:

o   Shared perceptions of *what* is important in an organization, and

o   Shared values and beliefs about *why* those things are important.

o   An essential feature of a service-oriented culture is a strong belief in the importance of delivering superior value and service excellence. It builds employee understanding and support for the organization's goals that lead to those outcomes.

o   Exemplary leaders understand the powerful, unifying effect of focusing on customers and creating a service culture with values that inspire, energize, and guide service providers.

LO13 ▶ A *service climate* is the surface layer on top of the culture. Climate is culture translated into the more concrete aspects that can be experienced by employees. It includes the policies, practices, and procedures of HR, operations, marketing, and IT. Climate also represents the shared perceptions of employees about the practices and behaviors that get rewarded in an organization.

LO14 ▶ Service leaders should have the following qualities:

o   Love for the business

o   A set of core values related to service excellence and performance, which they pass on to the organization

o   A strong belief in the people who work for them and recognition of the importance of the front line

o   Ability to ask great questions and get answers from their teams

o   Ability to role model the behaviors they expect from their teams

o   Effective communication skills that allow leaders to inspire the organization to create success

LO15 ▶ A leadership style that focuses on the basics and details creates a strong climate for service. Leaders should demonstrate a commitment to quality, set high standards, recognize and remove obstacles, and ensure the availability of the resources required to do it. This kind of leadership seems mundane compared to the transformational leadership that sets strategy and drives change, but both are needed to create a strong climate for service.

A strong service culture focuses on the front line. Leaders show by their actions that what happens at the front line is crucially important to them. The role of top and middle management is to support the front line in delivering service excellence to the firm's customers.

PART III

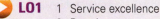

UNLOCK YOUR LEARNING

These keywords are found within the sections of each Learning Objective (LO). They are integral to understanding the services marketing concepts taught in each section. Having a firm grasp of these keywords and how they are used is essential to helping you do well on your course, and in the real and very competitive marketing scene out there.

LO1
1. Service excellence
2. Brand
3. Customer loyalty
4. Personalized relationships
5. Productivity
6. Front-line employees
7. Service firm
8. Service-Profit Chain
9. Differentiation
10. Service value
11. People
12. Competitive advantage

LO2
1. Boundary spanning
2. Emotional labor
3. Inter-client conflict
4. Organization/Client conflict
5. Person/Role conflict
6. Organizational behavior
7. Role stress
8. Role conflict
9. Two-bosses dilemma
10. Service sweatshops

LO3
1. Customer Cycle of Failure
2. Cycle of Failure
3. Cycle of Mediocrity
4. Cycle of Success
5. Employee Cycle of Failure
6. Cost variables
7. Revenue variables

LO4
1. Human resource management
2. Service Talent Cycle

LO5
1. Hire the right people
2. Multiple, structured interviews

3. Observe candidate behavior
4. Personality tests
5. Preferred employer
6. Recruitment advertising
7. Employment analytics
8. Realistic job preview
9. Employee–brand fit
10. Selection methods
11. Value proposition
12. Labor market

LO6
1. Interpersonal skills
2. Organizational culture
3. Product knowledge
4. Service knowledge
5. Technical skills
6. Training
7. Emotional commitment
8. Career-development program

LO7
1. Internal communications
2. Professionalizing the front line
3. Internal marketing

LO8
1 Employee involvement
2 Employee self-direction
3 Empowerment
4 Production-line approach
5 High involvement
6 Job involvement
7 Suggestion involvement
8 Control model
9 Involvement model
10 Service sweethearting
11 Power
12 Information
13 Rewards
14 Knowledge

LO9
1 Goals
2 Effective teamwork
3 Feedback
4 Service-delivery team
5 Goal achievement

LO10
1 Functional areas
2 Departments
3 Team integration

4 Service experience management
5 Cross-functional teams
6 Cross-departmental teams

LO11
1 Energize
2 Staff performance
3 Performance appraisal
4 Job content
5 Motivate
6 Recognition

LO12
1 Service-oriented culture

LO13
1 Organizational climate

LO14
1 Leadership

LO15
1 Inverted organizational pyramid
2 Leadership styles
3 Management of the "basics"
4 Transformational leadership

How well do you know the language of services marketing? Quiz yourself!

PART III

⚠ **Not for the academically faint-of-heart**

For each keyword you are able to recall without referring to earlier pages, give yourself a point (and a pat on the back). Tally your score at the end and see if you earned the right to be called—a *services marketeer*.

SCORE

01 – 12 Services Marketing is done a great disservice.

13 – 24 The midnight oil needs to be lit, pronto.

25 – 36 I know what you *didn't* do all semester.

37 – 48 By George! You're getting there.

49 – 60 Now, go forth and market.

61 – 73 There should be a marketing concept named after you.

KNOW YOUR SERVICES MARKETING

Review Questions

1. Why are service personnel so important for service firms?

2. What is emotional labor? Explain the ways in which it may cause stress for employees in specific jobs. Illustrate with suitable examples.

3. What are the key barriers for firms to break the Cycle of Failure and move into the Cycle of Success? How should an organization trapped in the Cycle of Mediocrity proceed?

4. List five ways in which investment in hiring and selection, training, and ongoing motivation of employees will have a positive impact on customer satisfaction for organizations such as (a) a restaurant, (b) an airline, (c) a hospital, and (d) a consulting firm.

5. Describe the key components of the Service Talent Cycle.

6. What can a service firm do to become a preferred employer and receive a large number of applications from the best potential candidates in the labor market?

7. How can a firm select the best suited candidates from a large number of applicants?

8. What are the key types of training service firms should conduct?

9. Identify the factors needed to make service teams successful in (a) an airline, (b) a restaurant, and (c) a customer contact center. What are the factors that favor a strategy of employee empowerment?

10. How can front-line employees be effectively motivated to deliver service excellence?

11. How can a service firm build a strong service culture that emphasizes service excellence and productivity?

12. What is the relationship among organizational culture, climate for service, and leadership?

13. Why is role modeling a desirable quality in service leaders?

WORK YOUR SERVICES MARKETING

Application Exercises

1. An airline runs a recruiting advertisement for cabin crew that shows a picture of a small boy sitting in an airline seat and clutching a teddy bear. The headline reads: "His mom told him not to talk to strangers. So what's he having for lunch?" Describe the types of personalities that you think would be (a) attracted to apply for the job by that ad and (b) discouraged from applying.

2. Use the Service Talent Cycle as a diagnostic tool on a successful and an unsuccessful service firm you are familiar with. What recommendations would you prescribe to each of these two firms?

3. Think of two organizations you are familiar with—one that has a very good climate for service and one that has a very poor service climate. Describe the

factors that shaped those climates. What factors do you think contributed the most? Why?

4. Which issues do you see as most likely to create boundary-spanning problems for employees in a customer-contact center at a major internet service provider? Select four issues and indicate how you would mediate between operations and marketing to create a satisfactory outcome for all three groups.

5. Identify the factors needed to make service teams successful in (a) an airline, (b) a restaurant, and (c) a customer contact center.

6. Profile an individual whose leadership skills have played a significant role in the success of a service organization, identifying personal characteristics that you consider important.

END**NOTES**

1. Adapted from: Leonard L. Berry, *Discovering the Soul of Service: The Nine Drivers of Sustainable Business Success* (New York: The Free Press, 1999): 156–159.

2. Liliana L. Bove and Lester W. Johnson, "Customer Relationships with Service Personnel: Do We Measure Closeness, Quality or Strength?" *Journal of Business Research* 54 (2001): 189–197; Magnus Söderlund and Sara Rosengren, "Revisiting the Smiling Service Worker and Customer Satisfaction," *International Journal of Service Industry Management* 19, no. 5 (2008): 552–574; Anat Rafaeli, Lital Ziklik, and Lorna Doucet, "The Impact of Call Center Employees' Customer Orientation Behaviors and Service Quality," *Journal of Service Research* 10, no. 3 (2008): 239–255.

3. The following study established the link between extra-role effort and customer satisfaction: Carmen Barroso Castro, Enrique Martín Armario, and David Martín Ruiz, "The Influence of Employee Organizational Citizenship Behavior on Customer Loyalty," *International Journal of Service Industry Management* 15, no. 1 (2004): 27–53.

4. James L. Heskett, Thomas O. Jones, Gary W. Loveman, W. Earl Sasser Jr., and Leonard A. Schlesinger, "Putting the Service Profit Chain to Work," *Harvard Business Review* 72 (March–April 1994): 164–174.

5. Benjamin Schneider and David E. Bowen, "The Service Organization: Human Resources Management Is Crucial," *Organizational Dynamics* 21, no. 4 (Spring 1993): 39–52.

6. "Just a Little Excitement on My Flight Today," http://www.fiveguysproductions.com/2010/08/just-little-excitement-on-my-flight.html, posted on August 9, 2010 by Phil Catelinet; accessed May 11, 2015.

7. Benjamin Schneider and David E. Bowen, "Boundary-Spanning Role Employees and the Service Encounter: Some Guidelines for Management and Research," in J. A. Czepiel, M. R. Solomon, and C. F. Surprenant (eds.), *The Service Encounter* (Lexington, MA: Lexington Books, 1985): 127–148.

8. Vaikakalathur Shankar Mahesh and Anand Kasturi, "Improving Call Centre Agent Performance: A UK-India Study Based on the Agents' Point of View," *International Journal of Service Industry Management* 17, no. 2 (2006): 136–157.

9. Arlie R. Hochschild, *The Managed Heart: Commercialization of Human Feeling* (Berkeley: University of California Press, 1983).

10. Panikkos Constanti and Paul Gibbs, "Emotional Labor and Surplus Value: The Case of Holiday 'Reps'," *The Service Industries Journal* 25 (January 2005): 103–116.

11. Arlie Hochschild, "Emotional Labor in the Friendly Skies," *Psychology Today* (June 1982): 13–15.

12. Michel Rod and Nicholas J. Ashill, "Symptoms of Burnout and Service Recovery Performance," *Managing Service Quality* 19, no. 1 (2009): 60–84; Jody L. Crosno, Shannon B. Rinaldo, Hulda G. Black, and Scott W. Kelley, "Half Full or Half Empty: The Role of Optimism in Boundary-Spanning Positions," *Journal of Service Research* 11, no. 3 (2009): 295–309.

13. Dan Moshavi and James R. Terbord, "The Job Satisfaction and Performance of Contingent and Regular Customer Service Representatives: A Human Capital Perspective," *International Journal of Service Industry Management* 13, no. 4 (2002): 333–347.

14. Mahesh and Kasturi, "Improving Call Centre Agent Performance," 136–157.

15. The terms "Cycle of Failure" and "Cycle of Success" were coined by: Leonard L. Schlesinger and James L. Heskett, "Breaking the Cycle of Failure in Services," *Sloan Management Review* (Spring 1991): 17–28. The term "Cycle of Mediocrity" comes from: Christopher H. Lovelock, "Managing Services: The Human Factor," in W. J. Glynn and J. G. Barnes (eds.), *Understanding Services Management* (Chichester, UK: John Wiley & Sons, 1995): 228.

16. Schlesinger and Heskett, "Breaking the Cycle of Failure," 17–28.

17. Jim Collins, *Good to Great: Why Some Companies Make the Leap . . . and Others Don't* (HarperBusiness, 2001).

18. Tor W. Andreassen and Even J. Lanseng, "Service Differentiation: A Self-Image Congruency Perspective on Brand Building in the Labor Market," *Journal of Service Management* 21, no. 2 (2010): 212–236.

19. Kathleen A. Keeling, Peter J. McGoldrick, and Henna Sadhu, "Staff Word-of-Mouth (SWOM) and Retail Employee Recruitment," *Journal of Retailing* 89, no. 1 (2013): 88–104.

20. www.glassdoor.com, accessed May 7, 2015.

21. Charles A. O'Reilly III and Jeffrey Pfeffer, *Hidden Value: How Great Companies Achieve Extraordinary Results with Ordinary People* (Boston, Massachusetts: Harvard Business School Press, 2000): 1.

22. Nancy J. Sirianni, Mary Jo Bitner, Stephen W. Brown, and Naomi Mandel, "Branded Service Encounters: Strategically Aligning Employee Behavior with the Brand Positioning," *Journal of Marketing* 77, no. 6 (2013): 108–123; Birgit Löndorf and Adamantios Diamantopoulos, "Internal Branding: Social Identity and Social Exchange Perspectives on Turning Employees into Brand Champions," *Journal of Service Research* 17, no. 3 (2014): 310–325.

23. Scott A. Hurrell and Dora Scholarios, "'The People Make the Brand': Reducing Social Skills Gaps through Person-Brand Fit and Human Resource Management Practices," *Journal of Service Research* 17, no. 1 (2014): 54–67.

24. Bill Fromm and Len Schlesinger, *The Real Heroes of Business* (New York: Currency Doubleday, 1994): 315–316.

25. Jim Collins, "Turning Goals into Results: The Power of Catalytic Mechanisms," *Harvard Business Review* (July–August 1999): 77.

26. Thomas H. Davenport, Jeanne Harris, and Jeremy Shapiro, "Competing on Talent Analytics," *Harvard Business Review* (October 2010): 52–58.

27. This section was adapted from: Benjamin Schneider and David E. Bowen, *Winning the Service Game* (Boston, MA: Harvard Business School Press, 1995): 115–126.

28. John Wooden, *A Lifetime of Observations and Reflections on and off the* Court (Chicago: Lincolnwood, 1997): 66.

29. For a review of this literature see: Benjamin Schneider, "Service Quality and Profits: Can You Have Your Cake and Eat It, Too?" *Human Resource Planning* 14, no. 2 (1991): 151–157.

30. Tom J. Brown, John C. Mowen, D. Todd Donovan, and Jane W. Licata, "The Customer Orientation of Service Workers: Personality Trait Effects on Self- and Supervisor Performance Ratings," *Journal of Marketing Research* 39, no. 1 (2002): 110–119; John E. G. Bateson, Jochen Wirtz, Eugene F. Burke, and Carly J. Vaughan, "Sifting to Efficiently Select the Right Service Employees," *Organizational Dynamics* 43 (2014): 312–320.

31. Serene Goh, "All the Right Staff," and Arlina Arshad, "Putting Your Personality to the Test," *The Straits Times*, Singapore, September 5, 2001, H1.

32. Have a look at SHL's website at http://ceb.shl.com to see the tests that are available.

33. This section was adapted from: Leonard L. Berry, *On Great Service: A Framework for Action* (New York: The Free Press, 1995): 181–182.

34. Donald W. Jackson Jr. and Nancy J. Sirianni, "Building the Bottomline by Developing the Frontline: Career Development for Service Employees," *Business Horizons* 52 (2009): 279–287.

35. Yukari Iwatani Kane and Ian Sherr, "Secrets from Apple's Genius Bar: Full Loyalty, No Negativity," *Wall Street Journal*, June 15, 2011, http://www.wsj.com/articles/SB10001424052702304563104576364071955678908, accessed May 11, 2015.

36. Schneider and Bowen, *Winning the Service Game*, 131.

37. Berry, *Discovering the Soul of Service*, 161; Pep Simo, Mihaela Enache, Jose M. Sallan, and Vicenc Fernandez, "Relations between Organizational Commitment and Focal and

Discretionary Behaviors," *The Service Industries Journal* 34, no. 5 (2014): 422–438.

38. Disney Institute, *Be Our Guest: Perfecting the Art of Customer Service*, updated edition (Disney Enterprises, 2011).

39. David A. Tansik, "Managing Human Resource Issues for High Contact Service Personnel," in D. E. Bowen, R. B. Chase, T. G. Cummings, and associates (eds.), *Service Management Effectiveness* (San Francisco: Jossey-Bass, 1990): 152–176; Kelly M. Wilder, Joel E. Collier, and Donald C. Barnes, "Tailoring to Customers' Needs: Understanding How to Promote an Adaptive Service Experience with Frontline Employees," *Journal of Service Research* 17, no. 4 (2014): 446–459.

40. Joseph A. Mitchelli, *The New Gold Standard: 5 Leadership Principles for Creating a Legendary Customer Experience Courtesy of The Ritz-Carton Hotel Company* (McGraw Hill, 2008): 61–66, 191–197.

41. Paul Hemp, "My Week as a Room-Service Waiter at the Ritz," *Harvard Business Review* 80 (June 2002): 8–11.

42. Parts of this section are based on: David E. Bowen and Edward E. Lawler III, "The Empowerment of Service Workers: What, Why, How and When," *Sloan Management Review* (Spring 1992): 32–39.

43. Michael K. Brady, Clay M. Voorhees, and Michael J. Brusco, "Service Sweethearting: Its Antecedents and Customer Consequences," *Journal of Marketing* 76, no. 2 (2012): 81–98.

44. Dana Yagil, "The Relationship of Customer Satisfaction and Service Workers' Perceived Control: Examination of Three Models," *International Journal of Service Industry Management* 13, no. 4 (2002): 382–398.

45. Graham L. Bradley and Beverley A. Sparks, "Customer Reactions to Staff Empowerment: Mediators and Moderators," *Journal of Applied Social Psychology* 30, no. 5 (2000): 991–1012.

46. Bowen and Lawler, "The Empowerment of Service Workers," 32–39.

47. Schneider and Bowen, *Winning the Service Game*, 250.

48. The system is described in: Serguei Netessine and Valery Yakubovich, "The Darwinian Workplace," *Harvard Business Review* 90 (May 2012): 25–28; Karan Girotra and Serguei Netessine, "Four Paths to Business Model Innovation: The Secret to Success Lies in Who Makes the Decisions When and Why," *Harvard Business Review* 92, no. 7/8 (2014): 96–103.

49. Jun Ye, Detelina Marionova, and Jagdip Singh, "Bottom-Up Learning in Marketing Frontlines: Conceptualization, Processes, and Consequences," *Journal of the Academy of Marketing Science* 40, no. 6 (2012): 821–844.

50. Jon R. Katzenbach and Douglas K. Smith, "The Discipline of Teams," *Harvard Business Review* (March–April, 1993): 112.

51. For the effects and drivers of alignment between leaders and their service delivery teams, see: Alexander Benlian, "Are We Aligned . . . Enough? The Effects of Perceptual Congruence between Service Teams and Their Leaders on Team Performance," *Journal of Service Research* 17, no. 2 (2014): 212–228.

52. Berry, *On Great Service*, 131.

53. O'Reilly and Pfeffer, *Hidden Value*, 9.

54. Mike Osheroff, "Teamwork in the Global Economy," *Strategic Finance* 88, no.8 (February 2007): 25, 61.

55. Robert J. Kwortnik Jr. and Gary M. Thompson, "Unifying Service Marketing and Operations with Service Experience Management," *Journal of Service Research* 11, no. 4 (2009): 389–406.

56. Adapted from: Kevin Freiberg and Jackie Freiberg, *Nuts! Southwest Airlines' Crazy Recipe for Business and Personal Success* (New York: Broadway Books, 1997): 165–168.

57. This section is based on: Schneider and Bowen, *Winning the Service Game*, 145–173.

58. Linda Nasr, Jamie Burton, Thorsten Gruber, and Jan Kitshoff, "Exploring the Impact of Customer Feedback on the Well-Being of Service Entities: A TSR Perspective," *Journal of Service Management* 25, no. 4 (2014): 531–555.

59. Adam M. Grant, "How Customers Can Rally Your Troops," *Harvard Business Review* (June 2011): 96–103.

60. O'Reilly and Pfeffer, *Hidden Value*, 232.

61. This section is based in part on: Schneider and Bowen, *Winning the Service Game*; Benjamin Schneider and David E. Bowen, "A Service Climate Synthesis and Future Research Agenda," *Journal of Service Research* 17, no. 1 (2014): 5–22.

62. Berry, *On Great Service*, 236–237; Leonard L. Berry and Kent D. Seltman, *Management Lessons from Mayo Clinic: Inside One of the World's Most Admired Service Organizations* (McGraw Hill, 2008).

63. For an excellent review of the extant service-climate literature and related constructs, see: Bowen and Schneider, "Service Climate Synthesis and Future Research Agenda," 5–22.

64. Hans Kasper, "Culture and Leadership in Market-Oriented Service Organisations," *European Journal of Marketing* 36, no. 9–10 (2002): 1047–1057; Ronald A. Clark, Michael D. Hartline, and Keith C. Jones, "The Effects of Leadership Style on Hotel Employees' Commitment to Service Quality," *Cornell Hospitality Quarterly* 50, no. 2 (2009): 209–231.

65. James L. Heskett, W. Earl Sasser Jr., and Leonard A. Schlesinger, *The Service Profit Chain* (New York: The Free Press, 1997): 236

66. Berry, *Discovering the Soul of Service*, 44, 47.

67. J. Hamm, "The Five Messages Leaders Must Manage," *Harvard Business Review* (May 2006): 115–123.

68. D. Blagg and S. Young "What Makes a Leader?" *Harvard Business School Bulletin* (February 2001): 31–36.

69. This section was adapted from: Bowen and Schneider, "Service Climate Synthesis and Future Research Agenda," 5–22. This article provides a detailed review of the research that underlies this section.

70. Heskett, Jones, Loveman, Sasser, and Schlesinger, "Putting the Service Profit Chain to Work," 164.

71. Thomas J. Peters and Robert H. Waterman, *In Search of Excellence* (New York: Harper & Row, 1982): 122.

72. From Rik Kirkland, "Leading in the 21st Century: An Interview with Hertz CEO Mark Frissora," © 2013 McKinsey & Company.

73. Catherine DeVrye, *Good Service Is Good Business* (Upper Saddle River, NJ: Prentice Hall, 2000): 11.

74. Tony Hsieh, *Delivering Happiness: A Path to Profits, Passion and Purpose* (New York: Business Plus, 2010): 153.

THE *ESM* FRAMEWORK

PART I

Understanding Service Markets, Products, and Customers

- Introduction to Services Marketing
- Consumer Behavior in a Services Context
- Positioning Services in Competitive Markets

PART II

Applying the 4 Ps of Marketing to Services

- Developing Service Products and Brands
- Distributing Services through Physical and Electronic Channels
- Setting Prices and Implementing Revenue Management
- Promoting Services and Educating Customers

PART III

Managing the Customer Interface

- Designing Service Processes
- Balancing Demand and Capacity
- Crafting the Service Environment
- Managing People for Service Advantage

PART IV

Developing Customer Relationships

- Managing Relationships and Building Loyalty
- Complaint Handling and Service Recovery

PART V

Striving for Service Excellence

- Improving Service Quality and Productivity
- Building a World-Class Service Organization

Developing Customer Relationships

Part IV focuses developing customer relationships through building loyalty and effective complaint handling and service recovery for the long term profitability. It consists of the following two chapters:

Chapter 12 Managing Relationships and Building Loyalty

Focuses on achieving profitability through creating relationships with customers from the right segments and then finding ways to build and reinforce their loyalty using the Wheel of Loyalty as an organizing framework. This chapter closes with a discussion of customer relationship management (CRM) systems.

Chapter 13 Complaint Handling and Service Recovery

Examines how effective complaint handling and professional service recovery can be implemented. It starts with a review of consumer complaining behavior and principles of effective service recovery. Service guarantees are discussed as a powerful way of institutionalizing effective service recovery and as an effective marketing tool signaling high quality service. The chapter also discusses how to deal with jaycustomers who take advantage of service recovery policies and abuse the service in other ways.

LEARNING OBJECTIVES (LOs)

By the end of this chapter, the reader should be able to:

▶ **LO 1** Recognize the important role customer loyalty plays in driving a service firm's profitability.

▶ **LO 2** Calculate the life-time value (LTV) of a loyal customer.

▶ **LO 3** Understand why customers are loyal to a particular service firm.

▶ **LO 4** Know the core strategies of the Wheel of Loyalty that explain how to develop a loyal customer base.

▶ **LO 5** Appreciate why it is so important for service firms to target the "right" customers.

▶ **LO 6** Use service tiering to manage the customer base and build loyalty.

▶ **LO 7** Understand the relationship between customer satisfaction and loyalty.

▶ **LO 8** Know how to deepen the relationship through cross-selling and bundling.

▶ **LO 9** Understand the role of financial and non-financial loyalty rewards in enhancing customer loyalty.

▶ **LO 10** Appreciate the power of social, customization, and structural bonds in enhancing loyalty.

▶ **LO 11** Understand what factors cause customers to switch to a competitor and how to reduce such switching.

▶ **LO 12** Know why loyalty programs and customer relationship management (CRM) systems are important enablers of delivering loyalty strategies.

▶ **LO 13** Understand the part played by CRM systems in delivering customized services and building loyalty.

OPENING VIGNETTE

Caesars Entertainment's Customer Relationship Management[1]

Caesars Entertainment (formerly Harrah's Entertainment) is the world's largest gaming company, with a number of key brands including Caesars, Harrah's, Horseshoe, and the London Clubs family of casinos. It is a leader in the use of highly sophisticated loyalty programs. Harrah's was the first company to launch a tiered customer loyalty program in the gaming industry. The program now covers Caesars Entertainment's other brands as well and is integrated across nearly all its properties and services. It has four tiers—Gold, Platinum, Diamond, and Seven Stars (by invitation only). Customers identify themselves (and earn points) at every touch point throughout the company, ranging from its gaming tables, restaurants, and hotels to its gift shops and shows. The points collected can be used to obtain cash, merchandise, lodging, show tickets, and vacations.

What is special about Caesars Entertainment is not its loyalty program but what it does with the information it gleans from its customers when they use their cards to earn points. At the back end, the firm has linked all its databases from casino management, hotel reservations, and events. This allows it to have a holistic view of each customer. The company now has detailed data on tens of millions of customers and knows each customer's preferences and behaviors. These range from how much they spend on each type of game and what food and drinks they like to the kind of entertainment and lodging they prefer. All this information about the customer is captured in real time.

Caesars Entertainment uses this data to drive its marketing and on-site customer service. For example, if a Diamond card holder on slot machine 278 signals for service, a Caesars associate is able to ask, "The usual, Mr. Jones?" He can then track the time it takes for a server to fulfill the guest's request. When a customer wins a jackpot, Caesars can tailor a customer-specific reward to celebrate that win. Caesars also

Figure 12.1 Caesars hit the jackpot with its technological innovation in developing customer relationships.

knows when a customer is approaching his maximum gaming limit on a particular evening and when he is likely to stop playing. Just before the limit is reached, Caesars can offer him a heavily discounted ticket in real time via text message for a show with available seats. This special deal keeps the customer on the premises (thereby encouraging him to spend more money) and makes him feel valued. At the same time, it helps the company to use otherwise wasted capacity in its shows and restaurants.

Likewise, when a customer makes a call to Caesars' call center, the staff members obtain detailed real-time information about his preferences and spending habits. They can then tailor promotions that cross-sell or up-sell the company's services. Caesars does not do blanket promotions that target all its customers at the same time. This is, according to Caesars' Chairman, President, and CEO Gary Loveman, "a margin eroding nightmare." Rather, it uses highly targeted promotions that create the right incentives for each of its different customers. It also uses control groups to measure the success of a promotion in dollars and cents and to further fine-tune its campaigns.

With its data-driven CRM, Caesars is able to personalize and differentiate customer interactions. Harrah's, the first brand in the group to launch the Total Rewards Program, has increased the share of wallet of its Total Rewards card holders from 34% (when the CRM program was first implemented) to an impressive 50%.

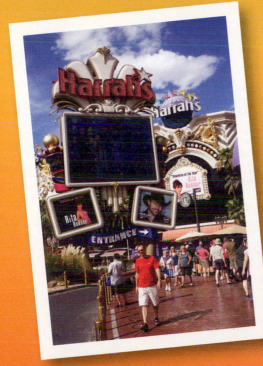

Figure 12.2 From high rollers to casual gamblers, the glittering lights of Harrah's promise customer satisfaction.

Importance of Customer Loyalty to Firm Profitability

- Higher purchases, share-of-wallet, and cross-buying
- Reduced customer service costs
- Positive word-of-mouth and referrals
- Lower price sensitivity
- Amortization of acquisition costs over a longer period

Customer Loyalty

Value Analysis

- Lifetime value computation
- Gap analysis between actual and potential customer value

Loyalty Drivers

- Confidence benefits
- Social benefits
- Special treatment benefits

Customer Loyalty Strategies: The Wheel of Loyalty

Foundation for Loyalty

- Target the right customers, match firm capabilities with customer requirements
- Search for value, not just volume
- Use tiering of the customer base to focus resources and attention on the firm's most valuable customers
- Deliver service quality to win behavioral (share-of-wallet) and attitudinal loyalty (share-of-heart)

Loyalty Bonds

- Deepen the relationship through bundling and cross-selling
- Offer loyalty rewards
  - Financial rewards (hard benefits); e.g., points, frequent flyer miles, free upgrades
  - Non-financial rewards (soft benefits), e.g., priority waitlisting, upgrading, early check-in, etc.; special recognition and appreciation; implicit service guarantee
- Higher-level loyalty bonds
  - Social bonds
  - Customization bonds
  - Structural bonds

Reduce Customer Churn

- Churn analysis
- Address key churn drivers
- Effective complaint handling and service recovery
- Increase switching costs
  - Positive switching costs (soft lock-in strategies) from adding value (see loyalty bonds)
  - Contractual and other hard lock-in strategies (e.g., early cancellation fees)

Enablers of Customer Loyalty Strategies

Frontline Employees and Account Managers

Membership-type Relationships

- Achieved through loyalty programs even for transaction-type services
- Loyalty programs provide a unique identifier of the customer that facilitates an integrated view of the customer across all channels, branches, and product lines

CRM Systems

- Strategy development (e.g., customer strategy, including target segments, tiering of customers, design of loyalty bonds)
- Value creation for customers and the firm (e.g., customer benefits through tiering, customization and priority service, and higher share-of-wallet for firm)
- Multi-channel integration (e.g., provide a unified customer interface)
- Information management (e.g., deliver customer data to all touchpoints)
- Performance assessment of strategy

Figure 12.3 Organizing framework for managing relationships and building loyalty.

THE SEARCH FOR CUSTOMER LOYALTY

Targeting, acquiring, and retaining the "right" customers are at the core of many successful service firms. In Chapter 3, we discussed segmentation and positioning. In this chapter, we emphasize the importance of focusing on desirable, loyal customers within the chosen segments and taking pains to build and maintain their loyalty through well-conceived relationship marketing strategies. The objective is to build relationships and to develop loyal customers who will do a growing volume of business with the firm in the future. Figure 12.3 provides the organizing framework for this chapter.

Why Is Customer Loyalty So Important to a Firm's Profitability?

"Few companies think of customers as annuities," says Frederick Reichheld, author of *The Loyalty Effect* and a major researcher in this field.[2] However, that is what a loyal customer can mean to a firm—a consistent source of revenue over a period of many years. How much is a loyal customer worth in terms of profits? In a classic study, Reichheld and Sasser analyzed the profit per customer in different service businesses. Customers were categorized on the basis of the number of years they had been with the firm. The study showed that the longer customers remained with a firm in each of the chosen industries, the more profitable they became. Annual profit increases per customer for a few sample industries, which have been indexed over a five-year period for easier comparison, are summarized in Figure 12.4. The industries studied (with average profits from a first-year customer shown in parentheses) were credit cards ($30), industrial laundry ($144), industrial distribution ($45), and automobile servicing ($25).

Underlying this profit growth are several factors that work to the supplier's advantage to create incremental profits. In order of magnitude at the end of seven years, these factors are:[3]

LO 1

Recognize the important role customer loyalty plays in driving a service firm's profitability.

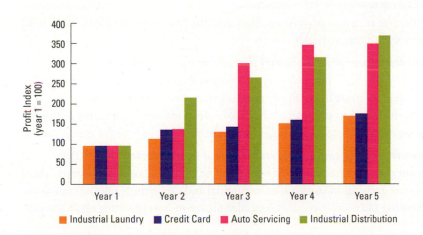

Figure 12.4 How much profit a customer generates over time.

SOURCE

From Frederick F. Reichheld and W. Earl Sasser, Jr., " Zero Defections: Quality Comes to Services," © 1990 Harvard Business School.

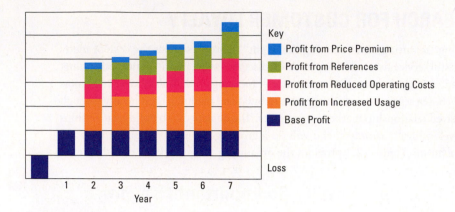

Figure 12.5 Why customers become more profitable over time.

SOURCE

From Frederick F. Reichheld and W. Earl Sasser, Jr., " Zero Defections: Quality Comes to Services," © 1990 Harvard Business School.

1) ***Profit derived from increased purchases (or, in a credit card and banking environment, higher account balances).*** Over time, business customers often grow larger and need to purchase in greater quantities. Individuals may also purchase more as their families grow or as they become more affluent. Both types of customers may be willing to consolidate their purchases with a single supplier who provides high-quality service, resulting in what we call a high share of wallet.[4]

2) ***Profit from reduced customer service costs.*** As customers become more experienced, they make fewer demands on the supplier (for instance, they have less need for information and assistance and make more use of self-service options). They may also make fewer mistakes when involved in operational processes and thereby contribute to greater productivity.

3) ***Profit from referrals to other customers.*** Positive word-of-mouth recommendations are like free sales and advertising. They save the firm from having to invest a lot of money in these activities.

4) ***Profit from lower price sensitivity that allows a price premium.*** New customers often benefit from introductory promotional discounts, whereas long-term customers are more likely to pay regular prices. When they are highly satisfied, they tend to be less price sensitive.[5] Moreover, customers who trust a supplier may be more willing to pay higher prices at peak periods or for express work.

5) ***Acquisition costs can be amortized over a longer period.*** Furthermore, the upfront costs of attracting these buyers can be amortized over many years. These customer acquisition costs can be substantial and can include sales commissions, advertising and promotion costs, and administrative costs of setting up an account.

Figure 12.5 shows the relative contribution of each of these different factors over a seven-year period, based on an analysis of 19 different product categories (both goods and services). Reichheld argues that the economic benefits of customer loyalty noted above often explain why one firm is more profitable than a competitor. As a response, Reichheld and Sasser popularized the term *zero defections* to describe a company that keeps every customer it can serve profitably.[6]

Assessing the Value of a Loyal Customer

One of the challenges that you are likely to face in your work is to determine the costs and revenues associated with serving customers in different market segments at different points in their customer life cycles and to predict future profitability. For insights on how to calculate customer value, see the box, "Worksheet for Calculating Customer Lifetime Value."[7]

Worksheet for Calculating Customer Lifetime Value

LO 2
Calculate the life-time value (LTV) of a loyal customer.

Calculating customer value is an inexact science that is subject to a variety of assumptions. You may want to try varying these assumptions to see how it affects the final figures. Generally speaking, revenues per customer are easier to track on an individualized basis than are the associated costs of serving a customer, unless (1) no individual records are kept and/or (2) the accounts served are very large and all account-related costs are individually documented and assigned.

Acquisition Revenues Less Costs

If individual account records are kept, the initial application fee paid and initial purchase (if relevant) should be found in these records. Costs, by contrast, may have to be based on average data. For instance, the marketing cost of acquiring a new client can be calculated by dividing the total marketing costs (advertising, promotions, selling, etc.) devoted toward acquiring new customers by the total number of new customers acquired during the same period. If each acquisition takes place over an extended period of time, you may want to build in a lagged effect between when marketing expenditures are incurred and when new customers come on board. The cost of credit checks—where relevant—must be divided by the number of new customers, not the total number of applicants, because some applicants will probably fail this hurdle. Account set-up costs will also be an average figure in most organizations.

Annual Revenues and Costs

If annual sales, account fees, and service fees are documented on an individual-account basis, account revenue streams (ex-

cept referrals) can be easily identified. The first priority is to segment your customer base by the length of its relationship with your firm. Depending on the sophistication and precision of your firm's records, annual costs in each category may be directly assigned to an individual account holder or averaged for all account holders in that age category.

Value of Referrals

Computing the value of referrals requires a variety of assumptions. To get started, you may need to conduct surveys to determine (1) what percentage of new customers claim that they were influenced by a recommendation from another customer and (2) what other marketing activities also drew the firm to that individual's attention. From these two items, estimates can be made of what percentage of the credit for all new customers should be assigned to referrals.

Net Present Value

Calculating net present value (NPV) from a future profit stream will require choice of an appropriate annual discount figure. (This could reflect estimates of future inflation rates.) It also requires assessment of how long the average relationship lasts. The NPV of a customer, then, is the sum of the anticipated annual profit on each customer for the projected relationship lifetime, suitably discounted each year into the future.

ACQUISITION		YEAR 1	YEAR 2	YEAR 3	YEAR n
Initial Revenue	*Annual Revenues*				
Application fee[a]	Annual account fee[a]				
Initial purchase[a]	Sales				
	Service fees[a]				
	Value of referrals[b]				
Total Revenues					
Initial Costs	*Annual Costs*				
Marketing	Account management				
Credit check[a]	Cost of sales				
Account setup[a]	Write-offs (e.g., bad debts)				
Less total costs					
Net Profit (Loss)					

[a] If applicable.
[b] Anticipated profits from each new customer referred (could be limited to the first year or expressed as the net present value of the estimated future stream of profits through year *n*); this value could be negative if an unhappy customer starts to spread negative word-of-mouth that causes existing customers to defect.

The Gap between Actual and Potential Customer Value

For profit-seeking firms, the potential profitability of a customer should be a key driver in marketing strategy. As Alan Grant and Leonard Schlesinger declare, "Achieving the full profit potential of each customer relationship should be the fundamental goal of every business . . . Even using conservative estimates, the gap between most companies' current and full potential performance is enormous."[8] They suggest analysis of the following gaps between the actual and potential value of customers:

▶ What is the current purchasing behavior of customers in each target segment? What would be the impact on sales and profits if they exhibited the ideal behavior profile of (1) buying all services offered by the firm, (2) using these to the exclusion of any purchases from competitors, and (3) paying full prices?

▶ How long, on average, do customers remain with the firm? What impact would it have if they remained customers for life?

Management's task is to design and implement marketing programs that increase loyalty (including share of wallet, up-selling, and cross-selling), identify the reasons why customers defect, and then take corrective action. The active management of the customer base and customer loyalty is also referred to as *customer asset management*.[9]

LO 3
Understand why customers are loyal to a particular service firm.

Why Are Customers Loyal?

After understanding how important loyal customers can be for the bottom line of a service firm, let's explore what makes a customer loyal. Customers are not automatically loyal to any one firm. Rather, the firm needs to give its customers a reason to buy from it and then stay with it.

Relationships can create value for individual consumers through factors such as inspiring greater confidence, offering social benefits, and providing special treatment (see Service Insights 12.1).

LO 4
Know the core strategies of the Wheel of Loyalty that explain how to develop a loyal customer base.

THE WHEEL OF LOYALTY

Building customer loyalty is difficult. Just try and think of all the service firms you are loyal to. Most people cannot think of more than a handful of firms they truly like and go back to repeatedly. This shows that although firms put enormous amounts of money and effort into loyalty initiatives, they are often unsuccessful in building true customer loyalty. We use the Wheel of Loyalty shown in Figure 12.6 as an organizing framework for thinking about how to build customer loyalty.

How Customers See Relational Benefits in Service Industries

What benefits do customers see themselves receiving from an extended relationship with a service firm? Researchers seeking answers to this question conducted two studies. The first consisted of in-depth interviews with 21 respondents from a broad cross-section of backgrounds. Respondents were asked to identify service providers that they patronized on a regular basis and discuss any benefits they received as a result of being a regular customer. Among the comments were:

- "I like him [hair stylist]… He's really funny and always has lots of good jokes. He's kind of like a friend now."
- "I know what I'm getting—I know that if I go to a restaurant that I regularly go to, rather than taking a chance on all of the new restaurants, the food will be good."
- "I often get price breaks. The little bakery that I go to in the morning, every once in a while, they'll give me a free muffin and say, 'You're a good customer, it's on us today.'"
- "You can get better service than drop-in customers … We continue to go to the same automobile repair shop because we have gotten to know the owner on a kind of personal basis, and he … can always work us in."
- "Once people feel comfortable, they don't want to switch to another dentist. They don't want to train or break a new dentist in."

After evaluating and grouping the comments, the researchers designed a second study in which they collected 299 survey questionnaires. The respondents were told to select a specific service provider with whom they had a strong, established relationship. The questionnaire then asked them to assess the extent to which they received each of the 21 benefits (derived from analysis of the first study) as a result of their relationship with the specific provider they had identified. Finally, they were asked to assess the importance of these benefits for them. A factor analysis of the results showed that most of the benefits that customers derived from relationships could be grouped into three categories. The first and most important group involved what the researchers labeled confidence benefits. These were followed by social benefits and special treatment benefits.

- *Confidence benefits* included customers' feeling that in an established relationship there was less risk of something going wrong. There was also greater confidence in correct performance and a greater ability to trust the provider. Customers experienced lowered anxiety when purchasing because they knew what to expect, and they typically received the firm's highest level of service.
- *Social benefits* embraced mutual recognition between customers and employees, such as being known by name, being on friendly terms with the service provider, and enjoying certain social aspects of the relationship.
- *Special treatment benefits* included better prices, discounts on special deals that were unavailable to most customers, extra services, higher priority when there was a wait, and faster service than most customers.

SOURCE

Source: From Kevin P. Gwinner, Dwayne D. Gremler, and Mary Jo Bitner, "Relational Benefits in Services Industries: The Customer's Perspective," *Journal of the Academy of Marketing Science* 26(2): 101–114. © 1998 Springer.

PART IV

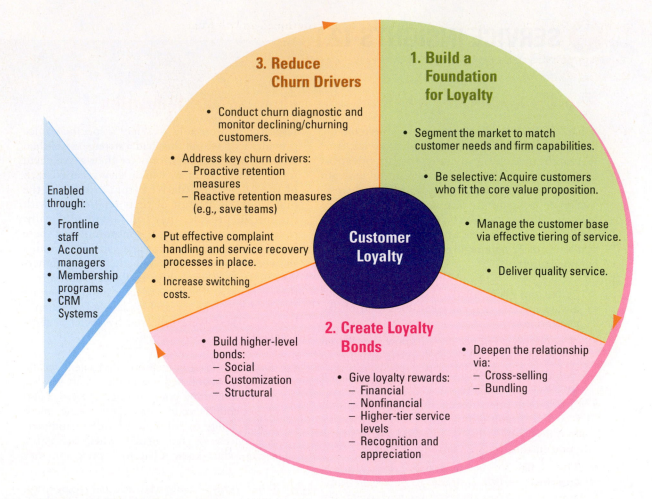

Figure 12.6 The Wheel of Loyalty.

The wheel contains the following sections:

Customer Loyalty (center)

1. Build a Foundation for Loyalty
- Segment the market to match customer needs and firm capabilities.
- Be selective: Acquire customers who fit the core value proposition.
- Manage the customer base via effective tiering of service.
- Deliver quality service.

2. Create Loyalty Bonds
- Deepen the relationship via:
  - Cross-selling
  - Bundling
- Give loyalty rewards:
  - Financial
  - Nonfinancial
  - Higher-tier service levels
  - Recognition and appreciation
- Build higher-level bonds:
  - Social
  - Customization
  - Structural

3. Reduce Churn Drivers
- Conduct churn diagnostic and monitor declining/churning customers.
- Address key churn drivers:
  - Proactive retention measures
  - Reactive retention measures (e.g., save teams)
- Put effective complaint handling and service recovery processes in place.
- Increase switching costs.

Enabled through:
- Frontline staff
- Account managers
- Membership programs
- CRM Systems

BUILDING A FOUNDATION FOR LOYALTY

In this section, we emphasize the importance of focusing on serving several desirable customer segments and then taking pains to build and maintain their loyalty through carefully thought-out relationship marketing strategies.

LO 5

Appreciate why it is so important for service firms to target the "right" customers.

Target the Right Customers

Loyalty management starts with segmenting the market to match customer needs and firm capabilities. "Who should we be serving?" is a question that every service business needs to raise periodically. Companies need to be selective about the segments they target if they want to build successful customer relationships. Managers must think carefully about how customer needs relate to such operational elements as speed and quality and the physical features and appearance of service facilities.

Leaders are picky about acquiring only the right customers; i.e., the customers for whom their firms have been designed to deliver truly special value. Acquiring the right customers often brings long-term revenues and continued growth from referrals. It can also enhance employee satisfaction, as the daily jobs of employees are improved when they deal with appreciative customers. The result of carefully targeting customers by matching the company capabilities and strengths with customer needs should be a superior service offering in the eyes of those customers who value what the firm has to offer.

Search for Value, Not Just Volume

Too many service firms continue to focus on the *number* of customers they serve without giving sufficient attention to the *value* of each customer.[10] Starwood Hotels & Resorts, for example, found that the top 2% of their guests generated a whopping 30% of their profits![11] Generally speaking, heavy users who buy more frequently and in larger volumes are more profitable than occasional users. Roger Hallowell makes this point nicely in a banking context:

Figure 12.7 A company that is able to exceed customer expectations will win their loyalty.

> A bank's population of customers undoubtedly contains individuals who either cannot be satisfied, given the service levels and pricing the bank is capable of offering, or will never be profitable, given their banking activity (their use of resources relative to the revenue they supply). Any bank would be wise to target and serve only those customers whose needs it can meet better than its competitors in a profitable manner. These are the customers who are most likely to remain with that bank for long periods, who will purchase multiple products and services, who will recommend that bank to their friends and relations, and who may be the source of superior returns to the bank's shareholders.[12]

Ironically, the firms that are highly focused and selective in their customer acquisition often grow very fast over long periods. Service Insights 12.2 shows how the Vanguard Group, a leader in the mutual funds industry, designed its products and pricing to attract and retain the right customers for its business model. Moreover, relationship customers are by definition not buying commodity services. Service customers who strictly buy on the basis of lowest price (a minority in most markets) are not good target customers for relationship marketing in the first place. They are deal-prone, continuously seek the lowest price on offer, and switch brands easily.

However, managers shouldn't assume that the "right customers" are always big spenders. Depending on the service business model, the right customers may come from a large group of people that no other supplier is doing a good job of serving. Many firms have built successful strategies on serving customer segments that had previously been neglected by established players which didn't see them as being "valuable" enough. Examples include Enterprise Rent-A-Car, which targets customers who need a temporary replacement car. It avoids the more traditional segment of business travelers targeted by its principal competitors. Similarly, Charles Schwab focuses on retail stock buyers, and Paychex provides small businesses with payroll and HR services.[13]

SERVICE INSIGHTS 12.2

Vanguard Discourages the Acquisition of "Wrong" Customers

The Vanguard Group is a growth leader in the mutual fund industry that built its $3.0 trillion in managed assets by 2015 by painstakingly targeting the right customers for its business model. Its share of new sales, which was around 25%, reflected its share of assets or market share. However, it had a far lower share of redemptions (customer defections in the fund context), which gave it a market share of net cash flows of 55% (new sales minus redemptions) and made it the fastest growing mutual fund in its industry.

How did Vanguard achieve such low redemption rates? The secret was in its careful acquisition of the "right" customers and its use of product and pricing strategies that facilitated this process.

John Bogle, Vanguard's founder, believed in the superiority of index funds and realized that their lower management fees would lead to higher returns over the long run. He offered Vanguard's clients the lowest management fees through a policy of not trading (its index funds hold the market they are designed to track), not having a sales force, and only spending a fraction of what its competitors did on advertising. The company also kept its costs low by discouraging the acquisition of customers who were not long-term index holders.

Bogle attributes the high customer loyalty Vanguard has achieved to a great deal of focus on customer redemptions. "I watched them like a hawk," he explained. He analyzed them more carefully than new sales to ensure that Vanguard's customer acquisition strategy was on course. Low redemption rates meant that the firm was attracting the right kind of loyal, long-term investors. The inherent stability of its loyal customer base has been key to Vanguard's cost advantage. Bogle's pickiness became legendary. He scrutinized individual redemptions with a fine-tooth comb to see who let the wrong kind of customers on board. When an institutional investor redeemed $25 million from an index fund bought only nine months earlier, he regarded the acquisition of this customer as a failure of the system. He explained, "We don't want short-term investors. They muck up the game at the expense of the long-term investor." At the end of his

chairman's letter to the Vanguard Index Trust, Bogle repeated: "We urge them [short-term investors] to look elsewhere for their investment opportunities."

This care and attention to acquiring the right customers is famous. For example, Vanguard once turned away an institutional investor who wanted to invest $40 million. The firm suspected that the customer would churn the investment within the next few weeks, creating extra costs for existing customers. The potential customer complained to Vanguard's CEO, who not only supported the decision but also used it as an opportunity to reinforce to his teams why they needed to be selective about the customers they accepted.

Furthermore, Vanguard introduced a number of changes to industry practices that discouraged active traders from buying its funds. For example, it did not allow telephone transfers for index funds. Redemption fees were added to some funds, and the standard practice of subsidizing new accounts at the expense of existing customers was rejected because it was considered disloyal to the firm's core investor base. These product and pricing policies turned away heavy traders but made the fund extremely attractive for long-term investors.

Finally, Vanguard's pricing was set up to reward loyal customers. For many of its funds, investors pay a one-time fee upfront. This goes into the funds (and not to Vanguard) to compensate all current investors for the administrative costs of selling new units. In essence, this fee subsidizes long-term investors and penalizes short-term investors. Another novel pricing approach was the creation of its Admiral shares for loyal investors, which carried a lower expense fee than ordinary shares (0.15% instead of 0.18% per year).

Manage the Customer Base through Effective Tiering of Services

LO 6
Use service tiering to manage the customer base and build loyalty.

Marketers should adopt a strategic approach to retaining, upgrading, and even ending relationships with customers. Customer retention involves developing long-term, cost-effective links with customers for the mutual benefit of both parties. However, these efforts need not necessarily target all the customers of a firm with the same level of intensity. Research has confirmed that customer profitability and return on sales can be increased by focusing a firm's resources on top-tier customers.[14] Furthermore, different customer tiers often have quite different service expectations and needs. According to Valarie Zeithaml, Roland Rust, and Katharine Lemon, it's critical for service firms to understand the needs of customers within different profitability tiers and adjust their service levels accordingly.[15]

Just as service product categories can be tiered to reflect the level of value included (e.g., first, business, and economy class in air travel; see Chapter 4), so can groups of customers. In the latter instance, service tiers can be developed around the levels of profit contribution of different groups of customers, their needs (including sensitivities to variables such as price, comfort, and speed), and identifiable personal profiles such as demographics. Zeithaml, Rust, and Lemon illustrate this principle through a four-level pyramid (Figure 12.8).

▶ *Platinum.* These customers form a very small percentage of a firm's customer base but are heavy users and tend to contribute a large share of the profits. They are usually less price-sensitive, but they expect higher service levels in return and are likely to be willing to invest in and try new services.

▶ *Gold.* The gold tier includes a larger percentage of customers than the platinum tier, but individual customers contribute less profit. They tend to be slightly more price sensitive and less committed to the firm.

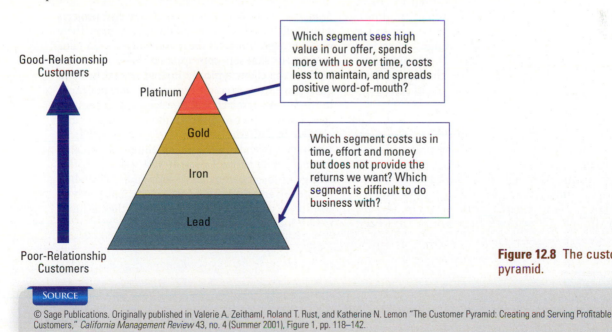

Figure 12.8 The customer pyramid.

> **Iron.** These customers provide the bulk of the customer base. Their numbers give the firm economies of scale. Hence, they are important for a firm to build and maintain a certain capacity level and infrastructure, which are often needed for serving gold and platinum customers well. However, iron customers in themselves may only be marginally profitable. Their level of business is not enough to justify special treatment.

> **Lead.** Customers in this tier tend to generate low revenues for a firm but often require the same level of service as iron customers. This turns them into a loss-making segment from the firm's perspective.

The precise characteristics of customer tiers vary from one type of business to another and even from one firm to another. Service Insights 12.3 provides an illustration from the marketing research industry.

SERVICE INSIGHTS 12.3

Tiering the Customers of a Market Research Agency

Tiering its clients helped a leading U.S. market research agency understand its customers better. The agency defined *platinum clients* as large accounts who were not only willing to plan a certain amount of research work during the year but were also able to commit to the timing, scope, and nature of their projects. This made capacity management and project planning much easier for the research firm. The acquisition costs for projects sold to these clients were only 2–5% of project values (compared to as much as 25% for clients who required extensive proposal work and project-by-project bidding). Platinum accounts were also more willing to try new services and buy a wider range of services from their preferred provider. These customers were generally very satisfied with the research agency's work and were willing to act as references for potential new clients.

Gold accounts had a similar profile to platinum clients, except that they were more price sensitive and more inclined to spread their budgets across several firms. Although these accounts had been clients for many years, they were not willing to commit to their research work a year in advance even though the research firm would have been able to offer them better quality and priority in capacity allocation.

Iron accounts spent moderate amounts on research and commissioned work on a project basis. Selling costs were high, as these clients tended to send out requests for proposals (RFPs) to a number of firms for all their projects. They sought the lowest price and often did not give the research firm sufficient time to perform a good-quality job.

Lead accounts sought only isolated, low-cost projects which tended to be "quick and dirty" in nature. There was little opportunity for the research firm to add value or apply its skill sets appropriately. Sales costs were high, as the client typically invited several firms to quote. Furthermore, as these firms were inexperienced in conducting research and in working with research agencies, selling a project often took several meetings and required multiple revisions to the proposal. Lead accounts also tended to be high maintenance because they did not understand research work well. They often changed project parameters, scope, and deliverables midstream and then expected the research agency to absorb the cost of any rework. This further reduced the profitability of the engagement.

SOURCE

Source: Adapted from Valarie A. Zeithaml, Roland T. Rust, and Katharine N. Lemon, "The Customer Pyramid: Creating and Serving Profitable Customers," *California Management Review* 43(4) (Summer 2001): 127–128.

Customer tiers are typically based on profitability and service needs. Each segment receives a service level that is customized on the basis of its requirements and its value to the firm. For example, the platinum tier receives some exclusive benefits that are not available to other segments. The benefit features for platinum and gold customers should be designed to encourage them to remain loyal, as they are the ones competitors would like to steal most.

Marketing efforts can be used to encourage an increased volume of purchases, upgrade the type of service used, or cross-sell additional services to any of the four tiers. However, these efforts have different thrusts for the different tiers, as their needs, usage behaviors, and spending patterns are usually very different.

Lead-tier customers at the bottom of the pyramid can be dealt with in two ways. The firm can either move them to the iron segment or end the relationship with them. Migration can be achieved via a combination of strategies, including up-selling, cross-selling, setting base fees, increasing prices, and/or cutting service costs. For example, imposing a minimum fee that is waived when a certain level of revenue is generated may encourage customers who use several suppliers to consolidate their buying with a single firm instead. Another way to move customers from the lead tier to the iron tier is to encourage them to use low-cost service delivery channels. For instance, lead-tier customers may be charged a fee for face-to-face interactions, but the fee may be waived when these customers use electronic channels. In the cellular telephone industry, for example, light mobile phone users can be encouraged to use pre-paid packages that do not require the firm to send out bills and collect payment. This also eliminates the risk of bad debts on such accounts.

Figure 12.9 Capital One 360 offers high interest rates that keep customers happy.

Divesting or terminating customers comes as a logical consequence of the realization that not all existing customer relationships are worth keeping.[16] Some relationships may no longer be profitable for the firm because they cost more to maintain than the contributions they generate. Some customers no longer fit the firm's strategy, either because that strategy has changed or because the customers' behavior and needs have changed.

Occasionally customers are "fired" outright (although concern for due process is still important). Capital One 360 is the fast-food model of consumer banking and is about as no-frills as it gets. It only has a handful of basic products, and it lures low-maintenance customers with no minimum balance or fees. It also has slightly higher interest rates for its savings accounts and lower interests on its home loans (Figure 12.9). To offset that generosity, its business model pushes its customers toward online transactions, and the bank routinely fires customers who don't fit its business model. When a customer calls too often (the average customer phone call costs the bank $5.25 to handle) or wants too many exceptions to the rule, the bank's sales associates terminate the relationship by advising the customer to employ the services of a community bank instead. As a result, the bank's cost per account is much lower than the industry average.[17]

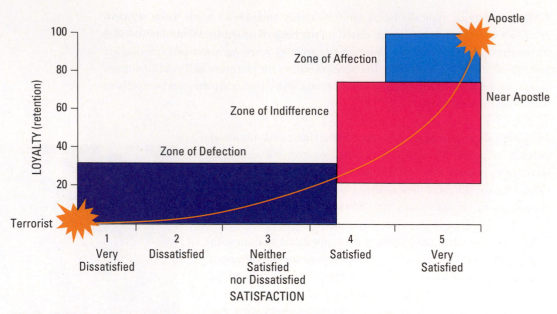

Figure 12.10 The customer satisfaction–loyalty relationship.

LO 7

Understand the relationship between customer satisfaction and loyalty.

Customer Satisfaction and Service Quality Are Prerequisites for Loyalty

The foundation for building true loyalty lies in customer satisfaction. Highly satisfied or even delighted customers are more likely to consolidate their buying with one supplier, spread positive word of mouth, and become loyal apostles of a firm.[18] Dissatisfaction, in contrast, drives customers away and is a key factor in switching behavior.

The satisfaction–loyalty relationship can be divided into three main zones: defection, indifference, and affection (Figure 12.10). The *zone of defection* occurs at low satisfaction levels. Customers will switch providers unless switching costs are high or there are no viable or convenient alternatives. Extremely dissatisfied customers can turn into "terrorists" for the service provider by spreading negative word of mouth in abundance.[19] The *zone of indifference* is found at moderate satisfaction levels. Here, customers are willing to switch if they find a better alternative. Finally, the *zone of affection* is located at very high satisfaction levels, where customers have such high attitudinal loyalty that they do not look for alternative service providers. Customers who praise the firm in public and refer others to the firm are described as "apostles."

True loyalty is often defined as combining both behavioral and attitudinal loyalty, also referred to as "share of wallet" and "share of heart" respectively. Behavioral loyalty includes behaviors such as buying again, contributing a high share of wallet, and providing positive word of mouth. Attitudinal loyalty refers to a true liking of and an emotional attachment to the firm, service, and brand.

It is important to note that satisfaction can be seen as a necessary but not a sufficient driver of true customer loyalty. Satisfaction alone does not explain a large amount of variance in loyalty behaviors. It has to be seen in combination with other factors such as switching costs,[20] the firm's competitive position (e.g., if a firm is seen as offering a better value proposition than the alternative provider,[21] switching makes little sense), and loyalty bonds (which we will discuss next).

STRATEGIES FOR DEVELOPING LOYALTY BONDS WITH CUSTOMERS

Having the right portfolio of customer segments, attracting the right customers, tiering the service, and delivering high levels of satisfaction are a solid foundation for creating customer loyalty (as shown in the Wheel of Loyalty in Figure 12.6). However, firms can use a variety of other strategies to "bond" more closely with their customers. These include (1) deepening the relationship through cross-selling and bundling; (2) creating loyalty rewards; and (3) building higher-level bonds such as social, customization, and structural bonds.[22] We will discuss each of these three strategies next.

Deepen the Relationship

Firms can build closer ties with their customers by bundling and/or cross-selling services. For example, banks like to sell as many financial products to an account or household as possible. Once a family has a checking account, credit card, savings account, safe deposit box, car loan, mortgage, and so on with the same bank, the relationship is so deep that switching becomes a major exercise and is unlikely unless the customers are extremely dissatisfied with the bank.

Often, there is also added value for the customer when he/she buys all particular services from a single provider. One-stop shopping is typically more convenient than buying individual services from different providers.

Encourage Loyalty through Financial and Non-financial Rewards

Few customers buy from only one supplier. This is especially true in situations where service delivery involves separate transactions (as in a car rental) instead of being continuous in nature (as with insurance coverage). In many instances, consumers are loyal to several brands (sometimes described as "polygamous loyalty") but avoid others. In such cases, the marketing goal is to strengthen the customer's preference for one brand over others and to gain a greater share of the customer's spending in that service category. Once acquired, it tends to be the reward-based bonds (often offered through a loyalty program) that entice customers to spend more money and increase a firm's share of wallet.[23] Incentives that offer rewards based on the frequency of purchase, value of purchase, or a combination of both represent a basic level of customer bonding. These rewards can be *financial* and *non-financial* in nature.

Financial Rewards. Financial rewards are customer incentives that have a financial value (also called "hard benefits"). These include discounts on purchases, loyalty program rewards such as frequent flier miles (Figure 12.11), and the cash-back programs provided by some credit card issuers.

▶ **LO 8**
Know how to deepen the relationship through cross-selling and bundling.

▶ **LO 9**
Understand the role of financial and non-financial loyalty rewards in enhancing customer loyalty.

PART IV

Figure 12.11 American Airlines tries to make its loyalty program enticing.

Grahame Dowling and Mark Uncles argue that marketers need to examine three psychological effects to assess the potential of a loyalty program to alter normal patterns of behavior:[24]

- *Brand loyalty versus deal loyalty*. To what extent are customers loyal to the core service (or brand) rather than to the loyalty program itself? Marketers should focus on loyalty programs that directly support the value proposition and positioning of the product in question.

- *How buyers value rewards*. Several elements determine a loyalty program's value to customers:
  - o The cash value of the redemption rewards (if customers had to purchase them)
  - o The range of choice among rewards (for instance, a selection of benefits rather than just a single benefit)
  - o The aspirational value of the rewards (something exotic that the consumer would not normally purchase may have greater appeal than a cash-back offer)
  - o Whether the amount of usage required to obtain a reward places it within the realm of possibility for any given consumer
  - o The ease of using the program and making redemptions
  - o The psychological benefits of belonging to the program and accumulating points.

- *Timing*. Deferred gratification tends to weaken the appeal of a loyalty program. One solution is to send customers periodic statements of their account status. This indicates progress toward reaching a particular milestone and promotes the rewards that might be forthcoming when that point is reached.

Of course, even well-designed rewards programs are by themselves not enough to keep a firm's most desirable customers. If you are dissatisfied with the quality of service or believe that you can get better value from another provider, you may quickly become disloyal. No service business that has instituted a rewards program for frequent users can ever afford to lose sight of its broader goals of offering high service quality and good value relative to the price and other costs incurred by customers.[25] Some customers will remain loyal if the firm simply delivers the basic service well, meets their needs, and solves their problems quickly and easily.[26]

Financial rewards-based programs can sometimes frustrate customers and breed dissatisfaction instead of creating loyalty and goodwill. This can happen (1) if customers feel they are excluded from a reward program because of low balances or volume of business, (2) if the rewards are seen as having little or no value, (3) if the customers cannot redeem their loyalty points because of black-out dates during high demand periods, and (4) if redemption processes are too troublesome and time-consuming.[27] Some customers already have so many loyalty cards in their wallet that they are simply not interested in adding more cards to that pile (especially if they see these cards as only marginally valuable).

Non-financial Rewards. Non-financial rewards (also called "soft benefits") provide benefits that cannot be translated directly into monetary terms. Examples include giving priority to loyalty program members on reservation wait lists and virtual queues in call centers.

Important intangible rewards include special recognition and appreciation. Customers tend to value the extra attention given to their needs and appreciate the efforts to meet their occasional special requests. High-tier loyalty program members also tend to enjoy an implicit service guarantee. When things go wrong, front-line employees pay extra attention to their most valuable customers and see that the service is recovered to their satisfaction.

Many loyalty programs also provide important status benefits to customers in the top tiers who feel part of an elite group (e.g., the Seven Stars card holders with Caesars in our opening vignette) and enjoy their special treatment. Tiered loyalty programs, in particular, can provide powerful incentives and motivation for customers to achieve the next higher level of membership, which often leads to higher share of wallet for the preferred provider.

Non-financial rewards, especially if linked to higher-tier service levels, are typically more powerful than financial ones as the former can create tremendous value for customers. Unlike financial rewards, non-financial rewards directly relate to the firm's core service and improve the customers' experience and value perception. In the hotel context, for example, redeeming loyalty points for free gifts does nothing to enhance the guest experience. However, getting priority for reservations, early check-in, late check-out, upgrades, and special attention make your stay more pleasant, leave you with the warm and fuzzy feeling that this firm appreciates your business, and make you want to come back.[28]

Service Insights 12.4 describes how British Airways has designed its Executive Club, effectively combining financial and non-financial loyalty rewards.

Small businesses often don't run formal loyalty programs but can still employ effective bonds. For example, they can use informal loyalty rewards. These may take the form of periodically giving regular customers a small treat as a way of thanking them, reserving their favorite table in a restaurant context, paying them special attention, and the like.

SERVICE INSIGHTS 12.4

Rewarding Value of Use, Not Just Frequency, at British Airways

Unlike some frequent flyer programs in which customer usage is measured simply in miles, British Airways' Executive Club members receive both *air miles* toward redemption of air travel rewards and *points* towards silver or gold tier status for travel on the airline. With the creation of the OneWorld alliance with American Airlines, Qantas, Cathay Pacific, and other airlines, Executive Club members have been able to earn miles (and sometimes points) by flying these partner airlines too.

As shown in Table 12.1, silver and gold card holders are entitled to special benefits, such as priority reservations and a superior level of on-the-ground

service. For instance, even if a gold-card holder is traveling in economy class, he or she will be entitled to first-class standards of treatment at check-in, in the airport lounges, and during boarding. Miles will not expire as long as the frequent flyer account has at least one transaction in every 36 months. However, tier status is valid only for 12 months beyond the membership year in which it was earned. This means that the right to special privileges must be re-earned each year. The objective of awarding tier status is to encourage passengers who have a choice of airlines to concentrate their travel on British Airways rather than join several frequent flyer programs and collect mileage awards from all of them. Few passengers travel often enough to be able to obtain the benefits of gold tier status (or its equivalent) on more than one airline.

The points given also vary according to the class of service. Longer trips earn more points than shorter ones. However, tickets at deeply discounted prices may earn fewer miles and no points at all. Passengers who purchase higher-priced tickets can earn points at up to 2.5 times the economy rate if they travel in club (business class) and up to triple the rate in first class.

Although the airline makes no promises about complimentary upgrades, members of British Airways' Executive Club are more likely to receive such invitations than other passengers. Tier status is an important consideration when employees decide who to upgrade on an overbooked flight. Unlike many airlines, British Airways tends to limit upgrades to situations in which a lower class of cabin is overbooked. They do not want frequent travelers to believe that they can plan on buying a less expensive ticket and then automatically receive an upgrade.

British Airways has even created a Household Account that allows up to six family members who live at the same address to pool their miles and make full use of the collective balance.

Table 12.1 Selected benefits offered by British Airways to its most valued passengers.

Benefit	Bronze Tier Members	Gold Tier Members
Reservations		Dedicated gold phone line
Reservation assurance		If flight is full, a guaranteed seat in economy when booking full fare ticket at least 24 hours in advance and checking in at least one hour in advance
Priority wait list and standby	Higher priority	Highest priority
Check-in desk	According to class of travel	First (regardless of travel class)
Lounge access	According to class of travel	First class departure lounge for passenger and one guest, regardless of travel class; use of arrivals lounges; lounge access any time; allowing use of lounges even when not flying BA intercontinental flights
Special services assistance		Dedicated direct line to customer support staff; problem solving beyond that accorded to other BA travelers
Bonus air miles	+25%	+100%
Upgrade for two		Free upgrade to next cabin for member and companion after earning 2,500 tier points in one year; another upgrade for two after 3,500 points in same year
Partner cards		Upon reaching 5,000 points, the member will receive two Executive Club Silver cards and one Gold Partner so that the benefits can be shared with loved ones.
Special privilege		Concorde Room access at Heathrow Terminal 5 and New York JFK Terminal 7 after earning 5,000 points
Lifetime membership		Upon earning 35,000 points, Gold membership status will be awarded for life.

Build Higher-Level Bonds

▶ **LO 10**

Appreciate the power of social, customization, and structural bonds in enhancing loyalty.

One objective of loyalty rewards is to motivate customers to combine their purchases with one provider or at least make it the preferred provider. However, rewards-based loyalty programs are quite easy for other suppliers to copy. As a result, they rarely provide the kind of sustained competitive advantage offered by higher-level bonds. We will now discuss the three main types of higher-level bonds, which are (1) social, (2) customization, and (3) structural bonds.

Social Bonds. Social bonds and the related personalization of services are usually based on personal relationships between providers and customers. Social bonds are more difficult to build than financial bonds and may take longer to achieve, but they are also harder for other suppliers to replicate for that same customer. A firm that has created social bonds with its customers has a better chance of retaining them for the long term because of the trust the customers place in the staff.[29] When social bonds include shared relationships (Figure 12.12) or experiences between customers, such as in country clubs or educational settings, they can be a major loyalty driver for the organization.[30]

Figure 12.12 A knowledgeable and charismatic lecturer helps build social bonds with students.

Customization Bonds. These bonds are built when the service provider succeeds in providing customized service to its loyal customers. For example, Starbucks's employees are encouraged to learn their regular customers' preferences and customize their service accordingly (Figure 12.13). Many large hotel chains capture the preferences of their customers through their loyalty program databases. Firms offering customized service are likely to have more loyalty customers. For example, when customers arrive at their hotel, they find that their individual needs have already been anticipated, from preferred room type (e.g., smoking vs. non-smoking) and bed type (e.g., twins or king size) to the kind of pillow they like and the newspaper they want to read in the morning. Amongst many other benefits, Fairmont Hotels & Resorts' loyalty program provides its members with jogging shoes and apparel of the right size. Guests also find yoga mats and stretch bands waiting in their rooms on their arrival.[31] When a customer becomes used to this special service level, he/she may find it difficult to adjust to another service provider who is not able to customize the service (at least immediately, as it takes time for the new provider to learn about someone's needs and preferences).[32]

Structural Bonds. Structural bonds are frequently seen in B2B settings. They are created by getting customers to align their way of doing things with the supplier's own processes, thus linking the customer to the firm. This makes it more difficult for competitors to draw the customers away. Examples include joint investments in projects and the sharing of information, processes, and equipment.

PART IV

Figure 12.13 Starbucks's employees are encouraged to learn their customers' preferences.

LO 11
Understand what factors cause customers to switch to a competitor and how to reduce such switching.

Structural bonds can be created in a B2C environment as well. For instance, some car rental companies offer travelers the opportunity to create a customized account on the firm's website and mobile app where they can retrieve details of past trips, including pick-up and return locations, the types of cars used, insurance coverage, billing address, credit card details, and so on. This simplifies the task of making new bookings.

Have you noticed that while all these bonds tie a customer closer to the firm, they also deliver the confidence, social, and special treatment benefits that customers desire (refer to Service Insights 12.1)? In general, bonds will not work well in the long term unless they generate value for the customer.

STRATEGIES FOR REDUCING CUSTOMER DEFECTIONS

So far, we have discussed drivers of loyalty and ways of tying customers more closely to the firm. A complementary approach is to understand the drivers of customer defections (also called customer churn) and work on eliminating or at least reducing those drivers.

Analyze Customer Defections and Monitor Declining Accounts

The first step is to understand the reasons for customer switching. Susan Keveaney conducted a large-scale study across a range of services and found several key reasons why customers switch to another provider (Figure 12.14).[33] These were:

▶ Core service failures (44% of respondents)

▶ Dissatisfactory service encounters (34%)

▶ High, deceptive, or unfair pricing (30%)

▶ Inconvenience in terms of time, location, or delays (21%)

▶ Poor response to service failure (17%)

Many respondents decided to switch after a series of related incidents, such as a service failure followed by an unsatisfactory service recovery. Other important factors that drive switching include overall dissatisfaction with the current service provider and the perception that it has an inferior performance on important attributes compared to the best alternative provider.[34]

Progressive service firms regularly conduct *churn diagnostics* to gain a better understanding of why customers defect. This includes the analysis of data from churned and declining customers, exit interviews (call-center staff often have a short set of questions they ask when a customer cancels an account), and in-depth interviews of former customers by a third-party research agency, which typically yield a more detailed understanding of churn drivers.[35]

Some firms even try to predict churn of individual accounts. For example, cell-phone service providers use *churn-alert systems,* which monitor the activity in individual

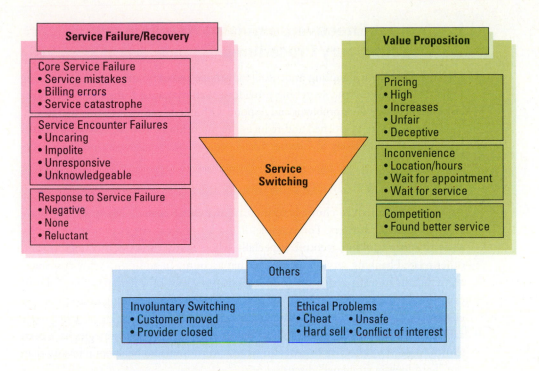

Figure 12.14 What drives customers to switch to a different service firm?

SOURCE

Journal of Marketing, American Marketing Association; American Marketing Society; National Association of Marketing Teachers, reproduced with permission of American Marketing Association.

customer accounts with the objective of predicting impending customer switching. Important accounts at risk are flagged and efforts are made to keep the customer, such as sending a voucher and/or having a customer service representative call the customer to check on the health of the customer relationship and initiate corrective action if needed.

Address Key Churn Drivers

Susan M. Keaveney's findings underscore the importance of addressing some general churn drivers by delivering quality service (see Chapter 14), minimizing inconvenience and other non-monetary costs, and having fair and transparent pricing (Chapter 6). In addition to these generic drivers, there are often industry-specific churn drivers as well. For example, handset replacement is a common reason for cell-phone service subscribers to discontinue an existing relationship, as new subscription plans usually come with heavily subsidized brand-new handsets. To prevent handset-related churn, many providers now offer proactive handset replacement programs, where their current subscribers are offered heavily discounted handsets at regular intervals. Some providers even provide handsets to high-value customers for free or against redemption of loyalty points.

In addition to such proactive retention measures, many firms also use reactive measures. These include the use of specially trained call-center staff (called *save teams*) to deal with customers who intend to cancel their accounts. The main job of save-team employees is to listen to customer needs and issues and try to address them with the key focus of retaining the customer.

Implement Effective Complaint Handling and Service Recovery Procedures

Effective complaint handling and excellent service recovery are crucial for keeping unhappy customers from switching providers. Well-managed firms make it easy for customers to voice their problems and respond with suitable service-recovery strategies. This keeps customers satisfied and reduces the intention to switch.[36] We will discuss how to do that effectively in Chapter 13.

Increase Switching Costs

Another way to reduce churn is to increase switching costs.[37] Many services have natural switching barriers. For example, it is a lot of work for customers to change their primary banking account, especially when many direct debits, credits, and other related banking services are tied to that account. In addition, many customers are reluctant to learn about the products and processes of a new provider.[38] Firms can increase these switching costs further by focusing on providing added value to customers through increased convenience, customization, and priority (collectively called "positive switching costs" or "soft lock-in strategies"). Such strategies have been shown to be more effective in generating both attitudinal and behavioral loyalty than the "hard lock-in strategies" discussed next.[39]

Hard lock-in strategies refer to switching costs that are created by having contractual penalties for switching, such as the transfer fees payable to some brokerage firms for moving shares and bonds to another financial institution. Cell-phone service providers often impose contractual penalties if a contract is cancelled during a lock-in period. However, firms need to be careful so that they are not seen as holding their customers hostage. A firm with high switching barriers and poor service quality is likely to generate negative attitudes and bad word of mouth. At some point, the last straw is reached, and the customer switches to a different service provider even if there are significant switching costs. Alternatively, he/she may switch at the first opportune moment when a contract expires.[40]

LO 12

Know why loyalty programs and customer relationship management (CRM) systems are important enablers of delivering loyalty strategies.

ENABLERS OF CUSTOMER LOYALTY STRATEGIES

As you can see, most strategies discussed in the Wheel of Loyalty require an in-depth understanding of one's customers. Enablers of customer loyalty strategies provide this understanding and include the creation of 'membership-type' relationships, such as through loyalty programs cum CRM systems, account managers, and front-line employees. Before discussing these enablers, let's focus on the fundamental difference between strategies intended to produce a single transaction (i.e., transaction marketing) and those designed to create extended relationships with customers (i.e., relationship marketing).

Customer Loyalty in a Transactional Marketing Context

A *transaction* is an event during which an exchange of value takes place between two parties. One transaction or even a series of transactions doesn't necessarily constitute a relationship, which requires mutual recognition and knowledge between the parties. When each transaction between a customer and a supplier is essentially discreet and anonymous, with no long-term record kept of a customer's purchasing history and little or no mutual recognition between the customer and employees, then no meaningful marketing relationship can be said to exist. This is true for many services (ranging from passenger transport and food service to visits to a movie theater) in which each purchase and use is a separate event.

Customer loyalty strategies in a transactional marketing context have to focus mostly on the foundational strategies of the Wheel of Loyalty, such as segmenting the market, matching customer needs with firm capabilities, and delivering high service quality.

Relationship Marketing

The term *relationship marketing* has been widely used to describe the type of marketing activity designed to create extended relationships with customers. Ideally, both the firm and the customer have an interest in deeper engagement and higher value-added exchange. A firm may have transactions with some customers who have neither the desire nor the need to make future purchases, but it must also work hard to move other customers up the loyalty ladder.[41]

Relationship marketing requires a membership-type relationship. The next section shows that some service industries naturally have a membership-type relationship, whereas others have to work hard to create them.

Creating 'Membership-type' Relationships as Enablers for Loyalty Strategies

The nature of the current relationship with customers can be analyzed by asking a few questions. First: Does the supplier enter into a formal "membership" relationship with customers, as with telephone subscriptions, banking, and the family doctor? Or is there no defined relationship? Second: Is the service delivered on a continuous basis, as in

Table 12.2 Relationships with Customers.

Benefit	Type of Relationship between the Service Organization and Its Customers	
Nature of Service Delivery	Membership Relationship	No Formal Relationship
Continuous delivery of service	Insurance	Radio station
	Cable TV subscription	Police protection
	College enrollment	lighthouse
	Banking	Public highway
Discrete transactions	Long-distance calls from subscriber phone	Car rental
	Theater series subscription	Mail service
	Travel on commuter ticket	Toll highway
	Repair under warranty	Pay phone
	Health treatment for HMO member	Movie theater
		Public transportation
		Restaurant

insurance, broadcasting, and police protection? Or is each transaction recorded and charged separately? Table 12.2 shows the matrix resulting from this categorization, with examples in each category. A *membership relationship* is a formalized relationship between the firm and an identifiable customer that often provides special benefits to both parties.

Discrete transactions, in which each use involves a payment to the service supplier by an essentially "anonymous" consumer, are typical of services such as transport, restaurants, cinemas, and shoe repairs. The problem for marketers of such services is that they tend to be less informed about who their customers are and what use each customer makes of the service than their counterparts in membership-type organizations. Managers in businesses that sell discrete transactions have to work a little harder to establish relationships.

In small businesses such as hair salons, frequent customers are (or should be) welcomed as "regulars" whose needs and preferences are remembered. Keeping formal records of customers' needs, preferences, and purchasing behavior is useful even for small firms. It helps employees avoid having to ask the same questions on each service occasion, allows them to personalize the service given to each customer, and also enables the firm to anticipate future needs.

In large companies with substantial customer bases, transactions can still be transformed into relationships by offering extra benefits to customers who choose to register with the firm. Having a loyalty program in place enables a firm to know who its current customers are and to capture their service transactions and preferences. This is valuable information because it allows the customization of service delivery and the segmentation and tiering of service.

Novices often equate loyalty points with loyalty programs. However, the most valuable aspects of loyalty programs for both the customer and the firm are often all the other benefits a firm's loyalty strategy brings with it. As discussed in the context of the Wheel of Loyalty, the benefits of the loyalty program that enhance the core service (from priority to customization) often have the highest value. You may ask: Why then don't firms do away with the points and focus on these other benefits? The answer has to do with consumer psychology. We all need a little incentive to sign up, install an app, provide information, and carry a loyalty card. For a firm to gain a system-wide view across outlets (often across countries), channels, services, etc., the only unique identifier that is reliable is typically a loyalty card (or card number) or a mobile app connected to a cell-phone number. All other unique identifiers such as name, passport numbers, and address have been shown to be problematic as names and addresses can be misspelled and passport numbers change. Therefore, it is often good to view the points (or air miles) of a loyalty program as a little incentive for customers to sign up and identify themselves at reservation, check-in, purchases, etc., through their loyalty-program membership number (card or mobile app). However, the real customer (and firm) benefits are delivered through the other bonds described in the Wheel of Loyalty.

Of course, the loyalty program and loyalty strategies have to be delivered, and that typically happens through CRM systems that capture, analyze, and deliver the relevant information to front-line employees and account managers (in B2B contexts or top-tier consumer segments). Front-line employees were discussed in Chapter 11, and the role of CRM systems in delivering loyalty strategies is discussed in the next section.

CUSTOMER RELATIONSHIP MANAGEMENT

LO 13

Understand the part played by CRM systems in delivering customized services and building loyalty.

Service marketers have understood for some time the power of customer relationship management, and certain industries have applied it for decades. Examples include the corner grocery store, the neighborhood car-repair shop, and providers of banking services to high-net-worth clients. However, if you mention CRM, costly and complex IT systems and infrastructure immediately come to mind. In reality, CRM signifies the whole process by which relations with the customers are built and maintained.[42] It should be seen as enabling the successful implementation of the Wheel of Loyalty. Let's first look at CRM systems before we move to a more strategic perspective.

Common Objectives of CRM Systems

Many firms have large numbers of customers (sometimes tens of millions) and many different touch points (e.g., tellers, call-center staff, self-service machines, apps, and websites) at multiple geographic locations. At a single large facility, it's unlikely that a customer will be served by the same front-line staff on two *consecutive* visits. Historically, managers lacked the tools to practice relationship marketing in such situations. Today, CRM systems allow customer information to be captured and delivered to the various touch points. Well-implemented CRM systems can offer a unified customer interface that delivers customization and personalization. They also allow the company to better understand, segment, and tier its customer base; better target promotions and cross-selling; and even implement churn alert systems that signal if a customer is in danger of defecting.[43] Service Insights 12.5 highlights some common CRM applications.

SERVICE INSIGHTS 12.5

Common CRM Applications

- **Data collection.** The system captures customer data such as contact details, demographics, purchasing history, service preferences, and the like.

- **Data analysis.** The data captured is analyzed and grouped by the system according to criteria set by the firm. This is used to tier the customer base and tailor service delivery accordingly.

- **Sales-force automation.** Sales leads and opportunities for cross-selling and up-selling can be effectively identified and processed. The entire sales cycle from lead generation to close of sales and after-sales service can also be tracked and facilitated through the CRM system.

- **Marketing automation.** Mining of customer data allows the firm to target its market. A good CRM system enables the firm to achieve one-to-one marketing and cost savings, often in the context of loyalty and retention programs. This increases the return on investment (ROI) on the firm's marketing expenditure. CRM systems also allow firms to assess the effectiveness of marketing campaigns through the analysis of responses.

- **Call-center automation.** Call-center staff members have customer information at their fingertips and can improve their service levels to all customers. Furthermore, caller ID and account numbers allow call centers to identify the customer tier the caller belongs to and tailor the service accordingly. For example, platinum callers get priority in waiting loops.

PART IV

What Does a Comprehensive CRM Strategy Include? [44]

Rather than viewing CRM as a technology, we subscribe to a more strategic view of CRM that focuses on the profitable development and management of customer relationships. Figure 12.15 provides an integrated framework of five key processes involved in a CRM strategy:

1. *Strategy development.* This involves the assessment of business strategy, including articulation of the company's vision, industry trends, and competition. The business strategy is typically the responsibility of top management. For CRM to have a positive impact on a firm's performance, the firm's strategy is crucial.[45] Therefore, business strategy should guide the development of customer strategy, including the choice of target segments, customer-base tiering, the design of loyalty bonds, and churn management (as discussed in the Wheel of Loyalty).

2. *Value creation.* This involves the translation of business and customer strategies into specific value propositions for customers and the firm. The value created for customers includes all the benefits that are delivered through priority tiered

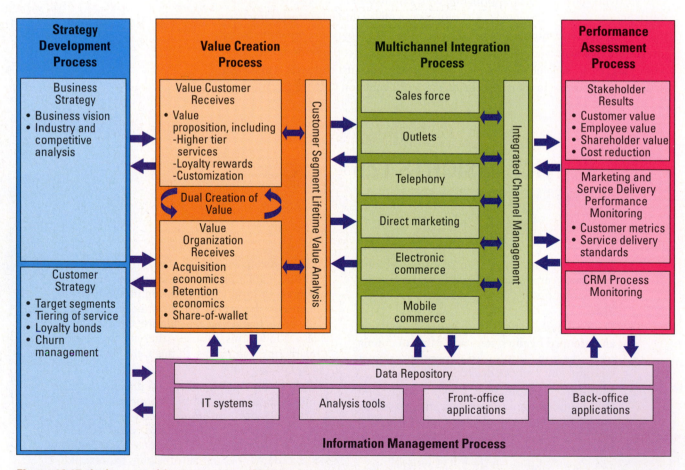

Figure 12.15 An integrated framework for a CRM strategy.

SOURCE

Journal of Marketing, American Marketing Association; American Marketing Society; National Association of Marketing Teachers, reproduced with permission of American Marketing Association.

services, loyalty rewards, and customization and personalization. The value created for the firm includes reduced customer acquisition and retention costs, increased share of wallet, and reduced customer serving costs. Customers need to participate in CRM (e.g., by volunteering information) to benefit from the firm's CRM strategy. For instance, if your driver's license, billing address, credit card details, and car and insurance preferences are stored in a car rental's CRM system, then you benefit from the increased convenience of not having to provide this data for each reservation. CRM is most successful when there is a win-win situation for the firm and its customers.[46]

3. *Multi-channel integration.* Most service firms interact with their customers through a multitude of channels. It has become a challenge for firms to serve customers well across many potential interfaces and offer a unified customer interface that delivers customization and personalization. CRM's channel integration addresses this challenge.

4. *Information management.* Service delivery across many channels depends on the firm's ability to collect customer information from all channels, integrate it with other relevant information, and make this information available to the front line (or to the customer in a self-service context) at the various touch points (Figure 12.16). The information-management process includes:

Figure 12.16 Airport self-check-in kiosks represent another service touch point that needs to be integrated into an airline's CRM system.

o The data repository, which contains all the customer data
o IT systems, including IT hardware and software
o Analytical tools such as data mining packages
o Specific application packages such as campaign management analysis, credit assessment, customer profiling, churn-alert systems, and even customer fraud detection and management
o Front-office applications, which support activities that involve direct customer contact, including sales-force automation and call-center management applications
o Back-office applications, which support internal customer-related processes, including logistics, procurement, and financial processing

5. *Performance assessment* must address three critical questions:

o Is the CRM strategy creating value for its key stakeholders (i.e., customers, employees, and shareholders)?
o Are the marketing objectives (ranging from customer acquisition and share of wallet to retention and customer satisfaction) and service delivery performance objectives (e.g., call-center service standards such as call waiting, abortion, and first-time resolution rates) being achieved?
o Is the CRM process itself performing up to expectations? (Are the relevant strategies being set? Is customer and firm value being created? Is the information management process working effectively? Is integration across customer service channels being achieved effectively?) The performance-assessment process should drive the continuous improvement of the CRM strategy itself.

Common Failures in CRM Implementation[47]

Unfortunately, the majority of CRM implementations have failed in the past. A key reason for this high failure rate is the misconception that the mere installation of CRM systems amounts to having a customer relationship strategy. Furthermore, CRM cuts across many departments and functions (e.g., from customer contact centers and online services to branch operations, employee training, and IT departments), programs (ranging from sales and loyalty programs to launching of new services and cross-selling initiatives), and processes (e.g., from credit line authorization all the way to complaint handling and service recovery). The wide-ranging scope of CRM implementation makes it challenging for firms to get it right. Another unfortunate reality is that it is often the weakest link that determines the success of a CRM implementation. Common reasons for CRM failures include:

▶ **Viewing CRM as a technology initiative.** It's easy to let the focus shift towards technology and its features, with the result that the IT department rather than top management or marketing takes the lead in devising the CRM strategy. This often results in a lack of strategic direction and an inadequate understanding of customers and markets during implementation.

▶ **Lack of customer focus.** Many firms implement CRM without the ultimate goal of enhancing the service value and enabling consistent service delivery for valued customers across all customer service processes and delivery channels.

▶ **Insufficient appreciation of customer life-time value (LTV).** The marketing of many firms is not sufficiently structured around the vastly different profitability of different customers.

▶ **Inadequate support from top management.** Without ownership and active involvement from top management, the CRM strategic intent will not survive the implementation intact.

▶ **Failing to re-engineer business processes.** It is nearly impossible to implement CRM successfully without redesigning customer service and back-office processes. Many implementations fail because CRM is fitted into existing processes. The focus should be on redesigning the processes to fit a customer-centric CRM implementation.

▶ **Underestimating the challenges in data integration.** Firms frequently fail to integrate customer data that are usually scattered all over the organization. A key to unlocking the full potential of CRM is to make customer knowledge available in real time to all employees who need it.

Finally, firms can put their CRM strategies at substantial risk if customers believe that CRM is used in a way that is harmful to them.[48] Examples include customers' feeling that they are not being treated fairly (e.g., if attractive pricing or promotions are offered to new accounts but not to existing customers) and potential privacy concerns.

How to Get CRM Implementation Right

Despite the many horror stories of millions of dollars being lost in unsuccessful CRM projects, more and more firms are getting it right. "No longer a black hole, CRM is becoming a basic building block of corporate success," argue Darrell Rigby and Dianne Ledingham.[49] Rather than transforming entire businesses through the wholesale implementation of the CRM model shown in Figure 12.15, service firms should focus on clearly defined problems within their customer relationship cycle. These narrow CRM strategies often reveal additional opportunities for further improvements which, when taken together, can evolve into broad CRM implementation extending across the entire company.[50] Likewise, Rigby, Reichheld, and Schefter recommend focusing on the customer strategy and not the technology. They pose the following question:

> If your best customers knew that you planned to invest $130 million to increase their loyalty…, how would they tell you to spend it? Would they want you to create a loyalty card or would they ask you to open more cash registers and keep enough milk in stock? The answer depends on the kind of company you are and the kinds of relationships you and your customers want to have with one another.[51]

Among the key issues managers should debate when defining their customer relationship strategy for a potential CRM system implementation are:

1) How should our value proposition be changed to increase customer loyalty?

2) How much customization or one-to-one marketing and service delivery is appropriate and profitable?

3) What is the incremental profit potential of increasing the share of wallet with our current customers? How much does this vary by customer tier and/or segment?

4) How much time and resources can we allocate to CRM right now?

5) If we believe in CRM, why haven't we taken more steps in that direction in the past? What can we do today to develop customer relationships without spending a lot on technology?[52]

Figure 12.17 CRM can help companies create two-way channels with customers.

Answering these questions may lead to the conclusion that a CRM system may currently not be the best investment or highest priority, or that a scaled-down version may suffice to deliver the intended customer strategy. In any case, we emphasize that the system is merely a tool to drive the strategy and must therefore be tailored to deliver that strategy.

CHAPTER SUMMARY

LO 1 ▶ Customer loyalty is an important driver of a service firm's profitability. The profits derived from loyal customers come from (1) increased purchases, (2) reduced operation costs, (3) referral of new customers, and (4) price premiums. In addition, customer acquisition costs can be amortized over a longer period of time.

LO 2 ▶ To understand the profit impact of the customers, firms need to learn how to calculate the life-time value (LTV) of their customers. LTV calculations need to include (1) acquisition costs, (2) revenue streams, (3) account-specific servicing costs, (4) expected number of years the customer will stay with the firm, and (5) discount rate for future cash flows.

LO 3 ▶ Customers are only loyal if they benefit in some way. Common benefits customers see in being loyal include:

o *Confidence benefits*, including the feeling that there is less risk of something going wrong and the ability to trust the provider

o *Social benefits*, including being known by name, being on friendly terms with the service provider, and enjoying certain social aspects of the relationship

o *Special treatment benefits*, including better prices, extra services, and higher priority

LO 4 ▶ It is not easy to build customer loyalty. The *Wheel of Loyalty* offers a systematic framework that guides firms on how to do so. The framework has three components that follow a sequence.

o First, firms need to build a *foundation for loyalty*, without which loyalty cannot be achieved. The foundation delivers confidence benefits to its loyal customers.

o Once the foundation has been laid, firms can create *loyalty bonds* to strengthen the relationship. Loyalty benefits include social and special treatment benefits.

o Finally, firms also have to work on reducing *customer churn*.

To build the foundation for loyalty, firms need to:

LO 5 ▶ Segment the market and *target the "right" customers*. A firm needs to choose its target segments carefully and match them to its own capabilities. It also needs to focus on customer value and fit rather than only on customer volume.

LO 6 ▶ Manage the customer base via *service tiering*, which divides the customer base into different value tiers (e.g., platinum, gold, iron, and lead). It helps the firm to tailor strategies to the different service tiers. The higher tiers offer higher value for

the firm but also expect higher service levels. For the lower tiers, the focus should be on increasing profitability by building volume, increasing prices, cutting service costs, and sometimes even ending unprofitable relationships.

LO 7 ▶ Understand that the foundation for loyalty lies in *customer satisfaction*. The satisfaction–loyalty relationship can be divided into three main zones: defection, indifference, and affection. Only highly satisfied or delighted customers who are in the zone of affection will be truly loyal. True loyalty covers both behavioral loyalty (share of wallet and referral behavior) and attitudinal loyalty (share of heart).

Loyalty bonds are used to build relationships with customers. There are three different types of customer bonds:

LO 8 ▶ The relationship bonds with customers can be deepened through cross-selling and bundling, which make switching more difficult and increase convenience through one-stop shopping.

LO 9 ▶ Reward-based loyalty programs aim at building share of wallet through *financial rewards* (e.g., loyalty points) and *non-financial rewards* (e.g., higher-tier service levels, priority service, recognition, and appreciation).

LO 10 ▶ Higher level bonds include *social, customization, and structural bonds*. Competing firms usually find these bonds more difficult to copy than reward-based bonds.

LO 11 ▶ The final step in the Wheel of Loyalty is to understand what causes customers to leave and then systematically reduce these *churn drivers*.

o Common causes for customers to switch include core service failures and dissatisfaction, deceptive and unfair pricing, inconvenience, poor response to service failures, and the overall perception that the provider has an inferior performance on key attributes compared to the best alternative provider.

o To prevent customers from switching, firms should (1) analyze and address the key reasons why their customers leave them, (2) have good complaint-handling and service-recovery processes in place, and (3) increase "positive" customer switching costs.

LO 12 ▶ Most strategies discussed in the Wheel of Loyalty require an in-depth understanding of customers to actively improve loyalty. For example, unless a firm knows the consumption behavior of individual customers, it cannot apply tiering of service, customization, personalization, and churn management. In such cases, "membership-type" relationships are needed. These can be created even for transaction-type services through loyalty programs cum CRM systems.

LO 13 ▶ Finally, CRM systems should be seen as enabling the successful implementation of the Wheel of Loyalty. CRM systems are particularly useful when firms have to serve large numbers of customers across many service delivery channels. An effective CRM strategy includes five key processes:

o *Strategy development*, including choice of target segments, tiering of service, and design of loyalty rewards

o *Value creation*, including delivering benefits to customers through tiered services and loyalty programs (e.g., priority wait listing and upgrades)

o *Multi-channel integration* to provide a unified customer interface across many different service delivery channels (e.g., from the website to the branch office)

o *Information management*, which includes the data repository, analytical tools (e.g., campaign management analysis and churn-alert systems), and front- and back-office applications.

o *Performance assessment*, which has to address three questions:

(1) Is the CRM creating value for the customers and the firm?

(2) Are its marketing objectives being achieved?

(3) Is the CRM system itself performing according to expectations?

o Performance assessment should lead to the continuous improvement of the CRM strategy and system.

UNLOCK YOUR LEARNING

These keywords are found within the sections of each Learning Objective (LO). They are integral to understanding the services marketing concepts taught in each section. Having a firm grasp of these keywords and how they are used is essential to helping you do well on your course, and in the real and very competitive marketing scene out there.

LO 1
1. Customer loyalty
2. Loyalty effect
3. Price premium
4. Profitability
5. Referrals
6. Amortization
7. Purchases
8. Share of wallet
9. Customer service costs
10. Price sensitivity
11. Zero defections
12. Acquisition costs

LO 2
1. Actual customer value
2. Customer life cycles
3. Customer life-time value
4. Potential customer value
5. Customer asset management

LO 3
1. Confidence benefits
2. Relational benefits
3. Social benefits
4. Special treatment benefits

LO 4
1. Build a foundation for loyalty
2. Create loyalty bonds
3. Reduce churn drivers
4. Wheel of Loyalty

LO 5
1. Relationship marketing
2. Search for value
3. Targeting
4. Customer acquisition

LO 6
1. Customer base
2. Customer pyramid
3. Customer retention
4. Gold
5. Iron
6. Lead
7. Migrate customers
8. Platinum
9. Tiering of service
10. Terminate customers

LO 7
1. Customer satisfaction
2. Satisfaction–loyalty relationship
3. Service quality
4. Zone of affection
5. Zone of defection
6. Zone of indifference
7. Share of heart
8. Attitudinal loyalty
9. Behavioral loyalty

LO 8
1. Deepen the relationship
2. Cross-selling
3. Bundling

LO 9
1. "Polygamous loyalty"
2. "Hard benefits"
3. Financial rewards
4. Non-financial rewards
5. Loyalty program
6. Timing
7. "Soft benefits"

LO 10
1. Customization bonds
2. Higher-level bonds
3. Social bonds
4. Structural bonds

LO 11
1. Churn diagnostics
2. Churn drivers
3. Churn management
4. Complaint handling
5. Customer churn
6. Customer defections
7. Declining accounts
8. Service recovery
9. Switching costs
10. Churn-alert systems

LO 12
1. Enablers of customer loyalty strategies
2. "Membership-type" relationships
3. Transaction marketing

LO 13
1. CRM applications
2. CRM implementation
3. CRM strategy
4. CRM systems
5. Customer life-time value
6. Customer relationship management
7. Data integration
8. Failures in CRM
9. Information management
10. Multi-channel integration
11. Performance assessment
12. Strategy development
13. Value creation

How well do you know the language of services marketing? Quiz yourself!

⚠ **Not for the academically faint-of-heart**

For each keyword you are able to recall without referring to earlier pages, give yourself a point (and a pat on the back). Tally your score at the end and see if you earned the right to be called—a *services marketeer*.

SCORE

01 – 12   Services Marketing is done a great disservice.
13 – 24   The midnight oil needs to be lit, pronto.
25 – 36   I know what you *didn't* do all semester.
37 – 48   By George! You're getting there.
49 – 60   Now, go forth and market.
61 – 73   There should be a marketing concept named after you.

PART IV

Review Questions

1. Why is customer loyalty an important driver of profitability for service firms?

2. Why is targeting the 'right customers' so important for successful customer relationship management?

3. How can you estimate a customer's life-time value (LTV)?

4. How do the various strategies described in the Wheel of Loyalty relate to one another?

5. How can a firm build a foundation for loyalty?

6. What is tiering of services? Explain why it is used. What are its implications for firms and their customers?

7. Identify some key measures that can be used to create customer bonds and encourage long-term relationships with customers.

8. Why are benefits related to the core service (e.g., customization, transaction convenience, and service priority) generally more effective in building loyalty than rewards that are unrelated to the core service (e.g., air miles)?

9. What is the role of churn management in an effective loyalty strategy, and what tools can be used to understand and reduce customer churn?

10. Why are loyalty programs often important for a customer loyalty strategy?

11. What is the role of CRM in delivering a customer relationship strategy?

WORK YOUR SERVICES MARKETING

Application Exercises

1. Identify three service businesses that you buy from on a regular basis. For each business, complete the following sentence: "I am loyal to this business because . . ."

2. What conclusions do you draw about (a) yourself as a consumer, and (b) the performance of each of the businesses in Exercise 1? Assess whether any of these businesses managed to develop a sustainable competitive advantage through the way it won your loyalty.

3. Identify two service businesses that you used several times in the past but no longer buy from (or that you plan to stop patronizing soon). Complete the sentence: "I stopped using (or will soon stop using) this organization as a customer because . . ."

4. What conclusions do you draw about yourself and the firms in Exercise 3? How could each of these firms avoid your defection? What could each of these firms do in the future to avoid the defection of customers with a profile similar to yours?

5. Evaluate the strengths and weaknesses of two loyalty programs, each one from a different service industry. Assess how each program could be improved further.

6. Design a questionnaire and conduct a survey about two loyalty programs. The first should be about a membership/loyalty program that keeps your classmates or their families loyal to a particular firm. The second should be about a loyalty program that is not well perceived and does not seem to add value for the customer. Use open-ended questions, such as "What motivated you to sign up in the first place?", "Why are you using this program?", "Has participating in the program changed your purchasing/usage behavior in any way?", "Has it made you less likely to use competing suppliers?", "What do you think of the rewards available?", "Did membership in the program lead to any immediate benefits in the use of the service?", "What are the three things you like best about this loyalty program?", "What did you like least?", and "What are some suggested improvements?" Analyze which features make loyalty/membership programs successful, and which features do not achieve the desired results. Use the Wheel-of-Loyalty framework to guide your analysis and presentation.

7. Approach service employees in two or three firms with implemented CRM systems. Ask the employees about their experience in interfacing with these systems and whether or not the CRM systems (a) help them understand their customers better, and (b) lead to improved service experiences for their customers. Ask them about potential concerns and improvement suggestions they may have about their organizations' CRM systems.

ENDNOTES

1. James L. Heskett, W. Earl Sasser Jr., and Joe Wheeler, *The Ownership Quotient* (Boston: Harvard Business Press, 2008): 9–13; www.totalrewards.com, accessed June 30, 2015. Note that Caesars placed Caesars Entertainment Operating Co. into a pre-packaged Chapter 11 bankruptcy in January 2015, which was largely caused by the company's high level of debt due to its privatization and follow-on acquisitions. Have a look at how the court ruling panned out for Caesars.

2. Frederick F. Reichheld and Thomas Teal, *The Loyalty Effect* (Boston: Harvard Business School Press, 1996).

3. The first four factors were proposed by Frederick F. Reichheld and W. Earl Sasser Jr., "Zero Defections: Quality Comes to Services," *Harvard Business Review* (October 1990): 105–111. The fifth factor was added by the authors of this book.

4. Share of wallet (SOW) refers to the percentage of a customer's total spending on a product category that is captured by a business. For example, if a customer spends a total of $6,000 per annum on air travel, of which $2,400 goes to airline A, then airline A's share of wallet is 40%.

5. Christian Homburg, Nicole Koschate, and Wayne D. Hoyer, "Do Satisfied Customers Really Pay More? A Study of the Relationship between Customer Satisfaction and Willingness to Pay," *Journal of Marketing* 69 (April 2005): 84–96.

6. Reichheld and Sasser, "Zero Defections," 105–111.

7. For a discussion on how to evaluate the customer base of a firm, see: Sunil Gupta, Donald R. Lehmann, and Jennifer Ames Stuart, "Valuing Customers," *Journal of Marketing Research* 41, no.1 (2004): 7–18.

8. From Alan W.H. Grant and Leonard A. Schlesinger, "Realize Your Customers' Full Profit Potential," © 1995 Harvard Business School.

9. Ruth Bolton, Katherine N. Lemon, and Peter C. Verhoef, "The Theoretical Underpinnings of Customer Asset Management: A Framework and Propositions for Future Research," *Journal of the Academy of Marketing Science* 32, no. 3 (2004): 271–292.

10. Yuping Liu, "The Long-Term Impact of Loyalty Programs on Consumer Purchase Behavior and Loyalty," *Journal of Marketing* 71, no. 4 (October 2007): 19–35.

11. Mark R. Vondrasek, "Redefining Service Innovation at Starwood," *McKinsey Quarterly* (February 2015).

12. From Roger Hallowell, "The Relationships of Customer Satisfaction, Customer Loyalty, and Profitability: An Empirical Study," *International Journal of Service Industry Management,* 7(4) pp. 27–42, © 1996 MCB University Press.

13. David Rosenblum, Doug Tomlinson, and Larry Scott, "Bottom-Feeding for Blockbuster Business," *Harvard Business Review* (March 2003): 52–59.

14. Christian Homburg, Mathias Droll, and Dirk Totzek, "Customer Prioritization: Does It Pay Off, and How Should It Be Implemented?" *Journal of Marketing* 72, no. 5 (2008): 110–130.

15. Valarie A. Zeithaml, Roland T. Rust, and Katharine N. Lemon, "The Customer Pyramid: Creating and Serving Profitable Customers," *California Management Review* 43, no. 4 (Summer 2001):118–142.

16. Vikras Mittal, Matthew Sarkees, and Feisal Murshed, "The Right Way to Manage Unprofitable Customers," *Harvard Business Review* (April 2008): 95–102.

17. Elizabeth Esfahani, "How to Get Tough with Bad Customers," *ING Direct* (October 2004), https://home.ingdirect.com/index.html, accessed August 5, 2011. Capital One Financial Corporation purchased ING Direct in 2012 and rebranded it as Capital One 360 in 2013. The positioning of the firm remained unchanged and focuses on saving customers time and money by offering simple products at low costs; see https://home.capitalone360.com, accessed June 30, 2015.

18. Not only is there a positive relationship between satisfaction and share of wallet, but

the greatest positive impact is seen at the upper extreme levels of satisfaction. For details, refer to: Timothy L. Keiningham, Tiffany Perkins-Munn, and Heather Evans, "The Impact of Customer Satisfaction on Share-of-Wallet in a Business-to-Business Environment," *Journal of Service Research* 6, no. 1 (2003): 37–50.

19. Florian V. Wangenheim, "Postswitching Negative Word of Mouth," *Journal of Service Research* 8, no. 1 (2005): 67–78.

20. For a review of the satisfaction–loyalty link, see: V. Kumar, Ilaria Dalla Pozza, and Jaishankar Ganesh, "Revisiting the Satisfaction–Loyalty Relationship: Empirical Generalizations and Directions for Further Research," *Journal of Retailing* 89, no. 3 (2013): 246–262.

21. Absolute satisfaction scores are less important in determining loyalty behaviors than being seen as the best or preferred provider. See: Timothy L. Keiningham, Lerzan Aksoy, Alexander Buoye, and Bruce Cooil, "Customer Loyalty Isn't Enough. Grow Your Share-of-Wallet," *Harvard Business Review* 89, no. 10 (2011): 29–31; Timothy L. Keiningham, Lerzan Aksoy, Luke Williams, and Alexander Buoye, *The Wallet Allocation Rule: Winning the Battle for Share* (Hoboken, New Jersey: John Wiley & Sons, 2015).

22. Leonard L. Berry and A. Parasuraman, "Three Levels of Relationship Marketing," in *Marketing Services: Competing through Quality* (New York: The Free Press, 1991), 136–142; Valarie A. Zeithaml, Mary Jo Bitner, and Dwayne D. Gremler, Chapter 7, *Services Marketing*, 6th ed. (New York: McGraw-Hill, 2012).

23. Heiner Evanschitzky, B. Ramaseshan, David M. Woisetschlager, Verena Richelsen, Markus Blut, and Christof Backhaus, "Consequences of Customer Loyalty to the Loyalty Program and to the Company," *Journal of the Academy of Marketing Science* 40, no. 5 (2012): 625–638; Michael Lewis, "The Influence of Loyalty Programs and Short-Term Promotions on Customer Retention," *Journal of Marketing Research* 41 (August 2004): 281–292; Jochen Wirtz, Anna S. Mattila, and May Oo Lwin, "How Effective Are Loyalty Reward Programs in Driving Share-of-Wallet?" *Journal of Service Research* 9, no. 4 (2007): 327–334.

24. Grahame Dowling and Mark Uncles, "Do Customer Loyalty Programs Really Work?" *Sloan Management Review* 38, no. 4 (1997): 71–82.

25. See for example: Iselin Skogland and Judy Siguaw, "Are Your Satisfied Customers Loyal?" *Cornell Hotel and Restaurant Administration Quarterly* 45, no. 3 (2004): 221–234.

26. Matthew Dixon, Karen Freeman, and Nicholas Toman, "Stop Trying to Delight Your Customers," *Harvard Business Review* (July–August 2010): 116–122.

27. Bernd Stauss, Maxie Schmidt, and Adreas Schoeler, "Customer Frustration in Loyalty Programs," *International Journal of Service Industry Management* 16, no. 3 (2005): 229–252.

28. Concrete benefits related to the core service (e.g., priority early check-in and priority wait listing) are more effective in driving customer gratitude and sales growth than status elevation without concrete benefits (i.e., the status is mostly symbolic). The latter can have a negative effect on profitability as it is more likely to increase customer entitlement perceptions, which in turn result in higher service costs. See: Hauke A. Wetzel, Maik Hammerschmidt, and Alex R. Zablah, "Gratitude versus Entitlement: A Dual Process Model of the Profitability Implications of Customer Prioritization," *Journal of Marketing* 78, no. 2 (2014): 1–19.

29. Paolo Guenzi, Michael D. Johnson, and Sandro Castaldo, "A Comprehensive Model of Customer Trust in Two Retail Stores," *Journal of Service Management* 20, no. 3 (2009): 290–316; Dwayne Ball, Pedro S. Coelho, and Manuel J. Vilares, "Service Personalization and Loyalty," *Journal of Services Marketing* 20, no. 6 (2006): 391–403.

30. Mark S. Rosenbaum, Amy L. Ostrom, and Ronald Kuntze, "Loyalty Programs and a Sense of Community," *Journal of Services Marketing* 19, no. 4 (2005): 222–233.

31. https://www.fairmont.com/fpc/benefits, accessed July 20, 2015.

32. Rick Ferguson and Kelly Hlavinka, "The Long Tail of Loyalty: How Personalized Dialogue and Customized Rewards Will Change Marketing Forever," *Journal of Consumer Marketing* 23, no. 6 (2006): 357–361.

33. Susan M. Keaveney, "Customer Switching Behavior in Service Industries: An Exploratory Study," *Journal of Marketing* 59 (April 1995): 71–82.

34. Jochen Wirtz, Ping Xiao, Jeongwen Chiang, and Naresh Malhotra, "Contrasting Switching Intent and Switching Behavior in Contractual Service Settings," *Journal of Retailing* 90, no. 4 (2014): 463–480.

35. For a more detailed discussion of situation-specific switching behavior, refer to: Inger Roos, Bo Edvardsson, and Anders Gustafsson, "Customer Switching Patterns in Competitive and Noncompetitive Service Industries," *Journal of Service Research* 6, no. 3 (2004): 256–271.

36. Gianfranco Walsh, Keith Dinnie, and Klaus-Peter Wiedmann, "How Do Corporate Reputation and Customer Satisfaction Impact Customer Defection? A Study of Private Energy Customers in Germany," *Journal of Services Marketing* 20, no. 6 (2006): 412–420.

37. Jonathan Lee, Janghyuk Lee, and Lawrence Feick, "The Impact of Switching Costs on the Consumer Satisfaction–Loyalty Link: Mobile Phone Service in France," *Journal of Services Marketing* 15, no. 1 (2001): 35–48; Shun Yin Lam, Venkatesh Shankar, M. Krishna Erramilli, and Bvsan Murthy, "Customer Value, Satisfaction, Loyalty, and Switching Costs: An Illustration from a Business-to-Business Service Context," *Journal of the Academy of Marketing Science* 32, no. 3 (2004): 293–311; Michael A. Jones, Kristy E. Reynolds, David L. Mothersbaugh, and Sharon Beatty, "The Positive and Negative Effects of Switching Costs on Relational Outcomes," *Journal of Service Research* 9, no. 4 (2007): 335–355.

38. Simon J. Bell, Seigyoung Auh, and Karen Smalley, "Customer Relationship Dynamics: Service Quality and Customer Loyalty in the Context of Varying Levels of Customer Expertise and Switching Costs," *Journal of the Academy of Marketing Science* 33, no. 2 (2005):

169–183; Markus Blut, Sharon E. Beatty, Heiner Evanschitzky, and Christian Brock, "The Impact of Service Characteristics on the Switching Cost–Customer Loyalty Link," *Journal of Retailing* 90, no. 2 (2014): 275–290.

39. Arvind Malhotra and Claudia Kubowicz Malhotra, "Exploring Mobile Switching Behavior of U.S. Mobile Service Customers," *Journal of Services Marketing* 27, no. 1 (2013): 13–24; Liane Nagengast, Heiner Evanschitzky, Markus Blut, and Thomas Rudolph, "New Insights in the Moderating Effect of Switching Costs on the Satisfaction–Repurchase Behavior Link," *Journal of Retailing* 90, no. 3 (2014): 408–427.

40. Lesley White and Venkat Yanamandram, "Why Customers Stay: Reasons and Consequences of Inertia in Financial Services," *International Journal of Service Industry Management* 14, no. 3 (2004): 183–194.

41. Johnson and Selnes proposed a typology of exchange relationships that included "strangers," "acquaintances," "friends," and "partners" and derived implications for customer portfolio management. For details see: Michael D. Johnson and Fred Selnes, "Customer Portfolio Management: Towards a Dynamic Theory of Exchange Relationships," *Journal of Marketing* 68, no. 2 (2002): 1–17.

42. For an overview on CRM, see: V. Kumar and Werner J. Reinartz, *Customer Relationship Management: A Database Approach* (Hoboken, New Jersey: John Wiley & Sons, 2006); B. Ramaseshan, David Bejou, Subhash C. Jain, Charlotte Mason, and Joseph Pancras, "Issues and Perspective in Global Customer Relationship Management," *Journal of Service Research* 9, no. 2 (2006): 195–207; V. Kumar, Sarang Sunder, and B. Ramaseshan, "Analyzing the Diffusion of Global Customer Relationship Management: A Cross-Regional Modeling Framework," *Journal of International Marketing* 19, no. 1 (2011): 23–39.

43. Kevin N. Quiring and Nancy K. Mullen, "More Than Data Warehousing: An Integrated View of the Customer," in John G. Freeland (ed.), *The Ultimate CRM Handbook: Strategies & Concepts for Building Enduring Customer Loyalty & Profitability* (New York: McGraw-Hill, 2002): 102–108.

44. This section is adapted from: Adrian Payne and Pennie Frow, "A Strategic Framework for Customer Relationship Management," *Journal of Marketing* 69 (October 2005): 167–176.

45. Martin Reimann, Oliver Schilke, and Jacquelyn S. Thomas, "Customer Relationship Management and Firm Performance: The Mediating Role of Business Strategy," *Journal of the Academy of Marketing Science* 38, no. 3 (2010): 326–346. The authors found that the effect of CRM is fully mediated by the two basic strategic postures of firms: differentiation versus cost leadership. Furthermore, their study found that the effects of CRM on differentiation are stronger in highly commoditized industries than in highly differentiated industries.

46. William Boulding, Richard Staelin, Michael Ehret, and Wesley J. Johnston, "A Customer Relationship Management Roadmap: What is Known, Potential Pitfalls, and Where to Go," *Journal of Marketing* 69, no. 4 (2005): 155–166.

47. This section is based on: Sudhir H. Kale, "CRM Failure and the Seven Deadly Sins," *Marketing Management* (September–October 2004): 42–46.

48. Boulding, Staelin, Ehret, and Johnston, "A Customer Relationship Management Roadmap," 155–166.

49. Darrell K. Rigby and Dianne Ledingham, "CRM Done Right," *Harvard Business Review* (November 2004): 118–129.

50. Rigby and Ledingham, "CRM Done Right," 118–129.

51. From Darrell Rigby, Fred Reichheld, and Phil Schefter, "Avoid the Four Perils of CRM," © 2002 Harvard Business Review.

52. Rigby, Reichheld, and Schefter, "Avoid the Four Perils of CRM," 108.

13

complaint handling and
SERVICE
RECOVERY

LEARNING OBJECTIVES (LOs)

By the end of this chapter, the reader should be able to:

LO 1 Recognize the actions that customers may take in response to service failures.

LO 2 Understand why customers complain.

LO 3 Know what customers expect from the firm when they complain.

LO 4 Understand how customers respond to effective service recovery.

LO 5 Explain the service recovery paradox.

LO 6 Know the principles of effective service recovery systems.

LO 7 Be familiar with the guidelines for front-line employees on how to handle complaining customers and recover from a service failure.

LO 8 Recognize the power of service guarantees.

LO 9 Understand how to design effective service guarantees.

LO 10 Know when firms should not offer service guarantees.

LO 11 Be familiar with the seven groups of jaycustomers and understand how to manage them effectively.

Figure 13.1 JetBlue's reputation for customer service excellence was temporarily grounded.

Too Little, Too Late—JetBlue's Service Recovery[1]

A terrible ice storm in the East Coast of the United States caused hundreds of passengers to be trapped for 11 hours inside JetBlue planes at the John F. Kennedy International Airport in New York. These passengers were furious because JetBlue personnel did nothing to get them off the planes. In addition, JetBlue cancelled more than 1,000 flights over six days, leaving even more passengers stranded. This incident cancelled out much that JetBlue had done right to become one of the strongest customer service brands in the United States. The company was going to be ranked number four by *Business Week* in a list of top 25 customer service leaders but was pulled from the rankings due to this service failure. What happened?

There was no service recovery plan. No one—not the pilot, the flight attendants, or the station manager—had the authority to get the passengers off the plane. JetBlue's offer of refunds and travel vouchers did not seem to reduce the anger of the passengers who had been stranded for so many hours. David Neeleman, JetBlue's CEO at the time, sent a personal e-mail to all customers in the company's database to explain what caused the problem, apologize profusely, and detail its service recovery efforts. He even appeared on late-night television to apologize, and he admitted that the airline should have had better contingency planning. However, the airline still had a long way to go to repair the damage done.

Gradually, JetBlue rebuilt its reputation, starting with its new Customer Bill of Rights. The bill required the airline

Figure 13.2 JetBlue's new Customer Bill of Rights and publicity campaigns involving the Simpsons were measures taken to win customers back.

to provide vouchers or refunds in certain situations when flights were delayed. Neeleman also changed JetBlue's information systems to keep track of the locations of its crew and trained staff at the headquarters to help out at the airport when needed. All these activities were aimed at helping the company climb its way back up to the heights it fell from. By 2014, JetBlue Airways was back on the list of J. D. Power Customer Service Champions for many consecutive years. (J. D. Power and Associates conducts customer satisfaction research based on survey responses from millions of customers worldwide.) This showed that JetBlue's customers had finally forgiven its service failure and were supporting its efforts to deliver continued service excellence.

Customer Responses to Service Failure

- Take public action (complain to the firm, to a third party, take legal action)
- Take private action (switch provider, spread negative word-of-mouth)
- Take no action

Customer Expectations Once a Complaint Is Made

Customers expect fair treatment along three dimensions:
- Procedural justice: Customers expect a convenient, responsive, and flexible service recovery process
- Interactional justice: The recovery effort must be seen as genuine, honest, and polite
- Outcome justice: The restitution has to reflect the customer loss and inconveniences suffered

Customer Complaining

Why do customers complain?
- Obtain restitution or compensation
- Vent anger
- Help to improve the service
- For altruistic reasons

What proportion of unhappy customers complains?
- 5%–10% complain

Why don't unhappy customers complain?
- It takes time and effort
- The payoff is uncertain
- Complaining can be unpleasant

Who is most likely to complain?
- Higher socio-economic class customers
- Customers with more product knowledge

Where do customers complain?
- The vast majority of complaints are made at the point-of-service provision (face to face or over the phone)
- Only a small proportion of complaints is sent via email, social media, websites, or letters

Customer Responses to an Effective Service Recovery

- Avoids switching, restores confidence in the firm
- The Service Recovery Paradox: An excellent recovery can even result in higher satisfaction and loyalty than if a service was delivered as promised

Principles of Effective Service Recovery Systems

- Make it easy for customers to provide feedback and reduce customer complaint barriers
- Enable effective service recovery: Make it (1) proactive, (2) planned, (3) trained, and (4) empowered
- Establish appropriate compensation levels: Set based on the (1) positioning of the firm, (2) severity of the service failure, and the (3) importance of the customer. Target for "well-dosed generosity."

Dealing with Complaining Customers:
- Act fast
- Acknowledge customer's feelings
- Don't argue
- Show understanding
- Clarify the facts
- Give customer the benefit of the doubt
- Propose steps to solve the problem
- Consider compensation
- Persevere to regain customer goodwill
- Improve the service system
- Keep the customer informed

Service Guarantees

- Institutionalize professional complaint handling and service recovery
- Drive improvement of processes
- Design: (1) unconditional, (2) easy to understand, (3) meaningful, (4) easy to invoke, (5) easy to collect on, and (6) credible
- Unsuitable for firms with (1) a reputation for excellence, (2) poor quality service, and (3) uncontrollable quality due to external factors (e.g., weather)

Jaycustomers

There are 7 types of jaycustomers:
- The Cheat
- The Thief
- The Rule Breaker
- The Belligerent
- The Family Feuders
- The Vandal
- The Deadbeat

- Jaycustomers cause problems for firms and can spoil the service experience of other customers.
- Firms need to keep track and manage their behavior, including, as a last resort, blacklisting them from using the firm's facilities.

Figure 13.3 Organizing framework for managing complaints and service recovery.

CUSTOMER COMPLAINING BEHAVIOR

The first law of service quality and productivity might be: Do it right the first time. However, we can't ignore the fact that failures continue to occur, sometimes for reasons outside the organization's control (such as the ice storm that caused the JetBlue incident in our opening vignette). Many "moments of truth" in service encounters are vulnerable to breakdowns. Such distinctive service characteristics as real-time performance, customer involvement, and people as part of the product greatly increase the probability of service failures. A firm's ability to handle complaints and resolve problems frequently determines whether it builds customer loyalty or watches its customers take their business elsewhere. An overview of this chapter is provided in Figure 13.3.

Customer Response Options to Service Failure

It is likely that you're not always satisfied with some of the services you receive. How do you respond to your dissatisfaction with these services? Do you complain informally to an employee, ask to speak to the manager, or file a formal complaint? Or do you just mutter darkly to yourself, grumble to your friends and family, and choose an alternative supplier the next time you need a similar type of service?

If you choose not to complain to the firm about poor service, you are not alone. Research around the globe has shown that most people decide not to complain, especially if they think it will do no good. Figure 13.4 suggests at least three major courses of action a customer may take in response to a service failure:

1) Take some form of public action (e.g., complaining to the firm or to a third party, such as a customer advocacy group, a consumer affairs or regulatory agency, or even civil or criminal court).

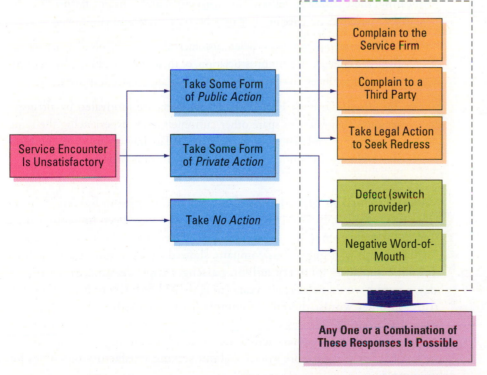

Figure 13.4 Customer response categories to service failures.

LO 1

Recognize the actions that customers may take in response to service failures.

2) Take some form of private action (e.g., abandoning the supplier).

3) Take no action (Figure 13.5).

It's important to remember that a customer can take any one action or a combination of actions. Managers need to be aware that the impact of a defection can go far beyond the loss of that customer's future revenue stream. Angry customers often tell many other people about their problems.[2] The internet allows unhappy customers to reach thousands of people by posting complaints on bulletin boards and blogs and even setting up their own websites to talk about their bad experiences with specific organizations.

LO 2

Understand why customers complain.

Understanding Customer Complaining Behavior

To be able to deal effectively with dissatisfied and complaining customers, managers need to understand key aspects of complaining behavior, starting with the questions posed below.

Why Do Customers Complain? In general, studies of consumer complaining behavior have identified four main purposes for complaining:

1) *To obtain restitution or compensation.* Consumers often complain to recover some economic loss by seeking a refund or compensation and/or to have the service performed again.[3]

2) *To vent their anger.* Some customers complain to rebuild self-esteem and/or to release their anger and frustration. When service processes are bureaucratic and unreasonable or when employees are rude, deliberately intimidating, or apparently uncaring, the customers' self-esteem, self-worth, and sense of fairness can be negatively affected. As a result, they may become angry and emotional.

3) *To help to improve the service.* When customers are highly involved with a service (e.g., at a college, an alumni association, or their main banking connection), they give feedback to try and contribute toward service improvements.

4) *For altruistic reasons.* Finally, some customers are motivated by altruistic reasons. They want to spare other customers from experiencing the same shortcomings, and they may feel bad if they fail to draw attention to a problem that will raise difficulties for others if it remains uncorrected.

What Proportion of Unhappy Customers Complain? Research shows that on average, only 5%–10% of customers who have been unhappy with a service actually complain.[4] Sometimes the percentage is far lower. A review of the records of a public bus company showed that there were about three formal complaints for every million passenger trips. Assuming two trips a day, a person would need 1,370 years (roughly 27 lifetimes) to make a million trips. In other words, the rate of complaints was incredibly low, especially since public bus companies are rarely known for service excellence. However, there's evidence that consumers across the world are becoming better informed, more self-confident, and more assertive about seeking satisfactory outcomes for their complaints.

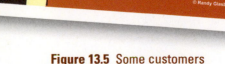

Figure 13.5 Some customers may be frustrated but do not take any action to complain, as seen here in an interaction with an online service.

Why Don't Unhappy Customers Complain? A number of studies have identified some of the reasons why customers don't complain. Customers may not want to take the time to write a letter, send an e-mail, fill in a form, or make a phone call, particularly if they don't see the service as being important enough to be worth the effort. Many customers see the pay-off as uncertain and believe that no one would be concerned about their problem or willing to deal with it. In some situations, people simply don't know where to go or what to do. Moreover, many people feel that complaining is unpleasant and fear confrontation, especially if the complaint involves someone they know and may have to deal with again (Figure 13.6).[5]

Figure 13.6 Customers often view complaining as difficult and unpleasant.

Who Is Most Likely to Complain? Research findings consistently show that people in higher socio-economic levels are more likely to complain than those in lower levels. Their better education, higher income, and greater social involvement give them the confidence, knowledge, and motivation to speak up when they encounter problems.[6] Furthermore, those who complain also tend to be more knowledgeable about the product in question.

Where Do Customers Complain? Studies show that the majority of complaints are made at the place where the service was received. One of the authors of this book completed a consulting project for developing and implementing a customer feedback system. He found that an amazing 99% of customer feedback was given face to face or over the phone to customer service representatives. Less than 1% of all complaints were submitted via the firm's website, social media pages, e-mail, letters, or feedback cards. A survey of airline passengers found that only 3% of respondents who were unhappy with their meal actually complained about it, and they all complained to the flight attendant. No one complained to the company's headquarters or to a consumer affairs office.[7] Moreover, although customers tend to use interactive channels such as face-to-face encounters or the telephone when they want a problem to be fixed, they use non-interactive channels to complain (e.g., e-mail or websites) when they mainly want to vent their anger and frustration.[8]

In practice, managers often don't hear about the complaints made to front-line employees. Without a formal customer feedback system, only a tiny proportion of the complaints may reach corporate headquarters.[9] If unhappy customers have already used other channels of complaint but their problem has not been solved, they are more likely to turn to online public complaining. This is due to "double deviation." The service performance already caused dissatisfaction in the first instance, and the firm's attempt to resolve the problem also failed.[10]

What Do Customers Expect Once They Have Made a Complaint?

LO 3
Know what customers expect from the firm when they complain.

Whenever a service failure occurs, people expect to be treated fairly. However, research has shown that many customers feel that they have neither been treated fairly nor given adequate compensation. When this happens, their reactions tend to be immediate, emotional, and enduring. In contrast, outcomes that are perceived as fair have a positive impact on customer satisfaction.[11]

PART IV

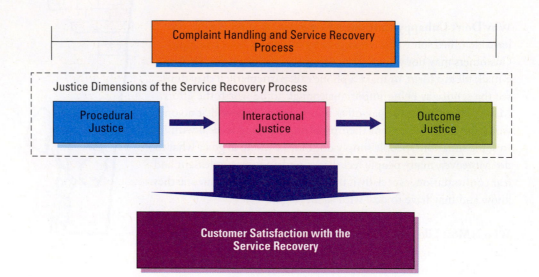

Figure 13.7 Three dimensions of perceived fairness in service recovery processes.

Stephen Tax and Stephen Brown found that as much as 85% of the variation in satisfaction with a service recovery was determined by three dimensions of fairness (see Figure 13.7):[12]

▶ *Procedural justice* refers to the policies and rules that any customer has to go through to seek fairness. Customers expect the firm to take responsibility, which is the key to the start of a fair procedure. This should be followed by a convenient and responsive recovery process that takes into account the flexibility of the system and the customer inputs into the recovery process.

▶ *Interactional justice* involves the employees of the firm who provide the service recovery and their behavior toward the customer. It is important to give an explanation for the failure and to make an effort to resolve the problem. Furthermore, the recovery effort must be seen as genuine, honest, and polite.

▶ *Outcome justice* concerns the restitution or compensation that a customer receives as a result of the losses and inconveniences caused by the service failure. This includes compensation not only for the failure but also for the time, effort, and energy spent during the process of service recovery.

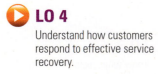

LO 4

Understand how customers respond to effective service recovery.

CUSTOMER RESPONSES TO EFFECTIVE SERVICE RECOVERY

"Thank Heavens for Complainers" was the provocative title of an article about customer complaining behavior. The article featured a successful manager exclaiming, "Thank goodness I've got a dissatisfied customer on the phone! The ones I worry about are the ones I never hear from."[13] Customers who do complain give the firm a chance to correct problems (including some the firm may not even know it has), restore relationships with the complainer, and improve future satisfaction for all customers.

Service recovery is a term used to describe the systematic efforts made by a firm to correct a problem following a service failure and retain a customer's goodwill. Service recovery efforts play an important role in achieving (or restoring) customer satisfaction and loyalty.[14] In every organization, incidents that have a negative impact on relationships with customers may occur. The true test of a firm's commitment to satisfaction and service quality isn't in the advertising promises it makes but in the way it responds when things go wrong for the customer. At times, complaints tend to have a negative effect on service personnel's commitment to customer service. However, employees with a positive attitude toward service and their own jobs are more likely to view complaints as a potential source of improvement and explore additional ways in which they can help customers.[15]

Impact of Effective Service Recovery on Customer Loyalty

When complaints are resolved satisfactorily, there is a very high chance that the customers involved will remain loyal. In fact, research has shown that complainants who are satisfied with the service recovery are 15 times more likely to recommend a company than dissatisfied complainants.[16] Research by TARP, a customer satisfaction and measurement firm, found that intentions to repurchase for different types of products ranged between 9%–37% when customers were dissatisfied but did not complain. For a major complaint, the retention rate increased from 9% if the dissatisfied customer did not complain to 19% if the company offered a sympathetic ear to the customer's complaint but was unable to resolve it to the satisfaction of the customer. If the complaint was resolved to the satisfaction of the customer, the retention rate jumped to 54%. The highest retention rate of 82% was achieved when problems were fixed quickly—typically on the spot![17]

We can conclude that complaint handling should be seen as a profit center rather than a cost center. When a dissatisfied customer defects, the firm loses more than just the value of the next transaction. It may also lose a long-term stream of profits from that customer and from anyone else who is deterred from patronizing that firm as a result of negative comments from an unhappy friend. However, many organizations are yet to understand that it pays to invest in service recovery designed to protect long-term profits.[18]

The Service Recovery Paradox

The *service recovery paradox* describes the phenomenon where customers who experience an excellent service recovery after a failure feel even more satisfied than customers who had no problem in the first place.[19] For example, a passenger may arrive at the check-in counter in an airport and find that they lost their confirmed seat due to overbooking. To recover the service, the airline upgrades the passenger to a business-class seat at no additional charge. The customer ends up being delighted and even more satisfied than before the problem occurred.

The service recovery paradox may lead to the thinking that it may be good for customers to experience service failure so that they can be delighted as a result of an excellent service recovery. However, this approach would be too expensive for the firm. It is also important to note that the service recovery paradox does not always apply. In fact,

LO 5
Explain the service recovery paradox.

PART IV

research has shown that the service recovery paradox is far from universal.[20] For example, a study of repeated service failures in a retail banking context showed that the service recovery paradox held for the first service failure that was recovered to customers' full satisfaction.[21] However, if a second service failure occurred, the paradox disappeared. This indicates that customers may forgive a firm once but become disillusioned if failures recur. The study also showed that customers' expectations were raised after they experienced a very good recovery (i.e., they began to expect the same standard of recovery for dealing with future failures).

The severity and "recoverability" of the service failure may also determine whether the customer comes out of the service recovery process delighted. No one can replace spoiled wedding photos or a ruined holiday, or eliminate the consequences of a debilitating injury caused by service equipment. In such situations, it's hard to imagine anyone being truly delighted even when a most professional service recovery is conducted. Contrast these examples with a lost hotel reservation, for which the recovery is an upgrade to a better room or even a suite. When poor service is recovered by the delivery of a superior product, the customer is usually delighted and may even hope for another lost reservation in the future.

The best strategy, of course, is to do it right the first time. As Michael Hargrove puts it, "Service recovery is turning a service failure into an opportunity you wish you never had."[22] Unfortunately, empirical evidence shows that some 40% to 60% of customers reported dissatisfaction with the service recovery processes they experienced.[23]

LO 6

Know the principles of effective service recovery systems.

PRINCIPLES OF EFFECTIVE SERVICE RECOVERY SYSTEMS

Managers need to recognize that current customers are a valuable asset base and develop effective procedures for service recovery following unsatisfactory experiences. We discuss three guiding principles to get it right: (1) make it easy for customers to give feedback, (2) enable effective service recovery, and (3) establish appropriate compensation levels. A fourth principle—learning from customer feedback and driving service improvements—will be discussed in Chapter 14 in the context of customer feedback systems. The components of an effective service recovery system are shown in Figure 13.8.[24]

Make It Easy for Customers to Give Feedback

How can managers overcome unhappy customers' reluctance to complain about service failures? The best way is to address the reasons for their reluctance directly. Table 13.1 gives an overview of potential measures that can be taken to overcome the reasons we identified earlier in this chapter. Many companies have improved their complaint-collection procedures by adding special toll-free phone lines (see Figure 13.9 for a tongue-in-cheek example of what not to do!), links on their websites and social media pages, and clearly displayed customer comment cards in their branches. In their customer communications, some companies feature service improvements that were the direct result of customer feedback under the motto "You told us, and we responded."

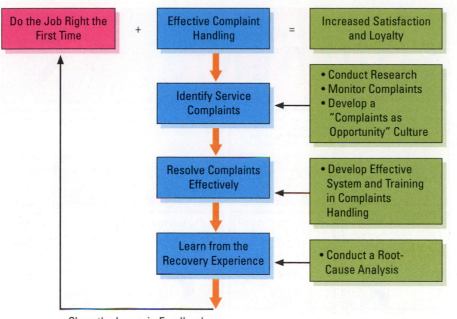

Figure 13.8 Components of an effective service recovery system.

SOURCE

From Christopher Lovelock, Paul Patterson, and Jochen Wirtz, *Services Marketing: An Asia-Pacific and Australian Perspective*, 6th ed, Pearson Australia, 2015.

Enable Effective Service Recovery

It takes more than just pious expressions of determination to recover from service failures or resolve any problems that may occur. Commitment, planning, and clear

Table 13.1 Strategies to reduce customer complaint barriers.

Complaint Barriers for Dissatisfied Customers	Strategies to Reduce These Barriers
Inconvenience • Difficult to find the right complaint procedure • Effort; e.g., writing and mailing a letter	Make feedback easy and convenient: • Put customer service hotline numbers, e-mail addresses, the website, and /or postal addresses on all customer communications materials (letters, bills, brochures, the website, phone book, yellow pages listings, etc.)
Doubtful payoff • Uncertain whether any or what action will be taken by the firm to address the issue the customer is unhappy with	Reassure customers that their feedback will be taken seriously and will pay off: • Have service recovery procedures in place and communicate this to customers; e.g., in the customer newsletter and the website. • Feature service improvements that resulted from customer feedback.
Unpleasantness • Fear of being treated rudely • Fear of being hassled • Feeling embarrassed	Make providing feedback a positive experience: • Thank customers for their feedback (can be done publicly and in general by addressing the entire customer base). • Train service employees not to hassle and to make customers feel comfortable. • Allow for anonymous feedback.

Figure 13.9 How not to treat unhappy customers.

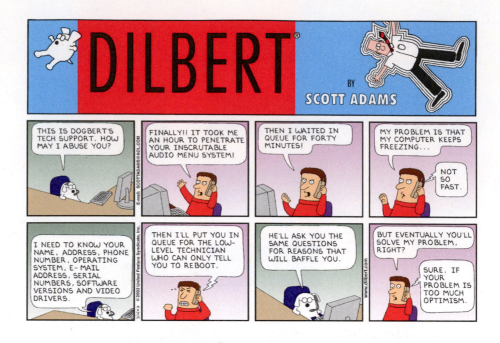

guidelines are necessary. Specifically, effective service recovery should be (1) proactive, (2) planned, (3) trained, and (4) empowered.

Service Recovery Should Be Proactive. Service recovery is ideally initiated on the spot, preferably before customers have a chance to complain (see Service Insights 13.1). Service personnel should be sensitive to signs of dissatisfaction so that they can ask whether customers might be experiencing a problem. For example, the waiter may ask a guest who has only eaten half of his dinner, "Is everything all right, sir?" The guest may say, "Yes, thank you, I am not very hungry," or "The steak is well done but I had asked for medium-rare." The second response gives the waiter a chance to recover the service rather than have an unhappy diner leave the restaurant and potentially not return.

Recovery Procedures Need to Be Planned. Contingency plans have to be developed for service failures, especially for those that occur regularly and cannot be designed out of the system.[25] For example, revenue management practices in the travel and hospitality industries often result in overbooking. Travelers are denied boarding, and hotel guests are "walked" even though they had confirmed seats or reservations. To simplify the task of front-line staff, firms should identify the most common service problems (such as overbooking) and then develop solution sets for employees to follow. In contact centers, the customer service representatives prepare scripts to guide them in a service recovery situation.

Recovery Skills Must Be Taught. As a customer, you may quickly feel insecure at the point of service failure because things are not turning out as you had expected. So you look to an employee for assistance. But are the employees willing and able to help you? Effective training on how to handle recovery solution sets for routine service failures (as in our hotel example in Service Insights 13.1) as well as non-routine ones builds confidence and competence among front-line staff, enabling them to turn distress into delight.[26]

Recovery Requires Empowered Employees. Service recovery efforts should be flexible, and employees should be empowered to use their judgment and communication skills to develop solutions that will satisfy complaining customers.[27] This is especially true for out-of-the-ordinary failures for which a firm may not have developed and trained solution sets. Employees need to be able to make decisions and spend money in order to resolve service problems promptly and recover customer goodwill. In this day and age, when online public complaining is gaining popularity, employees may even be empowered to respond online. For example, if complaints are made in the form of tweets, employees may tweet back with solutions to resolve the problems.[28]

SERVICE INSIGHTS 13.1

Effective Service Recovery in Action

The lobby is deserted. It's not hard to overhear the conversation between the front-desk receptionist at the Marriott Long Wharf Hotel in Boston and the late-arriving guest.

"Yes, Dr. Jones, we've been expecting you. I know you are scheduled to be here for three nights. I'm sorry to tell you, sir, but we are booked solid tonight. A large number of guests we assumed were checking out did not. Where is your meeting tomorrow, sir?"

The doctor tells the receptionist where it is.

"That's near the Omni Parker House! That's not very far from here. Let me call them and get you a room for the evening. I'll be right back."

A few minutes later, the receptionist returns with the good news.

"They're holding a room for you at the Omni Parker House, sir. And, of course, we'll pick up the tab. I'll forward any phone calls that come here for you. Here's a letter that will explain the situation and expedite your check-in, along with my business card so you can call me directly here at the front desk if you have any problems."

The doctor's mood is moving from exasperation toward calm. However, the receptionist is not finished with the encounter. He reaches into the cash drawer. "Here is a $50 bill. That should more than cover your cab fare from here to the Parker House and back again in the morning. We don't have a problem tomorrow night, just tonight. And here's a coupon that will get

you complimentary continental breakfast on our concierge level on the fifth floor tomorrow morning . . . and again, I am so sorry this happened."

As the doctor walks away, the hotel's night manager turns to the receptionist, "Give him about 15 minutes and then call to make sure everything went okay."

A week later, when it is still a peak period for hotels in that city, the same guest who had overheard the exchange is in a taxi, en route to the same hotel. Along the way, he tells his companion about the great service recovery episode he had witnessed the week before. The two travelers arrive at the hotel and make their way to the front desk, ready to check in.

They are greeted with unexpected news: "I am so sorry gentlemen. I know you were scheduled here for two nights. But we are booked solid tonight. Where is your meeting scheduled tomorrow?"

The would-be guests exchange a rueful glance as they give the receptionist their future plans. "That's near the Méridien. Let me call over there and see if I can get you a room. It won't but take a minute." As the receptionist walks away, the tale teller says, "I'll bet he comes back with a letter and a business card."

Sure enough, the receptionist returns to deliver the solution; it's not a robotic script, but all the elements from the previous week's show are on display. What the tale teller thought was pure initiative from the front-desk receptionist the previous week turns out to be a predetermined response to a specific category of service problem.

SOURCE

Ron Zemke, "Knock Your Socks Off Service Recovery," reproduced with permission of AMACOM Books.

How Generous Should Compensation Be?

Clearly, vastly different costs are associated with possible recovery strategies. How much compensation should a firm offer when there has been a service failure? Would an apology be sufficient instead? The following rules of thumb can help managers to answer these questions:

▶ **What is the positioning of your firm?** If a firm is known for service excellence and charges a premium price for quality, customers will expect service failures to be rare. The firm should therefore make a demonstrable effort to recover the few failures that do occur and be prepared to offer something of significant value. However, in a mass-market business, customers are likely to accept an apology and a rework of the service.

▶ **How severe was the service failure?** The general guideline is: "Let the punishment fit the crime." Customers expect little for minor inconveniences (here, a sincere apology will do), but a much more significant compensation is required if the failure caused major damage in terms of time, effort, annoyance, or anxiety.

▶ **Who is the affected customer?** Long-term customers and those who spend heavily at a service provider expect more, and it is worth making an effort to save their business. One-time customers tend to be less demanding and have less economic importance to the firm. Hence, compensation can be less but should still be fair. There is always the possibility that a first-time user will become a repeat customer if he or she is treated well.

The overall rule of thumb for compensation at service failures should be "well-dosed generosity." Being perceived as stingy adds insult to injury, and the firm will probably be better off apologizing rather than offering a minimal compensation. Overly generous compensation is not only expensive but may also be interpreted negatively by customers. It may raise questions in their minds about the soundness of the business and cause them to become suspicious about the underlying motives. They may worry about the implications of such generosity for the employee as well as for the business. Moreover, excessive generosity does not seem to result in higher repeat-purchase rates than when fair compensation is offered.[29] There is a risk, too, that a reputation for over-generosity may encourage dishonest customers to actively "seek" service failures.[30] In fact, what customers really want is often just a satisfactory solution to their service problem rather than bells and whistles![31]

LO 7

Be familiar with the guidelines for front-line employees on how to handle complaining customers and recover from a service failure.

Dealing with Complaining Customers

Both managers and front-line employees must be prepared to deal with distressed customers, including jaycustomers who can become confrontational and behave in unacceptable ways toward service personnel who often aren't at fault. (Jaycustomers will be discussed later in this chapter.)

Good interactive skills combined with training and on-the-spot thinking are critical for front-line employees to deal with such situations. Service Insights 13.2 provides specific guidelines for effective problem resolution. These guidelines are designed to help calm upset customers and to deliver a resolution that they will see as fair and satisfying.

"Who picked 'I Can't Get No Satisfaction' to be our on-hold music?"

SERVICE INSIGHTS 13.2

Guidelines for the Front Line: How to Handle Complaining Customers and Recover from a Service Failure

1 *Act fast*. If the complaint is made during service delivery, then time is of the essence to achieve a full recovery. When complaints are made after the fact, many companies have established policies of responding within 24 hours or sooner. Even when full resolution is likely to take longer, fast acknowledgment remains very important.

2 *Acknowledge the customer's feelings.* This must be done either tacitly or explicitly (for example, "I can understand why you're upset"). It helps to build rapport, which is the first step in rebuilding a bruised relationship.

3 *Don't argue with customers.* The goal should be to gather facts to reach a mutually acceptable solution, not to win a debate or prove that the customer is wrong. Arguing gets in the way of listening and seldom diffuses anger.

4 *Show that you understand the problem from each customer's point of view.* Seeing situations through the customers' eyes is the only way to understand what they think has gone wrong and why they're upset. Service personnel should avoid jumping to conclusions with their own interpretations.

5 *Clarify the facts and sort out the cause.* A failure may result from service inefficiency, misunderstanding by customers, or misbehavior by a third party. If you've done something wrong, apologize immediately in order to win the understanding and trust of the customer. The more the customer can forgive you, the less he/she will expect to be compensated. Don't be defensive; acting defensively may suggest that the organization has something to hide or is reluctant to look fully into the situation.

6 *Give customers the benefit of the doubt.* Not all customers are truthful, and not all complaints are genuine. However, customers should be treated as though they have a valid complaint until clear evidence proves the contrary. If a lot of money is at stake (as in insurance claims or potential lawsuits), careful investigation needs to be carried out. If the amount involved is small, it may not be worth haggling over a refund or other compensation. However, it's still a good idea to check records

to see if there is a past history of dubious complaints by the same customer.

7 *Propose the steps needed to solve the problem.* When instant solutions aren't immediately available, tell customers how the firm intends to take action to deal with the problem. This also sets expectations about the time involved, so firms should be careful not to over-promise!

8 *Keep customers informed of progress*. Nobody likes being left in the dark. Uncertainty causes people to be anxious and stressed. People tend to be more accepting if they are kept informed about what's going on and receive periodic progress reports.

9 *Consider compensation*. When customers do not receive the service outcomes they believe they have paid for, or when they suffer serious inconvenience and/or loss of time and money due to the failure of the service, either a monetary payment or some other compensation in kind (e.g., an upgrade on a flight or free dessert in a restaurant) is appropriate. This type of recovery strategy may also reduce the risk of legal action by an angry customer. Service guarantees often lay out in advance what such compensation will be, and the firm should ensure that all guarantees are met.

10 *Persevere to regain customer goodwill.* When customers have been disappointed, one of the hardest things to do is to restore their confidence and keep the relationship going. Perseverance may be required to defuse customers' anger and to convince them that actions are being taken to avoid a recurrence of the problem. Truly exceptional recovery efforts can be extremely effective in building loyalty and referrals.

11 *Self-check the service delivery system and improve it.* After the customer has left, you should check to see whether the service failure was caused by accidental mistakes or system defects. Take advantage of every complaint to perfect the whole service system. Even if the complaint is found to be a result of a misunderstanding by the customer, it implies that some part of the communication system is ineffective.

Figure 13.10 Language is important in appeasing upset customers.

SERVICE GUARANTEES

One way for particularly customer-focused firms to institutionalize professional complaint handling and effective service recovery is by offering service guarantees. In fact, a growing number of companies offer customers a service guarantee, promising that if service delivery fails to meet pre-defined standards, the customer will be entitled to one or more forms of compensation (such as an easy-to-claim replacement, refund, or credit). A well-designed service guarantee not only facilitates effective service recovery but also institutionalizes the practice of learning from service failures and ensuring subsequent system improvements.[32]

LO 8

Recognize the power of service guarantees.

The Power of Service Guarantees

Service guarantees are powerful tools for promoting as well as achieving service quality:[33]

1) Guarantees force firms to focus on what their customers want and expect in each element of the service.

2) Guarantees set clear standards, telling customers and employees alike what the company stands for. Payouts to compensate customers for poor service cause managers to take guarantees seriously, because they highlight the financial costs of quality failures.

3) Guarantees require the development of systems for generating meaningful customer feedback and acting on it.

4) Guarantees force service organizations to understand why they fail and encourage them to identify and overcome potential fail points.

5) Guarantees build "marketing muscle" by reducing the risk of the purchase decision and building long-term loyalty.

From the customer's perspective, the primary function of service guarantees is to lower the perceived risks associated with purchase.[34] The presence of a guarantee may also make it easier and more likely for customers to complain. They will anticipate a readiness on the part of front-line employees to resolve the problem and provide appropriate compensation.

The benefits of service guarantees can be seen clearly in the case of Hampton Inn's "100% Hampton Guarantee": "If you're not 100% satisfied, you don't pay". As a business-building program, Hampton's strategy of offering to refund the cost of the room to a guest who expresses dissatisfaction has not only attracted new customers but also served as a powerful retention device. People choose to stay at a Hampton Inn because they are confident that they will be satisfied. The guarantee has also become a vital tool to help managers identify new opportunities for quality improvement.

Figure 13.11 Hampton Inn's advertising often includes its "100% satisfaction guaranteed."

How to Design Service Guarantees

Some guarantees are simple and unconditional. Others appear to have been written by lawyers and contain many restrictions. Ideally, service guarantees should be designed to meet the following criteria:[35]

LO 9

Understand how to design effective service guarantees.

1) **Unconditional.** Whatever is promised in the guarantee must be totally un-conditional, and there should not be any element of surprise for the customer.

2) **Easy to understand and communicate.** The customer must be clearly aware of the benefits that can be gained from the guarantee.

3) **Meaningful to the customer.** The guarantee must be on something that is important to the customer, and the compensation should be more than adequate to cover the service failure.

4) **Easy to invoke.** It should be easy for the customer to invoke the guarantee.

5) **Easy to collect on.** If a service failure occurs, the customer should be able to easily collect on the guarantee without any problems.

6) **Credible.** The guarantee should be believable (Figure 13.12).

Is Full Satisfaction the Best You Can Guarantee?

Full-satisfaction guarantees have generally been considered the best possible design. However, it has been suggested that the ambiguity associated with such guarantees can lead to discounting of their perceived value. For example, customers may raise questions such as "What does full satisfaction mean?" or "Can I invoke a guarantee when I am dissatisfied even if the fault does not lie with the service firm?"[36] Attribute-specific guarantees (e.g., guaranteed delivery within 24 hours) are highly specific and therefore don't suffer from ambiguity. However, their coverage is not comprehensive, and this limits their appeal. A hybrid version of the full-satisfaction and attribute-specific guarantees, called the "combined guarantee," addresses this issue. It combines the wide scope of a full-satisfaction guarantee with the low uncertainty of attribute-specific performance standards. The combined guarantee has been shown to be superior to the pure full-satisfaction or attribute-specific guarantee designs.[37] Specific performance standards are guaranteed (e.g., on-time delivery), but the full-satisfaction coverage of

Figure 13.12 To leave a clear stamp of service quality on customers, the guarantee must be unconditional, meaningful, credible, easily understood, invoked, and collectable.

the combined guarantee applies if the consumer is dissatisfied with any other element of the service. Table 13.2 shows examples of the various types of guarantees.

LO 10

Know when firms should not offer service guarantees.

Is It Always Beneficial to Introduce a Service Guarantee?

Managers should think carefully about their firm's strengths and weaknesses when deciding whether or not to introduce a service guarantee. There are a number of situations in which a guarantee may not be appropriate:[38]

▶ Companies that already have a strong reputation for service excellence may not need a guarantee. In fact, it can be incongruent with their image to offer one, as it might confuse the market.[39] Rather, best practice service firms will be expected to do what's right without offering a service guarantee.

▶ In contrast, a firm whose service is currently poor must first work to improve quality to a level above what is guaranteed. Otherwise, too many customers will invoke the guarantee, and this will have serious cost implications for the firm.

▶ Service firms whose quality is truly uncontrollable because of external forces would be foolish to consider a guarantee. For example, when Amtrak realized that it was paying out substantial refunds because it lacked sufficient control over its rail-road infrastructure, it was forced to drop a service guarantee that included reimbursement of fares in the event of unpunctual train service.

▶ In a market in which consumers see little financial, personal, or physiological risk associated with purchasing and using a service, a guarantee adds little value but still costs money to design, implement, and manage.

Table 13.2 Types of service guarantees.

Term	Guarantee Scope	Example
Single attribute-specific guarantee	One key attribute of the service is covered by the guarantee.	"Any of three specified popular pizzas is guaranteed to be served within 10 minutes of ordering on working days between 12 a.m. and 2 p.m. If the pizza is late, the customer's next order is free."
Multiattribute-specific guarantee	A few important attributes of the service are covered by the guarantee.	Minneapolis Marriott's guarantee: "Our quality commitment to you is to provide: • a friendly, efficient check-in • a clean, comfortable room, where everything works • a friendly efficient check-out If we, in your opinion, do not deliver on this commitment, we will give you $20 in cash. No questions asked. It is your interpretation."
Full-satisfaction guarantee	All aspects of the service are covered by the guarantee. There are no exceptions.	Lands' End's guarantee: "If you are not completely satisfied with any item you buy from us, at any time during your use of it, return it and we will refund your full purchase price. We mean every word of it. Whatever. Whenever. Always. But to make sure this is perfectly clear, we've decided to simplify it further. GUARANTEED. Period."
Combined guarantee	All aspects of the service are covered by the full-satisfaction promise of the guarantee. Explicit minimum performance standards on important attributes are included in the guarantee to reduce uncertainty.	Datapro Information Services guarantees "to deliver the report on time, to high quality standards, and to the contents outlined in this proposal. Should we fail to deliver according to this guarantee, or should you be dissatisfied with any aspect of our work, you can deduct any amount from the final payment which is deemed as fair."

SOURCE

From Jochen Wirtz and D. Kum, "Designing Service Guarantees—Is Full Satisfaction the Best You Can Guarantee?" *Journal of Services Marketing* 15(14): 282–299, © 2002 Emerald Group Publishing Ltd.

PART IV

Furthermore, in markets where there is little perceived difference in service quality among competing firms, the first firm to institute a guarantee may be able to obtain a first-mover advantage and create value differentiation for its services. If more than one competitor already has guarantees in place, offering a guarantee may become a qualifier for the industry. In such cases, the only real way to make an impact is to launch a highly distinctive guarantee that goes beyond what is already offered by competitors.

Discouraging Abuse and Opportunistic Customer Behavior

Throughout this chapter, we advocate that firms should welcome and even encourage complaints and invocations of service guarantees. However, we have to acknowledge that not all complaints are honest. When firms have generous service recovery policies or offer guarantees, there is always the fear that some customers may take advantage of them. Moreover, not all complaining customers are right or reasonable in their behavior, and some may actually be the cause of complaints by other customers. We refer to such people as *jaycustomers*.

Every service has its share of jaycustomers. Jaycustomers are undesirable. At best, a firm should avoid attracting them in the first place. At worst, a firm needs to control or prevent their abusive behavior. Let us first describe the main types of jaycustomers before we discuss how to deal with them.

 LO 11

Be familiar with the seven groups of jaycustomers and understand how to manage them effectively

Seven Types of Jaycustomers[40]

We've identified seven broad categories and given them generic names, but many customer-contact personnel have come up with their own special terms.

The Cheat. There are many ways in which customers can cheat service firms. Cheating ranges from writing complaint letters with the sole purpose of exploiting service recovery policies and cheating on service guarantees to inflating or faking insurance claims and "wardrobing" (e.g., using an evening dress or tuxedo for an evening and then returning it to the retailer). The following quotes describe the thinking of these customers nicely in other contexts:

> On checking in to a hotel I noticed that they had a "100% satisfaction or your money back" guarantee, I just couldn't resist the opportunity to take advantage of it, so on checking out I told the receptionist that I wanted a refund as the sound of the traffic kept me awake all night. They gave me a refund, no questions asked. These companies can be so stupid they need to be more alert.[41]

> I've complained that service was too slow, too quick, too hot, too cold, too bright, too dark, too friendly, too impersonal, too public, too private . . . it doesn't matter really, as long as you enclose a receipt with your letter, you just get back a standard letter and gift coupon.[42]

Firms cannot easily check whether a customer is faking dissatisfaction or is truly unhappy. At the end of this section, we will discuss how to deal with this type of consumer fraud.

The Thief. The thief jaycustomer has no intention of paying and sets out to steal goods and services (or to pay less than full price by switching price tickets or contesting bills on baseless grounds). Shoplifting is a major problem in retail stores. For those with technical skills, it's sometimes possible to bypass electricity meters, access telephone lines free of charge, or bypass normal cable-TV feeds. Riding free on public transportation, sneaking into movie theaters, and not paying for restaurant meals are also popular. Finding out how people steal a service is the first step in preventing theft, catching thieves, and (where appropriate) prosecuting them. However, managers should try not to alienate honest customers by degrading their service experiences. Provisions must also be made for honest but absent-minded customers who forget to pay.

The Rulebreaker. Many service businesses need to establish rules of behavior for customers to guide them safely through the various steps of the service process. Some of these rules are imposed by government agencies for health and safety reasons. Air travel provides one of the best examples of rules designed to ensure safety.

Rules set by service firms facilitate smooth operations, avoid unreasonable demands on employees, prevent misuse of products and facilities, protect the firms legally, and discourage individual customers from misbehaving. Ski resorts, for instance, are getting tough on careless skiers who pose risks to themselves as well as others. Collisions can cause serious injury and even kill. Ski patrol members must be safety-oriented and may even be required to take on a policing role. Just as dangerous drivers can lose their licenses, dangerous skiers can lose their lift tickets (Figure 13.13).

There are risks attached to making lots of rules. Fewer rules help to make the most important ones clearer.

The Belligerent. You've probably seen them shouting angrily in a store, at the airport, or in a hotel or restaurant; or perhaps with insults, threats, and obscenities. Service personnel are often abused, even when they are not to blame. If an employee lacks the power to resolve the problem, the belligerent may become madder still, even to the point of physical attack. Unfortunately, when angry customers rant at service personnel, the latter sometimes respond in kind, thus escalating the confrontation and reducing the likelihood of resolution (Figure 13.14).

What should an employee do when an aggressive customer brushes off attempts to defuse the situation? In a public environment, one priority should be to move the person away from other customers. Sometimes, supervisors may have to settle disagreements between customers and staff members; at other times, they need to support the employee's actions. If a customer has physically attacked an employee, it may be necessary to summon security officers or the police.

Rudeness over the telephone poses a different challenge. One approach for handling a customer who continues to shout at a telephone-based employee is for the latter to say firmly, "This conversation isn't getting us anywhere. Why don't I call you back in a

Figure 13.13 Dangerous skiers are rule breakers who pose a danger to others and need to be policed.

Figure 13.14 Confrontations between customers and service employees can easily escalate.

few minutes when you've had time to digest the information?" In many cases, a break to think (and cool down) is exactly what's needed.

The Family Feuders. People who get into arguments with members of their own family—or worse, with other customers—make up a sub-category of belligerents we call "family feuders." Employee intervention may either calm the situation or make it worse. Some situations require detailed analysis and a carefully thought-out response. Others, such as customers starting a food fight in a nice restaurant (yes, such things do happen!), require an almost immediate response. Service managers in these situations need to be prepared to think on their feet and act fast.

The Vandal. Soft drinks are poured into bank cash machines; graffiti are scrawled on both interior and exterior surfaces; burn holes from cigarettes scar carpets, tablecloths, and bedcovers; bus seats are slashed and hotel furniture broken; customers' cars are vandalized; glass is smashed and fabrics are torn. The list is endless. Customers don't cause all of the damage, of course. Bored or drunk young people are the source of much exterior vandalism. However, much of the problem does originate with paying customers who choose to misbehave (Figure 13.15).

The best cure for vandalism is prevention. Improved security discourages some vandals. Good lighting and the open design of public areas also help. Companies can choose vandal-resistant surfaces, protective coverings for equipment, and rugged furnishings. Educating customers to use equipment properly (rather than fighting with it) and providing warnings about fragile objects can reduce the likelihood of abuse or careless handling. Finally, there are economic sanctions: security deposits or signed agreements in which customers agree to pay for any damage that they cause.

The Deadbeat. They are the ones who delay payment. Once again, preventive action is better than a cure. A growing number of firms insist on pre-payment. Any form of ticket sale is a good example of this. Direct-marketing organizations ask for your credit card number as they take your order. The next best thing is to present the customer with a bill immediately on completion of service. If the bill is to be sent by mail, the firm should send it fast while the service is still fresh in the customer's mind.

Customers may have a good reason for the delay, and acceptable payment arrangements can be worked out. There may be other considerations, too. If the client's problems are only temporary ones, what is the long-term value of maintaining the relationship? Will it create positive goodwill and word of mouth to help the customer work things out? These decisions are judgment calls, but if creating and maintaining long-term relationships is the firm's ultimate goal, they bear exploration.

Dealing with Customer Fraud

Dishonest customers may steal from the firm, refuse to pay for the service, fake dissatisfaction, purposefully cause service failures to occur, or overstate losses at the

We treat our customers like family.

GLASBERGEN

"Sometimes you have to treat them like a *dysfunctional* family."

Figure 13.15 Treating customers like family is not always the best response by a service manager.

time of genuine service failures. What steps can a firm take to protect itself against opportunistic customer behaviors?

The working assumption should be, "If in doubt, believe the customer." However, as Service Insights 13.3 shows, it's crucial to keep track of customers who repeatedly "experience service failures" and ask for compensation or invoke the firm's service guarantee. For example, one Asian airline found that the same customer lost his suitcase on three consecutive flights. As the chances of this truly happening are probably lower than winning the national lottery, front-line staff members were made aware of this individual. The next time he checked in his suitcase, the check-in staff followed the video image of the suitcase almost from check-in to pick-up at the baggage claim carrousel at the traveler's destination. It turned out that a companion collected the suitcase and took it away while the traveler again made his way to the lost-baggage counter to report his missing suitcase. This time, the police were waiting for him and his friend.

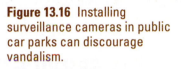

Figure 13.16 Installing surveillance cameras in public car parks can discourage vandalism.

In another example, Continental Airlines consolidated some 45 separate customer databases into a single data warehouse to improve service as well as to detect customer fraud. The airline found one customer who received 20 bereavement fares in 12 months off the same dead grandfather!

To be able to effectively detect consumer fraud, the firm must maintain a central database of all compensation payments, service recoveries, returned goods, and any other benefits given to customers based on special circumstances (i.e., such transactions cannot be retained only at the local or branch level but must be captured in a centralized system). It is important to merge customer data across departments and channels for detecting unusual transactions and the systems that allow them.[43]

Research has shown that customers who think they were treated unfairly in any way (see our earlier discussion regarding distributive, procedural, and interactive fairness) are much more likely to take advantage of a firm's service recovery effort. In addition, consumers tend to take advantage of large firms more often than small ones; they think that large firms can easily afford the recovery costs. One-time customers are also much more likely to cheat than loyal customers, and customers who do not have a personal relationship with service employees are more likely to take advantage of service recovery policies.

Service guarantees are often used as payouts in service recovery, and it has been shown that the amount of a guarantee payout (e.g., whether it is a 10% or 100% money-back guarantee) has no effect on consumer cheating. It seems that customers who cheat for a 100% refund also cheat for 10%, and that customers who do not cheat for 10% don't do so for 100% either. However, repeat purchase intention significantly reduces cheating intent. Another finding shows that customers are more reluctant to cheat if the service quality provided is truly high compared to when it is just satisfactory.[44]

These findings suggest a number of important managerial implications:

1) Firms should ensure that their service recovery procedures are fair.

2) Large firms should recognize that consumers are more likely to cheat them and have robust fraud-detection systems in place.

3) Firms can implement and thus reap the bigger marketing benefits of 100% money-back guarantees without worrying that the large payouts would increase cheating considerably.

4) Guarantees can be offered to regular customers or as part of a membership program, because repeat customers are unlikely to cheat on service guarantees.

5) Truly excellent services firms don't have to worry as much about cheating as the average service provider.

SERVICE INSIGHTS 13.3

Tracking Down Guests Who Cheat

As part of its guarantee-tracking system, Hampton Inn has developed ways to identify guests who appeared to be cheating. Guests showing high invocation trends receive personalized attention and follow-up from the company's Guest Assistance Team. Wherever possible, senior managers telephone these guests to ask about their recent stays. The conversation might go as follows: "Hello, Mr. Jones. I'm the director of guest assistance at Hampton Inn, and I see that you've had some difficulty with the last four properties you've visited. Since we take our guarantee very seriously, I thought I'd give you a call and find out what the problems were."

The typical response is dead silence! Sometimes the silence is followed with questions about how headquarters could possibly know about their problems. These calls have their humorous moments as well. One individual, who had invoked the guarantee 17 times in what appeared to be a trip that took him across the United States and back, was asked, "Where do you like to stay when you travel?" "Hampton Inn," came the enthusiastic response. "But," said the executive making the call, "our records show that the last seventeen times you have stayed at a Hampton Inn, you have invoked the 100% Satisfaction Guarantee." "That's why I like them!" proclaimed the guest (who turned out to be a long-distance truck driver on a per diem for his accommodation expenses).

LO 1 ▶ When customers are dissatisfied, they have several alternatives. They can:

- Take some form of public action (e.g., complain to the firm or a third party or even take legal action).
- Take some form of private action (e.g., switch to another provider and/or spread negative word of mouth).
- Take no action.

LO 2 ▶ To effectively recover from a service failure, firms need to understand customer complaining behavior and motivations as well as what customers expect in response.

- Customers typically complain for any combination of the following four reasons: (1) to obtain restitution or compensation, (2) to vent their anger, (3) to help to improve the service, and (4) to spare other customers from experiencing the same problems (i.e., they complain for altruistic reasons).
- In practice, most dissatisfied customers do not complain as (1) they may not know where to complain, (2) they think it requires too much effort and is unpleasant, and (3) they perceive the payoffs of their effort as uncertain.
- The people who are most likely to complain tend to be better educated, have higher incomes, are more socially involved, and have more knowledge about the product.
- Customers are most likely to complain at the point-of-service provision (face to face and over the phone). Only a small proportion of complaints is made via other channels such as e-mail, social media, websites, or letters.

LO 3 ▶ Once customers make a complaint, they expect firms to deal with it in a fair manner along three dimensions of fairness:

- Procedural fairness: Customers expect the firm to have a convenient, responsive, and flexible service recovery process.
- Interactional justice: Customers expect an honest explanation, a genuine effort to solve the problem, and polite treatment.
- Outcome justice: Customers expect a compensation that reflects the loss and inconvenience suffered as a result of the service failure.

LO 4 ▶ Effective service recovery can, in many cases, avoid customer switching and restore confidence in the firm. When customers complain, they give the firm a chance to correct problems, restore the relationship with the complainer, and improve future satisfaction. Service recovery is therefore an important opportunity to retain a valued customer.

LO 5 ▶ The *service recovery paradox* describes the phenomenon where customers who experience an excellent service recovery after a failure feel even more satisfied than customers who had no problem in the first place. However, it is important to note that this paradox does not always apply. It is best to get the service right the first time rather than provide expensive service recovery.

LO 6 ▶ Effective service recovery systems should:

- Make it easy for customers to give feedback (e.g., provide hotline numbers, e-mail addresses, and social media channels on all communications materials) and encourage them to provide feedback.
- Enable effective service recovery by making it (1) proactive, (2) pre-planned, (3) trained, and (4) empowered.
- Establish appropriate compensation levels. Compensation should be higher if (1) a firm is known for service excellence, (2) the service failure is serious, and (3) the customer is important to the firm.

LO 7 ▶ The guidelines that front-line employees should follow to handle customer complaints and recover the service effectively include: (1) act fast; (2) acknowledge the customer's feelings; (3) don't argue with the customer; (4) show that you understand the problem from the customer's point of view; (5) clarify the truth and sort out the cause; (6) give customers the benefit of the doubt; (7) propose the steps needed to solve the problem; (8) keep customers informed of progress; (9) consider compensation; (10) persevere to regain customer goodwill; and (11) self-check the service delivery system and improve it.

LO 8 ▶ Service guarantees are a powerful way to institutionalize professional complaint handling and service recovery. Service guarantees set clear standards for the firm. They also reduce customers' risk perceptions and can build long-term loyalty.

PART IV

LO 9 ▶ Service guarantees should be designed to be: (1) unconditional, (2) easy to understand and communicate, (3) meaningful to the customer, (4) easy to invoke, (5) easy to collect on, and (6) credible.

LO 10 ▶ Not all firms stand to gain from service guarantees. Specifically, firms should be careful offering service guarantees when: (1) they already have a reputation for service excellence, (2) service quality is too low and has to be improved first, (3) aspects of service quality are uncontrollable because of external factors (e.g., the weather), and (4) customers perceive low risk when buying the service.

LO 11 ▶ Not all customers are honest, polite, and reasonable. Some may want to take advantage of service recovery situations, while others may inconvenience and stress front-line employees and other customers. Such customers are called jaycustomers.

o   There are seven groups of jaycustomers: (1) the Cheat, (2) the Thief, (3) the Rulebreaker, (4) the Belligerent, (5) the Family Feuders, (6) the Vandal, and (7) the Deadbeat.

o   Different types of jaycustomers cause different problems for firms and may spoil the service experience of other customers. Hence, firms need to manage their behavior, even if that means keeping track of how often a customer invokes a service guarantee or (as a last resort) blacklisting them from using the firm's facilities.

UNLOCK YOUR LEARNING

These keywords are found within the sections of each Learning Objective (LO). They are integral to understanding the services marketing concepts taught in each section. Having a firm grasp of these keywords and how they are used is essential to helping you do well on your course, and in the real and very competitive marketing scene out there.

LO 1
1. Complain
2. Defection
3. No action
4. Private action
5. Public action
6. Service failure

LO 2
1. "Double deviation"
2. Anger
3. Compensation
4. Concern for others
5. Customer complaining behavior
6. Customer feedback system
7. Dissatisfied customers
8. Interactive channels
9. Non-interactive channels
10. Online public complaining
11. Restitution
12. Socio-economic levels

LO 3
1. Interactional justice
2. Outcome justice
3. Perceived fairness
4. Procedural justice

LO 4
1. Complaint handling
2. Customer satisfaction
3. Customer loyalty
4. Service recovery

LO 5
1. Full satisfaction
2. Repeated service failures
3. Service recovery paradox

LO 6
1. Affected customer
2. Complaint-collection procedures
3. Customer complaint barriers
4. Empowered
5. Fair compensation
6. Feedback
7. Contingency plans
8. Overly generous compensation
9. Planned
10. Positioning
11. Proactive
12. Revenue management practices

13. Service recovery systems
14. Severity of service failure
15. Trained

LO 7
1. Confrontational customers
2. Effective problem resolution

LO 8
1. "Marketing muscle"
2. Perceived risks
3. Service guarantees
4. Standards

LO 9
1. "Combined guarantee"
2. Attribute-specific guarantee
3. Credible
4. Easy to invoke
5. Easy to understand
6. Meaningful
7. Full-satisfaction guarantee
8. Unconditional

LO 10 1 Distinctive guarantee
2 Service excellence
3 Service quality

 LO 11 1 100% money-back
guarantees
2 Customer fraud
3 Delay payment
4 Employee intervention

5 Fake returns
6 Faking dissatisfaction
7 Jaycustomers
8 Misuse
9 Physical abuse
10 Rudeness
11 Shoplifting
12 The Belligerent

13 The Cheat
14 The Deadbeat
15 The Family Feuders
16 The Rulebreaker
17 The Thief
18 The Vandal

How well do you know the language of services marketing? Quiz yourself!

⚠ **Not for the academically faint-of-heart**

For each keyword you are able to recall without referring to earlier pages, give yourself a point (and a pat on the back). Tally your score at the end and see if you earned the right to be called—a *services marketeer*.

SCORE

01 – 12 Services Marketing is done a great disservice.

13 – 24 The midnight oil needs to be lit, pronto.

25 – 36 I know what you *didn't* do all semester.

37 – 48 By George! You're getting there.

49 – 60 Now, go forth and market.

61 – 73 There should be a marketing concept named after you.

Review Questions

1. How do customers typically respond to service failures?

2. Why don't many more unhappy customers complain? What do customers expect the firm to do once they have filed a complaint?

3. Why would a firm prefer its unhappy customers to come forward and complain?

4. What is the service recovery paradox? Under what conditions is this paradox most likely to hold? Why is it best to deliver the service as planned, even if the paradox does hold in a specific context?

5. How can a firm make it easy for dissatisfied customers to complain?

6. Why should a service recovery strategy be proactive, planned, trained, and empowered?

7. How generous should compensations related to service recovery be?

8. How should service guarantees be designed? What are the benefits of service guarantees over and above a good complaint handling and service recovery system?

9. Under what conditions is it not suitable to introduce a service guarantee?

10. What are the different types of jaycustomers? How can a service firm deal with such customers?

Application Exercises

1. Think about the last time you experienced a less-than-satisfactory service experience. Did you complain? Why? If you did not complain, explain why not.

2. When was the last time you were truly satisfied with an organization's response to your complaint? Describe in detail what happened and what made you satisfied.

3. What would be an appropriate service recovery policy for a wrongly bounced check for (a) your local savings bank, (b) a major national bank, and (c) a private bank for high net-worth individuals? Please explain your rationale and also compute the economic costs of the alternative service recovery policies.

4. Design an effective service guarantee for a service with high perceived risk. Explain (a) why and how your guarantee would reduce perceived risk of potential customers and (b) why current customers would appreciate being offered this guarantee although they are already a customer of that firm and therefore are likely to perceive lower levels of risk.

5. How generous should compensation be? Review the following incident and comment. Then evaluate the available options, comment on each, select the one you recommend, and defend your decision.

   "The shrimp cocktail was half frozen. The waitress apologized and didn't charge me for my dinner,"

   was the response of a very satisfied customer about the service recovery he received. Consider the following range of service recovery policies a restaurant chain could set, and try to establish the costs for each policy:

   Option 1: Smile and apologize, defrost the prawn cocktail, return it, and smile and apologize again.

   Option 2: Smile and apologize, replace the prawn cocktail with a new one, and smile and apologize again.

   Option 3: Smile and apologize, replace the prawn cocktail, and offer a free coffee or dessert.

   Option 4: Smile and apologize, replace the prawn cocktail, and waive the bill of $80 for the entire meal.

   Option 5: Smile and apologize, replace the prawn cocktail, waive the bill for the entire dinner, and offer a free bottle of champagne.

   Option 6: Smile and apologize, replace the prawn cocktail, waive the bill for the entire dinner, offer a free bottle of champagne, and give a voucher for another dinner to be redeemed within three months.

6. Identify the possible behavior of jaycustomers for a service of your choice. How can the service process be designed to minimize or control the behavior of jaycustomers?

END**NOTES**

1. "An Extraordinary Stumble at JetBlue," *Business Week*, March 5, 2007, http://www.bloomberg.com/bw/stories/2007-03-04/an-extraordinary-stumble-at-jetblue, accessed August 22, 2015.

2. Roger Bougie, Rik Pieters, and Marcel Zeelenberg, "Angry Customers Don't Come Back, They Get Back: The Experience and Behavioral Implications of Anger and Dissatisfaction in Service," *Journal of the Academy of Marketing* Science 31, no. 4 (2003): 377–393; Florian V. Wangenheim, "Postswitching Negative Word of Mouth," *Journal of* Service *Research* 8, no. 1 (2005): 67–78.

3. For research on cognitive and affective drivers of complaining behavior, see: Jean-Charles Chebat, Moshe Davidow, and Isabelle Codjovi, "Silent Voices: Why Some Dissatisfied Consumers Fail to Complain," *Journal of Service Research* 7, no. 4 (2005): 328–342.

4. Stephen S. Tax and Stephen W. Brown, "Recovering and Learning from Service Failure," *Sloan Management Review* 49, no. 1 (Fall 1998): 75–88.

5. A large body of literature has examined consumer complaining behavior. Important studies include: Jean-Charles Chebat, Moshe Davidow and Isabelle Codjovi, "Silent Voices: Why Some Dissatisfied Consumers Fail to Complain," *Journal of Service Research*, 7, no. 4 (2005): 328–342; Nancy Stephens and Kevin P. Gwinner, "Why Don't Some People Complain? A Cognitive-Emotive Process Model of Consumer Complaining Behavior," *Journal of the Academy of Marketing Science* 26, no. 3 (1998): 172–189; Kelli Bodey and Debra Grace, "Segmenting Service 'Complainers' and 'Non-Complainers' on the Basis of Consumer Characters," *Journal of Services Marketing* 20, no. 3 (2006): 178–187.

6. Nancy Stephens, "Complaining," in Teresa A. Swartz & Dawn Iacobucci (eds.), *Handbook of Services Marketing and Management* (Thousand Oaks, California: Sage Publications, 2000), 291; Alex M. Susskind, "Communication Richness: Why Some Guest Complaints Go Right to the Top—and Others Don't," *Cornell Hospitality Quarterly* 56, no. 3 (2015): 320–331.

7. John Goodman, "Basic Facts on Customer Complaint Behavior and the Impact of Service on the Bottom Line," *Competitive Advantage* (June 1999): 1–5.

8. Anna Mattila and Jochen Wirtz, "Consumer Complaining to Firms: The Determinants of Channel Choice," *Journal of Services Marketing* 18, no. 2 (2004): 147–155; Kaisa Snellman and Tiina Vihtkari, "Customer Complaining Behavior in Technology-Based Service Encounters," *International Journal of Service Industry Management* 14, no. 2 (2003): 217–231; Terri Shapiro and Jennifer Nieman-Gonder, "Effect of Communication Mode in Justice-Based Service Recovery," *Managing Service Quality* 16, no. 2 (2006): 124–144.

9. Technical Assistance Research Programs Institute (TARP), *Consumer Complaint Handling in America: An Update Study, Part II* (Washington D.C.: TARP and US Office of Consumer Affairs, 1986).

10. Thomas M. Tripp and Yany Gregoire, "When Unhappy Customers Strike Back on the Internet," *MIT Sloan Management Review* 52, no. 3 (Spring 2011): 37–44; Sven Tuzovic, "Frequent (Flier) Frustration and the Dark Side of Word-of-Web: Exploring Online Dysfunctional Behavior in Online Feedback Forums," *Journal of Services Marketing* 24, no. 6 (2010): 446–457.

11. Kathleen Seiders and Leonard L. Berry, "Service Fairness: What It Is and Why It Matters," *Academy of Management Executive* 12, no. 2 (1990): 8–20.

12. Tax and Brown, "Recovering and Learning from Service Failure," 75–88.

13. Oren Harari, "Thank Heavens for Complainers," *Management Review* (March 1997): 25–29.

14. Tom DeWitt, Doan T. Nguyen, and Roger Marshall, "Exploring Customer Loyalty Following Service Recovery," *Journal of Service Research* 10, no. 3 (2008): 269–281.

15. Simon J. Bell and James A. Luddington, "Coping with Customer Complaints," *Journal of Service Research* 8, no. 3 (February 2006): 221–233.

PART **IV**

16. Customer Care Measurement & Consulting (CCMC), *2007 National Customer Rage Study* (Customer Care Alliance, 2007).

17. Technical Assistance Research Programs Institute (TARP), *Consumer Complaint Handling in America: An Update Study, Part II* (Washington D.C.: TARP and US Office of Consumer Affairs, April 1986). Since this study, the CCMC and W. P. Carey School of Business at Arizona State University (ASU) have conducted six follow-on studies known as the "Customer Rage Studies" to explore important, emerging trends in the customer experience related to complaining behavior and service recovery. For highlights of the latest study, "The 2013 Customer Rage Study," see http://www.customercaremc.com/wp/wp-content/uploads/2014/01/KeyFindingsFrom2013NationalCustomerRageSurvey.pdf.

18. For a discussion on how to quantify complaint management profitability, see: Bernd Stauss and Andreas Schoeler, "Complaint Management Profitability: What Do Complaint Managers Know?" *Managing Service Quality* 14, no. 2–3 (2004): 147–156. For a comprehensive treatment of all aspects of effective complaint management, see Bernd Stauss and Wolfgang Seidel, *Complaint Management: The Heart of CRM* (Mason, Ohio: Thomson, 2004) and Janelle Barlow and Claus Móller, *A Complaint Is a Gift*, 2nd ed. (San Francisco, CA: Berrett-Koehler Publishers), 2008.

19. Celso Augusto de Matos, Jorge Luiz Henrique, and Carlos Alberto Vargas Rossi, "Service Recovery Paradox: A Meta-Analysis," *Journal of Service Research* 10, no. 1 (2007): 60–77; Randi Priluck and Vishal Lala, "The Impact of the Recovery Paradox on Retailer-Customer Relationships," *Managing Service Quality* 19, no. 1 (2009): 42–59.

20. Stefan Michel and Matthew L. Meuter, "The Service Recovery Paradox: True but Overrated?" *International Journal of Service Industry Management* 19, no. 4 (2008): 441–457.

21. James G. Maxham III and Richard G. Netemeyer, "A Longitudinal Study of Complaining Customers' Evaluations of Multiple Service Failures and Recovery Efforts," *Journal of Marketing* 66, no. 4 (2002): 57–72.

22. Michael Hargrove, cited in Ron Kaufman, *Up Your Service!* (Singapore: Ron Kaufman Plc. Ltd., 2005): 225.

23. Tax and Brown, "Recovering and Learning from Service Failure," 75–88; Stephen S. Tax, Stephen W. Brown, and Murali Chandrashekaran, "Customer Evaluation of Service Complaint Experiences: Implications for Relationship Marketing," *Journal of Marketing* 62, no. 2 (Spring 1998): 60–76.

24. For a discussion on how to quantify complaint management profitability, see: Stauss and Schoeler, "Complaint Management Profitability," 147–156.

25. Christian Homburg and Andreas Fürst, "How Organizational Complaint Handling Drives Customer Loyalty: An Analysis of the Mechanistic and the Organic Approach," *Journal of Marketing* 69 (July 2005): 95–114.

26. Ron Zemke and Chip R. Bell, *Knock Your Socks off Service Recovery* (New York: AMACOM, 2000), 60.

27. Barbara R. Lewis, "Customer Care in Services," in W. J. Glynn and J. G. Barnes (eds.) *Understanding Services Management* (Chichester, UK: Wiley, 1995), 57–89.

28. Josh Bernoff and Ted Schadler, "Empowered," *Harvard Business Review* (July–August 2010): 95–101.

29. Rhonda Mack, Rene Mueller, John Crotts, and Amanda Broderick, "Perceptions, Corrections and Defections: Implications for Service Recovery in the Restaurant Industry," *Managing Service Quality* 10, no. 6 (2000): 339–46.

30. Jochen Wirtz and Janet R. McColl-Kennedy, "Opportunistic Customer Claiming during Service Recovery," *Journal of the Academy of Marketing Science* 38, no. 5 (2010): 654–675.

31. Matthew Dixon, Karen Freeman, and Nicholas Toman, "Stop Trying to Delight Your Customers: To Really Win Their Loyalty, Forget the Bells and Whistles and Just Solve Their Problems," *Harvard Business Review* 88, nos 7–8 (2010): 116–122.

32. For an excellent review of extant academic literature on service guarantees, see: Jens Hogreve and Dwayne D. Gremler, "Twenty Years of Service Guarantee Research," *Journal of Service Research* 11, no. 4 (2009): 322–343.

33. Christopher W. L. Hart, "The Power of Unconditional Service Guarantees," *Harvard Business Review* (July–August 1988): 54–62.

34. L. A. Tucci and J. Talaga, "Service Guarantees and Consumers' Evaluation of Services," *Journal of Services Marketing* 11, no. 1 (1997): 10–18; Amy Ostrom and Dawn Iacobucci, "The Effect of Guarantees on Consumers' Evaluation of Services," *Journal of Services Marketing* 12, no. 5 (1998): 362–378.

35. Hart, "The Power of Unconditional Service Guarantees." 55-56.

36. Gordon H. McDougall, Terence Levesque, and Peter VanderPlaat, "Designing the Service Guarantee: Unconditional or Specific?" *Journal of Services Marketing* 12, no. 4 (1998): 278–293; Jochen Wirtz, "Development of a Service Guarantee Model," *Asia Pacific Journal of Management* 15, no. 1 (1998): 51–75.

37. Jochen Wirtz and Doreen Kum, "Designing Service Guarantees: Is Full Satisfaction the Best You Can Guarantee?" *Journal of Services Marketing* 15, no. 4 (2001): 282–299.

38. Amy L. Ostrom and Christopher Hart, "Service Guarantee: Research and Practice," in T. Schwartz and D. Iacobucci (eds.), *Handbook of Services Marketing and Management* (Thousand Oaks, California: Sage Publications, 2000), 299–316.

39. Jochen Wirtz, Doreen Kum, and Khai Sheang Lee, "Should a Firm with a Reputation for Outstanding Service Quality Offer a Service Guarantee?" *Journal of Services Marketing* 14, no. 6 (2000): 502–512.

40. This section is adapted and updated from: Christopher Lovelock, *Product Plus* (New York: McGraw-Hill, 1994), Chapter 15. For an additional discussion of jaycustomers, see: Leonard L. Berry and Kathleen Seiders, "Serving Unfair Customers," *Business Horizons* 51, no. 1 (2008): 29–37.

41. Kate L. Reynolds and Lloyd C. Harris, "When Service Failure Is Not Service Failure: An Exploration of the Forms and Motives of 'Illegitimate' Customer Complaining," *Journal of Services Marketing* 19, no. 5 (2005): 326.

42. From Kate L. Reynolds and Lloyd C. Harris, "When Service Failure Is Not Service Failure: An Exploration of the Forms and Motives of 'Illegitimate' Customer Complaining," *Journal of Services Marketing* 19(5): 321-335, © 2005 Emerald Group Publishing Limited.

43. Jill Griffin, "What Your Worst Customers Teach You about Loyalty," January 24, 2006, http://www.marketingprofs.com/6/griffin5.asp, accessed August 22, 2015.

44. Jochen Wirtz and Doreen Kum, "Consumer Cheating on Service Guarantees," *Journal of the Academy of Marketing Science* 32, no. 2 (2004): 159–175; Wirtz and McColl-Kennedy, "Opportunistic Customer Claiming during Service Recovery," 654–675.

PART IV

PART V

THE *ESM* FRAMEWORK

PART I

Understanding Service Markets, Products, and Customers

- Introduction to Services Marketing
- Consumer Behavior in a Services Context
- Positioning Services in Competitive Markets

PART II

Applying the 4 Ps of Marketing to Services

- Developing Service Products and Brands
- Distributing Services through Physical and Electronic Channels
- Setting Prices and Implementing Revenue Management
- Promoting Services and Educating Customers

PART III

Managing the Customer Interface

- Designing Service Processes
- Balancing Demand and Capacity
- Crafting the Service Environment
- Managing People for Service Advantage

PART IV

Developing Customer Relationships

- Managing Relationships and Building Loyalty
- Complaint Handling and Service Recovery

PART V

Striving for Service Excellence

- Improving Service Quality and Productivity
- Building a World-Class Service Organization

Striving for Service Excellence

Part V focuses on service quality and productivity, and how firms can achieve service leadership. It consists of the following two chapters:

Chapter 14 Improving Service Quality and Productivity

Both productivity and quality are necessary and related to financial success in services. Chapter 14 covers diagnosing quality shortfalls using the gaps model, and reviewing strategies to close quality gaps. Customer feedback systems are introduced as an effective tool for systematically listening to and learning from customers. Productivity is concerned with bringing down costs, and key approaches for increasing productivity are discussed.

Chapter 15 Building a Service Organization that Wins

This chapter covers the characteristics of world class service organizations and introduces four levels of service performance (i.e., service loser, nonentity, professional, and service leader). An audit tool is provided that helps to assess the performance level of an organization. We discuss how to move a service organization to higher levels of performance. The chapter closes with a discussion of the impact of customer satisfaction on financial performance and shareholder value.

LEARNING OBJECTIVES (LOS)

By the end of this chapter, the reader should be able to:

▶ **LO 1** Explain the relationships between service quality, productivity, and profitability.

▶ **LO 2** Be familiar with the different perspectives of service quality.

▶ **LO 3** Demonstrate how to use the Gaps Model for diagnosing and addressing service quality problems.

▶ **LO 4** Differentiate between hard and soft measures of service quality.

▶ **LO 5** Explain the common objectives of effective customer feedback systems.

▶ **LO 6** Describe key customer feedback collection tools.

▶ **LO 7** Be familiar with hard measures of service quality and control charts.

▶ **LO 8** Select suitable tools to analyze service problems.

▶ **LO 9** Understand return on quality and determine the optimal level of reliability.

▶ **LO 10** Define and measure service productivity.

▶ **LO 11** Understand the difference between productivity, efficiency, and effectiveness.

▶ **LO 12** Recommend the key methods to improve service productivity.

▶ **LO 13** Know how productivity improvements impact quality and value.

▶ **LO 14** Understand how to integrate all the tools to improve the quality and productivity of customer service processes.

▶ **LO 15** Explain how TQM, ISO 9000, Six Sigma, and the Malcolm Baldrige and EFQM approaches relate to managing and improving service quality and productivity.

Improving Service Quality in a Ferry Company[1]

Sealink British Ferries, whose routes linked Britain to Ireland and several European countries, was a poor service quality provider. Its top-down, military-style structure focused on the operational aspects of ship movements, not the quality of customers' experiences. Sealink was acquired by the Swedish company Stena Line, which is one of the world's largest car-ferry operators today. In contrast to Sealink, Stena had a whole department devoted to improving its service quality.

Before the takeover, Sealink did not focus on punctual or reliable operations, and ferries were often late. Customer complaints were ignored, and there was little pressure from customer service managers to improve the situation. After the takeover, things started to change. The ferry operator solved the problem of late departures and arrivals by concentrating on individual problem areas. On one route, for instance, the port manager involved all operational staff and gave each person responsibility over a particular aspect of the improvement process, thus creating employee "ownership." They kept detailed records of each sailing, together with reasons for late departures. They also kept track of competitors' performance. Staff members in different job positions had close links with each other. Customer service staff also learnt from experience. Within two years, the Stena ferries on this route were operating at close to 100% punctuality.

On-board service was another area singled out for improvement. Historically, customer service managers did what was convenient for staff rather than customers, such as scheduling meal breaks at times when customer demand for service was greatest. As one observer noted, "customers were ignored during the first and last half hour on board, when facilities were closed . . . Customers were left to find their own way around [the ship] . . . Staff only responded to customers when [they] initiated a direct request and made some effort to attract their attention."

Personnel from each on-board functional area had to work in small groups to improve service quality and productivity in that area. Initially, some teams were more successful than others, resulting in inconsistent levels of service from one ship to another. Subsequently, managers shared ideas and experiences, learned from each other's successes and failures, and made further changes on their individual ships. Key changes during the first two years contributed to eventual success in achieving consistent service levels on all sailings and all ferries. Together, the employees have come up with almost 1,500 improvement ideas since 2006.

By 2015, Stena Line had become one of the world's largest ferry operators, with 35 ships sailing on 22 routes, carrying over 7 million passengers and 1.5 million vehicles each year. A leader in all its markets, Stena emphasizes constant service and product improvement. Says the company's website:

> Customers must have the best possible experience when they choose Stena Line for travel, holidays, relaxation, or freight transport. The focus is firmly on constantly improving the service by, among other things, developing new and innovative products and services that create value for customers.

PART V

Integrating Service Quality and Productivity

- Quality and productivity are twin paths to creating value for customers and firms
- Service quality and productivity can reinforce, be independent or even counter each other's impact on profitability

What Is Service Quality?

- Customer defined
- Consistently meeting or exceeding customer expectations

The Gaps Model

The Gaps Model helps to identify the causes of quality problems at the macro level through a gap analysis:

- Gap 1: The Knowledge Gap
- Gap 2: The Policy Gap
- Gap 3: The Delivery Gap
- Gap 4: The Communications Gap
- Gap 5: The Perceptions Gap
- Gap 6: The Service Quality Gap

Each of the gaps has distinct causes. Prescriptions are provided on how to address the causes of each gap.

Measuring Service Quality

Customer Feedback

- Referred to as "soft measures"

Objectives:
- Assess and benchmark performance
- Improve performance by cementing strengths and improving weaknesses)
- Create a customer-oriented service culture and a culture for change

Use a mix of tools to obtain reliable and actionable feedback, such as:
- Surveys, feedback cards and online/ mobile messages, complaints and compliments
- Mystery shopping
- Focus groups and service reviews
- Online reviews and discussions

Operational Measures

- Process and outcome measures
- Referred to as "hard measures"
- Relate to process activities and outcomes that can be counted, timed or measured (e.g., system uptime, on-time departure, service response time, and failure rates)

Analysis, Reporting, and Dissemination of Customer Feedback and Operational Measures

- Daily morning briefings to the frontline
- Monthly service performance updates to process owners and service teams
- Quarterly service performance reviews to middle management and process owners
- Annual service performance reports to top management and the entire firm

Analyzing Service Quality Problems

Analytical tools:
- Fishbone diagram to conduct root cause analysis
- Pareto charts to identify key fail points and root causes
- Blueprinting

Return on quality:
- Assess costs and benefits of quality initiatives
- Importance-performance matrix
- Optimal level of reliability depends on cost of service recovery

Defining, Measuring, and Improving Service Productivity

- Productivity: output/input
- Efficiency: compared to a standard (i.e., "do things right")
- Effectiveness: compared to a goal (i.e., "do the right things")
- All three have to be balanced

Productivity improvement strategies:
- Generic strategies (i.e., "doing the same things better, faster, cheaper")
- Customer-driven approaches (e.g., shifting time of demand, using lower-cost delivery channels, and self-service)
- Outsourcing to third parties
- Monitor potential customer implications of productivity enhancement

Systematic Approaches to Improving Service Quality and Productivity

Nine-step approach to service process improvement:
1. Determine priority processes for improvement
2. Set targets for (a) customer satisfaction, (b) defects, (c) cycle-time, and (d) productivity improvements
3. Identify key elements of quality
4. Assess process performance
5. Identify quality gaps
6. Identify root causes of gaps
7. Improve process performance
8. Control and fine-tune
9. Start again; the journey is the destination...

Widely used organization-wide systematic approaches:
- Total Quality Management (TQM)
- ISO 9000 certification
- Six Sigma (including DMAIC)
- Malcolm Baldrige and EFQM approaches

Figure 14.1 Improving service quality and productivity.

INTEGRATING SERVICE QUALITY AND PRODUCTIVITY STRATEGIES

▶ **LO 1**

Explain the relationships between service quality, productivity, and profitability.

The Stena Line success story in the opening vignette is an excellent example that shows how improving service quality and productivity can turn a failing business around. We will learn in this chapter that quality and productivity are twin paths toward the creation of value for both customers and organizations. An overview of this chapter is provided in Figure 14.1.

Let's now dig deeper and examine the relationships between service quality, productivity, and profitability.

Service Quality, Productivity, and Profitability[2]

The individual relationships between service productivity, customer satisfaction (i.e., excellence), and profitability are shown in Figure 14.2. When examining the individual links, one can see that, everything being equal, higher customer satisfaction should improve the bottom line through higher repeat purchase, share of wallet, and referrals. Likewise, higher productivity should lead to higher profitability as costs are reduced.

The relationship between productivity and customer satisfaction is more complex. There is the general notion of a service productivity–customer satisfaction trade-off. However, although the relationships between productivity, service quality, and profitability can conflict, there are examples where productivity gains and customer satisfaction are aligned. For example, if a service firm redesigns customer service processes to be leaner, faster, and more convenient, then both productivity and customer satisfaction improve, and both have a direct and indirect positive effect on profitability. An example would be serve-it-yourself yogurt stores, which substitute relatively inexpensive and easy-to-use self-service machines for multiple customer-contact personnel.

In contrast, if productivity improvements result in changes in the service experience that customers do not like, customer satisfaction will drop. For example, replacing a

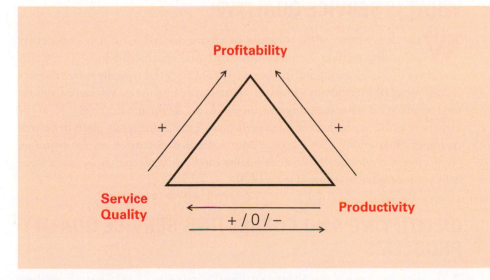

Figure 14.2 The Service Quality–Productivity–Profit Triangle.

Figure 14.3 Service quality can be difficult to manage for the fussy diner.

human agent in a customer-contact center with an interactive voice response system to reduce head count, doubling class sizes to increase the productivity of university professors, and reducing the frequency of trains to increase load factors can all have negative implications for the customer experience. In these cases, productivity enhancements have an immediate and direct positive effect on profitability. However, they also result in lower customer satisfaction, which over the medium to long term is likely to lead to lower customer loyalty and referrals.

Likewise, marketing strategies designed to improve customer satisfaction can prove costly and disruptive if the implications for operations and human resources have not been carefully thought through. For example, increasing head count in a customer-contact center or increasing the frequency of trains for the convenience of passengers will have direct and positive medium- to long-term effects on profitability via customer loyalty. However, these changes will also have an immediate, negative, and indirect effect on profitability via reduced productivity. The net result on profitability in both cases depends on the relative impact of the direct and indirect effects.

Finally, some quality improvements may not have any implications for productivity (e.g., improving a process in the front office that does not change the cost of providing it) and vice versa (e.g., improving the efficiency of back-office operations that do not have implications for customer touch points). In these cases, there is only a single positive effect of productivity or quality improvements on profitability.

One can therefore see that the relationship between productivity and customer satisfaction can be positive, neutral, or negative. In broad terms, quality focuses on the benefits created for the customer's side of the equation, and productivity addresses the financial costs incurred by the firm. If not properly integrated, these two foci can be in conflict. The bottom line is that strategies for improving service quality and productivity must be considered jointly rather than in isolation. Let's first examine how to improve service quality before we turn to productivity.

◯ LO 2

Be familiar with the different perspectives of service quality.

WHAT IS SERVICE QUALITY?

What do we mean when we speak of service quality? Common perspectives on quality include the manufacturing-based approach, which is primarily concerned with engineering and manufacturing practices and typically means delivery against measurable standards within certain tolerance levels (e.g., tolerance levels for weld seams in car manufacturing). In this book, we define service quality from the user's perspective as a high standard of performance that consistently meets or exceeds customer expectations. (See Chapter 2 for a detailed discussion on the customer perspective of service quality.) Service quality can be difficult to manage, even when failures are tangible in nature (Figure 14.3).

IDENTIFYING AND CORRECTING SERVICE QUALITY PROBLEMS

Let us explore a model that allows us to identify and correct service quality problems at the overall firm level.

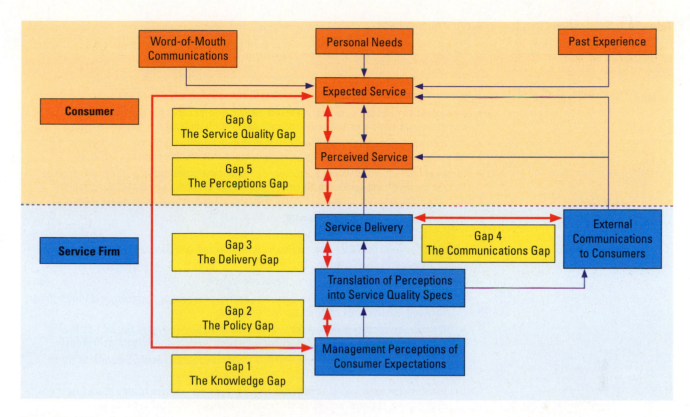

Figure 14.4 The Gaps Model.

SOURCE

Adapted and extended from: Valarie A. Zeithaml, A. Parasuraman, and Leonard L. Berry, *Delivering Service Quality: Balancing Customer Perceptions and Expectations*. New York: The Free Press, 1990, Chapters 4–7; and Valarie A. Zeithaml, Mary Jo Bitner, and Dwayne D. Gremler, *Services Marketing: Integrating Customer Focus across the Firm*, 5th ed. New York: McGraw-Hill, 2013, Chapter 2. The remaining prescriptions were developed by the authors.

The Gaps Model in Service Design and Delivery

Valarie Zeithaml, A. Parasuraman, and Leonard Berry identified four potential gaps within the service organization that may lead to the fifth and most serious gap—the difference between what customers expected and what they perceived was delivered.[3] Figure 14.4 extends and refines their framework to identify six types of gaps that can occur at different points during the design and delivery of a service performance. Let's explore the six gaps in greater detail:

▶ **Gap 1:** The **knowledge gap** is the difference between what senior management believes customers expect and what customers actually need and expect.

▶ **Gap 2:** The **policy gap** is the difference between the management's understanding of customers' expectations and the service standards they set for service delivery. We call it the policy gap because the management has made a policy decision not to deliver what they think customers expect. Reasons for setting standards below customer expectations are typically cost and feasibility considerations.

▶ **Gap 3:** The **delivery gap** is the difference between specified service standards and the service delivery teams' actual performance on these standards.

LO 3

Demonstrate how to use the Gaps Model for diagnosing and addressing service quality problems.

PART V

Table 14.1 Suggestions for closing service quality gaps.

Types of Quality Gap	Proposed Solutions
Gap 1: The Knowledge Gap	*Suggestion: Educate Management about What Customers Expect* • Implement an effective customer feedback system that includes satisfaction research, complaint and compliment content analysis, customer panels, and online monitoring. • Sharpen market research procedures (including questionnaire and interview design, sampling, and field implementation) and repeat research studies once in a while. • Increase interactions between customers and senior management (e.g., programs such as "day in the field" and senior management taking calls in customer-contact centers). • Improve upward communications, and facilitate and encourage communication between front-line employees and management.

Gap 2: The Policy Gap	*Suggestion: Establish the Right Service Products, Processes, and Standards That Are Based on Customer Needs and Expectations*
	• Get the products and customer service processes right:
	  – Use a rigorous, systematic, and customer-centric process for designing and redesigning service products and customer service processes.
	  – Standardize repetitive work tasks to ensure consistency and reliability by substituting hard technology for human contact and improving work methods (soft technology).
	• Set, communicate, and reinforce measurable customer-oriented service standards for all work units:
	  – Establish for each step in service delivery a set of clear service quality goals that are challenging, realistic, and explicitly designed to meet customer expectations.
	  – Ensure that employees understand and accept goals, standards, and priorities.
	• Develop tiered service products that meet customer expectations:
	  – Consider premium, standard, and economy-level products to allow customers to self-segment according to their needs, or
	  – Offer customers different levels of service at different prices.

Gap 3: The Delivery Gap	*Suggestion: Ensure That Performance Meets Standards*
	• Ensure that customer service teams are motivated and able to meet service standards:
	  – Improve recruitment with a focus on employee–job fit; select employees for the abilities and skill needed to perform their job well.
	  – Train employees on the technical and soft skills needed to perform their assigned tasks effectively, including interpersonal skills, especially for dealing with customers under stressful conditions.
	  – Clarify employee roles, and ensure that employees understand how their jobs contribute to customer satisfaction; teach them about customer expectations, perceptions, and problems.
	  – Build cross-functional service teams that can offer customer-centric service delivery and problem resolution, including effective service recovery.
	  – Empower managers and employees in the field by pushing decision-making power down the organization.
	  – Measure performance; provide regular feedback; and reward customer service team performance as well as individual employees and managers for attaining quality goals.
	• Install the right technology, equipment, support processes, and capacity:
	  – Select the most appropriate technologies and equipment for enhanced performance.
	  – Ensure that employees working on internal support jobs provide good service to their own internal customer, the front-line personnel.
	  – Balance demand against productive capacity.
	• Manage customers for service quality:
	  – Educate customers so that they can perform their roles and responsibilities in service delivery effectively.

Types of Quality Gap	Proposed Solutions

Gap 3: The Delivery Gap (*continued*)	• Effectively align intermediaries and third parties involved in service delivery:
	  – Align objectives, performance, costs, and rewards with intermediaries (as in outsourced service delivery in customer-contact centers or airline check-in counters).
	  – Monitor and incentivize service quality.

Gap 4: The Communications Gap	*Suggestion: Close the Internal and External Communications Gaps by Ensuring That Communication Promises Are Realistic and Correctly Understood by Customers*
	• Ensure that communications content sets realistic customer expectations, and educate managers responsible for sales and marketing communications about operational capabilities:
	  – Seek inputs from front-line employees and operations personnel when new communications programs are developed.
	  – Let service providers preview advertisements and other communications before customers are exposed to them.
	  – Get sales staff to involve operations staff in face-to-face meetings with customers.
	  – Develop internal educational and motivational campaigns to strengthen understanding and integration among the marketing, operations, and human resource functions and to standardize service delivery across different locations.
	• Align incentives for sales teams with those of service delivery teams. This will avoid the problem where the sale teams focus exclusively on generating sales (e.g., through over-promising) and neglect customer satisfaction (e.g., through disappointed expectations).
	• Be specific with promises, and manage customers' understanding of communication content:
	  – Pre-test all advertising, brochures, telephone scripts, and website content prior to external release to see if the target audience interprets them as the firm intends (if not, revise and retest). Make sure that the advertising content reflects those service characteristics that are most important to customers. Let them know what is and is not possible and why.
	  – Identify and explain, in real time, the reasons for shortcomings in service performance, highlighting those that cannot be controlled by the firm.
	  – Document beforehand what tasks and performance guarantees are included in an agreement or contract.

Gap 5: The Perception Gap	*Suggestion: Tangibilize and Communicate the Service Quality Delivered*
	• Make service quality tangible and communicate the service quality delivered:
	  – Develop service environments and physical evidence cues that are consistent with the level of service provided.
	  – For complex and credence services, keep customers informed during service delivery on what is being done, and give debriefings after the delivery so that customers can appreciate the quality of service they received.
	  – After completion of the work, explain what work was performed in relation to a specific billing statement.
	  – Provide physical evidence (e.g., for repairs, show customers the damaged components that were removed).

Gap 6: The Service Gap	*Suggestion: Close Gaps 1 to 5 to Consistently Meet Customer Expectations* • Gap 6 is the accumulated outcome of all the preceding gaps. It will be closed when Gaps 1 to 5 have been addressed.

▶ **Gap 4:** The **communications gap** is the difference between what the company communicates and what the customer understands and subsequently experiences. This gap is caused by two sub-gaps.[4] First, the *internal* communications gap is the difference between what the company's advertising and sales personnel think the product's features, performance, and service quality level are and what the company is actually able to deliver. Second, the *external* communications gap (also referred to as the over-promise gap) can be caused by advertising and sales personnel being assessed by the sales they generate. This can lead them to over-promise in order to generate sales.

▶ **Gap 5:** The **perceptions gap** is the difference between what is actually delivered and what customers feel they have received because they are unable to judge service quality accurately.

▶ **Gap 6:** The **service quality gap** is the difference between what customers expect to receive and their perception of the service that is actually delivered.

In this model, Gaps 1, 5, and 6 represent external gaps between the customer and the organization. Gaps 2, 3, and 4 are internal gaps occurring between various functions and departments within the organization.

Key Ways to Close the Gaps in Service Quality

Gaps at any point in service design and delivery can damage relationships with customers. The service quality gap (Gap 6) is the most critical. Hence, the ultimate goal in improving service quality is to close or narrow this gap as much as possible. However, to achieve this, service organizations usually need to work on closing the other five gaps depicted in Figure 14.4.

The strength of the Gaps Model is that it offers generic insights and solutions that can be applied across industries. We summarize a series of generic prescriptions for closing the six quality gaps in Table 14.1. These prescriptions are a good starting point to think about how to close specific gaps in an organization. Later in this chapter, we will discuss the nuts and bolts of how to do this at the micro or process level.

MEASURING SERVICE QUALITY

It is commonly said that "what is not measured is not managed." Without measurement, managers cannot be sure whether service quality gaps exist, let alone what types of gaps, where they exist, and what potential corrective actions should be taken.

LO 4

Differentiate between hard and soft measures of service quality.

Soft and Hard Service Quality Measures

Customer-defined standards and measures of service quality can be grouped into two broad categories: "soft" and "hard." Soft standards and their measures are those that cannot be easily observed and are typically collected by talking to customers. Soft standards "provide direction, guidance, and feedback to employees on how to achieve customer satisfaction, and they can be quantified by measuring customer perceptions and beliefs."[5] SERVQUAL (see Chapter 2) is an example of a sophisticated soft measurement system. We will discuss a variety of other customer feedback tools later in this chapter.

Hard standards and measures, in contrast, are typically process activities and outcomes that can be counted, timed, or measured. Such measures may include the number of orders that were filled correctly, the time required to complete a specific task, and the number of minutes customers had to wait in line at a particular stage in the service delivery. Standards are often set with reference to the percentage of occasions on which a particular measure is achieved. The challenge for service marketers is to ensure that operational measures of service quality reflect customer needs and wants (Figure 14.5).

Figure 14.5 Social media such as Facebook and Twitter have been deployed by organizations to gather valuable feedback from customers.

LEARNING FROM CUSTOMER FEEDBACK[6]

How can companies measure their performance against soft standards of service quality? Let's first review the objectives of measurement before we turn to the different types of measures.

Key Objectives of Effective Customer Feedback Systems

▶ **LO 5**
Explain the common objectives of effective customer feedback systems.

"It is not the strongest species that survive, nor the most intelligent, but the ones most responsive to change," wrote Charles Darwin. Similarly, many strategists have concluded that in increasingly competitive markets, the best competitive advantage for a firm is to learn and change faster than the competition.[7]

Customer feedback is a key input for becoming and remaining a customer-driven learning organization, and effective customer feedback systems facilitate fast learning. Their objectives typically fall into the following three main categories:

1) **Assessment and Benchmarking of Service Quality and Performance.** The objective is to answer the question, "How satisfied are our customers?" This includes learning about how well a firm has performed in comparison to its main competitor(s) or in comparison to the previous year (or quarter, or month), whether investments in certain service aspects have paid off in terms of customer satisfaction, and where the firm wants to be the following year. Often, a key objective of comparison against other units (branches, teams, service products, competitors) is to motivate managers and service staff to improve performance, especially when the results are linked to compensation.

2) **Customer-Driven Learning and Improvements.** Here, the objective is to answer the questions, "What makes our customers happy or unhappy?" and "What are the strengths we want to cement and the weaknesses we need to improve on?" More specific or detailed information on processes and products is required to guide a firm's service improvement efforts.

3) **Creating a Customer-Oriented Service Culture.** This objective is concerned with bringing the "voice of the customer" into the organization, focusing the organization on customer needs and customer satisfaction, and rallying the entire organization toward a service quality culture. It also includes fostering a culture of continuous improvement and change.

Table 14.2 Strengths and weaknesses of key customer feedback collection tools.

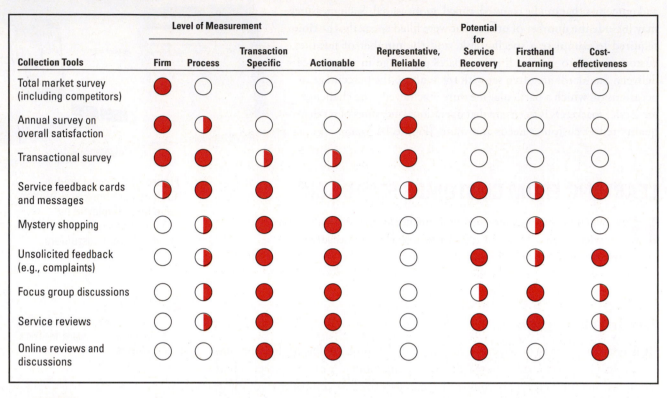

Collection Tools	Level of Measurement			Actionable	Representative, Reliable	Potential for Service Recovery	Firsthand Learning	Cost-effectiveness
	Firm	Process	Transaction Specific					
Total market survey (including competitors)	●	○	○	○	●	○	○	○
Annual survey on overall satisfaction	●	◐	○	○	●	○	○	○
Transactional survey	●	●	◐	◐	●	○	○	○
Service feedback cards and messages	◐	●	◐	●	◐	●	●	●
Mystery shopping	○	◐	●	●	○	○	◐	○
Unsolicited feedback (e.g., complaints)	○	◐	●	●	○	●	◐	●
Focus group discussions	○	◐	●	●	○	◐	●	◐
Service reviews	○	◐	●	●	○	●	●	◐
Online reviews and discussions	○	○	●	●	○	●	○	●

Legend: ● meets requirements fully; ◐ moderately; ○ hardly at all

SOURCE

From Jochen Wirtz and Monica Tomlin, "Institutionalizing Customer-driven Learning through Fully Integrated Customer Feedback Systems," *Managing Service Quality* 10(4): 210, © 2000 Emerald Group Publishing Ltd.

LO 6

Describe key customer feedback collection tools.

Use a Mix of Customer Feedback Collection Tools

Renee Fleming, soprano and America's beautiful voice, once said: "We singers are unfortunately not able to hear ourselves sing. You sound entirely different to yourself. We need the ears of others—from outside." Likewise, firms need to listen to the voice

Figure 14.6 Qualitative and quantitative feedback collection tools complement each other.

of the customer. Table 14.2 gives an overview of typically used feedback tools and their ability to meet various requirements. Recognizing that different tools have different strengths and weaknesses, service marketers should select a mix of customer feedback collection tools that jointly deliver the needed information (Figure 14.6). As Leonard Berry and A. Parasuraman observed, "Combining approaches enables a firm to tap the strengths of each and compensate for weaknesses."[8]

Total Market, Annual, and Transactional Surveys. *Total market surveys* and *annual surveys* typically measure satisfaction with all major customer service processes and products.[9] The level of measurement is usually high, with the objective of obtaining a global index or indicator of overall service satisfaction for the entire firm. Overall indices such as these tell us how satisfied customers are but not why they are happy or unhappy. There are limits to the number of questions that can be asked about each individual process or product. For example, a typical retail bank may have 30–50 key customer service processes (e.g., from car loan applications and cash deposits at the teller to online banking). Due to the sheer number of processes, many surveys have room for only one or two questions per process (e.g., how satisfied are you with our ATM services?) and cannot address issues in greater detail.

In contrast, *transactional surveys*, also called intercept surveys, are typically conducted after customers have completed a specific transaction (Figure 14.7). At this point, if time permits, they may be queried about the process in some depth. In the case of a bank, all key attributes and aspects of ATM services could be included in the survey, including some open-ended questions such as "liked best," "liked least," and "suggested improvements." Such feedback is more actionable, can tell the firm why customers are happy or unhappy with the service, and usually yields specific insights on how customer satisfaction can be improved.

Figure 14.7 Transactional surveys are typically conducted after service delivery.

Figure 14.8 Point-of-transaction terminals have become common in airports, hotels, and government offices around the world.

Many market research agencies offer cost-effective e-mail, SMS, electronic terminal, and app-based transactional survey tools. For example, after checking out of a hotel, guests receive an automated e-mail or message with a link to an online survey. Monthly online reports are then automatically generated for the hotel group at the overall level, for each of the individual hotels in a chain, and even for individual units within each hotel (e.g., front desk, rooms, room service, restaurants, spa, and gym). Such solutions are fully automated and can therefore be provided at a low cost (as low as $100 per hotel per month in a large chain).

Similarly, point-of-transaction surveys on terminals allow the measurement of customer satisfaction on key attributes immediately after a transaction has taken place (Figure 14.8). Again, the collection, analysis, and reporting are fully automated and cost-effective. The analysis can even be broken down to the individual service employee as they sign out of their service terminal.

All three survey types are representative and reliable when designed properly. Representativeness and reliability are required for:

1) Accurate assessments of where a company, process, branch, team, or individual stands relative to quality goals. It is important to have a representative and reliable sample so as to ensure that observed changes in quality scores are not the result of sample biases and/or random errors.

2) Evaluations of individual service employees, service delivery teams, branches, and/or processes, especially when incentive schemes are linked to such measures. The methodology has to be water-tight if employees are to trust and buy into the results, especially when surveys deliver bad news.

The potential for service recovery is important and should, if possible, be designed into feedback collection tools. However, many surveys promise anonymity, making it impossible to identify and respond to dissatisfied respondents.

Service Feedback Cards, Online and Mobile Messages. These powerful and inexpensive tools involve providing customers the opportunity to use feedback cards, online forms, e-mail, text messaging, or apps[10] to provide feedback, typically to a central customer feedback unit (Figure 14.9). For example, a feedback card can be attached to each housing loan approval letter or to each hospital invoice. These cards are a good indicator of process quality and yield specific feedback on what works well and what doesn't. However, customers who are delighted or very dissatisfied are likely to be over-represented among the respondents, and this affects the reliability and representativeness of the tool.

Figure 14.9 The widespread use of SMS text messaging allows for convenient mobile feedback.

Mystery Shopping. Service businesses often use "mystery shoppers" to determine whether front-line staff displays desired behaviors (see Service Insights 14.1). Banks, retailers, car-rental firms, and hotels are among the industries making active use of mystery shoppers. For example, the central reservation offices of a global hotel chain may appoint a research agency to conduct a large-scale monthly mystery-caller survey to assess the skills of individual associates in relation to the phone sales process. Actions such as the correct positioning of the various products, up-selling and cross-selling, and closing the deal are measured. The survey also examines the quality of the phone conversation on such dimensions as "a warm and friendly greeting" and "establishing rapport with the caller." Mystery shopping provides highly actionable and in-depth insights for coaching, training, and performance evaluation.

SERVICE INSIGHTS 14.1

Customers as Quality Control Inspectors?

Mystery shopping is a good method for checking whether front-line employees display the desired and trained behaviors and follow the specified service procedures, but customer surveys should not be used for this purpose. Ron Kaufman, founder of Up Your Service! College, describes a service experience:

"We had a wonderful ride in the hotel car from the airport. The driver was so friendly. He gave us a cold towel and a cool drink. He offered a choice of music, talked about the weather, and made sure we were comfortable with the air conditioning. His smile and good feelings washed over us, and I liked it!"

"At the hotel, I signed the guest registration and gave my credit card. Then the counter staff asked me to complete another form." It read:

Limousine Survey

To consistently ensure the proper application of our quality standards, we value your feedback on our limousine service:

1.	Were you greeted by our airport representative?	YES/NO
2.	Were you offered a cold towel?	YES/NO
3.	Were you offered cold water?	YES/NO
4.	Was a selection of music available?	YES/NO
5.	Did the driver ask you about the air conditioning?	YES/NO
6.	Was the driver driving at a safe speed?	YES/NO

Room Number: _____

Limo Number: _____

Date: _____

Kaufman continued: "As I read the form, all the good feelings fell away. The driver's enthusiasm suddenly seemed a charade. His concern for our well-being became just a checklist of actions to follow. His good mood was merely an act to meet the standard, not a connection with his guests. I felt like the hotel's quality control inspector, and I did not like it. If the hotel wants my opinion, make me an advisor, not an inspector. Ask me: What did you enjoy most about your ride from the airport? (I'd told them about their wonderful driver). What else could we do to make your ride even more enjoyable? (I'd have recommended offering the use of a cell phone)."

As the number of mystery calls or visits is typically small, no individual survey is reliable or representative. However, if a particular staff member performs well (or poorly) month after month, managers can infer with reasonable confidence that this person's performance is good (or poor).

Unsolicited Customer Feedback. Customer complaints, compliments, and suggestions can be transformed into a stream of information that can be used to monitor quality and highlight necessary improvements to the service design and delivery.

Like feedback cards, unsolicited feedback is not a reliable measure of overall customer satisfaction, but it is a good source of ideas for improvement. If the main objective of collecting feedback is to get ideas on what to improve (rather than for benchmarking and/or assessing staff), reliability and representativeness are not essential. More qualitative tools such as complaints, compliments, or focus groups generally suffice.

Furthermore, detailed customer complaint and compliment letters, recorded telephone conversations, and direct feedback from employees can serve as an excellent tool for communicating internally what customers want. They allow employees and managers at all levels to "listen" to customers first hand. Such learning is much more powerful for shaping the thinking and customer orientation of service staff than using "clinical" statistics and reports. For example, Singapore Airlines prints excerpts from complaint and compliment letters in its monthly employee magazine, *Outlook*. Seeing actual customers giving comments about their service (positive and negative) leaves a much deeper and lasting impression on staff members than any statistical analysis and encourages them to improve further.

For complaints, suggestions, and inquiries to be useful as research input, they have to be funneled into a central collection point, logged, categorized, and analyzed.[11] This requires a system for capturing customer feedback where it is made and then reporting it to a central unit. Some firms use a simple intranet site to record all feedback received by any staff member. Coordinating such activities is not a simple matter because of the many entry points, including the firm's own front-line employees who may be in contact with customers face to face, by telephone, via mail or e-mail, or through intermediary organizations acting on behalf of the original supplier. Managers normally work back stage, but they may be contacted by a customer seeking higher authority.

Focus Group Discussions and Service Reviews. Both tools give specific insights on potential service improvements and ideas. Typically, focus groups are organized by key customer segments or user groups to drill down on the needs of these users. Service reviews are in-depth, one-on-one interviews that are usually conducted once a year with a firm's most valuable customers (Figure 14.10). Typically, a senior executive of the firm visits the customer and discusses issues such as how well the firm performed the previous year and what should be maintained or changed. The senior executive then goes back to the organization and discusses the feedback with account managers. Subsequently, both write a letter to the client detailing how the firm will respond to their service needs and how the account will be managed the following year.

Figure 14.10 Service reviews being conducted with an important B2B customer.

Apart from providing an excellent learning opportunity (especially when the reviews across all customers are compiled and analyzed), service reviews focus on retention of the most valuable customers and get high marks for service recovery potential.

Online Reviews and Discussions. User-generated content and data can increasingly provide rich insights into the quality perceptions of a firm and its competitors. They also show how these comparisons vary over time at an increasingly granular attribute and temporal level.[12] Sentiment analysis of postings and automated text processing often allow real time insights into changes in consumer perceptions.[13] As one study showed, monitoring online sentiments has been shown to be a leading indicator of offline brand tracking surveys and even stock market prices.[14] Online monitoring tools combined with big data analytics allow real-time sensing of information. Location-based and user-generated content will be analyzed increasingly using techniques such as text mining, image processing and classification, social geo-tagging, human annotations, and geo-mapping.[15]

However, such analyses should be seen as augmenting more traditional tools such as surveys and focus groups. Consider the following example. A high-quality, high-priced grab-and-go-food business showed high growth (i.e., their customers must have loved what they offer), but online reviews were critical (e.g., "If you have money to spare, you could do worse" and "The prices are seriously whacked"), and its rating on an important review website was only three out of five stars.

One of the co-owners then attended a meeting of elite reviewers of this site and, to his surprise, found that these reviewers looked nothing like their customers, who tended to be professionals in their 30s or older. These reviewers were mostly in their 20s, had ample spare time to write free reviews, and seemed much less affluent than the firm's customers. The co-owner learned from his conversations with these reviewers

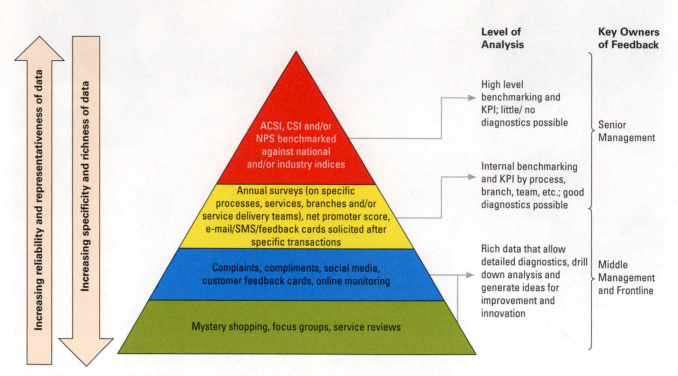

Legend: ACSI = American Customer Satisfaction Index; CSI = Customer Satisfaction Index, typically at the firm level; NPS = Net Promoter Score.

Figure 14.11 Mapping reporting of tools to levels of management.

that they were highly price-sensitive and were not willing to pay premium prices for premium food. These factors undoubtedly colored their reviews. In fact, they liked the food, but they downgraded the business as they felt the price was too high. The management of this firm responded to these findings with increasing investment in traditional focus groups to ensure that they respond to the needs of their core market.[16] Not relying too much on online user-generated content seems especially important if a firm's core target segments are expected to differ from those people who post online comments.

Analysis, Reporting, and Dissemination of Customer Feedback

Choosing the relevant feedback tools and collecting customer feedback is meaningless if the company is unable to disseminate the information to the relevant parties and take action. Hence, to drive continuous improvement and learning, a reporting system needs to deliver feedback and its analysis to front-line staff, process owners, branch or department managers, and top management. Figure 14.11 provides an overview on the types of information that should go to different key stakeholders in the organization. It also illustrates how the different tools complement each other: the top-level tools provide the benchmarking over time and against competition, and the lower-level tools help to identify which ratings go up or down and generate insights and ideas on how the service can be improved.

The feedback loop to the front line should be immediate for complaints and compliments, as is practiced in a number of service businesses where complaints, compliments, and suggestions are discussed with staff during a daily morning brief. In addition, we recommend three types of service performance reports to provide the information necessary for service management and team learning:

1) A monthly *Service Performance Update* provides process owners with timely feedback on customer comments and operational process performance. Here, the verbatim feedback should be passed on to the process managers, who can in turn discuss it with their service delivery teams.

2) A quarterly *Service Performance Review* provides process owners and branch or department managers with trends in process performance and service quality.

3) An annual *Service Performance Report* gives top management a representative assessment of the status and long-term trends relating to customer satisfaction with the firm's services.

These reports should be short and reader-friendly, focus on key indicators, and provide an easily understood commentary for the people in charge to act on. In addition to customer feedback, these reports should also contain key operational measures (as discussed in the next section).

HARD MEASURES OF SERVICE QUALITY

> **LO 7**
> Be familiar with hard measures of service quality and control charts.

Having learnt about the various tools for collecting soft service quality measures, let's explore hard measures in greater detail. Hard measures typically refer to operational processes or outcomes and include such data as uptime, service response times, and failure rates. In a complex service operation, multiple measures of service quality will be recorded at many different points. In low-contact services in which customers are not deeply involved in the service delivery process, many operational measures apply to back-stage activities that have only a second-order effect on customers.

FedEx was one of the first service companies to understand the need for a firm-wide index of service quality that embraced all the key activities that affect customers. By publishing a single, composite index on a frequent basis, senior managers hoped that all FedEx employees would work toward improving quality. The firm recognized the danger of using percentages as targets, because they might lead to complacency. In an organization as large as FedEx, which ships millions of packages a day, even delivering 99.9% of packages on time (which would mean one in 1,000 packages is delivered late) or having 99.999% of flights arrive safely would lead to horrendous problems. Instead, the company decided to approach quality measurement from the baseline of zero failures (see Service Insights 14.2). As noted by a senior executive:

> It's only when you examine the types of failures, the number that occur of each type, and the reasons why, that you begin to improve the quality of your service. For us the trick was to express quality failures in absolute numbers. That led us to develop the Service Quality Index or SQI [pronounced "sky"], which takes each of 12 different events that occur every day, takes the numbers of those events and multiplies them by a weight . . . based on the amount of aggravation caused to customers—as evidenced by their tendency to write to FedEx and complain about them.[17]

PART V

FedEx's Approach to Listening to the Voice of the Customer

As a company, FedEx believed in the beginning that service quality must be mathematically measured. The company has a commitment to clear quality goals and continuously measures its progress against those goals. This practice forms the foundation of its approach to quality.

FedEx initially set two ambitious quality goals: 100% customer satisfaction for every interaction and transaction and 100% service performance on every package handled. Customer satisfaction was measured by the percentage of on-time deliveries, which referred to the number of packages delivered on time as a percentage of total package volume. However, as things turned out, percentage of on-time delivery was an internal standard that was not synonymous with customer satisfaction.

Since FedEx had systematically cataloged customer complaints, it was able to develop a "Hierarchy of Horrors." This referred to the eight most common complaints by customers: (1) wrong-day delivery, (2) right day, late delivery, (3) pick-up not made (4) lost package, (5) customer misinformed, (6) billing and paperwork mistakes, (7) employee performance failures, and (8) damaged packages. In other words, the design of this "hard" index reflected the findings of extensive "soft" customer research. The "Hierarchy of Horrors" was the foundation on which FedEx built its customer feedback system.

FedEx refined the list of "horrors" and developed its SQI, a 12-item measure of satisfaction and service quality from the customers' viewpoint. The raw numbers of each event are multiplied by a weight that highlights the seriousness of that event for customers (see Table 14.3). The result is a point score for each item. The points are then added up to generate that day's index. Like a golf score, the lower the index, the better the performance. However, unlike golf, the SQI involves substantial numbers—typically six figures—reflecting the huge numbers of packages shipped daily. The total SQI and all its 12 items are tracked daily, so that a continuous index can be computed.

An annual goal is set for the average daily SQI, based on reducing the occurrence of failures from the previous year's total. To ensure a continuing focus on each

Table 14.3 Composition of the FedEx Service Quality Index (SQI) in an early rendition.

Failure Type	Weighting Factor × No. of Incidents = Daily Points
Late delivery—right day	1
Late delivery—wrong day	5
Tracing requests unanswered	1
Complaints reopened	5
Missing proofs of delivery	1
Invoice adjustments	1
Missed pickups	10
Lost packages	10
Damaged packages	10
Aircraft delays (minutes)	5
Overgoods (packages missing labels)	5
Abandoned calls	1
Total failure points (SQI)	XXX,XXX

separate component of the SQI, FedEx established 12 Quality Action Teams, one for each component. The teams were charged with understanding and correcting the root causes underlying the observed problems.

In addition to the SQI, which has been modified over time to reflect changes in procedures, services, and customer priorities, FedEx uses a variety of other ways to capture feedback.

Loyalty and Satisfaction Survey. This electronic survey is conducted annually with several thousand shippers and recipients who are randomly selected and stratified into key business as well as geographic segments. The results are relayed to senior management.

Targeted Customer Satisfaction Surveys (Moments of Truth). There are a number of ongoing customer surveys that measure specific customer processes with periodic reporting. These surveys target customers with a recent specific experience with particular aspects of FedEx processes.

Online Customer Feedback Surveys. FedEx conducts specific online customer surveys of people who have interacted with various aspects of the FedEx website and other forms of technology.

Customer Service. Customer service monitors the types of and reasons for phone calls to the FedEx toll-free number for purposes of evaluating and measuring problem phone calls.

Ad Hoc Research. FedEx conducts ad hoc research to determine acceptance of new products, testing of potential products and services, brand and reputation analysis, and advertising research.

The information from these various customer feedback measures has helped FedEx to maintain a leadership role in its industry. It has also played an important role in enabling the company to receive the prestigious Malcolm Baldrige National Quality Award.

SOURCE

"Blueprints for Service Quality: The Federal Express Approach," *AMA Management Briefing* (New York: American Management Association, 1991), 51–64; Linda Rosencrance, "BetaSphere Delivers FedEx Some Customer Feedback," *Computerworld* 14, no. 14 (2000): 36; Madan Birla, *Fedex Delivers: How the World's Leading Shipping Company Keeps Innovating and Outperforming the Competition* (John Wiley, 2005), 91–92; Madan Birla, *FedEx Delivers: How the World's Leading Shipping Company Keeps Innovating and Outperforming the Competition* (Wiley, 2013).

How can we show performance on hard measures? *Control charts* are a simple method of displaying performance over time against specific quality standards. The charts can be used to monitor and communicate individual variables or an overall index. Since they are visual, trends are easily identified. Figure 14.12 shows an airline's performance

Flights Departing within 15 Minutes of Schedule

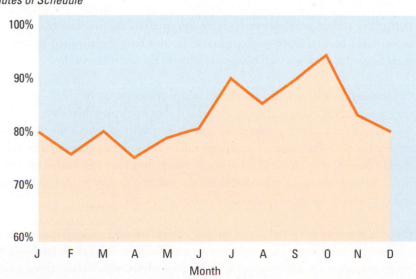

Figure 14.12 Control chart for departure delays showing percentage of flights departing within 15 minutes of schedule

on the important hard standard of on-time departures. The trends displayed suggest that this issue needs to be addressed by management, as performance is erratic and not very satisfactory. Of course, control charts are only as good as the data on which they are based.

LO 8

Select suitable tools to analyze service problems.

TOOLS TO ANALYZE AND ADDRESS SERVICE QUALITY PROBLEMS

After having assessed service quality using soft and hard measures, how can we drill deeper to identify common causes of quality shortfalls and take corrective actions? When a problem is caused by controllable, internal forces, there's no excuse for allowing it to recur. After all, maintaining customers' goodwill after a service failure depends on keeping promises made to the effect that "we're taking steps to ensure that it doesn't happen again!" With prevention as a goal, let's look briefly at some tools for determining the root causes of specific service quality problems.

Root Cause Analysis: The Fishbone Diagram

Cause-and-effect analysis uses a technique first developed by the Japanese quality expert, Kaoru Ishikawa. Managers and staff brainstorm all the possible reasons that might cause a specific problem. The reasons are then grouped into one of five categories—Equipment, Manpower (or People), Material, Procedures, and Other—on a cause-and-effect chart, popularly known as a fishbone diagram because of its shape. This technique was initially used in manufacturing but is now widely used for services.

To apply this tool better to service organizations, we show an extended framework that has eight rather than five groupings.[18] "People" has been further broken down into "Front-Stage Personnel" and "Back-Stage Personnel." This highlights the fact that front-stage service problems are often experienced directly by customers, whereas back-stage failures tend to show up more obliquely through a ripple effect.

In addition, "Information" has been separated from "Procedures," recognizing the fact that many service problems result from information failures. For example, failures often occur because front-stage personnel do not have the required information at their fingertips or do not tell customers what to do and when to do it.

"Customers" have been added as a further source of root causes. In a high-contact service, they are involved in front-stage operations. If they don't play their own role correctly, they may reduce service productivity and cause quality problems for themselves and other customers. For instance, an aircraft can be delayed if a passenger tries to board at the last minute with an oversized suitcase, which then has to be loaded into the cargo hold. An example of the extended fishbone is shown in Figure 14.13, displaying 27 possible reasons for late departures of passenger aircraft.[19]

Once all the main potential causes for flight delays have been identified, it is necessary to assess the impact that each cause has on actual delays. This can be established using frequency counts in combination with Pareto analysis, which is discussed next.

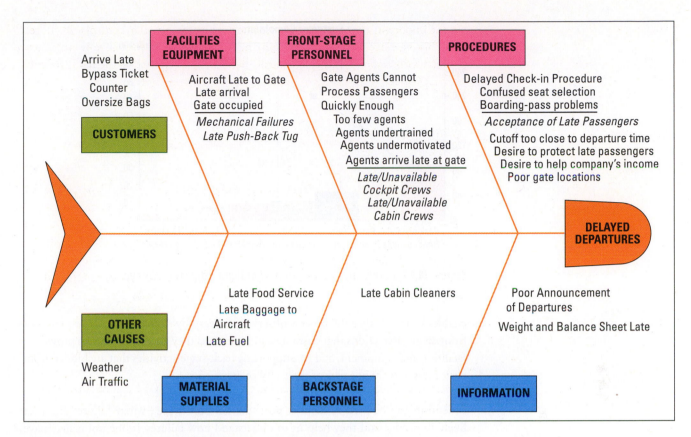

Figure 14.13 Cause-and-effect chart for flight departure delays.

Pareto Analysis

Pareto Analysis (so named after the Italian economist who first developed it) identifies the main causes of observed outcomes. It separates the important from the trivial and helps a service firm to focus its improvement efforts on the most important problem areas. This type of analysis underlies the so-called 80/20 rule, because it often reveals that around 80% of the value of one variable (in this instance, number of service failures) is caused by only 20% of the causal variables (i.e., number of possible causes as identified by the fishbone diagram). By combining the fishbone diagram and Pareto analysis, we can identify the main causes of service failure.

In the airline example, findings showed that 88% of late departures from the airports served by the company were caused by only four (15%) of all the possible factors (see Figure 14.14). In fact, more than half the delays were caused by a single factor: acceptance of late passengers (i.e., situations when the staff held a flight for one more passenger who was checking in after the official cut-off time). Further analysis, however, showed significant variations in the reasons from one airport to another (see Figure 14.15). This finding suggests that the individual airport teams should set slightly different priorities for improvements.

Blueprinting—A Powerful Tool for Identifying Fail Points

Fishbone diagrams and Pareto analyses tell us the causes and importance of quality problems. Blueprints allow us to probe further and identify where exactly in a service process the problem was caused. As described in Chapter 8, a well-constructed blueprint

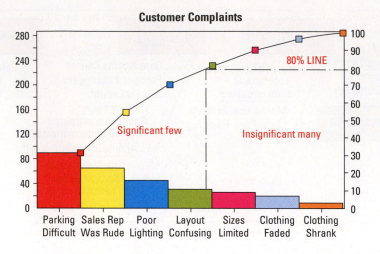

Customer Complaints

Significant few

Insignificant many

80% LINE

Parking Difficult | Sales Rep Was Rude | Poor Lighting | Layout Confusing | Sizes Limited | Clothing Faded | Clothing Shrank

Figure 14.14 Pareto analysis of causes of flight departure delays.

enables us to visualize the process of service delivery by showing (1) the sequence of front-stage interactions that customers experience as they encounter service providers, facilities, and equipment; and (2) supporting back-stage activities that are hidden from customers and are not part of their service experience.

Blueprints can be used to identify potential fail points (i.e., where failures are most likely to occur), and they help us to understand how failures at one point may have a ripple effect on later stages of the process. By adding frequency counts to the fail points in a blueprint, managers can identify the specific types of failures that occur most frequently and thus need urgent attention. Knowing what things can go wrong and where is an important first step in preventing service quality problems.

One desirable solution is to design fail points out of the system. (See Chapter 8 for a discussion of the poka-yokes technique on how to approach this.) In the case of

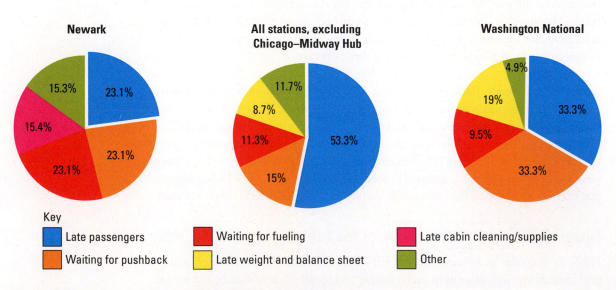

Figure 14.15 Analysis of causes of flight departure delays by station.

failures that cannot be easily designed out of a process or are not easily prevented (such as problems related to weather or the public infrastructure), solutions may revolve around the development of contingency plans and service recovery guidelines (See Chapter 13 on how to design service recovery policies and procedures.)

RETURN ON QUALITY

 **LO 9**
Understand return on quality and determine the optimal level of reliability.

We now understand how to drill down to specific quality problems, and we can use what we learnt from Chapter 8 on how to design and redesign improved service processes. However, the picture remains incomplete without an understanding of the financial implications related to quality improvements. Many firms pay a lot of attention to the improvement of service quality; however, quite a few of them have been disappointed by the results. Even firms recognized for service quality efforts have sometimes run into financial difficulties. This is partly because they spent too lavishly on quality improvements that customers did not value or even recognize. In other instances, such results indicated poor or incomplete execution of the quality program itself.

Assess Costs and Benefits of Quality Initiatives

A return-on-quality (ROQ) approach assesses the costs and benefits of quality initiatives. This is based on the assumptions that (1) quality is an investment, (2) quality efforts must make sense financially, (3) it is possible to spend too much on quality, and (4) not all quality expenditures are equally justified.[20] Hence, expenditures on quality improvement must be related to anticipated increases in profitability.

To determine the feasibility of new quality improvement efforts, they must be carefully costed in advance and then related to anticipated customer response. With good documentation, it is sometimes possible for a firm that operates in a number of locations to examine past experience and judge the strength of a relationship between specific

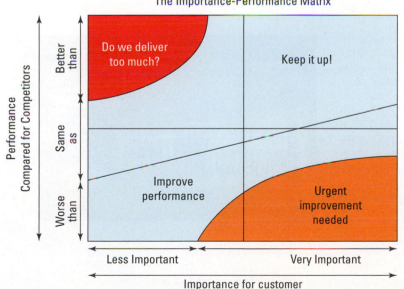

Figure 14.16 The importance-performance matrix compares a firm's service performance against competition and customer needs.

service quality improvements and revenues (see Service Insights 14.3). Methods that can help to identify the improvements with the greatest impact on customer satisfaction and purchase behaviors include the importance-performance matrix (see Figure 14.16 for an example), multiple regression analyses that establish the attributes with the highest impact on overall satisfaction, and a new method called marginal utility analysis (MUA), which uses direct questioning of customers on their improvement priorities (e.g., "if you could make an improvement . . . which four would be your top priorities ?").[21]

SERVICE INSIGHTS 14.3

Quality of Facilities and Room Revenues at Holiday Inn

To find out the relationship between product quality and financial performance in a hotel context, Sheryl Kimes analyzed three years of quality and operational performance data from 1,135 franchised Holiday Inn hotels in the United States and Canada.

Indicators of product quality came from the franchisor's quality assurance reports. These reports were based on unannounced, semi-annual inspections by trained quality auditors who were rotated among different regions and who inspected and rated the different quality dimensions of each hotel. Sheryl Kimes used 12 of these quality dimensions in her study: two relating to the guest rooms (bedroom and bathroom) and 10 relating to commercial areas (exterior, lobby, public restrooms, dining facilities, lounge facilities, corridors, meeting area, recreation area, kitchen, and back of house). Each quality dimension usually included 10–12 individual items that could be passed or failed. The inspector noted the number of defects for each dimension and the total number for the entire hotel.

Holiday Inn Worldwide also provided data on revenue per available room (RevPAR) at each hotel. To adjust for differences in local conditions, Kimes analyzed sales and revenue statistics obtained from thousands of U.S. and Canadian hotels and reported in the monthly Smith Travel Accommodation Reports (a widely used service in the travel industry). This data enabled Kimes to calculate the RevPAR for the immediate mid-scale competitors of each Holiday Inn hotel. The results were then used to make the RevPARs comparable across all Holiday Inns in the sample. The average daily room rate at the time was about $50.

For the purposes of the research, if a hotel had failed at least one item in an area, it was considered "defective" in that area. The findings showed that as the number of defects in a hotel increased, the RevPAR decreased. Quality dimensions that showed quite a strong impact on RevPAR were the exterior, the guest room, and the guest bathroom. Even a single defect resulted in a statistically significant reduction in RevPAR. However, the combination of defects in all three areas showed an even larger effect on RevPAR over time. Kimes calculated that the average annual revenue impact on a defective hotel was a revenue loss of $204,400 compared to a non-defective hotel.

Using a return-on-quality perspective, the results showed that the main focus of increased expenditure on housekeeping and preventive maintenance should be the hotel exterior, the guest rooms, and the bathrooms.

SOURCE

Source: Sheryl E. Kimes, "The Relationship between Product Quality and Revenue per Available Room at Holiday Inn," *Journal of Service Research* 2 (November 1999): 138–144.

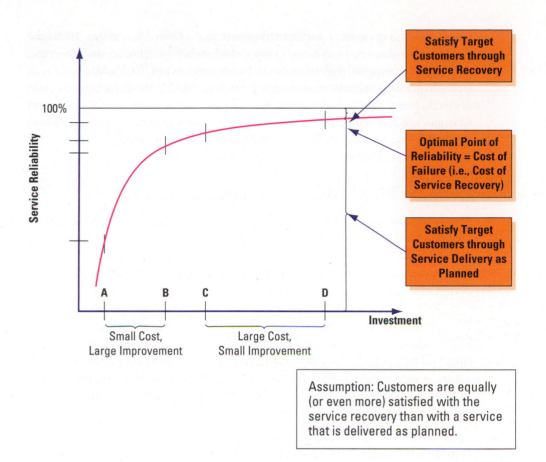

Figure 14.17 When does improving service reliability become uneconomical?

Determine the Optimal Level of Reliability

How far should we go in improving service reliability? A company with poor service quality can often achieve big jumps in reliability with relatively modest investments in improvements. As illustrated in Figure 14.17, initial investments in reducing service failure often bring dramatic results. However, at some point, diminishing returns set in as further improvements require increasing levels of investment (and can even become prohibitively expensive). What level of reliability should we target?

Typically, the cost of service recovery is lower than the cost of an unhappy customer. This suggests that service firms should increase reliability up to the point at which the incremental improvement equals the cost of service recovery (which is the actual cost of failure). Although this strategy results in a service that is less than 100% failure free, the firm can still aim to satisfy 100% of its target customers. This can be done by ensuring that they either receive the service as planned or obtain a satisfying service recovery if a failure occurs.

DEFINING AND MEASURING PRODUCTIVITY

LO 10
Define and measure service productivity.

Historically, services have lagged behind manufacturing in productivity growth. However, research by the McKinsey Global Institute shows that five of the seven largest contributors to labor productivity growth in the United States since 2000 have been service industries. These include retail and wholesale trade, finance and insurance, administrative support, and scientific and technical services.[22] Clearly, advances in technology enable dramatic improvements in productivity! In the introductory section of this chapter, we highlighted the need to look at quality and productivity improvement strategies together rather than in isolation. A firm needs to ensure that it can deliver quality experiences more efficiently to improve its long-term profitability. Let us first discuss what productivity is and how it can be measured.

Defining Productivity in a Service Context

Simply defined, productivity measures the amount of output produced relative to the amount of input used. Hence, improvements in productivity are reflected by an increase in the ratio of outputs to inputs. Such an increase may be achieved by cutting the resources required to create a given volume of output and/or by increasing the output obtained from a given level of inputs.

What do we mean by "input" in a service context? Input varies according to the nature of the business. It may include labor, materials, energy, and capital (consisting of land, buildings, equipment, information systems, and financial assets). The intangible nature of service performances makes it more difficult to measure the productivity of service industries than that of manufacturing. The problem is especially acute for information-based services.

Measuring Productivity

Measuring productivity is difficult in services because the output is often difficult to define. In a people-processing service such as a hospital, we can look at the number of patients treated in the course of a year and the hospital's "census" or average bed occupancy. However, how do we take into account the different types of medical activities performed, such as the removal of cancerous tumors, the treatment of diabetes, or the setting of broken bones? What about differences between patients? Standardized medical procedures offering highly predictable outcomes are relatively few in number.

The measurement task is perhaps simpler in possession-processing services, since many of these are provided by quasi-manufacturing organizations that perform routine tasks with easily measurable inputs and outputs. Examples include garages that change a car's oil and rotate its tires or fast-food restaurants that offer limited and simple menus. However, the task gets more complicated when the garage mechanic has to find and repair a water leak or when we are dealing with a French restaurant known for its varied and exceptional cuisine.

"If you're losing patience with our endless automated system and need to run outside and scream, press 44. If you're feeling better now and wish to continue, press 45..."

Figure 14.18 Productivity for the firm may result in customer frustration when they cannot easily talk to service personnel.

Independent of these more detailed considerations, labor productivity (e.g., revenue per employee, value added per employee, and number of customers served per employee) and asset productivity (e.g., return on assets) are frequently used measures to capture productivity at a high level.

Service Productivity, Efficiency, and Effectiveness

As already indicated, when we look at the issue of productivity, we need to distinguish between productivity, efficiency, and effectiveness.[23] *Productivity* refers to the output that one can get from a certain amount of inputs (e.g., labor and asset productivity). *Efficiency* is a measure of how well you do things and involves comparison to a standard that is usually time-based. For example, how long does it take for an employee to perform a particular task compared to the industry average or some other standard? The faster the task can be completed, the higher the efficiency. *Effectiveness* can be defined as the degree to which an organization meets its goals and desired outcomes, which would typically include customer satisfaction. Peter Drucker expressed it succinctly: "Efficiency is doing the thing right. Effectiveness is doing the right thing."

Classical techniques of productivity and efficiency measurement focus on outputs and benchmarking rather than outcomes. This means that productivity and efficiency are stressed, but effectiveness is neglected. In freight transport, for instance, a ton-mile of output for freight that is delivered late is treated in the same way for productivity purposes as a similar shipment delivered on time. Similarly, suppose a hairdresser usually serves three customers per hour. However, they can increase their output to one every 15 minutes by reducing conversation with the customers and by rushing them. Even if the haircut itself is just as good, the delivery process may be perceived as functionally inferior, leading customers to rate the overall service experience less positively (Figure 14.18). In this example, productivity and efficiency have been achieved, but not effectiveness.

In the long run, organizations that are more effective in consistently delivering outcomes desired by customers should be able to command higher prices for their output and build a loyal and profitable customer base. Therefore, there is a need to stress effectiveness and outcomes in addition to productivity and efficiency. (Figure 14.19)

Figure 14.19 A counselor needs to take his time in a session so that patients can gain greater benefit from their group therapy.

IMPROVING SERVICE PRODUCTIVITY

Intense competition in many service sectors pushes firms to continually seek ways to improve their productivity.[24] This section discusses various possible approaches to and sources of productivity gains.

Generic Productivity Improvement Strategies

Traditionally, operations managers have been in charge of improving service productivity, and their focus can be summed up as achieving the same output "better, faster, and cheaper." This approach typically centers on actions such as:

1) Controlling costs carefully at every step in the process. Many senior managers subscribe to the saying, "Costs are like fingernails: You have to cut them constantly."

2) Reducing the waste of materials and labor.

3) Training and motivating employees to do things faster, better, and more efficiently.

PART V

4) Broadening the variety of tasks that a service worker can perform (which may require revised labor agreements). This allows managers to eliminate bottlenecks and wasteful downtime by deploying workers wherever they are needed most.

5) Improving capacity utilization through better matching of supply and demand and/or matching productive capacity to average levels of demand rather than peak levels. This ensures that workers and equipment are not underemployed for extended periods.

6) Using machines, equipment, technology, and data that enable employees to work faster and/or achieve a higher level of quality.

7) Installing expert systems that allow paraprofessionals to take on work previously performed by more experienced individuals earning higher salaries.

8) Redesigning customer service processes to be more productive and effective (e.g., through Lean Six Sigma).

9) Replacing service employees by automated machines and customer-operated self-service technologies (SSTs).

10) Tiering service levels to allocate resources better to more important customers.

11) Outsourcing non-core activities that can be provided more cost-effectively by third parties.

Although improving productivity can be approached incrementally, major gains often require the redesign of customer service processes. For example, it's time for service process redesign when customers face unbearably long wait times, as happens often in healthcare (Figure 14.20). We discussed service process redesign in depth in Chapter 8.

Customer-Driven Approaches to Improve Productivity

In situations where customers are deeply involved in the service production process, operations managers should also examine how customer inputs can be made more

Figure 14.20 Long waiting times often indicate a need for service process redesign.

productive. Marketing managers should be thinking about the marketing strategies that may be used to influence customers to behave in more productive ways. Some of these strategies include:

▶ **Change the Timing of Customer Demand.** By encouraging customers to use a service outside peak periods and offering them incentives to do so, managers can make better use of their productive assets and provide better service. The issues that relate to managing demand in capacity-constrained service businesses are discussed in detail in Chapter 9; revenue management strategies are explored in Chapter 6.

▶ **Encourage Use of Lower-Cost Service Delivery Channels and Self-Service.** Shifting transactions to more cost-effective service delivery channels, such as the internet, apps, or self-service machines, improves productivity. Many technological innovations are designed to get customers to perform tasks previously undertaken by service employees (Figure 14.21). The issues related to customers playing a more active role as co-producers of the service are discussed in detail in the context of service process design in Chapter 8.

▶ **Ask Customers to Use Third Parties.** In some instances, managers may be able to improve service productivity by delegating one or more service support functions to third parties. Specialist intermediaries may enjoy economies of scale that allow them to perform the task more cheaply than the core service provider. This allows the service provider to focus on quality and productivity in its own area of expertise.

How Productivity Improvements Impact Quality and Value

Managers would do well to examine productivity enhancements from the broader perspective of the business processes used to transform resource inputs into the

LO 13
Know how productivity improvements impact quality and value.

Figure 14.21 Self-service pumps with credit card readers have increased gas station productivity.

PART V

outcomes desired by customers. This is especially important for processes that not only cross departmental and sometimes geographic boundaries but also link the back-stage and front-stage areas of the service operation. Hence, as firms make productivity improvements, they need to examine the impact on customer experience. (See also our discussion on the service quality–productivity–profitability triangle at the beginning of this chapter.)

Front-Stage Efforts to Improve Productivity. In high-contact services, many productivity improvements are quite visible. Some changes simply require acceptance by customers, while others require them to adopt new patterns of behavior in their dealings with the organization. If substantial changes are proposed, then it makes sense to conduct market research first to determine how customers may respond. Failure to consider the effects on customers may result in a loss of business and cancel out anticipated productivity gains. (Refer back to Chapter 8 on how to manage and overcome customers' reluctance to change in service processes.)

How Back-Stage Changes May Impact Customers. The marketing implications of back-stage changes depend on whether they affect or are noticed by customers. If airline mechanics develop a procedure for servicing jet engines more quickly without incurring increased wage rates or material costs, the airline has obtained a productivity improvement that has no impact on the customer's service experience.

Other back-stage changes, however, may have ripple effects that extend to the front stage and affect customers. Marketers should be abreast of proposed back-stage changes not only to identify such ripples but also to prepare customers for them. At a bank, for instance, the decision to install new computers and printer peripherals may be due to plans to improve internal quality controls and reduce the cost of preparing monthly statements. However, this new equipment may change the appearance of bank statements and the time of the month when they are posted. If customers are likely to notice such changes, an explanation may be warranted. If the new statements are easier to read and understand, the change may be worth promoting as a service improvement.

A Caution on Cost-Reduction Strategies. In the absence of new technology, most attempts to improve service productivity tend to center on efforts to eliminate waste and reduce labor costs. Cutbacks in front-stage staffing mean either that the remaining employees have to work harder and faster or that there are insufficient personnel to serve customers promptly at busy times. Although employees may be able to work faster for a brief period of time, few can maintain a rapid pace for extended periods. Workers who are trying to do two or three things at once—serving a customer face to face while simultaneously answering the telephone and sorting papers, for example—may do a poor job of each task. Excessive pressure breeds discontent and frustration, especially among customer-contact personnel who are caught between trying to meet customer needs and attempting to achieve management's productivity goals.

A better way is to search for service process redesign opportunities that lead to drastic improvements in productivity and at the same time increase service quality. Biometrics is set to become a new technology that may allow both (see Service Insights 14.4).

Biometrics: The Next Frontier in Driving Productivity and Service Quality?

Intense competitive pressures and razor-thin margins in many service industries do not allow firms the luxury of increasing costs to improve quality. Rather, the trick is to constantly seek ways to achieve great improvements in service quality and efficiency simultaneously. The internet and service apps have in the past allowed many firms to do just that and have redefined industries such as financial services, music distribution, and travel agencies. Biometrics may be the next major technology driving further service and productivity improvements in the service sector.

Biometrics is the authentication or identification of individuals based on a physical characteristic or trait. Physical characteristics include fingerprints, facial recognition, hand geometry, and the structure of the iris, and traits include signature formation, keystroke patterns, and voice recognition. Biometrics, as something you are, is more convenient and more secure than something you know (passwords or pieces of personal information) or something you have (card keys, smart cards, or tokens). There is no risk of forgetting, losing, copying, loaning, or getting your biometrics stolen (Figure 14.22).

Applications of biometrics include controlling access to service facilities (used by Disney World to provide access to season-pass holders), implementing voice recognition at call centers (used by the Home Shopping Network and Charles Schwab to enable fast and hassle-free client authentication), allowing self-service access to safe deposit vaults in banks (used by the Bank of Hawaii and First Tennessee Bank), cashing checks in supermarkets (used by Kroger, Food 4 Less, and BI-LO), and issuing library books and debiting catering accounts in schools (based on the child's finger-scan). The use of biometrics will become more prevalent.

Biometrics clearly has exciting applications that are generally more secure. However, if handled

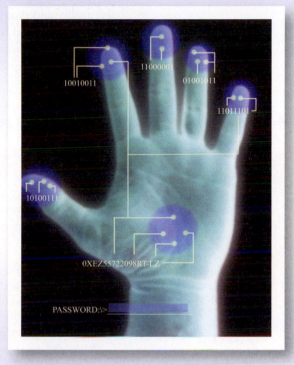
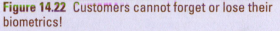

Figure 14.22 Customers cannot forget or lose their biometrics!

wrongly, the potential damage could also be far more serious. Even biometrics can be cloned. For example, fingerprints can be replicated (or "spoofed") from something a person has touched. Resetting a compromised password is merely a hassle, but what will happen if someone stole the digital version of your fingerprint or your retina? Perhaps biometrics will be supplemented by additional safety features for the highest risk applications. Future service innovation will show where biometrics can add the highest value to service organizations and their customers.

LO 14

Understand how to integrate all the tools to improve the quality and productivity of customer service processes.

INTEGRATION AND SYSTEMATIC APPROACHES TO IMPROVING SERVICE QUALITY AND PRODUCTIVITY

We have discussed a number of tools and concepts on how to improve service quality and productivity. Table 14.4 integrates the key tools discussed into a generic nine-step framework that you can use to structure your approach to improve the quality and productivity of a single customer service process. Such projects are typically conducted by experienced in-house teams or outside consultants. However, the continual improvement of a process (as described in Step 9) should typically be the responsibility of the process owner.

Table 14.4 An integrated nine-step approach to customer service process improvement.

Step	Objectives	Potential Tools to Apply
1	Determine priority processes for improvement and redesign.	• Use frequency count of process occurrence and number of complaints per process to identify priority processes. • Use prioritization matrix (ease of implementation vs potential business impact) to identify "low-hanging fruits" with which to start a service improvement initiative.
2	For the shortlisted processes, set targets for (1) customer satisfaction, (2) defects, (3) cycle time, and (4) productivity improvements.	• Benchmark internally, against competition, the best in class and world class to determine targets for all four priorities. • Decide the target level of performance (e.g., do you aim to be the best in your industry or to just catch up with industry average on those four priorities?). • Use a project charter to formalize the objectives of this customer service process redesign project.
3	Identify key elements of quality in priority service processes and determine customer needs and expectations.	• Use blueprinting to identify all touch points of a customer journey and the line of visibility to understand the customer view of a process. • For each touch point, determine what quality means in the customer's eyes (e.g., use the five dimensions of service quality [see Chapter 2] to cover all important areas, review customer feedback [including content analysis of compliments and complaints to understand drivers of customer delight and disgust], and conduct focus groups).
4	Assess process performance.	• Review hard, operational process measures (e.g., cycle times, customer waiting times, one-time resolution, etc.). • Measure customer perceptions of process performance (e.g., process-specific customer satisfaction surveys). • Interview front-line employees to obtain their views on what works, what doesn't work, and what needs urgent improvement.
5	Identify performance shortfalls and quality gaps.	• Map customer needs and wants from the process against process performance measures to determine important performance and quality gaps. • Identify the main performance gaps (e.g., map frequency counts of service failures and/or complaints on service blueprints to understand where exactly service processes fail).
6	Identify root causes of quality gaps.	• Use the Gaps Model to capture all possible sources of gaps in customers' service quality perceptions. • Use TQM tools to drill down on specific gaps (e.g., use Pareto charts to understand which fail points to focus on; use fishbone diagrams to identify the exact causes of key fail points; use Pareto charts again to identify the main root causes to be designed out of the processes).

Step	Objectives	Potential Tools to Apply
7	Improve process performance.	• Use prescriptions from the Gaps Model to close each of the six gaps (see Table 14.1). • Use customer service design and redesign tools. (See Chapter 8, which discusses how fail points may be designed out of the system through the use of poka yokes.) • Plan service recovery for fail points that cannot be designed out of the system (i.e., make it proactive, pre-planned, trained, and empowered; see Chapter 13)
8	Control and continuously fine tune the process to improve it further.	• Monitor the performance of the redesigned process using operational measures and customer feedback. • Make it a routine process at the new, high level of performance. • Ask the process owner to fine tune the process through incremental improvements (e.g., use Kaizen or other tools to get the process team to monitor and continually improve the process it is responsible for).
9	Start again; the journey is the destination . . .	• Create a culture of customer centricity, process improvement, and change by continuously working and redesigning customer service processes; become a customer-driven learning organization.

Systematic Approaches to Improving Service Quality and Productivity

LO 15

Explain how TQM, ISO 9000, Six Sigma, and the Malcolm Baldrige and EFQM approaches relate to managing and improving service quality and productivity.

There are certain systematic approaches that help service firms to achieve an organization-wide culture of focusing on customers, service quality, and productivity. In fact, many of the ideas, tools, and concepts introduced in this chapter originate from these approaches. A short overview of key approaches is presented below.

Total Quality Management (TQM) was originally developed in Japan. It is probably the most widely known approach to continuous improvement in manufacturing and (more recently) service firms. TQM can help organizations to attain service excellence, increase productivity, and create value continuously through innovative process improvements.[25] Many of the tools discussed in this chapter originate from TQM, including control charts, Pareto analysis, blueprints, and fishbone diagrams.

ISO 9000 Certification[26] is all about quality management and comprises requirements, definitions, guidelines, and related standards to provide an independent assessment and certification of a firm's quality management system. ISO 9000 uses many TQM tools and internalizes their use in participating firms. It also uses W. Edwards Deming's PDCA Cycle (i.e., Plan-Do-Check-Act Cycle).

Six Sigma was embraced by many service firms that have high-volume processes to reduce defects and cycle times and improve productivity.[27] Statistically, Six Sigma means achieving a quality level of only 3.4 defects per million opportunities (DPMO). To understand how stringent this target is, consider mail deliveries. If a mail service delivers with 99% accuracy, it misses 3,000 items out of 300,000 deliveries. However, if it achieves a Six Sigma performance level, only one item out of this total goes astray. The most popular Six Sigma improvement tool for analyzing and improving business processes is the Define-Measure-Analyze-Improve-Control (DMAIC) model, shown in Table 14.5.

Striving for Service Excellence **479**

Table 14.5 Applying the DMAIC model to process improvement and redesign.

	Process Improvement	Process Design/Redesign
Define	• Identify the problem • Define requirements • Set goals	• Identify specific or broad problems • Define goal/change vision • Clarify scope and customer requirements
Measure	• Validate problem/process • Refine problem/goal • Measure key steps/inputs	• Measure performance to requirements • Gather process efficiency data
Analyze	• Develop causal hypothesis • Identify root causes • Validate hypothesis	• Identify best practices • Assess process design • Refine requirements
Improve	• Develop ideas to measure root causes • Test solutions • Measure results	• Design new process • Implement new process, structures, and systems
Control	• Establish measures to maintain performance • Correct problems as needed	• Establish measures and reviews to maintain performance • Correct problems as needed

SOURCE

Reproduced from P. Pande, R. P. Neuman, and R. R. Cavanagh, *The Six Sigma Way* (New York: McGraw-Hill, 2000).

The Malcolm Baldrige National Quality Award (MBNQA) was developed by the National Institute of Standards and Technology (NIST) with the goal of promoting best practices in quality management and recognizing and publicizing quality achievements among U.S. firms. Countries other than the United States have similar quality awards, of which the most widely used is probably the European Foundation for Quality Management (EFQM) approach.[28]

Major service firms that have won the award include PricewaterhouseCoopers, Ritz-Carlton, FedEx, University of Wisconsin, Xerox Business Services, Boeing Aerospace Support, Caterpillar Financial Services Corp, and AT&T.

The Malcolm Baldrige model assesses firms in seven areas:

1) Leadership commitment to a service quality culture

2) Planning priorities for improvement, including service standards; performance targets; and measurement of customer satisfaction, defects, cycle time, and productivity

3) Information and analysis that will aid the organization to collect, measure, analyze, and report strategic and operational indicators

4) Human resources management that enables the firm to deliver service excellence, ranging from hiring the right people to development, involvement, empowerment, and motivation

5) Process management, including monitoring, continuous improvement, and process redesign

6) Customer and market focus that allows the firm to determine customer requirements and expectations

7) Business results[29]

Which Approach Should a Firm Adopt?

As we have seen, there are various approaches to systematically improving a firm's service quality and productivity. Which approach should the firm adopt—TQM, ISO 9000, the Malcolm Baldrige model, or Six Sigma? It is best to see these

Figure 14.23 When commitment and constant improvement meet the challenge of changing markets, technology, and environments head-on, success is more likely.

approaches as complementary and building on one another. TQM can be applied at differing levels of complexity, and basic tools such as flowcharting, frequency charts, and fishbone diagrams should probably be adopted by all service firms. Six Sigma and ISO 9000 seem to suit the next level of commitment and complexity and focus on process improvements and compliance to performance standards. This is followed by the Malcolm Baldrige model and the European Foundation for Quality Management (EFQM) approach, which offer comprehensive frameworks for organizational excellence.

Any one of the approaches can be a useful framework for understanding customer needs, analyzing processes, and improving service quality and productivity. Firms can choose a particular program, depending on their own needs and desired level of sophistication. Each program has its own strengths, and firms can use more than one program to gain additional benefits. For example, the ISO 9000 program can be used for standardizing the procedures and documenting processes. The Six Sigma and Malcolm Baldrige programs can then be used to improve processes and to focus on performance improvement across the organization.

A key success factor is how well the particular quality improvement program fits in with the overall business strategy. Service champions make best practices in service quality management a core part of their organizational culture.[30] The National Institute of Standards and Technology (NIST), which organizes the Malcolm Baldrige Award program, has an index of Malcolm Baldrige Award winners called the "Baldrige Index." It was observed that winners always outperformed the S&P 500 index![31]

Ironically, however, the two-time winner of the award and Six Sigma pioneer, Motorola, suffered financially and lost market share, partly due to the firm's failure to keep up with new technology. Moreover, firms which implement one of these programs due to peer pressure or just as a marketing tool are less likely to succeed than firms which view these programs as important development tools.[32] Clearly, success cannot be taken for granted. Commitment, implementation, and constant improvement that follow changing markets, technologies, and environments are keys for sustained success (Figure 14.23).

LO 1 ▶ Quality and productivity are twin paths for creating value for customers and the firm. However, the relationship between productivity and customer satisfaction (and the net effects on profitability) can be positive, neutral, or negative and therefore needs to be managed carefully.

LO 2 ▶ There are different definitions of service quality. In this book, we adopt the customer-focused definition of service quality as consistently meeting or exceeding customer expectations.

LO 3 ▶ The Gaps Model is an important tool to diagnose and address service quality problems at a macro level. We identified six gaps that can be the cause of quality shortfalls:

o Gap 1—the knowledge gap

o Gap 2—the policy gap

o Gap 3—the delivery gap

o Gap 4—the communications gap

o Gap 5—the perceptions gap

o Gap 6—the service quality gap (This is the most important gap. In order to close Gap 6, the other five gaps have to be closed first.)

We summarized a series of potential causes for each of the gaps and provided generic prescriptions for addressing these causes and thereby closing the gaps. These prescriptions take a holistic organization perspective.

LO 4 ▶ There are both soft and hard measures of service quality. *Soft measures* are usually based on perceptions of and feedback from customers and employees. *Hard measures* relate to processes and their outcomes.

LO 5 ▶ Feedback from customers (i.e., mostly soft measures) should be systematically collected via a customer feedback system (CFS). The key objectives of a CFS include:

o Assessment and benchmarking of service quality and performance

o Customer-driven learning and improvement

o Creating a customer-oriented service culture and a culture of change

LO 6 ▶ Firms can use a variety of tools to collect customer feedback, including: (1) total market surveys; (2) annual surveys on overall satisfaction; (3) transactional surveys; (4) service feedback cards and other transaction-specific feedback tools such as text-messaging, e-mails, and social media; (5) mystery shopping; (6) unsolicited customer feedback (e.g., compliments and complaints); (7) focus group discussions; (8) service reviews; and (9) online and social media monitoring.

o A reporting system is needed to channel feedback and its analysis to the relevant parties so that they may take action.

LO 7 ▶ *Hard measures* relate to operational processes and outcomes and can be counted, timed, or observed. *Control charts* are a simple method of displaying performance on hard measures over time against specific quality standards.

LO 8 ▶ Key tools to analyze and address important service quality problems are:

o *Fishbone diagrams* to identify the causes of quality problems

o *Pareto analysis* to assess the frequency of quality problems and identify the most common causes

o *Blueprinting* to determine the exact location of fail points in a customer service process and then help to redesign the process

LO 9 ▶ There are financial implications of service quality improvements. A return-on-quality (ROQ) approach assesses the costs and benefits of specific quality initiatives. Firms should increase service reliability up to the point at which the incremental improvement equals the cost of service recovery (which is the actual cost of failure). When a service failure occurs, customers should receive a satisfying service recovery.

LO 10 ▶ Productivity measures the amount of output produced relative to the amount of inputs used. An improvement in this ratio can be achieved by cutting the resources required to create a given volume of output and/or by increasing the output obtained from a given level of input. Key inputs vary according to the industry and can include labor, materials, energy, and assets.

LO 11 ▶ It is important to differentiate between these three concepts:

1. *Productivity* involves the amount of outputs based on a given level of inputs (e.g., input/output ratio).

2. *Efficiency* is usually time-based and compared to a standard such as industry average (e.g. speed of delivery).

3. *Effectiveness* refers to the degree to which a firm meets its goals (such as customer satisfaction).

Productivity and efficiency cannot be separated from effectiveness. Firms that strive to be more productive, efficient, and effective in consistently delivering customer satisfaction will be more successful.

LO 12 ► Generic methods to improve productivity include:

1. Controlling costs

2. Reducing waste of materials and labor

3. Training employees to work more productively

4. Broadening the job scope of employees to reduce bottlenecks and downtime

5. Improving capacity utilization

6. Providing employees with equipment and information that enable them to work faster and better

7. Installing expert systems so that para-professionals can do the work previously done by higher-paid experts

8. Replacing service employees with automated machines and customer-operated self-service technologies (SSTs)

9. Tiering service levels to allocate resources better to more important customers

10. Outsourcing non-core activities that can be provided more cost-effectively by third parties

Customer-driven methods to improve productivity include:

1. Changing the timing of customer demand to better match capacity to demand

2. Encouraging the use of lower-cost service delivery channels and replacing labor with machines and SSTs

3. Getting customers to use more cost-effective third parties for parts of the service delivery

LO 13 ► While making improvements to productivity, firms need to bear in mind that both front-stage and back-stage improvements can have an impact on service quality and the customer experience.

LO 14 ► A nine-step approach can be used to improve customer service processes:

1. Determine priority processes for improvement (e.g., through a frequency count of process occurrence and number of complaints and the use of the prioritization matrix).

2. Set targets for customer satisfaction, defects, cycle time, and productivity improvements (e.g., through benchmarking and a project charter).

3. Identify key elements of quality (e.g., through blueprinting to identify touch points and the use of the five dimensions of quality together with customer and employee feedback to understand what quality means in the eyes of the customer).

4. Assess process performance (e.g., through hard operational measures and soft customer feedback measures).

5. Identify performance shortfalls and quality gaps (e.g., map customer needs and wants against process performance; map frequency count of service failures on service blueprints to understand where exactly service processes fail).

6. Identify root causes of gaps (e.g., use the Gaps Model to capture all possible sources of gaps; use TQM tools such as the fishbone diagram, Pareto charts, and service blueprints to drill down on specific gaps).

7. Improve process performance (e.g., use the prescriptions of the Gaps Model for closing the quality shortfalls; use customer service process redesign tools as discussed in Chapter 8 and plans for service recovery as covered in Chapter 13).

8. Control and fine tune (i.e., monitor the performance of the redesigned process and fine tune it further).

9. Start again; the journey is the destination . . .

LO 15 ► TQM, ISO 9000, Six Sigma, Malcolm Baldrige, and European Foundation for Quality Management (EFQM) are systematic and complementary approaches to managing and improving service quality and productivity. They integrate many of the tools discussed in this chapter.

UNLOCK YOUR LEARNING

These keywords are found within the sections of each Learning Objective (LO). They are integral to understanding the services marketing concepts taught in each section. Having a firm grasp of these keywords and how they are used is essential to helping you do well on your course, and in the real and very competitive marketing scene out there.

LO 1
1. Profitability
2. Productivity
3. Service quality
4. Repeat purchase
5. Customer satisfaction
6. Customer loyalty
7. Share of wallet
8. Referrals
9. Customer service processes
10. Customer experience

LO 2
1. Customer expectations
2. Performance

LO 3
1. External communications gap
2. Internal communications gap
3. Delivery gap
4. Knowledge gap
5. Perceptions gap
6. Policy gap
7. Service quality gap
8. Gaps Model
9. Service design
10. Service recovery
11. Intermediaries
12. Service delivery

LO 4
1. Hard measures
2. Hard standards
3. Soft measures
4. Soft standards

LO 5
1. Assessment
2. Benchmarking
3. Customer feedback systems
4. Customer-driven improvements
5. Customer-driven learning
6. Customer-oriented service culture

LO 6
1. Annual surveys
2. Customer feedback collection tools
3. Feedback loop
4. Focus group discussion
5. Mystery shopping
6. Service feedback cards
7. Service performance report
8. Service performance review
9. Service performance update
10. Service reviews
11. Total market surveys
12. Transactional surveys
13. Unsolicited customer feedback
14. Representativeness
15. Reliability

LO 7
1. Zero failures
2. Operational processes
3. Control charts
4. Service quality index (SQI)
5. Uptime
6. Failure rates
7. Service response times

LO 8
1. Blueprinting
2. Cause-and-effect analysis
3. Fishbone diagram
4. Pareto analysis
5. Return on quality
6. Root-cause analysis
7. Service quality problems
8. Information failures
9. Fail points

LO 9
1. Assess benefits
2. Assess costs
3. Quality improvement
4. Quality initiatives
5. Return on quality
6. Service reliability

LO 10
1. Labor productivity
2. Inputs
3. Asset productivity
4. People-processing services
5. Possession-processing services
6. Outputs

LO 11
1. Effectiveness
2. Efficiency

LO 12
1. Capacity utilization
2. Tiering
3. Training
4. Outsourcing
5. Reducing waste
6. Third parties
7. Cost control
8. Self-service technologies

LO 13
1. Back-stage changes
2. Biometrics
3. Cost-reduction strategies
4. Front-stage changes
5. Physical characteristics
6. Traits

LO 14
1. Prioritization matrix
2. Process performance
3. Line of visibility
4. Customer service process improvement
5. Cycle time
6. Priority processes
7. Performance shortfalls

LO 15
1. European Foundation for Quality Management (EFQM)
2. Define-Measure-Analyze-Improve-Control (DMAIC) model
3. ISO 9000 Certification
4. Malcolm Baldrige model
5. Six Sigma
6. Total Quality Management (TQM)
7. Plan-Do-Check-Act (PDAC) cycle

How well do you know the language of services marketing? Quiz yourself!

⚠ **Not for the academically faint-of-heart**

For each keyword you are able to recall without referring to earlier pages, give yourself a point (and a pat on the back). Tally your score at the end and see if you earned the right to be called—a *services marketeer*.

SCORE

01 – 12	Services Marketing is done a great disservice.
13 – 24	The midnight oil needs to be lit, pronto.
25 – 36	I know what you *didn't* do all semester.
37 – 48	By George! You're getting there.
49 – 60	Now, go forth and market.
61 – 73	There should be a marketing concept named after you.

Review Questions

1. Explain the relationships between service quality, productivity, and profitability.

2. Identify the gaps that can occur in service quality and the steps that service marketers can take to prevent them.

3. Why are both soft and hard measures of service quality needed?

4. What are the main objectives of an effective customer feedback system?

5. What are the key customer feedback collection tools? What are the strengths and weaknesses of each of these tools?

6. What are the main tools service firms can use to analyze and address service quality problems?

7. Why is productivity more difficult to measure in service than in manufacturing firms?

8. How can you integrate all the tools in a nine-step approach to improve the quality and productivity of customer service processes?

9. How do concepts such as TQM, ISO 9000, Six Sigma and the Malcolm Baldrige and EFQM approaches relate to managing and improving service quality and productivity?

WORK YOUR SERVICES MARKETING

Application Exercises

1. Consider your own recent experiences as a service consumer. On which dimensions of service quality have you most often experienced a large gap between your expectations and your perceptions of the service performance? What do you think the underlying causes might be? What steps should management take to improve quality?

2. Collect a few customer feedback forms and tools (customer feedback cards, questionnaires, online forms, and apps), and explain how the information gathered with those tools can be used to achieve the main objectives of effective customer feedback systems.

3. What key measures could be used for monitoring service quality, productivity, and profitability for a large pizza restaurant chain? Specifically, what measures would you recommend for such a firm, taking administration costs into consideration? Who should receive what type of feedback on the results and why? On which measures would you base a part of the salary scheme of branch-level staff and why?

4. In what ways can you, as a consumer, help to improve productivity for at least three service organizations that you patronize? Which distinctive characteristics of each service make some of these actions possible?

5. Do a literature search, and identify the critical factors for a successful implementation of ISO 9000 or (Lean) Six Sigma in service firms.

ENDNOTES

1. Adapted from: Audrey Gilmore, "Service Marketing Management Competencies: A Ferry Company Example," *International Journal of Service Industry Management* 9, no. 1 (1998): 74–92; www.stenaline.com, accessed September 1, 2015.

2. This section was adapted from: Jochen Wirtz and Valarie Zeithaml, "Cost-Effective Service Excellence: Developing a Conceptual Framework," in Silke Bartsch and Christian Blümelhuber (eds.), *Always Ahead im Marketing: Offensiv, Digital, Strategisch* (Wiesbaden, Germany: Gabler Verlag, 2015), 547–557.

3. A. Parasuraman, Valarie A. Zeithaml, and Leonard L. Berry, "A Conceptual Model of Service Quality and Its Implications for Future Research," *Journal of Marketing* 49 (Fall 1985): 41–50; Valarie A. Zeithaml, Leonard L. Berry, and A. Parasuraman, "Communication and Control Processes in the Delivery of Services," *Journal of Marketing* 52 (April 1988): 36–58.

4. The sub-gaps in this model are based on the 7-gaps model in: Christopher Lovelock, *Product Plus: How Product + Service = Competitive Advantage* (New York: McGraw-Hill, 1994): 112.

5. Valarie A. Zeithaml, Mary Jo Bitner, and Dwayne D. Gremler, *Services Marketing: Integrating Customer Focus across the Firm*, 5th ed. (New York: McGraw-Hill, 2013), 261.

6. This section is based partially on: Jochen Wirtz and Monica Tomlin, "Institutionalizing Customer-Driven Learning through Fully Integrated Customer Feedback Systems," *Managing Service Quality* 10, no. 4 (2000): 205–215.

7. W. E. Baker and J. M. Sinkula, "The Synergistic Effect of Market Orientation and Learning Orientation on Organizational Performance," *Journal of the Academy of Marketing Science* 27, no. 4 (1999): 411–427.

8. Leonard L. Berry and A. Parasuraman provide an excellent overview of all key research approaches discussed in this section plus a number of other tools in their paper, "Listening to the Customer: The Concept of a Service Quality Information System," *Sloan Management Review* 38 (Spring 1997): 65–76.

9. For a discussion on suitable satisfaction measures, see: Jochen Wirtz and Lee Meng Chung, "An Examination of the Quality and Context-Specific Applicability of Commonly Used Customer Satisfaction Measures," *Journal of Service Research* 5 (May 2003): 345–355.

10. Highly cost-effective mobile apps that can track customers' experiences in real time and supply instant information have been developed; see: Emma K. Macdonald, Hugh N. Wilson, and Umut Konuş, "Better Customer Insight—in Real Time," *Harvard Business Review* 90, no. 9 (2012): 90, 102–108.

11. Robert Johnston and Sandy Mehra, "Best-Practice Complaint Management," *Academy of Management Executive* 16, no. 4 (2002): 145–154.

12. Seshadri Tirunillai and Gerard J. Tellis, "Mining Marketing Meaning from Online Chatter: Strategic Brand Analysis of Big Data Using Latent Dirichlet Allocation," *Journal of Marketing Science* 51, no. 4 (2014): 463–479.

13. Advanced analytical tools allow analysis and visualization of online posted reviews; see: Thomas Y. Lee and Eric T. Bradlow, "Automated Marketing Research Using Online Customer Reviews," *Journal of Marketing Research* 48, no. 5 (2011): 881–894.

14. Note, however, that there are differences across online media. For example, sentiments expressed in blogs tend to be more positive than those posted in other media such as forums; see: David A. Schweidel and Wendy W. Moe, "Listening in on Social Media: A Joint Model of Sentiment and Venue Format Choice," *Journal of Marketing Research* 51, no. 4 (2014): 387–402.

15. Roland T. Rust and Ming-Hui Huang, "The Service Revolution and the Transformation of Marketing Science," *Marketing Science* 33, no. 2 (2014): 206–221; Anindya Ghose, Panagiotis G. Ipeirotis, and Beibei Li, "Designing Marketing Ranking Systems for Hotels on Travel Search Engines by Mining User-Generated and Crowdsourced Content," *Marketing Science* 31, no. 3 (2012): 493–520.

16. Duncan Simester, "When You Shouldn't Listen to Your Critics," *Harvard Business Review* 89, no. 6 (2011): 42.

17. Comments by Thomas R. Oliver, then senior vice president, sales and customer service, Federal Express; reported in: Christopher H. Lovelock, *Federal Express: Quality*

Improvement Program (Lausanne: International Institute for Management Development, 1990).

18. Lovelock, *Product Plus*, 218.

19. These categories and the research data that follow have been adapted from information in: D. Daryl Wyckoff, "New Tools for Achieving Service Quality," *Cornell Hotel and Restaurant Administration Quarterly* (August–September 2001): 25–38.

20. Roland T. Rust, Anthony J. Zahonik, and Timothy L. Keiningham, "Return on Quality (ROQ): Making Service Quality Financially Accountable," *Journal of Marketing* 59 (April 1995): 58–70; Roland T. Rust, Christine Moorman, and Peter R. Dickson, "Getting Return on Quality: Revenue Expansion, Cost Reduction, or Both?" *Journal of Marketing* 66 (October 2002): 7–24.

21. Marginal utility analysis was found to outperform analyses based on importance-performance and regression analyses; see: Donald R. Bacon, "Understanding Priorities for Service Attribute Improvement," *Journal of Service Research* 15, no. 2 (2012): 199–214.

22. Martin Neil Baily, Diana Farrell, and Jaana Remes, "Where US Productivity Growing," *McKinsey Quarterly*, no. 2 (2006): 10–12. For EU data, see: Kristian Uppenberg and Hubert Strauss, *Innovation and Productivity Growth in the EU Services Sector* (European Investment Bank, 2010); the publication is available at: http://www.eib.org/attachments/efs/efs_innovation_and_productivity_en.pdf.

23. Kenneth J. Klassen, Randolph M. Russell, and James J. Chrisman, "Efficiency and Productivity Measures for High Contact Services," *Service Industries Journal* 18 (October 1998): 1–18; James L. Heskett, *Managing in the Service Economy* (New York: The Free Press, 1986). For a review and discussion on service productivity, see: Christian Grönroos and Katri Ojasalo, "Service Productivity: Towards a Conceptualization of the Transformation of Inputs into Economic Results in Services," *Journal of Business Research* 57, no. 4 (2004): 414–423.

24. For a more in-depth discussion on service productivity, refer to: Cynthia Karen Swank, "The Lean Service Machine," *Harvard Business Review* 81, no. 10 (2003): 123–129.

25. C. Mele and M. Colurcio, "The Evolving Path of TQM: Towards Business Excellence and Stakeholder Value," *International Journal of Quality and Reliability Management* 23, no. 5 (2006): 464–489; C. Mele, "The Synergic Relationship between TQM and Marketing in Creating Customer Value," *Managing Service Quality* 17, no. 3 (2007): 240–258.

26. See the official website of the International Organization for Standardization (ISO) for detailed information on ISO: http://www.iso.org. The ISO 9000 family of standards is described at: http://www.iso.org/iso/home/standards/management-standards/iso_9000.htm, and an introduction is provided in the publication: ISO Central Secretariat, *Selection and Use of the ISO 9000 Family of Standards* (ISO, 2009). This book can be downloaded for free from the ISO 9000 website.

27. Jim Biolos, "Six Sigma Meets the Service Economy," *Harvard Business Review* 80 (November 2002): 3–5.

28. The official website for the Malcolm Baldrige Award is http://www.nist.gov/baldrige. The official website for the European Foundation for Quality Management (EFQM) is http://www.efqm.org, and an overview of the EFQM model is provided at http://www.efqm.org/sites/default/files/overview_efqm_2013_v1.1.pdf.

29. Allan Shirks, William B. Weeks, and Annie Stein, "Baldrige-Based Quality Awards: Veterans Health Administration's 3-Year Experience," *Quality Management in Health Care* 10, no. 3 (2002): 47–54; National Institute of Standards and Technology, "Baldrige FAQs," http://www.nist.gov/baldrige/about/baldrige_faqs.cfm, accessed September 1, 2015.

30. Cathy A. Enz and Judy A. Siguaw, "Best Practices in Service Quality," *Cornell Hotel and Restaurant Administration Quarterly* (October 2000): 20–29.

31. Eight NIST Stock Investment Study (USA: Gaithersburg, National Institute of Standards and Technology, March 2002).

32. Gavin Dick, Kevin Gallimore, and Jane C. Brown, "ISO 9000 and Quality Emphasis: An Empirical Study of Front-Room and Back-Room Dominated Service Industries," *International Journal of Service Industry Management* 12, no. 2 (2001): 114–136; Adrian Hughes and David N. Halsall, "Comparison of the 14 Deadly Diseases and the Business Excellence Model," *Total Quality Management* 13, no. 2 (2002): 255–263.

PART V

building a world-class
SERVICE
ORGANIZATION

LEARNING OBJECTIVES (LOs)

By the end of this chapter, the reader should be able to:

 LO 1 Know the characteristics of world-class service organizations and be familiar with the four levels of service performance.

 LO 2 Understand what is required for transforming a service firm from a service loser to a service leader.

 LO 3 Know the long-term impact of customer centricity on profitability and shareholder value.

INTRODUCTION

You are almost at the end of this book and presumably also at the tail end of your services marketing course. In this final chapter, we integrate many of the topics you have studied and provide you with a summary of what a world-class service organization looks like. You can use this summary as an assessment tool. This is followed by a discussion of the financial impact of being a service leader. The chapter closes with a call to action on your part!

CREATING A WORLD-CLASS SERVICE ORGANIZATION

▶ **LO 1**

Know the characteristics of world-class service organizations and be familiar with the four levels of service performance.

How would one describe a breakthrough service organization? Having worked in the field of services marketing for decades, we have observed that a number of characteristics are necessary (but may not be sufficient) for becoming and remaining a breakthrough service organization. Let's now explore in a more comprehensive analysis (1) how firms can be categorized into four performance levels and (2) how they can move up the performance ladder.

From Losers to Leaders: Four Levels of Service Performance

Service leadership is not based on outstanding performance within a single dimension. Rather, it reflects excellence across multiple dimensions. In an effort to capture this performance spectrum, we need to evaluate the organization within each of the three functional areas described earlier—marketing, operations, and human resources. Table 15.1 categorizes service performers into four levels: loser, non-entity, professional, and leader.[1] At each level, there is a brief description of a typical organization across 12 dimensions.

Under the marketing function, we look at the role of marketing, competitive appeal, customer profile, and service quality. Under the operations function, we consider the role of operations, service delivery (front-stage), back-stage processes, productivity, and introduction of new technologies. Finally, under the human resources function, we examine the role of human resource management, the workforce, and front-line management. Obviously, there are overlaps among these dimensions and across functions. There may also be differences in the relative importance of some dimensions in different industries and across different delivery systems. For instance, human resource management tends to play a more prominent strategic role in high-contact services. The goal of this overall service performance framework is to generate insights into how service leaders perform so well and what needs to be changed in organizations that are not performing as well as they might.

If you want to do an in-depth appraisal of a company in a specific industry, you may find it useful to view Table 15.1 as a point of departure. You can modify some of the elements to create a customized assessment tool.

Service Losers. These firms are at the bottom of the barrel from customer, employee, and managerial perspectives and get failing grades in marketing, operations, and HRM.

PART V

Table 15.1 Four levels of service performance.

Level	1. Loser	2. Nonentity
Marketing Function		
Role of marketing	Tactical role only; advertising and promotions lack focus; no involvement in product or pricing decision.	Uses mix of selling and mass communication, using simple segmentation strategy; makes selective use of price discounts and promotions; conducts and tabulates basic satisfaction surveys.
Competitive appeal	Customers patronize a firm for reasons other than performance.	Customers neither seek nor avoid the firm.
Customer profile	Unspecified; a mass market to be served at a minimum cost.	One or more segments whose basic needs are understood.
Service quality	Highly variable, usually unsatisfactory. Subservient to operations priorities.	Meets some customer expectations; consistent on one or two key dimensions, but not all.
Operations Function		
Role of operations	Reactive; cost oriented.	The principal line management function creates and delivers product, focuses on standardization as key to productivity, and defines quality from internal perspective.
Service delivery (front-stage)	A necessary evil. Locations and schedules are unrelated to preferences of customers, who are routinely ignored.	Sticklers for tradition; "If it ain't broke, don't fix it"; tight rules for customers; each step in delivery run independently.
Back-stage operations	Divorced from front-stage operations; cogs in a machine.	Contributes to individual front-stage delivery steps but organized separately; unfamiliar with customers.
Productivity	Undefined; managers are punished for failing to stick within budget.	Based on standardization; rewarded for keeping costs below budget.
Introduction of new technology	Late adopter, under duress, when necessary for survival.	Follows the crowd when justified by cost savings.
Human Resources Function		
Role of human resources	Supplies low-cost employees who meet minimum skill requirements for the job.	Recruits and trains employees who can perform competently.
Workforce	Negative constraint: poor performers, do not care, disloyal.	Adequate resource, follows procedures but uninspired; turnover often high.
Frontline management	Controls workers.	Controls the process.

3. Professional	4. Leader	Assessment Score
Marketing Function		
Has clear positioning strategy against competition; uses focused communications with distinctive appeals to clarify promises and educate customers; pricing is based on value; monitors customer usage and operates loyalty programs; uses a variety of research techniques to measure customer satisfaction and obtain ideas for service enhancements; works with operations to introduce new delivery systems.	Innovative leader in chosen segments, known for marketing skills; brands at product/process level; conducts sophisticated analysis of relational databases as inputs to one-to-one marketing and proactive account management; uses state-of-the-art research techniques; uses concept testing, observation, and lead customers as inputs to new-product development; close to operations/HR.	
Customers seek out the firm based on its sustained reputation for meeting customer expectations.	Company's name is synonymous with service excellence; its ability to delight customers raises expectations to levels that competitors can't meet.	
Groups of individuals whose variation in needs and value to the firm are clearly understood.	Individuals are selected and retained based on their future value to the firm, including their potential for new service opportunities and their ability to stimulate innovation.	
Consistently meets or exceeds customer expectations across multiple dimensions.	Raises customer expectations to new levels; improves continuously.	
	Subtotal	
Operations Function		
Plays a strategic role in competitive strategy; recognizes a trade-off between productivity and customer-defined quality; willing to outsource; monitors competing operations for ideas and threats.	Recognized for innovation, focus, and excellence; an equal partner with marketing and HR management; has in-house research capability and academic contacts; continually experimenting.	
Driven by customer satisfaction, not tradition; willing to customize and embrace new approaches; emphasis on speed, convenience, and comfort.	Delivery is a seamless process organized around the customer; employees know whom they are serving; focuses on continuous improvement.	
Process is explicitly linked to front-stage activities; sees role as serving "internal customers," who, in turn, serve external customers.	Closely integrated with front-stage delivery, even when geographically far apart; understands how own role relates to the overall process of serving external customers; continuing dialog.	
Focuses on reengineering backstage processes; avoids productivity improvements that will degrade customers' service experience; continually refining processes for efficiency.	Understands the concept of return on quality; actively seeks customer involvement in productivity improvement; ongoing testing of new processes and technologies.	
An early adopter when IT promises to enhance service for customers and provide a competitive edge.	Works with technology leaders to develop new applications that create first-mover advantage; seeks to perform at levels competitors cannot match.	
	Subtotal	
Human Resources Function		
Invests in selective recruiting, ongoing training; keeps close to employees, promotes upward mobility; strives to enhance the quality of working life.	Sees the quality of employees as a strategic advantage; the firm is recognized as outstanding place to work; HR helps top management to nurture culture.	
Motivated, hard-working, allowed some discretion in choice of procedures, offers suggestions.	Innovative and empowered; very loyal, committed to the firm's values and goals; creates procedures.	
Listens to customers; coaches and facilitates workers.	Source of new ideas for top management; mentors workers to enhance career growth, value to firm.	
	Subtotal	
	Total Score	

Legend: Score each area from '1' to '4' depending on the performance level of the organization that is being assessed. Average the scores for each function, and then average the functions to obtain the total assessment score.
A score of "3.5 and above" indicates excellent performance; a score from "2.5 to 3.4" indicates good performance, a score from "1.5 to 2.4" indicates average to poor performance, and a score of "1.4 and lower" indicates very poor performance.
Note: This framework was inspired by, and expands upon, work in service operations management by Richard Chase and Robert Hayes.

PART V

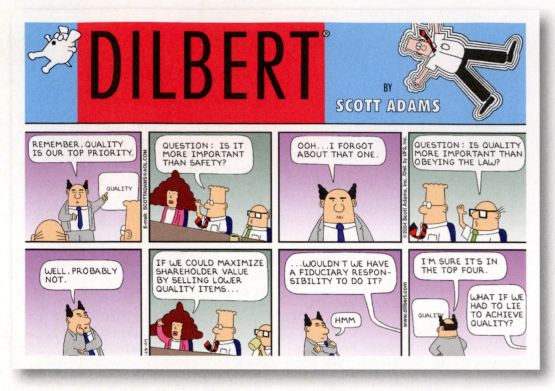

Figure 15.1 Dilbert's boss loses focus—and his audience.

Customers patronize them for reasons other than performance (typically because there is no viable alternative). Managers of such organizations may even see service delivery as a necessary evil. New technology is introduced only under duress, and the uncaring workforce is a negative constraint on performance.

Service Non-entities. Although their performance still leaves much to be desired, service non-entities have eliminated the worst features of losers. Non-entities are dominated by a traditional operations mindset that is typically based on achieving cost savings through standardization. Their marketing strategies are unsophisticated, and the roles of human resources and operations might be summed up, respectively, by the philosophies "adequate is good enough" and "if it ain't broke, don't fix it." Managers may talk about improving quality and other goals but are unable to set clear priorities to have a clear direction or gain the respect and commitment of their employees (Figure 15.1). Several such firms are often found competing in a lackluster fashion within a given marketplace, and you might have difficulty distinguishing one from the others. Periodic price discounts tend to be the primary means of trying to attract new customers.

Service Professionals. Service professionals are in a different league from non-entities and have a clear market positioning strategy. Customers within the target segments seek out these firms based on their sustained reputation for consistently meeting expectations. Marketing is sophisticated, using targeted communications and pricing based on value to the customer. Research is used to measure customer satisfaction and obtain ideas for service enhancement. Operations and marketing work together to introduce new delivery systems and to recognize the trade-off between productivity and customer-defined quality. There are explicit links between back-stage and front-stage activities; and the firm has a much more proactive, investment-oriented approach to HRM than is found among non-entities.

Service Leaders. These are breakthrough service organizations that are regarded as the *crème de la crème* of their respective industries. While service professionals are good, service leaders are outstanding. When we think of service leaders, we think of Amazon, McKinsey, Ritz Carlton, Southwest Airlines, Starbucks, and Zappos. Their company names are synonymous with service excellence and an ability to delight customers. Service leaders are recognized for their innovation in each functional area of management as well as for their superior internal communications and coordination among these three functions. The latter is often the result of a relatively flat organizational structure and the extensive use of teams. Service delivery is therefore a seamless process organized around the customer (Figure 15.2).

Marketing efforts by service leaders make extensive use of customer relationship management (CRM) systems that offer strategic insights about customers, who are often addressed on a one-to-one basis. Concept testing, observation, and contacts with lead customers are employed in the development of new, breakthrough services that respond to previously unrecognized needs. Operations specialists work with technology leaders around the world to develop new applications that will create a first-mover advantage and enable the firm to perform at levels that competitors cannot hope to reach for a long time to come. Senior executives see the quality of employees as a strategic advantage. HRM works on building and maintaining a service-oriented culture and creating an outstanding working environment that simplifies the task of attracting and retaining the best people (Figure 15.2).[2] The employees themselves are committed to the firm's values and goals. As they are engaged, empowered, and quick to embrace change, they are an ongoing source of new ideas and drive continuous improvement.

Figure 15.2 Service excellence is often underpinned by effective use of teams.

Moving to a Higher Level of Performance

Almost all companies want to be service leaders. We want to win our customers' loyalty, and we want our customers to say good things about us. If we can achieve these objectives, we will increase our market share, our shareholder value, and our share of community goodwill. Thus, there are powerful reasons for moving to a higher performance level. This view is becoming widely accepted, and in most markets we can find companies that are moving up the performance ladder through conscious efforts to improve and coordinate their marketing, operations, and HRM functions. This helps them to establish more favorable competitive positions and better satisfy their customers.

It requires human leaders at all levels of an organization to take a service firm in the right direction, set the right strategic priorities, and ensure that the relevant strategies are implemented throughout the organization. We have discussed ways of achieving these goals in the various chapters throughout this book. You now have the tools, concepts, and theories that will help you become an agent of change in your organization.

CUSTOMER SATISFACTION AND CORPORATE PERFORMANCE

The philosophy of this book has been all about customer centricity and creating value for customers as a long-term core strategy. This perspective permeates many of the key concepts and models you have learned in this book, including the Service-Profit

LO 2

Understand what is required for transforming a service firm from a service loser to a service leader.

LO 3

Know the long-term impact of customer centricity on profitability and shareholder value.

PART V

SERVICE INSIGHTS 15.1

Customer Satisfaction and Wall Street—High Returns and Low Risk!

Does a firm's customer satisfaction levels have anything to do with its stock price? This was the research question Claes Fornell and his colleagues wanted to answer. More specifically, they examined whether investments in customer satisfaction led to excess stock returns (see Figure 15.3)and, if so, whether these returns were associated with higher risks (as would be predicted by finance theory).

The researchers built two stock portfolios—one hypothetical back-dated portfolio and a real-world portfolio that tracked stock market performance in real time over several years. Both portfolios consisted only of firms that did well in terms of their customer satisfaction ratings, as measured by the American Customer Satisfaction Index (ACSI).

The ACSI-based portfolios were rebalanced once a year on the day when the annual ACSI results were announced. Only firms in the top 20% in terms of customer satisfaction ratings were included. (Firms were either retained if they were already in the top 20% last year, or they were added to the portfolio if they improved their satisfaction ranking to enter the top 20%.) Firms that fell below the 20% cut-off were sold. The return and risk of both portfolios were measured, and their risk-adjusted returns were then compared to broad market indices such as the S&P 500 and NASDAQ.

The findings are striking for managers and investors alike! Fornell and his colleagues discovered that the ACSI-based portfolios generated significantly higher risk-adjusted returns than their market benchmark indices and outperformed the market. Changes in the ACSI ratings of individual firms were significantly related to their future stock price movement and (as another study showed) even CEO compensation.[5]

However, simply publishing the latest data on the ACSI index did not immediately move share prices as efficient market theory would have predicted. Instead, share prices seemed to adjust slowly over time as firms published other results (perhaps earnings data or other "hard" facts that may lag behind changes in customer satisfaction). A recent study in a retail context confirmed this time lag. Increases in customer satisfaction were shown to lag operational improvements, and profits lagged increases in customer satisfaction. Therefore, becoming a service champion requires a long-term perspective.[6]

Firms that reacted faster than the market to changes in the ACSI index generated excess stock returns.

Figure 15.3 Can customer satisfaction data help to outperform the market?

This return represents a stock market imperfection, but it is consistent with research in marketing which holds that satisfied customers improve the level and the stability of cash flow.

In a later study, Lerzan Aksoy and her colleagues built on these findings and confirmed that a portfolio based on ACSI data outperformed the S&P 500 index over a 10-year period and delivered risk-adjusted abnormal returns.

For marketing managers, the findings of both studies confirm that investments (or "expenses" if you talk to accountants) into the management of customer relationships and the cash flows they produce are fundamental to the firm's, and therefore the shareholders', value creation.

Although the results are convincing, you should be careful if you want to exploit this apparent market inefficiency and invest in firms that show high increases in customer satisfaction in future ACSI releases. Your friends in finance will tell you that efficient markets learn fast! You will know this has happened when you see stock prices move in response to future ACSI releases. You can learn more about the ACSI at www.theacsi.org.

Chain, the Cycle of Success, the Service Talent Cycle, the Wheel of Loyalty, and the Gaps Model. We therefore feel it is fitting to end this book with a final piece of evidence which shows that a long-term perspective and customer centricity pay off financially.

There's convincing evidence of strategic links between the level of customer satisfaction with a firm's service offerings and overall firm performance. Researchers from the University of Michigan found that on average, every 1% increase in customer satisfaction is associated with a 2.4% increase in a firm's return on investment (ROI).[3] The analysis of companies' scores on the American Customer Satisfaction Index (ACSI) shows that, on average, among publicly traded firms, a 5% change in the ACSI score is associated with a 19% change in the market value of common equity.[4] In other words, by creating more value for the customer (as measured by increased satisfaction), the firm creates more value for its owners (see Service Insights 15.1).

CONCLUSION AND WRAP-UP

You are at the end of this book. We hope it exceeded your expectations, gave you new insights into the marketing (and management) of services, and provided you with the tools and skills you need to succeed. Transforming an organization and maintaining service leadership is no easy task even for the most gifted leader. We hope that working through this book will help you to become a more effective marketer and leader in any service organization. We also hope that we have managed to equip you not only with the necessary knowledge, understanding, and insights but also with the beliefs and attitudes about what propels a firm to service leadership. If this book has motivated and excited you to become a service champion, we as authors have achieved our objectives.

If you have feedback and suggestions on how to improve this book further, do contact us via www.JochenWirtz.com or sg.linkedin.com/in/jochenwirtz. We'd love to hear from you!

We would like to finish the book with a final quote by Tony Robins: "It's not knowing what to do, it's doing what you know." On this note, we wish you enjoyment, fulfillment, and success in applying what you've learned.

LO 1 ▶ There are four levels of service performance, and only the last two follow the key lessons from this book:

- o **Service losers.** They are poor performers in marketing, operations, and HRM. Service losers survive because monopoly situations give customers little choice other than to buy from them.

- o **Service non-entities.** Their performance leaves much to be desired, but they have eliminated the worst features of service losers.

- o **Service professionals.** They have a clear market position, and customers in target segments seek them out on the basis of their sustained reputation for meeting expectations. They are solid performers in marketing, operations, and HR, and the functions are tightly integrated.

- o **Service leaders.** They are the breakthrough service champions that are regarded as the *crème de la crème* of their respective industries. Their company names are synonymous with service excellence and an ability to delight customers.

- o We contrasted the description and actions of a service leader against professionals, non-entities, and losers along the three functional areas in Table 15.1. Service leadership requires high performance across a number of dimensions. These may include the use of sophisticated marketing, the management and motivation of employees, and the continuous improvement of service quality and productivity.

LO 2 ▶ It requires human leaders at all levels of an organization to take a service firm in the right direction and ensure that the relevant strategies are implemented throughout the organization. We have discussed ways of achieving these goals in the various chapters throughout this book. You now have the tools, concepts, and theories that will help you become an agent of change in your organization.

LO 3 ▶ A service leader's adoption of a long-term perspective and customer centricity pay off financially. There is solid empirical evidence that high customer satisfaction (compared to an organization's peer group) leads to superior financial returns.

UNLOCK YOUR LEARNING

These keywords are found within the sections of each Learning Objective (LO). They are integral to understanding the services marketing concepts taught in each section. Having a firm grasp of these keywords and how they are used is essential to helping you do well on your course, and in the real and very competitive marketing scene out there.

LO 1
1. Performance ladder
2. Operations
3. Performance levels
4. Marketing
5. World-class service organization
6. Competitive appeal
7. Human resources
8. Customer profile
9. Front-line management
10. Service delivery
11. Back-stage processes
12. Service losers
13. Customer relationship management (CRM)
14. Service professionals
15. Service non-entities
16. Service leaders

LO 2
1. Shareholder value
2. Market share
3. Human leaders
4. Community goodwill
5. Strategic priorities

LO 3
1. Customer centricity
2. Long-term perspective
3. Customer satisfaction
4. Corporate performance
5. Return on investment (ROI)
6. American Customer Satisfaction Index (ACSI)

How well do you know the language of services marketing? Quiz yourself!

⚠ **Not for the academically faint-of-heart**

For each keyword you are able to recall without referring to earlier pages, give yourself a point (and a pat on the back). Tally your score at the end and see if you earned the right to be called—a *services marketeer*.

SCORE

0 – 6	Services Marketing is done a great disservice.
7 – 13	The midnight oil needs to be lit, pronto.
14 – 19	I know what you *didn't* do all semester.
20 – 25	By George! You're getting there.
26 – 31	Now, go forth and market.
32 – 34	There should be a marketing concept named after you.

Review Questions

1. How are the four levels of service performance defined? Based on your own service experiences, provide an example of a company for each category.

2. Is there evidence that improving customer satisfaction leads to improved financial returns for shareholders?

WORK YOUR SERVICES MARKETING

Application Exercises

1. Select a company you know well, and obtain additional information from a literature review, website, company publication, blog, and so on. Evaluate the company on as many dimensions of service performance as you can, identifying where you believe it fits on the service performance spectrum shown in Table 15.1.

2. Based on all you've learned working throughout this book, what do you believe are the key drivers of success for service organizations? Try to develop an integrative causal model that explains the important drivers of success for a service organization.

END**NOTES**

1. The operations perspective was originally developed by: Richard B. Chase and Robert H. Hayes, "Beefing Up Operations in Service Firms," *Sloan Management Review* (Fall 1991): 15–26. The framework showed in this chapter has been significantly extended and updated to incorporate the marketing and HR functions.

2. Claudia H. Deutsch, "Management: Companies Scramble to Fill Shoes at the Top," *The New York Times*, nytimes.com (accessed November 1, 2000).

3. Eugene W. Anderson and Vikas Mittal, "Strengthening the Satisfaction-Profit Chain," *Journal of Service Research* 3 (November 2000): 107–120.

4. Claes Fornell, Sunil Mithas, Forrest V. Morgeson III, and M. S. Krishnan, "Customer Satisfaction and Stock Prices: High Returns, Low Risk," *Journal of Marketing* 70 (January 2006): 3–14.

5. A large-scale empirical study based on the ACSI showed that CEOs benefit if their firms outperform their peer group in terms of customer satisfaction. The benefits take the form of higher annual bonuses over and above what was explained by typical financial performance metrics and key control variables. See: Vincent O'Connel and Don O'Sullivan, "The Impact of Customer Satisfaction on CEO Bonuses," *Journal of the Academy of Marketing Science* 39, no. 6 (2011): 828–845.

6. The authors estimated that a 20% increase in operational investments to improve service resulted in an immediate drop in operating profits. However, the very next year, there was an increase in profit that amounted to twice the drop experienced in the year of investment. See: Heiner Evanschitzky, Florian V. Wangenheim, and Nancy V. Wünderlich, "Perils of Managing the Service Profit Chain: The Role of Time Lags and Feedback Loops," *Journal of Retailing* 88, no. 3 (2012): 356–366.

Sullivan Ford Auto World

Christopher H. Lovelock

A young healthcare manager unexpectedly finds herself running a family-owned car dealership in financial trouble. She is very concerned about the poor performance of the service department and wonders whether a turnaround is possible.

Viewed from Wilson Avenue, the Sullivan Ford Auto World dealership presented a festive sight. Flags waved, and strings of triangular pennants in red, white, and blue fluttered gaily in the late afternoon breeze. Rows of new model cars and trucks gleamed and winked in the sunlight. Geraniums graced the flower beds outside the showroom entrance. A huge rotating sign at the corner of Wilson Avenue and Route 78 sported the Ford logo and identified the business as Sullivan Ford Auto World. The banners below urged, "Let's Make a Deal!"

Inside the handsome, high-ceilinged showroom, four of the new model Fords were on display—a dark-green Explorer SUV, a red Mustang convertible, a white Focus sedan, and a red Ranger pick-up truck. Each vehicle was polished to a high sheen. Two groups of customers were chatting with salespeople, and a middle-aged man sat in the driver's seat of the Mustang, studying the controls.

Upstairs, in the comfortably furnished general manager's office, Carol Sullivan-Diaz finished running another spreadsheet analysis on her laptop. She felt tired and depressed. Her father, Walter Sullivan, had died of a sudden heart attack four weeks earlier at the age of 56. As executor of his estate, the bank had asked her to temporarily assume the position of general manager of the dealership. The only visible change that she had made to her father's office was the installation of an all-in-one laser printer, scanner, copier, and fax machine. However, she had been very busy analyzing the current position of the business.

Sullivan-Diaz did not like the look of the numbers on the printout. Auto World's financial situation had been deteriorating for 18 months and running in the red for the first half of the current year. New car sales had declined, dampened in part by the poor macroeconomic environment. Margins had been squeezed by promotions and other efforts to move new cars off the lot. Reflecting rising fuel prices, industry forecasts of future sales were discouraging, and so were Sullivan-Diaz's own financial projections for Auto World's sales department. Service revenues, which were below average for a dealership of this size, had also declined, although the service department still made a small surplus.

Had she made a mistake the previous week, Carol wondered, in turning down Bill Froelich's offer to buy the business? Admittedly, the amount was substantially lower than the offer from Froelich that her father had rejected two years earlier, but the business had been more profitable at that time.

THE SULLIVAN FAMILY

Walter Sullivan purchased a small Ford dealership in 1993, renamed it Sullivan's Auto World, and built it up to make it one of the best-known car dealerships in the metropolitan area. In 2009, he borrowed heavily to purchase the current site at a major suburban highway intersection in an area of the city with many new housing developments.

There had been a dealership on the site, but the buildings were 30 years old. Sullivan retained the service and repair bays but tore down the showroom in front of them and replaced it with an attractive modern facility. On moving to the new location, which was substantially larger than the old one, he renamed his business Sullivan Ford Auto World.

Everybody seemed to know Walter Sullivan. He was a consummate showman and entrepreneur, appearing in his own radio and television commercials. He was also quite active in community affairs. His approach to car sales emphasized promotions, discounts, and deals in order to maintain volume. He was never happier than when making a sale.

Carol Sullivan-Diaz, aged 28, was the eldest of Walter and Carmen Sullivan's three daughters. After obtaining a bachelor's degree in economics, she went on to take an MBA degree and then embarked on a career in health-care management. She was married to Dr. Roberto Diaz, a surgeon at St. Luke's Hospital. Her 20-year-old twin sisters, Gail and Joanne, who were students at the state university, lived with their mother.

In her own student days, Sullivan-Diaz had worked part time in her father's business on secretarial and book-keeping tasks and as a service writer in the service department. Thus, she was quite familiar with the operations of the dealership. At business school, she decided on a career in healthcare management. After graduation, she worked as an executive assistant to the president of St Luke's, a large teaching hospital. Two years later, she joined Heritage Hospitals, a large multi-hospital facility that also provided long-term care, as the assistant director of marketing, a position she had held for almost three years. Her responsibilities included designing new services, handling complaints, conducting market research, and introducing an innovative day-care program for hospital employees and neighborhood residents.

Carol's employer had given her a six-week leave of absence to put her father's affairs in order. She doubted that she would be able to extend that leave much beyond the two weeks still remaining. Neither she nor her other family members were interested in making a career of running the dealership. However, she was prepared to take time out from her healthcare career to work on a turnaround if that seemed a viable proposition. She had been successful in her present job and believed it would not be difficult to find another health-management position in the future.

THE DEALERSHIP

Like other car dealerships, Sullivan Ford Auto World operated both sales and service departments, often referred to in the trade as "front end" and "back end" respectively. Both new and used vehicles were sold, since a high proportion of new car and van purchases involved trading in the purchaser's existing vehicle. Auto World would also buy well-maintained used cars at auctions for re-sale. Purchasers who decided that they could not afford a new car would often buy a "pre-owned" vehicle instead, while shoppers who came in looking for used cars could sometimes be persuaded to buy new ones. Before being put on sale, used vehicles were carefully serviced, with parts being replaced as needed. They were then thoroughly cleaned

by a detailer whose services were hired as required. Dents and other blemishes were removed at a nearby body shop, and the vehicle's paint work was occasionally re-sprayed as well.

The front end of the dealership employed a sales manager, seven salespeople, an office manager, and a secretary. One of the salespeople had given notice and would be leaving at the end of the following week. The service department, when fully staffed, consisted of a service manager, a parts supervisor, nine mechanics, and two service writers. The Sullivan twins often worked part-time as service writers, filling in during busy periods, when one of the other writers was sick or on vacation, or when—as currently—there was an unfilled vacancy. The job entailed scheduling appointments for repairs and maintenance, writing up each work order, calling customers with repair estimates, and assisting customers when they returned to pick up their cars and pay for the work that had been done.

Sullivan-Diaz knew from her own experience as a service writer that it could be a stressful job. Few people liked to be without their car, even for a day. When a car broke down or had problems, the owner was often nervous about how long it would take to get it fixed and, if the warranty had expired, how much the labor and parts would cost. Customers could be quite unforgiving if a problem was not fixed completely on the first attempt, thereby requiring them to return their vehicle for further work.

Major mechanical failures were usually not difficult to repair, although the costs of replacing parts could be quite high. It was often the "little" things, such as water leaks and wiring problems, that were the hardest to diagnose and correct. Moreover, it was sometimes necessary for the customer to return two or three times before such a problem could be resolved. In these situations, parts and material costs were relatively low, but labor costs mounted up quickly, being charged out at US$75 an hour. Customers could sometimes be quite abusive, yelling at service writers over the phone or arguing with service writers, mechanics, and the service manager in person.

Turnover in the service-writer job was high, which was one reason why Carol—and more recently her sisters—had often been pressed into service by their father, to "hold the fort," as he described it. More than once, she had seen an exasperated service writer respond sharply to a complaining customer or hang up on one who was being abusive over the telephone. Gail and Joanne were currently taking turns to cover the vacant position, but there were times when both of them had classes and the dealership had only one service writer on duty.

By national standards, Sullivan Ford Auto World stood toward the lower end of medium-sized dealerships, selling around 1,100 cars a year, equally divided between new and used vehicles. In the most recent year, its revenues totaled US$26.6 million from new and used car sales and US$2.9 million from service and parts—down from US$30.5 million and US$3.6 million, respectively, in the previous year. Although the unit value of car sales was high, the margins were quite low, with margins for new cars being substantially lower than those for used ones. Industry guidelines suggested that the contribution margin (known as the departmental selling gross) from car sales should be about 5.5% of sales revenues and around 25% of revenues from service. In a typical dealership, 60% of the selling gross would traditionally come from sales and 40% from service, but the balance was shifting from sales to service. The selling gross was then applied to fixed expenses, such as administrative salaries, rent or mortgage payments, and utilities.

For the most recent 12 months at Auto World, Sullivan-Diaz had determined that the selling gross figures were 4.6% and 24% respectively. Both these figures were lower than those of the previous year and insufficient to cover the dealership's fixed expenses. Sullivan-Diaz's father had made no mention of financial difficulties, and she had been shocked to learn from the bank after his death that Auto World had been two months behind in mortgage payments on the property. Further analysis also showed that accounts payable had risen sharply in the previous six months. Fortunately, the dealership held a large insurance policy on Sullivan's life, and the proceeds from this were more than sufficient to bring mortgage payments up to date, pay down all overdue accounts, and leave some funds for future contingencies.

OUTLOOK

The opportunities for expanding new car sales did not appear promising, given declining consumer confidence and recent layoffs at several local plants, which were expected to hurt the local economy. However, promotional incentives had reduced the inventory to manageable levels. From discussions with Larry Winters, Auto World's sales manager, Sullivan-Diaz had concluded that costs could be cut by not replacing the departing sales representative, maintaining

inventory at its current reduced level, and trying to make more efficient use of advertising and promotion. Although Winters did not have Walter's exuberant personality, he had been Auto World's leading sales representative before being promoted and had shown strong managerial capabilities in his current position.

As she reviewed the figures for the service department, Sullivan-Diaz wondered what potential might exist for improving its sales volume and selling gross. Her father had never been very interested in the parts-and-service business, seeing it simply as a necessary adjunct of the dealership. "Customers always seem to be miserable back there," he had once remarked to her. "But here in the front end, everybody's happy when someone buys a new car." The service facility was hidden behind the showroom and therefore not easily visible from the main highway. Although the building looked old and greasy, the equipment itself was modern and well maintained. There was sufficient capacity to handle more repair work, but a higher volume would require the hiring of one or more new mechanics.

Customers were required to bring cars in for servicing before 8:30 a.m. After parking their cars, customers entered the service building by a side door and waited for their turn to see the service writers, who occupied a cramped room with peeling paint and an interior window overlooking the service bays. Customers stood while work orders for their cars were prepared. Ringing telephones frequently interrupted the process. Filing cabinets containing customer records and other documents lined the far wall of the room.

If the work was of a routine nature, such as an oil change or a tune-up, the customer was given an estimate immediately. For more complex jobs, customers would be called with an estimate later in the morning once the car had been examined. They were required to pick up their cars by 6:00 p.m. on the day the work was completed. On several occasions, Carol had urged her father to computerize the service work-order process, but he had never acted on her suggestions, so all orders continued to be handwritten on large yellow sheets, with carbon copies.

Rick Obert, who was in his late forties, had held the position of Service Manager since Auto World had opened at its current location. The Sullivan family considered him to be technically skilled, and he managed the mechanics effectively. However, his manner with customers could be gruff and argumentative.

CUSTOMER SURVEY RESULTS

Another set of data that Sullivan-Diaz had studied carefully was the results of the customer satisfaction surveys that were mailed to the dealership every month by a research firm retained by Ford USA.

Purchasers of all new Ford cars were sent a questionnaire by mail within 30 days of making the purchase and asked to use a five-point scale to rate their satisfaction with the dealership sales department, vehicle preparation, and the characteristics of the vehicle itself.

The questionnaire asked the purchasers how likely they were to recommend the dealership, the salesperson, and the manufacturer to someone else. It also asked if the customers had been introduced to the dealer's service department and been given explanations on what to do if their cars needed service. Finally, there were some classification questions relating to customer demographics.

A second survey was sent to new car purchasers nine months after they bought their cars. This questionnaire began by asking customers if they were satisfied with the vehicle and if they had taken it to the selling dealer for service of any kind. If the response to the second question was affirmative, respondents were asked to rate the service department on 14 different attributes—ranging from the attitudes of service personnel to the quality of the work performed—and then to rate their overall satisfaction with the service from the dealer.

The questionnaire also asked customers where they would go in the future for maintenance service, minor mechanical and electrical repairs, major repairs in those same categories, and bodywork. The options listed for service were the selling dealer, another Ford dealer, "some other place," or "do it yourself." Finally, there were questions about the customers' overall satisfaction with the dealer's sales department and the dealership in general as well as the likelihood of their purchasing another Ford product and from the same dealership or elsewhere.

Dealers received monthly reports summarizing customer ratings of their dealership for the most recent month as well as for several previous months. To provide a comparison of how other Ford dealerships were performing, the reports also included regional and national rating averages. After analysis, completed questionnaires were returned to the dealership. Since these included each customer's name, a dealer could see which customers were satisfied and which were not.

In the 30-day survey of new purchasers, Auto World achieved better-than-average ratings on most dimensions. One finding that puzzled Carol was that almost 90% of respondents answered "yes" when asked if someone from Auto World had explained what they had to do if they needed service, but less than a third said that they had been introduced to someone in the service department. She resolved to ask Larry Winters about this discrepancy.

The nine-month survey findings disturbed her. Although vehicle ratings were in line with national averages, the overall level of satisfaction with service at Auto World was consistently low, placing it in the bottom 25% of all Ford dealerships. The worst ratings for service concerned promptness of writing up orders, convenience of scheduling the work, convenience of service hours, and appearance of the service department. On length of time to complete the work, availability of needed parts, and quality of work done ("Was it fixed right?"), Auto World's rating was close to the average. For interpersonal variables such as attitude of service-department personnel, politeness, understanding of customer problems, and explanation of work performed, its ratings were relatively poor.

When Sullivan-Diaz reviewed the individual questionnaires, she found that there was a wide degree of variation between customers' responses on these interpersonal variables, ranging all the way across a five-point scale from "completely satisfied" to "very dissatisfied." Curious, she went to the service files and examined the records for several dozen customers who had recently completed the nine-month surveys. At least part of the ratings could be explained with reference to the specific service writer the customer had dealt with. Those who had been served two or more times by her sisters, for instance, gave much better ratings than those who had dealt primarily with Jim Fiskell, the service writer who had recently quit.

Perhaps the most worrying responses were those relating to how likely customers were to use Auto World's service department in the future. More than half indicated that they would use another Ford dealer or "some other place" for maintenance service (such as oil change, lubrication, or tune-up) or for minor mechanical and electrical repairs. About 30% would use another source for major repairs. The rating for overall satisfaction with the selling dealer after nine months was below average, and the customer's likelihood of purchasing from the same dealership again was a full point below that of buying another Ford product.

OPTIONS

Sullivan-Diaz pushed aside the spreadsheets she had printed out and shut down her laptop. It was time to go home for dinner. She saw the options for the dealership as basically twofold: either prepare the business for an early sale at what would amount to a distress price, or take a year or two to try to turn it around financially. In the latter instance, if the turnaround succeeded, the business could subsequently be sold at a higher price than it presently commanded, or the family could install a general manager to run the dealership for them.

Bill Froelich, owner of another dealership located nearby plus three more dealerships in neighboring cities, had offered to buy Auto World for a price that represented a fair valuation of the net assets, according to Auto World's accountants, plus $250,000 in goodwill. However, the rule of thumb when the auto industry was enjoying good times was that goodwill should be valued at $1,200 per vehicle sold each year. Carol knew that Froelich was eager to develop a network of dealerships in order to achieve economies of scale. His prices on new cars were very competitive, and his nearest dealership clustered several franchises—Ford, Lincoln-Mercury, Volvo, and Jaguar—on a single large property.

AN UNWELCOME DISTURBANCE

As Carol left her office, she spotted the sales manager coming up the stairs leading from the showroom floor. "Larry," she said, "I've got a question for you."

"Fire away!" replied the sales manager.

"I've been looking at the customer satisfaction surveys. Why aren't our sales reps introducing new customers to the folks in the Service Department? It's supposedly part of our sales protocol, but it only seems to be happening about one-third of the time!"

Larry Winters shuffled his feet. "Well, Carol, basically I leave it to their discretion. We tell them about service, of course, but some of the guys on the floor feel a bit uncomfortable taking folks over to the service bays after they've been in here. It's quite a contrast, if you know what I mean."

Suddenly, the sound of shouting arose from the floor below. A man of about 40, wearing a windbreaker and jeans, was standing in the doorway yelling at one of the salespeople.

The two managers could catch snatches of what he was saying, in between various obscenities:

"... three visits ... still not fixed right ... service stinks ... who's in charge here?" Everybody else in the showroom stopped what they were doing and turned to look at the newcomer.

Winters looked at his young employer and rolled his eyes. "If there was something your dad couldn't stand, it was guys like that, yelling and screaming in the showroom and asking for the boss. Walt would go hide out in his office! Don't worry, Tom'll take care of that fellow and get him out of here. What a jerk!"

"No," said Sullivan-Diaz, "I'll deal with him! One thing I learned when I worked at St. Luke's was that you don't let people yell about their problems in front of everybody else. You take them off somewhere, calm them down, and find out what's bugging them."

Exhibit 1: Marketing cars is a different proposition than marketing services for the same vehicles.

She stepped quickly down the stairs, wondering to herself, "What else have I learned in healthcare that I can apply to this business?"

STUDY QUESTIONS

1. How does marketing cars differ from marketing service for cars?

2. Compare and contrast the sales and service departments at Auto World.

3. From a consumer's perspective, what useful parallels do you see between operating a car sales and service dealership and operating health services?

4. What advice would you give to Carol Sullivan-Diaz?

Dr. Beckett's Dental Office

Lauren K. Wright

A dentist seeks to differentiate her practice on the basis of quality. She constructs a new office and redesigns the practice to deliver high quality service to her patients and to improve productivity through increased efficiency. However, it's not always easy to convince patients that her superior service justifies higher fees that may not be covered by insurance.

MANAGEMENT COMES TO DENTISTRY

"I just hope the quality differences are visible to our patients," mused Dr. Barbro Beckett as she surveyed the new office that housed her well-established dental practice. She had recently moved to her current location from an office that she felt was too cramped to allow her staff to work efficiently—a factor that was becoming increasingly important as the costs of providing dental care continued to rise. While Dr. Beckett realized that productivity gains were necessary, she did not want to compromise the quality of service her patients received.

The classes Dr. Beckett took in dental school taught her a lot about the technical side of dentistry but nothing about the business side. She received no formal training in the mechanics of running a business or understanding customer needs. In fact, professional guidelines discouraged marketing or advertising of any kind. This had not been a major problem 22 years earlier when Dr. Beckett had started her practice, since profit margins had been good back then. However, the dental care industry had changed dramatically. Costs had increased as a result of labor laws, malpractice insurance, and the constant need to invest in equipment updates and staff training as new technologies were introduced. Dr. Beckett's overhead was now between 70%–80% of revenues (without accounting for her wages or office rental costs).

At the same time, there was a movement in the United States to reduce healthcare costs for insurance companies, employers, and patients by offering "managed healthcare" through large health maintenance organizations (HMOs). The HMOs set the prices for various services by putting an upper limit on the amount that their doctors and dentists could charge for various procedures. The advantage to patients was that their health insurance covered virtually all costs. However, the price limitations meant that HMO doctors and dentists would not be able to offer certain services that could provide better-quality care but were too expensive. Dr. Beckett had decided not to become an HMO provider, because the reimbursement rates were only 80%–85% of what she normally charged for treatment. At these rates, she felt that she could not provide high-quality care to patients.

These changes presented some significant challenges to Dr. Beckett, who wanted to offer the highest level of dental care rather than be a low-cost provider. With the help of a consultant, she decided that her top priority was differentiating the practice on the basis of quality. She and her staff developed an internal mission statement that reflected this goal. The mission statement (prominently displayed in the back office) read, in part: "It is our goal to provide superior dentistry in an efficient, profitable manner within the confines of a caring, quality environment."

Since higher quality care was more costly, Dr. Beckett's patients often had to pay fees for costs that were not covered by their insurance policies. Thus, if the quality differences were not substantial, these patients could decide to switch to an HMO dentist or another lower-cost provider.

REDESIGNING THE SERVICE DELIVERY SYSTEM

The move to a new office gave Dr. Beckett a unique opportunity to rethink almost every aspect of her service. She wanted the work environment to reflect her own personality and values and provide a pleasant place for her staff to work.

Facilities and Equipment

Dr. Beckett first looked into the office spaces that were available in the Northern California town where she practiced. She didn't find anything she liked, so she hired an architect from San Francisco to design a contemporary office building with lots of light and space. This increased the building costs by $100,000, but Dr. Beckett felt that it would be a critical factor in differentiating her service.

Dr. Beckett's new office was Scandinavian in design, reflecting her Swedish heritage and her attention to detail. The waiting room and reception area were filled with modern furniture in muted shades of brown, grey, green, and purple. Live plants and flowers were abundant, and the walls were covered with art. Classical music played softly in the background. Patients could enjoy a cup of coffee or tea and browse through the large selection of current magazines and newspapers while waiting for their appointments.

The treatment areas were both functional and appealing. There was a small, sound-proof conference room in front of the office where children could watch movies or play with toys while their parents were being treated. Educational videos and readings were available here to demonstrate different dental procedures and to explain what patients needed to do to maximize their treatment outcomes.

The chairs in the examining rooms were covered in leather and were very comfortable. Each room had a large window that allowed patients to watch birds eating at the feeders that were filled each day. There were also attractive mobiles hanging from the ceiling to distract patients from the unfamiliar sounds and sensations they might be experiencing. Headphones were available with a wide selection of music.

The entire back-office staff (including Dr. Beckett) wore uniforms in cheerful shades of pink, purple, and blue that matched the office décor. Dr. Beckett's dental degrees were prominently displayed, along with certificates from various programs that she and her staff had attended to update their technical skills (Exhibit 1). All the equipment in the treatment rooms was very modern and spotlessly clean. Each room had a chair-side computer monitor, where both patients and staff could view digital X-rays and photos while discussing treatment options. The digital X-rays provided many benefits, including reduced radiation emissions (80% less than traditional X-rays), high-quality images

that could be viewed immediately, and digital storage and transmission capabilities. The hygienists used a tool called a DIAGNOdent during teeth cleaning procedures. The DIAGNOdent was a non-invasive laser that scanned teeth for decay and detected cavities that were starting to develop so that they could be treated at a very early stage.

Exhibit 1: A modern, state-of-the-art treatment room projects a professional image to visiting patients.

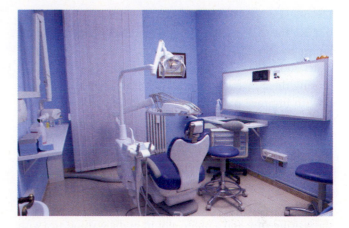

Service Personnel

There were eight employees in the dental practice, including Dr. Beckett (who was the only dentist). The seven staff members were separated by job function into "front-office" and "back-office" workers. Front-office duties (covered by two employees) included receptionist and secretarial tasks and financial/budgeting work. The back office was divided into hygienists and chair-side assistants.

The three chair-side assistants helped the hygienists and Dr. Beckett with treatment procedures. They had specialized training for their jobs but did not need a college degree. The two hygienists handled routine exams and teeth cleaning, plus some treatment procedures. In many dental offices, hygienists tend to act like "prima donnas" because of their education (a bachelor's degree plus specialized training) and experience. According to Dr. Beckett, such an attitude could destroy any possibility of team work among the office staff. She felt very fortunate that her hygienists viewed themselves as part of a larger team that worked together to provide quality care to patients.

Dr. Beckett valued her friendships with staff members and understood that they were a vital part of the service delivery. "90% of patients' perceptions of quality come from their interactions with the front desk and the other employees—

not from the staff's technical skills," she stated. When Dr. Beckett began to redesign her practice, she discussed her goals with the staff members and involved them in the decision-making process. The changes meant new expectations and routines for most employees, and some were not willing to adapt. There was some staff turnover (mostly voluntary) as the new office procedures were implemented. The current group worked very well as a team.

Dr. Beckett and her staff met briefly each morning to discuss the day's schedule and patients. They also had longer meetings every other week to discuss more strategic issues and resolve any problems that might have developed. During these meetings, employees made suggestions about how to improve patient care. Some of the most successful staff suggestions included "thank you" cards to patients who referred other patients; follow-up calls to patients after major procedures; a "gift" bag to give to patients after they'd had their teeth cleaned (containing a toothbrush, toothpaste, mouthwash, and floss); buckwheat pillows and blankets for patient comfort during long procedures; coffee and tea in the waiting area; and a photo album in the waiting area with pictures of staff and their families.

Exhibit 2: Service delivery is enhanced through customized interaction with patients, both young and old.

The expectations for staff performance (in terms of both technical competence and patient interactions) were very high. However, Dr. Beckett provided her employees with many opportunities to update their skills by attending classes and workshops. She also rewarded their hard work by giving monthly bonuses if business was good. Since she shared the financial data with her staff, they could see the difference in revenues if the schedule was slow or patients were dissatisfied. This provided an extra incentive to improve service delivery. The entire office also went on trips together once a year (paid for by Dr. Beckett); spouses were welcome to participate but had to cover their own trip expenses. Past destinations for these excursions had included Hawaii and Washington, D.C.

Procedures and Patients

With the help of a consultant, all the office systems (including billing, ordering, lab work, and patient treatment) were redesigned. One of the main goals was to standardize some of the routine procedures to reduce the occurrence of errors and ensure that all patients received the same level of care. Specific times were allotted for each procedure, and the staff worked very hard to see that these time requirements were met. Office policy specified that patients should be kept waiting no longer than 20 minutes without being given the option to reschedule, and employees often called patients in advance if they knew there would be a delay. They also attempted to fill in cancellations to make sure office capacity was maximized. Staff members substituted for each other when necessary or helped with tasks that were not specifically in their job descriptions in order to make things run more smoothly.

Dr. Beckett's practice included about 2,000 "active" patients (and many more who came infrequently). They were mostly white-collar workers with professional jobs (university employees, healthcare workers, and managers/owners of local establishments.) She did no advertising; all of her new business came from positive word of mouth by current patients. Dr. Beckett's practice was so busy that patients often had to wait 3–4 months for a routine cleaning and exam (if they didn't have their appointments automatically scheduled every six months), but they didn't seem to mind the delay.

The dentist believed that referrals were a real advantage, because new patients didn't come in "cold." She did not have to sell herself, because they had already been told about her service by friends or family. All new patients were required to have an initial exam so that Dr. Beckett could do a needs assessment and educate them about her service. She believed this was the first indication to patients that her practice was different from others they had experienced.

THE BIGGEST CHALLENGE

"Redesigning the business was the easy part," Dr. Beckett sighed. "Demonstrating the high level of quality to patients is the hard job." She said it was especially difficult since most people either disliked going to the dentist or felt that it was an inconvenience and came in with a negative attitude. Dr. Beckett tried to reinforce the idea that quality dental care depended on a positive long-term relationship between patients and the dental team. The website for the practice (www.chicogentledental.com) was designed to emphasize this concept. This philosophy was also reflected in a section of the patient mission statement hanging in the waiting area: "We are a caring, professional dental team serving motivated, quality-oriented patients interested in keeping healthy smiles for a lifetime. Our goal is to offer a progressive and educational environment. Your concerns are our focus."

Although Dr. Beckett enjoyed her work, she admitted that it could be difficult to maintain a positive attitude. The job required precision and attention to detail, and the procedures were often painful for patients. She often felt as though she were "walking on eggshells," because she knew

Exhibit 3: A team of closely-knit professionals working under the guidance of a clear, common mission statement can help overcome the most negative pre-conceived notions about visiting the dentist.

patients were anxious and uncomfortable, which made them more critical of her service delivery. It was not uncommon for patients to say negative things to Dr. Beckett even before treatment began (such as, "I really hate going to the dentist—it's not you, but I just don't want to be here!"). When this happened, she reminded herself that she was providing quality service whether patients appreciated it or not. "The person will usually have to have the dental work done anyway," she remarked, "So I just do the best job I can and make them as comfortable as possible." Even though patients seldom expressed appreciation for her services, she hoped that she had made a positive difference in their health or appearance that would benefit them in the long run.

STUDY QUESTIONS

1. Which of the seven elements of the Services Marketing Mix are addressed in this case? Give examples of each "P" you identify.

2. Why do people dislike going to the dentist? Do you feel Dr. Beckett has addressed this problem effectively?

3. How do Dr. Beckett and her staff educate patients about the service they are receiving? What else could they do?

4. What supplementary services are offered? How do they enhance service delivery?

5. Contrast your own dental care experiences with those offered by Dr. Beckett's practice. What differences do you see? Based on your review of this case, what advice would you give to (a) your current or former dentist and (b) Dr. Beckett?

6. Evaluate Dr. Beckett's website (www.chicogentledental. com). What strengths do you think the website has? What improvements would you suggest?

Uber: Competing as Market Leader in the United States versus Being a Distant Second in China

Jochen Wirtz and Christopher S. Tang

Uber allows people to book and share rides in private cars via their smart phones. With its headquarters in the United States, it operates in 60 countries and has a strong presence in the Asia-Pacific region. This case study explores Uber's development and growth in the United States as well as its global expansion and subsequent foray into China. Despite enjoying international success with deep penetration in major cities, Uber flopped in the Chinese market. What were the reasons for its failure in China, given its spectacular performance in many other countries?

INTRODUCTION

Uber was founded in 2009 by Travis Kalanick (the current CEO) and Garrett Camp in San Francisco. Its business model rested on the use of an app to call for a driver at any time and location (Exhibit 1). Uber managed to build a spectacular network of drivers and passengers in just three years. It thrives on what some people call an "instant-gratification economy," powered by the smart phone as the remote control for life. "If we can get you a car in five minutes, we can get you anything in five minutes," Kalanick said.[1]

Expanding outside the United States, Uber became a threat to taxi services in Europe and Asia, triggering protests in France, Germany, and India. Despite resulting government scrutiny, tighter regulations, and disputes with local taxi companies, Uber's disruptive business model successfully posed an effective challenge to taxi monopolies in the countries it operated in. As of August 2015, Uber has clinched the title of the most valuable start-up in the world, valued at $51 billion.

Enjoying first-mover advantage in app-enabled transportation services and ride sharing, Uber was far more successful in its number of users and drivers than its main American

competitor, Lyft. Lyft positioned itself as a more informal, community-centered way to travel. Drivers and shotgun-riding passengers were expected to strike up a conversation during the ride. However, entering the market three years after Uber, Lyft managed to commence operations in only 65 American cities by the end of 2015. In contrast, Uber had been operating in a total of 300 large cities in 60 countries. Both companies offered a myriad of services at different price points (Exhibit 2).

China, with a projection of 221 cities containing a population of one million or more, was a highly attractive market for any internationally minded taxi company. Uber pioneered its taxi service in Shanghai in 2013. Entering difficult markets was not new to Uber, which had already successfully navigated diverse markets in the United Kingdom, India, and South Africa. Nevertheless, Uber encountered unique roadblocks in China—strong competitors, existing low-cost taxi services, and a lack of know-how to navigate around local regulations and even corrupt officials. Uber also faced tough competition from a much larger local player, Didi-Kuaidi (known locally as 滴滴打车). Didi boasted more than one million drivers in 360 cities in China, whereas Uber only had about 100,000 drivers in 20 cities.

UBER'S GROWTH

The first conceptualization of Uber's business model started in Paris in 2008, when founders Kalanick and Camp could not get a cab while returning from a conference. The two discussed the idea of solving the problem with a mobile app—push a button and get a car.

Exhibit 1: Uber's business model.

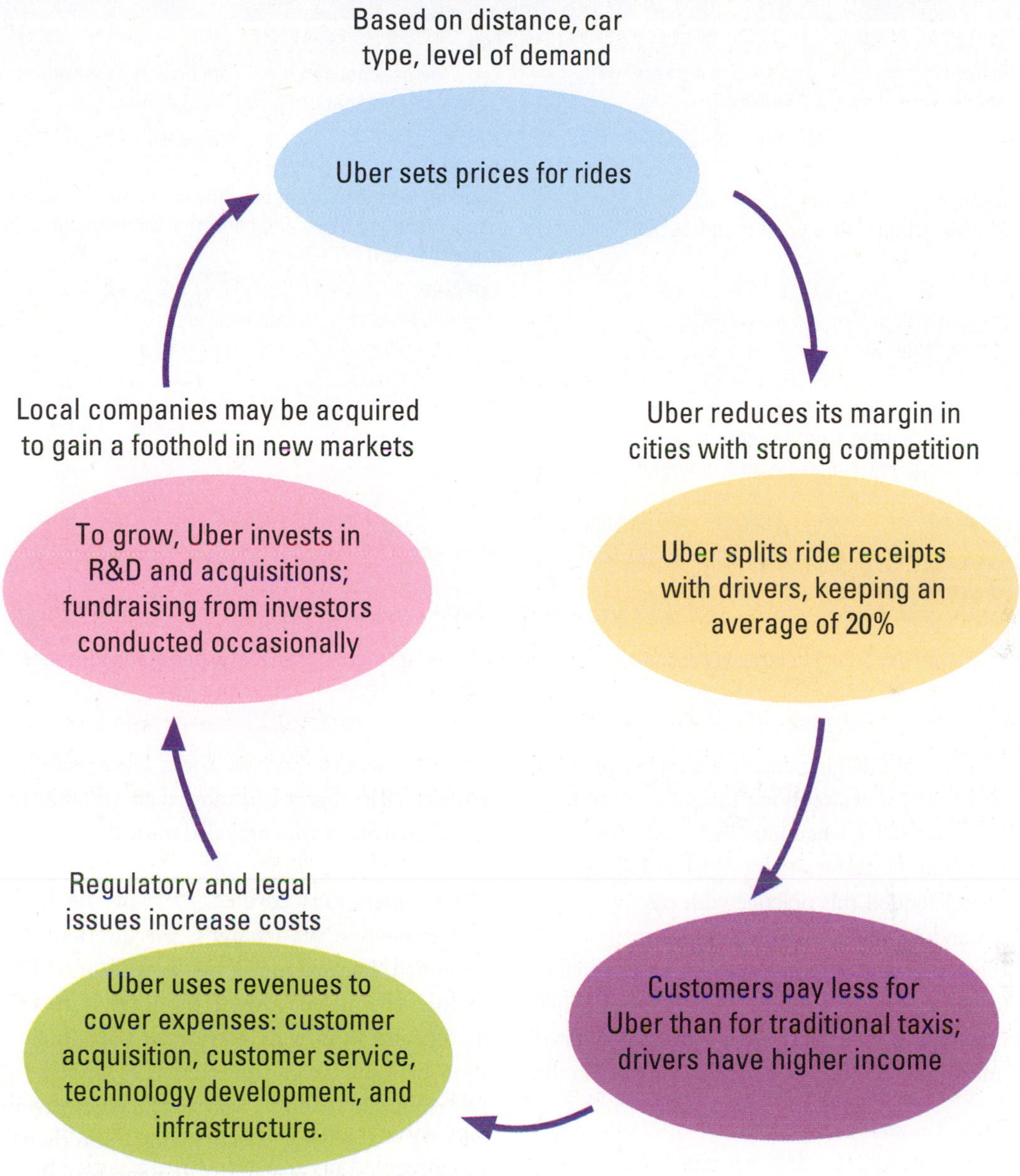

Based on distance, car
type, level of demand

Uber sets prices for rides

Local companies may be acquired
to gain a foothold in new markets

**To grow, Uber invests in
R&D and acquisitions;
fundraising from investors
conducted occasionally**

Uber reduces its margin in
cities with strong competition

**Uber splits ride receipts
with drivers, keeping an
average of 20%**

Regulatory and legal
issues increase costs

**Uber uses revenues to
cover expenses: customer
acquisition, customer service,
technology development, and
infrastructure.**

**Customers pay less for
Uber than for traditional taxis;
drivers have higher income**

Source: Forbes: http://www.forbes.com/sites/aswathdamodaran/2014/06/10/adisruptive-cab-ride-to-riches-the-uber
-payoff; accessed October 27, 2015.

In 2009, UberCab was born. After downloading its app, registering, and entering credit-card information, customers could summon a car with the press of a button. G.P.S. took care of the location, and the cost (including tips) was automatically charged to the customer's credit card. It did not take long for the company to run into regulatory issues. The San Francisco Municipal Transportation Agency objected to the use of "cab" in UberCab's name a few months after its launch, given its operation without a taxi license.

After changing its name to Uber, things went on an upward trajectory. Valued at $60 million after only six months of operation, Uber received support not only from angel investors and venture capitalists but also from prominent celebrities like Ashton Kutcher (founder of A-Grade Investments), Jay Z (co-founder of Roc-A-Fella Records), and Jeff Bezos (founder of Amazon).

Uber faced many obstacles and criticism in its early years. One criticism was directed at the "surge-pricing" model, which

Uber	Lyft
UberX The least expensive Uber service. Seats up to 4 passengers. Drivers use everyday cars that are 5 years old or less.	**Lyft** Lyft's lowest cost service. Seats up to 4 passengers. Drivers use everyday cars that are 5 years old or less.
UberXL Seats at least 6 passengers. An UberXL car will be a SUV or a Minivan. Higher fare price than UberX.	**Lyft Plus** Seats at least 6 passengers. Any six-seater vehicle can be used, including SUVs and minivans. Slightly higher fare price than Lyft.
UberPOOL A ridesharing service that pairs passengers with others who travel the same route. Similar to a carpool.	**Lyft Line** A ridesharing service that pairs passengers with others who travel the same route. Similar to a carpool.
UberPlus/UberSelect A luxury sedan that seats up to 4 passengers. Expect a BMW, Mercedes, Audi, and the like with a leather interior.	
UberBLACK Uber's 'executive' luxury service. Commercially registered and insured vehicles, typically a black SUV or luxury sedan.	

Note: Services are sorted according to fares in ascending order. Information adapted from http://www.ridesharingdriver.com

referred to the practice of charging customers higher prices at peak hours. It garnered a lot of attention during a snowstorm in New York in December 2013, when rates increased up to eight times the company's standard rates, attracting a flood of negative publicity. Kalanick defended this practice with economics—it reflected demand and supply at any given point in time and effectively allocated capacity to customers who were willing to pay even during super-peak periods. To ameliorate public outrage, Uber eventually tweaked its pricing model and limited fare hikes to a maximum of 2.8-times the normal fares in the face of snowstorms in New York.[2] Uber proudly announced in January 2015 that it had more than 160,000 active drivers in the United States who provided more than a million rides a day.

Uber's operations covered 75% of the U.S. population, and even as it set its sights on international markets, it remained focused on growth at home. Its efforts were mainly channeled toward building a strong network of drivers and improving service for consumers. These efforts soon paid off. Forty thousand U.S. drivers joined Uber in December 2014 alone. Service efficiency saw improvements with 91% of UberX rides arriving in less than 10 minutes in Philadelphia. Moreover, the demand for Uber peaked when people celebrated and consumed alcohol, testifying to Uber's position as a "better late-night option." Uber also started to pay more attention to corporate social responsibility. For example, its program UberMILITARY led to the hiring of 10,000 veterans—ex-military personnel—as drivers. In addition, it was calculated that the use of UberPOOL saved more than 13,000 gallons of fuel each month in San Francisco alone.[3] By stretching its network of drivers to different demographic segments in society, offering alternative ride-sharing options, and reducing waiting time, Uber was able to build on network effects for drivers and loyalty among consumers, making it difficult for competitors to enter and grow in its markets.

Exhibit 3: Lyft's pink carstache.

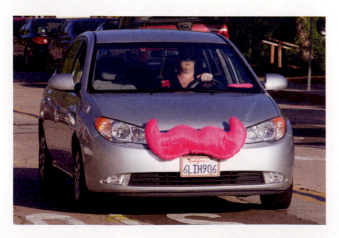

Exhibit 4: Average income of Uber and Lyft drivers per trip in selected cities.

Seattle
UberX: $13.17
Lyft: $11.21

San Francisco
UberX: $14.65
Lyft: $13.42

Dallas
UberX: $11.45
Lyft: $11.19

New York City
UberX: $29.34
Lyft: $28.62

Miami
UberX: $14.38
Lyft: $12.30

Source: Adapted from http://time.com/money/3959091/uber-lyft-priceper-trip; accessed October 27, 2015.

LYFT'S RISE AND RIVALRY

Lyft was launched in 2012 by John Zimmer and Logan Green, primarily as a low-cost competitor to Uber. Its focus was on short, urban rides. Lyft logged an impressive 2.2 million rides in December 2014, with revenues for that year estimated at $130 million. In May 2015, Lyft was valued at $2.5 billion,[4] its promising growth bolstered by estimates of 2015 revenues to be $796 million, an impressive 512% jump from 2014.

While Uber touted its iconic black cars to differentiate its luxury services for professionals (Exhibit 2), Lyft adorned its cars with a pink moustache (Exhibit 3), which became an identifying factor for the company in the streets of San Francisco.[5] This was accompanied by the greeting of all Lyft passengers with a fist bump. While these tongue-in-cheek communications were successful in positioning Lyft differently, Lyft's top management announced plans to tone down the "carstache" and scrap the fist-bump practice in January 2015. This decision was made with the realization that what worked in the West Coast would not necessarily be compatible with Lyft's plans to expand to other cities in the United States or even internationally.

Despite toning down its practices, Lyft still prided itself on its friendliness and laidback driving experience when compared to Uber. An internal presentation from March 2015 that was leaked to Bloomberg revealed its criticisms of Uber's "top-down model," "exclusive mentality," and "anti-social culture."[6] On the other hand, Lyft claimed its growth to be bottom-up and led by drivers (32% of whom were female) through positive word-of-mouth marketing. All in all, Lyft believed itself to be a "trusted brand" delivering a "social experience" with memorable quirks—the carstache being one of them.

Exhibit 5: Average income of Uber and Lyft drivers per trip in selected cities.

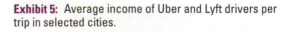

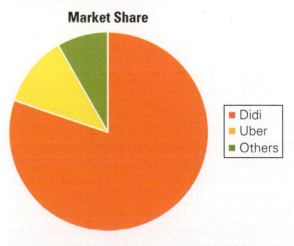

Market Share

Didi
Uber
Others

Source: Adapted from http://fortune.com/2015/09/30/will-china-be-ubers-waterloo, accessed October 10, 2015.

Apart from its more relaxed brand image, Lyft mainly positioned itself as a lower-cost alternative to Uber. In 2014, the company announced big price cuts—20% in early 2014 and an additional 10% in May.[7] Lyft also used a surge-pricing model. However, to ward off potential criticism, it provided discounts of 10%–15% during off-peak hours. While both companies engaged in aggressive price-cutting strategies whenever they operated in the same city, Lyft drivers typically charged—and earned—less than Uber drivers (Exhibit 4).

While Lyft enjoyed strong branding and was expected to spend a generous 60.5% of its revenue on marketing in December 2015, its operations were not as entrenched as those of Uber. One example can be seen in its attempts to break into New York's tight network of taxis in July 2014. Uber had already been operating in New York for three years. A public exposé occurred just days before Lyft planned to commence operations in the city. The company was issued a cease-and-desist letter by the New York State Department of Financial Services for non-compliance with safety requirements and licensing criteria.[8] Uber also aggressively cut the price of its UberX service by 20% the week before Lyft entered the market. The bottom line was that Uber enjoyed a first-mover advantage and, having established a presence in major cities beforehand, benefited from network effects and sufficient margins. This allowed it to cut prices when needed, erect barriers to entry, and slow down the growth of competitors. Uber's significantly higher market valuation also helped to raise more capital in each funding round. It raised $1 billion in July 2015, while Lyft raised only half the amount in the same year. This helped sustain any losses in operations in an era of price cuts.

Finally, Lyft tried to expand fast—it raised $250 million in 2014 and another $530 million by March 2015. Its main goal was to expand internationally and enter less competitive markets without already-entrenched competitors.

DIDI

In China, Uber found itself in the position of the much smaller late entrant. Here, Didi was the clear leader. Didi-Kuaidi, referred to as Didi by the public, was the product of a merger between Didi Dache and Kuaidi Dache, two of China's leading taxi-hailing apps. In February 2015, the merged entity was valued at $6 billion, and it doubled to $12 billion by September in the same year.[9] Didi's services covered 80% of China's huge market of 800 million city dwellers (Exhibit 5). It was a wealthy and dominant player reaping the network-leveraging dividends of having drivers and customers hooked on to its product early.

Didi was also far more successful than Uber in the aspect of legal legitimacy, which it acquired from its local connections.[10] Didi enjoyed the backing of powerful Chinese government investors, the most notable one being the China Investment Corporation, China's sovereign fund in charge of managing foreign exchange reserves. These well-connected investors opened up opportunities for Didi (such as the advantage of working with regulators) at the expense of its competitors. Didi tasted its first success in October 2015, when it became the first car-hailing app to be awarded an official license in Shanghai. This authorization was hailed as a landmark decision, allowing Didi to operate its ride-hailing business in the city without any fear of legal infringements.[11] It assuaged concerns among taxi drivers, such as the one revealed by a driver in September 2015, "I worry all the time about being caught and fined by the government. My biggest concern is policy uncertainties." With this formal recognition, more drivers were sure to sign on with Didi *vis-à-vis* its competitors, which could not provide the same level of regulatory security.

From the beginning, Didi pursued an aggressive strategy to lure as many drivers to its app as possible. It spent $700 million on rewards to taxi drivers between 2013 and 2014. Monetary incentives were used not only to attract new drivers but also to encourage drivers from existing taxi companies to switch to Didi. The sales team in Didi even went to the streets to promote their app to cabbies. By allowing taxi drivers to use its mobile apps as an additional channel to attract more passengers, Didi sought to persuade these drivers to work for them exclusively during peak hours. All these measures allowed Didi to swiftly convert a large number of taxi drivers and scale its operations in other cities. They also highlight the main difference between the business models of Didi and Uber. Didi started out by encouraging taxi drivers to adopt its app before adding non-traditional transport services to its portfolio. In contrast, Uber started out with the intention of disrupting the taxi industry by replacing its services altogether.

Part of Didi's fast growth was also due to the company's practice of tweaking and expanding its business model to meet unique local demands. For example, urban dwellers frequently looked for a compromise between overcrowded public transportation and the high cost of driving to work. This led Didi to introduce a new service offering in its app called Hitch, which allowed groups to share rides along pre-set routes. Hitch was for casual drivers who wanted to recoup some gas money and toll fees on their daily commute. Once the drivers entered their start and end points into the app,

Hitch connected them with nearby passengers heading in the same direction, allowing them to share the ride. This was different from the more traditional taxi-type service, as drivers had control over where the ride ended. Moreover, they did not make a profit off the service—passengers only paid for the cost of gas and tolls. This allowed for fares that were 30%–40% lower than those of regular taxis. Hitch encouraged consumers to try Didi's services at a low cost, thereby opening a pathway for them to convert to the more expensive for-profit taxi service eventually.

Clearly, Didi understood the local market's needs well enough to carry out effective customer segmentation and target the differentiated needs in its product development. This allowed for the building of customer loyalty to the main corporate brand and the greater willingness to try and switch between Didi's various services, depending on the occasion of travel.

UBER'S RESPONSE TO DIDI'S MULTIPLE SERVICE OFFERINGS

Uber had prioritized China as a key market for expansion, and it was befuddling to the company to be in a distantly second position. Uber was to Didi in China what Lyft was to Uber in the United States. In a cruel twist of fate, Didi invested $100 million in Lyft in September 2015, forming an international ride-sharing partnership.

Uber managed to capture only 11.5% of the Chinese market, but experts did not find it surprising in the context of China's unique institutional structures. Greg Tarr, partner at CrossPacific Capital, commented, "When you have great technology and a great business model but don't understand some of those local business premises . . . West Coast aggressiveness will only get you so far. China is such a different animal in terms of dealing with the local culture, the protectionism and the fact that you don't have local investors." This demonstrated the need for Uber to better understand the Chinese market instead of merely transplanting its San Francisco model of attracting American drivers and dealing with local regulations. Uber thus attempted to work closely with China's Ministry of Transport. It set up servers in China in an effort to obtain an internet-service company license by sharing data with local transport authorities.

Reformation in Uber's marketing strategy in China was a priority, and steps were taken to set up local teams to determine logistics, including language and support services. At consumers' requests, Uber strategically partnered with the Chinese search giant Baidu. It ditched Google Maps and incorporated Baidu Maps into its app. In turn, Baidu advertised Uber on its main page and incorporated a prominent "Get a Car" button that linked the website to Uber's app. Partnerships with Alibaba also allowed Uber to use the simpler and non-credit-card-based payment mechanism of Alipay.[12] This was important, as many Chinese residents did not own credit cards.

Uber and Didi competed vigorously on many other fronts to attract drivers to sign on with their respective companies. Both offered bonuses for drivers who hit ride targets in a bid to extend geographical coverage and reduce wait times. This was based on an industry-wide understanding that spending cash and leveraging on economies of scale to build an operational base as quickly as possible was the only way to win in China. As Didi's President, Jean Liu, revealed, "By using subsidies to get more cars on the road . . . waiting times were shortened, fares became cheaper, more users were drawn on to the platform and drivers on the platform. We have already created such a virtuous circle of increased orders, customer retention."[13]

To try and respond more effectively to Didi's diversification of services, Uber looked beyond its typical car-ordering model that had worked so well in other international markets. In August 2014, Uber announced the implementation of People's Uber. This incentive allowed drivers to offer "non-profit" rides to carpooling passengers, who only paid for the cost of gas and maintenance. It was Uber's version of Didi's Hitch, competing directly to attract people who wanted low-cost rides.

Uber seemed to be playing catch-up rather than setting trends in the Chinese market. The race to grab market share was critical, because it was understood that whoever got ahead first would remain the dominant player for a long time. Uber had to decide how to effectively compete with a much larger competitor, where to side-step competition and innovate new services, and where and how to go head-on with Didi.

STUDY QUESTIONS

1. How can Uber retain its dominant position in the U.S. market? Are there services and/or geographic niche markets where Uber should accommodate Lyft?

2. How can Uber effectively compete with Didi? Should it compete head-on in China, or should it side-step competition by focusing on niche markets through service innovation and geographic expansion within the country?

ENDNOTES

1. *Vanity Fair* covered an interview with Travis Kalanick in December 2014; this article's insights can be found throughout the Uber case study: http://www.vanityfair.com/news/2014/12/uber-travis-kalanick-controversy.

2. *The Guardian* covered the revision in surge pricing by Uber in http://www.theguardian.com/technology/2015/jan/26/uber-surge-pricing-new-york-snowstorm.

3. Uber Expansion, not officially affiliated with Uber, provides a range of statistics pertaining to Uber's expansion in this page: http://uberexpansion.com/2015-uber-data-stats.

4. The *Business Insider* website reported on the $2.5 billion valuation on 15 May 2015; the whole article can be found here: http://www.businessinsider.sg/carl-icahn-invests-150-million-in-lyft-2015-5/#.VicRavkrLIV.

5. The magazine *Wired* reports on the changing of Lyft's most prominent quirks in January 2015, with reasons: http://www.wired.com/2015/01/lyft-finally-ditching-furry-pink-mustache.

6. Eric Newcomer and Leslie Picker, "Leaked Lyft Document Reveals a Costly Battle with Uber," *Bloomberg Businessweek* (2015). Retrieved from http://www.bloomberg.com/news/articles/2015-04-30/leaked-lyft-document-reveals-a-costly-battle-with-uber.

7. *Vator* talks about Lyft's model with respect to prices and Uber's response in two articles written in 2014: http://vator.tv/news/2014-04-24-lyft-takes-off-hits-24-new-cities-in-one-day and http://vator.tv/news/2014-03-18-lyft-counters-surge-pricing-by-reducing-off-peak-fares.

8. To follow Lyft's saga in New York City in July 2014 and the time period during which it decided to offer its services in Hong Kong, read *Bloomberg Businessweek*'s exposé on the issue: http://www.bloomberg.com/news/articles/2014-07-10/lyft-not-authorized-for-new-york-days-before-start-due.

9. Gerry Shih, "China Taxi Apps Didi Dache and Kuaidi Dache Announce $6 Billion Tie-Up," *Reuters* (2015). Retrieved from http://www.reuters.com/article/2015/02/14/us-china-taxi-merger-idUSKBN0LI04420150214.

10. Deborah Findling, "What Stands between Uber and Success in China?" *CNBC* (2015). Retrieved from http://www.cnbc.com/2015/09/15/what-stands-between-uber-and-success-in-china.htm.

11. *Wall Street Journal*, "In the Race for Legal Legitimacy," (2015). Retrieved from http://www.wsj.com/articles/chinas-didi-kuaidi-gets-license-to-ride-in-shanghai-1444288510?alg=y.

12. *The Market Mogul* covers Didi's triumph over Uber in the Chinese market in a short read: http://themarketmogul.com/didi-kuaidi-crushes-uber-in-the-chinese-market.

13. *Financial Times* reports on the intensive cash burning on subsidies in the China market by Didi and Uber in http://www.ft.com/intl/cms/s/0/e85cc5fa-5473-11e5-8642-453585f2cfcd.html#axzz3oPUktNrd.

Banyan Tree: Branding the Intangible

Jochen Wirtz

Banyan Tree Hotels & Resorts had become a leading player in the luxury resort and spa market in Asia. As part of its growth strategy, Banyan Tree had launched new brands and brand extensions that included resorts, spas, residences, destination club memberships, retail outlets, and even museum shops. Now, the company is preparing to aggressively grow its global footprint in the Americas, Caribbean, Europe and the Middle East while preserving its distinctive Asian identity and strong brand image.

A brand synonymous with private villas, tropical garden spas, and retail galleries promoting traditional craft, Banyan Tree Hotels & Resorts received its first guest in 1994 in Phuket, Thailand. Since then, it had grown into a leading manager and developer of niche and premium resorts, hotels, and spas in the Asia-Pacific region.

Despite having minimal advertising, Banyan Tree achieved a global exposure and a high level of brand awareness through the company's public relations and global marketing programs. Much interest was also generated by the company's socially responsible business values and practices caring for the social and natural environments. With a firm foothold in the medium-sized luxury resorts market, the company introduced a new and contemporary brand, Angsana, in 2000 to gain a wider customer base.

As the resorts market became increasingly crowded with similar competitive offerings, lured by the success of Banyan Tree, the company had to contemplate about expanding its business and preserving its distinct identity. Banyan Tree and Angsana resorts were expanding geographically outside of Asia and also into the urban hotel market in major cities throughout the world. With around 30 hotels and resorts scheduled to open over the next three years, Banyan Tree faced the challenge of translating and maintaining the success of a niche Asian hospitality brand into various market segments on a global scale.

© 2018 by Jochen Wirtz.

The support and feedback of the management of Banyan Tree Hotels & Resorts in the writing of this case are gratefully acknowledged.

The complete list of awards won by Banyan Tree can be found on the company's website at www.banyantree.com.

COMPANY BACKGROUND

By October 2015, Banyan Tree Holdings Ltd. (BTHR) managed and/or had ownership interests in 38 resorts and hotels, 67 spas, 79 retail galleries, and two golf courses in 28 countries. Since its establishment in 1994, the company's flagship brand, Banyan Tree, had won some 1,200 international tourism, hospitality, design, and marketing awards, some of which included "2014 Forbes Travel Guide Award," "Top 10 Hotels In Mexico" in 2014 by the US News for Banyan Tree Mayakoba, "Best Spa Resort in China" in 2014 for Banyan Tree Lijiang from the 7th Annual TTG China Travel Award, "National Geographic Traveler" award for Banyan Tree Yangshuo in 2014, and "Best Spa Operator" at the 25th Annual TTG Travel Awards 2014 (for the 10th consecutive year), for Banyan Tree Spa.

BTHR was founded by Ho Kwon Ping, a travel enthusiast and former journalist, and his wife Claire Chiang, a strong advocate of corporate social responsibility. Prior to entering the hotel and resort business, Ho spent some 15 years managing the family business, which was into everything imaginable, such as commodities, food products, consumer electronics, and property development. It competed mainly on cost and was not dominant in any particular either country or industry. Meanwhile, Chiang was deeply involved in sociology and social issues.

The closing of a factory in Thailand one year after its opening—because it lost out to other low-cost producers in Indonesia—was the last straw for Ho, who then realized that a low-cost strategy was not only difficult to follow but would also lead nowhere. Determined to craft something proprietary that would allow the company to become a price maker rather than a price taker, Ho decided that building a strong brand was the only way for him to maintain a sustainable competitive advantage.

The idea of entering the luxury resorts market was inspired by the gap in the hotel industry that giant chains such as the Hilton and Shangri-La could not fill. There was a market segment that wanted private and intimate accommodation but without the expectation of glitzy chain hotels. This was fueled by the sharp price gap between the luxurious Aman Resorts and other resorts in the luxury resorts market. For example, in 2004 the Amanpuri in Thailand, one of Aman's resorts, charged a rack rate for its villas ranging from US$650 to over US$7,000 a night, whereas the prices of other luxury resorts, such as the Shangri-La Hotel and Phuket Arcadia Beach Resort by Hilton in Thailand were priced below US$350.

Noticing the big difference in prices between Aman Resorts and the other resorts in the luxury resorts market, Ho saw

potential for offering an innovative niche product that could also bridge the price gap in this market. Ho and Chiang had backpacked throughout the world in their youth and were seasoned travelers themselves. Their extensive travel experience is evident in their non-conforming beliefs that resorts should provide more than just accommodation. Ho and Chiang hit upon the idea of building a resort comprising individual villas with locally inspired architectural design and positioned as a romantic and intimate escapade for guests. Banyan Tree moved its positioning into the higher end of the luxury market, and by 2015, its rack rates for its basic category were typically between US$600 and US$1,200 for the resort in Phuket, and between €600 and €3,500 for the resort in the Seychelles.

Operations at Banyan Tree began with only one resort in Phuket, situated on a former mining site once deemed too severely ravaged to sustain any form of development by a United Nations Development Program planning unit and the Tourism Authority of Thailand. It was a bold

Exhibit 1: Hotel Business - Outlook.

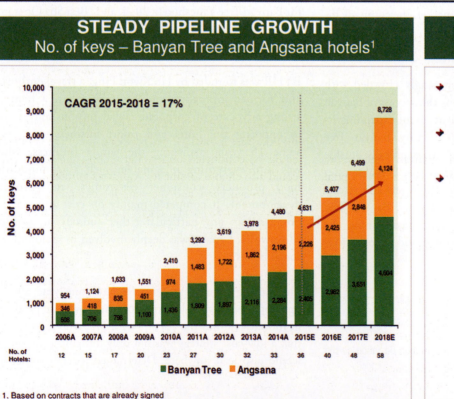

decision, but the company, together with Ho, Chiang, and Ho's brother Ho Kwon Cjan, restored it after extensive rehabilitation works costing a total of $250 million. The Banyan Tree Phuket was so successful when it was finally launched that the company worked quickly to build two other resorts, one at Bintan Island in Indonesia and the other at Vabbinfaru Island in the Maldives. The company has never looked back since. Even though Asia's travel industry experienced periodic meltdowns such as the Asian economic crisis in 1997/8, the September 11 attacks on the World Trade Center in 2001, the dot.com crisis in 2001–2, severe acute respiratory syndrome (SARS) in 2003, and the Indian Ocean tsunami on December 26, 2004, the World Economic Crisis in 2008/9, and the Euro Crisis from 2011 through to 2015, no employee was retrenched; instead, Banyan Tree grew its number of resorts and rooms aggressively, and its room rates rose steadily.

BRAND ORIGINS

Known as *Yung Shue Wan* in the local dialect, Banyan Tree Bay was a fishing village on Lamma Island in Hong Kong where Ho and his wife Chiang lived for three idyllic years before he joined the family business. Despite the village's modest and rustic setting, they remember it as a sanctuary of romance and intimacy. The large canopies of the Banyan Tree also resembled the shelter afforded by Asia's tropical rainforests. Ho and Chiang thus decided to name their resort Banyan Tree, and position it as a "Sanctuary for the Senses."

THE SERVICE OFFERING

Unlike most other resorts then, Banyan Tree resorts comprised individual villas that came with a private pool, Jacuzzi, or spa treatment room, each designed to offer guests exclusivity and the utmost privacy. For example, a guest could skinny-dip in the private pool within his villa without being seen by other guests, putting him in a world of his own (see Exhibit 2).

All Banyan Tree hotels and resorts were designed around the concept of providing "a sense of place" to reflect and enhance the culture and heritage of the destination. This is reflected in the architecture, furnishings, landscape, vegetation and the service offering. To create a sense of exotic sensuality and ensure the privacy of its guests, the resorts are designed to blend into the natural landscape of

Exhibit 2: A world of privacy in a double pool villa at Banyan Tree Phuket.

the surrounding environment and use the natural foliage and boulders as the privacy screen (see Exhibit 3 showing Banyan Tree Seychelles). The furnishings of Banyan Tree villas were deliberately native to convey the exoticism of the destination with its rich local flavor and luxurious feel. The spa pavilions in Seychelles were constructed around the large granite boulders and lush foliage to offer an outdoor spa experience in complete privacy. The resorts' local flavor was also reflected in the services offered, some of which were unique to certain resorts. Employees were allowed to vary the service delivery process according to local culture and practices, as long as these were consistent with the brand promise of romance and intimacy. Thus, in Phuket, for instance, a couple could enjoy dinner on a traditional Thai long tail boat accompanied by private Thai musicians while cruising instead of dining in a restaurant. Banyan Tree Phuket also offered wedding packages in which couples were blessed by Buddhist monks. In the Maldives, wedding ceremonies could be conducted underwater among the coral. Guests could also choose to dine in a castaway sandbank with only their private chefs and the stars for company, and watch the sunset while toasting champagne on a Turkish gulet returning from a trip watching a school of spinner dolphins.

Products and services were conceived with the desired customer experience in mind. Banyan Tree launched themed packages across their hotels, such as "Sense of Rejuvenation" with a focus on wellness, spa, and detox, and "Sense of Romance" for couples. These themed packages varied from resort to resort, to incorporate the unique experiences each location had to offer, but they would have some common features, such as a couple spa treatment, couple dining concepts, and the special decoration of the couples' villas

with lit candles, incense oil burners, flower petals spread throughout the room, and a chilled bottle of champagne or wine. The couple was presented with a variety of aromatic massage oils to further inspire those intimate moments.

Another draw of the resorts was the Banyan Tree Spa, found at every Banyan Tree property. The pioneer of the tropical garden spas concept, Banyan Tree Spas offered a variety of aromatic oil massages, and face and body beauty treatments using traditional Asian therapies, with a choice of indoor or outdoor treatment. The spa products used were natural, indigenous products made from local herbs and spices. Non-clinical in concept, Banyan Tree Spas relied mainly on the "human touch" instead of energy-consuming, high-tech equipment. The spa experience was promoted as a sensorial, intimate experience that would rejuvenate the "body, mind, and soul" and was mainly targeted at couples who would enjoy their treatments together.

Exhibit 4: Banyan Tree mainly targets its spa experiences at couples.

In line with Banyan Tree's ethos of conserving local culture and heritage and promoting cottage crafts, Chiang founded the Banyan Tree Gallery, a retail outlet showcasing indigenous crafts. Banyan Tree Gallery outlets were set up in each resort. Items sold were made by local artisans and included traditionally woven handmade fabrics, garments, jewelry, handicrafts, tribal art, and spa accessories, such as incense candles and massage oils, which guests could use at home to recreate the Banyan Tree experience.

Exhibit 5: Banyan Tree Gallery outlets sell indigenous crafts that guests can use at home to recreate the Banyan Tree experience.

Banyan Tree Gallery embarked on projects to support the various communities in the locations Banyan Tree resorts are situated and worked closely with village cooperatives and not-for-profit craft marketing agents to provide gainful employment to the artisans. While acting as a marketing channel for Asian crafts like basket weaving, hill tribe cross-stitching and lacquer ware, Banyan Tree Gallery also educated its customers about the crafts with an accompanying write-up. In the course of Banyan Tree Gallery's operations, the community outreach extended from across Thailand to Laos, Cambodia, India, Nepal, Sri Lanka, Indonesia, Malaysia, and Singapore.

The result of Banyan Tree's efforts was "a very exclusive, private holiday feeling", as described by one guest. Another guest commented, "It's a treat for all the special occasions like honeymoons and wedding anniversaries. It's the architecture, the sense of place and the promise of romance."

MARKETING BANYAN TREE

In the first two years after Banyan Tree was launched, the company's marketing communications was managed by an international advertising agency. The agency also designed the Banyan Tree logo shown in Exhibit 6 and, together with the management, came up with the marketing tagline "Sanctuary for the Senses."

Though furnished luxuriously, Banyan Tree resorts were promoted as providing romantic and intimate "smallish" hotel experiences rather than luxurious accommodation as touted by most competitors then. "Banyan Tree Experiences" was marketed as intimate private moments. The resorts saw themselves as setting the stage for guests to create those unforgettable memories.

When Banyan Tree was first launched, extensive advertising was carried out for a short period of time to gain recognition in the industry. Subsequently, the company scaled down on advertising and kept it minimal, mainly in high-end travel magazines in key markets. The advertisements were visual in nature with succinct copy or showcased the awards and accolades won.

Brand awareness for Banyan Tree was generated largely through public relations and global marketing programs. For example, relationships with travel editors and writers were cultivated to encourage visits to the resorts. This helped to increase editorial coverage on Banyan Tree, which management felt was more effective in conveying the "Banyan Tree Experience" from an impartial third-party perspective. Its website, www.banyantree.com, increasingly drove online bookings and provided vivid information about the latest offerings of Banyan Tree's fast-growing portfolio.

Exhibit 6: The Banyan Tree logo.

The management of marketing activities was centralized at its headquarters in Singapore in order to maintain consistency in brand building. BTHR appointed a few key wholesalers in each targeted market and worked closely with them to promote sales. Rather than selling through wholesale and retail agents that catered to the general market, BTHR chose to work only with agents specializing in exclusive luxury holidays targeted at wealthy customers. Global exposure was also achieved through Banyan Tree's membership in the Small Luxury Hotels and Leading Hotels of the World. Targeting high-end consumers, they represent various independent exclusive hotels and have sales offices in major cities around the world.

The end of 2007 marked a new stage of Banyan Tree's global expansion with the launch of its own GDS code "BY." GDS is a Global Distribution System that is used by travel providers to process airline, hotel, car rental reservations across 640,000 terminals of travel agents and other distribution partners around the world. Prior to BY, Banyan Tree was represented by its marketing partners, Leading Hotels of the World (LW) and Small Luxury Hotels (LX). Thereafter, Banyan Tree had its unique identity on the GDS code, further strengthening its brand presence and customer ownership. Banyan Tree then had enough critical mass to ensure the economic feasibility of a GDS private label. The acquisition of its own GDS code meant that Banyan Tree was transitioning from a relatively small regional player to a global brand in the eyes of the travel industry.

BRAND VALUES

Banyan Tree embraced certain values, such as actively caring for the natural and human environment and revitalizing local communities, which in turn created pride and respect among staff. The company hoped to build the brand on values that employees and customers could identify with and support as part of their own life values. A dedicated corporate social responsibility committee, headed by Chiang and featuring general managers and valued associates from each resort, was formed to focus on these issues with both a regional overview and simultaneously local perspectives. Thus, the company worked actively to preserve, protect, and promote the natural and human environments in which Banyan Tree resorts were located. In 2009, Banyan Tree Global Foundation was launched as a separate entity to enhance governance and institutional safeguards for funding of sustainability projects.

PRESERVING THE ENVIRONMENT

Resorts were built using local materials as far as possible and, at the same time, minimizing the impact on the environment. At Banyan Tree Bintan, for example, the 70 villas located in a rainforest were constructed around existing trees, cutting down as few trees as possible, to minimize the impact the resort had on the natural environment. The villas were built on stilts and platforms to avoid cutting trees and possible soil erosion. At Banyan Tree Maldives Vabbinfaru and Banyan Tree Seychelles, fresh water supply was obtained by the more expensive method of desalination, instead of extracting water from the underground water table, which risked long-term disruption of the ecological system. Toiletries such as shampoo, hair conditioner, bath foam, and body lotion provided in the resorts were non-toxic and biodegradable and filled in reusable containers made from celadon or ceramic. Refuse was recycled where possible and treated through an in-house incinerator system otherwise. Waste water was also treated and recycled in the irrigation of resort landscapes.

Through the retail arm Banyan Tree Gallery, human environment efforts were evident in the active sourcing of traditional crafts from indigenous tribes to provide gainful employment. These employment opportunities provided a source of income for the tribes and, at the same time, helped preserve their unique heritage.

In line with the Banyan Tree Group's Green Imperative initiative, Banyan Tree Gallery constantly used eco-friendly and recycled materials in the development of its merchandise. Examples included photo frames made using discarded telephone directories, elephant dung paper stationary, and lead-free celadon and ceramic spa amenities. Unique collections like the black resin turtles stationery range and leaf-inspired merchandise were created to promote environmental awareness, and were accompanied by a write-up to educate the consumer on the targeted conservation campaign. In support of animal rights, the galleries did not carry products made from shell or ivory.

Besides trying to conduct business in an environmentally responsible manner, BTHR actively pursued a number of key initiatives, including its Greening Communities program. Greening Communities was launched in 2007 as a challenge for properties to raise awareness for climate change by planting 2,000 trees per year. It planted 28,321 trees in the first two years of the program. Banyan Tree Lijiang, for example, planted some 20,000 fruit trees to create additional income for families of the supporting community. While trees will absorb carbon dioxide and improve the quality of the environment, the main goal of this program was to engage local communities, associates, and guests to share the causes of climate change and actions that can reduce our collective carbon footprint. The program had planted 358, 885 trees by end-2014, far exceeding its target of 286, 272.

CREATING BRAND OWNERSHIP AMONG EMPLOYEES

All Banyan Tree employees were trained to the basic standards of five-star service establishments, which included greeting guests, remembering their first names, and anticipating their needs. In addition, some employees got a taste of the "Banyan Tree Experience" as part of their training. The management believed that the stay would help employees understand better what guests will experience and, in return, enhance their delivery of special experiences for the guests.

Although management imposed strict rules in the administration of the resorts, employees were empowered to exercise creativity and sensitivity. For example, the housekeeping teams were not restricted by a standard bed decoration. Rather, they were given room for creativity, though they had general guidelines for turning the bed to keep in line with the standards of a premium resort. Banyan Tree invested liberally in staff welfare: Employees were taken to and from work in air-conditioned buses and had access to various amenities, including good-quality canteens, medical services, and childcare facilities. Staff dormitories had televisions, telephones, refrigerators, and attached bathrooms.

The company's generous staff welfare policies apparently paid off. Ho said, "The most gratifying response is the sense of ownership that our staff began to have. It's not a sense of financial ownership, but they actually care about the property. In our business, service and service standards do not always mean the same thing as in a developed country, where standards are measured by efficiency and productivity by people who are already quite well versed in a service culture. We operate in places that, sometimes, have not seen hotels. People come from villages. What we need— more than exact standards—is for them to have a sense of hospitality, a sense that the guest is an honored person who, by virtue of being there, is able to give a decent livelihood to the people who work. This creates a culture in which everybody is friendly and helpful."

INVOLVING GUESTS IN ENVIRONMENTAL CONSERVATION

Part of the company's corporate social responsibility initiatives was designed to encourage environmental conservation and help ecological restoration. To create greater environmental awareness, Banyan Tree organized activities that involved interested guests in their research and environmental preservation work. In the Maldives, for instance, guests were invited to take part in the coral transplantation program (see Exhibit 5 for a picture of guest involvement in the long-running coral planting program). Guests who participated in the program were then encouraged to return several years later to see the progress of their efforts. Guests were also offered free marine biology sessions, allowing them to learn more about the fascinating marine life and its conservation. Guests also had an opportunity to take part in the Green Sea Turtle Headstarting Projects. The response from guests was tremendously positive.

In 2002, Banyan Tree established The Green Imperative Fund (GIF) to further support community-based and environmental initiatives in the regions where it has a presence. Guests were billed US$2 per room night at Banyan Tree properties and US$1 at Angsana properties (of which they could opt out if they wished) and the company matched dollar for dollar. Details of the program were communicated to guests through various methods, including sand-filled turtles and in-villa turndown gifts.

Guests were generally happy to know that their patronage contributed to meaningful causes, like the construction of new schools for the local community, the restoration of coral reefs, and ensuring the longevity of local village crafts.

Exhibit 7: Guests are invited to participate in planting corals at the Banyan Tree Maldives and Angsana Iharu.

INVOLVING THE LOCAL COMMUNITY

In addition to engaging local craftsmen to produce indigenous art and handicrafts for sale at its galleries, Banyan Tree also involved the local community in all aspects of its business, even as the resorts were being built. Villas were constructed with as much indigenous material as possible, most of which was supplied by local traders. Traditional arts and handicrafts that complemented the villas' aesthetics were also purchased from local artisans.

The company believed in building profitable resorts that would benefit the surrounding environment and contribute to local economies through the creation of employment and community development projects. Thus, besides providing employment for the local community, the company brought business to the local farmers and traders by making it a point to purchase fresh produce from them. Whenever possible, the company supported other regional tourism ventures that would benefit the wider local community and enhance the visitor's experience. The Banyan Tree Maldives Marine Laboratory is a prime example, being the first fully equipped private research facility to be fully funded and operated by a resort. The Lab seeks to lead conservation efforts in the Maldives to protect and regenerate coral and marine life for the future of the tourism industry as well as to promote awareness and education of this field to the local community.

Recognizing that the disparity in lifestyles and living standards between guests and the local community might create a sense of alienation within the local community, a Community Relations Department was set up to develop and manage community outreach programs. After consultations with community stakeholders, a number of funding scholarships for needy children were given, a school and childcare centre were built, lunches and parties for the elderly were hosted, and local cultural and religious activities were supported.

One of BTHR's formalized programs was Seedlings, which aimed to help young adults from local communities and motivate them and provide the means for completing their education to successfully enter the labor force as adults. This program benefited the community at large, as it provided the next generation with educational opportunities to break the poverty cycle.[2]

Detailed information on BTHR's CSR activities can be found at http://www.banyantree.com/csr.

GROWING BANYAN TREE

In 2002, BTHR took over the management of a city hotel in the heart of Bangkok from Westin Hotel Company. The hotel was rebranded as Banyan Tree Bangkok after extensive renovation works were completed to upgrade the hotel's facilities and build new additional spa amenities and a Banyan Tree Gallery. This was the first Banyan Tree hotel to be located in the city area, unlike the other beachfront Banyan Tree properties. Banyan Tree planned to open city hotels in Seoul, Shanghai, and Hangzhou, and Angsana and also expanded into Morocco and Laos.

As the Banyan Tree brand became established, the company began expanding its network of spas and retail outlets. Standalone Banyan Tree Spas and Banyan Tree Galleries were set up as separate ventures, independent of Banyan Tree hotels, cruise ships, and resorts, in various cities such as Singapore, Shanghai, Sydney, India, and Dubai, operating either in other hotels or as standalone outlets.

In addition to the Spa Academy in Phuket, which opened in 2001, and to support its fast-growing spa business, Banyan Tree opened two new spa academies in Lijiang, China, and Bangkok, Thailand, in 2007.

After establishing a foothold in the luxury resort market, BTHR introduced the Angsana brand in response to the demand from hotel operators in Asia that were keen to introduce spa services in their hotels. As the positioning of these hotels did not fit that of Banyan Tree, the company decided to launch a new brand, Angsana, a more contemporary and affordable brand than Banyan Tree, to run as standalone spa businesses in other hotels.

Exhibit 8: Extending the Banyan Tree Maldives experience on board the Banyan Velaa.

The first Angsana Spa was opened in 1999 at Dusit Laguna, one of several hotels at Laguna Phuket, an integrated resort development with shared facilities located at Bang Tao Bay in Thailand. The Angsana Spa was so well received that the company quickly set up five other such spas in various hotels in Thailand. In 2000, BTHR opened its first Angsana Resort & Spa, complete with an Angsana Gallery, located less than one kilometer away from Banyan Tree Bintan in Indonesia.

Exhibit 9: Angsana Maldives Ihuru.

In 2003, Banyan Tree launched The Museum Shop by Banyan Tree, a joint partnership with Singapore's National Heritage Board to showcase Asia's rich and diverse cultural heritage through unique museum-inspired merchandise. Designed to inspire and educate shoppers, The Museum Shop by Banyan Tree makes history more accessible and approachable to the layperson. Although it eventually disposed of all museum shops, Banyan Tree had 79 retail outlets, ranging from Banyan Tree Galleries, Heritage Collection by Banyan Tree Spa Galleries, Elements by Banyan Tree, and Angsana Galleries by 2015.

Banyan Tree Galleries are the retail outlets supporting the hotels, while Banyan Tree Spa Galleries support the spa outlets, selling more spa-focused merchandise such as signature aromatherapy amenities, essential oils, candles, and body care products.

THE ROAD AHEAD

To diversify its geographic spread, Ho had started to venture into locations in South America (the first resort in Mexico opened in 2009), southern Europe, and the Middle East, where he hoped to replicate Banyan Tree's rapid success.

However, given the higher costs of doing business in the Americas and Europe, would the same strategy that had brought fame and success to Banyan Tree in Asia be workable in the rest of the world? Ho's ultimate vision was "to string a necklace of Banyan Tree Resorts around the world; not quantity, but a number of jewels that form a chain around the world." By the second half of 2015, Banyan Tree had signed management contracts that would increase the total numbers to 66 hotels and resorts, 117 spas, and 115 galleries across 33 countries by 2019. Of the properties under development, the majority were resorts and/or integrated resorts.

While expanding the company's network of hotels and resorts, spas, and retail outlets, Ho had to be mindful of the brands' focus and be careful not to dilute the brands. He also had to consider the strategic fit of the company's portfolio of brands, which comprised Banyan Tree and Angsana. (Exhibit 9), and more recently, a significant property arm that develops and sells villas and serviced apartment units that are typically in close proximity of its resorts. As part of this property development, it launched a new brand, Cassia, an exciting and bold new proposition in the serviced apartment sector which targets the Asian middle class.

Banyan Tree certainly stood out among its competitors in the resorts industry when it was first launched. Since then, its success had attracted various competitors that offer similar products and services. Thus, it was imperative that Banyan Tree retained its competitive advantage to prevent losing its distinctive position in the market.

STUDY QUESTIONS

1. What are the main factors that contributed to Banyan Tree's success?

2. Evaluate Banyan Tree's brand positioning and communication strategies. Can Banyan Tree maintain its unique positioning in an increasingly overcrowded resorts market?

3. Discuss whether the brand portfolio of Banyan Tree, Angsana, and Cassia, as well as the product portfolio of beach resorts, services residences, city hotels, spas, galleries, and museum shops fit as a family. What are your recommendations to Banyan Tree for managing these brands and products in the future?

4. What effect does the practice of corporate social responsibility have on brand equity?

5. What potential problems do you foresee bringing Banyan Tree to the Americas, Europe and the Middle East? How could Banyan Tree address those issues?

Kiwi Experience

Mark Colgate

How do you manage a business where customers are unlikely to buy again? Answer: the Kiwi Experience way! This case explores how to truly get inside the heads of your target market, how to build a culture of service excellence, and how other customers can add as much to the service experience as the employees—but only if you encourage them to do so.

"**A**re you ready for a most excellent adventure?" shouted Rob, the driver of the Kiwi Experience bus as it climbed to the top of an extinct volcano on a beautiful sunny morning in Auckland. It was the start of another trip around New Zealand for the driver and the bus as well as for the 40 like-minded travelers who were unprepared for the burst of enthusiasm as the panoramic view unveiled itself.

Virtually all of the travelers were unsure of what to expect from this trip. They had never traveled on Kiwi Experience before, although all of them had heard of the company through various media before buying their tickets. This knowledge had somewhat reduced their uncertainty.

One of the passengers, Rory Gillies, a 23-year-old Scotsman, had heard much about Kiwi Experience while traveling around Australia. He was curious to find out what made this bus service so successful and so different from the others that were offered in New Zealand. As they boarded the bus after taking in the sights of Auckland, Rory approached Rob the driver.

"Have you been busy this summer?" Rory asked. "I haven't stopped," replied Rob, "and what's more, I can only remember one or two instances when my bus was not full!" "So what does Kiwi Experience do that makes it so successful?" continued Rory. "If I told you, it would ruin the trip for you," Rob suggested, "but jump on and maybe I'll give you a few ideas along the way."

© 2018 by Mark Colgate.

Mark Colgate is Professor of Service Excellence at the Gustavson School of Business, University of Victoria. The support and feedback of the management of Kiwi Experience in the writing of this case is gratefully acknowledged. All statistics on New Zealand's tourism industry were taken from http://www.stats.govt.nz/tourism.

COMPANY BACKGROUND

Kiwi Experience (KE) is an adventure transport network that was formed in December 1988 by three partners. The first bus left in late 1989. The company recently celebrated its 25th birthday, and over 400,000 passengers have now had a Kiwi Experience.

The fundamental concept behind the venture was to create a coach transport network that was neither an express point-to-point service nor an inflexible coach tour. Instead, Kiwi Experience set out to create a transport tour experience that had the advantages of both. This meant that it was going to offer the flexibility of the traditional express service (in that customers could get on or off the bus where they wanted) in addition to the guidance, information, and access to excitement-orientated places that a good adventure tour would offer, without the inherent drawbacks of either.

This was an innovation in the marketplace and the first of its kind in the world. In fact, the concept was so original that staff at Kiwi Experience initially had to spend much of their time explaining it to potential customers. They had to clarify to their clients that passengers could get on and off the coach wherever they liked (on a pass that lasted for six months) and still be part of an adventure trip that would take them to places off the beaten track. In fact, more than 90% of customers break their journey at some point, which proves that this concept has been popular with travelers. Today, many copies of the Kiwi Experience concept can be seen all over the world.

Neil Geddes, one of the founders of the company, outlines the concept:

> I have always thought that a coach was a great way to get around, as meeting people is one of the fun things about traveling. But I could never understand the fact that everyone is stuck on one coach and you

all had to do the same things. I don't believe you can create the ideal holiday for more than just the one person—this is why KE was invented.

The company's service offering is specifically designed for backpackers, adventurers, and other like-minded travelers. This means that Kiwi Experience is developed around the high-volume, low-margin business where minimizing costs is key.

Although Kiwi Experience has no specific target market in terms of age (the company believes that a backpacker tends to be defined in terms of lifestyle rather than age), it is the 18–30 age group which travels with the company the most, with 18–22 being the most common age range. Similarly, people of many nationalities travel on Kiwi Experience, with backpackers from the United Kingdom, Germany, the United States, Canada, Denmark, Switzerland, and the Nordic countries making up the bulk of customers. Less than 1% of all customers actually come from New Zealand.

NEW ZEALAND AS A TOURIST DESTINATION

In 2015, New Zealand hosted a total of 3 million international visitors aged 15 years and above (compared to 1.6 million in 1999 and 2.5 million in 2014). This number has increased dramatically since 2014 due to the efforts of New Zealand Tourism to recover from the 2007 financial crisis that hit it hard. Total international visitor expenditure in 2014 reached NZ$10.3 billion; this was up from NZ$9.6 billion in 2013. New Zealand's current share of international tourism is small at only 1%–2%; but given the size of the country, they do incredibly well.

New Zealand is marketed abroad as a "clean, green" adventure playground with beautifully natural destinations such as Milford Sound, Abel Tasman National Park, and the Tongariro Alpine Crossing. Activities such as bungee jumping or whale watching exemplify typical tourist attractions marketed primarily to individual and small-group travelers. Of course, the *Lord of the Rings* movies and *The Hobbit* have also added to New Zealand's international attraction as a tourist destination.

As a growing labor-intensive industry, tourism generates an increasingly wide range of jobs for New Zealanders. The number of equivalent full-time jobs supported directly by tourism in New Zealand was approximately 168,000 in 2014, constituting about 7.8% of the work force.

GROWTH OF KIWI EXPERIENCE

Kiwi Experience has grown rapidly since its creation. Although this is partly due to the general increase in the number of visitors to New Zealand, the percentage increase of passengers traveling on Kiwi Experience is well above the percentage increase in overseas visitors. In fact, the number of Kiwi Experience passengers has increased faster than the growth of international visitors. Kiwi Experience is clearly taking a larger slice of a growing market.

Kiwi Experience has now grown to a size that the original owners had never thought possible; they assumed they had reached market saturation a few years ago. However, over the last few years, the popularity of backpacking holidays has increased immensely among different types of people, and the company now has 30 buses and over 40 drivers. The directors of Kiwi Experience have had to broaden their limited definition of backpacking to encompass the demographic who now travel with the company. For instance, professionals who only have three weeks' holiday are now opting for a backpacker-style tour around New Zealand.

Exhibit 1: Kiwi Experience has expanded its offerings to cater to backpackers.

The success of Kiwi Experience is due to many factors besides the growth of the backpacking market.

THE "EXPERIENCE"

"How did you enjoy Waitomo Caves?" Rob asked Rory at a stop en route to Rotorua. "Amazing," he replied. "I saw the caves while black water rafting, and I really enjoyed the candlelight walk you took us all on through the Ruakuri Scenic Reserve to see the glow worms. It didn't stop there though; later on, a group of us from the coach went down to the Waitomo Tavern for a few drinks—I feel a bit rough today!" Rob laughed. Rory, he thought, was slowly coming to grips with what the Kiwi Experience was all about.

The Kiwi Experience concept is based on being the best in the market for those people who want to see the real New Zealand. Backpacking is all about traveling, meeting other people, getting value for money, and getting involved in the local environment and culture. The service Kiwi Experience offers allows the passengers to do just that. It allows backpackers to choose where and on what they want to spend their money at a price they can afford.

When Neil Geddes was asked what makes the Kiwi Experience so good, he had a simple reply.

> We ensure we give the customer what they want better than anyone else. Our service is not designed around what is good for the drivers; it is designed around what is good for the customer. We are close to our market, we are proud to be close to our market. When we [the directors of KE] travel, we stay in backpackers hostels, so as to learn and understand what the market wants. That is how we ensure that we always offer the best possible service for our clients. That is our core strength.

Kiwi Experience encourages all the people working within the business to interact with customers. For example, there was a BBQ at a backpackers' hostel in Auckland recently, at which Kiwi Experience had its accountants and other staff meet the guests. This group of staff did not usually come in direct contact with customers, but the event gave them a better understanding of who the company's customers were and where they came from.

Being first in the marketplace has also allowed Kiwi Experience to gain a lead in understanding what its target market wants and how it can service these needs effectively. This understanding has led the company's staff to realize that it is both the driver of the coach and the interactions among backpackers that help create the "Kiwi Experience."

THE DRIVERS

"The drivers are the single most important people in our company, we know that," states Neil Geddes. Their market research has shown that the driver can make or break a Kiwi Experience trip. This is why the company undertakes a very comprehensive and strict selection process for its drivers, along with a very thorough training program.

The first thing the directors look for when selecting drivers is a certain type of person—fun, young, and adventurous. They must have an outgoing personality and be proud to show off New Zealand. While this means that most drivers are from New Zealand, this is not always the case. Secondly, they must have extensive driving experience, as it is critical that they be safe drivers.

Kiwi Experience receives hundreds of applications for its driver jobs, and one of the reasons for this is the pay. The drivers are rewarded nicely for doing their job well, particularly through the bonuses and commission they receive at the end of each trip. However, very few drivers fit the strict selection criteria that the company has. The drivers must undergo a series of driving tests and interviews before they are selected. Even then they may not necessarily get the job.

All prospective drivers are then taken on a "dummy" trip around New Zealand. They are asked to take notes of the various activities that are on offer and record any other information that may assist them in doing their job effectively. After this initial training, they are taken on a proper Kiwi Experience trip, where they observe how an experienced driver operates. The prospective drivers could be asked to take over the driving or the commentary at any moment in time. They are taken on as Kiwi experience staff members only if they perform satisfactorily in these two tests.

Driving a Kiwi Experience bus is a highly rewarding job but a stressful one as well. The driver has many responsibilities besides having to safely drive 40 people around the whole of New Zealand. These include:

▶ Providing informative and knowledgeable commentary

▶ Booking all accommodation every night

▶ Ensuring that people on the bus interact as much as possible

▶ Socializing as much as possible among the passengers

▶ Organizing group meals and other group activities

▶ Organizing paid excursions

▶ Undertaking regular checks and maintenance (e.g., cleaning) of the bus

▶ Listening to and responding to customer complaints

Exhibit 2: A Kiwi Experience costume party organized by one of its drivers.

Due to the above factors, drivers of Kiwi Experience buses rarely last three years within the company. Not all leave because of the intensive nature of the job; many leave because they obtain other jobs elsewhere.

Each driver is debriefed by an operations manager after each trip. This enables the operations manager to determine how tired the driver is and whether they should be taken off the duty roster for a couple of weeks. An exhausted driver cannot provide the best service for the customers on the bus, and this will harm the reputation of the driver as well as Kiwi Experience in the long run. An experienced operations manager can easily spot when a certain driver needs rest. The drivers are also required to fill out a survey at the end of each trip, detailing how the trip went and the problems they encountered. The survey includes a section that allows the driver to make recommendations to improve the overall quality of the Kiwi Experience.

It is clear, therefore, that the drivers are the single most important asset that Kiwi Experience possesses. Their enthusiasm, knowledge, and personality have a huge impact on customers' perceptions of the quality of the trip and of Kiwi Experience as a whole.

CUSTOMER INTERACTION

Market research has shown that the interaction between the customers on the bus is the second most important part of a Kiwi Experience trip. Backpackers generally enjoy meeting other like-minded people. In fact, many backpackers travel for the specific purpose of making new friends and acquaintances. It is important for Kiwi Experience to ensure this by managing customer interactions well.

Kiwi Experience does several things to achieve the correct customer mix on its buses and ensure that the customers interact well together (beyond the normal interaction that would occur). Firstly, it ensures, as best as it can, that its booking agents do not book people who would not be suited to the kind of experience offered by the company. For example, older travelers may not be interested in some of the things that Kiwi Experience does. This strategy is important as it prevents potential customers from having a negative experience on the trip. Such an experience could influence the enjoyment of other customers on the same bus and ultimately lead to negative word of mouth for the company.

The company enforces this strategy in a number of ways. To begin with, it sends representatives from its booking agents on tour to help them understand the types of people who would enjoy traveling with Kiwi Experience. Secondly, the drivers are trained to notice any passengers on the bus who might be affecting the quality of the service other passengers are receiving. They are also empowered to take appropriate action. For example, in extreme cases, a driver may ask certain passengers to leave the bus and offer a full refund to encourage them to do so. Kiwi Experience has realized that if certain people undermine the enjoyment of a significant proportion of other customers, it is important to remove them from the bus.

Finally, the driver encourages social interaction among the customers on the bus and enables them to form bonds and friendships at an early stage within the trip. This should have a positive impact on the quality of customers' experiences on the bus and the impression that they have of the overall trip. The drivers usually encourage interaction through group meals and social activities in the evening (e.g., fancy dress competitions; see Exhibit 2).

ADVERTISING AND WORD OF MOUTH

"Why did you choose Kiwi Experience anyway?" Rob asked Rory as the inter-Islander ferry pulled away from the Wellington Harbour on its three-and-a-half hour trip to Picton in the South Island. "I never really planned to; before I left Scotland, I'd always planned to hire a campervan," replied Rory.

"So what made you change your mind then?" quizzed Rob. "I kept hearing of KE when I was traveling around Australia," said Rory. "Every time I stopped at a backpackers', I'd meet at least one person who would have a Kiwi Experience story to tell. Then when I came to New Zealand, KE did a slide show in the backpackers' I was staying at, and that really swung it for me!"

Many service organizations can rely on repeat purchases to maintain and enhance their profitability. For example, airlines often have passengers who have already flown with them many times. For Kiwi Experience, however, this is not the case. It is very unusual for passengers to travel with the company for a second time. Kiwi Experience relies heavily on new and referral customers for virtually all of its sales. Promoting the company and stimulating word of mouth are therefore vitally important.

Kiwi Experience promotes heavily in its target market and attempts to stimulate word of mouth wherever possible. It has also recognized the importance of advertising overseas. Backpackers often start searching for information well before they have left their own country to come to New Zealand, a fact that Neil Geddes acknowledges:

> A significant amount of our customers look for travel options well before they come near New Zealand. Most people mistakenly believe that backpackers turn up and make up their mind when they get in New Zealand. In fact, around 25% of customers buy their KE ticket overseas. For us, therefore, it is important to advertise overseas.

Other research that Kiwi Experience has undertaken shows that 75% of customers hear of the company before they enter New Zealand. This assists sales, since customers are familiar with the service before they purchase it. Word of mouth accounts for some of these cases, but a large percentage of customers hear of Kiwi Experience through advertising. For example, Kiwi Experience places leaflets in backpackers' and youth hostels located along destinations that backpackers commonly visit before they come to New Zealand, such as Hawaii, Sydney, Bangkok, and Fiji.

The advertising really starts once the backpackers are in New Zealand. Kiwi Experience uses people called "street fighters" (backpackers who hand out brochures at railway terminals, bus stations, etc.) throughout the gateway cities of Auckland and Christchurch. It also spreads the word through backpackers' hostels. It prefers recruiting backpackers who

have had the "Experience," as they are informed, motivated, and credible communicators who can sell the service better than anyone else. It seems that Kiwi Experience really does fight for every customer it gets.

The distinctive branding that Kiwi Experience uses on its leaflets and brochures certainly helps it to get its advertisements noticed. The company's brand research revealed a profile of its target market, which helped to shape its new brand:

> 18–35-year old men and women. They have a sense of anticipation; they crave the unknown and are seeking total adventure. The thought of meeting new people is an essential criteria in their choice of holiday . . . They spend time wondering what the dynamic of the group might be, and the 'unknown' is a thrill for them. They are free of the day-to-day rat race and they yearn to be their hedonistic selves. Each day is a new feeling, a new experience . . . There is little time for thinking on this holiday, only time for doing! These men and women love a laugh—they love the sensation of not taking anything too seriously (there will be other times in their life when they will have to be grown-up) . . . Right now life is about living—to the max.

Kiwi Experience also holds slide shows in backpackers' hostels in Auckland and Christchurch to persuade consumers who are still unsure about which mode of transport to use around New Zealand. These slide shows are an attempt to make the service more tangible and to reduce the perceived risk customers may have about taking the trip.

Kiwi Experience creates its own propaganda letters called "Bullsheets," which it sends to its major booking agents in New Zealand. This enables agents to be better informed about the service it offers. Finally, Kiwi Experience tries to ensure that its service is mentioned in popular travel guides such as Lonely Planet, which is widely read by backpackers (although the most recent write-up about Kiwi Experience was less than complimentary).

Kiwi Experience tries to ensure positive word of mouth by monitoring the performance of its service at all times. It does this by surveying customers on every single bus. One of the directors and the operations manager read these surveys to monitor what is happening. They then use these surveys to improve the service for their customers. Although the core experience basically remains the same, they continuously try and add value to the service.

This strategy has worked, says Neil Geddes:

> We have always had a strong and loyal customer following that is proud to have traveled with us, and proud to tell other people about KE. That is the one good thing about the backpacker market, they enjoying giving good information to other travelers. We rely on a huge rate of first time users and we achieve that by having good word-of-mouth.

In essence, therefore, Kiwi Experience attempts to create positive word of mouth by offering a consistently high quality of service at all times.

COMPETITION

"There goes our rivals," screamed Rob, as another bus whisked past the Kiwi Experience bus as they approached Franz Joseph Glacier. A huge "Boooo" was released from the passengers, and various faces were pulled as the competition disappeared in the distance. "They weren't hanging about," said Rory. "They have got to get back to Auckland as soon as possible; no time to look at the scenery!" replied Rob. "Yeah right, it is not as if it's important or anything," laughed Rory.

The competition Kiwi Experience faces comes from many places. Direct competition comes from other national backpacker coach services, several "regional" backpacker buses, and other tour buses and coach services that travel around New Zealand. In the past, Kiwi Experience's single biggest competition was the alternative national backpacking bus, Magic Bus. This bus service was created by the national coach company, whose market had been diminished by the introduction of Kiwi Experience. In 2013, Kiwi Experience purchased Magic Bus and began to dominate the market even more.

However, a new national competitor called Stray Bus has emerged. Its target market is slightly older and the trips a little longer than those of Kiwi Experience, but the services offered are quite similar. Exhibit 3 shows a comparison of some of the similar trips and prices the two companies offer. The debate about which bus company to take or how to travel around New Zealand is a heated one among travelers. See http://backpackercompare.com/nz-backpacker-bus/ for updated discussions on Stray Bus versus Kiwi Experience!

Exhibit 3: Kiwi Experience and Stray Bus: Comparison of trips and prices for 2015.

Company	Pass	Length of Trip	Price in NZ$
Kiwi Experience	All of New Zealand	25	1,895
Stray Bus	All of New Zealand	30	1,995
Kiwi Experience	Auckland to Christchurch	22	1,696
Stray Bus	Auckland to Christchurch	21	1,445

The other backpacking bus services that exist operate in other very specific regions of New Zealand; there are currently three of these in operation. Most of these bus services had been in existence before Kiwi Experience was created. Since the introduction of Kiwi Experience and the competition that followed, these buses have been hit badly, as passengers have favored a national bus pass over a regional one.

The third type of competition comes from other national bus companies that either offer express services to different points in New Zealand or specific tours around New Zealand. Passengers are not allowed to get on and off the bus wherever they desire. These buses pose a lesser threat to Kiwi Experience than the backpacking buses, as they tend to attract different market segments.

The fourth type of competition comes from other modes of transport that can be taken around New Zealand. The main sources of this type of competition are rental campervans and cars. A large number of these vehicles are "dumped" into the market in winter. However, the customers who are likely to use them have different psychographic, behavioral, and demographic (particularly in terms of income) variables than those who use backpacker buses.

The domestic airlines in New Zealand are not a major threat to Kiwi Experience as it is a relatively small country; they really only pose a threat over longer distances. In fact, Kiwi Experience has attempted to overcome any possible threat from the airlines by creating strategic alliances with them. For example, one of the national passes it offers includes an Air New Zealand flight from Christchurch to Auckland. The railway network in New Zealand offers little competition as it is limited in its coverage.

The final form of competition to Kiwi Experience is from other countries. Most travelers have a limited amount of time to spend on holidays and must therefore make decisions on where to spend their time. New Zealand competes for this time with countries such as Australia, the United States, Fiji, Thailand, and most recently South Africa, which has become a larger threat. Staff members at Kiwi Experience are aware that they must promote New Zealand as well as the company itself.

ADVENTURE ACTIVITIES

Rory's face was white as he approached the bus. "Are you ready to go?" asked Rob. "Just about; the skydiving was incredible, but I feel a bit dizzy," replied Rory. "Wait until you do the bungee in Queenstown, then you'll know what

Exhibit 3: Kiwi Experience offers a large range of activities to its passengers.

dizzy means," Rob said. "No thanks," said Rory, "I think I've had enough excitement to last me a lifetime."

One of Kiwi Experience's major appeals is the enormous number of paid excursions and activities that are on offer. From swimming with dolphins to aerobatic flights, the list is almost endless. By purchasing a bus ticket, a passenger is also entitled to discounts on many activities throughout New Zealand.

The activities offered are important to the organization for a variety of reasons. Firstly, it helps Kiwi Experience differentiate itself from its competitors, since some activities and discounts are exclusive to it. It also allows the company to exceed the expectations that customers may have at the start of the trip. Secondly, backpackers are usually adventurers who are looking for excitement and activities that will challenge them. By offering various activities, Kiwi Experience is fulfilling these customer needs. Finally, the activities also provide an additional source of revenue for the company in the form of commissions from the service operators. This enables Kiwi Experience to earn incremental income from its passengers.

One risk is that these activities do not always match the quality of service that Kiwi Experience offers. If an activity recommended by Kiwi Experience turns out to be of low quality, it will reflect poorly on the company. It is therefore important for Kiwi Experience to protect its brand image by ensuring that a consistently excellent standard of quality is maintained. Neil Geddes explains how Kiwi Experience attempts to achieve this:

> We assess every single activity that we offer, and we monitor their performance continuously. We ask questions on a customer questionnaire regarding the paid excursions they undertook. We also ensure every activity is up to adequate safety standards, beyond those of legal requirements, and we get feedback from our drivers on the quality of these activities.

MEMORABILIA

"Okay, everyone, squeeze in together!" shouted the photographer along the Queenstown waterfront. All the passengers on the bus shuffled together to ensure that they would appear in the photo. "Rob, jump in at the front!" shouted Rory, "We can't have a group photograph without you!" Rob was reluctantly pushed into the photograph, and the picture was taken. Queues quickly formed to order a copy of the photo.

Souvenirs and memories of each trip are a small but important part of Kiwi Experience. They provide additional revenue for the organization and are also positive reminders of the trip, helping to generate loyalty and positive word of mouth for a long time. Memorabilia can take the form of many things, such as T-shirts, sweatshirts, baseball caps, and group photographs.

FLEXIBILITY AND VALUE FOR MONEY

"I'm going to leave the bus here in Queenstown," said Rory to Rob. "A group of us are going to hang around here for a few weeks and take in the amazing scenery." "Great idea," said Rob. "Make sure you book yourself on the bus; one comes through here every day in the summer." "Thanks for a great time," added Rory, "Maybe you'll be driving the next bus we catch!"

If there is one thing that the management of Kiwi Experience constantly strives for, it is to increase the frequency of its bus services. They have realized that the more often the buses operate, the more flexible their service becomes. This increases its attractiveness to potential customers.

Kiwi Experience offers daily departures for about four months of the year (January–April) and 4–5 times a week throughout the rest of the year (although some of the more off-beat routes run less frequently). However, the company has learned to stay flexible and change its departure dates quickly. As it is in a high-volume, low-margin business, it must always be very fluid in the way it operates. This has sometimes led to customers being stuck in various places longer than they had planned.

One way that this flexibility is created is through the reservation system, which can tell Kiwi Experience where its customers are, where they got off the bus, and for how long. This enables customer flows to be managed effectively and ensures that the buses are as full as possible. This is important to Kiwi Experience, as the company only makes any significant amount of profit on the last 15% of its business. This is due to the fact that it works on very fine break-evens that are significantly higher than those for traditional package tours. However, the reservation system is not faultless, and over-booking and under-booking (when a backpacker is told that the bus is full when it is in fact not) occur every now and then.

Market research has shown that value for money is the third most important aspect of the Kiwi Experience trip. The price of the tickets, the activities offered, and the flexibility and the quality of the service prompt many backpackers to feel that they are obtaining value from Kiwi Experience. To date, the company has managed to maintain this perception, and it is one of the fundamental reasons for its success.

However, Kiwi Experience does not intend to stand still. Neil Geddes knows that in order to stay ahead of the competition, the company must always improve its service offering:

> We are our own biggest threat, being seen as mainstream, or not leading edge, or by becoming a service that is perceived as not being for independent travelers. We must continually move with the market to ensure we offer the best possible experience for our customers.

The challenges for Kiwi Experience are clear and present. It needs to be seen as leading edge but not mainstream. It also needs to avoid being labeled a "booze bus"—a problem that its competitor, Contiki, suffers from. The need to find high-quality bus drivers is a constant source of worry, as is the reservation system.

"Hey, Rory!" shouted Rob, as Rory walked toward his backpackers. "Did you ever work out the answer to your question?" Rory turned around and looked puzzled. "What question?" he said. "Oh you mean the one about why Kiwi Experience is so successful?"

"That's it! Did you ever work it out?" asked Rob. "Yeah I think I did . . . no, I know I did," Rory said forcefully. "It's just difficult to express it all. Maybe one day I'll put it down on paper," he said.

"Well, don't forget to mention me if you ever do," laughed Rob.

STUDY QUESTIONS

1. How does Kiwi Experience maintain a continuous customer focus?

2. What role does culture and leadership play in the success of Kiwi Experience?

3. Brainstorm on how other service companies might get customers to play a more active role in the service experience.

The Accra Beach Hotel: Block Booking of Capacity during a Peak Period

Sheryl E. Kimes and Jochen Wirtz

Cherita Howard, sales manager for the Accra Beach Hotel, a 175-room hotel on the Caribbean island of Barbados, was debating what to do about a request from the West Indies Cricket Board. The Board wanted to book a large block of rooms during some of the hotel's busiest periods more than six months in advance and was also asking for a discount. In return, it promised to promote the Accra Beach as the host hotel in all advertising materials and television broadcasts of the upcoming West Indies Cricket Series, an important international sporting event.

THE HOTEL

The Accra Beach Hotel and Resort had a prime beach-front location on the south coast of Barbados, just a short distance from the airport and the capital city of Bridgetown. Located on 3½ acres of tropical landscape and fronting one of the best beaches on Barbados, the hotel featured rooms offering panoramic views of the ocean, pool, or island.

The centerpiece of its lush gardens was the large swimming pool, which had a shallow bank for lounging and a swim-up bar. In addition, there was a squash court and a fully equipped gym. Golf facilities were also available only 15 minutes away at the Barbados Golf Club, with which the hotel was affiliated.

The Accra Beach had two restaurants and two bars as well as extensive banquet and conference facilities. It offered state-of-the-art conference facilities to local, regional, and international corporate clientele and had hosted a number of large summits in recent years. Three conference rooms, which could be configured in a number of ways, served as the setting for large corporate meetings, training seminars, product displays, dinners, and wedding receptions. A business center provided guests with internet access, faxing capabilities, and photocopying services.

The hotel's 141 standard rooms were categorized into three groups—island view, pool view, and ocean view. There were also 24 ocean-view junior suites, 4 two-bedroom suites, and 6 penthouse suites, each decorated in tropical pastel prints and handcrafted furniture. All rooms were equipped with a cable/satellite TV, air conditioning, ceiling fans, a hair dryer, a coffee percolator, a direct-dial telephone, a bath tub/shower, and a balcony.

Exhibit 1: The Accra Beach Hotel offers panoramic views of the beach.

Standard rooms were configured with either a king-size bed or two twin beds in the island and ocean view categories, while the pool view suites had two double beds. The eight penthouse suites and four two-bedroom suites, all of which offered ocean views, contained the features listed for the standard rooms plus added comforts. They were built on two levels, featuring a living room with a bar area on the third floor of the hotel and a bedroom accessed by an internal stairway on the fourth floor. These suites also had a bathroom containing a Jacuzzi, a shower stall, a double vanity basin, and a skylight.

The 24 junior suites were fitted with a double bed or two twin beds, plus a living room area with a sofa that could be converted to another bed.

HOTEL PERFORMANCE

The Accra Beach enjoyed a relatively high occupancy rate, with the highest rates achieved from January through March and the lowest generally achieved during the summer (Exhibit 2). The average room rates followed a similar pattern—they were highest (US$150–$170) from December through March and relatively low (US$120) during the summer months Exhibit 3). The hotel's RevPAR (revenue per available room—a product of the occupancy rate and the average room rate) showed even more variation, exceeding $140 from January through March but falling to less than $100 from June through October (Exhibit 4). The rates on the penthouse suites ranged from $310 to $395, while those on the junior suites ranged from $195 to $235.

The hotel had traditionally promoted itself as a resort destination, and its clientele had been dominated by tourists from the United Kingdom and Canada. However, the composition of hotel guests had changed drastically over the past few years. The percentage of business customers increased dramatically after the hotel started promoting its convenient location. Cherita Howard, the hotel's sales manager, worked extensively with tour operators and corporate travel managers. The majority of hotel guests were corporate clients from companies such as Barbados Cable & Wireless and the Caribbean International Banking Corporation (Exhibit 5), who usually came for business meetings with local companies. The Accra Beach Hotel had been named Hotel of the Year by the Barbados Hotel Association twice.

Sometimes, guests who were on vacation (particularly during the winter months) felt uncomfortable finding themselves surrounded by business people. As one vacationer put it, "There's just something weird about being on vacation and going to the beach and then seeing suit-clad business people chatting on their cell phones." However, the hotel achieved a higher average room rate from business guests than vacationers and had found the volume of corporate business to be much more stable than that from tour operators and individual guests.

THE WEST INDIES CRICKET BOARD

Cherita had been approached by the West Indies Cricket Board (WICB) about the possibility of the Accra Beach Hotel serving as the host hotel for next spring's West Indies Cricket Home Series, an important international sporting event among cricket-loving nations. The location of this event rotated among several different Caribbean nations. Barbados would be hosting the next one, which would feature visiting teams from India and New Zealand.

Exhibit 2: Accra Beach Hotel: Monthly occupancy rate.

Year	Month	Occupancy
2 years ago	January	87.7%
2 years ago	February	94.1%
2 years ago	March	91.9%
2 years ago	April	78.7%
2 years ago	May	76.7%
2 years ago	June	70.7%
2 years ago	July	82.0%
2 years ago	August	84.9%
2 years ago	September	64.7%
2 years ago	October	82.0%
2 years ago	November	83.8%
2 years ago	December	66.1%
Last year	January	87.6%
Last year	February	88.8%
Last year	March	90.3%
Last year	April	82.0%
Last year	May	74.7%
Last year	June	69.1%
Last year	July	76.7%
Last year	August	70.5%
Last year	September	64.7%
Last year	October	71.3%
Last year	November	81.7%
Last year	December	72.1%

Exhibit 3: Accra Beach Hotel: Average daily room rate.

Year	Month	Average room rate (in US$)
2 years ago	January	$159.05
2 years ago	February	$153.73
2 years ago	March	$157.00
2 years ago	April	$153.70
2 years ago	May	$144.00
2 years ago	June	$136.69
2 years ago	July	$122.13
2 years ago	August	$121.03
2 years ago	September	$123.45
2 years ago	October	$129.03
2 years ago	November	$141.03
2 years ago	December	$152.87
Last year	January	$162.04
Last year	February	$167.50
Last year	March	$158.44
Last year	April	$150.15
Last year	May	$141.79
Last year	June	$136.46
Last year	July	$128.49
Last year	August	$128.49
Last year	September	$127.11
Last year	October	$132.76
Last year	November	$141.86
Last year	December	$151.59

Exhibit 4: Accra Beach Hotel: Revenue per available room (RevPAR).

Year	Month	Revenue per available room (in US$)
2 years ago	January	$139.49
2 years ago	February	$144.66
2 years ago	March	$144.28
2 years ago	April	$120.96
2 years ago	May	$110.45
2 years ago	June	$96.64
2 years ago	July	$100.15
2 years ago	August	$102.75
2 years ago	September	$79.87
2 years ago	October	$105.80
2 years ago	November	$118.18
2 years ago	December	$101.05
Last year	January	$141.90
Last year	February	$148.67
Last year	March	$143.02
Last year	April	$123.12
Last year	May	$105.87
Last year	June	$94.23
Last year	July	$98.55
Last year	August	$90.59
Last year	September	$82.24
Last year	October	$94.62
Last year	November	$115.89
Last year	December	$109.24

Note: RevPAR refers to revenue per available room and is computed by multiplying the room occupancy rate (see Exhibit 3) with the average room rate (Exhibit 4).

Exhibit 5: Accra Beach Hotel: Market segments.

Accra Beach Hotel: Market Segments

Individual Travelers
Corporate
Tour Operators

Exhibit 6: Standard room sales and average daily room rates for same periods in previous year.

Date of WICB Home Series	Standard rooms sold in previous year during the same period	Average daily room rate (ADR) in US$
Part 1		
4/24	141	$129
4/25	138	$120
4/26	135	$128
4/27	134	$135
4/28	123	$133
4/29	128	$124
4/30	141	$119
5/1	141	$124
5/2	141	$121
5/3	139	$122
5/4	112	$118
5/5	78	$126
5/6	95	$130
5/7	113	$138
Part II		
5/27	99	$131
5/28	114	$132
5/29	114	$136
5/30	125	$136
Part III		
6/17	124	$125
6/18	119	$122
6/19	112	$126
6/20	119	$111
6/21	125	$110
6/22	116	$105
6/23	130	$106
6/24	141	$101
6/25	141	$110
6/26	125	$115

Both Cherita and Jon Martineau, the general manager of the hotel, thought that the marketing exposure associated with hosting the teams would be very beneficial for the hotel. However, they were concerned about accepting the business because they knew from past experience that many of the desired dates were usually very busy days for the hotel. They were sure that the rate the WICB was willing to pay would be lower than the average rate of US$140–$150 they normally achieved during the period in question. In contrast to regular guests, who could usually be counted on to have a number of meals at the hotel, team members and officials would be less likely to dine at the hotel because they would be on a per diem budget. Cherita and Jon Martineau were also worried about how the hotel's other guests might react to the presence of the cricket teams. Nevertheless, the marketing potential for the hotel was substantial. The WICB had promised to list the Accra Beach as the host hotel in all promotional materials as well as during the televised matches.

The West Indies Home Series was divided into three parts, and each would require bookings at the Accra Beach Hotel. The first part pitted the West Indies team against the Indian team and would run from April 24 to May 7. The second part featured the same teams and would run from May 27 to May 30. The final part showcased the West Indies team against the New Zealand team and would run from June 17 to June 26.

The WICB wanted 50 standard rooms for the duration of each part and was willing to pay US$110 per night per room. It also specified that each team had to be housed on a single floor of the

hotel. In addition, the WICB insisted that laundry service for team uniforms (cricket teams typically wear all-white clothing) and practice gear be provided at no additional charge for all team members. Cherita estimated that it would cost the hotel about $20 per day if they could do the laundry in-house but about $200 per day if they had to send it to an outside source.

Cherita called Ferne Armstrong, the reservations manager of the hotel, and asked her what she thought. Like Cherita, Ferne was concerned about the possible displacement of higher-paying customers but offered to conduct further investigation into the expected room sales and associated room rates for the desired dates. Since the dates were over six months in the future, Ferne had not yet developed forecasts. However, she was able to provide data on room sales and average room rates from the same days of the previous year (Exhibit 6).

Soon after Cherita returned to her office to analyze the data, she was interrupted by a phone call from the head of the WICB, who wanted to know the status of his request. She promised to have an answer for him before the end of the day. As soon as she hung up, Jon Martineau called and chatted about the huge marketing potential of being the host hotel.

Cherita shook her head and wondered, "What should I do?"

STUDY QUESTIONS

1. What factors lead to variations in demand for rooms at a hotel such as the Accra Beach?

2. Identify the various market segments currently served by the hotel. What are the pros and cons of seeking to serve customers from several segments?

3. What are the key considerations facing the hotel as it reviews the booking requests from the West Indies Cricket Board? (For simplification of calculations, assume that each room will hold only one occupant; i.e., 50 rooms equate to 50 cricket players.)

4. What action should Cherita Howard take, and why?

Revenue Management of Gondolas: Maintaining the Balance between Tradition and Revenue

Sheryl E. Kimes

A ride on a gondola, one of the historical black boats of Venice, is considered by many to be part of the quintessential Venice experience. However, while the demand for gondolas is extremely high, the number of boats has dropped from several thousand gondolas in the 18th century to about 400 today. In addition, there is pressure to maintain some of the tradition associated with the gondolas, thereby making it tricky to increase revenue. The question is, how can a balance between tradition and revenue be maintained?

Although Venice is considered to be one of the most beautiful and romantic cities in the world, modern Venice has faced many challenges, including a loss of population to other parts of Italy and physical damage from flooding, pollution, and age. The basis of the Venetian economy is tourism. The beauty of the architecture and canals and the many artistic and cultural attractions of Venice draw over 20 million visitors per year from around the world.

Venice is set on over 100 islands interconnected by about 150 canals. All transportation within the city is either by boat or on foot. A ride on a gondola, one of the historical black boats of Venice, is considered by many to be part of the quintessential Venice experience. Although the demand for gondola rides is extremely high, the number of boats has dropped from several thousand gondolas in the 18th century to about 400 today. Gondolas are regulated by the City of

Venice, and there is a strong desire to maintain their tradition. However, at the same time, the economic impact on the city and its population is considerable. The question is how best to balance the maintenance of tradition with the economic impact on the gondolier and the city.

TOURISM IN VENICE

In 2010, Venice received an average of 60,000 tourists per day, of which less than half spent the night. About 85% of the tourists come from outside of Italy. Venice has one of the highest ratios of tourists to local residents (89 visitors for every 100 Venetians—the highest in Europe). During busy periods (the summer, over Christmas, and during Carnivale), even more people enter the city. Americans represent the largest proportion of overnight tourists, followed by the British, the French, and Germans.

THE GONDOLA

The first mention of the gondola was in 1094, but gondolas became popular during the 15th century and helped people better maneuver the canals of Venice. Gondolas are designed to navigate the shallow and narrow canals of Venice and are strictly bound by tradition. They are 11 m long, 1.4 m wide, and weigh about 500 kg. The left side is higher than the right side by 24 cm, and the bottoms are flat so that they can function in the very shallow water (sometimes much less than a meter deep). The gondolas are constructed of 280 pieces of 8 different types of wood and only have metal in the head and stem. They are traditionally black and take about 3–6 months to build at a cost of approximately €20,000 to €30,000.

Exhibit 1: Gondola traffic at the Grand Canal in Venice.

Gondoliers. Gondolas are owned and steered by gondoliers. Their numbers have dropped from several thousand in the 18th century to only 425 today. Gondoliers are usually male and must have been born in Venice. Traditionally, the profession of the gondolier was passed from one generation to the next. However, this has changed in recent years, because many young people have decided to take more lucrative and less physically demanding jobs. To become a gondolier, potential applicants must take a test that measures their boat-handling skills, their language ability, their knowledge of the city, and their ability to work with tourists.

Gondoliers are divided into 10 *traghetti* (or ferry stations). Each *traghetto* elects *barcali* who represent the *traghetto* to the government. Gondola rides are available at about eight *stazi* (ferry stations) throughout the city.

THE ROLE OF GONDOLAS IN TOURISM

Gondolas were once the primary mode of transportation in Venice. However, with the advent of faster and cheaper motorboats and *vaporetti* (a form of water-based bus), gondolas have become more of a tourist activity than a mode of transportation.[1] During the 1920s, it was thought that gondolas would disappear. A lively debate ensued, with even Mussolini chiming in that the gondola tradition needed to be preserved. Even in the late 19th century, Mark Twain commented that gondolas were little more than an anachronism.

As mass tourism increased, the design and operation of gondolas were altered so that they could accommodate more tourists and generate additional revenue. The boats were lengthened and narrowed, and a more elaborate oar link was developed so that the gondola could be steered by one oarsman. These modifications, along with a few other design changes, provided more space for passengers. However, as the amount of motorized boat traffic increased, it became more difficult to maneuver the gondolas safely through the narrow canals.

Pricing and Distribution. By 1930, tour guides such as Baedeker's listed gondola prices by the hour and by the trip. By 1945, the gondola trips were based more on the experience rather than actual transportation to a destination.

1 Much of the discussion on the next two pages is taken from Robert C. Davis and Garry R. Marvin, *Venice: The Tourist Maze* (Berkeley, California: University of California Press, 2004).

Exhibit 2: Venetian gondolier dressed in a traditional outfit.

Since World War II, the tourist demand for gondola rides has been extremely high, and the posted rates have increased accordingly. Whereas the posted rate was $0.42 for 50 minutes in 1930, it reached $1.00 by 1945, $5.00 by 1965, and $70 by 1999.

The price of gondola rides is regulated by the city. Day rates are €80 for 40 minutes for a maximum of 6 passengers, while night rates (7 p.m.–8 a.m.) are €20 higher. Although the rates are regulated, they are not always followed, and many prices are set through negotiation. Due to the popularity of gondola rides, it is quite possible to share the gondola with strangers.

Gondolas are typically booked in one of three ways: directly with the gondolier, through a hotel, or through a third-party travel agency. Hotels and travel agencies often package the gondola ride with other services (such as dinner or music) and take a sizable commission.

About 80% of gondola business comes from tour operators. Typically, tour operators either package the gondola ride with other travel options (such as hotel rooms, bus tours, and transfers) or sell them separately. In the former case, customers do not even know the cost of the gondola ride, because it is included in the package price.

Even when customers can see the price, it does not seem exorbitant as it is generally on a per-person basis. That being said, the rates are based on six people per gondola. Given that tour operator rates range from €35 to over €80 per person, the revenue associated with one 40-minute gondola ride is substantial. The tour operator passes on some of this revenue to the *stazi*, who in turn distribute it to the gondolas. However, the tour operator is able to maintain a very good profit margin even after covering costs.

The gondoliers seem to like working with the tour operators because of the guaranteed and steady stream of business. In addition, much of the tour operator business arrives en masse, which makes it easier and more efficient to fill and dispatch gondolas. Nevertheless, the tour operator profit margin is high, and there may be opportunities for the *stazi* to increase revenue.

Carovane (caravans) of multiple gondolas (sometimes up to 30) are often used to keep groups together and to increase efficiency. Sometimes an accordionist and singer are provided for the entire *carovana* (at a cost of about €150). Sending out a large *carovana* requires a great deal of coordination because of the need to quickly load and unload customers. Gondolas are not the most stable of boats for customers to board, and retired gondoliers are assigned to assist with loading and unloading.

The *carovane* follow a set route and can easily return to the dock within 50 minutes for the next group of passengers. Each of the *stazi* has different routes that are designed to ensure a smooth flow and to avoid traffic tie-ups with *vaparettos* and other commercial boats.

Demand and Revenue. Firm statistics on the number of gondola rides do not exist, but it is estimated that about a quarter of all tourists take a gondola ride. In 2004, it was estimated that there were at least 3 million gondola rides. Even with a rate of $20 per person, this is a sizable business.

Gondolas generate income not only for the gondoliers, the *ganzeri* (usually retired gondoliers who help with the boats), and the group leaders of the *stazi* but also for the boat construction trade (including the boat yard, the oar makers, the smiths, and the gilders). In addition, they provide jobs and revenue for hat makers and tailors (who supply the traditional gondolier uniform) and generate a sizable amount of souvenir sales.

THE DILEMMA

Although the demand for gondola rides is extremely high, capacity issues seem to be constraining the number of rides that can be offered. This, combined with the pressure to maintain some of the traditions associated with the gondolas, makes it tricky to increase revenue. Nevertheless, the revenue provided by the gondola industry is substantial and plays an important role in the Venice economy. How should the business proceed?

INTERESTING WEBSITES ON GONDOLAS:

▶ http://www.gondolavenezia.it/history_tariffe.asp?Pag=43

▶ http://www.venicewelcome.com/servizi/tour-ing/venicewalktours.htm

▶ http://researchnews.osu.edu/archive/venice.htm

▶ http://www.independent.co.uk/news/world/europe/the-death-of-venice-corrupt-officials-mass-tourism-and-soaring-property-prices-have-stifled-life-in-10251434.html

STUDY QUESTIONS

1. What can be done to increase the capacity of gondolas? What revenue impact would this have?

2. How can you balance revenue maximization with the maintenance of cultural heritage? Is it possible? If so, what would you recommend?

3. Consider the pricing structure of the gondolas. What sort of changes would you recommend? How would customers react? What revenue impact would your recommendations have?

Aussie Pooch Mobile

Lorelle Frazer

After creating a mobile service that washes dogs outside their owners' homes, a young entrepreneur has successfully franchised the concept. Her firm now has almost 200 franchises in many parts of Australia as well as up to 30 in other countries. She and her management team are debating how best to plan future expansion.

Elaine and Paul Beale drew up in their four-wheel drive outside 22 Ferndale Avenue, towing a bright blue trailer with red and white lettering. As Aussie Pooch Mobile franchisees whose territory covered four suburbs of Brisbane, Australia, they were having a busy day. It was only 1 p.m., and they had already washed and groomed 16 dogs at 12 different houses. Now they were at their last appointment—a "pooch party" of 10 dogs at Number 22, where five other residents of the street had arranged to have their dogs washed on a bi-weekly basis.

Prior to their arrival outside the house, there had been ferocious growling and snarling from a fierce-looking Rottweiler. However, when the animal caught sight of the brightly colored trailer, he and two other dogs in the yard bounded forward eagerly to the chain-link fence in a flurry of barking and wagging tails.

Throughout the residential areas of Brisbane and in a number of other Australian cities, dogs of all shapes and sizes were being washed and groomed by Aussie Pooch Mobile franchisees. By mid-2015, the company had grown to over 165 franchisees and claimed to be "Australia's premier mobile dog wash and care company." A key issue facing its managing director, Christine Taylor, and members of the management team was how to plan and shape future expansion (see Exhibit 1).

FOUNDING AND EXPANSION

Located in Burpengary, Queensland, just north of Brisbane, Aussie Pooch Mobile Pty Ltd (APM) was founded in 1991 by Christine Taylor, then aged 22. Taylor had learned customer service early, working in her parents' bait-and-tackle shop from the age of eight. Growing up in an environment with dogs and horses as pets, she knew she wanted to work with

Exhibit 1: Christine Taylor with dogs.

animals and learned dog-grooming skills from working in a local salon. At 16, Taylor left school and began her own grooming business on a part-time basis using a bathtub in the family garage. As she was still too young to drive, her parents would take her to pick up the dogs from their owners. She washed and groomed the animals at home and then returned them.

Once Taylor had learned to drive and bought her own car, she decided to take her service to the customers. So she went mobile, creating a trailer in which the dogs could be washed outside their owners' homes. She named this fledgling venture "The Aussie Pooch Mobile." Soon, it became a full-time job. Eventually, she found that she had more business than she could handle alone, so she hired assistants. The next step was to add a second trailer. Newly married, she and her husband David McNamara ploughed their profits into the purchase of additional trailers and gradually expanded until they had six mobile units.

The idea of franchising came to Taylor when she found herself physically constrained by a difficult pregnancy:

> David would go bike riding or head to the coast and have fun with the jet ski and I was stuck at home

and felt like I was going nuts, because I'm a really active person. I was hungry for information on how to expand the business, so I started researching other companies and reading heaps of books and came up with franchising as the best way to go, since it would provide capital and also allow a dedicated group of small business people to help expand the business further.

As existing units were converted from employees to franchisee operations, Taylor noticed that they quickly became about 20% more profitable. Initially, Aussie Pooch Mobile focused on Brisbane and the surrounding region of southeast Queensland. Subsequently, it expanded into New South Wales and South Australia in 1995; Canberra, Australian Capital Territory (ACT) in 1999; and Victoria in 2000 (Exhibit 2). Expansion into Western Australia came in mid-2004.

In 1996, a New Zealand division of the firm was launched in Tauranga, a small city 200 km southeast of Auckland, under the name Kiwi Pooch Mobile. In 2000, Taylor expanded operations into New Caledonia through a master franchise agreement, launching "La Pooch Mobile." In 2001, The Pooch Mobile was launched in the United Kingdom, beginning with a town in northern England. Soon, there were four operators under a master franchisee. The following year saw the official launch of The Pooch Mobile Malaysia, also under a master franchisee. When setting up the company's presence in the United States in 2006, Taylor offered the master franchise to a top-performing Australian master franchisee to provide them with further opportunities to grow.

By mid-2015, the company had 167 mobile units in Australia, with 60 located in Queensland, 52 in New South Wales, 19

Exhibit 2: Map image.

in Victoria, 14 in South Australia, 14 in Western Australia, and 8 in the Australian Capital Territory. The Aussie Pooch Mobile group bathed more than 20,000 dogs each month and had an annual turnover of approximately $7.5 million.

Aussie Pooch Mobile was a member of the Franchise Council of Australia and complied with the Franchising Code of Conduct. The management team consisted of Christine Taylor as the managing director and David McNamara as the director responsible for overseeing trailer design and systems support. Each state had its own manager and training team. The central support office also housed staff who provided further assistance to managers and franchisees.

Aussie Pooch Mobile's expansion benefitted from the leverage provided by several master franchisees who had obtained the rights to work a large territory and sell franchises within it. Said Taylor:

> I look at the business as if it's my first child. I see it now starting to come of age where it wants to go alone, but still needs me to hold its hand a little bit, whereas initially it needed me there the whole time. With the support staff we have in place, the business is now gaining the support structure it needs to work without me. This is what I am aiming towards. I appreciate that a team of people can achieve much more than one person alone.

THE SERVICE CONCEPT

Unlike retail pet service stores that required customers to bring their animals to the store or kennel, Aussie Pooch Mobile specialized in taking its dog washing services to customers' homes. Dogs were washed in a hydrobath installed in a specially designed trailer that was parked in the street. The trailer had partially open sides and a roof to provide protection from sun and rain (Exhibit 3). The use of hydrobath equipment (in which warm, pressurized water was pumped through a shower head) enabled operators to clean dogs more thoroughly than would be possible with a garden hose. The bath was designed to rid the dog of fleas and ticks, improve its skin condition, clean its coat, and eliminate smells. Customers supplied water and electrical power.

Apart from flea-control products and a few grooming aids, Aussie Pooch Mobile did not attempt to sell dog food and other pet supplies initially. The company had resisted the temptation to diversify into other fields so that it could

Services offered in 1990	Services offered in 2015
Hydrobath	Hydrobath
Brush	Brush
Nail cut	Nail cut
Ear clean	Ear clean
Eye clean	Eye clean
Chamois dry	Chamois dry
Deodorize	Deodorize
Own brand solutions	Own brand solutions (expanded)
	Blow dry
	Retail own-brand products
	Retail products
	Medicated washes
	De-worming
	Massage for dogs
	Aromatherapy for dogs
	Doggy facials
	Clipping (hair cutting)

focus on its niche in the dog-bathing industry. "We did not want to be a jack of all trades because you'll never be good at anything," declared Taylor. "We now have an exclusive range of products that customer demand has driven us to providing, but we still work closely with vets and pet shops and are by no means a pet shop on wheels. We are more like a specialist dog care service that provides needed items with professional advice."

The fee paid by customers varied from $22–$70 per dog, depending on breed and size, condition of coat and skin, behavior, and geographic location, with discounts for multiple animals at the same address. At "pooch parties," a concept developed at Aussie Pooch Mobile, the home owner acting as host typically received a discount on their dog wash at the discretion of the operator. Additional services, for which an extra fee was charged, included aromatherapy baths, doggy facials, and doggy massages. These services ranged from $4–$10. Additional dog grooming and clipping were available for $10–$50 per dog, depending on the breed and condition of the animal.

Operators also offered free advice to customers about their dogs' diet and health care, including such issues as ticks and skin problems. They encouraged customers to have their dogs bathed on a regular basis. Most customers made appointments once every two or four weeks.

A SATISFIED CUSTOMER

The process of bathing a dog involved a sequence of carefully coordinated actions, as exemplified by Elaine Beal's treatment of Zak the Rottweiler. "Hello my darling, who's a good boy?" crooned Elaine as she patted the enthusiastic dog, placed him on a leash, and led him out through the gate to the footpath on this warm, sunny day. Paul busied himself connecting hoses and electrical cords to the house, while Elaine began back-combing Zak's coat in order to set it up for the water to get underneath. She then led the now placid dog to the hydrobath inside the trailer, where he sat patiently while she removed his leash and clipped him to a special collar in the bath for security. Meanwhile, the water had been heating to the desired temperature.

Over the next few minutes, Elaine bathed the dog, applied a medicated herbal shampoo to his coat, and rinsed him thoroughly with the pressure-driven hose. After releasing Zak from the special collar and reattaching his leash, she led him out of the hydrobath and onto the footpath, where she wrapped him in a chamois cloth and dried him. Next, she cleaned the dog's ears and eyes with disposable baby wipes, all the time continuing to talk soothingly to him. She checked his coat and skin to ensure that there were no ticks or skin problems, gave his nails a quick clip, and sprayed a herbal conditioner and deodorizer onto Zak's now gleaming coat and brushed it in. Returning Zak to the yard and removing the leash, Elaine patted him and gave him a large biscuit, specially formulated to protect the animal's teeth.

THE AUSTRALIAN MARKET

Australia's population of 23.7 million in 2015 was small in relation to the country's vast land area of 7.7 million km². A federal nation, Australia is divided into six states—New South Wales (NSW), Victoria, Queensland, South Australia, Western Australia, and the island of Tasmania—plus two territories: the large but thinly populated Northern Territory and the small Australian Capital Territory (ACT), which contained the federal capital, Canberra, and its suburbs. The average annual earning for employed persons was $77,000.

With much of the interior of the continent uninhabitable and many other areas inhospitable to permanent settlement, most of the Australian population was concentrated in a narrow coastal band running clockwise from Brisbane on the southeast coast through Sydney and Melbourne to Adelaide, the capital of South Australia. Some 2,700 km (1,600 miles) to the west lay Perth, known as the most isolated city in the world. A breakdown of the population by state and territory is shown in Exhibit 4. The northern half of the country was in the tropics; Brisbane and Perth enjoyed a sub-tropical climate; and the remaining major cities had a temperate climate. Melbourne was known for its sharp fluctuations in temperature.

There were about 3.4 million domestic dogs in the country in 2009, and approximately 36% of the nation's eight million households owned at least one dog. Western Australia had the lowest proportion of dogs per population, while Tasmania had the highest. In 2011, it was estimated that Australians spent approximately $3.6 billion on dog-related goods and

Exhibit 4: Population of Australia by State and Territory, March 2011.

State/Territory	Population (000)
New South Wales	7,618.2
Victoria	5,938.1
Queensland	4,779.4
South Australia	1,698.6
Western Australia	2,591.6
Tasmania	516.6
Australian Capital Territory	390.8
Northern Territory	244.6
Australia Total	23,781.2

Source: Australian Bureau of Statistics, 2015.

services, of which 30% went to dog food, 37% to veterinary services, 15% to dog products and equipment, and 17% to other services, including washing and grooming (Exhibit 5).

FRANCHISING IN AUSTRALIA

Australia was home to a number of internationally known franchise operators, including Hertz Rent-a-Car, Avis, McDonald's, KFC, Pizza Hut, Subway, Kwik Kopy, and Snap-on Tools. By contrast, most Burger King outlets operated under the name Hungry Jack's, an acquired Australian chain with significant brand equity.

By the beginning of the 21st century, the Australian franchising sector had reached a stage of early maturity. McDonald's, KFC, and Pizza Hut opened their first outlets in Australia in the 1970s. These imported systems were followed by many home-grown business-format franchises such as Just Cuts (hairdressing), Snap Printing, Eagle Boys Pizza, and VIP Home Services. All of these grew into large domestic systems and then expanded internationally, principally to New Zealand and Southeast Asia.

In 2014, Australia boasted more than 1,100 business-format franchise systems holding an estimated 79,000 outlets. Although the United States had many more systems and outlets, Australia had more franchisors per capita, reflecting the relative ease of entry into franchising in this country.

Most of the growth in franchising occurred in business-format franchising as opposed to product franchising. Business-format franchises provided franchisees with a full business system and the rights to operate under the franchisor's brand name, whereas product franchises merely allowed independent operators to supply a manufacturer's product (such as car dealerships or soft-drink bottlers).

Exhibit 5: Distribution of consumer expenditures on dog-related goods and services, 2010.

Product/Service	Allocation
Dog food	31%
Vet charges	44%
Dog services	21%
Pet purchases	4%
Total dog-related expenditure	$3.6 billion

Source: Australian Companion Animal Council, *Contribution of the Pet Care Industry to the Australian Economy, Report,* 7th ed. (2010).

Typically, franchisees were required to pay an up-front franchise fee (averaging $30,000 in service industries and $40,000 in retailing) for the right to operate under the franchise system within a defined geographic area. This initial fee was included in the total start-up cost of the business (ranging from around $89,000 in the service sector to more than $275,000 in the retail industry). In addition, franchisees paid a royalty on all sales and an ongoing contribution toward advertising and promotional activities designed to build brand awareness and preference. Would-be franchisees who lacked sufficient capital might be able to obtain bank financing against personal assets such as property or an acceptable guarantor.

FRANCHISING TRENDS

The rapid growth of franchising globally had been stimulated in part by demographic trends. For instance, the increase in dual-income families had led to greater demand for outsourcing of household services such as lawn mowing, house cleaning, and pet grooming. Some franchise systems offered multiple concepts under a single corporate brand name. An example was VIP Home Services, which had separate franchises available in lawn mowing, cleaning, car washing, and rubbish removal. Additional growth came from conversion of existing individual businesses to a franchise format. For instance, Eagle Boys Pizza had often approached local pizza operators and offered them the opportunity to join this franchise. Almost half the franchise systems in Australia were in retail trade (27% non-food and 18% food). Other large and growing industries were administration and support services (15%) and other services (11%), as shown in Exhibit 6. Most franchisees were former white-collar workers or blue-collar supervisors who craved independence and a life-cycle change.

Over the years, Australia's franchising sector had experienced a myriad of regulatory regimes. Finally, in 1998, in response to perceived problems in many franchising systems, the federal government introduced a mandatory Franchising Code of Conduct, administered under what is now the Competition and Consumer Act 2011 (formerly the Trade Practice Act). Among other things, the Code required that potential franchisees be given full disclosure about the franchisor's background and operations prior to signing a franchise agreement. In contrast, the franchising sector in the United States faced an inconsistent set of regulations that varied from one state to another. In the United Kingdom, there were no specific franchising regulations beyond those applying to all corporations operating in designated industries.

Exhibit 6: Distribution of franchise systems in Australia by industry.

Industry	Percentage
Retail trade	27.1
Accommodation and food services (includes food retail, fast food, coffee shops, etc.)	18.1
Administration and support services (includes travel agencies, office services, domestic and industrial cleaning, gardening services, lawn mowing, etc.)	14.7
Other services (includes personal services, pet services, auto repairs and servicing, IT services, etc.)	10.5
Education and training	6.9
Rental, hire, and real-estate services	6.4
Arts and recreation services	3.4
Financial and insurance services	3.3
Professional, scientific, and technical services	2.9
Construction	2.1
Transport, postal, and warehousing	1.2
Information media and telecommunications	1.0
Healthcare and social assistance	1.0
Wholesale trade	0.6
Manufacturing	0.4
Electricity, gas, water, and waste services	0.4
Total	**100.0**

Source: Franchising Australia 2014, Asia-Pacific Centre for Franchising Excellence, Griffith University.

Master franchising arrangements had become common in Australian franchise systems. Under master franchising, a local entrepreneur was awarded the rights to sub-franchise the system within a specific geographic area, such as an entire state. Due to Australia's vast geographic size, it was difficult for a franchisor to monitor franchisees who were located far from the head office. The solution was to delegate many of the tasks normally handled by the franchisor to master franchisees instead. This made them responsible for recruiting, selecting, training, and monitoring franchisees in their territories as well as overseeing marketing and operations.

Not all franchisees proved successful, and individual outlets periodically failed. The main reasons for failure appeared to be poor choice of location or territory and a franchisee's own shortcomings. In addition to the technical skills required in a given field, success often hinged on the franchisees' sales and communication abilities. Disputes in franchising were not uncommon but could usually be resolved internally without recourse to legal action. The causes of conflict most frequently cited by franchisees related to franchise fees and alleged misrepresentations made by the franchisor. By contract, franchisors cited conflicts based on lack of compliance with the system by franchisees.

FRANCHISING STRATEGY AT AUSSIE POOCH MOBILE

New Aussie Pooch Mobile franchisees were recruited through newspaper advertisements and "advertorials" as well as by word of mouth. The concept appealed to individuals who sought to become self-employed on their own. Interested individuals were invited to meet with a representative of the company to learn more. If they wished to proceed further, they had to complete an application form and submit a refundable deposit of $250 to hold a particular area for a maximum of four weeks. During this period, the applicant could further investigate the characteristics and prospects of the designated territory. The fee was credited to the purchase cost of the franchise if the applicant decided to proceed or returned if the applicant withdrew the application. A new franchise in 2015 cost $35,820, excluding the federal goods and services tax (GST) (up from $34,700 in 2010, $24,000 in 2002, and $19,500 in 1999). Exhibit 7 identifies how Aussie Pooch Mobile costed out the different elements.

SELECTION REQUIREMENTS FOR PROSPECTIVE FRANCHISEES

Aussie Pooch Mobile had set a minimum educational requirement of passing Year 10 of high school (or its equivalent) for prospective franchisees. Taylor noted that successful applicants tended to be outdoors people who shared four characteristics:

They are motivated and outgoing. They love dogs, and they want to work for themselves. Obviously, being great with dogs is one part of the business—our franchisees understand that the dog's even an extended member of the customer's family—but it's really important that they can handle the bookwork side of the business as well, because that's basically where your bread and butter is made.

Other desirable characteristics included people skills, patience, and a good telephone manner. Would-be franchisees also required a valid driver's license, access to a vehicle that was capable of towing a trailer, and the ability to do this type of driving in an urban setting. Originally, Taylor had expected that most franchisees would be relatively young people with

Exhibit 7: Aussie Pooch Mobile: Breakdown of franchise purchase cost.

Item		Cost (2015)
Initial training		$2,500.00
Initial franchise fee and documents		803.88
Guaranteed income		4,800.00
Exclusive territory plus trailer registration		10,900.00
Fixtures, fittings, stock, insurance, etc.:	12,064.30	
Aussie Pooch Mobile trailer and hydrobath	2,000.00	
Consumables (shampoo, conditioner, etc.)	350.00	
Retail products	300.00	14,714.30
Insurance		2,000.00
Initial advertising		100.00
Communications levy		
Total franchise cost (excluding GST)		**$35,818.18**

parents who were willing to buy them a franchise and set them up with a job. However, in fact, only about half of all franchisees were aged 21–30. 40% were aged 31–40, and 10% were in their forties or fifties. About 60% were female.

Potential franchisees were offered a trial work period with an operator to see if they liked the job and were suited to the business. They were also required to have good skills with animals and people as well as sufficient physical fitness.

HOW THE FRANCHISE WORKED

In return for the franchise fee, successful applicants received the rights to a geographically defined franchise, typically comprising about 12,000 homes. Franchisees also obtained an Aussie Pooch Mobile trailer with all the necessary products and solutions to service the first 100 dogs, plus red uniform shirts and caps, advertising material, and stationery. The trailer was built to industrial-grade standards. Its design included many refinements developed by Aussie Pooch Mobile in consultation with franchisees to simplify the process of dog washing and enhance the experience for the animal. Operators were required to travel with a mobile phone, which they had to pay for themselves.

In addition to franchised territories, Aussie Pooch Mobile had approximately 30 company-owned outlets. These were operated by representatives who leased the territory and equipment and in return paid the company 25% of the gross weekly revenues (including GST). The reps were generally individuals who either could not afford the start-up cost at present or who were evaluated by the company for their suitability as franchisees. Typically, reps either became franchisees within about twelve months or left the company.

ASSISTING FRANCHISEES, OLD AND NEW

The franchisor provided two weeks' pre-opening training for all new franchisees. Representatives also spent time with each franchisee to help them open their new territories. Training topics included operational and business procedures, effective use of the telephone, hydrobathing techniques, dog grooming techniques, and information on dog health and behavior. Franchisees were given a detailed operations manual containing instructions on running the business in accordance with company standards.

To help new franchisees get started, Aussie Pooch Mobile placed advertisements in local newspapers for a period of 10 weeks. It also prepared human interest stories for distribution to these newspapers. Advertising on Facebook, Google AdWords, and other websites was carried out. Other promotional activities at the time of launch included distributing pamphlets in the territory and writing to local vets and pet shops to inform them of the business. Aussie Pooch Mobile guaranteed new franchisees a weekly income of $600 for the first eight weeks and paid for a package of insurance policies for six months, after which the franchisee became responsible for the coverage.

Ongoing support by the franchisor included marketing efforts, Facebook networking within their area, monthly newsletters, a telephone hotline service for advice, an insurance package, regular (but brief) field visits, and additional training. If a franchisee fell sick or wished to take a vacation, Aussie Pooch Mobile would offer advice on how to deal with this situation best. Wherever possible, it would provide a trained person to help out. It also organized periodic meetings for franchisees in the major metropolitan areas, at which guest presenters spoke on topics relating to franchise operations. Previous guest speakers included veterinarians, natural therapists, pharmacists, and accountants. Once a year, a conference with trade stalls and guest speakers from within as well as outside the group was organized. New products, systems, and services were introduced at this conference.

To further support individual franchisees, Aussie Pooch Mobile created a Facebook forum, allowing operators to share ideas among themselves. However, a team leader kept an eye on things to ensure that the forum remained positive. Each franchisee was assigned to a franchise area development manager (FADM). The FADM facilitated communications between franchisees and the support office. Face-to-face contact, group meetings, phone conversations, and e-mail exchanges allowed regular interaction and the discussion of different issues within the company. The FADMs undertook bi-annual training to help improve systems and communications within the franchise. They were provided with strategies and training to help support their groups and ensure that all their key performance indicators (KPIs) were met.

FEES

In return for these services and support from the franchisors, franchisees paid a royalty fee of 10% of their gross weekly income, plus $34 (including GST) flat fee per week. Prior to 2014, franchisees had to pay an advertising levy of 2.5% instead of the flat fee component. Income was reported on a weekly basis, and fees had to be paid weekly. In addition to these fees, operating costs for a franchisee included car-related expenses and purchase of consumable products such as shampoo, insurance, telephone, and stationery. Exhibit 8 shows the average weekly costs that a typical franchisee might expect to incur.

Franchisees often included several couples (like the Beals). However, Taylor believed that although having two operators work together could be companionable, it was not really efficient. Paul Beal, a retired advertising executive, had other interests and did not always accompany Elaine. Some couples split the work, with one operating three days a week and the

Exhibit 8: Average annual operating expenses for an Aussie Pooch Mobile franchisee based on $55,000 turnover.

Expense Categories	Cost
Consumable products	$2,880
Car registration	430
Car insurance	500
Fuel	3,360
Insurances	1,151
Repairs and maintenance	1,104
Phones, stationery, etc.	1,920
Communications levy	624
Franchise royalties	5,500
Flat fee	1607
Total	**$19,076**

other three or even four days. All franchisees were required to be substantially involved in the hands-on running of the business. Some had more than one territory and employed additional operators to help them.

ADVERTISING AND MARKETING

Aussie Pooch Mobile had a national website and Facebook page and paid for Google AdWords to promote the national website. It promoted a single telephone number staffed by an answering service 24 hours a day, seven days a week throughout Australia. Customers only had to pay a local call charge of 25 cents to access this number. They could leave their name and telephone number, which would then be electronically sorted and forwarded via alphanumeric pagers to the appropriate franchisee. The franchisee would then return the call to arrange a convenient appointment time. Customers could also send a message directly to an operator from the website.

Aussie Pooch Mobile offered its franchisees expert advice on local advertising and promotions. It also made promotional products and advertising templates available to franchisees and encouraged them to set up their own Facebook pages. Other corporate communications activities included maintaining the website (www.aussiepm.com.au); distributing public relations releases to the media; and controlling all aspects of corporate identity, such as trailer design, business cards, and uniforms.

"I try to hold the reins pretty tightly on advertising matters," said Taylor. Aussie Pooch Mobile's franchise agreement required individual franchisees to submit their plans regarding promotional activity for corporate approval. Taylor shook her head as she remembered an early disaster involving an unauthorized campaign by a franchisee who had placed an offer of a free dog wash in a widely distributed coupon book. Unfortunately, this promotion had set no expiration date or geographic restriction, with the result that customers were still presenting the coupon more than a year later across several different franchise territories.

With Aussie Pooch Mobile's approval, some franchisees had developed additional promotional ideas. For example, Elaine and Paul Beal wrote informative articles and human interest stories about dogs for their local newspaper. When a client's dog died, Elaine sent a sympathy card and presented the owner with a small tree to plant in memory of the pet. Franchisees also provided a Pet Report Card accompanied by a retail promotional flyer to their clients.

DEVELOPING A TERRITORY

Obtaining new customers and retaining existing ones was an important aspect of each franchisee's work. The brightly colored trailer often attracted questions from passers-by and presented a useful opportunity to promote the service. Operators could ask satisfied customers to recommend the service to their friends and neighbors. Encouraging owners to increase the frequency of washing their dogs was another way to build business. Knowing that a dog might become lonely in the absence of its owner and could even develop behavioral problems, Elaine Beal sometimes recommended the acquisition of a "companion pet." As Paul remarked, "Having two dogs is not twice the trouble, it halves the problem!"

However, to maximize profitability, franchisees also had to operate as efficiently as possible, minimizing time spent in non-revenue producing activities such as travel, set up, and socializing. As business grew, some franchisees employed additional operators to handle the excess workload. This allowed the trailer to be in service for extended hours seven days a week. Eventually, a busy territory could be split, with a portion sold off to a new franchisee.

Aussie Pooch Mobile encouraged this practice. The company had found that franchisees reached a comfort zone at about 50 to 80 dogs a week, after which their business stopped growing as they could not physically wash any more dogs. Franchisees could set their own price when selling all or part of a territory, and Aussie Pooch Mobile helped them to coordinate the sale. When a territory was split, a franchisee was usually motivated to rebuild the remaining half to its maximum potential.

COMPETITION

Although many dog owners had traditionally washed their animals themselves (or had not even bothered), there was a growing trend toward paying a third party to handle this task. Dog washing services fell into two broad groups. One consisted of fixed-site operations to which dog owners brought their animals for bathing. The locations for these businesses included retail sites in suburban shopping areas, kennels, and service providers' own homes or garages. The second type of competition, which had grown in popularity in recent years, consisted of mobile operations that travelled to customers' homes.

With few barriers to entry, there were numerous dog washing services in most major metropolitan areas. The majority of dog washing services in Australia were believed to be standalone operations, but there were other franchisors in addition to Aussie Pooch Mobile. Of these, the most significant appeared to be Jim's Dogwash and HydroDog.

JIM'S DOGWASH

One of Australia's best-known locally developed franchisors was the Melbourne-based Jim's Group, which described itself as a company providing quality mobile grooming and care for dogs throughout Australia and New Zealand. The company had originated with a mowing service started by Jim Penman in Melbourne in 1982 when he abandoned ideas of an academic career after his PhD thesis was rejected. In 1989, Penman began franchising the service, known as Jim's Mowing, as a way to facilitate expansion. The business grew rapidly, using master franchisees in different regions to recruit and manage individual franchisees. Over the following years, an array of other home-related services were launched under the Jim's brand, including Jim's Fencing, Jim's Pool Care, Jim's Cleaning, Jim's Bookkeeping, and Jim's Car Detailing.

Jim's Dogwash made its debut in 1996, employing a bright red, fully enclosed trailer emblazoned with a logo that showed Jim with a dog. It had 57 franchises in Australia and two franchisees in New Zealand. Jim's expansion strategy had been achieved in part by creating smaller territories than Aussie Pooch Mobile and pricing them relatively inexpensively in order to stimulate the recruitment of new franchisees.

A territory, typically encompassing about 6,000 residences, sold from $13,000 up to $19,000 (including GST). A trailer could be purchased for $18,500 or rented at $400 per month (both including GST). Ongoing franchise fees included a flat monthly royalty (rather than royalties being calculated on a percentage of sales) of $438; an advertising levy, also set as a flat monthly fee of $165; and a $7 per lead fee (all the figures include GST). Jim's fee for washing and blow drying averaged $65 per dog. In recent years, Jim's Dogwash started offering aromatherapy and also sold pet food and accessories.

BLUE WHEELERS

Another franchised dog washing operation was Blue Wheelers (formerly Hydrodog), based on the Gold Coast in Queensland. Hydrodog commenced operations in 1994 and sold its first franchise in 1996. In 2012, the franchise renamed itself Blue Wheelers and diversified its brand by introducing a new franchise called Dash Dog Wash. While the latter only provided a straight dog wash service, Blue Wheelers continued to offer the full range of dog washing and grooming services. By 2015, Blue Wheelers had 178 franchise units across Australia, with one master franchisee operating in Western Australia. Dash Dog Wash was still in the "puppy" stage of development with only three units operating. The distribution of franchise units across both franchises was broken down as follows:

State/Territory	Blue Wheelers	Dash Dog Wash
ACT	4	0
New South Wales	51	1
Northern Territory	4	1
Queensland	40	0
South Australia	18	0
Tasmania	3	0
Victoria	36	1
Western Australia	22	0
Total	178	3

A new Hydrodog franchise unit cost $24,950 (including GST) in 2002, of which $10,800 was accounted for by the initial franchise fee for a 10,000-home territory. By 2011, the franchise fee had increased to $41,950 plus GST; this included the trailer, equipment, launch promotions, and everything a franchisee needed to start their business. The territory size had also changed, with a minimum of 5,000 homes, although most territories included more than that number and were based on a designated suburb. By 2015, the Blue Wheelers franchise fee was $46,990 based on a minimum of 5,000 homes. The Dash Dog Wash franchise fee was $29,990 based on 10,000 homes. On average, the company washed about 45,000 dogs per month, with average earnings per franchisee between $1,100 and $2,500 per week.

Blue Wheeler's dog grooming services, which included blow drying, ranged in price from $35 to $90. In addition to their dog grooming services, franchisees sold dog food products (including dry biscuits and processed meats such as pork, chicken, beef, or kangaroo) as well as dog toys and other accessories. They did not offer aromatherapy, facials, or massages. Both franchises charged franchisees a flat management fee instead of a royalty: $140 (+GST) per week for Dash Dog Wash and $175 (+GST) per week for Blue Wheelers.

DEVELOPING A STRATEGY OF GROWTH FOR THE FUTURE

For the directors of Aussie Pooch Mobile, managing continued expansion presented an ongoing challenge. However, as Christine Taylor pointed out, "You can be the largest but you may not be the best. Our focus is on doing a great job and making our franchisees successful."

To facilitate expansion outside its original base of southeast Queensland, Aussie Pooch Mobile appointed a franchise sales manager in Sydney for the New South Wales market and another in Melbourne for both Victoria and South Australia. One question was whether to adopt a formal strategy of appointing master franchisees. Currently, there are master franchises in Queensland (Gold Coast), New South Wales (Wollongong and Campbelltown), and Western Australia.

In addition, Taylor had long been attracted by the idea of expanding internationally. In 1996, the company had licensed a franchisee in New Zealand to operate a subsidiary named Kiwi Pooch Mobile. However, there was only one unit operating by early 2002, and Taylor wondered how best to increase this number. Another subsidiary had been established as a master franchise in the French province of New Caledonia, a large island northeast of Australia. Launched in late 2000 under the name of La Pooch Mobile, it had one unit. A third master franchise territory had been established in Malaysia in late 2001, and there were two units operating by 2002.

In 2001, Aussie Pooch Mobile had granted exclusive rights for operation in the United Kingdom to a British entrepreneur who operated under the name The Pooch Mobile. Thus far, twelve units were operating in the English county of Lincolnshire, 200 km (125 miles) north of London. This individual noted that English people traditionally washed their dogs very infrequently, often as little as once every two to three years. However, once they had tried The Pooch Mobile, they quickly became monthly clients, primarily for the hygiene benefits.

In 2004, the regional master franchisee from the Gold Coast in Queensland moved to Denver, Colorado, to open The Pooch Mobile in the United States. The Pooch Mobile has since expanded to Las Vegas and Hawaii. The United States market is strong, and dog owners have readily embraced the dog washing concept.

As the company grew, the directors knew it was likely to face increased competition from other providers of dog washing services. However, as one successful franchisee remarked, "Competition keeps us on our toes. It's hard being in the lead and maintaining the lead if you haven't got anybody on your tail."

STUDY QUESTIONS

1. How did Christine Taylor succeed in evolving the local dog washing service she developed as a teenager into an international franchise business?

2. Compare and contrast the tasks involved in recruiting new customers and new franchisees.

3. From a franchisee's perspective, what is the advantage of belonging to the Aussie Pooch Mobile franchise rather than working alone?

4. In planning for future expansion, how should Christine Taylor evaluate the market potential of Australia versus that of overseas countries? What strategies do you recommend, and why?

Shouldice Hospital Limited (Abridged)

James Heskett and Roger Hallowell

Two shadowy figures, enrobed and in slippers, walked slowly down the semi-darkened hall of Shouldice Hospital. They did not notice Alan O'Dell, the hospital's Managing Director, and his guest. Once they were out of earshot, O'Dell remarked good naturedly, "By the way they act, you'd think our patients own this place. And while they're here, in a way they do." Following a visit to the five operating rooms, O'Dell and his visitor once again encountered the same pair of patients still engrossed in discussing their hernia operations, which had been performed the previous morning.

HISTORY

An attractive brochure that had been printed recently, although neither dated nor distributed to prospective patients, described Dr. Earle Shouldice, the founder of the hospital:

> Dr. Shouldice's interest in early ambulation stemmed, in part, from an operation he performed in 1932 to remove the appendix from a seven-year-old girl and the girl's subsequent refusal to stay quietly in bed. In spite of her activity, no harm was done, and the experience recalled to the doctor the postoperative actions of animals upon which he had performed surgery. They had all moved about freely with no ill effects.

Professor James Heskett prepared the original version of this case, "Shouldice Hospital Limited," HBS No. 683-068. This version was prepared jointly by Professor James Heskett and Roger Hallowell (MBA 1989, DBA 1997). HBS cases are developed solely as the basis for class discussion. Cases are not intended to serve as endorsements, sources of primary data, or illustrations of effective or ineffective management.

1 Most hernias, known as external abdominal hernias, are protrusions of some part of the abdominal contents through a hole or slit in the muscular layers of the abdominal wall, which is supposed to contain them. Well over 90% of these hernias occur in the groin area. Of these, by far the most common are inguinal hernias, many of which are caused by a slight weakness in the muscle layers brought about by the passage of the testicles in male babies through the groin area shortly before birth. Aging also contributes to the development of inguinal hernias. Due to the cause of the affliction, 85% of all hernias occur in males.

By 1940, Shouldice had given extensive thought to several factors that contributed to early ambulation following surgery. Among them were the use of a local anesthetic, the nature of the surgical procedure itself, the design of a facility to encourage movement without unnecessarily causing discomfort, and the post-operative regimen. With these things in mind, he began to develop a surgical technique for repairing hernias[1] that was superior to others; word of his early success generated demand.

Dr. Shouldice's medical license permitted him to operate anywhere, even on a kitchen table. However, as more and more patients requested operations, Dr. Shouldice created new facilities by buying a rambling 130-acre estate with a 17,000-square-foot main house in the Toronto suburb of Thornhill. After some years of planning, a large wing was added to provide a total capacity of 89 beds.

Dr. Shouldice died in 1965. At that time, Shouldice Hospital Limited was formed to operate both the hospital and clinical facilities under the surgical direction of Dr. Nicholas Obney. In 1999, Dr. Casim Degani, an internationally recognized authority, became surgeon-in-chief. By 2004, 7,600 operations were being performed per year.

THE SHOULDICE METHOD

Only external (vs internal) abdominal hernias were repaired at Shouldice Hospital. Thus, most first-time repairs, also called "primaries," were straightforward operations requiring about 45 minutes. The remaining procedures involved patients who were suffering recurrences of hernias previously repaired elsewhere.[2] Many of the recurrences and very difficult hernia repairs required 90 minutes or more.

In the Shouldice method, the muscles of the abdominal wall were arranged in three distinct layers, and the opening was repaired, each layer in turn, by overlapping its margins as the edges of a coat might be overlapped when buttoned. The end result reinforced the muscular wall of the abdomen with six rows of sutures (stitches) under the skin cover, which was then closed with clamps that would be removed later. (Other methods often did not separate muscle layers and involved fewer rows of sutures. Sometimes, screens and meshes were also inserted under the skin.)

A typical first-time repair could be completed with the use of pre-operative sedation (sleeping pills) and analgesics (pain killers) plus a local anesthetic (an injection of Novocain in the region of the incision). This allowed immediate post-operative patient ambulation and facilitated rapid recovery.

The Patients' Experience

Most potential Shouldice patients learned about the hospital from previous Shouldice patients. Although thousands of doctors often referred patients, they were less likely to recommend Shouldice because of the generally regarded simplicity of the surgery, often considered a "bread-and-butter" operation. Typically, many patients had their problem diagnosed by a personal physician and then contacted Shouldice directly. Many more made this diagnosis themselves.

The process experienced by Shouldice patients depended on whether or not they lived close enough to the hospital to visit the facility and obtain a diagnosis. Approximately 10% of Shouldice patients came from outside the province of Ontario, and most of them were from the United States. Another 60% of patients lived beyond the Toronto area. These out-of-town patients were often diagnosed by mail using the Medical Information Questionnaire shown in Exhibit 1. Based on information in the questionnaire, a Shouldice surgeon would determine the type of hernia the respondent had and indicating signs indicating that some risk might be associated with surgery. (For example, surgery could be risky if the patient was overweight, had a heart condition, or had suffered a heart attack or a stroke in the

past year. The surgeon would also have to decide whether a general or a local anesthetic was required.) At this point, a patient was given an operating date and sent a brochure describing the hospital and the Shouldice method. If necessary, a sheet outlining a weight-loss program prior to surgery was also sent. A small proportion was refused treatment. This could happen if the patient was overweight, represented an undue medical risk, or did not have a hernia at all.

Arriving at the clinic between 1:00 p.m. and 3:00 p.m. the day before the operation, a patient joined other patients in the waiting room. Each patient was soon examined in one of the six examination rooms staffed by surgeons who had completed their operating schedules for the day. This examination required no more than 20 minutes, unless the patient needed reassurance. (Patients typically exhibited a moderate level of anxiety until their operation was completed.) At this point, it was occasionally discovered that some patients had not corrected their weight problems. Others might be found not to have a hernia at all. In either case, the patient was sent home.

After administrative details had been checked, patients were directed to the room numbers shown on their wrist bands about an hour after arriving at the hospital. Throughout the process, they were asked to keep their luggage (usually light) with them.

All patient rooms at the hospital were semi-private, containing two beds. Patients with similar jobs, backgrounds, or interests were assigned to the same room as far as possible. Upon reaching their rooms, patients busied themselves unpacking, getting acquainted with room mates, shaving themselves in the area of the operation, and changing into pajamas.

At 4:30 p.m., a nurse's orientation provided the group of incoming patients with information about what to expect, including the need for exercise after the operation and the daily routine. According to Alan O'Dell, "Half are so nervous they don't remember much." Dinner was then served, followed by further recreation as well as tea and cookies at 9:00 p.m. Nurses emphasized the importance of attendance at that time, because it provided an opportunity for pre-operative patients to talk to other patients whose operations had been completed earlier that same day.

Patients to be operated on early were awakened at 5:30 a.m. to be given pre-op sedation. An attempt was made to schedule operations for room mates at approximately the

---

2 Based on tracking of patients over more than 30 years, the gross recurrence rate for all operations performed at Shouldice was 0.8%. Recurrence rates reported in the literature for these types of hernia varied greatly. However, one text stated, "In the United States, the gross rate of recurrence for groin hernias approaches 10%."

same time. Patients were taken to the pre-operation room, where the circulating nurse administered the analgesic Demerol 45 minutes before surgery. A few minutes prior to the first operation at 7:30 a.m., the surgeon assigned to each patient administered Novocain, a local anesthetic, in the operating room. This was in contrast to the typical hospital procedure, in which patients were sedated in their rooms and then taken to the operating rooms.

Upon completion of their operation, during which a few patients were "chatty" and fully aware of what was going on, patients were invited to get off the operating table and walk to the post-operation room with the help of their surgeons. According to the Director of Nursing:

> 99% accept the surgeon's invitation. While we use wheelchairs to return them to their rooms, the walk from the operating table is for psychological as well as physiological [blood pressure, respiratory] reasons. Patients prove to themselves that they can do it, and they start their all-important exercise immediately.

Throughout the day after their operation, patients were encouraged by nurses and housekeepers alike to exercise. By 9:00 p.m. on the day of their operations, all patients were ready and able to walk down to the dining room for tea and cookies, even if it meant climbing stairs, to help indoctrinate the new "class" admitted that day. On the fourth morning, patients were ready for discharge.

During their stay, patients were encouraged to take advantage of the opportunity to explore the premises and make new friends. Some members of the staff felt that the patients and their attitudes were the most important element of the Shouldice program. According to Dr. Byrnes Shouldice, son of the founder, a surgeon on the staff, and a 50% owner of the hospital:

> Patients sometimes ask to stay an extra day. Why? Well, think about it. They are basically well to begin with. But they arrive with a problem and a certain amount of nervousness, tension, and anxiety about their surgery. Their first morning here, they're operated on and experience a sense of relief from something that's been bothering them for a long time. They are immediately able to get around, and they've got a three-day holiday ahead of them with a perfectly good reason to be away from work with no sense of guilt. They share experiences with other patients, make friends easily, and have the run of the hospital. In summer, the most common

after-effect of the surgery is sunburn.

The Nurses' Experience

Thirty-four full-time-equivalent nurses staffed Shouldice each 24-hour period. However, during non-operating hours, only six full-time-equivalent nurses were on the premises at any given time. While the Canadian acute-care hospital average ratio of nurses to patients was 1:4, at Shouldice, the ratio was 1:15. Shouldice nurses spent an unusually large proportion of their time on counseling activities. As one supervisor commented, "We don't use bedpans." According to a manager, "Shouldice has a waiting list of nurses wanting to be hired, while other hospitals in Toronto are short-staffed and perpetually recruiting."

The Doctors' Experience

The hospital employed 10 full-time surgeons and eight part-time assistant surgeons. Two anesthetists were also on site. The anesthetists floated among cases, except when general anesthesia was in use. Each operating team required a surgeon, an assistant surgeon, a scrub nurse, and a circulating nurse. The operating load varied from 30 to 36 operations per day. As a result, each surgeon typically performed three or four operations each day.

A typical surgeon's day started with a scrubbing shortly before the first scheduled operation at 7:30 a.m. If the first operation was routine, it was usually completed by 8:15 a.m. At its conclusion, the surgical team helped the patient walk from the room and summoned the next patient. After scrubbing, the surgeon could be ready to operate again at 8:30 a.m. Surgeons were advised to take a coffee break after their second or third operation. Even so, a surgeon could complete three routine operations and a fourth involving a recurrence and still be finished in time for a 12:30 p.m. lunch in the staff dining room.

Upon finishing lunch, surgeons not scheduled to operate in the afternoon examined incoming patients. A surgeon's day ended by 4:00 p.m. In addition, a surgeon could expect to be on call one week-day night in 10 and one week end in 10. Alan O'Dell commented that the position appealed to doctors who "want to watch their children grow up. A doctor on call is rarely called to the hospital and has regular hours." According to Dr. Obney:

> When I interview prospective surgeons, I look for experience and a good education. I try to gain some

Exhibit 1: Medical information questionnaire.

SHOULDICE HOSPITAL

7750 Bayview Avenue
Box 379, Thornhill, Ontario L3T 4A3 Canada
Phone (418) 889-1125

(Thornhill - One Mile North Metro Toronto)

MEDICAL

INFORMATION

Patients who live at a distance often prefer their examination, admission and operation to be arranged all on a single visit — to save making two lengthy journeys. The whole purpose of this questionnaire is to make such arrangements possible, although, of course, it cannot replace the examination in any way. Its completion and return will not put you under any obligation.

Please be sure to fill in both sides.

This information will be treated as confidential.

(continued on next page)

FAMILY NAME (Last Name) | FIRST NAME | MIDDLE NAME

STREET & NUMBER (or Rural Route or P.O. Box) | Town/City | Province/State

County | Township | Zip or Postal Code | Birthdate: Month | Day | Year

Telephone
Home _____ If none, give
Work _____ neighbour's number _____

Married or Single | Religion

NEXT OF KIN: Name | Address | Telephone #

Date form completed

INSURANCE INFORMATION: Please give name of Insurance Company and Numbers.

HOSPITAL INSURANCE: (Please bring hospital certificates) | OTHER HOSPITAL INSURANCE

O.H.I.P. BLUE CROSS
Number _____ Number _____

Company Name _____
Policy Number _____

SURGICAL INSURANCE: (Please bring insurance certificates) | OTHER SURGICAL INSURANCE

O.H.I.P. BLUE SHIELD
Number _____ Number _____

Company Name _____
Policy Number _____

WORKMEN'S COMPENSATION BOARD | Approved | Social Insurance (Security) Number

Claim No. | Yes | No

Occupation | Name of Business | Are you the owner? If Retired – Former Occupation
Yes | No

How did you hear about Shouldice Hospital? (If referred by a doctor, give name & address)

Are you a former patient of Shouldice Hospital? | Yes | No | Do you smoke? | Yes | No

Have you ever written to Shouldice Hospital in the past? | Yes | No

What is your preferred admission date? (Please give as much advance notice as possible)

No admissions Friday, Saturday or Sunday.

FOR OFFICE USE ONLY

Date Received | Type of Hernia | Weight Loss
lbs.

Consent to Operate ☐ | Special Instructions | Approved
Heart Report ☐

Referring Doctor Notified | Operation Date

Exhibit 1: (Continued)

THIS CHART IS FOR EXPLANATION ONLY

Ordinary hernias are mostly either
at the navel ("belly-button") - or just above it

or down in the groin area on either side

An "Incisional hernia" is one that bulges through
the scar of any other surgical operation that has
failed to hold – wherever it may be.

THIS IS YOUR CHART – PLEASE MARK IT!

(MARK THE POSITION OF EACH HERNIA
YOU WANT REPAIRED WITH AN "X")

APPROXIMATE SIZE...
Walnut (or less)
Hen's Egg or Lemon
Grapefruit (or more)

ESSENTIAL EXTRA INFORMATION
Use only the sections that apply to your hernias and put a ✓ in each
box that seems appropriate.

NAVEL AREA (AND JUST ABOVE NAVEL) ONLY
Is this navel (bellybutton) hernia your FIRST one?   Yes ☐   No ☐

If it's NOT your first, how many repair attempts so far?   ☐

GROIN HERNIAS ONLY

	RIGHT GROIN		LEFT GROIN	
	Yes	No	Yes	No
Is this your FIRST GROIN HERNIA ON THIS SIDE?	☐	☐	☐	☐

How many hernia operations in this groin already?   Right ☐   Left ☐

DATE OF LAST OPERATION ☐

INCISIONAL HERNIAS ONLY (the ones bulging through previous operation scars)
Was the original operation for your Appendix? ☐ , or Gallbladder? ☐ ,
or Stomach? ☐ , or Prostate? ☐ , or Hysterectomy? ☐ , or Other?..........

How many attempts to repair the hernias have been made so far?   ☐

PLEASE BE ACCURATE!: Misleading figures, when checked on a
admission day, could mean postponement of your operation till your weight
is suitable.

HEIGHT..........ft...........ins.   WEIGHT...........lbs.Nude   Recent gain?...........lbs.
or just pyjamas   Recent loss?...........lbs

Waist (muscles relaxed)................ins.   Chest (not expanded)...............ins.

GENERAL HEALTH

Age..........years   is your health now GOOD ☐ ,   FAIR ☐ ,   or POOR ☐

Please mention briefly any severe past illness – such as a
"heart attack" or a "stroke", for example, from which you
have now recovered (and its approximate date)...............

We need to know about other present conditions, even though your admission is
NOT likely to be refused because of them.

Please tick ☑ any condition
for which you are having regular
treatment:

Blood Pressure ☐
Excess body fluids ☐
Chest pain ("angina") ☐
Irregular Heartbeat ☐
Diabetes ☐
Asthma & Bronchitis ☐
Ulcers ☐
Anticoagulants ☐
(to delay blood-clotting
or to "thin the blood")
Other............... ☐

Name of any prescribed
pills, tablets or capsules you
take regularly -

Did you remember to MARK AN "X" on your body chart to show us where
each of your hernias is located?

insight into their domestic situation and personal interests and habits. I also try to find out why a surgeon wants to switch positions. And I try to determine if he's willing to perform the repair exactly as he's told. This is no place for prima donnas.

Dr. Shouldice added:

Traditionally, a hernia is often the first operation that a junior resident in surgery performs. Hernia repair is regarded as a relatively simple operation compared to other major operations. This is quite wrong, as is borne out by the resulting high recurrence rate. It is a tricky anatomical area and occasionally very complicated, especially to the novice or those doing very few hernia repairs each year. But, at Shouldice Hospital, a surgeon learns the Shouldice technique over a period of several months. He learns when he can go fast and when he must slow down. He develops a pace and a touch. If he encounters something unusual, he is encouraged to consult immediately with other surgeons. We teach each other and try to encourage a group effort. And he learns not to take risks to achieve absolute perfection. Excellence is the enemy of good.

Chief Surgeon Degani assigned surgeons to an operating room on a daily basis by noon of the preceding day. This allowed surgeons to examine the specific patients on whom they were to operate. Surgeons and assistants were rotated every few days. Cases were assigned to give doctors a non-routine operation (often involving a recurrence) several times a week. More complex procedures were assigned to more senior and experienced members of the staff. Dr. Obney commented:

If something goes wrong, we want to make sure that we have an experienced surgeon in charge. Experience is most important. The typical general surgeon may perform 25 to 50 hernia operations per year. Ours perform 750 or more.

The 10 full-time surgeons were paid a straight salary, typically $144,000.[3] In addition, bonuses to doctors were distributed monthly. These depended on profit, individual productivity, and performance. The total bonus pool

paid to the surgeons in a recent year was approximately $400,000. Total surgeon compensation (including benefits) was approximately 15% more than the average income for a surgeon in Ontario.

Training in the Shouldice technique was important, because the procedure could not be varied. It was accomplished through direct supervision by one or more of the senior surgeons. The rotation of teams and frequent consultations allowed for an ongoing opportunity to appraise performance and take corrective action. Wherever possible, former Shouldice patients suffering recurrences were assigned to the doctor who had performed the first operation "to allow the doctor to learn from his mistake." Dr. Obney commented on being a Shouldice surgeon:

A doctor must decide after several years whether he wants to do this for the rest of his life because, just as in other specialties—for example, radiology—he loses touch with other medical disciplines. If he stays for five years, he doesn't leave. Even among younger doctors, few elect to leave.

THE FACILITY

The Shouldice Hospital contained two facilities in one building—the hospital and the clinic. On its first level, the hospital contained the kitchen and dining rooms. The second level contained a large, open lounge area, the admission offices, patient rooms, and a spacious glass-covered Florida room. The third level had additional patient rooms and recreational areas. Patients could be seen visiting each others' rooms, walking up and down hallways, lounging in the sunroom, and making use of light recreational facilities ranging from a pool table to an exercycle. Alan O'Dell pointed out some of the features of the hospital:

The rooms contain no telephone or television sets. If a patient needs to make a call or wants to watch television, he or she has to take a walk. The steps are designed specially with a small rise to allow patients recently operated on to negotiate the stairs without undue discomfort. Every square foot of the hospital is carpeted to reduce the hospital feeling and the possibility of a fall. Carpeting also gives the place a smell other than that of disinfectant.

This facility was designed by an architect with input from Dr. Byrnes Shouldice and Mrs. W. H. Urquhart

---

3 All monetary references in the case are to the Canadian dollar. US$1 equaled C$1.33 on February 23, 2004.

(the daughter of the founder). The facility was discussed for years, and many changes in the plans were made before the first concrete was poured. A number of unique policies were also instituted. For example, parents accompanying children here for an operation stay free. You may wonder why we can do it, but we learned that we save more in nursing costs than we spend for the parent's room and board.

Patients and staff were served food prepared in the same kitchen, and staff members picked up food from a cafeteria line placed in the very center of the kitchen. This provided an opportunity for everyone to chat with the kitchen staff several times a day and allowed the hospital staff to eat together. According to O'Dell, "We use all fresh ingredients and prepare the food from scratch in the kitchen."

The Director of Housekeeping pointed out:

I have only three on my housekeeping staff for the entire facility. One of the reasons for so few housekeepers is that we don't need to change linens during a patient's four-day stay. Also, the medical staff doesn't want the patients in bed all day. They want the nurses to encourage the patients to be up socializing, comparing notes [for confidence], encouraging each other, and walking around, getting exercise. Of course, we're in the rooms straightening up throughout the day. This gives the housekeepers a chance to josh with the patients and to encourage them to exercise.

The clinic housed five operating rooms, a laboratory, and the patient-recovery room. In total, the estimated cost to furnish an operating room was $30,000. This was considerably less than that for other hospitals, which require a bank of equipment with which to administer anesthetics for each room. At Shouldice, two mobile units were used by the anesthetists when needed. In addition, the complex had one "crash cart" per floor for use if a patient should suffer a heart attack or a stroke.

---

4 The chart in Exhibit 2 was prepared by the case writer on the basis of conversations with hospital personnel.

5 This figure included a provincially mandated return on investment.

6 The latter figure included the bonus pool for doctors.

ADMINISTRATION

Alan O'Dell described his job:

We try to meet people's needs and make this as good a place to work as possible. There is a strong concern for employees here. Nobody is fired. [This was later reinforced by Dr. Shouldice, who described a situation involving two employees who confessed to theft in the hospital. They agreed to seek psychiatric help and were allowed to remain on the job.] As a result, turnover is low.

Our administrative and support staff are non-union, but we try to maintain a pay scale higher than the union scale for comparable jobs in the area. We have a profit-sharing plan that is separate from the doctors'. Last year, the administrative and support staff divided up $60,000.

If work needs to be done, people pitch in to help each other. A unique aspect of our administration is that I insist that each secretary is trained to do another's work and in an emergency is able to switch to another function immediately. We don't have an organization chart. A chart tends to make people think they're boxed in jobs.[4] I try to stay one night a week, having dinner and listening to the patients, to find out how things are really going around here.

Operating Costs

The 2004 budgets for the hospital and clinic were close to $8.5 million[5] and $3.5 million respectively.[6]

THE MARKET

Hernia operations were among the most commonly performed operations on males. In 2000, an estimated 1,000,000 such operations were performed in the United States alone. According to Dr. Shouldice:

When our backlog of scheduled operations gets too large, we wonder how many people decide instead to have their local doctor perform the operation. Every time we've expanded our capacity, the backlog has declined briefly, only to climb once again. Right now, at 2,400, it is larger than it has ever been and is growing by 100 every six months.

Exhibit 2: The organization chart

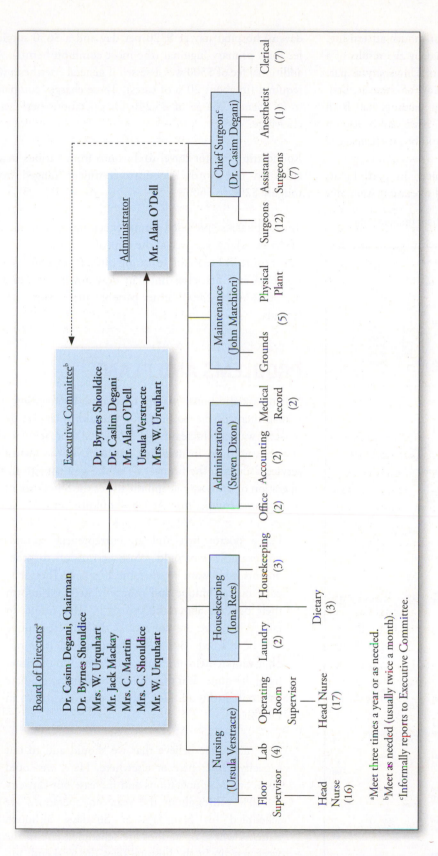

Board of Directors[a]

Dr. Casim Degani, Chairman
Dr. Byrnes Shouldice
Mrs. W. Urquhart
Mr. Jack Mackay
Mrs. C. Martin
Mrs. C. Shouldice
Mr. W. Urquhart

Executive Committee[b]

Dr. Byrnes Shouldice
Dr. Caslim Degani
Mr. Alan O'Dell
Ursula Verstracte
Mrs. W. Urquhart

Administrator
Mr. Alan O'Dell

Chief Surgeon[c]
(Dr. Casim Degani)

Nursing
(Ursula Verstracte)

- Floor Supervisor
  - Head Nurse (16)
- Lab (4)
- Operating Room Supervisor
  - Head Nurse (17)

Housekeeping
(Iona Rees)

- Laundry (2)
- Housekeeping (3)
  - Dietary (3)

Administration
(Steven Dixon)

- Office (2)
- Accounting (2)
- Medical Record (2)

Maintenance
(John Marchiori)

- Grounds
- Physical Plant (5)

- Surgeons (12)
- Assistant Surgeons (7)
- Anesthetist (1)
- Clerical (7)

[a]Meet three times a year or as needed.
[b]Meet as needed (usually twice a month).
[c]Informally reports to Executive Committee.

The hospital relied entirely on word-of-mouth advertising, the importance of which was suggested by the results of a poll carried out by students of DePaul University as part of a project (Exhibit 3 shows a portion of these results). Although little systematic data about patients had been collected, Alan O'Dell remarked that "if we had to rely on wealthy patients only, our practice would be much smaller."

Patients were attracted to the hospital, in part, by its reasonable rates. Charges for a typical operation were four days of hospital stay at $320 per day and a $650 surgical fee for a primary inguinal (the most common hernia). An additional fee of $300 was assessed if general anesthesia was required (in about 20% of cases). These charges compared to an average charge of $5,240 for operations performed elsewhere.

Round-trip fares for travel to Toronto from various major cities on the North American continent ranged from roughly $200 to $600.

The hospital also provided annual check-ups to alumni, free of charge. Many occurred at the time of the patient reunion. The most recent reunion, featuring dinner and a floor show, was held at a first-class hotel in downtown Toronto and was attended by 1,000 former patients, many from outside Canada.

PROBLEMS AND PLANS

When asked about major questions confronting the management of the hospital, Dr. Shouldice cited a desire to seek ways of increasing the hospital's capacity while, at the same time, maintaining control over the quality of service delivered, the future role of the government in the operation of the hospital, and the use of the Shouldice name by potential competitors. As Dr. Shouldice put it:

> I'm a doctor first and an entrepreneur second. For example, we could refuse permission to other doctors who want to visit the hospital. They may copy our technique and misapply it or misinform their patients about the use of it. This results in failure, and we are concerned that the technique will be blamed. But we're doctors, and it is our obligation to help other surgeons learn. On the other hand, it's quite clear that others are trying to emulate us. Look at this ad. [The advertisement is shown in Exhibit 4.]

> This makes me believe that we should add to our capacity, either here or elsewhere. Here, we could go to Saturday operations and increase our capacity by 20%. Throughout the year, no operations are scheduled for Saturdays or Sundays, although patients whose operations are scheduled late in the week remain in the hospital over the weekend. Or, with an investment of perhaps $4 million in new space, we could expand our number of beds by 50%

Exhibit 3: Shouldice Hospital's annual patient reunion data.

Exhibit 4: Advertisement by a Shouldice competitor.

The Canadian Hernia Clinic

Hernias (Ruptures) Required Under local anesthesia as by Canadian method.

No Overnight Hospital Stay.

Consultations Without Charge

23061 St. Rd. 7
BOCA RATON, FLA. 33433
482-7755

Exhibit 5: The Shouldice Hospital grounds are a haven for rest and recuperation.

and schedule the operating rooms more heavily.

However, given government regulations, do we want to invest more in Toronto? Or should we establish another hospital with similar design, perhaps in the United States? There is also the possibility that we could diversify into other specialties offering similar opportunities such as eye surgery, varicose veins, or diagnostic services (e.g., colonoscopies).

For now, we're also beginning the process of grooming someone to succeed Dr. Degani when he retires. He's in his early 60s, but, at some point, we'll have to address this issue. And for good reason, he's resisted changing certain successful procedures that I think we could improve on. We had quite a time changing the schedule for the administration of Demerol to patients to increase their comfort level during the operation. Dr. Degani has opposed a Saturday operating program on the premise that he won't be here and won't be able to maintain proper control.

Alan O'Dell added his own concerns:

How should we be marketing our services? Right now, we don't advertise directly to patients. We're even afraid to send out this new brochure we've put together, unless a potential patient specifically requests it, for fear it will generate too much demand. Our records show that just under 1% of our patients are medical doctors, a significantly high percentage. How should we capitalize on that? I'm also concerned about this talk of Saturday operations. We are already getting good utilization of this facility. And if we expand further, it will be very difficult to maintain the same kind of working relationships and attitudes. Already there are rumors floating around among the staff about it. And the staff is not pleased.

The matter of Saturday operations had been a topic of conversation among the doctors as well. Four of the older doctors were opposed to it. While most of the younger doctors were either indifferent or supportive, at least two who had been at the hospital for some time were particularly concerned about the possibility that the issue would drive a wedge between the two groups. As one put it, "I'd hate to see the practice split over the issue."

STUDY QUESTIONS

1. What is the market for the service offered by Shouldice Hospital? How successful is the hospital?

2. Define the service model for Shouldice. How does each of its elements contribute to the hospital's success?

3. As Dr. Shouldice, what actions, if any, would you like to take to expand the hospital's capacity? How would you implement such changes?

Red Lobster

Christopher H. Lovelock

A peer review panel of managers and service workers from a restaurant chain must decide whether or not a waitress has been unfairly fired from her job.

"**I**t felt like a knife going through me!" declared Mary Campbell, 53, after she was fired from her waitressing job at a restaurant in the Red Lobster chain. Instead of suing for what she considered unfair dismissal after 19 years of service, Campbell called for a peer review, seeking to recover her job and three weeks of lost wages.

Three weeks after the firing, a panel of employees from different Red Lobster restaurants was reviewing the evidence and trying to determine whether the server had, in fact, been unjustly fired for allegedly stealing a guest comment card completed by a couple of customers whom she had served.

PEER REVIEW AT DARDEN INDUSTRIES

Red Lobster was owned by Darden Industries, which also owned other restaurant chains such as Olive Garden, Longhorn Steakhouse, The Capital Grill, Bahama Breeze, and Seasons 52. The company had about 1,900 restaurants serving 400 million meals a year. Red Lobster, which had more than 180,000 employees, had adopted a policy of encouraging peer reviews of disputed employee firings and disciplinary actions several years earlier. The company's key objectives were to limit worker lawsuits and ease workplace tensions.

Advocates of the peer review approach, which had been adopted at several other companies, believed that it was a very effective way of constructively channeling the pain and anger that employees felt after being fired or disciplined by their managers. By reducing the incidence of lawsuits, a company could also save on legal expenses.

A Darden spokesperson stated that the peer review program had been "tremendously successful" in protecting valuable employees from unfair dismissal. Each year, about 100 disputes ended up in peer review, with only 10 subsequently resulting in lawsuits. Red Lobster managers and many employees also credited peer review with reducing racial tensions. Campbell, who said she had received dozens of calls of support, chose peer review over a lawsuit not only because it was much cheaper but also because she "liked the idea of being judged by people who know how things work in a little restaurant."

THE EVIDENCE

The review panel included a general manager, an assistant manager, a server, a hostess, and a bartender. All of them had volunteered to review the circumstances of Mary Campbell's firing. Each panelist had undergone peer review training and was receiving regular wages plus travel expenses. Panelists were simply instructed to do what they felt was fair.

Campbell, who worked as a restaurant server at the Red Lobster in Marston, had been fired by Jean Larimer, the general manager of this outlet. The reason given for the firing was that Campbell had asked the restaurant's hostess, Eve Taunton, for the key to the guest comment box and had stolen a card from it. The card had been completed by a couple of guests whom Campbell had served and who seemed dissatisfied with their experience at the restaurant. Subsequently, the guests learned that their comment card, which complained that their prime rib of beef was too rare and that their waitress was "uncooperative," had been removed from the box.

Jean Larimer's testimony. Larimer, who supervised 100 full- and part-time employees, testified that she had dismissed Campbell after one of the two customers complained angrily to her and her supervisor. "She [the guest] felt violated," declared the manager, "because her card was taken from the box and her complaint about the food was ignored." Larimer drew the panel's attention to the company rule book, pointing out that Campbell had violated the policy that forbade removal of company property.

Mary Campbell's testimony. Campbell testified that the female customer had requested that her prime rib be cooked "well done" and had subsequently complained that it was fatty and undercooked. The waitress told the panel that she had politely suggested that "prime rib always has fat on it" but had arranged to have the meat cooked a little more. However, the woman still seemed unhappy. She poured some steak sauce over the meat but then pushed away her plate without eating all the food. When the customer remained displeased, Campbell offered her a free dessert. However, the guests decided to leave, paid the bill, filled out the guest comment card, and dropped it in the guest comment box.

Admitting she was consumed by curiosity, Campbell asked Eve Taunton, the restaurant's hostess, for the key to the box. After removing and reading the card, she pocketed it. Her intent, she declared, was to show the card to Jean Larimer, who had been concerned earlier that the prime rib served at the restaurant was overcooked rather than undercooked. However, she forgot about the card and later threw it out accidentally.

Eve Taunton's testimony. At the time of the firing, Taunton, a 17-year-old student, was working at Red Lobster for the summer. "I didn't think it was a big deal to give her [Campbell] the key," she said. "A lot of people would come up to me to get it."

THE PANEL DELIBERATES

Having heard the testimony, the members of the review panel had to decide whether Jean Larimer had been justified in firing Mary Campbell. The panelists' initial reactions to the situation were split by rank, with the hourly workers supporting Campbell and the managers supporting Larimer. The debate began in earnest when an effort was made to reach consensus.

STUDY QUESTIONS

1. What are the marketing implications of this situation?

2. Evaluate the concept of peer review. What are its strengths and weaknesses? What type of environment is required to make it work well?

3. Review the evidence. Do you believe the testimony presented?

4. What decision would you make and why?

Exhibit 1: The restaurant scene becomes the testing ground for the validity of peer review.

Singapore Airlines: Managing Human Resources for Cost-Effective Service Excellence

Jochen Wirtz and Loizos Heracleous

We find the films you love, to make you feel at home.

A truly entertaining journey. There's more to it than just the latest movies. It's about finding culture and experiences from near and far, for you to enjoy. Because we understand that enriching moments make your flight just that much more meaningful. It's just one of the lengths we go to, to make you feel at home.

SINGAPORE AIRLINES
A great way to fly

A STAR ALLIANCE MEMBER

© 2018 by Jochen Wirtz and Loizos Heracleous.

This case is based on the following earlier publications: Loizos Heracleous and Jochen Wirtz, "Singapore Airlines' Balancing Act: Asia's Premier Carrier Successfully Executes a Dual Strategy: It Offers World-Class Service and Is a Cost Leader," *Harvard Business Review 88*, no. 7/8 (July–August 2010): 145–149; Loizos Heracleous, Jochen Wirtz, and Nitin Pangarkar, *Flying High in a Competitive Industry: Cost-Effective Service Excellence at Singapore Airlines* (Asia: McGraw-Hill Education, 2009); Jochen Wirtz, Loizos Heracleous, and Nitin Pangarkar, "Managing Human Resources for Service Excellence and Cost Effectiveness at Singapore Airlines," *Managing Service Quality 18*, no. 1 (2008): 4–19. It also draws on interviews conducted with Singapore Airlines personnel by Jochen Wirtz in 2015.

Singapore Airlines (SIA) has managed and organized its human resources (HR) to achieve sustainable competitive advantage and outperform other airlines in its peer group for decades. The case describes the role of HR in Singapore Airlines' simultaneous pursuit of the apparently conflicting objectives of service excellence and cost effectiveness through its approach to the recruitment, selection, training, motivation, and retention of its employees.

"At the end of the day, it's the software, people like us, who make the real difference."

Patrick Seow, senior rank trainer at
Singapore Airlines Training School and in-flight supervisor

"In Singapore, we always want to be the best in a lot of things. SIA is no different. . . . a lot of things that we have been taught from young, from our Asian heritage . . . filial piety, the care and concern, hospitality, and of course, the most important part is trying, if we can, to do whatever we can to please the customer. And how do we do it? Sometimes, people just wonder, 'How do you guys manage to do it with limited time and resources on a flight,' yet we manage to do it somehow. Call us magicians."

Lim Suet Kwee, assistant manager of
Cabin Crew Performance Management and former senior inflight supervisor

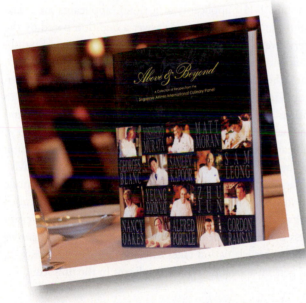

A cookbook based on recipes from SIA's International Culinary Panel.

SIA's new business class has the widest seats in the industry.

HR AND COST-EFFECTIVE SERVICE EXCELLENCE AT SINGAPORE AIRLINES

Over the past four decades, Singapore Airlines has earned a stellar reputation in the fiercely competitive commercial-aviation business by providing customers with high-quality service and dominating the business-travel segments. Singapore Airlines has been the most awarded airline in the world for many years. For example, it won the World's Best Airline Award from the prestigious U.K. travel magazine Condé Nast Traveler 23 out of the 24 times it was nominated. It also won Skytrax's Airline of the Year award three times over the past decade. These awards are a reflection of Singapore Airlines' customer focus. According to Tan Pee Teck, Senior Vice President of Cabin Crew, "It's not just consistency that we need to maintain, but also an overall elevation in the average standard of service to a higher threshold, because the expectations of frequent flyers especially will rise in tandem."

'One key element of Singapore Airlines' competitive success is that it manages to navigate skillfully between poles that most companies think of as distinct: delivering service excellence in a cost-effective way. Singapore Airlines' costs are lower than those of all other full-service airlines. In fact, its cost levels are so low that they are comparable to those of budget airlines. From 2001 to 2009, the airline's costs per available seat kilometer were just 4.6 cents. According to a 2007 International Air Transport Association study, the costs for full-service European airlines were 8 to 16 cents, for U.S. airlines 7 to 8 cents, and for Asian airlines 5 to 7 cents per available seat kilometer. Singapore Airlines had even lower costs than most low-cost carriers in Europe and the United States, which ranged from 4 to 8 cents and 5 to 6 cents respectively.

A key challenge of implementing business-level strategies, such as effective differentiation at Singapore Airlines through service excellence and innovation combined with superior levels of operational efficiency, is the alignment of functional strategies such as HR, marketing, and operations with the business-level strategy. The focus of this case is on how HR practices, a crucial aspect of most service businesses, contribute to Singapore Airlines' success by creating capabilities that support the company's strategy.

Figure 1: The five core elements of SIA's HR strategy.

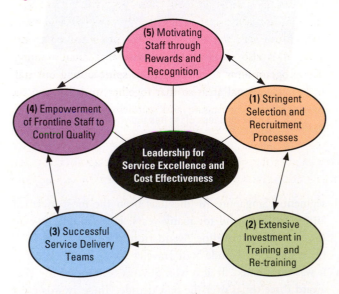

Source: This model was derived from the authors' interviews with SIA's senior management and service personnel.

Five inter-related and mutually supportive elements inherent in Singapore Airlines' HR strategy, along with leadership and role modeling by top management, play a key role in SIA's ability to deliver its business strategy of service excellence in a cost-effective way. Let us now take a closer look at how the five elements work and complement each other.

STRINGENT SELECTION AND RECRUITMENT PROCESS

HR strategy begins with recruitment, and Singapore Airlines adopts a highly rigorous and strict selection process. Senior managers emphasize the need for cabin crew who can empathize with passengers and are cheerful, friendly, and humble. Cabin crew applicants are required to meet a multitude of criteria, starting with an initial screening looking at age ranges, academic qualifications, and physical attributes.

The subsequent recruitment interviews comprise four rounds. In round 1 (10 applicants at a time), applicants are asked to introduce themselves and answer a question posed by the interviewers. They are assessed on their command of English, confidence, and grooming. In round 2 (six applicants at a time), the candidates are divided into two groups and given a topic to debate. Applicants are assessed on their ability to work as a team and present their arguments in a logical and convincing manner. For the second half of the interview, applicants are given passages to read so that their enunciation can be tested. In round 3, one-on-one interviews with management are carried out to assess the candidate's aptitude and suitability for the position. In the final round, also called the grooming round, a uniform test allows the interviewers to assess the look of the applicant in Singapore Airlines' *sarong kebaya*. This evaluation takes into account the posture, gait, and general appearance of the applicant in the uniform.

From the 18,000 applications received annually, only some 600 to 900 new cabin-crew members are hired to cover turnover rates of 10%. These include both voluntary and directed attrition and company growth. After the initial training, new crew members are carefully monitored for the first six months of flying. This is done through monthly reports from the in-flight supervisors throughout the probationary period. Usually around 85% of the new recruits are confirmed for an initial five-year contract. Some 10% have their probation extended, and the rest leave the company.

This meticulous selection process (with a selection rate of 3%–4% of the applicant pool) ensures with reasonable certainty that Singapore Airlines hires applicants with the desired attributes. Despite the stringent procedures and strict rules about appearance and behavior, many educated young people around the region apply to join Singapore Airlines due to the perceived social status and glamour associated with its cabin crew. Singapore Airlines' reputation as a service leader in the airline industry and an extensive and holistic developer of talent enables it to have its pick of applicants. Many school leavers and graduates see it as a desirable company to work for. They also get the opportunity to move to more lucrative jobs in other companies after having worked with Singapore Airlines (typically for two or more five-year contracts).

EXTENSIVE INVESTMENT IN TRAINING AND RE-TRAINING

Singapore Airlines places considerable emphasis on training, which is one of the focal points in its HR strategy. According to a senior manager of HR development, "SIA invests huge amounts of money in infrastructure and technology, but ultimately, you need people to drive it. At SIA, we believe that people actually do make a difference, so the company has in place a very comprehensive and holistic approach to developing our human resources. Essentially, we do two types of training, namely functional training and general management-type training." Almost half of Singapore Airlines' expenditure is on functional training and re-training.

Even though training is often emphasized as a key element of success in service industries, Singapore Airlines remains the airline with the highest emphasis on this aspect. Newly recruited cabin-crew members are required to undertake intensive 15-week training courses—the longest and most comprehensive in the industry. Singapore Airlines' training aims to enable cabin crew to provide gracious service, reflecting warmth and friendliness while maintaining an image of authority and confidence in the passengers' minds. Singapore Airlines' holistic training includes not only safety and functional issues but also grooming, gourmet food, wine appreciation, and the art of conversation. Even during economic downturns and crises, Singapore Airlines maintains its heavy emphasis on training. Goh Choon Phong, CEO of Singapore Airlines, said: "We will continue to invest heavily in the training and development of our people to bring out the best in them, even in the most difficult of times."

As Singapore Airlines' reputation for service excellence grows stronger, its customers' expectations are raised even further, and this increases the pressure on its front-line staff. According to a commercial training manager, the motto of Singapore Airlines is: "If SIA can't do it for you, no other airline can. The challenge is to help the staff deal with difficult situations and take the brickbats. The company helps its staff deal with the emotional turmoil of having to satisfy and even please very demanding customers without feeling that they are being taken advantage of." Former CEO Cheong Choong Kong also commented, "To the company, training is forever and no one is too young to be trained, nor too old."

Continuous training and re-training has been vital for sustaining service excellence at Singapore Airlines. Staff members are equipped with an open mindset that enables them to accept change and development and deliver the new services that the airline introduces regularly. The Singapore Airlines group has four training schools. The first is corporate learning, and the other three involve the core functional areas of cabin crew, flight operations, and engineering. Singapore Airlines' Corporate Learning Centre (CLC) offers general management training under the purview of its HR division. CLC provides executive and leadership programs for all staff members with the objective of generating effective managers and visionary leaders. It also drives customer-service training and functional training for commercial areas.

Singapore Airlines' training programs (about 70% of which are in-house) develop 12,000 people a year. Often, training is aimed at supporting internal initiatives such as the Transforming Customer Service (TCS) program, which involves staff in five key operational areas: cabin crew, engineering, ground services, flight operations, and sales support. According to a senior manager for HR development, "To ensure that the TCS culture is promoted company-wide, it is also embedded into all management training. The program aims at building team spirit among our staff in key operational areas so that together we will make the whole journey as pleasant and seamless as possible for our passengers. One has to realize that it is not just the ticketing or reservations people and the cabin crew who come into contact with our passengers. The pilots, station managers, and station engineers have a role in customer service as well, because from time to time, they do come into contact with passengers." She also added, "But TCS is not just about people. In TCS, there is the 40–30–30 rule, which is a holistic approach to people, processes (or procedures), and products. SIA focuses 40% of the resources on training and invigorating our people, 30% on reviewing processes and procedures, and 30% on creating new product and service ideas."

Singapore Airlines' leadership and relationship management with its staff play a key role in the success of its training initiatives. As a project manager in the airline's new service development program puts it, "I see myself first as a coach and second as a team player." Singapore Airlines managers often assume the role of mentors and coaches to guide new employees.

Singapore Airlines also adopts a job-rotation approach that allows management to obtain a more holistic picture of the organization. Rotating to other departments every two to three years enables managers to develop a deeper understanding of operations in other areas of the organization. This practice promotes a corporate outlook and reduces the likelihood of inter-departmental conflicts. It also facilitates change and innovation, as people bring fresh perspectives and approaches to their new roles. Constant job rotation is a core part of employee learning and development.

BUILDING HIGH-PERFORMANCE SERVICE DELIVERY TEAMS

The nature of the working environment on board requires people to work effectively as a team to deliver service excellence. In fact, effective teams are often a prerequisite to service excellence. In view of this, Singapore Airlines aims to create *esprit de corps* among its cabin crew. The 7,700 crew members are formed into "wards." Each ward consists of about 180 crew members led by a "ward leader," who acts as a counsellor to guide and develop the other members. Ward leaders issue newsletters for their teams and organize face-to-face sessions and activities with their ward members. These activities include inter-ward games, overseas bonding sessions, and full-day engagement sessions on the ground.

Each ward leader learns about their ward members' individual strengths and weaknesses and acts as a counselor to whom they can turn for help or advice. These ward leaders also play the roles of "inflight auditors," who often fly with the teams to inspect performance and generate feedback that can aid the team's development. According to an assistant manager of training, "Team leaders are able to monitor and point out what can be improved in the crew; team leaders are the ones to evaluate the crew, monitor staff development, staff performance, and supervise them. They see the feedback and monitor the performance."

According to Sim Kay Wee, former Senior Vice President of Cabin Crew, "The interaction within each of the teams is very strong. As a result, when team leaders do staff appraisal, they really know the staff. You would be amazed how meticulous and detailed each staff record is, even though there are 7,700 of them. We can pinpoint any staff's strengths and weaknesses easily. So, in this way, we have good control, and through this, we can ensure that the crew delivers the promise. If there are problems, we will know about them and we can send them for re-training. Those who are good will be selected for promotion."

In addition, Singapore Airlines organizes activities that reach out to the wider crew population. The management staff have frequent interactions with crew members at the Control Centre (where crew members report for work) over food and drinks. The senior crew members are invited for full-day engagement sessions with the management.

Singapore Airlines' cabin crew also engages in some seemingly unrelated activities. An example is the performing-arts circle for talented employees, which raised over half a million dollars for charity during the biennial cabin-crew gala dinner. Currently, there are 30 diverse groups whose activities cover arts, sports, music, dance, and community service. These interest groups provide an avenue for crew members to come together to pursue their passions outside work and to further develop team spirit. The company believes that such activities encourage empathy for others, an appreciation of the finer things in life, and camaraderie and teamwork. It therefore supports cabin-crew members who set up interest groups.

EMPOWERMENT OF THE FRONT LINE TO DELIVER SERVICE QUALITY

Over time, the soft skills of flight crew and other service personnel get honed, leading to service excellence that is difficult to replicate not only in terms of how the service is delivered but also in terms of the mindset that supports this delivery. Virtually all outstanding service firms have legendary stories of employees who recovered failed service transactions, walked the extra mile to make a customer's day, or averted some kind of disaster for a customer. A senior manager of crew performance shared such a story:

> This particular passenger was a wheelchair-bound lady in her eighties [who] was very ill, suffering from arthritis. She was traveling from Singapore to Brisbane. What happened was that a stewardess found her gasping for air owing to crippling pain. The stewardess used her personal hot-water bottle as a warm compress to relieve the passenger's pain

and knelt to massage the lady's legs and feet for 45 minutes. By that time, the lady's feet were actually swollen. The stewardess offered her a new pair of flight-support stockings without asking her to pay for them. She basically took care of the old lady throughout the trip, seven to eight hours. When the old lady got back to Brisbane, her son called the hotel in which the crew were staying to try and trace this stewardess to thank her personally. He then followed up with a letter to us. I don't know if training contributes to it, or if it is personal. I mean, you don't find people who'd do this purely as a result of training, I think. We find the right people, give them the right support, give them the right training, and with the right support, people will do this kind of thing.

Such thoughtful actions are part of the culture at Singapore Airlines. According to a senior manager of crew performance, the crew members "are very proud to be part of the SIA team, very proud of the tradition and very proud that SIA is held up as a company that gives excellent care to customers. So they want to live up to that."

Employees need to feel empowered in order to expend discretionary effort and make decisions independently. Front-line staff members frequently have to handle customers on their own, since it is not feasible or even desirable for managers to constantly monitor employees' actions. At Singapore Airlines, senior management emphasizes that staff members must have a clear concept of the boundaries of their authority. It is also the responsibility of the management to communicate and explain these empowerment limits. Empowerment of the front line is especially important during service-recovery processes and in situations where customers have special needs.

MOTIVATING STAFF THROUGH REWARDS AND RECOGNITION

Rewards and recognition are key levers that any organization can use to encourage appropriate behavior, emphasize positive as well as undesirable practices, and recognize excellence. Singapore Airlines employs various forms of rewards and recognition, including interesting and varied job content, symbolic actions, performance-based share options, and a significant percentage of variable-pay components linked to individual staff contributions and the company's financial performance. It keeps base salaries low by offering employees bonuses of up to 50% of their annual base salary. This formula is hardwired and depends on the airline's profitability. The numerous international accolades received by the airline over the years, including "Best airline," "Best cabin-crew service," and "Asia's most admired company," serve as further sources of motivation.

The company also holds company-wide meetings and circulates newsletters to keep staff updated about latest developments. As an assistant manager of cabin crew performance noted, "It's about communication. For example, if we add a new service at check-in, we will talk to the people involved before, during, and after implementation. We will discuss the importance and the value of it and make sure everyone is aware of what we are doing and why. It helps to give staff pride in what they do."

Communication also aids in recognizing service excellence. Staff members who go the extra mile receive recognition through honors such as the annual CEO Transforming Customer Service (TCS) Awards. A former senior vice president of cabin crew stressed the importance of recognition: "We know that a pat on the back, a good ceremony, photographs, and write-ups in the newsletters can be more motivating than mere financial rewards; hence, we put in a lot of effort to ensure that heroes and heroines are recognized for their commitment and dedication."

Finding the right people and creating a service-oriented culture are essential. A senior manager of crew performance said, "Here, there are some intangibles. I think what makes it special is a combination of many things. First, you've got to ensure that you find the right people for the job, and after that, training matters a great deal: the way you nurture them, the way you monitor them, and the way you reward them. The recognition you give need not necessarily be money. I think another very important ingredient is the overall culture of cabin crew, the fact that you have people who really are very proud of the tradition. And I think a lot of our senior people—and it rubs off on the junior crew—take pride in the fact that they helped build up the airline; they are very proud of it and they want to ensure that it remains that way." Another senior manager of crew performance added, "Among other contributing factors is a deeply ingrained service culture not just among the cabin crew but also in the whole company. I think it goes back to the early 1970s, when the airline was set up. A very, very strong service culture throughout the whole organization, very strong commitment from top management. We take every complaint seriously. We respond to every compliment and complaint. We try to learn from the feedback; it's a never-ending process."

Singapore Airlines' reward and evaluation system is highly aligned with the desired behaviors. The key element is "on-board assessment," which encompasses image (grooming and uniform turnout), service orientation (crew's interaction and passenger-handling capabilities), product knowledge and job skills, safety and security knowledge and adherence to procedures, and work relationship (spirit of team work). For the crew member in charge, the additional factors of people-management skills and pre-flight briefing sessions are very important. The Appendix provides information on how cabin crew members are evaluated.

Singapore Airlines offers average pay by Singaporean standards, which is low by global standards. Occasionally, there have been disputes between the Singapore Airlines group management and the labor unions. In 2007, the airline was in the spotlight again when the Air Line Pilots' Association Singapore (ALPA-S) disagreed with the management's proposed salary rate for pilots flying the Airbus A380. The case had to be settled by the Industrial Arbitration Court.

BEYOND HUMAN RESOURCES

For four decades, Singapore Airlines has managed to achieve what many others in the aviation industry can only dream of—cost-effective service excellence and sustained superior performance. Understanding the underpinnings of Singapore Airlines' competitive success has important implications for organizations in general. One of the key implications concerns strategic alignment, particularly the aligning of HR practices to the company's competitive strategy.

At Singapore Airlines, the HR management practices outlined above enable the development of service excellence, customer orientation, adaptability, and cost consciousness. In turn, these capabilities support the company's dual strategy of differentiation through service excellence and low cost.

The Singapore Airlines experience highlights how training and development should be employed in order to achieve a holistically developed work force that can effectively support the company's strategy. Key questions for leaders therefore include, What sort of behaviors and attitudes do our reward and evaluation systems encourage? Are these aligned with what is needed to support our strategy? Do we train and develop our people in a way that develops the right capabilities to support our strategy? Do we go beyond technical training to address attitudes and ways of thinking?

No organization can stand still. The recent socio-economic crises at the macro level and the fast growth of high-quality full-service airlines in the Middle East (e.g., Emirates, Etihad, and Qatar Airways) as well as Asian budget carriers (e.g., AirAsia) at the industry level mean that Singapore Airlines not only needs to sustain its focus on achieving cost-effective service excellence but also re-examine and re-invent some ingredients of its recipe for success.

STUDY QUESTIONS

1. Describe what is so special about the five elements of Singapore Airlines' successful HR practices.

2. Evaluate the effectiveness of each element's contribution toward Singapore Airlines' leadership in service excellence and cost effectiveness.

3. Despite evidence that such practices help service firms achieve higher company performance, many organizations have not managed to execute them as effectively. Why do you think that is the case?

4. Why do you think full-service airlines in the United States are largely undifferentiated low-quality providers? What are the reasons that none of the full-service airlines have positioned themselves as high service-quality providers?

5. Some of Singapore Airlines' HR practices would be frowned upon in the United States and Europe (e.g., having cabin crew on time-based contracts that are renewable every five years). Is this fair competition (i.e., desired competition between regulatory frameworks, as was favored by Margaret Thatcher, former Prime Minister of the United Kingdom), or is it arbitration of regulatory environments that encourage a "race to the bottom" in terms of employee rights?

6. How do people feel if they are working in a culture that focuses so intensely on customers but cuts costs to the bone internally?

7. View http://youtu.be/fNEJrd6GkSY (Across the World with the Singapore Girl) and http://youtu.be/P5sGKR6NJBw (Singapore Airlines SQ Girl), and discuss how these videos might be perceived by Singapore Airlines cabin crew.

APPENDIX: CABIN CREW PERFORMANCE MANAGEMENT (PM) QUESTIONS

1. How is the cabin-crew area structured, and how does this influence the performance management system?

Cabin-crew members are divided into 45 groups known as wards, each headed by a ward leader (WL). Each ward consists of approximately 180 crew members of all ranks. The ward leader is primarily responsible for monitoring performance, coaching and developing; establishing rapport and communication; and ensuring the welfare of crew members of CS rank and below. Ward leaders report to a ward management leader (WML), who typically supervises five ward leaders. In-flight supervisors (IFS) come under the management of ward management leaders.

2. Describe the performance management tool/process that you use to monitor your cabin crew.

The performance of a crew member is measured through "on-board assessments" (OBA) carried out by a more senior crew member on the same flight. The elements assessed are:

a) Image—grooming and uniform turnout

b) Service orientation—crew's interaction and passenger-handling capabilities

c) Product knowledge and job skills—crew's performance with the various bar and meal services and its familiarity with procedures/job and product knowledge

d) Safety and security—knowledge and adherence to safety and security procedures

e) Work relationship—to assess crew's general attitude and team work/team spirit

f) People-management skills—supervisory and management skills, development of junior crew, and the ability to plan and co-ordinate the various services

(Section f is applicable only to the crew-in-charge.)

3. How frequently do the assessments occur?

It varies on the basis of rank and is tracked over a financial year.

In-flight supervisor—two on-board assessments per financial year

All other cabin crew—six on-board assessments per financial year

4. What degree of alignment exists between the company values and the areas assessed?

The company's core values are embedded in the elements assessed in on-board assessments, such as service orientation and product knowledge (pursuit of excellence), safety and security (safety), and work relationship and people management (teamwork).

5. How do you train assessors, and what level of on-going training occurs to ensure rater consistency?

All crew members promoted to supervisory rank have to attend a one-day appraisal workshop where they are taught the basics of assessment and coached on the use of the on-board assessment form. There's also an ongoing process to review all assessments that have been improperly done and pick out appraisers who habitually give extreme ratings for follow-up by the ward leaders.

Dr. Mahalee Goes to London: Global Client Management

Christopher H. Lovelock

A senior account officer at an international bank is about to meet a wealthy Asian businessman who seeks funding for a buyout of his company. The prospective client has already visited a competing bank.

It was a Friday in mid-February. Dr. Kadir Mahalee, a wealthy businessman from the Southeast-Asian nation of Tailesia, was visiting London on a trip that combined business and pleasure. Mahalee held a doctorate from the London School of Economics and had earlier been a professor of international trade and a government trade negotiator. He was the founder of Eximsa, a major export company in Tailesia. Business brought him to London every 2–3 months. These trips provided him with the opportunity to visit his daughter Leona, the eldest of his four children, who lived in London. Several of his 10 grandchildren were attending college in Britain. He was especially proud of his grandson, Anson, who was a student at the Royal Academy of Music. In fact, he had scheduled this trip to coincide with a violin recital by Anson at 2 p.m. on this particular Friday.

The primary purpose of Mahalee's visit was to resolve a delicate matter regarding his company. He had decided to retire and wished to make arrangements for the company's future. His son, Victor, was involved in the business and ran Eximsa's trading office in Europe. However, Victor was in poor health and unable to take over the firm. Mahalee believed that a group of loyal employees were interested in buying his company if the necessary credit could be arranged.

Before leaving Tailesia, Mahalee discussed the possibility of a buyout with his trusted financial adviser Pascal Huet. Huet recommended that he talk to several banks in London because of the potential complexity of the business deal:

> The London banks are experienced in buyouts. Also, you need a bank that can handle the credit for the interested buyers in New York and London, as well as Asia. Once the buyout takes place, you'll have significant cash to invest. This would be a good time to review your estate plans as well.

Referring Mahalee to two competing firms, The Trust Company and Global Private Bank, Lee added:

> I've met an account officer from Global who called on me several times. Here's his business card; his name is Michael Johnston. I've never done any business with him, but he did seem quite competent. Unfortunately, I don't know anyone at The Trust Company, but here's their address in London.

After checking into the Savoy Hotel in London the following Wednesday, Mahalee telephoned Johnston's office. Since Johnston was out, Mahalee spoke to the account officer's secretary, described himself briefly, and arranged to stop by Global's Lombard Street office around mid-morning on Friday.

On Thursday, Mahalee visited The Trust Company. The two people he met were extremely pleasant and had spent some time in Tailesia. They seemed very knowledgeable about managing estates and gave him some good recommendations about handling his complex family affairs. However, they were clearly less experienced in handling business credit, which was his most urgent need.

The next morning, Mahalee had breakfast with Leona. As they parted, she said, "I'll meet you at 1:30 p.m. in the lobby of the Savoy, and we'll go to the recital together. We mustn't be late if we want to get front-row seats."

On his way to Global Private Bank, Mahalee stopped at Mappin & Webb's jewelry store to buy his wife a present for their anniversary. His shopping was pleasant and leisurely. He purchased a beautiful emerald necklace that he knew his wife would like. When he emerged from the jewelry store, he was caught in an unexpected snow flurry. He had difficulty finding a taxi and his arthritis started acting up, making it impossible for him to walk to the nearest Tube station. At last, he caught a taxi and arrived at the Lombard Street location of Global Bancorp around noon. After going into the street-level branch of Global Retail Bank, he was redirected by a security guard to the Private Bank offices on the second floor.

He arrived at the Private Bank's nicely appointed reception area at 12:15 p.m. The receptionist greeted him and contacted Johnston's secretary, who came out promptly to see Mahalee and declared:

> Mr. Johnston was disappointed that he couldn't be here to welcome you, Dr. Mahalee, but he had a lunch appointment with one of his clients that was scheduled over a month ago. He expects to return at about 1:30. In the meantime, he has asked another senior account officer, Sophia Costa, to assist you.

Exhibit 1: Receiving a client on short notice would require a bank's vice president to rely on all her expertise and experience to clinch the deal.

Sophia Costa, 41, was a vice president of the bank and had worked for Global Bancorp for 14 years (two years longer than Michael Johnston). She had visited Tailesia once but had not met Mahalee's financial adviser or any member of the Mahalee family. An experienced relationship manager, Costa was knowledgeable about off-shore investment management and fiduciary services. Michael Johnston had looked into her office at 11:45 a.m. and asked her if she would cover for him in case a prospective client—a Dr. Mahalee whom he had expected to see earlier—should happen to arrive. He told Costa that Mahalee was a successful Tailesian businessman planning for his retirement but clarified that he had never met the prospect personally. He then rushed off to lunch.

The phone rang in Costa's office, and she reached across the desk to pick it up. It was Johnston's secretary. "Dr. Mahalee is in reception, Ms. Costa."

STUDY QUESTIONS

1. Prepare a flowchart of Dr. Mahalee's service encounters.

2. Putting yourself in Dr. Mahalee's shoes, how do you feel (both physically and mentally) after speaking with the receptionist at Global? What are your priorities right now?

3. As Sophia Costa, what action would you take in your first five minutes with Mahalee?

4. What would be a good outcome of the meeting for both the client and the bank? How should Costa try to bring about such an outcome?

The Royal Dining Membership Program Dilemma

Sheryl E. Kimes, Rohit Verma, Christopher W. Hart, and Jochen Wirtz

The Royal Dining membership program is highly popular with diners and generates significant revenue. However, it might be displacing regular, full-price-paying customers and could have a negative effect on the painstakingly built and maintained high-end luxury image of the Hong Kong Grand Hotel. In addition, quite a few managers and servers have expressed unhappiness with the program, the conflicts it creates with diners, and the type of customers it attracts.

Erica Liu, Program Manager for the Royal Dining (RD) Membership Program at the Hong Kong Grand Hotel, hung up the phone after a call from a disgruntled customer. Just then, Jerome Tan, Vice President of Hotel Operations, walked into her office. "I tell you, Jerome," sighed Erica. "I've been getting calls from customers complaining about all the rules we have for the RD program. It's driving me nuts." "Tell me about it," Jerome replied. "These RD members really annoy our staff. All they're looking for is free stuff. I heard the ultimate one yesterday. Some guy walked into the Cantonese Café with 10 little kids and wanted them all to eat for free! Yes, we have a rule that kids under five can eat for free, but not the whole city! It turned out it was his son's birthday party. Can you believe that?" Erica sighed again. "I guess that means we're going to have to create another rule for members to complain about. I mean, I think it's a great program and all, and it definitely brings in a lot of business, but how are we going to deal with all these problems?"

THE HONG KONG GRAND LAUNCHES A DINING MEMBERSHIP PROGRAM

The Hong Kong Grand, a 140-room landmark hotel on Hong Kong Island, opened in the late 1800s and was considered a national monument. It was one of the world's well-known Grand hotels and had received numerous awards, including Best Luxury Hotel and Best Hotel in Asia. Its guest list included such luminaries as Queen Elizabeth II, Bill Gates, and James Michener, and it was one of the most photographed sites in Hong Kong. The hotel had four restaurants, ranging from the 56-seat Hollywood Road Deli to the fine-dining 112-seat Kabuki. All the restaurants took reservations and were open for lunch and dinner. The adjoining convention center, the second largest meeting space in Hong Kong, provided an ideal setting for upscale conferences. The adjoining shopping mall

Exhibit 1: The Hong Kong Grand's restaurants.

Restaurant name	Cuisine	Restaurant type	Average check (HK$)	Number of seats	À la carte or buffet	Average lunch duration (hours)	Average dinner duration (hours)	Hours of operation for each meal
Cantonese Café	Local/Buffet	Local/buffet	$76	106	Both	1.0	1.0	5
Kabuki	Japanese	Fine dining	$250	112	À la carte	1.0	1.5	5
Hollywood Road Deli	American style	Casual	$104	56	À la carte	0.5	0.5	5
Dragon Boat	International	Smart casual	$109	72	Both	1.0	1.0	5

offered a multitude of shopping and dining options. For more information on the Hong Kong Grand restaurants, see Exhibit 1.

The ownership of the Hong Kong Grand had changed recently. Previously, the company that owned the shopping center had also owned the hotel and had restricted the number of restaurants that operated in the mall. Once they sold the hotel, this restriction was lifted. The hotel restaurants therefore had to contend with much more vigorous competition and were often empty. As a response, the Hong Kong Grand launched the Royal Dining (RD) membership program.

The Royal Dining program was designed to encourage Hong Kong residents to dine in the restaurants at a discounted rate. With a food cost as a percentage of sales that averaged 32% of gross revenue, even a 50% discount yielded a reasonable gross margin. In addition, the program required the purchase of annual memberships, which provided a substantial revenue stream with practically no variable cost.

THE ROYAL DINING MEMBERSHIP PROGRAM

The Royal Dining membership program offered members the opportunity to receive discounted meals and rooms at the restaurants and bars located in the Hong Kong Grand. The program was an immediate hit. Within the first year, over 1,000 memberships were sold. Local residents welcomed the opportunity to dine at the four hotel restaurants at major discounts. The hotel's restaurant revenue increased sharply from the added sales. By 2015, the program had a total of 4,200 members.

The Royal Dining membership card gave customers a 50% discount when two adults dined at one table and ordered at least one dish per person (starter, main course, or set menu). Typically, members dined for free; their dining companions paid for the meal. If members dined alone, they received only a 10% discount. The discount was calculated on the total food bill and did not include beverages, taxes, or service charges. It was also unavailable for take-away orders or private dining events. Children dining with members received the discount as well. Children under five could even eat for free in the buffet restaurant. In addition, special children's menus were available in the à la carte restaurants. (See Exhibit 2 for the complete program rules.)

The card came with other benefits, including discounted room rates at the Hong Kong Grand (subject to availability),

Exhibit 2: Royal Dining membership rules.

Royal Dining annual membership fee: HKS$1,588 (ca. US$205)	
PRICE REDUCTION SCHEDULE:	
Member plus 1 guest (2 adults)	50% *
Member plus 2 guests (3 adults)	33%
Member plus 3 guests (4 adults)	25%
Member plus 4 guests or more (up to a total of 10 adults)	20%
Member dining alone	10%

* 50% discount is applicable only when there are two adult dining parties at a table and when a minimum of two food items are ordered (e.g., one set menu and one starter, or one main course and one starter). Two dining parties may not necessarily order a main course, but at least two starter orders are required. In the event that only one food item is ordered for sharing and there are two parties dining, a 10% discount is applicable instead of the 50% discount. Members and their guests have to order a dish per person in order to enjoy the varying discounts. Side dishes are excluded from this discount benefit.

Conditions:
- The price-reduction structure is calculated on the total food bill only, excluding beverages, government taxes, and service charge. Reduction does not apply to private dining and take-away.
- One card per table, per party, per occasion. Not valid with any other discounts or promotions.
- A 10% reduction will also be applied to bar snacks, where applicable.

OTHER BENEFITS
- A flat 20% discount will be given to members during Chinese New Year black-out dates when dining with a minimum of five or more people at one table at all restaurants except Kabuki.
- 1 Special Occasion voucher for 50% discount on total food bill in any one of the hotel's restaurants when dining in a party of 6–12 people. Not available during the Chinese New Year period (the eve to the 15th day of the Chinese New Year).
- Discounted room rates at the Hong Kong Grand (subject to availability)
- Birthday and wedding vouchers, and discounts at several stores in the hotel

birthday and wedding vouchers, and discounts at several stores. Members could not use the card on Valentine's Day, Mother's Day, Christmas Eve, Christmas Day, and the first few days of the Chinese New Year. Although Royal Dining program rules stated that the restaurants could restrict seating availability during busy periods, this was rarely done.

Exhibit 3: Royal Dining membership.

Membership type	Number of members	% active cards	Average visits p.a.	Average party size	Average % Discount
RD—Traditional	78	71%	6.7	2.4	35%
RD—Epicure	641	76%	6.5	2.7	38%
Credit Card—Traditional	3,214	28%	3.5	2.5	35%
Credit Card—Epicure	310	20%	2.5	2.6	32%
Totals	4,243	49%	4.8	2.5	35%

Types of Memberships. Two types of memberships were available: Royal Dining Traditional (HK$1,588 per year) and Royal Dining Epicure (HK$2,588 per year). The majority of members opted for the Epicure membership because it included a free room night at the hotel.

In addition, Royal Dining cards were given for free to all premium members of a well-known credit card company. This company paid the Hong Kong Grand a discounted rate of HK$275 per year for each member in the Traditional program and HK$400 per year for Epicure memberships. The latter were given only to their most valued customers. Both the Hong Kong Grand and the credit card company saw a mutually beneficial partnership evolving from the alliance of the two highly regarded brands. About 85% of all members were premium customers of the credit card company and therefore did not pay for their Royal Dining cards. Of the credit card members, 3,214 were Traditional members, and 310 were Epicure members (see Exhibit 3).

Not surprisingly, the purchased Royal Dining cards had a higher likelihood of being used (about 75%) and were used more frequently (about once every month-and-a-half) than those given to credit card holders. Only 25% of credit card members used their memberships at an average rate of once every four months. The average party size was comparable (about 2.5 customers), as was the average net revenue (HK$225). However, for the credit card Epicure members, the average revenue was HK$325. The average discount for all Royal Dining transactions was 35% (see Exhibit 3).[1]

The percentage of restaurant revenue derived from the Royal Dining program ranged from under 3% at the Hollywood Road Deli to over 60% at Kabuki. (See Exhibit 4.)

1 For a list of commonly used restaurant terminology, see Appendix A.

2 https://en.wikipedia.org/wiki/Hong_Kong_cuisine

Competing Programs. Food and dining out are important parts of Hong Kong's national identity. Along with shopping, eating out is often seen as a national pastime. Indeed, Hong Kong has frequently been referred to as a "gourmet paradise" and "the World's Fair of Food."[2] In response to the Royal Dining program, several other hotels had developed similar dining programs in an attempt to emulate the Hong Kong Grand and tie into the local passion for eating out.

THE PROGRAM DILEMMA

After finishing a meeting, Susan Li, Vice President of Finance, decided to stop by Erica Liu's office to say hello. Jerome Tan was present, and the two were in a heated conversation that stopped abruptly when she knocked. "Let me guess. The two of you are arguing about the RD program again!" Their looks confirmed her suspicion. "I don't see why you have so many

Exhibit 4: Royal Dining program share of restaurant revenue.

Restaurant	Last financial year revenue (millions of HK$)	% of revenue from:	
		Royal Dining members	Credit card members
Hollywood Road Deli	$23.3	3.4%	2.4%
Dragon Boat	$20.1	4.0%	5.9%
Kabuki	$53.5	42.8%	19.6%
Cantonese Café	$15.4	1.3%	1.4%

problems with it. It's produced a lot of incremental revenue that has boosted our bottom line." (See Exhibits 5 to 7.)

"But Susan," Jerome exclaimed, "the RD members are displacing lots of our regular customers, especially during busy periods, and we're practically giving meals away. I feel that we should develop other programs to fill the restaurants and increase revenue—without all these cheapskates." Erica jumped in. "Jerome, I keep telling you this, but you're forgetting about all the money these people spend to become members. That is pure profit—hardly any cost involved. And the members deserve to get value for their money—or they won't renew their annual memberships. What do we give them, though? More rules that make them feel like anything *but* members. I tell you, I can understand why they complain."

"Erica, you just don't know what it's like to be working in the restaurants," Jerome replied. "These RD members are so pushy and always ask for more, more, more—and they try to game the system. For example, remember that rule about how only one discount card per table can be presented, even if there are two parties and each of them is a member? Well, since we have so many members, it's pretty common for several people at the table to have membership cards. And then they all want to use their cards so they can save more money. When we tell them that it's against the rules, they say it's unfair because it penalizes people for dining together; that if they had come as couples and sat at separate tables, each table would have received a 50% discount. To get around the rule, guess what they're doing?" Pausing for effect, he said,

Exhibit 5: Table configuration of Hong Kong Grand restaurants.

Table size	Cantonese Café	Kabuki	Hollywood Road Deli	Dragon Boat
	Tables			
2	5	2	16	8
4	20	15	3	12
5	0	0	0	0
6	0	0	2	0
8	2	2	0	1
10	0	0	0	0
Bar		10		
Tempura		Table for 10		
Teppanyaki		Table for 12		

Exhibit 6: Number of customers for each restaurant by meal period and day of week.

	Cantonese Café	Kabuki	Hollywood Road Deli	Dragon Boat
Average number of lunch customers				
Monday	195	298	250	203
Tuesday	190	336	291	228
Wednesday	228	327	333	254
Thursday	228	344	333	269
Friday	244	370	375	277
Saturday	325	242	375	306
Sunday	244	225	354	337
Average number of dinner customers				
Monday	325	190	260	170
Tuesday	358	249	286	198
Wednesday	293	257	286	161
Thursday	341	272	286	246
Friday	317	372	312	359
Saturday	317	327	312	320
Sunday	325	301	234	218

"I'll tell you what they do. They show up separately and then ask to be seated at adjacent tables. Once seated, they push the tables together and try to get double the discount! How do you handle that situation if you're the server? Doesn't exactly fit with the ambience we're trying so hard to create, does it? And it does a number on the servers' attitudes." (See Exhibit 8 for sample comments.)

Jerome was getting visibly upset. The more upset he got, the more flustered Erica became. Her program was adversely affecting people whose attitudes and behavior were vital to creating the dining experience. As Susan tried to calm him down, Carmen Teo, Vice President of Marketing, walked in. "I heard you from my office around the corner! I thought I'd better come down before someone had to call security!" she said with a laugh. Erica quickly said, "What do you think of the RD program, Carmen?" Carmen thought for a long moment and then said, "I certainly can see the point of the program, but I just don't know. We spend so much money trying to build and maintain our luxury image—and then we offer a discount program that is very much at odds with

Exhibit 7: Average revenue for each restaurant by meal period and day of week.

	Cantonese Café	Kabuki	Hollywood Road Deli	Dragon Boat
Average lunch revenue				
Monday	$17,937	$39,107	$26,692	$25,563
Tuesday	$17,199	$42,576	$27,485	$30,170
Wednesday	$16,166	$38,231	$30,791	$29,003
Thursday	$16,751	$44,450	$32,208	$27,484
Friday	$18,052	$46,411	$35,783	$30,596
Saturday	$15,404	$40,234	$38,381	$28,890
Sunday	$19,227	$39,324	$41,110	$27,629
Average dinner revenue				
Monday	$20,754	$100,088	$21,437	$21,581
Tuesday	$25,671	$81,638	$25,738	$22,238
Wednesday	$24,438	$96,045	$20,451	$29,778
Thursday	$25,664	$109,375	$32,395	$28,136
Friday	$31,273	$113,909	$47,283	$31,160
Saturday	$28,678	$126,059	$40,559	$29,790
Sunday	$18,986	$112,027	$28,715	$24,368

Exhibit 8: Sample server comments about the Royal Dining program

"My RD customers love the program. For many of them, this is the only reason they come out to The Dragon Boat." – *Dragon Boat*

"I am sick of this program! I hate having to explain the rules to people trying to use multiple cards per table." – *Cantonese Café*

"While it's sometimes tough to have to explain rules to customers, I have to admit that the program benefits the restaurant and helps make my job more secure and earn more service fees and tips." – *Kabuki*

"I think it's embarrassing! I'm working at the Hong Kong Grand and I have to deal with tacky discounts?!" – *Kabuki*

"I'm sure it makes sense to management, but dealing with customers who don't understand how the program works is the worst. The rules should be more clear to the customers." – *Hollywood Road Deli*

"The RD discount ruins the tip. I work for half as much!" – *Dragon Boat*

it. I know it generates profits that we otherwise would never see, but what are the costs? Our guests pay a lot to be here and expect a wonderful experience. I don't know if we can provide this experience when we have coupon-wavers in there with them."

Jerome chimed in. "Especially when our customers have become so much more creative in getting around the rules." Erica agreed, saying, "Yes, and that's why we have so many rules now—and that's why I get so many calls complaining about them! Again, these people are spending a lot of money for their memberships and we're making it very difficult for them! I can see why they're annoyed."

Carmen said, "The question we need to think about is how to provide good value to our RD members that keeps the revenue flowing while protecting the hotel from possible abuses of the program and negative impact on the guest experience. The answers are anything but obvious."

Susan jumped in, "Let me give you an alternative view. We have owners who are very much focused on the bottom line. Imagine their reaction if we suddenly dumped the program. I'm thinking that maybe we should extend the discount to beverages, since our cost of sales is so much lower. Right now our food cost percentage is 32%, but the beverage cost percentage is only 24%. I think it would be a strong contributor to financial performance." Jerome groaned. "But Susan, one of the only things that I can possibly see as a good thing for this program is that while we're basically giving the food away, we at least get a decent profit from the beverages. That would cost us more money!"

Erica checked her watch and noticed that she and Jerome were due at another meeting. "Well, it's nice that we're all in agreement. Anyone want to take over my job?"

Erica shook her head as she walked out the door and thought about the meeting she had with the hotel executive committee in two days. Jerome, Carmen, and Susan were all members, and the future of the Royal Dining program was high on the meeting's agenda. She thought to herself, "I need to present a comprehensive analysis of the program's costs and benefits and recommendations about where to go from here. How will I resolve all the differing views?"

"Better get to work," Erica thought, as she reached for a bottle of aspirin.

STUDY QUESTIONS

1. If you were in Erica Liu's shoes, what would you present to the executive committee?

2. As Erica Liu, what analyses would you run to assess the financial performance of the Royal Dining membership program?

3. What effect does the Royal Dining membership program have on the brand and value perception of its local customers in Hong Kong and its full-paying hotel guests and diners? How could the hotel address these issues?

4. Review the rules set for the Royal Dining program. How would you go about setting rules for the program that would protect the hotel against abuse without making the members feel that the program is unnecessarily restrictive and difficult to use?

5. How could negative server attitudes toward Royal Dining customers be handled?

APPENDIX A

Restaurant Terminology

▶ Cover: A customer

▶ Average check: The average amount paid per customer

▶ Party: The number of customers at a particular table

▶ Total check: The total check amount from a party

▶ Server: A waiter or waitress

▶ Seat occupancy: The percentage of seats occupied during a given period

▶ Table occupancy: The percentage of tables occupied during a given period

▶ Revenue per available seat hour (RevPASH): Total revenue divided by the number of seat hours available

▶ Meal duration: The length of a meal. Varies based on the type of restaurant and the meal period (e.g., lunch, dinner). Dinners average 150% the time spent at lunch.

▶ Meal period: The length of time that the restaurant is open for a given meal. Depending upon the part of the world, most restaurants offer lunch from 11 a.m. to 2:30 p.m. or 3 p.m., while dinner is typically offered from 5:30 p.m. or 6 p.m. until 10 p.m.

▶ Restaurant types (in the context of the Hong Kong Grand):

o Fine dining: Full service, sit-down restaurant with a comprehensive menu and served in a fairly luxurious setting. High average check per person. The type of restaurant that most people visit a few times per year.

o Upscale casual: Full service, sit-down restaurant with a comprehensive menu and served in a casual setting. High average check per person. The type of restaurant that people might visit once a month.

o Casual: Full service, sit-down restaurant with a somewhat limited menu and served in a casual setting. Moderate average check per person. The type of restaurant that people might visit once a month.

o Fast casual: Limited service restaurant with a fairly limited menu. Customers can either take their food with them or eat it in the restaurant. These restaurants are fairly casual with a low to moderate average check. The type of restaurant that most people might visit a few times per month.

o Quick service (fast food): Limited service restaurant with a limited menu. Customers can either take their food with them or eat it at the restaurant. These restaurants are very casual, with a low average check. The type of restaurant that most people might visit on a weekly basis.

Customer Asset Management at DHL in Asia

Jochen Wirtz, Indranil Sen, and Sanjay Singh

DHL serves a wide range of customers, from global enterprises to the occasional customer who ships the odd one or two documents a year. To be able to effectively manage such a diverse customer base, DHL implemented a sophisticated customer-segmentation-cum-loyalty-management system. The focus of this system is to assess the profitability from its customers, reduce customer churn, and increase DHL's share of shipments.

COMPANY BACKGROUND AND MARKET ENVIRONMENT

DHL, the international air express and logistics company, serves a wide range of customers, from global enterprises with sophisticated and high volume supply-chain solutions shipping anything from spare parts to documents to the occasional customer who ships the odd one or two documents a year. Exhibits 1 and 2 show some of DHL's logistics operations. To be able to effectively manage such a diverse customer base, DHL implemented a sophisticated customer-segmentation-cum-loyalty-management system. The focus of this system is to assess the profitability from its customers, reduce customer churn, and increase DHL's share of shipments.

Exhibit 2: DHL logistics.

Exhibit 1: DHL logistics center warehouse facility in Hong Kong.

CUSTOMER SEGMENTATION

To achieve this, the first task was to divide its customers into actionable segments with distinct needs. DHL defined three main segments. First, "strategic customers" are extremely high-volume shippers with a full range of logistics solutions and express-shipment needs. This segment approximately includes DHL's top 250 customers worldwide, most of which are large multi-nationals. Second, the "relationship customers" segment consists of customers who use DHL to ship their products and documents regularly, but with a lower volume than the strategic customer segment. Moreover, its supply-chain needs are not as sophisticated. Finally, the "direct customers" segment ships infrequently with DHL. The customer segmentation can be represented in the form of the familiar customer pyramid in Exhibit 3.

These segments are further divided into sub-segments based on the kind of service required (Exhibit 4). The needs of direct customers and many of the relationship customers are often fully met by DHL's *basic products*. For relationship customers

Exhibit 3: The customer pyramid.

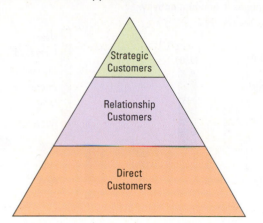

Exhibit 5: Segment Analysis.

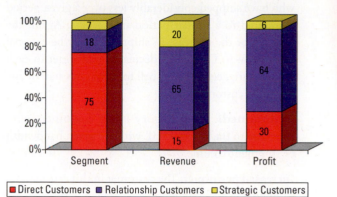

with special needs, DHL also offers some special programs such as direct distribution to its partners, test services, and parts distribution to fulfill these needs. Strategic customers almost always use customized solutions, such as providing bulk-breaking facilities and planned production support for precision delivery schedules. DHL also aims to meet their entire express delivery needs.

Customers using DHL's basic products find it easier to switch, because switching costs are low, and all its key competitors also offer similar products. The switching costs are significantly higher for customers with special programs and highest for clients using customized solutions.

Exhibit 5 shows some output of DHL's segmentation analysis for one of its country markets. The majority of revenue and profits were derived from only 18% of the customers, its relationship customers. The direct customer segment consisted of 75% of the total customer base and contributed only 15% of revenues and 30% of profits. The

Exhibit 4: Customer subsegmentation.

	Strategic Customers	Relationship Customers	Direct Customers
Basic Products	▨	▨	▨
Special Programs	▨	▨	
Customized Solutions	▨		

strategic customer segment contributed only 6% to profits. Similar patterns were observed for all countries where this analysis was conducted.

The verdict seems clear: Focus on the relationship customer segment for maximum profitability. However, this does not mean that DHL should neglect the other segments. Rather, it should deploy cutting-edge technology and best-practice infrastructure to maintain the loyalty of the strategic customer segment, because there is high future business potential for this group. Extra effort should also be put into upgrading the direct customers who have high volume potential and latent needs for special program products.

A LOYALTY MANAGEMENT SYSTEM: FURTHER CATEGORIZATION OF SEGMENTS

To focus on customer retention and development, it was necessary to get more information about DHL's customers. Each of these three segments was further classified into six categories, and the data was used to take corrective and proactive measures to enhance customer loyalty. These six categories were:

1. **Lost.** The customer in this category has stopped shipping with DHL. This could be for external reasons (such as a customer gone into liquidation) or internal reasons (such as service performance failure or an increase in prices). Once the reason has been identified, it is easier for DHL to control internal reasons and reduce customer churn. Sales and service staff can then focus on regaining potentially profitable accounts.

2. **Decreased performer.** This category refers to customers who have shipped considerably less over a given period compared to a similar period in the past. Again, the reasons for the decrease in shipments may be external or internal to DHL. The decreased performer in each segment triggers an alarm bell to warn sales staff of any potential customer churn.

3. **Maintained.** This category is for customers who continue to trade with DHL within a given bandwidth of shipment volume.

4. **Increased performer.** The customer in this category has shipped considerably more over a given period. Again, the reasons for increased performance may be external or internal. Sales staff follow up with the customer to identify the causes for increase in volumes and, in particular, to find out whether the increase in trading is a result of a DHL initiative. If so, the successful initiative is further improved to gain better results.

5. **New.** This category includes customers who have shipped for the first time with DHL. Special efforts are made by the sales staff to make them permanent customers.

6. **Regained.** This customer was previously "lost" but has recommenced shipping with DHL recently. The reasons for this renewed activity may be external, (e.g., renewed business activity of a lapsed customer) or internal (e.g., the shipment was made as a result of reactive measures by DHL to regain the customer).

The data collected is graphically represented for each segment (as given in Exhibit 6) and reported to sales, marketing, and customer service departments and senior management. This makes it easy to understand the impact of the change in

Exhibit 6: Segment analysis.

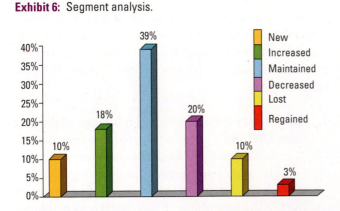

Exhibit 7: Relationship customers—estimated revenue—impact of changes in account activity.

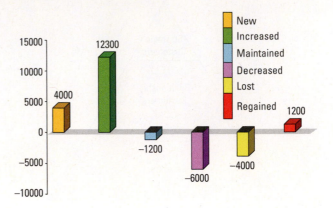

customer base. An increased percentage of decreased performers immediately prompts DHL's sales and customer service staff to take corrective action.

By classifying each customer and collecting data, the sales force is forewarned about potential customer defections. This means that DHL can take corrective action and identify any shortcomings in service performance as well as customer dissatisfaction, leading to more proactive measures in the future. The data also makes it possible to calculate (1) the defection rate of customers for each tier of the customer pyramid and (2) the life-time value of each segment. The change in life-time value of all customers gives the management an idea of the revenue and profit implications of its marketing and service initiatives.

The expected increase or decrease in revenue for the month is also calculated and represented graphically (as shown in Exhibit 7), illustrating the impact of the change in the customer segment portfolio on DHL's revenues.

Similarly, sales staff can study the reasons for up-trading for each customer and tap the remaining potential for further up-trading. This program also helps DHL to send targeted communication to the customers based on market segments instead of general communication to all customers, thereby making communication cost-effective.

A short period after implementation, this initiative had already been yielding impressive results, and further modules were being developed and pilot-tested for potential roll-out (Exhibit 8).

Exhibit 8: DHL delivery man.

STUDY QUESTIONS

1. What are the main challenges in implementing this segmentation in DHL's customer database?

2. How would you recommend DHL to address those challenges?

3. What are the various possible practical applications of this segmentation methodology in other functional departments (e.g. sales, customer service, etc.)?

Starbucks: Delivering Customer Service

Youngme Moon and John Quelch

Starbucks, the dominant specialty-coffee brand in North America, must respond to recent market research indicating that the company is not meeting customer expectations in terms of service. To increase customer satisfaction, the company is debating a plan that would increase the amount of labor in its stores and theoretically increase the speed of service. However, the impact of the plan (which would cost $40 million annually) on the company's bottom line is unclear.

In mid-2002, Christine Day, Starbucks' Senior Vice President of Administration in North America, sat in the seventh-floor conference room of Starbucks' Seattle headquarters and reached for her second cup of *toffee nut latte*. The hand-crafted beverage—a buttery, toffee-nut-flavored espresso concoction topped with whipped cream and toffee sprinkles—had become a regular afternoon indulgence for Day ever since its introduction earlier that year.

As she waited for her colleagues to join her, Day reflected on the company's recent performance. While other retailers were still reeling from the post-9/11 recession, Starbucks was enjoying its 11th consecutive year of 5%, or higher, comparable store-sales growth, prompting its founder and chairman, Howard Schultz, to declare, "I think we've demonstrated that we are close to a recession-proof product."[1]

Day, however, was not feeling nearly as sanguine, in part because Starbucks' most recent market research had revealed some unexpected findings. "We've always taken great pride in our retail service," said Day, "but according to the data, we're not always meeting our customers' expectations in the area of customer satisfaction."

As a result of these concerns, Day and her associates had come up with a plan to invest an additional $40 million annually in the company's 4,500 stores, which would allow each store to add the equivalent of 20 hours of labor per week. "The idea is to improve speed of service and thereby increase customer satisfaction," said Day.

In two days, Day was due to make a final recommendation to both Schultz and Orin Smith, Starbucks' CEO, about whether the company should move forward with the plan. "The investment is the EPS [earnings per share] equivalent of almost seven cents a share," said Day. In preparation for her meeting with Schultz and Smith, Day had asked one of her associates to help her think through the implications of the plan. Day noted, "The real question is, do we believe what our customers are telling us about what constitutes 'excellent' customer service? And if we deliver it, what will the impact be on our sales and profitability?"

COMPANY BACKGROUND

The story of how Howard Schultz managed to transform a commodity into an upscale cultural phenomenon had become the stuff of legends. In 1971, three coffee fanatics—Gerald Baldwin, Gordon Bowker, and Ziev Siegl—opened a small coffee shop in Seattle's Pike Place Market. The shop specialized in selling whole arabica beans to a niche market of coffee purists.

In 1982, Schultz joined the Starbucks marketing team. Shortly thereafter, he traveled to Italy, where he became fascinated with Milan's coffee culture; in particular, the role the neighborhood espresso bars played in Italians' everyday social lives. Upon his return, the inspired Schultz convinced the company to set up an espresso bar in the corner of its only downtown Seattle shop. As Schultz explained, the bar became the prototype for his long-term vision:

The idea was to create a chain of coffeehouses that would become America's "third place." At the time, most Americans had two places in their lives—home and work. But I believed that people needed another place, a place where they could go to relax and enjoy others, or just be by themselves. I envisioned a place that would be separate from home or work, a place that would mean different things to different people.

Schultz got his chance a few years later when Starbucks' founders agreed to sell him the company. As soon as Schultz took over, he began opening new stores. The stores sold whole beans and premium-priced coffee beverages by the cup and catered primarily to affluent, well-educated, white-collar patrons (skewed female) between the ages of 25 and 44. By 1992, the company had 140 such stores in the Northwest and Chicago and was successfully competing against other small-scale coffee chains such as Gloria Jean's Coffee Bean and Barnie's Coffee & Tea.

That same year, Schultz decided to take the company public. As he recalled, many Wall Street types were dubious about the idea: "They'd say, 'You mean, you're going to sell coffee for a dollar in a paper cup, with Italian names that no one in America can say? At a time in America when no one's drinking coffee? And I can get coffee at the local coffee shop or doughnut shop for 50 cents? Are you kidding me?'"[2]

Ignoring the skeptics, Schultz forged ahead with the public offering, raising $25 million in the process. The proceeds allowed Starbucks to open more stores across the nation.

By mid-2002, Schultz had unequivocally established Starbucks as the dominant specialty-coffee brand in North America. Sales had climbed at a compound annual growth rate (CAGR) of 40% since the company went public, and net earnings had risen at a CAGR of 50%. The company was now serving 20 million unique customers in well over 5,000 stores around the globe and was opening an average of three new stores a day. (See Exhibits 1–3 for company financials and store growth over time.)

What made Starbucks' success even more impressive was that the company had spent almost nothing on advertising to achieve it. North American marketing consisted primarily of point-of-sale materials and local-store marketing and was far less than the industry average. (Most fast-food chains had marketing budgets in the 3–6% range.)

For his part, Schultz remained the Chairman and Chief Global Strategist of the company. However, in 2002, he handed over day-to-day operations to CEO Orin Smith, a Harvard MBA (1967) who had joined the company in 1990.

THE STARBUCKS VALUE PROPOSITION

Starbucks' brand strategy was best captured by its "live coffee" mantra, a phrase that reflected the importance the company attached to keeping the national coffee culture alive. From a retail perspective, this meant creating an "experience" around the consumption of coffee, an experience that people could weave into the fabric of their everyday lives.

There were three components to this experiential branding strategy. The first component was the coffee itself. Starbucks prided itself on offering what it believed to be the highest-quality coffee in the world, sourced from Africa, Central and South America, and the Asia-Pacific region. To enforce its exacting coffee standards, Starbucks controlled as much of the supply chain as possible. It worked directly with growers in various countries of origin to purchase green coffee beans. It oversaw the custom-roasting process for the company's various blends and single-origin coffees. It controlled distribution to retail stores around the world.

The second brand component was service, or what the company sometimes referred to as "customer intimacy." "Our goal is to create an uplifting experience every time you walk through our door," explained Jim Alling, Starbucks' Senior Vice President of North American retail. "Our most loyal customers visit us as often as 18 times a month, so it could be something as simple as recognizing you and knowing your drink or customizing your drink just the way you like it."

The third brand component was atmosphere. "People come for the coffee," explained Day, "but the ambience is what makes them want to stay." For that reason, most Starbucks outlets had seating areas to encourage lounging and layouts that were designed to provide an upscale yet inviting environment for those who wanted to linger. "What we have built has [a] universal appeal," remarked Schultz. "It's based on the human spirit, it's based on a sense of community, the need for people to come together."[3]

Exhibit 1: Starbucks' financials, FY 1998 to FY 2002 (in million $).

	FY 1998	FY 1999	FY 2000	FY 2001	FY 2002
Revenue					
Co-owned North American	1,076.8	1,375.0	1,734.9	2,086.4	2,583.8
Co-owned Int'l (UK, Thailand, Australia)	25.8	48.4	88.7	143.2	209.1
Total company-operated retail	1,102.6	1,423.4	1,823.6	2,229.6	2,792.9
Specialty operations	206.1	263.4	354.0	419.4	496.0
Net revenues	**1,308.7**	**1,686.8**	**2,177.6**	**2,649.0**	**3,288.9**
Cost of goods sold	578.5	747.6	961.9	1,112.8	1,350.0
Gross profit	**730.2**	**939.2**	**1,215.7**	**1,536.2**	**1,938.9**
Joint-venture income[a]	1.0	3.2	20.3	28.6	35.8
Expenses:					
Store operating expense	418.5	543.6	704.9	875.5	1,121.1
Other operating expense	44.5	54.6	78.4	93.3	127.2
Depreciation and amortization expense	72.5	97.8	130.2	163.5	205.6
General and admin expense	77.6	89.7	110.2	151.4	202.1
Operating expenses	**613.1**	**785.7**	**1,023.8**	**1,283.7**	**1,656.0**
Operating profit	**109.2**	**156.7**	**212.3**	**281.1**	**310.0**
Net income	**68.4**	**101.7**	**94.5**	**181.2**	**215.1**
% Change in monthly comparable store sales[b]					
North America	5%	6%	9%	5%	7%
Consolidated	5%	6%	9%	5%	6%

Source: Adapted from company reports and Lehman Brothers, 5 November 2002.

a   Includes income from various joint ventures, including Starbucks' partnership with the Pepsi-Cola Company to develop and distribute Frappuccino and with Dreyer 's Grand Ice Cream to develop and distribute premium ice creams.

b   Includes only company-operated stores open 13 months or longer.

Exhibit 2: Starbucks' store growth.

	FY 1998	FY 1999	FY 2000	FY 2001	FY 2002
Total North America	**1,755**	**2,217**	**2,976**	**3,780**	**4,574**
Company-operated	1,622	2,038	2,446	2,971	3,496
Licensed stores[a]	133	179	530	809	1,078
Total international	**131**	**281**	**525**	**929**	**1,312**
Company-operated	66	97	173	295	384
Licensed stores	65	184	352	634	928
Total stores	**1,886**	**2,498**	**3,501**	**4,709**	**5,886**

Source: Company reports.

a   Includes kiosks located in grocery stores, book stores, hotels, airports, and so on.

Exhibit 3: Additional data for North American company-operated stores (FY2002).

	Average
Average hourly rate with shift supervisors and hourly partners	$9.00
Total labor hours per week, average store	360
Average weekly store volume	$15,400.00
Average ticket	$3.85
Average daily customer count, per store	570

Source: Company reports.

Channels of Distribution

Almost all of Starbucks' outlets in North America were company-operated stores located in high-traffic, high-visibility settings, such as retail centers, office buildings, and university campuses.[4] In addition to selling whole-bean coffees, these stores sold rich-brewed coffees, Italian-style espresso drinks, cold-blended beverages, and premium teas. Product mixes tended to vary depending on a store's size and location, but most stores offered a variety of pastries, sodas, and juices, along with coffee-related accessories and equipment, music CDs, games, and seasonal novelty items.

(About 500 stores even carried a selection of sandwiches and salads.)

Beverages accounted for the largest percentage of sales in these stores (77%); this represented a change from 10 years earlier, when about half of store revenues had come from sales of whole-bean coffees. (See Exhibit 4 for retail sales mix by product type; see Exhibit 5 for a typical menu board and price list.)

Starbucks also sold coffee products through non-company-operated retail channels; these so-called "specialty operations" accounted for 15% of net revenues. About 27% of these revenues came from North American food-service accounts, that is, sales of whole-bean and ground coffees to hotels, airlines, restaurants, and the like. Another 18% came from domestic retail store licenses that, in North America, were only granted when there was no other way to achieve access to desirable retail space (e.g., in airports).

The remaining 55% of specialty revenues came from a variety of sources, including international licensed stores, grocery stores and warehouse clubs (Kraft Foods handled marketing and distribution for Starbucks in this channel), and online and mail-order sales. Starbucks also had a joint venture with Pepsi-Cola to distribute bottled Frappuccino beverages in North America and a partnership with Dreyer's Grand Ice Cream to develop and distribute a line of premium ice creams.

Exhibit 4: Product mix for North American company-operated stores (FY2002).

	Percent of Sales
Retail Product Mix	
Coffee beverages	77%
Food items	13%
Whole-bean coffees	6%
Equipment and accessories	4%

Source: Company reports.

Day explained the company's broad distribution strategy:

> Our philosophy is pretty straightforward—we want to reach customers where they work, travel, shop, and dine. In order to do this, we sometimes have to establish relationships with third parties that share our values and commitment to quality. This is a particularly effective way to reach newcomers with our brand. It's a lot less intimidating to buy Starbucks at a grocery store than it is to walk into one of our coffeehouses for the first time. In fact, about 40% of our new coffeehouse customers have already tried the Starbucks brand before they walk through our doors. Even something like ice cream has become an important trial vehicle for us.

Starbucks Partners

All Starbucks employees were called "partners." The company employed 60,000 partners worldwide, of whom about 50,000 were in North America. Most were hourly-wage employees (called *baristas*) who worked in Starbucks retail stores. Alling remarked, "From day one, Howard has made clear his belief that partner satisfaction leads to customer satisfaction. This belief is part of Howard's DNA, and because it's been pounded into each and every one of us, it's become part of our DNA, too."

The company had a generous policy of giving health insurance and stock options even to entry-level partners, most of whom were between the ages of 17 and 23. Partly as a result of this, Starbucks' partner satisfaction rate consistently hovered in the 80%–90% range, well above the industry norm.[5] The company had recently been ranked 47th in the *Fortune* magazine list of best places to work, and this was quite an accomplishment for a company with so many hourly-wage workers.

In addition, Starbucks had one of the lowest employee turnover rates in the industry—just 70%, compared with fast-food industry averages as high as 300%. The rate was even lower for managers. As Alling noted, the company was always looking for ways to bring turnover down further: "Whenever we have a problem store, we almost always find either an inexperienced store manager or inexperienced baristas. Manager stability is key. It not only decreases partner turnover but also enables the store to do a much better job of recognizing regular customers and providing personalized service. So our goal is to make the position a lifetime job."

To this end, the company encouraged promotion from within its own ranks. About 70% of the company's store managers were ex-baristas, and about 60% of its district managers were ex-store managers. In fact, upon being hired, all senior executives had to train and succeed as baristas before being allowed to assume their positions in corporate headquarters.

DELIVERING ON SERVICE

Partners who were hired to work in one of Starbucks' North American retail stores had to undergo two types of training. The first type focused on "hard skills," such as learning how to use the cash register and mix drinks. Most Starbucks beverages were hand-crafted, and to ensure product quality, there was a pre-specified process associated with each drink. Making an espresso beverage, for example, required seven specific steps.

The other type of training focused on "soft skills." Alling explained:

> In our training manual, we explicitly teach partners to connect with customers—to enthusiastically welcome them to the store, to establish eye contact, to smile, and to try to remember their names and orders if they're regulars. We also encourage partners to create conversations with customers using questions that require more than a yes or no answer. So for example, "I noticed you were looking

Exhibit 5: Typical menu board and price list for a North American company-owned store.

Espresso Traditions Classic Favorites	Tall	Grande	Venti
Toffee Nut Latte	2.95	3.50	3.80
Vanilla Latte	2.85	3.40	3.70
Caffe Latte	2.55	3.10	3.40
Cappuccino	2.55	3.10	3.40
Caramel Macchiato	2.80	3.40	3.65
White Chocolate Mocha	3.20	3.75	4.00
Caffe Mocha	2.75	3.30	3.55
Caffe Americano	1.75	2.05	2.40

Espresso	Solo	Doppio	
Espresso	1.45	1.75	

Extras			
Additional Espresso Shot	.55		
Add flavored syrup	.30		
Organic milk and soy available upon request			

Frappuccino Ice Blended Beverages	Tall	Grande	Venti
Coffee	2.65	3.15	3.65
Mocha	2.90	3.40	3.90
Caramel Frappuccino	3.15	3.65	4.15
Mocha Coconut (limited offering)	3.15	3.65	4.15

Crème Frappuccino Ice Blended Crème	Tall	Grande	Venti
Toffee Nut Crème	3.15	3.65	4.15
Vanilla Crème	2.65	3.15	3.65
Coconut Crème	3.15	3.65	4.15

Tazo Tea Frappuccino Ice Blended Teas	Tall	Grande	Venti
Tazo Citrus	2.90	3.40	3.90
Tazoberry	2.90	3.40	3.90
Tazo Chai Crème	3.15	3.65	4.15

Brewed Coffee	Tall	Grande	Venti
Coffee of the Day	1.40	1.60	1.70
Decaf of the Day	1.40	1.60	1.70

Cold Beverages	Tall	Grande	Venti
Iced Caffe Latte	2.55	3.10	3.50
Iced Caramel Macchiato	2.80	3.40	3.80
Iced Caffe Americano	1.75	2.05	3.40

Coffee Alternatives	Tall	Grande	Venti
Toffee Nut Crème	2.45	2.70	2.95
Vanilla Crème	2.20	2.45	2.70
Caramel Apple Cider	2.45	2.70	2.95
Hot Chocolate	2.20	2.45	2.70
Tazo Hot Tea	1.15	1.65	1.65
Tazo Chai	2.70	3.10	3.35

Whole Beans: Bold Our most intriguing and exotic coffees		1/2 lb	1 lb
Gold Coast Blend		5.70	10.95
French Roast		5.20	9.95
Sumatra		5.30	10.15
Decaf Sumatra		5.60	10.65
Ethiopia Sidame		5.20	9.95
Arabian Mocha Sanani		8.30	15.95
Kenya		5.30	10.15
Italian Roast		5.20	9.95
Sulawesi		6.10	11.65

Whole Beans: Smooth Richer, more flavorful coffees		1/2 lb	1 lb
Espresso Roast		5.20	9.95
Decaf Espresso Roast		5.60	10.65
Yukon Blend		5.20	9.95
Café Verona		5.20	9.95
Guatemala Antigua		5.30	10.15
Arabian Mocha Java		6.30	11.95
Decaf Mocha Java/SWP		6.50	12.45

Whole Beans: Mild The perfect introduction to Starbucks coffees		1/2 lb	1 lb
Breakfast Blend		5.20	9.95
Lightnote Blend		5.20	9.95
Decaf Lightnote Blend		5.60	10.65
Colombia Narino		5.50	10.45
House Blend		5.20	9.95
Decaf House Blend		5.60	10.65
Fair Trade Coffee		5.95	11.45

Source: Starbucks location: Harvard Square, Cambridge, Massachusetts, February 2003.

at the menu board—what types of beverages do you typically enjoy?" is a good question for a partner to ask.

Starbucks' "Just Say Yes" policy empowered partners to provide the best service possible, even if it required going beyond company rules. "This means that if a customer spills a drink and asks for a refill, we'll give it to him," said Day. "Or if a customer doesn't have cash and wants to pay with a check (which we aren't supposed to accept), then we'll give her a sample drink for free. The last thing we want to do is win the argument and lose the customer."

Most barista turnover occurred within the first 90 days of employment; a barista who lasted beyond that was highly likely to stay for three years or more. "Our training ends up being a self-selection process," Alling said. Indeed, the ability to balance hard and soft skills required a particular type of person, and Alling believed the challenges had only grown over time:

> Back in the days when we sold mostly beans, every customer who walked in the door was a coffee connoisseur, and it was easy for baristas to engage in chitchat while ringing up a bag. Those days are long gone. Today, almost every customer orders a hand-crafted beverage. If the line is stretching out the door and everyone's clamoring for their coffee fix, it's not that easy to strike up a conversation with a customer.

The complexity of the barista's job had also increased over time; making a *venti tazoberry and crème*, for instance, required 10 different steps. "It used to be that a barista could make every variation of drink we offered in half a day," Day observed. "Nowadays, given our product proliferation, it would take 16 days of eight-hour shifts. There are literally hundreds of combinations of drinks in our portfolio."

This job complexity was compounded by the fact that almost half of Starbucks' customers customized their drinks. According to Day, this created a tension between product quality and customer focus for Starbucks:

> On the one hand, we train baristas to make beverages to our pre-established quality standards—this means enforcing a consistent process that baristas can master. On the other hand, if a customer comes in and wants it their way—extra vanilla, for instance— what should we do? Our heaviest users are always the most demanding. Of course, every time we customize, we slow down the service for everyone

else. We also put a lot of strain on our baristas, who are already dealing with an extraordinary number of sophisticated drinks.

One obvious solution to the problem was to hire more baristas to share the work load. However, the company had been extremely reluctant to do this in recent years, particularly given the economic downturn. Labor was already the company's largest expense item in North America (see Exhibit 3), and Starbucks stores tended to be located in urban areas with high wage rates. Instead, the company had focused on increasing barista efficiency by removing all non-value-added tasks, simplifying the beverage production process, and tinkering with the facility design to eliminate bottlenecks.

In addition, the company had recently begun installing automated espresso machines in its North American cafés. The verismo machines decreased the number of steps required to make an espresso beverage, reduced waste, improved consistency, and generated an overwhelmingly positive customer and barista response.

Measuring Service Performance

Starbucks tracked service performance using a variety of metrics, including monthly status reports and self-reported checklists. The company's most prominent measurement tool was a mystery-shopper program called the "Customer Snapshot." Under this program, every store was visited by an anonymous mystery shopper three times a quarter. Upon completing the visit, the shopper would rate the store on four "Basic Service" criteria:

▶ *Service*—Did the register partner verbally greet the customer?

Did the barista and register partner make eye contact with the customer? Say "thank you"?

▶ *Cleanliness*—Was the store clean? The counters?

The tables?

The restrooms?

▶ *Product quality*—Was the order filled accurately? Was the temperature of the drink within range? Was the beverage properly presented?

▶ *Speed of service*—How long did the customer have to wait?

The company's goal was to serve a customer within three minutes, from back-of-the-line to drink-in-hand. This benchmark was based on market research which indicated that the three-minute standard was a key component in how current Starbucks customers defined "excellent service."

In addition to Basic Service, stores were also rated on "Legendary Service," which was defined as "behavior that created a memorable experience for a customer, that inspired a customer to return often and tell a friend." Legendary Service scores were based on secret-shopper observations of service attributes such as partners initiating conversations with customers, partners recognizing customers by name or drink order, and partners being responsive to service problems.

During 2002, the company's Customer Snapshot scores had increased across all stores (see Exhibit 6), leading Day to comment, "The Snapshot is not a perfect measurement tool, but we believe it does a good job of measuring trends over the course of a quarter. In order for a store to do well on the Snapshot, it needs to have sustainable processes in place that create a well-established pattern of doing things right so that it gets 'caught' doing things right."

COMPETITION

In the United States, Starbucks competed against a variety of small-scale specialty-coffee chains, most of which were regionally concentrated. Each tried to differentiate itself from Starbucks in a different way. For example, Minneapolis-based Caribou Coffee, which operated more than 200 stores in nine states, differentiated itself on store environment. Rather than offer an upscale, pseudo-European atmosphere, its strategy was to simulate the look and feel of an Alaskan lodge, with knotty-pine cabinetry, fireplaces, and soft seating. Another example was California-based Peet's Coffee & Tea, which operated about 70 stores in five states. More than 60% of Peet's revenues came from the sale of whole beans. Peet's strategy was to build a super-premium brand by offering the freshest coffee on the market. One of the ways it delivered on this promise was by "roasting to order," that is, by hand-roasting small batches of coffee at its California plant and making sure that all of its coffee was shipped within 24 hours of roasting.

Starbucks also competed against thousands of independent specialty-coffee shops. Some of these independent coffee shops offered a wide range of food and beverages, including beer, wine, and liquor; others offered satellite televisions or internet-connected computers. Still others differentiated themselves by delivering highly personalized service to an eclectic clientele.

Finally, Starbucks competed against donut and bagel chains such as Dunkin Donuts, which operated over 3,700 stores in 38 states. Dunkin Donuts attributed half of its sales to coffee and, in recent years, had begun offering flavored coffee and non-coffee alternatives such as Dunkaccino (a coffee and chocolate combination available with various toppings) and Vanilla Chai (a combination of tea, vanilla, honey, and spices).

CAFFEINATING THE WORLD

The company's overall objective was to establish Starbucks as the "most recognized and respected brand in the world."[6] This ambitious goal required an aggressive growth strategy. In 2002, the two biggest drivers of company growth were retail expansion and product innovation.

Retail Expansion

Starbucks already owned close to one-third of America's coffee bars, more than its next five biggest competitors combined. (By comparison, Diedrich Coffee, the second-largest player in the United States, operated fewer than 400 stores.) However, the company had plans to open 525 company-operated and 225 licensed North American stores in 2003, and Schultz believed that there was no reason North America could not eventually expand to at least 10,000 stores. As he put it, "These are still the early days of the company's growth."[7]

The company's optimistic growth plans were based on a number of considerations:

▶ First, coffee consumption was on the rise in the United States following years of decline. More than 109 million people (about half of the U.S. population) now drank coffee every day, and an additional 52 million drank it occasionally. The market's biggest growth appeared to be among drinkers of specialty coffee,[8] and it was estimated that about one-third of all U.S. coffee consumption took place outside of the home, in places such as offices, restaurants, and coffee shops. (See Exhibit 7.)

▶ Second, there were still eight states in the United States without a single company-operated Starbucks. In

Exhibit 6: Customer Snapshot scores (North American stores). Source: Company information.

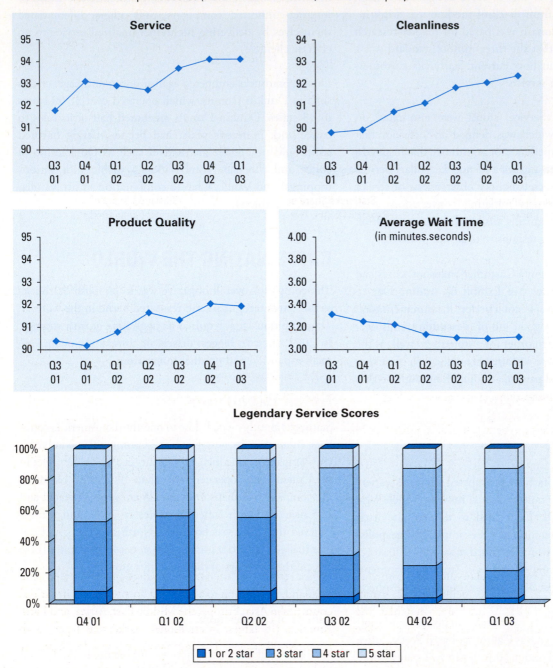

Legendary Service Scores

Legend: ■ 1 or 2 star ■ 3 star ■ 4 star □ 5 star

fact, the company was only in 150 of the roughly 300 metropolitan statistical areas in the nation.

▶ Third, the company believed it was far from reaching saturation levels in many existing markets. In the Southeast, for example, there was only one store for every 110,000 people (compared with one store for every 20,000 people in the Pacific Northwest). More generally, only seven states had more than 100 Starbucks locations.

Starbucks' strategy for expanding its retail business was to open stores in new markets while geographically clustering stores in existing markets. Although the latter often resulted in significant cannibalization, the company believed that this was more than offset by the total incremental sales associated with the increased store concentration. As Schultz readily conceded, "We self-cannibalize at least a third of our stores every day."[9]

Exhibit 7: Total U.S. retail coffee market (includes both in-home and out-of-home consumption).

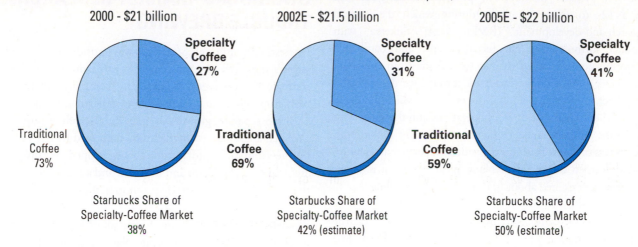

2000 - $21 billion

Specialty Coffee 27%

Traditional Coffee 73%

Starbucks Share of Specialty-Coffee Market 38%

2002E - $21.5 billion

Specialty Coffee 31%

Traditional Coffee 69%

Starbucks Share of Specialty-Coffee Market 42% (estimate)

2005E - $22 billion

Specialty Coffee 41%

Traditional Coffee 59%

Starbucks Share of Specialty-Coffee Market 50% (estimate)

Other estimates[a] for the U.S. retail coffee market in 2002:

- In the home, specialty coffee[b] was estimated to be a $3.2-billion business, of which Starbucks was estimated to have a 4% share.

- In the food-service channel, specialty coffee was estimated to be a $5-billion business, of which Starbucks was estimated to have a 5% share.

- In grocery stores, Starbucks was estimated to have a 7.3% share in the ground-coffee category and a 21.7% share in the whole-beans category.

- It was estimated that, over the next several years, the overall retail market would grow less than 1% per annum, but growth in the specialty-coffee category would be strong, with a compound annual growth rate (CAGR) of 9–10%.

- Starbucks' U.S. business was projected to grow at a CAGR of approximately 20% top-line revenue growth.

Source: Adapted from company reports and Lehman Brothers, 5 November 2002.

a   The value of the retail coffee market was difficult to estimate, given the highly fragmented and loosely monitored nature of the market (i.e., specialty coffee houses, restaurants, delis, kiosks, street carts, grocery and convenience stores, and vending machines).

b   Specialty coffee includes espresso, cappuccino, latte, café mocha, iced/ice-blended coffee, gourmet coffee (premium whole bean or ground), and blended coffee.

When it came to selecting new retail sites, the company considered a number of criteria, including the extent to which the demographics of the area matched the profile of the typical Starbucks drinker, the level of coffee consumption in the area, the nature and intensity of competition in the local market, and the availability of attractive real estate. Once a decision was made to move forward with a site, the company was capable of designing, permitting, constructing, and opening a new store within 16 weeks. A new store typically averaged about $610,000 in sales during its first year; same-store sales (comps) were strongest in the first three years and then continued to comp positively, consistent with the company average.

Starbucks' international expansion plans were equally ambitious. Starbucks already operated over 300 company-owned stores in the United Kingdom, Australia, and Thailand, in addition to about 900 licensed stores in various countries in Asia, Europe, the Middle East, Africa, and Latin America. (Its largest international market was Japan, with close to 400 stores.) The company's goal was to ultimately have 15,000 international stores.

Product Innovation

The second big driver of company growth was product innovation. Internally, this was considered one of the most significant factors in comparable store-sales growth, particularly since Starbucks' prices had remained relatively stable in recent years. New products were launched on a regular basis; for example, Starbucks introduced at least one new hot beverage every holiday season.

The new-product development process generally operated on a 12- to 18-month cycle, during which the internal research-and-development (R&D) team tinkered with product formulations, ran focus groups, and conducted in-store experiments and market tests. Aside from consumer acceptance, whether a product made it to market depended on a number of factors, including the extent to which the drink fit into the "ergonomic flow" of operations and the speed with which the beverage could be hand-crafted. Most importantly, the success of a new beverage depended on partner acceptance. "We've learned that no matter how great a drink it is, if our partners aren't excited about it, it won't sell," said Alling.

One of the company's most successful innovations was the 1995 introduction of a coffee and non-coffee-based line of Frappuccino beverages, which drove same-store sales primarily by boosting traffic during non-peak hours. The bottled version of the beverage (distributed by PepsiCo) became a $400-million[10] franchise; it managed to capture 90% of the ready-to-drink coffee category. This was due in large part to its appeal to non-coffee-drinking 20-somethings.

SERVICE INNOVATION

In terms of non-product innovation, Starbucks' stored-value card (SVC) was launched in November 2001. This pre-paid, swipeable smart card—which Schultz referred to as "the most significant product introduction since Frappuccino"[11]—could be used to pay for transactions in any company-operated store in North America. Early indications of the SVC's appeal were very positive. After less than one year on the market, about six million cards had been issued, and initial activations and reloads had already reached $160 million in sales. In surveys, the company learned that card holders tended to visit Starbucks twice as often as cash customers did and tended to experience reduced transaction times.

Day remarked, "We've found that a lot of the cards are being given away as gifts, and many of those gift recipients are being introduced to our brand for the first time. Not to mention the fact that the cards allow us to collect all kinds of customer-transaction data, data that we haven't even begun to do anything with yet."

The company's latest service innovation was its T-Mobile HotSpot wireless internet service, which it planned to introduce in August 2002. The service would offer high-speed access to the internet in 2,000 Starbucks stores in the United States and Europe, starting at $49.99 a month.

STARBUCKS' MARKET RESEARCH: TROUBLE BREWING?

Interestingly, although Starbucks was considered one of the world's most effective marketing organizations, it lacked a strategic marketing group. In fact, the company had no chief marketing officer, and its marketing department functioned as three separate groups—a market research group that gathered and analyzed market data requested by the various business units, a category group that developed new products and managed the menu and margins, and a marketing group that developed the quarterly promotional plans.

This organizational structure forced all of Starbucks' senior executives to assume marketing-related responsibilities. As Day pointed out, "Marketing is everywhere at Starbucks—it just doesn't necessarily show up in a line item called 'marketing.' Everyone has to get involved in a collaborative marketing effort." However, the organizational structure also meant that market- and customer-related trends could sometimes be overlooked. "We tend to be great at measuring things, at collecting market data," Day noted, "but we are not very disciplined when it comes to using this data to drive decision making." She continued:

> This is exactly what started to happen a few years ago. We had evidence coming in from market research that contradicted some of the fundamental assumptions we had about our brand and our customers. The problem was that this evidence was all over the place—no one was really looking at the "big picture." As a result, it took a while before we started to take notice.

Starbucks' Brand Meaning

Once the team did take notice, it discovered several things. First, despite Starbucks' overwhelming presence and convenience, there was very little image or product differentiation between Starbucks and the smaller coffee chains (other than Starbucks' ubiquity) in the minds of specialty-coffee-house customers. There *was* significant differentiation, however, between Starbucks and the independent specialty coffee houses (see Table A).

More generally, the market research team discovered that Starbucks' brand image had some rough edges. The number of respondents who strongly agreed with the statement "Starbucks cares primarily about making money" was up from 53% in 2000 to 61% in 2001, while the number of respondents who strongly agreed with the statement "Starbucks cares primarily about building more stores" was up from 48% to 55%. Day noted, "It's become apparent that we need to ask ourselves, 'Are we focusing on the right things? Are we clearly communicating our value and values to our customers, instead of just our growth plans?'" (see Table B)

The Changing Customer

The market research team also discovered that Starbucks' customer base was evolving. Starbucks' newer customers tended to be younger, less well-educated, and in a lower income bracket than Starbucks' more established customers. In addition, they visited the stores less frequently and had very different perceptions of the Starbucks brand compared to more established customers (see Exhibit 8).

Furthermore, the team learned that Starbucks' historical customer profile—the affluent, well-educated, white-collar female between the ages of 24 and 44—had expanded. For example, about half of the stores in southern California had large numbers of Hispanic customers. In Florida, the company had stores that catered primarily to Cuban-Americans.

Customer Behavior

With respect to customer behavior, the market research team discovered that, regardless of the market—urban

Table A: Qualitative brand meaning: Independents vs Starbucks

Independents:

- Social and inclusive
- Diverse and intellectual
- Artsy and funky
- Liberal and free-spirited
- Lingering encouraged
- Particularly appealing to younger coffee-house customers
- Somewhat intimidating to older, more mainstream coffee-house customers

Starbucks:

- Everywhere—the trend
- Good coffee on the run
- Place to meet and move on
- Convenience oriented; on the way to work
- Accessible and consistent

Source: Starbucks, based on qualitative interviews with specialty-coffee-house customers.

versus rural, new versus established—customers tended to use the stores in the same way. The team also learned that although the company's most frequent customers averaged 18 visits a month, the typical customer visited just five times a month (see Figure A).

Measuring and Driving Customer Satisfaction

Finally, the team discovered that, despite its high Customer Snapshot scores, Starbucks was not meeting

Table B: The top five attributes consumers associate with the Starbucks brand.

- Known for specialty/gourmet coffee (54% strongly agree)
- Widely available (43% strongly agree)
- Corporate (42% strongly agree)
- Trendy (41% strongly agree)
- Always feel welcome at Starbucks (39% strongly agree)

Source: Starbucks, based on 2002 survey.

expectations in terms of customer satisfaction. The satisfaction scores were considered critical because the team also had evidence of a direct link between satisfaction level and customer loyalty (see Exhibit 9 for customer satisfaction data).

While customer satisfaction was driven by a number of different factors (see Exhibit 10), Day believed that the customer satisfaction gap could primarily be attributed to a *service gap* between Starbucks scores on key attributes and customer expectations. When Starbucks had polled its customers to determine what it could do to make them feel more like valued customers, "improvements to service"—in particular, speed of service—had been mentioned most frequently (see Exhibit 11 for more information).

REDISCOVERING THE STARBUCKS CUSTOMER

Responding to the market research findings posed a difficult management challenge. The most controversial proposal was the one on the table before Day—it involved relaxing the labor-hour controls in the stores to add 20 hours of labor per week per store, at a cost of an extra $40 million

% OF STARBUCKS' CUSTOMERS WHO FIRST STARTED VISITING STARBUCKS . . .	
in the past year	27
1–2 years ago	20
2–5 years ago	30
5 or more years ago	23

Source: Starbucks, 2002. Based on a sample of Starbucks' 2002 customer base.

	New Customers (First Visited in the Past Year)	Established Customers (First Visited 5+ Years Ago)
Percent female	45	49%
Average age	36	40
Percent with college degree +	37	63
Average income	$65,000	$81,000
Average # cups of coffee/ week (includes at home and away from home)	15	19
Attitudes toward Starbucks:		
High-quality brand	34%	51%
Brand I trust	30%	50%
For someone like me	15%	40%
Worth paying more for	8%	32%
Known for specialty coffee	44%	60%
Known as the coffee expert	31%	45%
Best-tasting coffee	20%	31%
Highest-quality coffee	26%	41%
Overall opinion of Starbucks	**25%**	**44%**

Source: Starbucks, 2002. "Attitudes toward Starbucks" measured according to the percent of customers who agreed with the above statements.

per year. Not surprisingly, the plan was being met with significant internal resistance. "Our CFO is understandably concerned about the potential impact on our bottom line," said Day. "Each $6 million in profit contribution translates into a penny a share. But my argument is that if we move away from seeing labor as an expense to seeing it as a customer-oriented investment, we'll see a positive return." She continued:

> We need to bring service time down to the three-minute level in all of our stores, regardless of the time of day. If we do this, we'll not only increase customer satisfaction and build stronger long-term relationships with our customers, we'll also improve our customer throughput. The goal is to move each store closer to the $20,000 level in terms of weekly sales, and I think that this plan will help us get there.

In two days, Day was scheduled to make a final recommendation to Howard Schultz and Orin Smith about whether the company should roll out the $40 million plan in October 2002. In preparation for this meeting, Day had asked Alling to help her think through the implications of the plan one final time. She mused:

> We've been operating with the assumption that we do customer service well. But the reality is, we've started to lose sight of the consumer. It's amazing that this could happen to a company like us—after all, we've become one of the most prominent consumer brands

Exhibit 9: Starbucks' customer behavior, by satisfaction level.

	Unsatisfied Customer	Satisfied Customer	Highly Satisfied Customer
Number of Starbucks Visits/Month	3.9	4.3	7.2
Average Ticket Size/Visit	$3.88	$4.06	$4.42
Average Customer Life (Years)	1.1	4.4	8.3

Source: Self-reported customer activity from Starbucks survey, 2002.

Figure A: *Customer visit.*

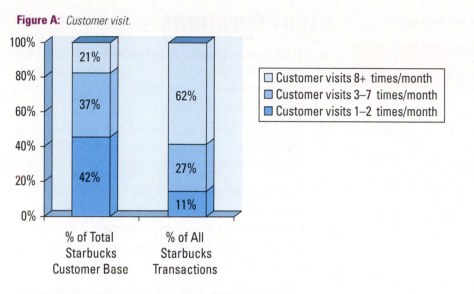

Legend:
- ☐ Customer visits 8+ times/month
- ☐ Customer visits 3–7 times/month
- ☐ Customer visits 1–2 times/month

% of Total Starbucks Customer Base: 21%, 37%, 42%

% of All Starbucks Transactions: 62%, 27%, 11%

Exhibit 10: Importance rankings of key attributes in creating customer satisfaction

To be read: 83% of Starbucks' customers rate a clean store as being highly important (90+ on a 100-point scale) in creating customer satisfaction.

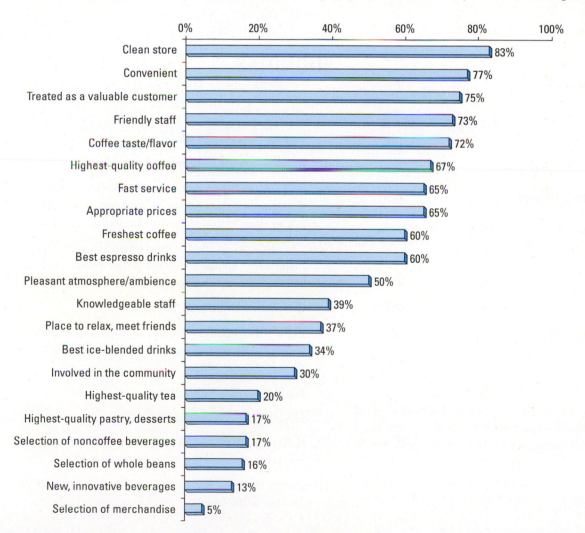

Attribute	Percentage
Clean store	83%
Convenient	77%
Treated as a valuable customer	75%
Friendly staff	73%
Coffee taste/flavor	72%
Highest-quality coffee	67%
Fast service	65%
Appropriate prices	65%
Freshest coffee	60%
Best espresso drinks	60%
Pleasant atmosphere/ambience	50%
Knowledgeable staff	39%
Place to relax, meet friends	37%
Best ice-blended drinks	34%
Involved in the community	30%
Highest-quality tea	20%
Highest-quality pastry, desserts	17%
Selection of noncoffee beverages	17%
Selection of whole beans	16%
New, innovative beverages	13%
Selection of merchandise	5%

Source: Self-reported customer activity from Starbucks survey, 2002.

Exhibit 11: Factors driving "valued customer" perceptions.

How could Starbucks make you feel more like a valued customer?	% Responses
Improvements to Service (total)	**34%**
Friendlier, more attentive staff	19%
Faster, more efficient service	10%
Personal treatment (remember my name, remember my order)	4%
More knowledgeable staff	4%
Better service	2%
Offer Better Prices/Incentive Programs (total)	**31%**
Free cup after X number of visits	19%
Reduce prices	11%
Offer promotions, specials	3%
Other (total)	**21%**
Better quality/variety of products	9%
Improve atmosphere	8%
Community outreach/charity	2%
More stores/more convenient locations	2%
Don't Know/Already Satisfied	**28%**

Source: Starbucks, 2002. Based on a survey of Starbucks' 2002 customer base, including highly satisfied, satisfied, and unsatisfied customers.

in the world. For all of our focus on building the brand and introducing new products, we've simply stopped talking about the customer. We've lost the connection between satisfying our customers and growing the business.

Alling's response was simple: "We know that both Howard and Orin are totally committed to satisfying our retail customers. Our challenge is to tie customer satisfaction to the bottom line. What evidence do we have?"

STUDY QUESTIONS

1. What factors accounted for Starbucks' success in the early 1990s, and what was so compelling about its value proposition? What brand image did Starbucks develop during this period?

2. Why have Starbucks' customer satisfaction scores declined? Has the company's service declined, or is it simply measuring satisfaction the wrong way?

3. How has Starbucks changed since its early days?

4. Describe the ideal Starbucks customer from a profitability standpoint. What would it take to ensure that this customer is highly satisfied? How valuable to Starbucks is a highly satisfied customer?

5. Should Starbucks make the $40 million investment in labor in the stores? What's the goal of this investment? Is it possible for a mega-brand to deliver customer intimacy?

ENDNOTES

1. Jake Batsell, "A Grande Decade for Starbucks," *Seattle Times*, 26 June 2002.

2. Batsell, "Grande Decade."

3. Batsell, "Grande Decade."

4. Starbucks had recently begun experimenting with drive-throughs. Less than 10% of its stores had drive-throughs, but in these stores, the drive-throughs accounted for 50% of all business.

5. Industrywide, employee satisfaction rates tended to be in the 50%–60% range. Source: Starbucks, 2000.

6. Starbucks 2002 Annual Report.

7. Dina ElBoghdady, "Pouring It On: The Starbucks Strategy? Locations, Locations, Locations," *Washington Post*, 25 August 2002.

8. National Coffee Association.

9. ElBoghdady, "Pouring it on."

10. Refers to sales at retail. Actual revenue contribution was much lower due to the joint-venture structure.

11. Stanley Holmes, "Starbucks' Card Smarts," *BusinessWeek*, 18 March 2002.

LUX*: Staging a Service Revolution in a Resort Chain

Jochen Wirtz and Ron Kaufman

LUX* was a successful hospitality group operating in the Indian Ocean as well as other locations. In its previous incarnation, the company suffered from poor financial performance, poor service quality, and a weak brand. A change in the leadership of the company prompted a transformation that showed positive results within 12 months. This case study describes a service revolution that led to rapid improvements in service culture and guest experience, which in turn led to sustained financial improvements on a quarter-on-quarter basis.

INTRODUCTION

With its headquarters in Mauritius, the LUX* hospitality group operated a portfolio of eight resorts and a private island in the Indian Ocean (Exhibit 1). The brand promised guests a celebration of life through its new value proposition—luxury resort hospitality that is "Lighter.Brighter."

What is the "Lighter.Brighter" hospitality? Established luxury hotels had come to be associated with stiff-upper-lipped service and stuffy opulence. Lighter hospitality meant breaking away from these precedents to offer a more effervescent experience without compromising on the hotel's upscale sensibilities. At the same time, LUX* wanted to brighten up guest experiences. For example, the company significantly lowered the prices of items in the mini-bar to encourage guests to just take what they fancied and enjoy themselves. Such measures allowed LUX* to ensure that both guests and business would benefit from its operations.

Although LUX* was launched only four years ago, the group's resorts have been doing exceptionally well. Within a short span of time, LUX* has successfully transformed its service

culture. The group has seen 16 consecutive quarter-on-quarter improvements in its financial performance. The group's resorts also enjoy a higher occupancy rate than the industry average in the destinations where they operate (measured quarterly by the Market Penetration Index, which compares the hotel's occupancy against its competitive set). The group's financial performance is reflected in the multiple accolades it has won for service excellence. These include the "Indian Ocean Leading Hotel" award for LUX* Maldives from World Travel Awards, the "Best Resort Hotel Mauritius" award for LUX* Belle Mare from International Hospitality Awards, and the "Reunion Island's Leading Hotel" award for LUX* Ile de la Réunion from World Travel Awards.

THE DARK AGES

However, things were not always this rosy. Before LUX* was launched in 2011, the group was known as Naiade Resorts, and the company suffered from poor financial health. None of its hotels were on the list of top 10 hotels on TripAdvisor in their geographic competitive sets. To top it off, the Naiade brand lacked clarity. Its brand name was used for nine different properties ranging from three to five stars, creating an unclear positioning in the minds of consumers. The problems in its positioning became apparent when the global financial crisis struck in 2008–2009, causing a large drop in occupancy and room rates (Exhibit 2). The group's troubles culminated in 2011 with a criminal case involving the high-profile murder of an Irish hotel guest.

Having witnessed prolonged economic turmoil and a criminal case, the motivation and morale of hotel employees were unprecedentedly low. Financially, the impact of these troubles cumulated in a downward trajectory in the company's performance from 2008 to 2010 (Exhibit 3). The company reported a loss in 2010.

© 2018 by Jochen Wirtz and Ron Kaufman. Jochen Wirtz is Professor of Marketing at the National University of Singapore. Ron Kaufman is founder and chairman of UP! Your Service Pte Ltd.

The support and feedback of the management of LUX* is gratefully acknowledged, including Paul Jones, CEO; Julian Hagger, Chief Sales & Marketing Officer and Executive Director; Marie-Laure-Ah-You, Chief Strategy Officer; Nicolas Autrey, Chief Human Resources Officer; Nitesh Pandey, General Manager and Group Chief Innovation Officer; and Smita Modak, Group Training Manager. The authors also thank Arthur Lee, who provided excellent assistance with the data collection, analysis, and writing of this case study.

All dollar amounts referred to in the text are in U.S. dollars unless otherwise indicated. The exchange rate used for all currency conversions is MUR100 to US$2.845.

Exhibit 1: Some of the LUX* resorts in the Indian Ocean.

LUX* Belle Mare's Pool

LUX* Belle Mare's Beach

LUX* Belle Mare's Villa

LUX* Le Morne

LUX* Le Morne's Beach

Note: LUX* owns eight seaside resorts by the Indian Ocean. Each of them are fitted with an expansive infinity pool, stylish bars and ocean themed furnishings.

After hitting rock bottom, the company's management had to move fast, and Naiade Resorts achieved a turnaround within a very short span of time. By mid-2011, Naiade Resorts saw an improvement in its service, and this quickly translated into improved financial performance. Since then, the company has witnessed substantive and consistent service culture improvement and financial performance growth. How did the group manage this turnaround so quickly?

LUX* TRANSFORMATION

The very first step in Naiade's transformation can be traced back to the second half of 2010. In dire straits then, the board of directors of Naiade Resorts made changes to the company's leadership and appointed Paul Jones as CEO in October 2010.

Under Jones's leadership, many changes were introduced to the organization within the first 12 months of his appointment. They were aimed at rapidly improving the profitability of the business and creating a world-class brand that could eventually expand internationally. However, this marked a difficult transitional period for Naiade Resorts, which was in financial doldrums. Every month, the company struggled to pay salaries. Some employees even wondered if the changes would sink the company further.

Observing how dire the situation was, Jones commented, "The numbers pre-2010 were alarming and the company was sinking fast and would have been bankrupt had it not been for the capital injection from shareholders. In addition, the properties were in poor shape and staff morale was exceedingly low."

Together with his team, Jones focused transformation efforts on four main areas through an integrated and congruent strategy (Exhibit 4). First, he looked into the company's core strategy as well as the company values. Naiade Resorts' business model was shifted from one of owning hotels to one of managing them following an asset-light strategy. This new model would reduce the company's cash outlay, as owning hotels can be highly capital extensive. For example, buying a modest-sized resort in Mauritius is estimated to cost upwards of 15 million. The new business model would reduce the company's risk exposure and allow it to expand at a faster rate. This shift provided a critical impetus for the company to concentrate on improving its service delivery.

To decide how to go forward, Paul Jones flew in the general managers from its resorts and the group's senior management from all over the world. The managers and executives from various levels made important decisions on the company. These include the company's new Vision, Purpose, and Values

Exhibit 2: Revenue, occupancy rates, and REVPAR.

Revenue (USD m)

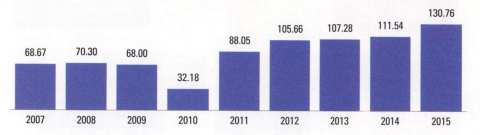

2007	2008	2009	2010	2011	2012	2013	2014	2015
68.67	70.30	68.00	32.18	88.05	105.66	107.28	111.54	130.76

Occupancy Rate (%)

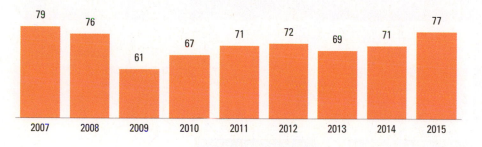

2007	2008	2009	2010	2011	2012	2013	2014	2015
79	76	61	67	71	72	69	71	77

RevPAR (USD)

2007	2008	2009	2010	2011	2012	2013	2014	2015
121	123	86	90	108	117	120	136	146

Exhibit 3: Financial performance of LUX*.

EBITDA (USD m)

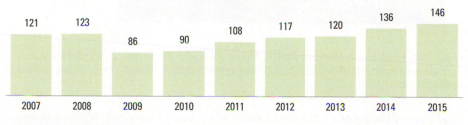

2007	2008	2009	2010	2011	2012	2013	2014	2015
21.26	14.20	10.55	2.73	18.92	18.98	22.02	25.10	29.56

Annual Profit (USD m)

2007	2008	2009	2010	2011	2012	2013	2014	2015
17.28	9.30	3.78	(0.68)	12.26	10.84	13.80	16.43	19.09

Note: Up till 2009, the financial year ended on 31 December. For 2010, all financial figures reported are for six months ending on 30 June 2010. From 2011 onwards, the financial year ended on 30 June.

Exhibit 4: LUX*'s four-pronged approach.

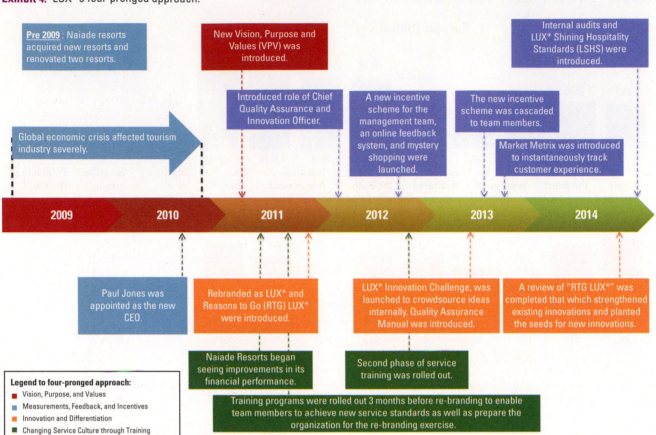

Pre 2009: Naiade resorts acquired new resorts and renovated two resorts.

New Vision, Purpose and Values (VPV) was introduced.

Internal audits and LUX* Shining Hospitality Standards (LSHS) were introduced.

Introduced role of Chief Quality Assurance and Innovation Officer.

A new incentive scheme for the management team, an online feedback system, and mystery shopping were launched.

The new incentive scheme was cascaded to team members.

Market Metrix was introduced to instantaneously track customer experience.

Global economic crisis affected tourism industry severely.

2009 2010 2011 2012 2013 2014

Paul Jones was appointed as the new CEO.

Rebranded as LUX* and Reasons to Go (RTG) LUX* were introduced.

LUX* Innovation Challenge, was launched to crowdsource ideas internally. Quality Assurance Manual was introduced.

A review of "RTG LUX*" was completed that which strengthened existing innovations and planted the seeds for new innovations.

Naiade Resorts began seeing improvements in its financial performance.

Second phase of service training was rolled out.

Training programs were rolled out 3 months before re-branding to enable team members to achieve new service standards as well as prepare the organization for the re-branding exercise.

Legend to four-pronged approach:
- Vision, Purpose, and Values
- Measurements, Feedback, and Incentives
- Innovation and Differentiation
- Changing Service Culture through Training

Note: LUX*'s service revolution can be encapsulated by a four-pronged approach. After a change of leadership, Jones and his team swiftly introduced important changes in multiple areas that proved to be critical in turning the company around. The company has since continued to build on this momentum to continually improve.

(VPV); a new name for the business; and the re-defining of service standards. Many of these changes were implemented almost immediately after being agreed upon. This allowed for a progressive roll-out of the company's new strategy.

Second, to engage and reinvigorate its staff in the transformation, the top management decided it had to build the company's service culture from scratch. This included extensive training across all levels of the organization, an alignment of expectations of service standards, and a psychological and tangible breakaway from the old Naiade Resorts.

Third, Jones leveraged a fledgling spirit of innovation to build an organization that is bold, open to ideas and experimentation, and willing to accept failure. This was aimed at enabling LUX* to differentiate its value proposition.

Lastly, as CEO, Jones also embedded various performance management tools to sustain transformation. These tools included

the measurement of service and the use of employee-incentive schemes to re-align a transformed organization.

In the review of this four-pronged approach, the first major change was the introduction of the new VPV.

VISION, PURPOSE, AND VALUES

Before any transformation could occur, Jones needed a guiding compass that would provide a foundation for the new Naiade Resorts. A professional credo would expound the company's aspirations and provide a fundamental rallying zeitgeist for the staff. The Vision, "We Make Each Moment Matter" and the Purpose, "Helping People Celebrate Life" were crafted, and the Values of "People, Passion, Integrity, Leadership, and Creativity" were selected. These tied in closely with how staff members were expected to behave and interact with guests.

Between February 2011 and August 2011, every team member of Naiade was called upon to participate in the VPV foundation

Exhibit 5: Actionable examples from employees on how they live by LUX*'s values.

People		Passion		Integrity		Leadership		Creativity	
Should Do	Should Not Do	Should Do	Should Not Do	Should Do	Should Not Do	Should Do	Should Not Do	Should Do	Should Not Do
Always thank guests when they are leaving.	Argue/ display a bad attitude/ be rude.	Go beyond expectations.	Allow laziness to take over.	Report any wrongdoing	Participate in any wrongdoing, no matter how insignificant.	Always take action.	Act irresponsibly.	Apply your own final touch.	Dismiss colleagues' ideas disrespectfully
Be available to replace a sick co-worker.	Challenge the guest.	Try to meet every guest request.	Act in a frustrated or angry manner.	Always say the truth regardless of circumstances	Not take responsibility for a mistake.	Be attentive and prompt to act.	Blame others when things go wrong.	Surprise guests.	Enter into a routine.
Always be polite, caring, and attentive.	Ignore colleagues because you are busy.	Care for the guest.	See problems instead of opportunities in situations.	Report every item found.	Be involved in dishonest acts.	Lead by example, be a role model and coach employees, colleagues, and team members.	Behave in an autocratic manner.	Go the extra mile by thinking out of the box, and try to be innovative.	Merely copy and replicate others' ideas.

Note: After the introduction of the new VPV, employees from each resort listed behaviors that they considered to epitomize LUX's values. A sampling of the examples provided is shown above, in no particular order of importance.

course. The course was rolled out over three phases. In the first phase, the CEO personally visited each hotel to share the new VPV with team members. Hand in hand with the CEO's visits, the general managers of the resorts organized engagement workshops involving all team members to ensure that everyone understood the VPV as the foundation of the group's operations. Finally, in the third phase, all staff members were asked to pledge to abide by the ideology.

To support this roll-out process, Naiade Resorts developed communication collaterals to support what the staff had heard from its leaders. For example, a visual mnemonic in the form of an open hand was created to represent the new values. In addition, the ideology of the group was translated into French, Creole, and Mandarin—the mother tongues of the majority of the employees. Beyond these initiatives, team members were encouraged to incorporate VPV into their lives outside of their work, such as making each moment matter for the staff's family and loved ones.

Even after its initial launch, VPV continued to be emphasized on a day-to-day basis. In many companies, missions and values are rarely looked at. However, at LUX*, they were lived out daily. Post-launch, team members from each resort

shared actionable examples of how they lived the values by listing down behaviors they should engage in as well as those they should avoid. These items were selected on the basis of observations regarding the behaviors that were needed to drive the new culture and those that had to be rejected (Exhibit 5). Another way in which this was operationalized was through the Quote of the Day. Every day, a quote linked to one of LUX*'s values was sent to team members to inspire them (Exhibit 6). This initiative was so well-received that when there were some operational hiccups during the initial roll-out, team members even asked why they did not receive the quote. This new VPV formed the foundation of the changes at LUX* that were to follow.

CHANGING THE SERVICE CULTURE THROUGH TRAINING

Guided by the VPV, a pervasive overhaul of Naiade Resorts' service culture was carried out in preparation for its re-branding. Extensive training was conducted across all levels of the company, and efforts were made to align all service-delivery expectations internally. A re-branding exercise also provided a much-needed psychological and tangible fresh start for the

Exhibit 6: An example of a Quote of the Day.

> **Our Value**
> Integrity
>
> **Quote**
> "Do the right thing. It will gratify some people and astonish the rest."
> –Mark Twain
>
> **Meaning**
> Do what's right always and you will never go wrong.
>
> **LUX* Shining Personality**
> Team Members have a thorough knowledge of the resort and local environment, and demonstrate pride and confidence by enthusiastically sharing this knowledge with others.

Note: A 'Quote of the Day' is sent to employees every day to remind them of LUX*'s values as well as to motivate and inspire them.

employees, and initiatives were introduced to sustain the transformation.

Comprehensive training permeated the company. Apart from the senior managers who met to deliberate on the desired service standards—benchmarking against different industries—LUX* partnered with an external service provider to design and deliver training on fundamental service principles. The first course delivered an actionable service education that enabled team members to deliver service valued by guests. As part of the course, employees were introduced to the building blocks of an uplifting service culture. By breaking down an abstract concept like culture into smaller and more tangible parts, it was easier for the organization to achieve its desired culture. Such a training helped LUX* to look beyond standard procedures in order to interact with guests and find out what they truly value. In doing so, LUX* was eventually able to deliver a unique experience to its guests.

Adarsh Grewal, HR and training manager at LUX* Le Morne, was one of the many employees who benefited from the training. He commented:

> When you break down everything you do daily and look at it from the eyes of your customer—internal or external; you begin to realize the value of every little step and the loopholes their absence might leave. Soon enough it becomes a habit to break down every service transaction and when it starts happening subconsciously, that is when we really start to "Make Each Moment Matter."

Nagassen Valadoo, villa manager of LUX* Belle Mare, shared his reflections on the training, echoing the change in culture at LUX*:

> As a team member who has gone through the course, I would say that it has been a very rich experience. I have learnt that "Taking Personal Responsibility" in everything that I undertake in my daily duties is of utmost importance. I have understood, we need to adapt our service according to each guest's needs in order to offer them an unbelievable experience of their stay. I have also learnt that the contribution of each of the team members in making "Each Moment Matter" for our guests is essential in making an experience memorable for them.

The training kicked off with an initiation workshop held for all 2,800 employees across the group. To roll out the training, more than 30 team members underwent a workshop to become certified course leaders. Hailing from diverse backgrounds, the trainers developed entirely in-house a customized version of the generic course materials from an external provider. This created the perception of the training as an internal LUX* product, improving receptivity from team members.

To make the materials more relatable for team members, the examples used were from best-practice organizations in the hospitality industry. For instance, case studies of companies such as Disney, The Ritz-Carlton, and Singapore Airlines were used to illustrate service excellence.

The way the training was structured also contributed to the success of re-building the company's service culture. The course was rolled out in two phases with a gap of four months between the end of the first phase and the beginning of the second (Exhibit 7). Such a course structure facilitated buy-in from staff members, as they were able to try out what they learnt in the first phase in their day-to-day work to see the value of the training. An example of this is the Perceptions Points analysis, which taught employees to focus on understanding guests' points of view and finding out what they value rather than be bound by internal procedures. This analytical tool was applied to what is now known as Reasons to Go (RTG) LUX*. For each reason, the importance of different touch points that contribute to overall guest experience was explained. The usefulness of such tools set the stage for a successful roll-out of the second phase of training.

A common service language is one of the building blocks of an uplifting service culture. During the training, employees

Exhibit 7: Training on service culture.

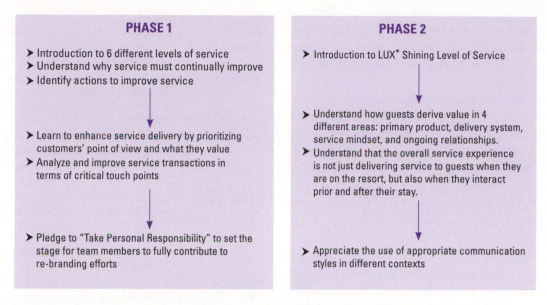

PHASE 1

➤ Introduction to 6 different levels of service
➤ Understand why service must continually improve
➤ Identify actions to improve service

↓

➤ Learn to enhance service delivery by prioritizing customers' point of view and what they value
➤ Analyze and improve service transactions in terms of critical touch points

↓

➤ Pledge to "Take Personal Responsibility" to set the stage for team members to fully contribute to re-branding efforts

PHASE 2

➤ Introduction to LUX* Shining Level of Service

↓

➤ Understand how guests derive value in 4 different areas: primary product, delivery system, service mindset, and ongoing relationships.
➤ Understand that the overall service experience is not just delivering service to guests when they are on the resort, but also when they interact prior and after their stay.

↓

➤ Appreciate the use of appropriate communication styles in different contexts

Note: To prepare the company for its new direction, employees underwent training in two different phases to learn more about building an uplifting service culture.

were introduced to a "Levels of Service" framework, which mapped out the different levels of service that LUX* can render. This provided employees with a common frame of reference when communicating with each other about service standards. For instance, when the general managers say, "Let's give that guest an unbelievable experience," team members understand exactly what they need to do. Notably, LUX* also added a 7th level of service entitled "LUX* SHINING is beyond unbelievable" to the original framework (Exhibit 8). In doing so, LUX* clearly communicated its vision for its

Exhibit 8: The 7 levels of service.

OUR COMMON SERVICE LANGUAGE
The 7 Levels of Service at LUX*

LUX* SHINING is beyond Unbelievable

UNBELIEVABLE is WOW

SURPRISING is something special

DESIRED is what guests prefer

EXPECTED is just average

BASIC is the bare minimum

CRIMINAL is below the bare minimum

Note: LUX* adapted the Levels of Service framework from its training partner, UP! Your Service College, and added a 7th superior Level of Service.

service levels to its employees. LUX* also helped its employees to connect VPV to the desired service standards, explaining why they needed to deliver on certain service standards based on their company beliefs. This took the form of a pledge that elegantly weaved VPV with service standards (Exhibit 9).

Three months after the launch of the course, Naiade Resorts was re-branded as LUX* Resorts and Hotels. On 3 December 2011, LUX* opened its doors to journalists and invited representatives of the finest magazines from around the world to stay in its resorts. A whole week of events was organized in Mauritius to celebrate the occasion. The launch of LUX* elicited a very positive response from its key partners and the media and helped to generate word of mouth.

Over time, the training became more comprehensive and covered five core areas (Exhibit 10). Service training continued to be delivered to new team members as well as veterans. New hires were introduced to the content of the course as part of LUX*'s orientation program. Almost 60%–65% of the orientation's content was dedicated to service delivery and the training of new team members to blend in seamlessly with experienced staff. For veterans, continual training on service culture helped to reinforce the learning. In follow-up sessions, participants talked about how they had put the core learning to practice. Together, these revamped and intensified training

Exhibit 10: LUX*'s areas of focus for training.

Area of Focus	Description
General training	Ensured that team members were equipped to deal with operations and guest issues.
Service culture	A large part of LUX*'s training efforts focused on building an uplifting service culture to deliver service that is truly world-class.
Technical	Focused on training needed for staff to perform their jobs efficiently in different departments. A large part of the technical training was done in-house.
Leadership	Specific leadership-development programs were targeted at different leadership levels in the company. Training was customized and delivered in partnership with training providers that had a strong focus on leadership.
Language	Language training was important to ensure that LUX* was able to customize their service experience to the changing market mix (especially the Chinese and Russian markets, which had seen fast growth in recent years).

and coaching programs helped to develop a strong learning culture and better-trained team members who contributed significantly to LUX*'s success.

INNOVATION AND DIFFERENTIATION

In order to deliver a truly "Lighter.Brighter" luxury-resort experience, LUX* had to cultivate a service DNA that embraced the invariable experimentation failures along the way. It also had to promote a culture that would continually innovate and differentiate itself from the competition. (See Exhibit 11 to understand how employees embraced creativity.)

During the development of LUX*, the management was bold and open to ideas. Paul Jones sought to instill in the LUX* DNA a spirit that is open to experimentation, continual innovation, and acceptance of failure. Many ideas were put to the test when the company re-branded and even after the launch of LUX*. The company saw the continual improvement of its service and performance as an imperative.

At the inception of LUX*, one idea that was experimented with was the use of the theatre as an analogy for the hotel. Team members of the hotel were thought of as actors who performed, while the general managers were the producers who directed the

Exhibit 9: Weaving VPV into levels of service.

As I believe in *'Consideration for People,'* I will always avoid **CRIMINAL** levels of service to my Guests and Colleagues.

As I believe in *'Serving with Passion,'* I cannot be satisfied with just giving **BASIC** level of service.

As I have pledged to *'Make Each Moment Matter'* for my Guests and Colleagues towards achieving our purpose of **'Helping People Celebrate Life,'** I must go beyond delivering only the **EXPECTED** level of service.

I expect myself and my colleagues always to be *Honest, Fair, Sincere and Authentic.* Together we will always *'Insist on Integrity.'*

Our belief *'Responsibility of Leadership'* will inspire me to **Lead by Example** in always delivering **DESIRED** level of service to my guests and colleagues.

My Curiosity and Imagination will drive my *'Creativity'* to deliver, when the opportunity arises, **SURPRISING** and **UNBELIEVABLE** levels of service to my guests and colleagues.

To uphold our promise and become a winning brand; I aim to deliver **LUX* SHINING** level of service to all our guests. I want to convince them that they have made a perfect choice for their vacation.

Exhibit 11: Employees exercise their own creativity in making guests feel special.

show. LUX* intended to use this analogy to motivate staff to give more of themselves to guests. However, they soon realized that it was difficult to bring this idea to fruition. The analogy was confusing to guests as well as team members.

On this matter, Sydney Pierre, Head of Worldwide Sales, said:

> The theatre analogy was a great concept and a game changer in terms of innovative operational approaches; however, the practicality of implementation was low and did not really make any difference to our tour operators.

Echoing Sydney's thoughts was Caroline Gaud, Marketing Communication Manager, who said:

> It was confusing for our partners and our guests; some of them expected to see a "show" playing at the resorts and were disappointed. The analogy was misunderstood and created too much confusion; therefore, we decided to get rid of it. Simplifying the brand concept was critical at this stage to raise awareness and attract guests.

The team coined the term RTG LUX*, which stands for "Reasons to Go LUX*" and refers to the unique selling points of LUX* resorts. It bore testament to LUX*'s innovative spirit and its willingness to try. When creating LUX*, the leadership team had initially set a bold target of creating 50 Reasons to Go LUX*. This ambitious goal was met with difficulty, as there were many other initiatives that were concurrently being rolled out.

One Reason to Go LUX* that was dropped was the Secret Bar, a pop-up bar. The bar was found in different parts of the resort at different times of the day and worked on an honor

system—guests poured their own drinks and recorded what they consumed. Conceptually, the idea was brilliant, but it was beset by operational challenges. For instance, spillage sometimes occurred when the guests were serving themselves, and this impacted the experience of subsequent guests. Although some properties were able to control the quality of the guest experience, it was difficult to achieve this across all properties. As a result, it had to be retired as a Reason to Go LUX*. Nonetheless, it continued to be offered as a service in some properties that managed to make it work.

Apart from quality, some of the Reasons to Go LUX* were withdrawn due to factors such as budget and logistics. Eventually, the list of Reasons to Go LUX* was organically narrowed down to 20. Some of these reasons became iconic and resonated very well with guests. One of the most documented Reasons to Go LUX* on social media and TripAdvisor was "Message in a Bottle."

XLuo, a TripAdvisor user, described his experience with Message in a Bottle as follows:

> We found a total of four secret bottles around the island that include free bottle of wine, free pizza for in-villa dining, and free cocktails. We woke up every day around 6:00 a.m. to jog around the island and spend time to find these bottles hidden all around the island, and it was really a fun way to start every day on the island.

Epitomizing LUX*'s emphasis on innovation was the decision to introduce the role of a Chief Quality Assurance and Innovation Officer. To stimulate innovation, the incumbent introduced the LUX* Innovation Challenge. Each year, a theme that revolves around business needs such as increasing the loyalty of guests and team members and improving revenue is set. Teams in each resort

Exhibit 12a: The impact of FIESTA; Exhibit 12b. The Global Index: Five dimensions of well-being at the work place.

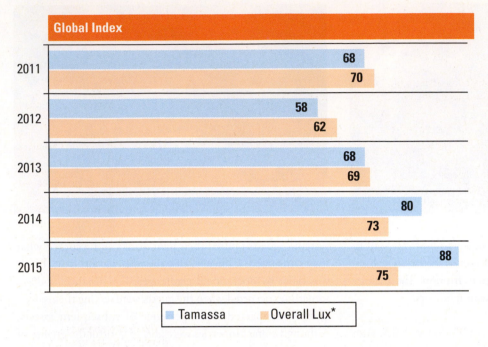

Global Index

Year	Tamassa	Overall Lux*
2011	68	70
2012	58	62
2013	68	69
2014	80	73
2015	88	75

■ Tamassa   ■ Overall Lux*

Note: FIESTA was introduced in Tamassa and its impact on the loyalty of team members is reflected in the trend in its Global Index in comparison to other LUX* resorts.

The Global Index is a weighted index of 5 Dimensions of well-being at the workplace that are measured by LUX* through its Team Member Satisfaction Survey. The higher the score of the index, the better the performance on these dimensions.

as well as the head office then propose ideas, which are rolled out upon approval. Toward the end of the year, the teams re-convene to present the results of their ideas to a jury. Subsequently, the winning idea is rolled out across all the resorts, along with other promising ideas that have come out of this challenge.

A particularly influential idea was FIESTA, which won the first place in the 2014 challenge on innovating to increase the loyalty of team members. FIESTA is a wide-ranging high-engagement program that allows employees to benefit from activities in the following areas: *F*itness, *I*nnovation, *E*tiquette and Morale Week, *S*pa, *T*hank you, and *A*ward.

For example, Etiquette and Morale Week, the main highlight of the program and also the world's first initiative of this type, brings together young children of team members for three days for a series of activities. Examples of these activities are tennis classes, mocktail classes, recycling of plastic products, and dedicating poem-writing to their parents to express gratitude. All in all, the event instills a sense of pride and respect in the children for the work their parents do. This ground-up initiative had a significant impact on team-member satisfaction (Exhibits 12a and 12b) and also went on to win the Best Initiative in Human Resources Award at the 15th Edition of the Worldwide Hospitality Awards.

LUX* was cognizant of the need to stay different and keep ahead of its competition. This spirit of constant innovation

is also exemplified by the decision to review its Reasons to Go LUX* three years after its launch. The review served to formally define what a Reason to Go LUX* is and critically evaluate the reasons by identifying what was done well, what was not so successful, and how further improvements could be made. The value of each reason was assessed using a 5D system (Exhibit 13) developed by LUX*.

After the review, the management decided to focus on 11 Reasons to Go LUX* (Exhibit 14). They appealed to different types of guests—families, couples, the young and young at

Exhibit 12b: The Global Index—5 Dimensions of well-being at the work placetraining.

Dimension	Description
Vital Dimension	Team-member morale (state of mind: tense, depressed, happy, etc.)
Existential Dimension	Personal and professional accomplishment (training, work load, and resources)
Social Dimension	Inter-relationships, sense of belonging and recognition
Material Dimension	Physical comfort at work, ergonomics, salary, benefits, fun and excitement
Organizational Dimension	Internal organization perception and degree of engagement with LUX* resorts' Vision, Purpose, and Values

Exhibit 13: The 5D System: Reasons to Go LUX*.

Evaluation Filter	Guiding Questions
1. Does it **DELIVER** the brand experientially on property?	Vision—Does it make a moment that matters? Purpose—Does it help people to celebrate life? Does it substantiate the promise of hospitality that is "Lighter.Brighter"?
2. Does it **DEMONSTRATE** our creative principles?	Does it banish thoughtless patterns? Is it simple, fresh, and sensory?
3. Does it **DRAMATIZE** the brand concept?	Does it celebrate "Locale Life," our nature and culture? Is it Light Luxury: light-weight and light-hearted?
4. Does it **DIFFERENTIATE** us from our competitors?	Is it quirky, charming, or cool? Is it generous, thoughtful, or surprising?
5. How well does it **DISSEMINATE** the word?	Is it PR-able? Is it sellable? Is it shareable?

Note: The 5D system was developed by LUX* to evaluate current and future Reasons to Go LUX*.

heart, as well as niche audiences. These Reasons to Go LUX* made guests feel different and special. While a single reason may not have encouraged guests to choose LUX*, the various reasons worked together to deliver an attractive proposition.

Another outcome of the review was an augmentation of the successful Reasons to Go LUX*. With Message in a Bottle (Exhibit 15), numerous improvements were made in various areas. Execution-wise, bottles were placed at different times to cater to guests with different sleep cycles.

To capture, develop, and disseminate new ideas, LUX* created the LUX* Ideas Bank, a depository where ideas could be placed, shared, discussed, measured, and tested. Ideas were contributed by team members and scored. Promising ideas were developed into prototypes and evaluated again. Those ideas that passed the rigorous testing process were finally screened by a senior operator task force that selected them for implementation. This process created an innovation pipeline, allowing the company to launch three new Reasons to Go LUX* every quarter and thereby drive continual innovation.

Exhibit 14: Eleven Reasons to Go LUX*.

Reasons to Go LUX*	Description
ICI	A holiday without ice cream isn't a holiday at all, so we created our own brand called "ICI." An array of exotic, island flavors are served from retro-styled parlors and mobile carts while a fresh waffle cone is baked right in front of your eyes. Crunch. Munch. Perfect after lunch.
Café LUX*	We believe that great coffee is a must and not a luxury; so at the heart of each resort, you'll find a Café LUX*. Enjoy our organic Island Blend, freshly roasted on-site, in a truly different café setting. Flat White or FrappeLux—they're perfect for a seaside sip and surf.
Phone Home	We believe that holidays should be stress and hassle-free, which is why if you explore our resorts you'll find a telephone box, and inside, a vintage VOIP phone. Here you can make local and international calls free of charge. We just ask one thing: Please do not call the office!
LUX* Me	LUX* Me is an integrated philosophy of wellbeing, offering a step-by-step path to an altogether healthier way of life. Naturally, in addition to al fresco classes, our personal trainers specialize in pilates, yoga, and meditation classes as well as tailoring programs to you and your requirements. Now stretch!
Scrucap	We love a good Burgundy or vintage Bordeaux, but the Indian Ocean's a long way from the vineyards of France, so we've tapped South Africa for its most exciting contemporary wines. Cape blends survive the short journey in mint condition. Introducing "Scrucap" and "Popcap." Not a corked wine in sight.

Reasons to Go LUX*	Description
Cinema Paradiso	A large screen, fastened between two palms, flickers into life and you're transported to another world—of blockbusters, family classics, and world cinema. It wouldn't be the movies without the nibbles, so there's fresh popcorn on the house, ICI ice cream, and drinks served right to your beanbag. Curtains Up!
Message in a Bottle	You spot a lonely bottle hidden in a bush beside a sandy path. Inside this mysterious vessel, you find a scroll of paper, which reveals a special treat waiting for one lucky guest. Stay alert, because it's only if you find the bottle that this daily surprise can be yours.
Thread Lightly	We can't always promise clear skies, but with your help, we can guarantee a clear conscience. LUX* cares about the destinations that are home to its properties. After all, memorable holidays shouldn't cost the earth, and that's why we are doing our best to "Thread Lightly" by offsetting 100% of the carbon emitted during your stay. It's one of a number of measures we're putting in place to help us leave a lighter footprint.

Reasons to Go LUX*	Description
Mamma Aroma	For as long as any of us can remember, amenities have been a staple in every hotel and resort bathroom around the world. Imagine hair lovingly nourished by deep conditioners; lazy baths scented with tropical oils; bodies gently burnished with a patina of sea salt scrub and sun-kissed skin glowing with the natural moisturizing properties of the island's products. LUX* Resorts & Hotels offers you, for your bath experience, something different: an element of surprise, a gasp of pleasure and a nod to simplicity are behind our selection. And being considerate to the environment, our products and their packaging are as light on the planet as they are on the body. We have also worked with renowned aroma therapist Shirley Page to create an exclusive range of essential oils using island ingredients—essences, flowers, and spices that combine to create a magical world of fragrance. Used in our LUX* Me spa, the oils are also present in interior and linen scents.

Exhibit 14b

Reasons to Go LUX*	Description
Tree of Wishes 	At every LUX* Resort & Hotel you'll find a specially commissioned Tree of Wishes sculpture made by local artisans. Upon check-in you'll be handed a unique ribbon featuring your initials and the date of your visit. Although not compulsory, you are invited to make a donation which will be made annually to a local children's charity. Tie the ribbon around one of the branches whilst making a wish. Whilst we can't guarantee your wish will come true, we can promise that once a year one lucky ribbon will be selected and the lucky person who placed it there will win a free holiday to LUX*.

Exhibit 15: Message in a bottle.

Note: LUX* staff places coupons for complimentary spa treatments, pedicure facial or massages in bottles around the beach. Some messages are written clues directing guests towards the Secret Bar, or offer an opportunity to enjoy a special dining experience for two on the beach. Guests who serendipitously stumble upon these bottles on the beach are in for a treat.

MEASUREMENT, FEEDBACK, AND INCENTIVES

In the transformation journey, measurement of service performance became a priority. Prior to Jones' tenure at LUX*, Naiade Resorts collected guest feedback using written forms, and a quality assurance coordinator was appointed in each resort. This system placed certain limitations on what the company could do with feedback. These included delays in terms of consolidating feedback, a lack of central coordination of quality assurance, low visibility among top management, and difficulty in measuring service performance within and between the different properties of the group.

While a basic customer feedback system was in place, service measurement and feedback had become much more sophisticated under Jones's leadership. Within a month of recruiting the Chief Quality Assurance and Innovation Officer, LUX* went online with its feedback form. Although LUX* could not afford to invest heavily in an online feedback system at that point in time, it saw a basic online platform as a step in the right direction. With an online platform, LUX* had visibility on how each resort was performing in terms of service quality, and it also motivated employees to provide better service.

Soon after, LUX* launched a quality-assurance manual based on standards of global best practices in hotel and hospitality management. It spelt out clear service targets in all areas of operations, right down to micro moments such as the amount of time that the restaurant should take to hand guests the restaurant menu. This was accompanied by a mystery-shopping audit to check that standards were met.

In terms of external measurements, the company paid close attention to customer feedback and ratings on TripAdvisor (Exhibit 16). For instance, qualitative feedback on TripAdvisor was monitored and personally responded to by the management. The feedback was also discussed with department heads within LUX* when it concerned their line of work. The ratings were even monitored and tracked as part of selected employees' key performance indicators (KPI).

Throughout the transformation, the impact of the changes introduced was seen in the improvements in their financial performance, such as the growth in their publicly reported quarterly revenue. This provided satisfaction for staff members in the form of indirect feedback for what they had accomplished. However, in 2012, LUX*'s management also realized that there were only a few incentive schemes in place. Sometimes, the incentives did not serve the purpose of getting team members to focus on the necessary areas. This prompted the management to review incentive plans to align the company in achieving its targets.

The new incentive schemes focused on three important things—guest experience; team-member engagement; and

Exhibit 16: LUX*'s Trip Advisor rankings within each resort.

TRIP ADVISOR RANKING

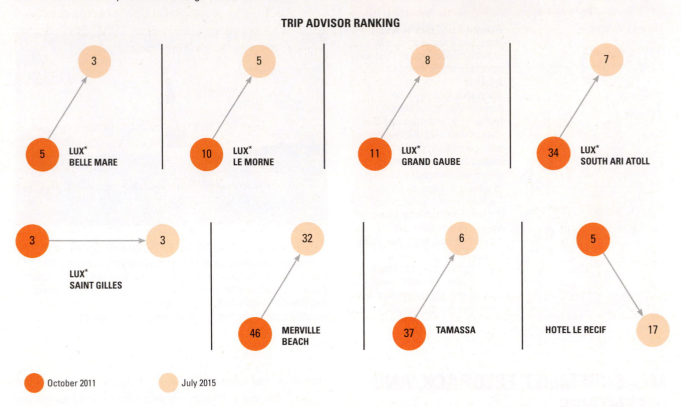

October 2011   July 2015

Note: This chart illustrates the change in ranking of LUX*s resorts, from 2011 to 2015. The resorts are segmented by country, with the relevant LUX* resort ranked against other resorts listed on TripAdvisor. Note that TripAdvisor's ranking methodology changed in 2015 for LUX* Saint Gilles and Hotel Le Recif, using a much wider geographic region for the ranking. This lead to many more resorts being included in the ranking and it explains the drop for Hotel Le Recif.

earnings before interest, taxes, depreciation, and amortization (EBITDA). This was first rolled out to the general managers of each resort in 2012. Subsequently, various schemes were developed for different groups of employees. A sample of the KPIs includes targeted EBITDA, targeted TripAdvisor scores, guest-satisfaction-related metrics, and a team-member-satisfaction index. In Mauritius, an incentive scheme was extended to all team members. Under this scheme, the performance of individual hotels was linked to rewards for 2,000 front-line employees in Mauritius. By 2015, team members were given targets for EBITDA, TripAdvisor ratings, as well as MarketMetrix scores (a measure of guest satisfaction). A bonus of 8% of the team member's basic monthly salary was paid when the KPIs were met. Paid out on a monthly basis, the bonus served as a tangible incentive to further motivate front-line staff to meet the company's goals.

While these tools served LUX* well, the group's ambitions have, in a few years, evolved from turning around the company to becoming a leading international player. This also meant that some of its management tools had to evolve.

One tool that evolved was the way LUX* measured customer satisfaction. In 2013, LUX*'s online system evolved from a fairly basic system to one that was much more sophisticated. By partnering with MarketMetrix, LUX* was able to track customer experience almost instantaneously on a daily basis. Aspects of customer experience that were tracked included check in and check out, room, food and beverage, and facilities and amenities. Customer feedback was also taken so seriously that the CEO received metrics on customer satisfaction on his smart phone on a daily basis. LUX*'s partnership with MarketMetrix allowed it to benchmark itself not only across its resorts but also with its key competitors. The strong focus on customer satisfaction helped the company to monitor and track its performance on a resort-by-resort basis and, within resorts, on a department-by-department level.

More recently, LUX* fine-tuned its internal quality standards and developed LUX* Shining Hospitality Standards (LSHS), which served as the brand's operational standards. In comparison to the LUX* Quality Assurance Manual, LSHS represented a shift from benchmarking against competitors to delivering service that was distinctively LUX*. For example, LSHS provided guidance to employees by grooming them and training them on how they should interact with guests. A company-wide standard, LSHS was adapted to each resort in the form of standard operating procedures. The company also changed the way it tracked these new standards. For instance, it began to use internal audits in place of mystery shopping.

FUTURE PLANS

Having successfully revolutionized its service through a four-pronged approach, LUX* was in a much better position to implement its asset-light strategy in 2015. It had already signed a number of long-term management agreements for upcoming hotels in the Maldives and China.

By the end of 2016, LUX* expects to have almost a third of its portfolio owned by third parties but managed by LUX*.

Finally, LUX* has entered into a franchise agreement to open Café LUX*, a Reason to Go LUX* concept, outside the hotel. With its strong service culture, LUX* aims to become a global company with a bigger footprint.

STUDY QUESTIONS

1. What were the main factors that contributed to LUX* Resorts' successful service revolution?

2. What key challenges did LUX* face while carrying out its transformation? How were they addressed, and what else could have been done?

3. What are the next steps that LUX* should take to cement its strong service culture, continue service innovation, and maintain its high profitability?

KidZania: Shaping a Strategic Service Vision for the Future

James L. Heskett, Javier Reynoso, and Karla Cabrera

Late in 2013, KidZania's management team, under the leadership of Xavier Lopez Ancona, held its latest meeting at the company's Mexico City headquarters to discuss the possible roll-out to other locations of new experiential learning concepts tested at its Cuicuilco kids' edutainment park.

The team had prepared itself over several months for what had become a complex discussion—based on 15 years of success developing and operating "parks" where children could role-play adult activities—about the direction the company should take. Having recently adopted experiential learning as its core strategy, the leadership team was challenged to understand what that meant in terms of priorities and tangible projects of the kind being brought to the company by potential partners as well as those tested at Cuicuilco. With initial operating results from Cuicuilco in hand, Lopez' team had evidence on which to base decisions about whether, where, and how experiential learning initiatives should be introduced elsewhere in the KidZania global network. One important decision concerned the format for the first KidZania location in the U.S. In addition, franchising opportunities continued to arise. The two latest proposals were from Doha and London.

Emeritus Professor James L. Heskett; Professor Javier Reynoso (Chair, Service Management Research & Education Group, EGADE Business School, Tecnologico de Monterrey, Mexico); and Senior Researcher Karla Cabrera (Service Management Research & Education Group, EGADE Business School, Tecnologico de Monterrey, Mexico) prepared this case with the assistance of Cammie Dunaway (KidZania Global CMO and US President). It was reviewed and approved before publication by a company designate. Funding for the development of this case was provided by Harvard Business School and not by the company. HBS cases are developed solely as the basis for class discussion. Cases are not intended to serve as endorsements, sources of primary data, or illustrations of effective or ineffective management.

HISTORY OF KIDZANIA

While working in the toy industry in 1996, Luis Javier Laresgoiti visited a small child care-center, located in Raleigh, North Carolina, that incorporated themed role-playing activities. The children pretended they were visiting real-life destinations and used fake money and groceries as part of their play. Upon returning to his home in Mexico, he formed a team with three of his friends to create a "city" for children that revolved around role-playing. Laresgoiti believed this concept would provide the perfect type of activity for the children of Mexico City who lacked an educational, fun, value-oriented and social entertainment center. The team formed a company and made plans to meet with developers and explore design options with architects.

After working together for a year, Laresgoiti introduced the group to Xavier Lopez Ancona, a friend from school who had attended business school at Northwestern University and was an executive at that time for GE Capital. Lopez's experience working with major corporations provided him with an extensive perspective for running a company. To make the envisioned city a reality from both a structural and financial standpoint, the group agreed that the concept had to be changed from a day-care center to an entertainment and educational center. It would have to be large (4,000 square meters or approximately 40,000 square feet), be able to accommodate 3,500 to 4,000 people per day over one or two shifts of eight hours each, be equally entertaining and educational, be built within a shopping mall (an existing, successful destination), and be created through a partnership with several established and highly recognizable companies functioning as sponsors. The sponsorship angle was particularly unique because it provided the group not only with the financial support it would need but also assistance in the design of activities, architecture, and interiors.

With significant investments from Lopez and a friend of his, the group began to implement its plan in February 1997. Soon after, they found an ideal site for the project in a major shopping center in the Santa Fe area of Mexico City. They hired an experienced design team to kick start the planning and development process while they presented the idea to potential sponsors using sketches, renderings, 3D models, and a dynamic graphic identity package for what was then known as *"La Ciudad de los Niños"* ("The City of Children"). By the end of 1997 Lopez had tested the idea with 16 potential sponsors, all of which were major companies and whose brands aligned well with the concept of the project. Half of the companies expressed immediate interest and willingness to participate in the project.

In 1998 the team worked to acquire sponsors, complete the project's design, and obtain all the necessary permits. All of the final touches came together in 1999 and on September 1st, "La Ciudad de los Niños" opened to the public. The park attracted 792,000 visitors during the first year (significantly more than the 400,000 that had been forecast), won industry accolades, and attracted investors, which in turn encouraged company growth. In part encouraged by the success of the concept, Larasgoiti sold his share in the venture and moved to Florida, where he opened a similar facility called Wannado. Ironically, it closed in 2011.

Based on ideas developed over more than five years in Mexico City, in February 2005 the team began working on a new city plan in Monterrey, Mexico's second-largest city, that enhanced the concept's environment, atmosphere, and activities. Many sponsors from Mexico City were eager to participate in the expanding company, and as plans for an updated location in Monterrey progressed, potential partners began contacting management with proposals for international opportunities. As a result, a franchise concept was developed, described in detail below. Under this program, the first franchise was granted to investors in Tokyo. Its facility became the first to open under the name of KidZania outside Mexico in October 2006.

As the company began to grow as an international entity, management, with the help of external consultants, arrived at the idea that each "city" (facility) could be part of a network comprising the "nation" of KidZania. This provided a framework for an expanded conceptual story of a nation founded by kids who saw how their parents had made many mistakes governing the real world; wrote a Declaration of Independence outlining six "rightz" to "be, know, create, share, care, and play"; composed both a national motto ("Get ready for a better world.") and a national anthem; and created a language. It also fueled the notion of franchise growth and an expansion of related project ideas. (See Exhibit 1 for a list of KidZania locations).

In 2012 the company introduced a new outdoor automotive-based concept, with a stronger emphasis on driver education and citizenship, in Cuicuilco, a suburb of Mexico City. A concept that began with a passion to create a place for Mexican children to play among themselves while making a difference in their lives had now become a business concept that could inspire, educate, entertain, and empower children around the world.

A NATION IS BORN: THE KIDZANIA SERVICE CONCEPT

KidZania was conceived as an edutainment concept that invited children to role-play adult activities in realistically themed environments, programmed to mimic real-life. Built to a size scaled for kids (two-thirds of normal size), these environments were designed to imitate the inner workings of a typical city through the integration of recognizable destinations, real world products, and a functioning economy.

A Visitor's Experience

Under the KidZania service concept, every visitor to KidZania had the choice to participate in role-play activities, eat, and shop. Participation in the activities was varied in type and number depending on whether the visitor was a kid or an adult.

To enter KidZania, visitors purchased a ticket (prices varied from $14 in Mexico City to $50 in Tokyo) at a branded airport ticket counter representing the entrance to each facility. Here children and parents or guardians received RFID-enabled ID bracelets. These bracelets allowed adults to monitor the location of their children within KidZania at booths that were set up both inside and outside the actual facility. Each kid received 50 "kidzos" (Kidzania currency).

Upon entering, kids began learning a new language: "kai" (for hi), two fingers of the right hand arrayed over the heart for a greeting, "zanks" (thanks), and "Z-U," among others. Each KidZania facility was modeled to resemble a fully functional and realistic city. Children were guided through each activity under the supervision of a KidZania employee or "Zupervisor". Each activity had a runtime of approximately 25 minutes and was carefully scripted for both Zupervisors and role-playing kids.

Those arriving at the park were classified into two categories: tourists and CitiZens. Tourists included children who were visiting KidZania for the first time as well as any adult. CitiZen,

Exhibit 1: Official KidZania States and International Locations, 1999–2013[a]

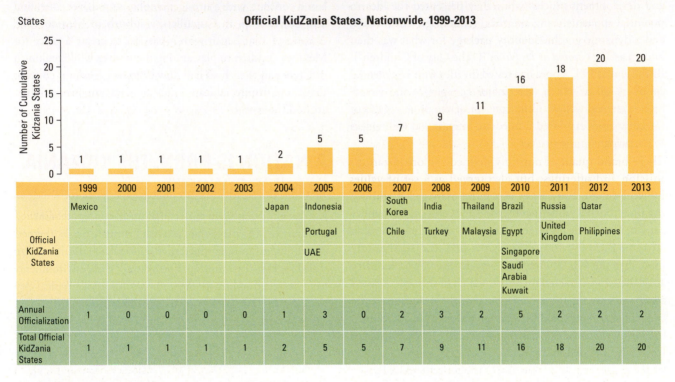

Official KidZania States, Nationwide, 1999-2013

States

Number of Cumulative KidZania States

	1999	2000	2001	2002	2003	2004	2005	2006	2007	2008	2009	2010	2011	2012	2013
Official KidZania States	Mexico					Japan	Indonesia		South Korea	India	Thailand	Brazil	Russia	Qatar	
							Portugal		Chile	Turkey	Malaysia	Egypt	United Kingdom	Philippines	
							UAE					Singapore			
												Saudi Arabia			
												Kuwait			
Annual Officialization	1	0	0	0	0	1	3	0	2	3	2	5	2	2	2
Total Official KidZania States	1	1	1	1	1	2	5	5	7	9	11	16	18	20	20

Source: Company documents

[a] Year indicates when the license has been signed.

a status for which children had to apply after their first visit, was a special designation solely for repeat visitors to KidZania. These children were also referred to as "KidZanians" and were issued a "pazzport" as part of B • KidZanian, the Company's loyalty program. KidZanians had their passports stamped each time they visited a facility and at each establishment. As KidZanians received more stamps, they earned benefits such as expedited entry, increased salaries when performing a job at KidZania, discounted products, and invitations to special events. The loyalty program provided the means to drive traffic, repeat visits, and increased revenue by engaging parents with targeted offers and personalized recognition of the achievements of their CitiZens. It also enabled management to track preferences for various activities by age group. To date, about 400,000 Pazzports had been issued.

Children from 4 to 14 participated as workers, customers, spectators, or explorers. Those younger than 4 and those above 14 and up to 16 years old did not participate in this manner. Instead, they participated in activities especially designed with their age group in mind. Adults with children over 8 had the option of dropping their children off at KidZania, but adults with children younger than that had to join them inside the facility. Adults who wished to share in their kid's experience could become involved with activities as participants or spectators. They could also choose to spend time independently of their kids at spaces specially designed just for them, like the parent's lounge.

Activities offered to visitors represented common businesses, services, and industries that contributed to a conventional city's economy. Most of the activities in KidZania were designed as completely hands-on to provide the most contextual and engaging learning experiences. From police officer to dentist to restauranteur, each KidZania offered nearly 100 role-playing activities with a range of difficulty to meet the abilities and interests of every child. Kids worked to earn kidZos, KidZania's own currency, so they could pay for goods and services in KidZania city. Pilots navigated airplanes, television anchors read the news, police officers performed detective work, and chefs cooked food. Getting started was simple: kids picked an occupation, learned about their job, donned a uniform, and started earning and spending kidZos, and, it was hoped, having fun.

When children and adults were ready to leave KidZania, they had to do so through the airport exit. This exit was a highly secure area in which the parent and child were cross-checked against the entry records before leaving.

The KidZania experience was reflected in fourteen "brand qualities" subscribed to by its management: kid-centered, role-play based, reality-based, interactive, fun, thrilling, educational, skill developer, value promoter, safe, detail oriented, keep current, accessible to all, and sustainable. These brand qualities not only defined the organization's mission and offerings, but also served as a set of values by which the organization was to be managed. Exhibit 2 contains several photos illustrating the KidZania service experience.

THE TARGET MARKET

KidZania's target visitor fell into one of four types of customer groups: young families with children 3 to 14 visiting mainly on weekends, holidays, and vacations; school groups attracted by the highly educational nature of the concept on weekdays; party groups attracted by special programming and food; and event groups that utilized KidZania after hours for gatherings, product launches, or for special programs such as summer camp.

KidZania catered to children ages 3 through 14 with most of its programming. It focused on kids from 5 to 11. Some of its programming was designed to be suitable for kids ages 11 to 14. Activities attractive to this older age group were generally more social in nature (e.g., Disco) or physically challenging (e.g., Climbing Building). KidZania also featured separate areas for toddlers, who were not yet ready for role-play, and adult visitors (parents, seniors and teachers) who could spend their time in activities ranging from viewing children in the theater productions to enjoying coffee and internet access in the special parents' lounge.

KidZania's primary audience was families of middle to high socioeconomic levels. Kids from low income families were also able to take advantage of price discounts that were offered as part of KidZania's corporate social responsibility program. All of KidZania's facilities and activities were designed to be accessible to visitors with mobility, viewing, hearing, or cognitive disabilities.

In addition, KidZania offered an alternative for educators to help children to use the expertise, skills, and values they acquired at school and practice them in a safe but realistic setting while sharing and cooperating with peers. Similarly, children who had experienced KidZania learning could practice this learning in their everyday lives.

The company was careful to direct all of its marketing activity to parents, not to kids. This helped dampen potential criticism of KidZania's role in introducing children to commercial activities.

Industry Partners

In addition to providing a valuable experience for children, the KidZania service concept also provided (and depended significantly upon) sponsorship opportunities for companies and institutions. Industry partners included corporations, non-governmental organizations (NGOs), and government institutions. Each contributed the economic resources for the design, build out, fit out, supplies, and know-how of one of the KidZania experiences. Partners brought the experience to life through the use of real products, services, processes, and technologies. KidZania's industry partners included many of the world's largest companies who additionally provided most of the supplies necessary for each activity, marketed and advertised the business and their association with it, and funded refurbishment. Industry partners ranged from major multinational brands like Coca Cola, Walmart, Toyota, DHL, and Sony to local companies like Telcel in Mexico (a major Telco), Yakult in Japan (a yogurt company), and Qatar Airlines in Kuwait. KidZania had relationships with over 800 brands around the world. In–kind contributions and fees from partners represented about 30% of the revenue of a typical KidZania facility and about 40%–50% of the capital investment required. Capital investment ranged from US$15 million (Monterrey and Jakarta, Indonesia) to US$30 million (Dubai and Tokyo).

Each KidZania began with research about what children would like to see in the city. Some activities like firefighting were consistent across all facilities while some reflected local interests. Once a list of desirable activities was developed, the KidZania experience team created an outline of the content. The search then began for industry partners who could be a good fit with that content and could provide the knowledge to make it even more authentic. For example, in the first KidZania the team knew they wanted an airplane activity. When they began meeting with American Airlines, the AA team decided it was necessary to provide a real airplane interior in which kids could work. Each partnership became a knowledge sharing activity between what KidZania's team

FIGURE 1 Airport ticket counters, KidZania Lisbon

FIGURE 2 Main plaza—Kids running, KidZania Tokyo

FIGURE 3 Withdrawing kidZos from ATM—KidZania Santa Fe, Mexico City

FIGURE 4 Building in flames—KidZania Seoul

FIGURE 5 Flight Simulator, KidZania Istanbul

Source: Company documents.

knew about kids and what the partner knew about the best ways to bring its business to life. A list of some of KidZania's industry partners, and the activities they supported, is shown in Exhibit 3.

THE SANTA FE OPERATION

The Santa Fe "Ciudad de los Niños" operated in roughly 40,000 square feet of space in the upscale Santa Fe shopping center in Mexico City.

The Offerings

The facility itself offered opportunities for role-playing of 80 different activities. Some of these required a minimum number of children to function properly. For example in the TV studio where kids aired a variety of programs including news reports, weather, and variety shows, kids were needed to operate the camera, work in the editing booth, and serve as reporters and news anchors. As a result, while an emphasis was placed on choice of activity by a child entering the facility, Zupervisors nevertheless were trained to suggest alternatives, depending on the need for role players in various activities and the desire to cut waiting times that reduced satisfaction.

Staffing

City staff were selected and encouraged to share eight qualities embedded in KidZania's core values: passion, creativity, quality, commitment, integrity, vision, motivation and result orientation. These guiding principles shaped KidZania's corporate culture.

The success of KidZania relied on the staff's ability to make "the magic" happen: getting children involved in the realistic, thrilling and fun experiences of being an adult. The KidZania "experience" was centered on Zupervisors, typically 18 to 24-year-old undergraduate students or recent college graduates. More recently, they also included retired adults with a strong interest and experience in working with children, good energy, patience and a service orientation, working on a half-time basis.

The KidZania experience relied on perfectly trained staff. As the organization grew and expanded internationally, KZ University was created to train local trainers with a focus on helping everyone understand the unique components of the KidZania brand experience as well as good customer service practices and operating procedures.

KidZania's turnover rate (83%) for frontline employees was lower than the average industry rate (120%). Efforts were ongoing to engage employees and encourage the sharing of best practice ideas. With that objective in mind, staff were rotated through various positions and had the opportunity to move between positions at an individual facility and headquarters, particularly in jobs that provided support to franchisees (described below).

Typically, a KidZania city required about 380 people to operate. About 130 of the employees were full time. They included staff members who worked in point-of-sale positions selling food or merchandise. Approximately 40 people worked in general services including security, maintenance and IT. There were typically 15–20 people working in administrative functions like finance and procurement and 5 in human resources. Each facility was led by a General Manager, called a Mayor who was responsible for the overall facility P&L.

In addition, 250 part time staff generally worked 4-hour shifts. They worked directly with the children to guide them through activities, communicate the key concepts, and help them to complete the job successfully. These "Zupervisors" also maintained their "establishment," doing light cleaning, restocking supplies and setting up for each group. Staff members had to be selected and trained very carefully, with special attention to energy level and love for children. Training typically involved several days of classroom courses as well as 3 weeks of on-the-job training. The part time staff received an hourly rate that ranged from the equivalent of $2 in Mexico to $10 in Japan. There were 3 levels each with different rates — a training level for three months followed by levels 1 and 2 Zupervisors. Labor costs were one of the most significant items on the unit level P&L, typically representing about 25%–30% of total revenue.

A chart showing the unit level organization for Santa Fe is presented in Exhibit 4. In its early years of operation, Santa Fe generated a great deal of publicity and benefitted from a positive word-of-mouth that helped it maintain the traffic levels shown in Exhibit 5.

THE SERVICE CONCEPT EVOLVES: CUICUILCO

The development of the Cuicuilco facility represented a milestone in the evolution of KidZania. It was started in 2009 as a project requested by a local municipal government interested in promoting children's driver education. It opened in June 2012.

Exhibit 3: A Partial List of KidZania's industry partners in Santa Fe

Establishment	Activity	Industry Partner
Culinary School	Learn the basics of the chef profession and learn and prepare a new recipe.	Herdez
Painting School	Learn an art discipline of choice, use authentic art supplies for painting a fresco on a wall or ceiling, paint on easels or color an illustration on paper.	Dixon Vinci
Secret Agent Training	Get training as an agent of the cities intelligence forces in a specially designed training facility and exercise the learned skills in a high rise building complex where a vertical descent down an elevator shaft is the final challenge.	Danone
University	Perform an enrollment process to get a student's ID and join a class of their choice in an undergraduate level. As students progress in their work experience, they can study a masters or a PhD degree, and receive higher salaries in KidZos as they finish higher degrees.	Anahuac University
City Bus Stop	At the bus stop, visitors board the city tour bus to know KidZania, its story, facts and its landmarks listening to a narration.	Cartoon Network
Bank	Cash kidZos checks provided at the airport's counters and perform bank transactions like opening an account, making a deposit or withdrawals and getting an account balance.	BBVA Bancomer
Hospital	Perform a liver transplant or a laparoscopy surgery in the operating rooms. Provide first aid services to an injured patient, taking her from the site of the accident to the emergency room in an ambulance. Bathe, change, dress and feed newborn babies at the nursery room. Perform a general health check and sight test to patients to ensure their good health condition.	Hospital Angeles
Bottling Plant	Learn and execute the steps for producing a soft drink, from cleaning and filling the bottles with carbonated water and adding syrup, to placing a cap and labeling it.	Coca-Cola
Chocolate Factory	Make a chocolate bar by mixing chocolate on a bowl, pouring it on a mold, cooling it down and packing it at the end of the process.	Nestlé
Newspaper	Get an assignment to write for a section in a newspaper. Interview people as assigned and take pictures on the field to illustrate the story. Then, write the story at the news room integrating text and images and print a copy of the newspaper for take away.	Reforma
TV Studio	Record a live TV program with audience on site, helping the cast to prepare for the program (wardrobe and makeup), performing in front of cameras, setting up the scenery, operating cameras on the floor or audio and video equipment in the control room.	Televisa
Beauty Salon	Provide customers with hairdressing, facials, makeup, and manicure services.	Jafra
Courier Service	Deliver and pick up parcels at different establishments around the city according to the assigned route. Kids also get the opportunity to send real letters to their friends or home.	DHL
Hotel	Welcome and check in hotel's guests at the front desk, set up a hotel room, make the bed and ensure all amenities are in place, or set tables in a banquet hall.	Fiesta Americana
Vet Clinic	Learn concepts of animal health and perform a veterinarian task such as prescribing medicated pet food or performing veterinary surgery.	Purina
Fire Station	Get training as fire fighter, then attend a fire alarm triggered at the Flamingo Hotel or a match factory, riding a fire truck along KidZania's streets to extinguish the fire with pressured-water hoses.	Seguros Bancomer
Burger Shop	Prepare a burger according to specified techniques for its ingredients and package.	McDonald's

(continued)

Exhibit 3 (*continued*)

Establishment	Activity	Industry Partner
Pizza Shop	Prepare an individual pizza, preparing the dough, pouring pizza sauce, and placing toppings according to specific instructions, then bake it, cut it, and package it.	Domino's
Department Store	Customers have the opportunity to find products from different departments and buy them with the kidZos earned and saved.	Liverpool
Supermarket	Employees attend cash registries, serve in the different sections in the supermarket, like meat and poultry, fruits, vegetables, and pharmacy, or restock shelves.	Walmart
Aviation Academy	Get aircraft pilot training in a state of the art flight simulator. Provide safety instructions to passengers in the cabin and provide them with the dining service.	American Airlines

Source: Company documents.

It was based on the core KidZania service concept but offered new experiences to its visitors: driving and various aspects of citizenship. The facility, the largest opened to date, was outdoors and oriented around a system of roads, with most of the facility's grounds covered by tenting in case of inclement weather. The roads were navigated by scaled-down cars, and each child was assigned to different vehicles depending on age and experience. Each vehicle was designed with a low maximum speed and high safety standards in order to maintain an accident-free environment. After sufficient driving experience, children were able to upgrade from cars to trucks and buses.

In addition to driver education, Cuicuilco emphasized health, civics, community, and the environment. To transmit these topics, activities were redesigned and augmented. New ones were created. For example, the supermarket, a traditional KidZania establishment, was redesigned to include an activity in which children shopped for their groceries in a completely dark environment simulating the reality of a blind person. The facility also included a recyclables drop-off center, wind turbines, solar panels, and an electric power plant where children could learn about alternative energies and their impact on the environment. KidZania's focus on developing children's global citizenship, being empathetic and inclusive with those with different abilities, and awareness of issues like taking care of the environment was intended to enrich the KidZania service concept. However, it required not only much more space but also new kinds of partnerships.

Compared to the original Santa Fe concept, the 2012 facility at Cuicuilco (largely outdoors) required more employees, about 300 full-time and 500 part-time. It also required 23,435 square meters (or roughly 220,000 square feet) of indoor and outdoor space, higher equipment costs, and personnel costs that were

20%–25% of revenues. But it generated a higher operating profit. Because ticket prices had to be higher at Cuicuilco ($17) and there were more revenues from Industry partners, EBITDA margins were about 40%. Operating comparisons between Santa Fe and Cuicuilco are shown in Exhibit 6.

Challenges faced in the first few months of operation of Cuicuilco included managing a greater number of activities and staff. This contrasted with Santa Fe, where the biggest challenges in its first months of operation were learning the basics of operating an edutainment facility. In its first 12 months of operation, Cuicuilco attracted 729,000 people, substantially more than had been projected.

The Santa Fe facility required an investment of US$8 million. It was financed with funds from Industry Partners (45%), equity (30%), and debt (25%). By comparison, Cuicuilco cost $38 million to build and equip. Its sources of financing were 30% from Industry Partners, 30% equity, and 40% debt.

FRANCHISING

The first KidZania franchised facility was opened in Tokyo in 2006. As franchised facilities began to develop along with those owned by KidZania, a detailed planning process, called "city planning," was refined. Excerpts from a document describing "city planning" are shown in Exhibit 7.

The original franchising agreement called for a payment by franchisees of $250,000 (later $650,000) in territory (countries or "nation states") fees, $250,000 (later $600,000) in facility fees and 5% of all ongoing revenue to KidZania. In return for the payments, KidZania agreed to provide intellectual

Exhibit 4: Organization Chart for Santa Fe

ORGANIZATIONAL CHART

KIDZANIA METROPOLITAN GOVERNMENT

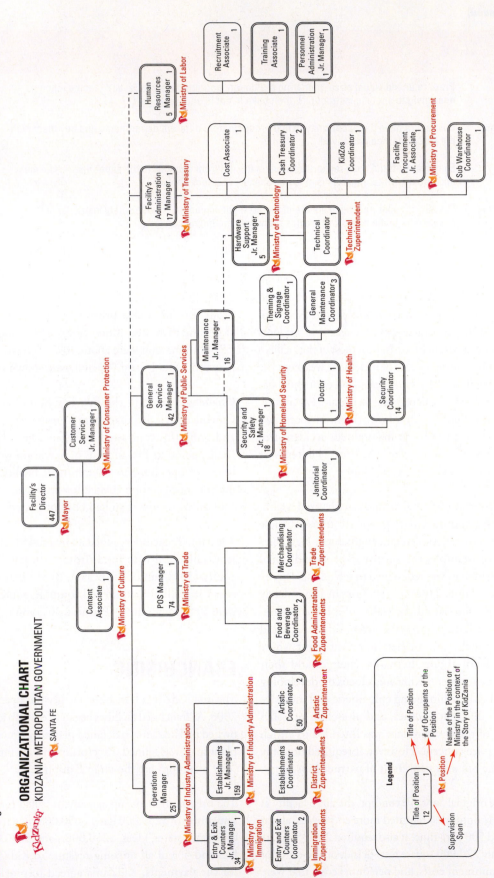

SANTA FE

Legend

Title of Position — Title of Position
# of Occupants of the Position
Position — Name of the Position or Ministry in the context of the Story of KidZania
Supervision Span

Source: Company documents.

Exhibit 5: Historical Attendance Information for Santa Fe.

Figures Expressed in MXP	1999	2000	2001	2002	2003	2004	HISTORICAL 2005	2006	2007	2008	2009	2010	2011	2012	2013
SANTA FE															
TOTAL ATTENDANCE	207,852	779,416	815,213	798,412	793,017	803,703	767,453	752,832	789,996	786,459	607,598	684,247	791,491	596,166	417,229
FAMILIES	156,215	493,529	462,723	433,367	452,091	460,411	430,669	421,364	426,173	417,510	319,650	341,677	365,940	306,636	246,771
SCHOOLS	28,430	211,458	289,839	289,136	263,395	271,801	277,236	286,900	287,668	281,248	217,166	240,567	296,491	218,077	112,013
PARTIES	9,877	26,084	18,511	16,287	16,388	18,620	17,419	17,720	18,717	19,706	20,534	25,171	25,445	22,613	17,716
CORPORATE	-	-	-	-	-	-	-	-	2,792	6,231	11,016	27,191	58,028	13,834	12,872
EVENTS	13,330	33,010	12,315	27,014	28,297	26,330	19,654	26,848	31,252	38,465	11,346	21,869	16,483	6,887	1,500
SUMMER CAMP	-	-	-	-	-	-	-	-	-	1,511	1,468	2,144	1,525	2,070	1,386
PRO BONO	-	15,335	31,825	32,608	32,846	26,541	22,475	-	23,394	21,788	26,418	25,628	27,579	26,049	24,971
REVENUE															
ADMISSIONS	13,134,013	53,768,451	59,375,167	62,058,597	64,125,926	71,557,792	75,112,221	74,145,220	76,029,215	77,820,118	60,517,605	68,633,065	81,245,834	65,415,720	47,480,274

Source: Company documents.

property (name, logos, characters, story, music and trademark registration); facility design (program development, master plan, design details, and theming); marketing materials; guidelines, manuals, and operating procedures; software; training; web design; and merchandise. Franchisees were required to secure the location, adapt the design locally, construct and fit out the facility, hire and train staff, market the concept and facility, secure industry partners, and operate the facility. There was significant supervision and oversight by KidZania during both development and ongoing operations. There was a system of regular audits and certifications that insured that the standards were consistently met. If there were significant breeches, the license could be revoked. This had not been necessary to date.

Interest among potential franchisees was strong. The first foreign entity to sign up was Japan, where KidZania was regarded as a good concept for Japanese families. Adjustments in the design of the park and the role-playing offerings to accommodate Japanese families included an even greater focus on educational content, including the addition of a University and a Kindergarten area for toddlers. These additions were a result of KidZania's ongoing research and commitment to continuous innovation. With each new facility the company aimed to enhance the experience. After a successful opening in Tokyo, the KidZania brand became known in Asia. Others began approaching the company expressing a desire to franchise.

Exhibit 6: Unit Financial Statements, Santa Fe and Cuicuilco, 2013

FIGURES IN MXN	Santa Fe		Cuicuico	
	TOTAL PY		TOTAL PY	
	$	%	$	%
TOTAL ATTENDANCE	417,229	100.0%	650,776	100.0%
TOTAL PAYING ATTENDANCE	392,258	94.0%	621,474	95.5%
FAMILIES	246,771	59.1%	342,242	52.6%
SCHOOLS	112,013	26.8%	185,245	28.5%
PARTIES	17,716	4.2%	28,717	4.4%
CORPORATE	14,372	3.4%	64,673	9.9%
EVENTS				
CAMPS	1,386	0.3%	597	0.1%
PRO BONO	24,971	6.0%	29,302	4.5%
TOTAL PER CAPITA	175.17	100.0%	228.31	100.0%
ADMISSION	121.04	69.1%	146.14	64.0%
FOOD AND BEVERAGE	31.64	18.1%	55.49	24.3%
MERCHANDISING	12.94	7.4%	17.60	7.7%
PHOTO	5.55	3.2%	4.89	2.1%
LOYALTY	1.19	0.7%	1.57	0.7%
OTHERS	2.80	1.6%	2.63	1.2%

(continued)

Exhibit 6 (*continued*)

REVENUE	111,347,208	100.0%	234,342,074	100.0%
OPERATING REVENUE	68,710,417	61.7%	141,891,567	60.5%
INDUSTRY PARTNERS REVENUE	42,636,792	38.3%	92,450,508	39.5%
FRANCHISE REVENUE				
RETAIL REVENUE				
BUSINESS UNITS REVENUE				
COST OF GOODS SOLD	20,043,752	18.0%	40,578,160	17.3%
OPERATING COST OF GOODS SOLD INDUSTRY PARTNERS COGS FRANCHISES COGS RETAIL COGS	14,476,392	21.1%	28,873,988	20.3%
ROYALTY COGS	5,567,360	5.0%	11,704,173	5.0%
GROSS PROFIT	91,303,456	82.0%	193,763,914	82.7%
OPERATING EXPENSES	70,225,166	63.1%	102,865,808	43.9%
PAYROLL	44,478,913	39.9%	68,780,304	29.4%
RENT	8,779,845	7.9%	9,168,413	3.9%
UTILITIES	3,598,985	3.2%	4,309,068	1.8%
INSURANCE	358,104	0.3%	577,152	0.2%
SUPPLIES	2,816,602	2.5%	2,208,247	0.9%
MAINTENANCE	4,562,468	4.1%	4,605,853	2.0%
EXTERNAL OPERATING SERVICES	1,356,889	1.2%	1,887,200	0.8%
EXTERNAL PROFESSIONAL SERVICES	680,232	0.6%	1,275,927	0.5%
OPERATING TAXES	6,371	0.0%	7,737	0.0%
ALLOWANCE FOR DOUBTFUL ACCOUNTS				
NON DEDUCTIBLE	31,315	0.0%	61,943	0.0%
ADVERTISING	3,533,762	3.2%	9,979,288	4.3%
TRAVEL EXPENSES	21,679	0.0%	4,677	0.0%
OTHER EXPENSES				
EQUIPMENT LEASING				
EBITDA	21,078,290	18.9%	90,898,106	38.8%

Source: Company documents.

Even though the KidZania philosophy challenged adult customs, beliefs, and even laws in some countries, franchisees had found ways of adapting it to achieve acceptance among adults. Female kids, for example, were permitted to perform "jobs" in KidZania's Middle Eastern parks that their elders were prohibited from performing in the real world. KidZania's Middle Eastern facilities were among its most successful, something that management attributed to partnership with local franchisees.

EXPERIENTIAL LEARNING

Competition that was increasing at a faster and faster pace globally (see below) combined with a more restrictive regulatory environment led KidZania's management to give increasing consideration to the expansion of the organization's mission and activities to include a greater emphasis on experiential learning. Experiential Learning involved education by direct experience or "doing" rather than rote or didactic learning. Research had shown that recall was higher after 3 weeks among people who had been told, shown, and experienced information as opposed to those who were only told or were told and shown. KidZania executives believed that its facilities' focus on role-play was particularly well aligned with the experiential learning approach to education. For example, rather than seeing a film on earning money and making decisions about spending, kids earned kidZos for the work they did, spent them on goods and services, and opened bank accounts where they could save kidZos and earn interest.

After the success of the educational and socially oriented ideas developed in Cuicuilco, KidZania's management adopted experiential learning as the core of the organization's service concept. As a result, experiential learning in KidZania was divided into two main blocks, general and specific learning. General learning fell into five main categories: How a City Works, Financial Literacy, The World of Work, Model CitiZenship, and Good Habits. Additionally, by participating in the activities and establishments, children were expected to develop expertise in understanding various industries and careers. It was hoped they would also develop necessary skills and good values. Specific learning areas were defined as: Expertise, Value Promotion and Skills Development.

It was hoped that an increased emphasis on experiential learning at KidZania would strengthen the attractiveness of the service concept for a different mix of industry partners, providing them with a unique "experiential marketing" platform. For example, rather than a focus on just signage with logos, they could become a more integral part of the "story." This interactive and immersive environment would ensure that product interactions would be more meaningful and entertaining, while providing kids with ample opportunity to create a connection to the brand. If designed properly, these activities would reinforce KidZania's mission and help to negate any criticism or misunderstanding about the commercialization of children.

For example, Walmart had been a partner for many years, sponsoring the grocery store in Santa Fe. This was a great way to teach children about the different sections of the supermarket as well as to practice adding up the cost of items as a customer or giving correct change as a clerk. Walmart wanted to go further, however, in helping kids understand the need to be empathetic to people with special needs. This was consistent with Walmart's own corporate goal to be a socially responsible company. As a result, at Cuicuilco KidZania created the Blind Awareness Center where customers could shop or work in Walmart with special goggles to stimulate the experience of being blind. To add to the children's experience, the Zupervisors who worked in the establishment were themselves visually impaired. Similarly, JAFRA, a multinational beauty company that had long been a KidZania partner in the beauty salon activity, decided it wanted to teach kids the science in creating its products. So now kids could work as chemical engineers in its "cosmetics lab" at Cuicuilco, manufacturing customized cosmetic products from development to packaging selection and decoration.

It was expected that experiential learning activities would require more detailed and complex design of activities. It would also require higher investments in media, complementary educational material (e.g., posters), and training. Designers faced the challenge of maintaining an optimal balance between learning and fun. Activities had to be adjusted to fit children's attention spans. While technology played a key role in the creation of children's experiences, one of the main objectives of experiential learning was promoting interaction among kids, avoiding the use of technology as a substitute for role-playing.

COMPETITION

While people inevitably compared KidZania with theme parks like Disney and Universal Studios, there were significant differences. For example, Disney was primarily a destination entertainment serving tourists who came from hundreds of

Selecting a Location

The market base for KidZania at city level requires a resident market size of three million people. The analysis of market size should consider the amount and type of competitors already operating in the city to reveal if the market's size can support additional development and explore pricing potential. It is also necessary to understand what the area's reputation is relative to tourism and what types of visitors are already frequenting businesses there. Also to be considered is if the area is appealing and considered an easy destination to get to.

KidZania facilities are best suited to a shopping mall that features an innovative tenant mix. Shopping malls are synergistic with the KidZania concept. They are strategically located and highly visible, offering good transport access and large areas for parking. A situation indoors is preferable over outdoor entry venues because the position offers protection from inclement weather, is easier to maintain and easier to exert safety control. However, outdoors locations, such as Cuicuilco, provide more realism and contribute to a more enjoyable experience.

The average size of a KidZania facility requires a footprint of four to five thousand square meters and a total construction area of six to eight thousand square meters. The size reflects a mixture of visitor area, programming and back-office space and must include at least fifty to sixty establishments. Each KidZania facility must accommodate eighteen hundred to two thousand visitors simultaneously, 3,500 to 4,000 visitors per day over one or two five-hour shifts of operation, and a yearly attendance of four to eight hundred thousand visitors, depending on the size of the facility.

Founding the City

After analyzing the market, an alliance is made with a local partner or a franchisee with global experience that provides the expertise to adapt the concept to local context. Every *Metropolis* (city) has a mixture of about 60 establishments, including mandatory (e.g., airport, hospital, bank), optional (selected depending on the space available, e.g., go-karts), recommended (most popular), and switchable.

For each establishment there are a number of fun and educative activities designed for the kids. Local partners look for industry partners, consider the available space (e.g., driving experience or the stadium requires bigger spaces), cultural specificities (e.g., not including dogs in the UK

facility) and, with the counseling of KidZania, make the final selection of establishments and activities.

All the activities are developed by KidZania to assure that the contents are attached to the experience learning guidelines and have a balance between learning and fun. Local partner input is crucial at this stage, and in some cases, its contributions led to the development of completely new experiences (e.g., Sleeping Institute in Korea).

The City Plan

The city's plan is one big environment made up of many small environments replicating a thematic mix of industry sectors. This is where the city comes to life. Establishments are the name for all the role-play locations independently if they take place at fabricated environments, in vehicular devices, or as part of independent activities within "common areas" of the city. The city plan is always arranged per four distinct city areas: city access, city center, suburbs, and industry clusters.

The role-play locations at KidZania are representative of the most common businesses, services, and industries that contribute to a conventional city's growing economy. These include: restaurants, retail, entertainment, media, public services, private services, transportation and manufacturing.

The design of these scenarios physically replicates relevant areas or aspects of role-playing as dictated by the functional purpose of the environment or vehicle and follows a specially designed storyline supported by thematic components. These components, collectively referred to as elements, are occupationally related and include props, costumes, consumables, specialized equipment, and furnishings, among others.

For each establishment, KidZania provides detailed information to serve as a database and guide of the experience: activities, architecture design, theming, and fixed and variable elements. During the design of the city, Experiential Learning fundamentals must be considered in order to provide the physical elements needed to create the experiences. For example, for the "University," a mandatory establishment in the city, KidZania specifies a foot print area between 50 and 60 m^2, provides a detailed description of all possible activities to be performed (e.g., "Bachelor degrees" in "Health," "Administration" or "Engineering" or "postgraduate education"), the roles of Zupervisors, children, and adults (e.g., "professor," "student," and "observer," respectively), the activity's duration (30 minutes), capacity (e.g., 12 children per hour), kidZo transactions (pay or purchase), giveaways (e.g., student card, career backpack), equipment (e.g. computers), uniforms for staff and children, theming props (e.g., human anatomy models), layout, accessibility components (e.g., wheel chair access for staff and visitors), etc. All these elements are aligned to offer children a fun experience while they learn about the role of a university in society, strengthen values (e.g., honesty, preparing for an examination, and taking a test without cheating) and develop skills (e.g., children as students will require analytical thinking while solving doubts and answering exams).

City Staff

KidZania's corporate culture, completely service- and kid-oriented, makes the collaborators' selection and training crucial. As the CEO has mentioned, "If we are going to be an exceptional company, it is because of our people."

As a nation, KidZania faces the challenges of being multicultural and inclusive. Some of the best practices developed worldwide have been adapted to different cultural particularities. For example, in Jeddha, all Zupervisors must be women because men are not allowed to be physically in touch with children. In Cuicuilco, there are some blind Zupervisors performing specific activities associated with an effort to create a sightless experience for kids.

Safety and Security

KidZania takes great care to ensure the safety of its CitiZens, visitors and city workers going above and beyond standard safety and security practices. These practices include supervised access and exit monitored by a surveillance system and managed by security personnel; a well-trained security force to look out for the safety needs of the city and its people; an identification system of wireless radio frequency bracelets with a special identity chip that offers location tracking; the city's master plan providing for optimal precautionary considerations that include emergency exiting and signage, ambulance access, first aid location and the position of each of its fire hydrants; in addition, all materials within the city are non-flammable or fire resistant and that nothing within reach features sharp textures, pointed corners, or expansive gaps that could cause injury. Areas frequented by KidZania's youngest visitors include the added consideration of non-toxicity in all materials specified.

Facility (Urban) Economics

Revenue. KidZania generates operating revenue through tickets (sold to families, schools, birthday parties, and corporations), food and beverage sales, photography, and merchandise. Admission prices vary based on relevant competitive and consumer factors, ranging from just over $15 in Monterrey to almost $60 per child in Japan. Prices also vary by age to provide discounts of ~35% to adults and toddlers who fall outside the target demographic. Children under the age of one enter free of charge, and school groups receive a discount on the regular admission price. KidZania features a pay-one-price admission policy for entry that provides its visitors free access to all activities. Only food and beverage and merchandise locations require additional spending. Additional revenue comes from industry partners who pay an initial investment, an annual investment, and remodeling fees when they wish to change or update their establishment design (see Capital Expenditures).

Expenses. General and administrative expenses consist of payroll costs composed of expenses from personnel working at the owned and operated facilities (see Exhibits 6 and 8) as well as employees at the corporate level; rent comprised of the rent paid for the owned and operated facilities located in the shopping malls as well as for the corporate offices in the US, Mexico, and Hong Kong; utilities and supplies including facility and office-related expenses such as telephones, internet, electricity, water, stationery, uniforms, etc.; marketing and PR expenses driven by marketing and PR initiatives at each facility and at the corporate level; travel primarily composed of the costs associated with the evaluation and development of both new owned and operated facilities as well as new licensed locations; external professional services primarily related to third-party consulting and outsourced development services as well as architecture, tax, legal, auditing, and other outsourced services; and other expenses including maintenance costs, services, insurance expenses, leases, and other miscellaneous costs.

Capital Expenditures. Annual capital expenditures ("capex") can be broken down into two categories: maintenance and new facilities. Maintenance capital expenditures for the owned and operated facilities consist of remodeling expenses. The industry partner model enables KidZania to keep its maintenance capex relatively low. Industry partners not only typically pay for the upkeep of their establishments but also for any redesigns, leaving the company to only maintain the common grounds of each facility. New facility capex is made up of the costs to plan, design, and build out new owned and operated facilities.

Source: Compiled from company documents.

miles away and stayed 3–5 days. Most families visited Disney only 1 or 2 times in their lifetime, spending large sums of money. KidZania drew from a resident market, with families staying 5 hours and coming multiple times during the year.

At Disney the focus was on family fun with children interacting only with their families and primarily through rides and shows. At KidZania children were largely free to pursue their own interests away from their parents. There was socialization and interaction with other children as they role-played together.

Disney focused on fantasy experiences and characters while KidZania focused on real life experiences. Because Disney was very capital intensive—with investment per facility of $1–$2 billion—growth opportunities were limited to a handful of markets that could provide the necessary attendance. As a result, much of Disney's revenue growth came from licensing characters or other types of entertainment like movies and online games. By way of contrast, KidZania's facilities typically cost between $10–$40 million and could thrive in markets with as few as 700,000 children in a 90-minute radius. That meant that growth could come from expanding to 90 to 100 cities that fit these criteria.

Both theme parks and KidZania did, however, compete with local establishments for visitors' time and money. Competing establishments included local operations such as zoos, movie theaters, concerts, sporting events, and museums. When potential customers decided where to spend time and money, they were influenced by such things as entertainment value, cost, time consumption, and proximity to home.

Perhaps KidZania's biggest source of competition was technology that fostered social networking among children. This could, however, present marketing opportunities. Cammie Dunaway, in charge of KidZania's global marketing, commented that "KidZania might be productively promoted to parents as a place for kids to get unplugged."[1] One Kidzanian remarked to a reporter in Kuwait that he would "much rather be at KidZania than in a virtual world . . . 'What a boring thing, just touching a screen,' another added."[2]

KidZania's success to date and the fact that role-play could not be protected as intellectual property led other parties to attempt to replicate the business model, especially in Asia (where there were more than 50 copycats). But no one had had the success of KidZania in offering experiential learning. Competitors generally offered lower quality properties. Without adequate corporate sponsorship

support, many of these struggled. They offered fewer, less frequently updated activities within their facilities. In addition, they often chose poor locations in small cities that could not support the traffic needed for the facilities to thrive. These more direct competitors were, however, getting savvier than in the past.

Other Challenges

In addition to increasing competition, KidZania faced a future characterized by changing market regulations, challenges in entering new markets, and the integration of new technologies. In particular, the digital revolution enveloping the world had significant implications for the organization and its service business concept. At the same time, the changing environment suggested the possibility of using new formats to introduce the public to KidZania. These shifting forces raised a number of questions in the minds of KidZania's leaders.

Market regulations There was growing potential for greater parental resistance to overt marketing to children. The current regulatory environment associated with children's marketing could make it difficult to secure partnerships from "traditional" child-focused brands. This raised the question: How could KidZania adapt its business model, including industry partners, to face market regulations without losing profitability?

Entering new markets What adjustments should KidZania make to enter more sophisticated and crowded markets? In bigger markets, should KidZania open more than one facility? Why? Are smaller markets an expansion alternative for KidZania? What implications and risks must be considered?

Technology integration Greater sophistication of children and age compression could require adjustments to the core concept, integrating greater use and availability of technology into KidZania facilities, especially those aimed at children over the age of 10. How far should KidZania go in the integration of technology in its activities? How could KidZania best capitalize on the interactive essence of role-play based on technology?

Digital experiences Questions were raised by KidZania's leaders about the possibility of entering services based on digital experiences. How could KidZania ensure that such digital experiences would maintain interactivity and experiential learning fundamentals? Without any prior expertise in digital experiences, what main aspects should KidZania consider before entering into a digital world?

Exhibit 8: Financial Statements for KidZania, 2010 through 2013 (in US$)

KZ CORPORATION FINANCIAL STATEMENTS	2010	2011	2012	2013
ATTENDANCE	4,361,530	4,466,003	5,510,268	6,472,533
TOTAL REVENUE	27,368,627	25,993,847	51,871,401	47,906,339
TOTAL OPERATION REVENUE	10,171,733	11,575,021	15,765,830	20,315,180
ADMISSION REVENUE	7,203,379	8,435,691	11,230,455	13,550,428
EVENTS REVENUE	172,550	-	-	-
FOOD AND BEVERAGE REVENUE	1,650,586	1,933,567	3,332,718	4,347,321
MERCHANDISING REVENUE	886,465	1,042,471	975,853	1,444,445
PHOTOGRAPHY REVENUE	-	-	-	460,659
LOYALTY REVENUE	-	-	-	139,894
OTHER REVENUE	258,752	163,292	226,804	372,434
TOTAL INDUSTRY PARTNER	7,168,339	5,948,797	19,319,321	13,592,690
INDUSTRY PARTNER INITIAL INVESTMENT	1,705,735	853,984	11,617,763	1,765,309
INDUSTRY PARTNER OTHER	119,756	36,052	144,949	259,617
INDUSTRY PARTNER ANNUAL FEE	5,184,892	5,016,918	7,417,568	11,473,351
INDUSTRY PARTNER REMODELING REVENUE	157,956	41,843	139,040	94,413
FRANCHISE REVENUE	10,028,555	8,148,006	13,238,324	11,673,977
FEES	3,310,388	1,877,069	4,192,830	1,889,151
ROYALTIES	6,634,303	6,214,890	8,790,736	9,116,266
OTHER REVENUE	83,864	56,047	254,758	591,344
LOYALTY REVENUE		-	-	77,216
MERCHANDISING REVENUE	-	322,024	3,547,926	2,324,492
MERCHANDISING REVENUE	-	322,024	874,505	1,618,459
REDEMPTION REVENUE	-	-	230,401	282,847
KEY MATERIALS REVENUE	-	-	2,443,020	423,186
COST OF GOODS SOLD	2,062,227	2,701,660	5,584,683	6,081,502
ESTABLISHMENT CONSUMABLES	546,352	754,633	761,801	989,328
REDEMPTION	30,220	49,976	57,008	13,851
LOYALTY	-	-	210,932	110,645
FOOD AND BEVERAGE	913,973	966,472	1,471,053	2,025,262
MERCHANDISING	436,927	685,623	3,018,024	2,507,370
PHOTOGRAPHY	-	-	-	309,008
EVENTS	97,538	-	-	-
FRANCHISES	37,217	244,956	65,866	126,037
ROYALTIES	-	-	-	-

(continued)

Exhibit 8 (*continued*)

KZ CORPORATION FINANCIAL STATEMENTS	2010	2011	2012	2013
GROSS PROFIT	**25,306,400**	**23,292,187**	**46,286,718**	**41,824,838**
% OF TOTAL REVENUE	92.5%	89.6%	89.2%	87.3%
OPERATION EXPENSES	**18,916,249**	**26,649,541**	**30,955,509**	**34,443,477**
PAYROLL	10,550,295	14,692,039	19,403,862	22,155,177
RENT	1,201,340	1,556,017	2,228,715	2,522,398
UTILITIES	711,779	858,946	1,058,839	1,193,109
SERVICES	463,176	507,357	683,300	684,013
MAINTENANCE	812,467	901,755	1,044,286	1,103,575
SUPPLIES	293,749	322,404	556,899	512,585
CORPORATE EXPENSES	3,094,223	4,291,190	2,677,478	3,575,182
MARKETING AND PR EXPENSES	653,604	2,030,493	2,121,172	1,609,734
DOUBTFUL ACCOUNTS	-	-	-	-
TRAVEL EXPENSE	808,669	1,422,323	1,157,473	1,058,751
LEASES	326,854	67,018	23,487	28,951
EBITDA	**6,390,151**	**(3,357,354)**	**15,331,208**	**7,381,361**
% OF TOTAL REVENUE	23.3%	−12.9%	29.6%	15.4%

*2011 Negative EBITDA: First Year State USA Expenses Start operations of KSLP CUI Preop Expenses.
Source: Company documents.

New formats The company was also exploring new ways to extend the service experience outside the park through new formats and communication channels. This raised the questions: What new alternatives could be explored to extend the experiential learning experience? How could new formats and channels leverage KidZania's strategy of becoming the leader in experiential learning content?

RESULTS

KidZania's revenues and profits exhibited steady growth, as shown in the financial statements contained in Exhibit 8 for the period 2010 through 2013. Both franchised and owned facilities continued to perform well, with franchising revenues comprising 25% of total revenues and a higher proportion of profits in 2013. This performance led to increasing expectations among the organization's major investors. It underlined the importance of initiatives to grow the KidZania Nation as well as those associated with experiential learning.

THE MANAGEMENT MEETING

Several items were on the agenda for the KidZania management meeting late in 2013. All were related to ways in which experiential learning could be expanded within KidZania's service concept and mission. First on the agenda was a consideration of the results of several tests of experiential learning activities at Cuicuilco. Management discussed the results of each to determine whether it should be rolled out to owned and franchised parks. It required an assessment of not only the financial potential of each but also the degree to which each activity enhanced experiential learning. The activities under consideration for inclusion in future KidZania "cities" were as follows:

1. The activities at Cuicuilco were divided into 5 theme areas: Driving Safety, Citizenship, Health and Wellness, Environmental Sensitivity, and Community. There was substantial support among members of the management group for including more government establishments as "partners." One benefit of this initiative would be

Exhibit 9: Information about Initiatives to Be Considered for Adoption at the December, 2013 KidZania Management Meeting

Establishment		Activities Program							Industry Partner			
Name	Ideal Footprint (sqm)	No. of Activities	Roles	Age Range	Duration (min)	Children per Hour	Adults per Hour	Staff Needed (regular season)	Industry Partner	Initial Fee (US$)	Annual Fee (US$)	2013 Attendance
Tax Office	20.00	2	– Tax contributor – Tax officer	7–16	10	48	0	1	SAT	100,400.00	57,900.00	28,768
Driving Street	190.00	1	– Driver	Children 4–9	10	72	0	2	AVIS	80,000.00	80,000.00	187,776
Natural Resources Research Lab	55.00	1	– Lab research assistant	Children 7–12	20	24	0	2	Seguros Bancomer	110,000.00	54,000.00	27,795
Supermarket	90.00	2	– Customer – Employee (cashier, aisles manager, shelf supply)	Children 4–12	20	15	0	2	Wal-Mart	95,000.00	95,000.00	26,783
Parents Spa	150.00	1	– Customer	Adults 16+	90	0	8	1	Fiesta Americana	176,000.00	99,000.00	3,351

Source: Company documents.

Exhibit 10: Information about KidZania's Two New Franchise Proposals

This exhibit shows information about two propositions to create a new franchise, the nature of the market, the proposed facility, a willingness to develop new experiential learning concepts, and estimates of potential traffic, revenue, and profit.

PROPOSAL A

The first proposal was to establish KidZania in a major market in Europe. The franchisee would be a newly established affiliate of a limited corporation led by two entrepreneurs who had previously developed a wide range of property and leisure businesses across the market including a 24-hour restaurant; an iconic private members club for the media and entertainment business; a health and fitness club housing an organic supermarket and café; and London's largest integrated medical center. The entrepreneurs were also involved in a number of charity projects ranging from education and wildlife conservation, to community sport and art.

The resident market size was over 20 million, with a children's population between 0–14 of 3.6 million. Future population growth was expected to be moderate. There was also a sizable tourism market. Attendance forecasts for KidZania were around 700,000 annually. Because of the relative affluence of the market, the expected children's ticket price would be approximately $41 in US currency.

The potential franchisees had identified a location in a well-located and desirable mall that received over 47 million visitors a year.

The market was highly competitive, with many entertainment and education offerings. Competition for school visits was extremely competitive, with many reputable museums providing free attendance to school groups.

Development costs and rents in the market would be high. Labor costs were also a concern. As opposed to other KidZania locations, which typically use a part-time staff schedule of 6 hours per day, 6 days a week, this type of schedule would not work in this market due to difficulty of finding people willing to travel to work 6 days a week and the need to certify employees who work with children every year.

PROPOSAL B

The second proposal came from a relatively small developing market in the Middle East. While the market would not normally fit KidZania's requirements, the potential franchisee had close government relationships and made convincing arguments about the country's commitment to educational experiences.

The market size was 1.9 million, with just over 290,000 children 0–14. The market, however, was growing rapidly and had one of the highest per capita average incomes in the world. Recently the government had created a specific plan to turn the country into a developed nation by 2030 with a focus on human, social, economic and environmental development. There was a major desire and commitment to create new educational experiences for children as there were currently very few enrichment opportunities outside the classroom.

The potential franchisees had identified a location in a shopping center that was receiving 1.2 million visitors a year. They believed they could attract approximately 218,000 visitors a year to KidZania and charge admission fees equivalent to approximately $35 in US currency. They were very excited about the new educational content at Cuicuilco and felt they could receive significant government support both in sponsoring establishments and endorsing school field trips.

A comparison of the proposals is presented below:

	Proposal A	Proposal B
Market size	20,000,000	1,900,000
Children 0–14	3,600,000	290,928
Assumed Penetration	3%	20%
Assumed Repeat		250%
Assumed Attendance	700,000	218,196
Location Footfall	47 Million	1.2 Million
Proposed Children's Ticket Price	$41	$35

Source: Company documents.

improved relationships with government agencies that could exercise control over KidZania's offerings. Experience had shown that the selling cycle for such partnerships was longer and more onerous and the contract period was shorter than KidZania's typical five-year contracts in other partnerships. A significant new initiative under consideration was the involvement of government agencies in creating activities centered around such entities as the tax office, customs, and the coin mint. Should it be added to offerings elsewhere?

2. The driving curriculum proved to be very popular at Cuicuilco. Should it be replicated elsewhere?

3. The Ecological House where children were to make environmentally friendly design decisions faced a lack of interest by industry partners at Cuicuilco. Did the idea warrant further exploration?

4. Should the blind Wal-Mart experience designed to sensitize children to a diverse range of personal differences be replicated elsewhere?

5. There was a proposal on the table to add a spa as part of the parents' lounge. Should it be explored further?

Supporting documentation for each of these initiatives is shown in Exhibit 9.

In addition, two new franchise proposals were before the group. They were for new facilities in Qatar and London. Information about each is contained in Exhibit 10. In addition to financial considerations, each would have to be assessed in terms of the degree to which they could carry out the demands created by the new emphasis on experiential learning and contribute further to the growth of the service concept.

Finally, further discussion was scheduled to determine which of the Santa Fe and Cuicuilco facility designs would be most suitable for KidZania's first facility in the U.S. It was anticipated that, unlike other non-Mexico parks, KidZania corporate would assume a significant share of the ownership of this facility.

STUDY QUESTIONS

1. Using service management best practices are criteria, which of the things KidZania is doing impressed you the most/the least, and why?

2. What are the risks in this business? How does KidZania's management ameliorate them?

3. What do you think are the main challenges and implications being faced regarding the changes in the service concept of KidZania, centered on experiential learning?

4. Considering the experience gained from all their current parks as well as the external forces including increasing competition, market regulations, diversity of potential new markets, and technology integration, what criteria should KidZania's management follow in selecting specific activities for its future "cities" to enhance experiential learning while remaining profitable?

ENDNOTES

1. Rebeca Mead, "When I Grow Up," *The New Yorker*, January 19, 2015, p. 27.

2. Ibid., p. 28.

Glossary

This glossary defines key terms used in this book and more generally in service marketing and management. For a broader coverage of marketing terms, see the glossaries in marketing management texts such as Philip Kotler and Kevin Lane Keller, *Marketing Management*, 15th ed. (Upper Saddle River, NJ: Prentice Hall, 2015) or consult the American Marketing Association's online dictionary of marketing terms *at* https://www.ama.org/resources/Pages/Dictionary.aspx).

You should be aware that not everyone attaches precisely the same meaning to the same term. That's why it's important that you know and can clarify your own understanding when using a particular word or phrase. As often happens in an evolving field, the same terms sometimes get defined and used in different ways by academics and practitioners and among managers in different industries. Even individual companies may attach distinctive meanings to specific terms.

A

activity-based costing (ABC): an approach to costing based on identifying the activities performed and then determining the resources that each consumes.

adequate service: the minimum level of service a customer will accept without being dissatisfied.

advertising: any paid form of nonpersonal communication by a marketer to inform, educate, or persuade members of target audiences.

ambient conditions: the atmosphere of a service environment that includes lighting, airquality, music, scents and color schemes.

arm's length transactions: interactions between customers and service suppliers in which mail or telecommunications minimize the need to meet face to face.

attitude: a person's consistently favorable or unfavorable evaluations, feelings, and action tendencies toward an object or idea.

auction: a selling procedure managed by a specialist intermediary in which the price is set by allowing prospective purchasers to bid against each other for a product offered by a seller.

augmented product: a core product (a good or a service) plus supplementary elements that add value for customers.

B

backstage (or technical core): those aspects of service operations hidden from customers.

banner ads: small, rectangular boxes on websites that contain text and perhaps a picture to support a brand.

benchmarking: the process of comparing an organization's products and processes to those of competitors or leading firms in other industries to find ways to improve performance, quality, and cost effectiveness.

benefit: an advantage or gain that customers obtain from performance of a service or use of a physical good.

blog: a publicly accessible "web log" containing frequently updated pages in the form of journals, diaries, news listings, etc.; authors—known as bloggers—typically focus on specific topics.

blueprint: a visual map of the sequence of activities required for service delivery that specifies front-stage and back-stage elements and the linkages between them.

boundary spanning positions: jobs that straddle the boundary between the external environment, where customers are encountered, and the internal operations of the organization.

brand: a name, phrase, design, symbol, or some combination of these elements that identifies a company's services and differentiates it from competitors.

business model: the means by which an organization generates income from sales and other sources through choice of pricing mechanisms and payors (e.g, user, advertiser or sponsor, other third parties), ideally sufficient to cover costs and create value for its owners. (Note: For nonprofits and public agencies, donations and designated tax revenues may be an integral part of the model.)

C

chain stores: two or more outlets under common ownership, control and brand name, selling similar goods and services.

chase demand strategy: adjusting the level of capacity to meet the level of demand at any given time.

churn: loss of existing customer accounts and the need to replace them with new ones.

clicks and mortar: a strategy of offering service through both physical stores and virtual storefronts via websites on the Internet.

climate for service: the shared believes of employees of the service practices, procedures, and behaviors that get rewarded by the organization.

competition-based pricing: the practice of setting prices relative to those charged by competitors.

competitive advantage: a firm's ability to perform in one or more ways that competitors cannot or will not match.

complaint: a formal expression of dissatisfaction with any aspect of a service experience.

complaint log: a detailed record of all customer complaints received by a service provider.

conjoint analysis: a research method for determining the utility values consumers attach to varying levels of a product's attributes.

consumption: the purchase and use of a service or good.

control charts: charts that graph quantitative changes in service performance on a specific variable relative to a predefined standard.

control model of management: an approach based on clearly defined roles, top-down control systems, a hierarchical organizational structure, and the assumption that management knows best.

core competency: a capability that is a source of competitive advantage.

corporate culture: the shared beliefs, norms, experiences, and stories that characterize an organization.

corporate design: the consistent application of distinctive colors, symbols, and lettering to give a firm an easily recognizable identity.

cost leader: a firm that bases its pricing strategy on achieving the lowest costs in its industry.

cost-based pricing: the practice of relating the price charged to the costs associated with producing, delivering, and marketing a product.

credence attributes: product characteristics that customers may not be able to evaluate even after purchase and consumption.

critical incident: a specific encounter between customer and service provider in which the outcome has proved especially satisfying or dissatisfying for one or both parties.

critical incident technique (CIT): a methodology for collecting, categorizing, and analyzing critical incidents that have occurred between customers and service providers.

CRM system: IT systems and infrastructure that support the implementation and delivery of a customer relationship management strategy.

cross-sell: get a customer to buy new products from the firm than in the past.

customer churn: customers canceling a contractual agreement who then sign a new contract, with either the same service provider or a new provider.

customer contact personnel: service employees who interact directly with individual customers, either in person or through mail and telecommunications.

customer equity: the total combined customer lifetime values of the company's entire customer base.

customer interface: all points at which customers interact with a service organization.

customer lifetime value (CLV): the net present value of the stream of future contributions or profits expected over each customer's purchases during his or her anticipated lifetime as a customer of the organization.

customer relationship management (CRM): the overall process of building and maintaining profitable customer relationships by delivering superior customer value and satisfaction.

customer satisfaction: a short-term emotional reaction to a specific service performance.

customer training: formal training courses offered by service firms to teach customers about complex service products.

customization: tailoring service characteristics to meet each customer's specific needs and preferences.

cyberspace: a term used to describe the absence of a definable physical location where electronic transactions or communications occur.

D

data mining: the extracting of useful information about individuals, trends, and segments from a mass of customer data.

data warehouse: a comprehensive database containing customer information and transaction data.

database marketing: the process of building, maintaining, and using customer databases and other databases for contacting, selling, cross-selling, up-selling, and building customer relationships.

defection: a customer's decision to transfer brand loyalty from a current service provider to a competitor.

delivery channels: the means by which a service firm (sometimes assisted by intermediaries) delivers one or more product elements to its customers.

demand curve: a curve that shows the number of units the market will buy at different prices.

demand cycle: a period of time during which the level of demand for a service will increase and decrease in a somewhat predictable way before repeating itself.

demographic segmentation: dividing the market into groups based on demographic variables such as age, gender, family lifecycle, family size, income, occupation, education, religion, and ethnic group.

desired service: the "wished for" level of service quality that a customer believes can and should be delivered.

discounting: a strategy of reducing the price of an item below the normal level.

dynamic pricing: a technique, employed primarily by e-tailers, to charge different customers different prices for the same products, based on information collected about their purchase history, preferences, and price sensitivity.

E

e-commerce: buying, selling, and other marketing processes supported by the Internet (*see also* **e-tailing**).

emotional labor: the act of expressing socially appropriate (but sometimes false) emotions toward customers during service transactions.

empowerment: authorizing employees to find solutions to service problems and make appropriate decisions about responding to customer concerns without having to ask a supervisor's approval.

enablement: providing employees with the skills, tools, and resources they need to use their own discretion confidently and effectively.

enhancing supplementary services: supplementary services that may add extra value for customers.

e-tailing: retailing through the Internet instead of through physical stores.

excess capacity: an organization's capacity to create service output is not fully utilized.

excess demand: demand for a service at a given time exceeds the organization's ability to meet customer needs.

expectations: internal standards that customers use to judge the quality of a service experience.

experience attributes: product performance features that customers can evaluate only during service delivery.

expert systems: interactive computer programs that mimic a human expert's reasoning to draw conclusions from data, solve problems, and give customized advice.

F

facilitating supplementary services: supplementary services that aid in the use of the core product or are required for service delivery.

fail point: a point in a process where there is a significant risk of problems that can damage service quality.

financial outlays: all monetary expenditures incurred by customers in purchasing and consuming a service.

fishbone diagram: a chart-based technique that relates specific service problems to different categories of underlying causes (also known as a cause-and-effect chart).

fixed costs: costs that do not vary with production or sales revenue.

flat-rate pricing: the strategy of quoting a fixed price for a service in advance of delivery.

flowchart: a visual representation of the steps involved in delivering service to customers (*see also* **blueprint**).

Flower of Service: a visual framework for understanding the supplementary service elements that surround and add value to the product core.

focus: the provision of a relatively narrow product mix for a particular market segment.

focus groups: groups of six to ten people carefully selected on certain characteristics (e.g., demographics, psychographics, or product ownership) who are convened by researchers for in-depth, moderator-led discussions on specific topics.

franchise: a contractual association between a franchiser (typically a manufacturer, wholesaler, or service organization) and independent businesspeople (franchisees) who buy the right to own and operate one or more units in the franchise system.

frequency programs (FPs): programs designed to reward customers who buy frequently and in substantial amounts.

front stage: those aspects of service operations and delivery that are visible or otherwise apparent to customers.

G

geographic segmentation: dividing a market into different geographical units such as countries, regions, or cities.

global industry: an industry in which the strategic positions of competitors in major geographic or national markets are fundamentally affected by their overall global positions.

goods: physical objects or devices that provide benefits for customers through ownership or use.

H

halo effect: the tendency for consumer ratings of one prominent product characteristic to influence ratings for many other attributes of that same product.

high-contact services: services that involve significant interaction among customers, service personnel, and equipment and facilities.

human resource management (HRM): the coordination of tasks related to job design, employee recruitment, selection, training, and motivation; it also includes planning and administering other employee-related activities.

I

image: a set of beliefs, ideas, and impressions held regarding an object.

impersonal communications: one-way communications directed at target audiences not in personal contact with the message source (including advertising, promotions, and public relations).

information processing: intangible actions directed at customers' assets.

information search: the stage of the buyer decision-making process in which the consumer searches for information to help make a purchase decision.

information-based services: all services in which the principal value comes from the transmission of data to customers (includes both mental stimulus processing and information processing).

in-process wait: a wait that occurs during service delivery.

inputs: all resources (labor, materials, energy, and capital) required to create service offerings.

intangibility: a distinctive characteristic of services that makes it impossible to touch or hold on to them in the same manner as physical goods.

intangible: something experienced that cannot be touched or preserved.

integrated marketing communications (IMC): a concept in which an organization carefully integrates and coordinates its many communications channels to deliver a clear, consistent, and compelling message about the organization and its products.

internal communications: all forms of communication from management to employees in a service organization.

internal customers: employees who receive services from an internal supplier (another employee or department) as a necessary input to performing their own jobs.

internal marketing: marketing by a service firm directed at its employees to train and motivate them and instill a customer focus.

internal services: service elements within any type of business that facilitate creation of, or add value to, its final output.

Internet: a large public web of computer networks that connects users from around the world to each other and to a vast information repository.

inventory: for *manufacturing*, physical output stockpiled after production for sale at a later date; for *services*, future output not yet reserved in advance, such as the number of hotel rooms still available for sale on a given day.

involvement model of management: an approach based on the assumption that employees are capable of self-direction and—if properly trained, motivated, and informed—can make good decisions concerning service operations and delivery.

iTV: (interactive television) procedures that allow viewers to alter the viewing experience by controlling TV program delivery (e.g., TiVo, video on demand) and/or content.

J

jaycustomer: a customer who acts in a thoughtless or abusive way, causing problems for the firm, its employees, and other customers.

L

levels of customer contact: the extent to which customers interact directly with elements of the service organization.

low-contact services: services that require minimal or no direct contact between customers and the service organization.

loyalty: a customer's commitment to continue patronizing a specific firm over an extended period of time.

M

market focus: the extent to which a firm serves few or many markets.

market segmentation: the process of dividing a market into distinct groups within which all customers share relevant characteristics that distinguish them from customers in other segments and who respond in a similar way to a given set of marketing efforts.

marketing communications mix: the full set of communication tools (both paid and unpaid) available to marketers, including advertising, sales promotion, events, public relations and publicity, direct marketing, and personal selling.

marketing implementation: the process that turns marketing plans into projects and ensures that such projects are executed in a way that accomplishes the plan's stated objectives.

marketing research: the systematic design, collection, analysis, and reporting of customer and competitor data and findings relevant to a specific marketing situation facing an organization.

marketplace: a physical location where suppliers and customers meet to do business.

mass customization: offering a service with some individualized product elements to a large number of customers at a relatively low price.

maximum capacity: the upper limit to a firm's ability to meet customer demand at a particular time.

medium-contact services: services that involve only a limited amount of contact between customers and elements of the service organization.

membership relationship: a formalized relationship between the firm and a specified customer the may offer special benefits to both parties.

mental intangibility: difficulty for customers in visualizing an experience in advance of purchase and understanding the process and even the nature of the outcome (*see also* **physical intangibility).**

mental stimulus processing: intangible actions directed at people's minds.

mission statement: succinct description of what the organization does, its standards and values, whom it serves, and what it intends to accomplish.

molecular model: a framework that uses a chemical analogy to describe the structure of service offerings.

moment of truth: a point in service delivery where customers interact with service employees or self-service equipment and the outcome may affect perceptions of service quality.

mystery shopping: a research technique that employs individuals posing as ordinary customers in order to obtain feedback on the service environment and customer-employee interactions.

N

needs: subconscious, deeply felt desires that often concern long-term existence and identity issues.

net value: the sum of all perceived benefits (gross value) minus the sum of all perceived outlays.

nonfinancial outlays: (*see* **nonmonetary costs**).

nonmonetary costs: the time expenditures, physical and mental effort, and unwanted sensory experiences associated with searching for, buying, and using a service.

O

opportunity cost: the potential value of the income or other benefits foregone as a result of choosing one course of action instead of other alternatives.

optimum capacity: the point beyond which a firm's efforts to serve additional customers will lead to a perceived decline in service quality.

organizational climate: employees' shared perceptions of the practices, procedures, and types of behaviors that get rewarded and supported in a particular setting.

organizational culture: shared values, beliefs, and work styles based on an understanding of what is important to the organization and why.

OTSU ("opportunity to screw up"): (*see* **fail point**).

outputs: the final outcomes of the service delivery process as perceived and valued by customers.

P

Pareto analysis: an analytical procedure to identify what proportion of problem events is caused by each of several different factors.

people: customers and employees involved in service production.

people processing: services that involve tangible actions to people's bodies.

perception: the process in which individuals select, organize, and interpret information to form a meaningful picture of the world.

perceptual map: a visual illustration of how customers perceive competing services.

permission marketing: a marketing communications strategy that encourages customers to volunteer permission to a company to communicate with them through specific channels so they may learn more about its products and continue to receive useful information and specific offers of value to them.

personal communications: direct communications between marketers and individual customers that involve two-way dialog (including face-to-face conversations, phone calls, and email).

personal selling: two-way communications between service employees and customers designed to directly influence the purchase process.

physical effort: undesired consequences to a customer's body resulting from involvement in the service delivery process.

physical evidence: visual or other tangible clues that provide evidence of service quality.

physical intangibility: service elements not accessible to examination by any of the five sense; elements that cannot be touched or preserved by customers.

place, cyberspace, and time: management decisions about when, where, and how to deliver services to customers.

positioning: establishing a distinctive place in the minds of customers relative to competing products.

possession processing: tangible actions to goods and other physical possessions belonging to customers.

postencounter stage: the final stage in the service purchase process where customers evaluate the service experienced and form their satisfaction/dissatisfaction judgment with the service outcome.

postprocess wait: a wait that occurs after service delivery has been completed.

posttransaction surveys: techniques to measure customer satisfaction and perceptions of service quality while a specific service experience is still fresh in the customer's mind.

predicted service: the level of service quality a customer believes a firm will actually deliver.

preprocess wait: a wait before service delivery begins.

prepurchase stage: the first stage in the service purchase process where customers identify alternatives, weigh benefits and risks, and make a purchase decision.

price and other user outlays: expenditures of money, time, and effort that customers incur in purchasing and consuming services.

price bucket: an allocation of service capacity (for instance, seats) for sale at a particular price.

price bundling: the practice of charging a base price for a core service plus additional fees for optional supplementary elements.

price elasticity: the extent to which a change in price leads to a corresponding change in demand in the opposite direction. (Demand is described as "price inelastic" when changes in price have little or no impact on demand.)

price leader: a firm that takes the initiative on price changes in its market area and is copied by others.

process: a particular method of operations or series of actions, typically involving steps that need to occur in a defined sequence.

product: the core output (either a service or a manufactured good) produced by a firm.

product attributes: all features (both tangible and intangible) of a good or service that can be evaluated by customers.

product elements: all components of the service performance that create value for customers.

productive capacity: the extent of the facilities, equipment, labor, infrastructure, and other assets available to a firm to create output for its customers.

productivity: how efficiently service inputs are transformed into outputs that add value for customers.

promotion and education: all communication activities and incentives designed to build customer preference for a specific service or service provider.

psychographic segmentation: dividing a market into different groups based on personality characteristics, social class, or lifestyle.

psychological burdens: undesired mental or emotional states experienced by customers as a result of the service delivery process.

public relations: efforts to stimulate positive interest in a company and its products by sending out news releases, holding press conferences, staging special events, and sponsoring newsworthy activities put on by third parties.

purchase process: the stages a customer goes through in choosing, consuming, and evaluating a service.

Q

quality: the degree to which a service satisfies customers by meeting their needs, wants, and expectations.

queue: a line of people, vehicles, other physical objects, or intangible items waiting their turn to be served or processed.

queue configuration the way in which a waiting line is organized.

R

rate fences: techniques for separating customers so that segments for whom the service offers high value are unable to take advantage of lower priced offers.

reciprocal marketing: a marketing communications tactic in which an online retailer allows its paying customers to receive promotions for another online retailer and vice versa, at no upfront cost to either party.

reengineering: the analysis and redesign of business processes to create dramatic performance improvements in such areas as cost, quality, speed, and customers' service experiences.

relationship marketing: activities aimed at developing long-term, cost-effective links between an organization and its customers for the mutual benefit of both parties.

reneging: a decision by a customer to leave a queue before reaching its end because the wait is longer or more burdensome than originally anticipated.

repositioning: changing the position a firm holds in a consumer's mind relative to competing services.

retail displays: presentations in store windows and other locations of merchandise, service experiences, and benefits.

retail gravity model: a mathematical approach to retail site selection that involves calculating the geographic center of gravity for the target population and then locating a facility to optimize customers' ease of access.

return on quality: the financial return obtained from investing in service quality improvements.

revenue management: a pricing and product design strategy based on charging different prices to different segments in order to maximize the revenue that can be derived from a firm's available capacity at any specific period of time (*also known as yield management*).

role: a combination of social cues that guides behavior in a specific setting or context.

role congruence: the extent to which both customers and employees act out their prescribed roles during a service encounter.

S

S-D Logic: (*see* **Service Dominant Logic**).

sales promotion: a short-term incentive offered to customers and intermediaries to stimulate quicker or greater purchase.

satisfaction: a person's feelings of pleasure or disappointment resulting from a consumption experience when comparing a product's perceived performance or outcome in relation to his or her expectations.

scripts: learned sequences of behaviors obtained through personal experience or communications with others.

search attributes: product characteristics that consumers can readily evaluate prior to purchase.

search engine optimization (SEO): enhances the visibility of a website or a web page in a search engine's unpaid results. It is often referred to as "organic" or "earned" results.

segment: a group of current or prospective customers who share common characteristics, needs, purchasing behavior, or consumption patterns.

sensory burdens: negative sensations experienced through a customer's five senses during the service delivery process.

SEO: (*see* **search engine optimization**).

service: an economic activity offered by one party to another, most commonly employing time-based performances to bring about desired results in recipients or in objects or other assets for which purchasers have responsibility. In exchange for their money, time, and effort, service customers expect to obtain value from access to goods, labor, professional skills, facilities, networks, and systems; but they do not normally take ownership of any of the physical elements involved.

service blueprint: (*see* **blueprint, flowchart**).

service delivery system: the part of the total service system where final "assembly" of the elements takes place and the product is delivered to the customer; it includes the visible elements of the service operation.

Service Dominant Logic: advocates that all products (goods and services) are valued for the service they provide and that value is co-created. For example, a razor ultimately provides a barbering service that is co-created with the user, and the value is derived by the service and not the good itself.

service encounter: a period of time during which customers interact directly with a service.

service encounter stage: the second stage in the service purchase process where the service delivery takes place through interactions between customers and the service provider.

service factory: the physical site where service operations take place.

service failure: a perception by customers that one or more specific aspects of service delivery have not met their expectations.

service focus: the extent to which a firm offers few or many services.

service guarantee: a promise that if service delivery fails to meet predefined standards, the customer is entitled to one or more forms of compensation.

service marketing system: the part of the total service system where the firm has any form of contact with its customers, from advertising to billing; it includes contacts made at the point of delivery.

service model: an integrative statement that specifies the nature of the service concept (what the firm offers, to whom, and through what processes), the service blueprint (how the concept is delivered to target customers), and the accompanying business model (how revenues will be generated sufficient to cover costs and ensure financial viability).

service operations system: the part of the total service system where inputs are processed and the elements of the service product are created.

service preview: a demonstration of how a service works to educate customers about the roles they are expected to perform in service delivery.

service-profit chain: a strategic framework that links employee satisfaction to performance on service attributes to customer satisfaction, then to customer retention, and finally to profits.

service quality: customers' long-term, cognitive evaluations of a firm's service delivery.

service quality information system: an ongoing service research process that provides timely, useful data to managers about customer satisfaction, expectations, and perceptions of quality.

service recovery: systematic efforts by a firm after a service failure to correct a problem and retain a customer's goodwill.

Service Science, Management and Engineering (SSME): combines management sciences (including services marketing), computer science, operations research, industrial engineering, social and cognitive sciences, legal sciences and others to innovate and design complex service systems.

service sector: the portion of a nation's economy represented by services of all kinds, including those offered by public and nonprofit organizations.

services marketing mix: seven strategic elements, each beginning with P, in the services marketing mix, representing the key ingredients required to create viable strategies for meeting customer needs profitably in a competitive marketplace.

servicescape: the design of any physical location where customers come to place orders and obtain service delivery.

SERVQUAL: a pair of standardized 22-item scales that measure customers' expectations and perceptions concerning five dimensions of service quality.

Seven (7) Ps: (*see* **services marketing mix**).

social marketing: makes use of social networks to increase a firm's online presence, ranging from advertising on social networking sites to viral marketing and providing social networking sites focused around the service promoted.

SSME: (*see* **Service Science, Management and Engineering**).

standardization: reducing variation in service operations and delivery.

stickiness: a website's ability to encourage repeat visits and purchases by providing users with easy navigation and problem-free execution of tasks and by keeping its audience engaged with interactive communication presented in an appealing fashion.

sustainable competitive advantage: a position in the marketplace that can't be taken away or minimized by competitors in the short run.

T

tangible: capable of being touched, held, or preserved in physical form over time.

target market: a part of the qualified available market with common needs or characteristics that a company decides to serve.

target segments: segments selected because their needs and other characteristics fit well with a specific firm's goals and capabilities.

third-party payments: payments to cover all of part of the cost of a service or good made by a party other than the user (who may or may not have made the actual purchase decision).

three-stage model of service consumption: a framework depicting how consumers move from a prepurchase stage (in which they recognize their needs, search for and evaluate alternative solutions, and make a decision) to a service encounter search (in which they obtain service delivery) and a postencounter stage (in which they evaluate service performance against expectations).

time expenditures: time spent by customers during all aspects of the service delivery process.

total costs: the sum of the fixed and variable costs for any given level of production.

transaction: an event during which an exchange of value takes place between two parties.

Twitter: a social networking and microblogging service that allows its users to send and read other users' updates, which are up to 140 characters in length and can send and receive via the Twitter website, short message service (SMS), or external applications.

U

undesirable demand: requests for service that conflict with the organization's mission, priorities, or capabilities.

up-sell: persuade a customer to buy something additional or a more expensive version of what the customer had requested.

V

value chain: The series of departments within a firm or external partners and subcontractors that carry out value-creating activities to design, produce, market, deliver, and support a product or service offering.

value exchange: transfer of the benefits and solutions offered by a seller in return for financial and other value offered by a purchaser.

value net (*or* value network): a system of partnerships and alliances a firm creates to source, augment, and deliver its service offering.

value proposition: the full set of benefits a company promises to deliver.

value-based pricing: the practice of setting prices based on what customers are willing to pay for the value they believe they will receive.

variability: a lack of consistency in inputs and outputs during the service production process.

variable costs: costs directly dependent on the volume of production or service transactions.

viral marketing: using the Internet to create word-of-mouth effects to support marketing efforts.

W

Wheel of Loyalty: a systematic and integrated approach to targeting, acquiring, developing, and retaining a valuable customer base.

word of mouth: positive or negative comments about a service made by one individual (usually a current or former customer) to another.

Y

yield: the average revenue received per unit of capacity offered for sale.

yield management (*see* revenue management).

Z

zone of tolerance: the range within which customers are willing to accept variations in service delivery.

Credits

Chapter 1 — p. 4: Andres Rodriguez/123RF; p. 5: Pavel L Photo and Video/Shutterstock; p. 8: Chris Howey/Shutterstock; p. 12: Used with permission by Randy Glasbergen; p. 13: Coleman Yuen/Pearson Education Asia Ltd; p. 15: Nippon News/Aflo Co. Ltd./Alamy Stock Photo; p. 16: Gosphotodesign/Shutterstock; p. 16: Dmitry Kalinovsky/Shutterstock; p. 17: Pavel Losevsky/123RF; p. 18: LDprod/Shutterstock; p. 21T: Stephen Coburn/Shutterstock; p. 21B: Yegor Korzh/Shutterstock; p. 22: Kullapol/Shutterstock; p. 23: Peter Horree/Alamy Stock Photo; p. 24: Arek_Malang/Shutterstock; p. 25: Nakamasa/Shutterstock.

Chapter 2 — p. 36: Antonio Balaguer Soler/123RF; p. 37: Christo/Shutterstock; p. 39: Mikadun/Shutterstock; p. 42: Natalia Bratslavsky/Shutterstock; p. 44T: Michaeljung/Shutterstock; p. 44B: Langstrup/123RF; p. 45: © Zurich Insurance Company Ltd. Credit: Nick Meek; p. 46: Kurhan/123RF; p. 47: Ulrich Perrey/dpa picture alliance archive/Alamy Stock Photo; p. 48: Mihai Simonia/Shutterstock; p. 49: Motmot/Shutterstock; p. 50: Used with permission by Randy Glasbergen; p. 51T: Erwinova/Shutterstock; p. 51B: Jack.Q/Shutterstock; p. 52T: Amble Design/Shutterstock; p. 52B: Wavebreakmedia/Shutterstock; p. 54: Scott Griessel/123RF.

Chapter 3 — p. 64: Anatols/123RF; p. 65: Anatols/123RF; p. 67: Jan Miks/123RF; p. 70T: William Perugini/Shutterstock; p. 70B: Bikeriderlondon/Shutterstock; p. 72: © Air Charter Team, Inc. All rights reserved; p. 73: Dmitry Kalinovsky/Shutterstock; p. 74: Andrew Gardner/Alamy Stock Photo; p. 75: Jenny Matthews/Alamy Stock Photo; p. 76: Used with permission by Randy Glasbergen; p. 77T: Mast3r/Shutterstock; p. 77B: Naki Kouyioumtzis/Pearson Education Ltd; p. 80: Martine Oger/123RF; p. 82: Syda Productions/Shutterstock.

Chapter 4 — p. 90: Zeljkodan/Shutterstock; p. 91T: James Boardman/Alamy Stock Photo; p. 91L: CartoonStock; p. 91R: CartoonStock; p. 96: Tyler Olson/Shutterstock; p. 97T: Corepics VOF/Shutterstock; p. 97B: Angellodeco/123RF; p. 98T: Yama/Shutterstock; p. 98B: Jules Selmes/Pearson Education Ltd; p. 99T: Lisa F. Young/Shutterstock; p. 99B: CartoonStock; p. 100T: Hemis/Alamy Stock Photo; p. 100B: Glasshouse Images/Alamy Stock Photo; p. 101T: Gelpi JM/Shutterstock; p. 101B: Jirkaejc/123RF; p. 102: Alex Segre/Alamy Stock Photo; p. 104T: CBsigns/Alamy Stock Photo; p. 104B: Robert Convery/Alamy Stock Photo; p. 109: Web Pix/Alamy Stock Photo; p. 110: © Space Adventures Ltd.; p. 112: Akio Kon/Bloomberg/Getty Images.

Chapter 5 — p. 118: Bloomua/Shutterstock; p. 119: WENN Ltd/Alamy Stock Photo; p. 122: Frank L Junior/Shutterstock; p. 123: Used with permission by Randy Glasbergen; p. 124: © Aggreko Plc; p. 126: Used with permission by Randy Glasbergen; p. 127: Halil Erdoğan/123RF; p. 128T: Kevpix/Alamy Stock Photo; p. 128B: Pudi Studio/Shutterstock; p. 129: Tito/123RF; p. 130: B Christopher/Alamy Stock Photo; p. 131: Zhu Difeng/Shutterstock; p. 136: Gareth Boden/Pearson Education Ltd; p. 138: Christian Lagerek/Shutterstock; p. 139: Le Moal Olivier/123RF; p. 140: Agencja Fotograficzna Caro/Alamy Stock Photo; p. 142: Alexeyboldin/123RF.

Chapter 6 — p. 152: Nagy-Bagoly Arpad/Shutterstock; p. 153: Cynthia Lindow/Alamy Stock Photo; p. 157: Jules Selmes/Pearson Education Ltd; p. 158T: Diego Cervo/Shutterstock; p. 158B: Goodluz/Shutterstock; p. 160T: CPC Collection/Alamy Stock Photo; p. 160B: Graphixmania/Shutterstock; p. 161: King Features. All rights reserved; p. 162T: Darl Hurst/123RF; p. 162B: Used with permission by Randy Glasbergen; p. 164: Szasz-Fabian Ilka Erika/Shutterstock; p. 165: Iofoto/123RF; p. 169: Agencja Fotograficzna Caro/Alamy Stock Photo; p. 172: Universal Uclick. A Division of Andrews McMeel Universal; p. 173T: Wavebreakmedia/Shutterstock; p. 173B: John Panella/Shutterstock; p. 176: Natalia Deksbakh/123RF; p. 180: Photoinnovation/Shutterstock; p. 181T: Kzenon/123RF; p. 181B: Used with permission by Randy Glasbergen; p. 182: Kzenon/Shutterstock; p. 183T: Pawan Kumar/Alamy Stock Photo; p. 183B: Dorling Kindersley Ltd/Alamy Stock Photo; p. 184: Aastock/Shutterstock.

Chapter 7 — p. 195TR: Kilronan Castle Estate; p. 195BR: Kilronan Castle Estate; p. 195BL: Kilronan Castle Estate; p. 195TL: Kilronan Castle Estate; p. 196: Matthew Chattle/Alamy Stock Photo; p. 200T: Maurusone/Thinkstock; p. 200CT: Coleman Yuen/Pearson Education Asia Ltd; p. 200CB: Tyler Olson/Shutterstock; p. 200B: Mama_Mia/Shutterstock; p. 201: Pressmaster/Shutterstock; p. 202T: NetPhotos/Alamy Stock Photo; p. 202B: Erik Tham/Alamy Stock Photo; p. 204T: Ssviluppo/123RF; p. 204B: Robert Kneschke/Shutterstock; p. 207: Bloomua/Shutterstock; p. 208T: Used with permission by Randy Glasbergen; p. 208B: Used with permission by Randy Glasbergen; p. 209: Victor Biro/Alamy Stock Photo; p. 210: WinMaster/Shutterstock; p. 211: Friedrich Stark/Alamy Stock Photo; p. 213L: Denso Wave Inc.; p. 213R: Kristoffer Tripplaar/Alamy Stock Photo; p. 216: Efrain Padro/Alamy Stock Photo; p. 217: Tobias Hase/dpa picture alliance/Alamy Stock Photo; p. 218: Konrad Bak/123RF; p. 219: rawpixel/123RF; p. 224: Kevin Foy/Alamy Stock Photo; p. 225TL: Valentino Visentini/Alamy Stock Photo; p. 225BL: Peter Probst/Alamy Stock Photo; p. 225TCL: Finnbarr Webster/Alamy Stock Photo; p. 225BCL: Maurice Savage/Alamy Stock Photo; p. 225TCR: Stuart Kelly/Alamy Stock Photo; p. 225BCR: Arterra Picture Library/Alamy Stock Photo; p. 225TR: PhotoEdit/Alamy Stock Photo; p. 225BR: 360b/Alamy Stock Photo.

Chapter 8 — p. 236: Aletia/Shutterstock; p. 237: Coleman Associates; p. 238: Lightpoet/Shutterstock; p. 241: Gemenacom/123RF; p. 242L: Wavebreak Media Ltd/123RF; p. 242C: Rui Santos/123RF; p. 242R: Alena Brozova/123RF; p. 243L: Heinz Leitner/123RF; p. 243CL: Christos Meimaroglou/123RF; p. 243CR: Denis Raev/123RF; p. 243R: Bowie15/123RF; p. 244L: 36clicks/123RF; p. 244C: Imagehit Limited/123RF; p. 244R: Phil Date/123RF; p. 245L: Phil Date/123RF; p. 245CL: Pixbox/123RF; p. 245CR: Tatjana Romanova/Shutterstock; p. 245R: Rui Santos/123RF; p. 246: RosaIreneBetancourt 7/Alamy Stock Photo; p. 247: CandyBox Images/Shutterstock; p. 249: Franck Boston/Shutterstock; p. 253: Natsuki Sakai/AFLO Co. Ltd./Alamy Stock Photo; p. 254: Ocskay Bence/Shutterstock; p. 256T: Used with permission by Randy Glasbergen; p. 256B: Kristina Afanasyeva/123RF; p. 257: Auremar/Shutterstock; p. 259: Arterra Picture Library/Alamy Stock Photo.

Chapter 9 — p. 268: Preve Beatrice/123RF; p. 269L: Martin Beebee/Alamy Stock Photo; p. 269R: Anton Oparin/123RF; p. 270: Iodrakon/Shutterstock; p. 272: Deklofenak/Shutterstock; p. 273: SeanPavonePhoto/Shutterstock; p. 274T: Alexptv/Shutterstock; p. 274: CandyBox Images/Shutterstock; p. 275T: Kasto/123RF; p. 275B: Monkey Business Images/Shutterstock; p. 276: Dmitry Kalinovsky/Shutterstock; p. 277: Meiqianbao/Shutterstock; p. 279: Staticnak/Shutterstock; p. 280: Karin Hildebrand Lau/123RF; p. 281: bikeriderlondon/Shutterstock; p. 282: RSBPhoto1/Alamy Stock Photo; p. 285T: Roman Milert/123RF; p. 285B: 123ucas/123RF; p. 286: deborah thompson/Alamy Stock Photo; p. 287: Used with permission by Randy Glasbergen; p. 288: Gemenacom/123RF; p. 289: Hongqi Zhang/123RF; p. 290: Robert Kneschke/Shutterstock.

Chapter 10 — p. 298: Jules Selmes. Pearson Education Ltd; p. 299: Jules Selmes/Pearson Education Ltd; p. 302TL: Edvard Nalbantjan/123RF; p. 302TR: 2009fotofriends/Shutterstock; p. 302B: Sean Pavone/Alamy Stock Photo; p. 303: Jessica Duley/Alamy Stock Photo; p. 304TL: 3208787/Shutterstock; p. 304TR: Andresr/Shutterstock; p. 304BL: michaeljung/Shutterstock; p. 304BR: 123RF; p. 305: 123RF; p. 306TL: Mark Hayes/Shutterstock; p. 306TR: Galina Barskaya/Shutterstock; p. 306BL: Maridav/123RF; p. 306BR: Oliveromg/Shutterstock; p. 310T: Hamsterman/123RF; p. 310B: Stokkete/123RF; p. 311: ximagination/123RF; p. 313: Pavel L Photo and Video/Shutterstock; p. 314T: truembie/123RF; p. 314BL: Friedrich Stark/Alamy Stock Photo; p. 314BR: Jochen Wirtz; p. 315: James Steidl/Shutterstock; p. 317: Serghei Starus/123RF; p. 318: Naki Kouyioumtzis/Pearson Education Ltd.

Chapter 11 — p. 326: Wavebreakmedia/Shutterstock; p. 327: Wavebreakmedia/Shutterstock; p. 330: © 2016 Hotel Lotte Co., Ltd. All Rights Reserved; p. 332T: Gstockstudio/123RF; p. 332B: © Universal Uclick. A Division of Andrews McMeel Universal; p. 333: Bikeriderlondon/Shutterstock; p. 334: Qwasyx/123RF; p. 336: Wavebreakmedia/Shutterstock; p. 338: Used with permission by Randy Glasbergen; p. 339: Used with permission by Randy Glasbergen; p. 340T: Racorn/Shutterstock; p. 340B: Used with permission by Randy Glasbergen; p. 341: RosaIreneBetancourt 5/Alamy Stock Photo; p. 344: MindStudio/Pearson Education Ltd; p. 345: Kadmy/123RF; p. 346T: Stuart Cox/Pearson Education Ltd; p. 346B: Used with permission by Randy Glasbergen; p. 347: Helen Sessions/Alamy Stock Photo; p. 351T: Used with permission by Randy Glasbergen; p. 351B: Poznyakov/Shutterstock; p. 353: ALMAGAMI/Shutterstock.

Chapter 12 — p. 372: kzenon/123RF; p. 373T: Shots Studio/Shutterstock; p. 373B: Travel Pictures/Alamy Stock Photo; p. 381: Stephen Coburn/Shutterstock; p. 382: Kristoffer Tripplaar/Alamy Stock Photo; p. 385: B Christopher/Alamy Stock Photo; p. 388: Newscast Online/Alamy Stock Photo; p. 391: stylephotographs/123RF; p. 392: RosaIreneBetancourt 7/Alamy Stock Photo; p. 399: Michaeljung/Shutterstock; p. 401: Nomad_Soul/Shutterstock.

Chapter 13 — p. 412: AR Images/Alamy Stock Photo; p. 413T: Gregg DeGuire/WireImage/Getty Images; p. 413B: Patti McConville/Alamy Stock Photo; p. 416: Used with permission by Randy Glasbergen; p. 417: Illustration Source; p. 422: © Universal Uclick; p. 425: Used with permission by Randy Glasbergen; p. 426: © Universal Uclick; p. 427: RosaIreneBetancourt 9/Alamy Stock Photo; p. 428: Zoom Team/Shutterstock; p. 431: Dmitry Kalinovsky/Shutterstock; p. 432: Xalanx/123RF; p. 432: Randy Glasbergen; p. 433: Dmitry Kalinovsky/123RF.

Name Index

A

A&W, 104
A380 Airbus, 47
AA333 Flight, 167
Aaker, D., 117
ABC Corp., 216
Abdullah, F., 149
Adams, S., 172, 191
Aggreko, 123, 124
Air Canada, 346
AirAsia, 212
Airport Plaza, 78, 79
Alba, J. W., 191
Alexander IV, 79
Allure, 119
Alwi, M. R., 149
Amazon, 110, 111, 179, 207,
    217, 257, 494
Ambtman, A., 233
American Airlines, 165, 167, 388, 389
AMEX, 139
Anand, P., 324
Anderson, E. W., 63, 501
Anderson, S. R., 191
Andreassen, T. W., 366
Andreessen, M., 111
Apple, 91, 111, 302
Armario, E. M., 365
Armstron, G., 233
Ashill, N. J., 365
Astous, A., 318
Au Bon Pain, 341, 342
Auh, S., 410
Aussie Pooch Mobile, 548
Avis, 104
Ayres, I., 191

B

Bachman, J., 325
Bacon, D. R., 489
Baer, R., 232
Baily, M. N., 489
Baker, J., 232, 296, 324
Baker, W. E., 488
Ball, D., 409
Banerjee, M., 149

Banyan Tree Hotels & Resorts,
    102, 521–529
Barlow, J., 442
Baron, S., 62
Barron, G., 296
Barry, T. E., 233
Bart, Y., 232
Bateson, J. E. G., 35, 62, 324
Bayon, T., 192
Beatty, S. E., 149
Bejou, D., 410
Bell, C. R., 442
Bell, S. J., 410, 441
Bell, T., 130
Bellizzi, J. A., 325
Benlian, A., 367
Berman, R., 232
Bernoff, J., 442
Berry, L. L., 35, 46, 57, 62, 107, 117,
    149, 191, 266, 324, 355, 365,
    366, 368, 409, 441, 457, 488
Bielen, F., 296
Bing, 210
Biolos, J., 489
Bitner, M. J., 35, 149, 233, 257,
    266, 267, 324, 366, 409, 488
Black, H. G., 365
Black, N. J., 149
Blagg, D., 368
Blair, E. A., 192
Blodgett, J., 232
Bloemer, J., 233
Blondie, 158
BMW, 287
Bodey, K., 441
Bogle, J., 382
Bolton, L. E., 191
Bolton, R. N., 408
Bond, J., 124
Bone, P. F., 325
Bone, S. A., 266
Boston Marathon, 317
Boudreau, K. J., 117
Bougie, R., 441
Boulding, W., 411
Bourdeau, B.L., 296
Bourgeoris, L., 299
Bove, L. L., 365
Bowen, D. E., 254, 255, 266,
    365, 366
Bradley, G. L., 367

Bradlow, E. T., 488
Brady, M. K., 367
Branson, R., 216
Bright Horizons, 65, 67, 76
Brin, S., 211
British Airways (BA), 104, 389–390
    Club (business class), 390
    Executive Club, 389, 390
    Gold Tier Members, 390
Brocato, E. D., 296
Broderick, A., 442
Brown, J. C., 489
Brown, L., 35
Brown, R., 65, 76, 87
Brown, S. W., 35, 149, 267,
    366, 441, 442
Brown, T. J., 233, 366
Brusco, M. J., 367
Brustein, J., 191
Bulte, C V, 233
Bureau of Economic Analysis, 9
Burger King, 37, 39, 40
Burj Al Arab, 77
Burke, K. G., 232
Burton, J., 367
Buzz Lightyear's Tomorrowland, 315
Byrnes, N., 87

C

Cabrera, K., 619
Caesar's, 373
Caldwell, C., 325
Canadian Rockies, 42
Candlewood Suites, 103
Canli, Z. G., 233
Cape Cod, 317
Caplan, J., 325
Carlo, T. E. De, 62
Carlzon, J., 48, 62
Casado Diaz, A. B., 296
Castaldo, S., 409
Castle, 79
Castle, K., 232
Castro, C. B., 365
Castrogiovanni, G. J., 149
Cathay Pacific, 389
Central Intelligence Agency, 7, 8
Cespedes, F. V., 149

Y

Yadav, M. S., 191
Yagil, D., 367
Yahoo, 209, 210
Yakubovich, V., 367
Yanamandram, V., 410
Yankelovich, D., 87
Young, R. F., 62

Young, S., 368
YouTube, 119, 201, 213

Z

Zahonik, A. J., 489
Zappos, 217, 219, 359, 494
Zeelenberg, M., 441

Zeithaml, V. A., 35, 46, 55, 57, 62,
    63, 157, 383, 384, 408,
    409, 451, 488
Zemke, R., 442
Zhang, Z. J., 232
Zhu, Z., 267
Ziklik, L., 365
Zimring, C., 305
Zollinger, H., 325
Zurich, 45

Subject Index